Praise for
REAGAN'S REVOLUTION

"This is an exhilarating story of political daring. It would be fascinating even if we did not know that the campaign Craig Shirley recounts was The Great Prologue. The world-shaping events of 1980–88 were made possible by what Ronald Reagan did in 1976."

—GEORGE F. WILL

"American politics can be described as B.R. and A.R.—Before Reagan and After Reagan. Shirley's fascinating inside account shows us how and why Reagan was able to redefine the broad outlines of American government and politics."

—LARRY J. SABATO, director,
University of Virginia Center for Politics

"The view from the canvas is highly educational. In this thoughtful and detailed book, Craig Shirley shows us how the seeds of Ronald Reagan's stunning political victory were sown in his only major defeat. Liberals, conservatives and everyone who wants to learn about toughness, tenacity and triumph will love this book."

—PAUL BEGALA, co-host,
CNN's *Crossfire*

"For at least a generation, Craig Shirley's unique blend of guile and charm has assisted his conservative brethren in confounding and confusing their liberal enemies. Now this consummate political insider has placed the outside world in his debt by opening a window on the internal workings of one of the most momentous presidential campaigns in recent history."

—ROBERT SHOGAN, author,
Constant Conflict: Politics, Culture and the Struggle for America's Future

"*Reagan's Revolution* is a must for anyone interested in reading about the beginning of the Ronald Reagan Prairie Fire. In many ways, this was the real campaign for the Presidency."

—MICHAEL K. DEAVER, vice chairman international,
Edelman Worldwide

"Shirley's is a story that has not been told before, and he tells it well."

—R. EMMETT TYRRELL JR., founder and editor in chief,
The American Spectator

"The 1976 Reagan campaign has been largely ignored by political scientists and historians, which makes Craig Shirley's thorough and definitive account an indispensable contribution to Reagan literature."

—STEVEN F. HAYWARD, author,
The Age of Reagan: The Fall of the Old Liberal Order

"Easy to read and well researched, Craig Shirley does a great job of taking advantage of the fact that many of the key and bit players—the behind-the-scenes people who give color and texture to events—are alive and still able to tell their stories. Shirley fills an important void and does it well."

—CHARLIE COOK, editor,
The Cook Political Report

"Craig Shirley masterfully explains how the 1976 Republican primary established the critical prerequisites for Ronald Reagan's successful race for the presidency in 1980."

—DR. RICHARD WIRTHLIN, CEO,
Wirthlin Worldwide

"Craig Shirley has written a fascinating account of a nearly forgotten campaign that paved the way for one of the most successful Presidencies in American history. Rich in detail and original reporting, *Reagan's Revolution* is required reading for anyone who seeks to understand fully how Ronald Reagan changed America and the world."

—WILLIAM SCHULZ, retired executive editor,
Reader's Digest

"Craig Shirley's *Reagan's Revolution* reminds us all that the revolution really began in 1976, not in 1980. It is my firm conviction after reading this book that if Reagan had won the Republican nomination against Jerry Ford in '76 he would have been swept into the White House that year in a landslide, America's economic collapse of the late 1970s would have been averted, and the Cold War would have ended a decade earlier. At least the Republicans finally got it right in 2000!"

—STEPHEN MOORE, president,
Club for Growth

"Craig Shirley has done an invaluable service for future generations by filling in the previously untold details of a key part of the Ronald Reagan story."

—DR. ART LAFFER, president,
Laffer Associates

REAGAN'S REVOLUTION

REAGAN'S REVOLUTION

THE UNTOLD STORY OF THE CAMPAIGN THAT STARTED IT ALL

CRAIG SHIRLEY

THOMAS NELSON
Since 1798

NASHVILLE DALLAS MEXICO CITY RIO DE JANEIRO

Published in Nashville, Tennessee, by Thomas Nelson. Thomas Nelson is a registered trademark of Thomas Nelson, Inc.

Thomas Nelson, Inc., titles may be purchased in bulk for educational, business, fund-raising, or sales promotional use. For information, please e-mail SpecialMarkets@ThomasNelson.com.

ISBN 978-1-59555-342-3 (TP)

Library of Congress Cataloging-in-Publication Data

Shirley, Craig.
Reagan's revolution : the untold story of the campaign that started it all / Craig Shirley.
p. cm.
ISBN 0-7852-6049-8
1. Presidents—United States—Election—1980. 2. United States—Politics and government—1977–1981. 3. Reagan, Ronald. 4. Political campaigns—United States—History—20th century. 5. Presidential candidates--United States—Biography. 6. Presidents United States—Biography. I. Title.
E875.S46 2005
324.973'0926—dc22

2004026809

Printed in the United States of America

10 11 12 13 14 RRD 5 4 3 2 1

This year-long effort would not have been possible without
the indulgent love, devoted encouragement and
unyielding support of my wife and best friend,
Zorine,
to whom this book is dedicated.

It is also dedicated to the four rocks of our life:
Matthew McGiveron, Andrew Abbott,
Taylor Mackintosh and Mitchell Boman Reagan Shirley.

And to Edward B. Shirley and Barbara S. Eckert,
who taught me about love and honor, patriotism,
the dignity of the private individual and the appealing intellectual
attributes of the conservative philosophy.

CONTENTS

CONTENTS

CAST OF CHARACTERS

CITIZENS FOR REAGAN

MARTIN ANDERSON: policy advisor
ERNIE ANGELO: Texas Campaign Co-Chairman
RAY BARNHART: Texas Campaign Co-Chairman
JEFF BELL: Research Director
CHARLIE BLACK: Midwest Field Director
MORTON BLACKWELL: state convention tactician; conservative activist
ANDY CARTER: Field Director
RON DEAR: Texas delegates for Reagan Chairman
MICHAEL DEAVER: public relations
DON DEVINE: state convention tactician; conservative activist
BRUCE EBERLE: direct mail strategist
TOM ELLIS: chief political strategist in North Carolina
ARTHUR FINKELSTEIN: North Carolina and Texas tactician
HUGH GREGG: New Hampshire Campaign Chairman and former Governor
PETER HANNAFORD: public relations
DAVID KEENE: Southern Field Director
JIM LAKE: New Hampshire Campaign Director; Communications Director
PAUL LAXALT: Nevada Senator; Campaign Chairman
EDWIN MEESE: "Kitchen Cabinet"; joined campaign, Summer 1976
BILLY MOUNGER: Reagan Chairman, Mississippi
LYN NOFZIGER: Press Secretary; California Campaign Chairman; Convention Manager
CHARLES PICKERING: incoming State Chairman, Mississippi
CLARKE REED: Mississippi State Republican Chairman
NANCY REYNOLDS: personal advance aide to the Reagans
RICHARD SCHWEIKER: Pennsylvania Senator; running mate
JOHN SEARS: Campaign Manager
LOREN SMITH: General Counsel

ROGER STONE: Youth for Reagan
TOMMY THOMAS: Florida Campaign Chairman
BOB WALKER: campaign strategist; conservative activist
FRANK WHETSTONE: Western Field Director
DICK WIRTHLIN: pollster
CARTER WRENN: North Carolina strategist

PRESIDENT FORD COMMITTEE

JAMES BAKER: Deputy Chairman of Delegate Operations
HOWARD "BO" CALLAWAY: Campaign Chairman, resigned March 1976
HARRY DENT: senior advisor; Southern strategist
PETER KAYE: Press Secretary, resigned August 1976
DREW LEWIS: Pennsylvania Chairman
ROGERS "ROG" C.B. MORTON: Campaign Chairman, April to August 1976
BOB MOSBACHER: Finance Director, beginning November 1975
DAVID PACKARD: Finance Director, resigned November 1975
STUART SPENCER: Deputy Chairman for Political Affairs
BOB TEETER: Deputy Chairman for Research
BOB VISSER: General Counsel
CLIFF WHITE: senior advisor

FORD ADMINISTRATION

DICK CHENEY: Deputy Chief of Staff; Chief of Staff, beginning November 1975
ROBERT HARTMANN: counselor to the President
HENRY KISSINGER: Secretary of State
RON NESSEN: Press Secretary
NELSON ROCKEFELLER: Vice President of the United States
DONALD RUMSFELD: Chief of Staff; Secretary of Defense, beginning November 1975

CONSERVATIVE AND GOP LEADERS

JIM BUCKLEY: New York Senator; conservative leader
FRANK DONATELLI: Executive Director, Young Americans for Freedom
BARRY GOLDWATER: Arizona Senator, 1964 Republican Presidential nominee

Stan Evans: Chairman, American Conservative Union
Jesse Helms: North Carolina Senator; North Carolina Reagan Campaign Chairman
Eddie Mahe: Executive Director, Republican National Committee
Richard "Rosey" Rosenbaum: New York State Republican Chairman
Meldrim Thomson: New Hampshire Governor; Reagan supporter
Richard Viguerie: direct mail strategist; conservative activist

JOURNALISTS

Fred Barnes: political reporter, *Washington Star*
William F. Buckley: editor, *National Review*
Lou Cannon: political reporter, *Washington Post*
Rowland Evans, Bob Novak: syndicated columnists
William Loeb: publisher, *Manchester Union-Leader*
Frank Reynolds: *ABC News* correspondent
William Rusher: author, *The Making of the New Majority Party*, columnist
William Safire: columnist, *New York Times*
Jules Witcover: political reporter, *Washington Post*
George Will: syndicated columnist, *Newsweek* contributor
Tom Winter, Allan Ryskind: co-editors, *Human Events*

FOREWORD

by Fred Barnes

The Presidential race of 1976 brought forth two new political stars, but the press was excited about only one of them. This was Jimmy Carter, the peanut farmer who emerged spectacularly in the Presidential primaries, won the Democratic nomination with ease, and captured the White House by defeating America's only unelected President, Gerald Ford.

Carter was a Southern pragmatist with moderate to liberal views and a crew of smart, young political advisers. He was seen by reporters and commentators not only as the savior of the Democratic Party, but as a political heavyweight capable of reshaping public policy in creative ways. Carter was the future, the vanguard of a progressive future.

The other star was Ronald Reagan, the former California Governor and conservative whose spirited challenge of Ford for the Republican Presidential nomination was viewed as his swan song. At sixty-five, his political career was over. He represented the past.

Such was the conventional political wisdom in 1976. And seldom has the press been so wrong. True, Carter left his mark on the nation, mostly by weakening it. The economy during his Presidency was beset by a new phenomenon called stagflation—high inflation and unemployment at the same time—that mystified Carter. And he was unable to slow the march of Soviet Communism around the world. But Carter had a political legacy, an inadvertent one. He paved the way for Ronald Reagan to be elected President and become the most event-making leader of the second half of the twentieth century.

More important, of course, was what Reagan himself achieved in 1976. While losing, he laid the foundation for his successful capture of the Presidency four years later. This is what Craig Shirley explains with such insight and thoroughness in *Reagan's Revolution.* It's a story that's never been fully told before.

As a young reporter for the *Washington Star,* I covered several episodes of the Reagan story in 1976: the North Carolina recovery, the Texas blowout, the convention speech that changed the Republican Party. By the time the North Carolina primary arrived, the Ford camp was cocky and confident and Reagan was reeling. The exceptions were two Reaganites, Republican Senator Jesse Helms and his sidekick Tom Ellis, who hadn't given up. To say Ford, having won the New Hampshire, Florida, and Illinois primaries, was shocked by North Carolina is putting it mildly. Neither he nor the press had any idea that Helms and Ellis might engineer a huge Reagan upset, a victory that kept him in the race.

Then came Texas. Ford had meticulously organized what few Republicans there were in the state. His chief Texas strategist, Jim Francis, persuaded me that despite Reagan's popularity with conservatives, Ford was poised to win the primary with a record turnout. So I wrote exactly that. It turned out to be the worst story I ever wrote. On primary day, Francis gave me the bad news. He knew Ford was in trouble when he arrived at his local precinct voting place and encountered a line filled with people he'd never laid eyes on. They weren't regular Republicans, that's for sure, but Reagan had attracted them. Ford actually got his record vote, but the turnout for Reagan swamped it. The Texas primary was the same day as the White House Correspondents' dinner in Washington, attended by Ford and all the bigwigs in his Administration and campaign. They were a glum lot at the dinner.

For me, the lesson from Texas was never underestimate Ronald Reagan. Texas was also significant for another reason. Reagan reached top form in campaigning in the weeks before the primary. To this day, I have never seen any candidate in America arouse crowds the way Reagan did. His riff about keeping the Panama Canal prompted his audiences to go practically berserk. Weeks earlier, I'd seen Reagan drop his note cards on the floor at a luncheon speech in Joliet, Illinois, then fail to put them back in the right order. His speech that day was dreary and incoherent. He looked like a loser. But in Texas, a different Reagan had stepped front and center, the Reagan we came to know as President and world leader.

He ran off a string of primary victories—Indiana, Georgia, Alabama—that left him close to Ford in delegates at the convention in Kansas City. Political reporters, including me, could scarcely believe it. But once the Mississippi delegation, led by conservative Clarke Reed, sided with Ford, it was clear Reagan couldn't win the nomination. However, he remained a major presence at the convention, which the Ford forces resented. They were delighted when Reagan sent word he didn't want to be considered as a Vice Presidential running mate. Ford was glad not to ask.

But then one of the most amazing and emotional moments I've ever witnessed in politics occurred. Ford, accepting the nomination, gave the best speech of his entire life. But that's not the moment I'm referring to. It came when Reagan, asked to say a few words, went to the podium. Ford and his allies expected Reagan to look like a loser, a humiliated foe. He didn't once he began speaking.

I now know from Craig Shirley that Reagan spoke without notes. But it didn't seem like that was the case at the time. I thought Reagan, because he was so clear in what he was saying, must be reciting the text of what would have been his acceptance speech had he won the nomination.

The audience—fifteen thousand people or so—was rapt. Some were weeping. Nobody got up. The arena was still. And Reagan was eloquent. It was obvious the delegates were his, both the Reaganites and the Ford delegates. The Ford people were locked into backing an incumbent President of their party. But their hearts were with Reagan. In the time it took for Reagan to speak, the Republican Party escaped the clutches of its moderate establishment and fell into Reagan's lap. He lost the nomination, but won the party—and ultimately the Presidency, the country, and the world.

After the convention, the future was obvious. The nomination was Reagan's in 1980 if he wanted it. But I guess this wasn't as clear to others. Some Reaganites from the 1976 campaign urged Jack Kemp to run, figuring Reagan would be too old in 1979 to win the nomination. Several others jumped to George Bush (the father). And the press, wrong once again, grabbed onto the idea that Senator Howard Baker of Tennessee, a moderate with great skill as a legislator, would emerge as the powerhouse in the 1980 race.

The media and the political community simply didn't understand the role 1976 had played in Reagan's advance to the White House. It escaped them that Reagan had achieved credibility as a candidate, developed a fervent national following, and created a lasting political organization. Worse, what they knew for sure about Reagan—that his conservatism was too extreme for most voters—was wrong. When it came to Reagan, the political cognoscenti didn't have a clue.

That leads me to Craig Shirley and *Reagan's Revolution.* I've known Craig for two decades. He is not a journalist or an historian or a political scientist or a professional writer. He's a Washington-based political consultant who knew and understood Reagan far better than the supposed experts. Craig has also proved to be a dogged reporter and researcher and a man of rare political insight. Even now, many who've written about Reagan don't know what to make of his appeal to so many people, not just conservatives. Some still insist Reagan was a boob propped up by a clever staff. Others claim it was merely his optimism and acting skill that made him a political success. Craig knows better. He knows it was Reagan's belief in America, his deep conservative convictions, and his faith in ordinary people that catapulted him to greatness. Raw political skill? He had that too.

The centrality of 1976 to the Reagan story has never been told before. I don't know why. There are books on Reagan's years as Screen Actor's Guild President, volumes on his Governorship, and monographs and memoirs touching on every aspect of his Presidency. But 1976 proved too elusive a subject for everyone except Craig. *Reagan's Revolution* fills a huge gap in the Reagan epic. It is, in fact, the missing chapter in the life and times of Reagan. Or I should say was. Thanks to Craig, that critical chapter is no longer missing.

PREFACE

"This is our challenge."

August 19, 1976.

In the sweltering Kemper Arena in Kansas City, Gerald Ford—the incumbent but unelected President of the United States—has just accepted the Republican nomination before the assembled perspiring Republican Party delegates, alternates, and journalists. Millions more Americans are watching at home. It is late in the evening, but half the crowd in the hall is still restless.

Ford's speech, by the standards of a John F. Kennedy or a Dr. Martin Luther King or his challenger, former California Governor Ronald Reagan, is passable. But for him, it is the best political speech of his life. Indeed, it is well received by many in the crowd and a press corps accustomed to his malapropisms, mangled syntax, and star-crossed Administration of the past two years.

However, the convention and the party are not healed following the long and brutal campaign between Ford and Reagan. The battle has resulted in Ford's nomination by only fifty-seven votes more than the 1,130 required to secure the nomination. This is out of the total 2,257 ballots cast by the delegates the previous night. Reagan's narrow loss of the nomination came on the heels of losing a critical rules fight on the floor of the convention. His supporters are angry and the animosity between the two warring camps is palpable.

Ironically it is Reagan and not Ford who has won a majority of the Republican primary votes over the previous eight months: 4,616,126 to 4,481,845. Reagan garnered 50.7 percent of the total primary vote, while Ford received 49.3 percent.[1] Wrote one journalist of Reagan's ascendancy, "His candidacy has been extraordinary. He was seen by many as shallow and simplistic and even dangerous. All but a handful of Senators and Congressmen shunned him. He was opposed by nearly every state organization. He had practically no editorial support. But when it was all over, Reagan—virtually alone—had collected several hundred thousand more votes than the President in the contested primaries. The popular explanation was that his opponent Ford was dull. But Reagan on his own had surely touched a public nerve."[2]

Ford's slim margin of victory in Kansas City is even less impressive when the *force majeure* behind him is considered. His incumbency, the advantages of the White House and the Republican Party infrastructure—including the Republican National Committee, most of the state and county party leadership, most of the GOP's elected officials, and Ford's own re-election committee, the President Ford Committee—have all been thrown into the fight against the former two-term Governor of California. Reagan's campaign subsisted only through the support of a few courageous elected officials and conservative activists.

Even Reagan's old movies, shown occasionally on late-night television in local markets, have been banned from airing after the Ford Committee filed complaints with the Federal Election Commission alleging illegal corporate contributions to Reagan under the new campaign finance laws. Once Reagan had declared himself in the running, the Federal Communication Commission had barred their broadcast entirely, as they violated the "equal time" provisions.

An Iowa straw poll had been conducted on January 19. Ford prevailed over Reagan, albeit narrowly, 264 to 248. There were sixty-two undecided voters, and a smattering of votes for other Republicans.[3] The *Des Moines Register* presciently reported, "The results of the poll sent a clear message to both camps that a good many partisan battles lie ahead, before the state's 36 delegates to the Republican National Convention are chosen."[4]

Iowa Governor Robert Ray, a moderate and a Ford supporter, told the *Register*, "I don't think our caucuses have the same meaning as the Democrats [which had chosen McGovern in 1972 and Carter in 1976]."[5] Maybe not. But given the arcane and complicated system the Iowa Republicans had created to choose their delegates, they certainly acted as if they cared. The straw poll at the time meant little.

But it did initiate the protracted process of choosing local delegates to Iowa's statewide Republican convention in June, where national delegates would be elected to proceed to the Republican National Convention in Kansas City in August. On the night of the critical procedural vote, these delegates gave Reagan and Ford eighteen votes apiece. The following night, when Ford seemed sure to win the nomination, the President won nineteen of Iowa's delegates, while Reagan took seventeen.

Ford's selection of Senator Robert Dole of Kansas as his running mate, a conservative with a wit and slashing tongue, has not assuaged the bitter feelings of Reagan's passionate supporters. Recognizing his slim chances against former Georgia Governor Jimmy Carter, whom Democrats chose as their nominee for

President at an uncharacteristic love fest in New York the previous month, the President knows he also needs a unified convention. So he beckons for Reagan and Mrs. Reagan to join him and Mrs. Ford, Senator Dole, Dole's wife Elizabeth, Vice President Nelson Rockefeller, and the rest of the thin and tattered ranks of what passes for the GOP's stars assembled at the podium.

Sources differ on whether Ford's invitation to Reagan was being staged. But if it was, someone must have forgotten to tell Reagan. He initially waves Ford off, believing it is Ford's night. While there is no love lost between the two men, Reagan is respectful of the office Ford holds and knows that the spoils go to the victor. Also, Reagan isn't acting. He really has little interest in sharing a platform with the President. The previous year has been too acrimonious, too bitter, and too closely fought for either man to simply overlook their differences now. This is especially true for Reagan, who has sometimes been the brunt of personal attacks by the Ford campaign.

The animosity between the supporters of the two runs deep. Brad Minnick, a young aide to Ford's Floor Manager, Senator Robert Griffin, said, "Some of the Ford people saw Reagan . . . was out for his own gain. Ford's team had no real love for him. They resented that Reagan didn't mention Ford in his speech and that he upstaged Ford. The resentment was both personal and ideological."[6]

But Ford insists, smiling, and Reagan waves him off again. Finally, as the arena thunders with applause and shouts for Reagan, he relinquishes and makes his way to the podium, where Ford asks him to make a few comments.

The old trouper hasn't forgotten how to make an entrance.

Some of Ford's forces, while not quite hoping Reagan falls on his face, still believe that Reagan is "just an actor," incapable of giving a good speech without his notes or a prepared text. This fact would only later be learned by his pollster, Dick Wirthlin. It is not quite a setup, but they would like to see Reagan fumble a bit at the lectern. Then his armor wouldn't look so shiny to his devoted followers.[7] Even after all the months of battling Reagan down to the wire for the GOP nomination, many on Ford's team still underestimate him and hope his vaunted reputation for public speaking will pale when compared to Ford's acceptance speech, which he spent hours practicing before a videotape machine, reviewing with a phalanx of speechwriters—including two joke writers on the White House payroll. No President before that even had one on payroll; Ford had two.

Reagan has no prepared remarks, but he has always been his own best speechwriter. With his God-given Irish humor, he would never need a professional joke writer even after he became President. Arriving at the podium before a stilled and hushed crowd, Reagan proves the Ford forces not only wrong but woefully wrong.

Reagan is masterful in his extemporaneous speech, and the hall is rapt with attention. "There were so many people crying," remembers journalist Terry Wade who was on the floor that night for Donrey Newspapers. Wade wrote a column the next day with a lead reflective of Kemper Arena this night: "Ford won the nomination, but Reagan won their hearts."[8] A twenty-six-year-old conservative, Frank Donatelli, who in 1975 and 1976 organized two separate but important independent efforts in support of Reagan for the Young Americans for Freedom and Young America's Foundation said, "It was simply the most bittersweet moment of my life."[9]

Unknown to all at the time, except Reagan himself, his speech signals the end of the old GOP order and its obsession with the past. Reagan's comments are not a "concession speech," they are a rallying cry for the beleaguered GOP that points not to the past but to the future. The American public has known of Reagan for years, through his movies, on television in the 1950s, as a Governor, and as a Presidential candidate. But these remarks, broadcast live on all three networks, constitute his first real introduction to the American people. They like what they see.

On the floor of the convention, Senator Paul Laxalt, the genial son of Nevada sheepherders for whom Will Rogers would have invented his famous phrase had they ever met, turned to his daughter, Michelle, and said, "this is probably the most exciting convention of your lifetime . . . mine too."[10]

For more than a year, Laxalt had been the Chairman of the campaign committee, Citizens for Reagan, and had traveled hundreds of thousands of miles to forty-five states on Reagan's behalf. When Reagan's mood drooped, or when he needed a kick in the pants, Laxalt was his unflinching and tireless corner man. At the time, the two most important people in Reagan's life were Nancy Reagan and Paul Laxalt.

Laxalt later wrote in his memoirs, "Then, for a magical few moments, Ron delivered the finest, most moving speech I've ever heard. He spoke of the realistic aspirations of all Americans, that America should be a 'shining city on a hill.'"[11]

In his comments, Reagan speaks of writing a letter for a time capsule that people would open a hundred years hence. He says, "They will know whether or not we met our challenge. Whether we will have the freedom that we have known up until now will depend on what we do here . . . and if we fail, they probably won't get to read the letter at all because it spoke of individual freedom, and they won't be allowed to talk of this or read of it. . . . This is our challenge." Reagan also uses words like "successful," "cause," "united," "determined," and, of course, "victory."[12]

Sam Donaldson, reporting for ABC, said, "The first real emotion of the night wasn't for the ticket, but for the man who wasn't on it."[13] Kenny Klinge, a grassroots organizer for Reagan in Virginia, North Dakota, and Iowa, was standing in an aisle next to a "big-time Ford supporter from Florida" when she exclaimed, "Oh my God, we've nominated the wrong man."[14]

As Reagan addresses the awed crowd of thousands in the Kemper Arena, only his nemesis, Henry Kissinger, and Kissinger's wife are not paying attention to him—talking with each other while she smokes a cigarette.

"I can't remember another instance where the defeated candidate is given the opportunity to make a major and . . . dominating performance. The President of the United States gives the best speech he had ever given, and in fact gave in his life, and he's upstaged by his opponent," Ford's media consultant Douglas Bailey recalled.[15]

Lou Cannon, who had covered Reagan and knew him better than anyone else in the media, said the speech, "revealed very, very deep convictions . . . it gave a glimpse of what a visionary Reagan was . . . it was Reagan's heart and it set him apart."[16]

Reagan probably didn't know it, but two years prior—within days of Ford's taking office following Richard Nixon's resignation—Ford's longtime aide Robert Hartmann asked the new President which Presidential portraits he would like to hang in the Cabinet Room of the White House. Nixon had chosen paintings of both Teddy Roosevelt and Woodrow Wilson but Hartmann believed that Ford needed to start making symbolic breaks with his predecessor.

Hartmann suggested a portrait of Andrew Jackson accompany the portraits of Abraham Lincoln and Dwight D. Eisenhower. Instead, Hartmann was surprised that Ford selected the likeness of Harry S. Truman.[17] Ford saw himself as Trumanesque—a simple, everyday man from the Midwest; plainspoken and scrupulously loyal while fanatically partisan. Further, Ford thought that he, like Truman, was a man thrust into the Presidency in difficult and unprecedented times. Both men were comfortable with the past and accepting of the present. Neither gave the future much thought.

By contrast, if Reagan had been given the choice of Douglas MacArthur or Harry Truman as a role model for himself, he would have chosen MacArthur without blinking an eye. Reagan, like MacArthur, saw himself as decisive, inner-directed, unafraid to make controversial decisions, and as a leader among men who was confident in the future. It is telling that Harry Truman and Douglas MacArthur despised each other. In 1976 and for sometime thereafter, Ronald Reagan and Gerald Ford also have little use for each other.

It is no surprise then that Reagan quotes five-star General MacArthur saying, "There is no substitute for victory." The crowd goes wild with the concluding remark of his seven-minute address. Ford partisans will bitterly note later that Reagan never mentions Ford's name.

Reagan's speech is a historic and course-altering moment when the GOP parted company with its past to embrace the future.

The difference between Ford's and Reagan's speeches in Kemper Arena could be compared to the anecdote of Demosthenes and Aeschines, two Athenian orators debating the coming conflict with Sparta, also known as the Peloponnesian War, 2,500 years earlier. Aeschines delivered a well-crafted, thoughtful speech aimed at persuading his people to welcome the invaders to avoid a protracted and bloody war. The audience applauded politely and it was reported, "How well he spoke." But Demosthenes, who delivered a rousing call to arms, expounding individual liberties and freedom as inherent rights, moved the Greeks to action. When he finished speaking, the Greeks said, "Let us march."

Like Aeschines, Ford's speech was also well received and well crafted. But when Reagan concluded his inspirational remarks, the delegates would have indeed marched for him.

Gerald Ford and his party were stuck in the past.

Ronald Reagan and his party will become rooted in the future.

INTRODUCTION

*"He was the most competitive son of a b—
who ever lived."*

Dozens of books have been authored about Ronald Reagan. Indeed, since his death, a veritable flood of tomes has become widely available about the now beloved President. Interest has grown in evaluations of his life, his many careers, and his Administration.

Yet Reagan, the conservative ideologue, was not always revered. Gerald Ford derided Reagan in 1974 at a Gridiron Club dinner, saying, "Governor Reagan does not dye his hair. That's ridiculous. He is just turning prematurely orange."[1] Reagan probably laughed when he learned of Ford's comment. But others inside and outside the GOP said and thought much worse things about him at the time. And few books were being written about him.

Certainly, several books have delved into the subject of Reagan's 1976 campaign for President. Jules Witcover's outstanding book *Marathon* is one of the best on all the candidates running that year. But it was published in 1977, so Witcover could not see the long-term effect Reagan's insurgent challenge to Gerald Ford would have on the Republican Party and the country. His book was an important source for *Reagan's Revolution: The Untold Story of the Campaign That Started It All,* as was his reporting for the *Washington Post* in 1976.

Another excellent book on the entire 1976 campaign is Elizabeth Drew's *American Journal.* Drew, the Washington correspondent for the *New Yorker,* did a masterful job of recording many public events. But her book was also published in 1977 and is limited in its perspective. Longtime Reagan scribe Lou Cannon has also written a number of well-received books, including *Reagan* and several others that contain important information about the 1976 campaign and were also useful sources for this book. Furthermore, his reportage in 1976 also contained critical information.

Other books that dealt with the 1976 campaign include those by longtime

Reagan aides. Peter Hannaford's *The Reagans* was written in 1983, and Lyn Nofziger's *Nofziger* was published in 1992. Both are important insider accounts of some of the events of 1976.

Yet in most books about Reagan, his 1976 campaign is limited to a page or two. Even Reagan himself in his autobiography, *An American Life*, devoted only a few pages to his 1976 quest. This is not to say that Reagan lacked a sense of history. He and John F. Kennedy probably had the most profound sense of history of any two Presidents of the twentieth century. Reagan's little attention in *An American Life* to his 1976 campaign shows just how fiercely competitive he was. Few people understood just how much Reagan hated to lose. He simply concealed it better than other politicians. Mike Deaver, Reagan's longtime aide and friend said, "He was the most competitive son of a b— who ever lived."

"Citizens for Reagan" is the campaign that started it all. Many political scholars point to Barry Goldwater's insurgent crusade in 1964 as the beginning of the conservative movement. Others go back even further and cite Senator Robert Taft's challenge to Dwight Eisenhower at the Republican convention in 1952 as the beginning. Others still point to the now famous rally in Madison Square Garden sponsored by the nascent Young Americans for Freedom in 1962.

Each of these events was among the important turning points in the development and growth of the conservative movement. But none left such a permanent legacy as Reagan's 1976 campaign. It marked the point when conservatives took over the Republican Party and changed its message and its ideology.

Conservatism—straight and without a chaser—was considered the province of the uninformed, the uneducated, the unknowing, the unwashed, the un-understanding ("You don't understand" was a favorite patronizing putdown of conservatives by liberals in those days), the un-Harvard, the un-Yale, the un-Americans for Democratic Action, the un-*New Republic*, the un-United Nations, the un-Georgetown cocktail circuit, the un-Manhattan, the un-Beverly Hills, the "un." Conservatives were accused, as Reagan pointed out in his 1964 speech, "of always being against things, we're never for anything."

Most national elections in the twentieth century were debates over which party could best manage government. The issues dividing the two parties and the two candidates typically pertained to internationalism, how quickly or slowly to grow the federal government, who could best manage it, and how far to allow its reach to extend. These debates were never about the threat the United States government itself posed to American freedoms. It was simply not logical. Not educated. Not sophisticated. Government was good, so it was good for you. And to some, more government was even better for you.

Issues like tax cuts, the role of government in our daily lives, aggressive anti-Communism, the projection of American military power to protect American interests, abortion, cutting government spending, the Strategic Defense Initiative, and of course Reagan's appeal to national pride and patriotism might never have come to the fore as acceptable positions for the Republican Party had Reagan not run for President in 1976.

Without Reagan's 1976 campaign, Americans would not have witnessed the reordering of the two major political parties and the shift in our political universe, with one party becoming predominately conservative and the other predominately liberal. One party became suspicious of the concentration of power. The other became addicted to it.

Dr. Donald Devine, a political scientist and a member of the first Reagan Administration, observed, "The Republican Party, absent the 1976 contest, would most likely have remained a moderate 'Tory' party that never becomes a majority governing party. The Democrats would have remained the majority party, and even if the GOP wins the Presidency in 1980, it would only be because of Jimmy Carter's incompetence. . . . A rejection of Carter by the voters, and the GOP would have only become a one or two term interregnum of a natural Democratic majority political system."[2] To paraphrase political writer Samuel Lubell, the GOP would have remained the moon to the Democrat's sun.

Those who knew Reagan best say he never would have run in 1980 had he not run—and lost—in 1976. His appetite was whetted and his pride was at stake. Losing in 1976 taught Reagan how to run and win the GOP nomination in 1980, thereby initiating one of the most polarizing campaigns in American history. As noted political writer Michael Barone said, "In most American Presidential campaigns in the twentieth century, the distinctions are blurred for the most part . . . 1980 was dramatically different because the choices were so stark and clear."[3] Rarely before had the choice been so clear between two competing candidates and two competing philosophies. As Nancy Gibbs and Matthew Cooper would write in *Time* years later, "We know a legacy when we see one. Ronald Reagan not only changed the landscape when he was in office, but he had also fundamentally changed his party."[4]

As Reagan mulled whether to challenge Gerald Ford for the Republican Presidential nomination in 1975, he was not the dominant figure in the party, and his conservatism was not widely embraced by the party's leadership. Reagan's stature in the world is taken for granted today, and so is the place of conservatism as the dominant ideology in the Republican Party. But this was not the case in 1975. While conservatives were never particularly enamored of Gerald Ford, there had been a glimmer of hope that he would be some kind of ideological improvement over Richard Nixon.

But conservatives' hopes were quickly dashed. Upon becoming President, Ford grossly misread and misunderstood the mood of the Republican Party and its ever-accelerating move to the right. Nixon met with the Soviets and signed agreements, so Ford went to Vladivostok, met with Soviet Premier Leonid Brezhnev, and signed an agreement. Nixon went to China and met with Mao, so Ford went to China and met with Deng Xiaoping. Nixon filled his Cabinet with moderates and liberals, and Ford did likewise. Nixon appointed liberal, activist judges to the federal bench, including the Supreme Court, and Ford did likewise. Nixon fiddled with the economy, so Ford proposed a tax increase and the "WIN" program ("Whip Inflation Now"), which provided the nation's comedians with fodder for months.

To the consternation of conservatives, Ford also chose former New York Governor Nelson Rockefeller as his Vice President in late August of 1974, who was confirmed by the Congress later that year. Conservatives had not forgotten his petulance at the 1964 convention in San Francisco when he lost the nomination to Goldwater. Conservatives were appalled at the announcement.

Many Republicans, including Republican National Committee Chairman Mary Louise Smith, George H.W. Bush's former Deputy, thought that the party should try to "broaden the base" and "move to the middle." Reagan and other conservatives interpreted these suggestions as a rebuke of conservatism and a selling out of their ideology. Sometimes their opposition to Reagan was personal.

For example, in 1975, Roger Stone, a young aide in the office of the Young Republicans, headquartered in the building owned by the Republican National Committee, hung a studio portrait of former Governor Reagan and Mrs. Reagan, much to the chagrin of the Ford supporters in the building. Stone was told by those on high to take down the offending photo immediately—or else the funding the national party provided the Young Republicans might be cut off.[5]

In addition to opposition within his own party over his conservatism, Reagan was thought by most of the liberal intelligentsia of the media and the academy to be "unqualified" to be President. It was neither the first nor the last time he would be underestimated.

"I suspect that the Ford White House was subject to what most of Washington was, a sort of dismissing the actor from the West Coast. They thought Ronald

Reagan was purely a production of Hollywood and not a very good actor quite frankly. I don't think there was a single person . . . who understood that this was not just a talented communicator . . . or that he was an avid reader or understood what the hell he was talking about," recalled GOP consultant and Ford aide Douglas Bailey.[6]

At the higher echelons, the Republican Party was in conflict over what it stood for. Longtime Reagan friend and counselor Ed Meese told PBS in a documentary about Reagan in 2001, "There was still a big government groundswell among the liberal element, and certainly the idea of conservatism as we know it today was not something that politicians embraced very eagerly. Nor did the voting public. So in that sense, Reagan was ahead of his time."[7]

As far back as 1967, then-liberal Republicans George Gilder and Bruce Chapman had written in *The Party that Lost Its Head*,

> As before the election, the party is most deeply and bitterly split in California, the nation's largest state, where Republicanism takes its most exotic and colorful shapes. Here the far right has retained most of its former strength and most of its former illusions. Reality is to be shut out altogether as the GOP eschews the problematical and mentally taxing world of politics for the more glamorous, exhilarating, free-floating world of entertainment. This is the home of the pop-politician, ruggedly handsome, blond, alliterative, Ronald Reagan—the party's hope to usurp reality with the fading world of the class-B movie. With his more moderate colleague George Murphy victorious before him both in show biz and pol-biz; with John Wayne eager to aid in the right-wing cause; with Roy Rogers and Dale Evans ready for one last right-wing roundup; and with Air Force Brigadier General James Stewart as Sky King—the Republican Party in California has become a Hollywood retirement home, where the stars of the past re-create in politics the fictitious glories of their antic youths."[8]

Such criticisms continued throughout the course of Reagan's political career.

At the 1976 Republican National Convention in Kansas City, Connecticut Republican Senator Lowell P. Weicker Jr. told the *Washington Post*, "As far as I'm concerned, I don't think what they're doing in Kansas City represents the Republican Party. They're not speaking for the party. They're destroying it." Added Glenn S. Gerstell, then president of the liberal Republican Ripon Society, conservatives had their "head in the sand" and would "push through their proposals regardless of the potential effect on the GOP's fortunes with the electorate."[9] The fight had been ongoing for some time inside the party, and its outcome and the victor would become clear shortly after 1976.

Reagan's Revolution; The Untold Story of the Campaign That Started It All is the comprehensive history of how Ronald Reagan's narrow and improbable loss to Gerald Ford for the 1976 Republican Presidential nomination changed the conservative movement, the Republican Party, America, and eventually the world.

Today, the conservative movement is a vibrant, respected, and far flung enterprise, encompassing political organizations, think tanks, publications, newsletters, cable television networks, authors, columnists, publishing houses, talk radio hosts, a significant presence on the Internet, and a myriad of other concerns.

Today, all Republicans are "Reagan Republicans," as Reagan's definition of "maximum freedom consistent with law and order" has become the basis of the party's philosophy. Furthermore, Reagan unleashed the most vigorous debates over the role of government in Americans' daily lives since the founding of the Republic. These debates and the ensuing transformation of the Republican Party started with Reagan's seemingly quixotic but most important campaign: his failed 1976 Presidential campaign.

Today, the Warsaw Pact no long exists. Today, the Soviet Union no longer exists. Today, millions of people across the globe live in freedom. Today, democratic capitalism is the accepted governing model the world over.

And much of this, if not most, is due to Ronald Reagan.

1

THE BEGINNING OF THE END

"Republicans are people too!"

By the late summer of 1974, the Republican Party was in its death throes. Bereft, bedraggled, unloved, and unwanted, it stood for nothing and antagonized everyone. If the GOP had been a stray cat, it would have been hauled away to the animal shelter and immediately euthanized—no one would have claimed it.

The many psychological problems of the Republican Party would have baffled a convention of psychiatrists—not that they would have wanted to cure the GOP anyway. It suffered from multiple personality disorder, an inferiority complex, delusions of persecution, and was committing slow suicide. The headquarters for this party of losers, the Republican National Committee on Capitol Hill in Washington, D.C., had actually produced buttons that idiotically proclaimed, "Republicans Are People Too!" As if to remove all doubt about the Republicans' insecurities and cowardice, the buttons were manufactured in a bright yellow.

Had there been a national referendum to institute a bounty on the heads of the few remaining Republican office holders, it probably would have passed overwhelmingly. In fact, one Republican who did have a bounty on his head at the time was mass murderer, Ted Bundy, the "Deliberate Stranger" who had once been a volunteer in several GOP campaigns in Washington State.

Laboring side by side in the bowels of the Republican National Committee were two junior staffers: Gary Bauer, who would go on to work for Ronald Reagan and later still become an important voice in the Christian Right, and Rita Carpenter who would go on to her own sort of fame by having sex with her husband, Democratic Congressman John Jenrette, on the steps of the U.S. Capitol and writing about it in a steamy memoir, *My Capitol Secrets*. After their marriage, Congressman Jenrette became ensnared in an FBI sting and went to jail. Mrs. Jenrette parlayed his misery into fifteen more minutes of fame. She also posed nude for *Playboy* (her own interpretation of "the body politic"), a stunt that would become a rite of passage for infamous women who were clinging and clamoring for attention. The Bauer/Jenrette dichotomy seemed to sum up the schizophrenic nature of the Republican Party.[1]

Talk was rampant among the burgeoning "New Right" that the Republican Party was through and what was needed was a new, third political party. Some of the "New Rightists" thought they had been badly treated by the country clubbers that made up the GOP, so a certain amount of payback was involved. Many conservatives had a chip on the shoulder when it came to the GOP.

Their desire to walk away made some sense. Conservatives had money, principles, energy, drive, organization, and—most important—ideas. The Republican Party had a humiliated ex-Vice President in seclusion, a President about to be driven from office, and the tattered remains of a once great party that included many liberals like Senator Jacob Javits of New York at one end and a few conservatives like Senator Jesse Helms of North Carolina at the other. These two Senators had virtually nothing in common except maybe that they both enjoyed the Navy Bean Soup in the Senate Dining Room. As for conservatives, they were held in "minimum high regard" by moderates in the party or, as long-time journalist Ralph Hallow noted, "No one respected conservatives at the time."[2] Yet, "Movement conservatives [Bill] Rusher, [William F.] Buckley, [Richard] Viguerie, Reagan, et al. were getting the upper hand. In Nixon's absence, especially, the initiatives of the early seventies were coming under attack," wrote Herbert Parmet.[3]

After Nixon's resignation, according to the Gallup organization, Republican Party identification continued to decline for the two years of Gerald Ford's Presidency while the Democrats continued to build on their two-to-one lead.[4]

The Democrats also had their ideological extremes, but they did have one core philosophy that had held them together since the 1930s: the spoils system. Office holders and bureaucrats took part in handing out federal, state, and local largess—from milk subsidies to tobacco allotments to federal appointments to contracts to largess for the cities—to people of all ideologies, all races, all creeds, and all regions. Their organizing principle had evolved into a finely tuned machine fed by power and money that would stanch a lot of wounds inside the Democratic Party.

Patronage was the glue that had held the Democrats together. Despite their accused image of "Rum, Romanism, and Rebellion," despite their quadrennial brawls, despite all their ideological, racial, cultural, and regional differences, the Democrats could always be counted on to circle the wagons in the end to protect the system that had enriched so many. They obediently followed the supposed advice of one of the less reputable popes, who upon ascension during the Dark Ages said, "Now that we have the Papacy, let us enjoy it."

The Republicans had nothing to hold them together. Through Nixon's criminal behavior and through his pursuit of liberal policies—including Keynesian economics, détente (which conservatives saw as Soviet appeasement), overtures to Communist China, abandoning Southeast Asia, cuts in defense spending, increasing social spending, appointing liberal jurists, instituting wage and price controls—the party had made a lot of enemies and alienated would-be friends.

Following Nixon's resignation in August of 1974 and Gerald Ford's pardon of the ex-President, the Republican Party was decimated in the fall elections. "In state after state after state, it was just wipeout time. It was a very depressing period," recalled GOP ad man Doug Bailey.[5] Watergate may not have bothered Lynyrd Skynyrd, but it did everybody else. Voters threw out dozens of Republican legislators in 1974. The GOP lost forty-three Representatives and four Senators in the off-year elections.[6]

By the spring of 1976, the Republican Party had only thirty-eight U.S. Senators who could not even mount an effective filibuster. In the House, they were outnumbered by better than two to one. Only thirteen of the nation's fifty Governors were Republicans. The state legislatures were even worse. In the summer of 1976, the *New York Times* wrote an editorial that reflected the prevailing thought at the time:

> There is one way, it seems to us, in which the Republicans could dig their own political grave for 1976 as surely as anything can be done in American politics. That is by capitulating to the far right wing of the party that forms the core support of Governor Reagan in his quest for the nomination. To put it in the crudest political terms, the far right of the G.O.P. has no place to go; yet the nomination of Governor Reagan for the Presidency (or, for that matter, even the Vice Presidency on a Ford ticket) would surely alienate the most important centrist and liberal segments of the Republican Party, without whose support it could not conceivably achieve national success.[7]

It was no wonder that many thought the GOP would go the way of the Whigs, and many conservatives wanted a new third party—one that could appeal to conservatives from both the Democrats and the Republicans. "We had commissioned Bob Teeter to do a poll for us after the 1974 off year elections," Ladonna Lee recalled. Lee was an assistant to Eddie Mahe, the Executive Director of the RNC. "Teeter didn't want to bring the results to Washington . . . too hot to handle. The results were devastating."[8]

Republicans, it seemed, could only win the Presidency when Democrats screwed up, as in 1968 and 1972, or when they nominated a popular war hero like Eisenhower.

America, from the time of Franklin Roosevelt on, was ideologically a conservative majority country. But politically, it was a Democratic Party majority country. Democrats were much more unified than Republicans, generally favoring government as the solution to the problems that Americans faced. Republicans were more schizophrenic; some of the more moderate and liberal elements supported government activism, while the more conservative elements opposed government action and favored a smaller centralized government and more freedom for the individual.

FDR had made the Democratic Party, through the New Deal and World War II, secure in the belief that government was the solution. Republicans really offered no alternative or choice for the American people except a watered-down version of what their counterparts were telling voters. In fact, it was FDR's political aide, Harry Hopkins, who had coined the phrase, when it came to the Democrats, "Tax and tax, spend and spend, elect and elect." The Republican rejoinder appeared to be, "Tax less than the other guys, spend less than the other guys, and elect less than the other guys."

Still, a small but growing chorus of conservatives within the GOP had expressed grave and growing concern over governmental power and its abuses. Historically, from Benjamin Disraeli to Ronald Reagan, conservatives came to their philosophy based on thousands of years of witnessing the abuses of concentrated, centralized power. From the pharaohs to Caesar to illicit popes in the Dark Ages to the English Monarchy to the Kremlin, conservatives had a well-founded suspicion about those who would have too much power; a healthy fear of the rule of men over the rule of law.

Since the late 1940s, the party had housed two competing personalities, with conservatives battling liberals in a pretty much perpetual state of equilibrium. In 1948, New York Governor Thomas Dewey, a moderate, won the Presidential nomination but lost the election to President Harry S. Truman. Truman was not a very good campaigner, but Dewey was even worse, offering nothing as an alternative to the "New Deal" and "Fair Deal" politics of the previous sixteen years. Truman also campaigned hard against the "do-nothing Congress" temporarily seized by Republicans in the 1946 off-year elections. Truman won convincingly over Dewey and ushered the Democrats back into control of Congress.

The debate between the two wings of the GOP picked up steam in the wake of the defeat. As historian Lewis Gould wrote,

> After Dewey's loss, the conservative and moderate wings of the party argued about the cause of the 1948 debacle in a debate that raged for another decade . . . Dewey himself contended in a speech that same month that the Republicans could not win national elections if they joined those "who honestly oppose farm price supports, unemployment insurance, old age benefits, slum clearance, and other social programs." Should the Republicans come out against these measures, "you can bury the Republican party as the deadest pigeon in the country." The Republicans allied with Dewey's point of view made speeches while the conservatives and their supporters worked at the grass roots to reaffirm their dominance within the party. Liberal Republicanism in its twentieth-century form always had an air of electoral expediency rather than real conviction about it. As a result, that faction's hold on the GOP was more tenuous than it seemed.[9]

The 1948 election also saw the victory of Gerald Ford for a House seat in Grand Rapids, Michigan, after he defeated an incumbent conservative Republican in the primary. Ford had been a football star at Michigan, a Yale law graduate, a war hero, and was married to an attractive former fashion model.

At the 1952 Republican National Convention, moderate Dwight D. Eisenhower defeated conservative darling Senator Robert Taft of Ohio, "Mr. Republican," who ironically had been tagged by the "can't win" label by two-time loser Dewey. Eisenhower won the nomination by successfully challenging Taft delegates' credentials, and he knew he needed to unify the party. So he chose the thirty-nine-year-old "Red-baiting" Senator from California, Richard M. Nixon—known to his friends as "Dick" and to his enemies as "Tricky Dick."

Republicans swept into office and took control of the White House and both houses of Congress for the first time in decades. Democratic Massachusetts Congressman John F. Kennedy had successfully fought the rising Eisenhower tide and defeated liberal Senator Henry Cabot Lodge, who was running for re-election. Kennedy's uphill win in the Republican state of Massachusetts put him on the national stage and began what would be his successful drive for the White House in 1960.

Republicans' success at gaining control of the Congress in 1952 was an anomaly. Two years later, Republicans would lose control of Congress and not regain it for forty years. The GOP won because of Ike's popularity, because of voters' dismay over the Korean War, because of President Truman's low standing with the American people and because the Democrats nominated a liberal egghead from Illinois, Governor Adlai Stevenson, as their candidate. Stevenson made his contempt known for the little people in various ways. Once while campaigning, a woman exclaimed to Stevenson, "All the intelligent people are voting for you!" To which he replied, "Yes ma'am, but I need a majority." His supporters also derided Ike by saying that he could not read if his lips were chapped.

By 1960, the sometime conservative Nixon, now the nominee of the Republican Party, picked Lodge as his running mate, after being prodded by Nelson Rockefeller into doing so—a curious choice because Lodge was the one man whom John Kennedy had defeated in political combat.

The best example of the problems of the Republican Party by 1960 were illustrated by one simple fact: at the Republican National Convention in Chicago, the party selected as a featured speaker former President Herbert Hoover, who had been run out of town on a rail twenty-eight years earlier and whose Presidency signaled the end of the era of Republican dominance in American politics. The GOP was the party of the past, the "eat your spinach" party. The Democrats were more fun, more intellectual, more relevant, more popular, and more interesting.

Also adding to conservatives' angst, around the time of the convention, Richard Nixon, the Vice President of the United States, the presumptive Presidential nominee of the Republican Party met in New York with Governor Nelson Rockefeller. Together, they produced the "Compact of Fifth Avenue" which steered the party and its nominee leftward in exchange for Rockefeller's support of the ticket. Arizona Senator Barry Goldwater, who never needed a map to find the jugular vein, said that if the compact became part of the GOP platform it "will live in history as the Munich of the Republican Party."[10]

Rockefeller symbolized everything that grassroots Republicans, becoming increasingly conservative, despised about the other wing of the party. Gould wrote,

> The problem was that Rockefeller seemed to think that his money and celebrity appeal entitled him to leadership and he made little secret of his disdain for the opinions of rank-and-file Republicans. Dominant in New York where his money and a divided Democratic Party helped him, Rockefeller was not a very good national politician. Along with indecision went a tin ear for Republican attitudes, and his casual approach to his wedding vows compounded his problems. But through an array of publicists and sympathetic journalists, he could make noise about Republican issues whenever he chose.[11]

The concession to Rockefeller angered both Eisenhower and Goldwater. Given their opposing views of Republicanism, this was no small feat. At the convention,

Goldwater's name was placed in nomination for Vice President, and he took the podium to decline the opportunity to be considered as a candidate. But he did initiate a sensational and prophetic moment in the history of the conservative movement and the Republican Party. Said Goldwater, "This great Republican Party is our historic house. This is our home."[12] And addressing those who had placed his name in nomination, the Arizonan said, "Let's grow up, conservatives. If we want to take this party back, and I think we can some day, let's go to work."[13] Four years later, Goldwater and his grassroots legions would do precisely that, much to the dismay of the "Eastern Elite" wing of the Republican Party.

In the 1960 general election campaign, John Kennedy saw a high-hanging fastball and hit it out of the park. Kennedy successfully tapped into the vein in the American electorate that was gravely concerned about the Soviet threat. He positioned himself to Nixon's right on the issue of anti-Communism, scorching his former House and Senate colleague over the rise of Fidel Castro, defending Quemoy and Matsu, and the "missile gap" where Kennedy accused the Eisenhower Administration of allowing the United States to fall behind the Soviet Union. Continuing the tradition of the Democratic Party as the party of the future and the party of "Happy Days Are Here Again," Kennedy also zapped Nixon as he urged the need "to get this country moving again."

In 1964, Kennedy's unlikely friend, Barry Goldwater, began the slow process of redefining the Republican Party—and hence the Democratic Party as well. Goldwater eschewed the traditional "ticket balancing" act embraced by Nixon and Eisenhower and picked a little known but equally conservative Congressman and Chairman of the Republican National Committee from Upstate New York, Bill Miller. In choosing Miller, Goldwater gave moderates and liberals little reason to stay in the party and a mass exodus occurred. Goldwater lost in a landslide to Lyndon Johnson. But he also began to attract conservative Democrats to the GOP, thus upsetting its equilibrium between conservatives and liberals.

Liberals like New York Mayor John Lindsay would eventually become Democrats, while Democrats, like South Carolina Senator Strom Thurmond and former Texas Governor John Connally, would become Republicans. Thereafter, Democrats would only nominate tickets that were either left of center or slightly left of center while Republicans would only nominate tickets that were either right of center or slightly right of center. It is instructive to remember that Ronald Reagan, perhaps seeing the handwriting on the wall, switched parties before Goldwater was nominated.

When asked later why he chose Miller, Goldwater said, "because he bugs Johnson." But someone who bugged conservatives more than Lyndon Johnson was Rockefeller. For years conservatives in the party had gagged on nominees like Wendell Wilkie, Tom Dewey, and, to a lesser extent, Dwight Eisenhower and Richard Nixon. Now, when conservatives actually won the Presidential nomination for one of their own, they had expected the moderates to "suck it up" and support their side as they had supported the other side. But they had no such luck in 1964. Rockefeller, New York Senator Jacob Javits, Pennsylvania Governor Bill Scranton, and other moderate-to-liberal Republicans took a walk on Goldwater. Conservatives would never forget nor forgive the traitorous Rockefeller. Bill Schulz, a founding member of the Young Americans for Freedom said, "Conservatives had always been good sports, rallying behind Eisenhower. Here was a situation where major figures of the party were not supporting the nominee."[14]

One major Republican figure did emerge unscathed from the 1964 Goldwater debacle: Reagan. He had given a nationally televised speech on behalf of the Republican nominee, and this introduced him to the American people as a conservative spokesman. Goldwater had initially opposed Reagan's giving the half-hour appeal. The Goldwater campaign wanted to bring in an outsider to make pitches for their candidate in California. But Holmes Tuttle—a California auto dealer, Goldwater supporter, and later a member of the now famous "Reagan Kitchen Cabinet"—resisted, telling the campaign he "had someone in California who could make those speeches." Tuttle's support for Reagan meant the campaign required him to provide the money for the speech.

The address Reagan delivered was billed as "A Time for Choosing," and a later record album of the address was called "Rendezvous with Destiny." As far as history is concerned, it is now simply known as "The Speech." Reagan's address raised millions for the Goldwater campaign and was described by many political scribes as the one bright spot in an otherwise bleak campaign.

In his own peculiar show of gratitude, Goldwater returned the favor years later when he endorsed Gerald Ford over Reagan in the 1976 GOP Presidential primaries. In fact, some years after Reagan left the Presidency and Goldwater had retired from the Senate, a documentary producer went to Arizona to interview Goldwater about Reagan's legacy. Goldwater answered just about every question by starting out, "Well you know he was just an actor . . ."[15]

Although Nixon tried to pull strings behind the scenes at the Republican National Convention in San Francisco to wrest the Presidential nomination away from Goldwater, the Arizonan had the delegates' hearts, minds, and votes. But Nixon did hit the trail for Goldwater and probably campaigned harder than any other national Republican figure in 1964, save Goldwater himself. Goldwater took note and would not forget his sometime friend's efforts. He had gotten over his animosity toward Nixon and was deeply appreciative of Nixon's tireless work after many moderate and liberal Republicans had abandoned him.

Despite Goldwater's triumph at the Cow Palace in San Francisco in 1964, his nomination did not immediately herald a new era for the GOP—especially in Washington. For many years before and after 1964, liberal and moderate Republican Senators met on Capitol Hill each week for lunch at what was called "The Wednesday Club." In 1967, following the GOP's midterm comeback, a large number of newly elected Senators joined with the incumbent Republican Senators to propose new government programs and controls while denouncing conservatives in the party as a "minority of a minority." Senators attending included Hugh Scott and Richard Schweiker of Pennsylvania, Chuck Percy of Illinois, Margaret Chase Smith of Maine, Ed Brooke of Massachusetts, Jacob Javits of New York, Charles Mathias of Maryland, Clifford Case of New Jersey, and Lowell Weicker of Connecticut, among others. In the 1960s and into the mid-seventies, the Wednesday Club was considered by many to be an important incubator for GOP progressive thought. Today, The Wednesday Club no longer exists. Without Reagan's 1976 challenge of the incumbent but unelected Ford, the Republican Party would most likely have continued its leftward drift.

Goldwater lost in a landslide due to the harshness of rhetoric, but also because of Lyndon Johnson's dirty campaign and the memory of a martyred President. Still, conservatives knew the Goldwater effort wasn't meaningless. The effort, for the first time, introduced real, conservative solutions to the problems faced by Americans.

The Republican National Committee, which previously had a direct mail house file of only 40,000 names, had over 600,000 direct mail contributors by the time of Goldwater's loss. Yet the elected leadership of the GOP was moving to the center, and GOP candidates running in 1966 did not run as the children of Goldwater. By and large, they ran as traditional Republicans who were defenders of the status quo. The one notable exception was the new Governor elected in California.

Reagan had won in a landslide primary over his liberal opponent, San Francisco Mayor George Christopher, and defeated incumbent Democrat Edmund G. "Pat" Brown in the general election by over a million votes. Brown had handily defeated Richard Nixon four years earlier, nearly destroying Nixon's political fortunes.

In both the primary and general election, Reagan continued to hammer at the existing order and hone the same message he had used in campaigning for Goldwater two years earlier. 1966 was a comeback year for the GOP, but not because of ideology or because the party was moving in a new direction. Instead, it was somewhat of a backlash year against then President Johnson. More importantly, GOP voters who had voted for Johnson in 1964 or did not participate in that election returned to the fold, voting in their natural and normal patterns for an off-year election.

Brown's campaign, misunderstanding Reagan's appeal, ran half-hour commercials of Brown, which included the Governor's telling a group of assembled schoolchildren, "and don't forget, it was an actor who shot Lincoln."[16] California voters were appalled, including Dan Blocker, who played Hoss Cartwright on the popular show *Bonanza.* Blocker renounced his endorsement of Brown, and Lyn Nofziger of the Reagan campaign did everything he could to exacerbate Brown's impolitic predicament with the media.

Separate from the Republican Party, an intellectual and political "conservative movement" was developing, though still in the nascent stages. In 1960, the Young Americans for Freedom was founded. Richard Viguerie, just starting his direct mail company, wrote to Reagan asking him to sign fundraising letters for YAF. Weeks passed with no reply, and Viguerie forgot about it until one day when he opened his mail. Viguerie found a crumpled copy of his letter to Reagan with a note from Reagan saying he would be delighted to help out. Reagan then sheepishly explained that he had found the letter in his son's toy box.[17]

These conservatives eschewed party labels and had wide and varying opinions on many issues. But on one issue, they were in firm agreement: all were staunch anti-Communists. This developing movement went largely unnoticed by the national media. When they did try to work with the Republican Party, they were treated like the hired help, as many of its established and influential organizations were decidedly liberal. Similar in influence to the Wednesday Club, the Ripon Society, the standard-bearing organization for liberals within the party, was flush with cash and oversaw many policy debates and decisions. Yet conservatives saw their influence grow steadily.

Almost immediately after Goldwater's loss, Nixon started plotting his comeback for 1968. He recounted the events following the 1964 election in his autobiography *RN: The Memoirs of Richard Nixon*:

> Goldwater took his defeat with grace, and Johnson resisted what must have been a great temptation to crow over his landslide. It was Nelson Rockefeller who tried to turn the disaster to his own advantage. The day after the election, he issued a statement aimed at reading Goldwater and

> his followers—and, by indirection, those like me who had supported Goldwater—out of the party. I had intended to make no comment on the results until after a "cooling-off" period, but Rockefeller's attack changed my mind.
>
> On November 5, I held a press conference. I complimented Goldwater saying he had fought courageously against great odds. I said that those who had divided the party in the past could now not expect to unite it in the future. At the end, I pulled out all the stops and said that Rockefeller was a spoilsport and a divider, and that there now was so much antipathy to him among Republicans throughout the country that he could no longer be regarded as a party leader anywhere outside New York.[18]

The Republican Party was changing dramatically beneath the surface during the mid-1960s. It was becoming more suburban and rural, more middle class, more blue-collar, and definitely more conservative. Nixon saw this trend before most others in the GOP.

Anyone who underestimated the resiliency of Nixon did so at his peril. Nixon carefully observed and understood the changes that were going on inside the GOP at the time. In preparation for another try at the White House following Goldwater's loss, Nixon had learned from two of his own losses: in 1960 to Kennedy and in 1962 to Pat Brown for Governor of California. In 1960, Kennedy got to his right on anti-Communism. In 1962, Nixon had faced a conservative primary opponent, Joe Shell, the Republican leader in the California State Assembly. Shell drew a surprising 36 percent of the vote and weakened Nixon for the fall election. Nixon knew if he were to win the nomination of an increasingly conservative party in 1968, he couldn't let another candidate get to his right. And if he was going to win the general election in 1968, no one was going to get to his right in that battle either.

In fact, Nixon had almost always been in good stead with the grassroots conservatives in the party. His aggressive pursuit of Alger Hiss and public comments about Julius and Ethel Rosenberg, his work with the House Un-American Activities Committee, his defeat of Helen Gahagan Douglas—wife of leftist actor Melvin Douglas—for the U.S. Senate seat in California in 1950, and his famous "Kitchen Debate" with Nikita Khrushchev, had all earned him the chops necessary to be acceptable to the American Right. And Nixon always talked a tough talk—bashing commies, liberals, and others whom he had once called members of the "Cowardly College of Communist Containment." The conservatives who made up the base of the Republican Party in the 1950s and 1960s generally liked

Dick Nixon. The same could not always be said about the leadership of various conservative groups.

Nixon undertook his spadework with the American Right beginning in 1965. He met with conservative groups, individuals, and writers. He also hired a young editorial writer from the *St. Louis Globe-Democrat* named Patrick J. Buchanan. Buchanan was a committed conservative who possessed a stiletto for a pen and a bellicose public manner that was belied by a genuine private shyness and sincerity. Nixon also hired a talented young lawyer from Indiana, Tom Charles Huston, who shared his understanding of the importance of conservatism in the context of the Republican Party. Goldwater's early endorsement of Nixon in 1965 for the 1968 nomination clearly helped Nixon's cause with the Right.

Nixon continued to work assiduously for the 1968 GOP nomination. The "New Nixon" model, which was unveiled in 1966, contained one interesting and telling change. For virtually his entire political career, he was referred to in public and private as "Dick Nixon." He even signed letters, "Dick Nixon." But the repackaged product became known as "Richard M. Nixon."

Roger Stone, a GOP consultant, had known Nixon for years and would later befriend the old President during his years of seclusion and derision. Stone helped with Nixon's partially successful reemergence after Watergate and was once asked by an acquaintance to ask Nixon to autograph four magazines featuring Nixon on the cover. Stone complied and several weeks later returned the magazines to his friend. But much to his surprise, only two of the four were autographed. "What gives?" asked the friend. Stone replied, "The two he autographed were from his Presidency and the two he didn't were from his Vice Presidency. Nixon totally blacked out that period in his life. He then thought of himself as 'Dick Nixon, political hatchet man.' But after that, it was 'Richard M. Nixon, World Statesman.' And only people who knew him from that period were allowed to call him 'Dick' and only to people from that era would he sign his name 'Dick.'"[19]

By 1968, Nixon had both a new image and the lion's share of conservative support heading into the Republican National Convention in Miami Beach.

Despite their ideological differences, Nelson Rockefeller and Ronald Reagan worked together to try to stop Nixon's nomination. As fellow Governors of the two most populous states, they were actually good friends who could cooperate when it served their purposes. Rockefeller and Reagan disagreed with each other's politics, and each thought his own ideology was best for the future of the GOP. But both men shared a deep concern about Nixon; they saw him as a deeply flawed man who had the capacity to wreck the party. While it was apparent that

Nixon was on his way to a first ballot nomination, both men floated eleventh hour candidacies, if only to stop Nixon. "For a 'rigid' and 'unimaginative' ideologue, Reagan could be quite pragmatic and obviously ambitious when it suited his purposes," said David Keene, a key aide in Reagan's eventual 1976 bid.[20]

Although Reagan and Rockefeller both held out hope of a brokered convention and worked behind the scenes to stop Nixon on the first ballot, they did not succeed. Ultimately, Nixon won the blessings of the delegates. And when the Wisconsin delegation put Nixon over the top, Reagan went to the lectern at the convention and asked the delegates to make Nixon's nomination unanimous. The California Governor's 1968 attempt to win the Republican nomination was ill-conceived, ill-timed, and too little, too late. Conservatives from Bill Buckley to Strom Thurmond were already supporting Nixon.

The result was never really in doubt. Liberal columnists had trumpeted the sometimes panting, sometimes Hamlet-like Rockefeller, Governor George Romney of Michigan, and Pennsylvania's Governor Bill Scranton. But all of them were, of course, liberals from the moderate Tom Dewey wing of the party. They were the essence of the "Me Too Republicans." They were Republicans who never really had any quarrel with the size or growth of government or higher taxes and never worried too much about Soviet expansionism. They were often proponents of a larger role of the state in the affairs of Americans. They favored higher taxes as a means to pay for that bigger state and were more interested in promoting trade with the Soviets than worrying about Russian missiles pointed at their children's and grandchildren's heads. Their main argument was simply that they could manage government better than their Democratic counterparts.

Conservatives were disappointed that Nixon chose the little known, moderately conservative Governor of Maryland, Spiro Agnew, as his running mate. But Agnew fit the bill for Nixon. He was a border state Governor who would not cause Nixon to look over his shoulder. Nixon remembered the insults Eisenhower piled on him when he was Vice President, and he confided to a campaign insider at the 1968 convention that he wanted to run without a Vice President.[21] He had nothing but funerals and presiding over the Senate in mind for his running mate. Nixon wanted someone who would mind his Ps and Qs and not cause him any concerns.

Nixon won the Presidency that fall by the narrowest of margins over Democratic nominee Vice President Hubert H. Humphrey of Minnesota and Alabama Governor George Wallace, who ran as an independent on the American Party ticket. John Mitchell, Nixon's law partner, friend, and incoming Attorney General, famously told reporters, "watch what we do, not what we say." Nervous conservative leaders, who had often been suspicious of the new President-elect over the years, planned on watching Richard Nixon too.

2

AWAKENING AMBITIONS

"No pale pastels."

Neither Ronald Reagan nor his most passionate conservative supporters could simply will him into the Presidential campaign of 1976. A fateful path had to first be cleared through the wilderness.

Richard Nixon's first term, beginning in 1969, was mostly a disaster for conservatives. His relations with the leadership of the conservative movement went from qualified support to grudging suspicion to outright hostility within the first three years of his Administration. The dam broke in 1971 when Daniel Patrick Moynihan, a liberal Democrat and Nixon White House aide, proposed to Nixon a federally mandated, minimum guaranteed household income—the very essence of socialism. Nixon, always trying to curry the favor of the liberal intelligentsia, agreed to the proposal.

This was too much for conservatives. A group of them met in Manhattan at the townhouse of Bill Buckley, founder and editor of the fortnightly *National Review.* The result of the meeting was a letter signed by what became known as the "Manhattan Twelve," which included activist Jeff Bell, Tom Winter of *Human Events,* Buckley, and others. They sent their letter to President Nixon and signaled the conservatives' intention to break with him and suspend their support in his re-election campaign.[1] But the cynical old politician knew he had "spoons" in his pocket with the grassroots right of the party to protect him against any primary challenge in 1972. The Manhattan Twelve wanted to make a point and launched the campaign of Congressman John Ashbrook of Ohio.

Ashbrook was a well-respected, solid conservative with the courage to challenge Nixon in the primaries. The effort was admirable but quixotic. Nixon administered a quick kill to the Ashbrook insurgency. Nonetheless, the campaign was important because it marked another struggle impelled by conservatives' desire to reshape the Republican Party. If they failed, they were quite willing to leave it and form a new political party. But a third party was not a realistic option in 1972.

Despite the leftward movement of the Republican Party leadership, the Democrats were moving even faster to the left, as evidenced by their nomination of the ultra-liberal George McGovern of South Dakota. Their party's platform in 1972 called for each American's inheritance to be limited, with the vast balance going to the government for "redistribution." The 1972 edition of the Democrats may have been the most pro-collectivism, anti-free enterprise political party since the American Socialist Party. McGovern's odd collection of malcontents truly made them the party of "acid, amnesty, and abortion" as Republicans chided.

Nixon trounced McGovern in the November election. The embarrassment at the Democratic Convention over McGovern's Vice Presidential choice of Senator Tom Eagleton of Missouri, who had failed to tell McGovern prior to coming aboard the ticket that he had been institutionalized in a mental hospital and undergone electro-shock therapy, paired with McGovern's extremist views made it easy to see why President Nixon, campaigning on peace and prosperity, carried forty-nine states with the notable exception of Massachusetts.[2]

With the easy re-election of Nixon and Agnew, it looked in the early days of 1973 as if Ronald Reagan's political career would end in Sacramento. Spiro Agnew was the man of the hour who made conservatives' hearts go pitter-patter. While Reagan too was liked by conservatives nationally, it was Agnew who had taken it to the Eastern Establishment and the liberal media. "Agnew was more esteemed than Reagan in 1973. Reagan hadn't pursued a national agenda at the time. And Agnew was hated by liberals," said Bill Schulz, a conservative of long standing who later would help edit Gerald Ford's autobiography while working as Washington Bureau Chief of *Reader's Digest*.[3]

Agnew had already begun his move to the right while Governor of Maryland, partially because the race riots of the 1960s and because the militant leadership of the Democratic Party appalled him. Like Nixon before him, Agnew had done his homework on the evolution of the GOP and came to realize that as a conservative Vice President in a liberal Nixon Administration, he would be viewed as the Right's oasis in the liberal desert of Washington.

In several speeches written for him by Pat Buchanan and William Safire, the Vice President lashed out against liberal editorial writers of the major newspapers, labeling them as an "effete corps of impudent snobs" and "nattering nabobs of negativism."[4] Agnew thus tapped into that raw nerve of "chip-on-the-shoulder-conservatives," who deeply resented the intellectual Left.

Agnew met regularly with conservatives, soliciting their advice and listening to their complaints about Nixon. He knew that Nixon wanted him off the ticket in 1972 in favor of Treasury Secretary John Connally, who had recently switched parties. So it served Agnew's ambitions to be the one defiantly conservative member of the Nixon Administration, as he knew conservatives would have gone ballistic had Nixon booted him off the ticket. Despite Nixon's preference for Connally, as 1976 Reagan strategist Roger Stone said, "The Republicans are a 'royalist party,' and Agnew was next in line."[5]

David Keene, an aide to Agnew at the time, said succinctly, "Agnew was the 800 pound gorilla. Nobody was going to stop Agnew from getting the nomination. No one, that is, except himself."[6] But neither Agnew nor Reagan nor their supporters could predict the political "perfect storm" that was about to envelop Washington and the Republican Party over the next two years. Unforeseen events were about to change the entire country's political landscape and alter for good or ill the political fortunes of men and women everywhere, especially Ronald Reagan.

The circumstances surrounding Watergate are well-documented as was their astonishing outcome. But one small, alleged event has never been reported to this day. And had things been different, Nixon, Agnew, Ford, Reagan, and America may well have been part of a drastically altered future.

On Friday, June 16, 1972—the night of the Watergate break-in—a uniformed police officer abandoned patrol of his assigned area, which included the Watergate Complex where the headquarters of the Democratic National Committee were located.[7] The officer went to a favorite watering hole for a drink—many drinks as it turned out. The co-owner of the establishment, which was a "swinging singles" bar at the time, recalled hearing from his brother bartender that the officer was drinking bourbon and Coke.[8]

Late into the evening, the police officer's handheld radio blared for him with an alert from the police dispatcher, ordering him to investigate curious goings on in the Watergate Complex. Frank Wills, the twenty-four-year-old security guard on duty at the time, reported the suspicious activity at the hotel to the D.C. police.[9] Too inebriated to respond, the officer—at the bartender's suggestion—radioed back that he was low on gas and proceeded to tell the dispatcher to send back-up.[10]

Around 2:00 Saturday morning the backup police officers arrived at the Watergate—the three undercover cops dressed as civilians, driving a beat-up car, were Sergeant Paul Leper and Officers John Barret and Carl Shollfer.[11] The spotter for the burglars, in the hotel across from the Watergate Complex, did not notify the team by walkie-talkie that a car containing three harmless "civilians" had arrived in front of the Watergate.

The "civilians," accompanied by Wills, made the famous arrest of the five Watergate burglars around 2:30 A.M. on June 17, 1972. "They were surprised at gunpoint by three plain-clothes officers of the metropolitan police department in a sixth-floor office at the plush Watergate . . . where the Democratic National Committee occupies the entire floor," wrote *Washington Post* police reporter Alfred E. Lewis. Eight reporters contributed to the story, including Bob Woodward and Carl Bernstein.[12]

One can only wonder how the world might be different today had a police car appeared with sirens wailing and lights flashing with a uniformed police officer there to investigate. It would have given the spotter plenty of time to reach the burglars on their walkie-talkies so they could make their escape. Instead, a civilian car with three undercover cops arrived, possibly changing the careers of thousands and the world for millions of people and transforming forever American history. Instead of becoming a mysterious and unsolved crime, earning maybe a small mention in the *Washington Post*, it became one of the biggest stories in the history of American journalism and would lead to the unprecedented resignation of a U.S. President.

Two other critical events led to Gerald Ford's ascension from Vice President to Chief Executive and helped to open a door to Reagan that had been welded shut. Michael McShane, a young aide to Congressman John Rooney, Democrat of New York, told of one late evening in 1974 when Congressman Rooney called him into his office to "sit down, shut up, and listen" to the tale of former Congressman Emanuel Celler.

Celler, who had been the Chairman of the House Judiciary Committee, had lost in a bitter and unexpected primary to Elizabeth Holtzman in 1972. Holtzman was a passionate liberal who despised Republicans, conservatives, and Richard Nixon. She successfully tapped into the liberal base in the district to upset Celler. Celler's political supporters urged him to run in the fall against Holtzman as an Independent, assuring him he would win with a bigger turnout, but Celler declined. Celler's departure from the Congress elevated Peter Rodino of New Jersey to the Chairmanship of the House Judiciary Committee, where he aggressively pursued the Watergate investigation.[13]

Celler told Rooney and the enraptured McShane that if he had stayed in Congress, he never would have pursued Watergate, fearing it would tear apart the country, which is precisely what it did. "John, if I were still chairman of the committee, I would not have held a single hearing. I would not have put the country through this. And John, there is no one in the House, including the Speaker, who could have forced me to hold a hearing," McShane remembered Celler declaring.[14] Of course, Celler had the luxury of addressing the issue in hindsight. Still, there is no doubt that Rodino was a fiercely partisan Democrat, much more so than Celler.

The third event that would lead to Reagan's 1976 campaign was the abrupt decision of Spiro Agnew to resign in the fall of 1973. Agnew had been accused of taking cash kickbacks for years from contractors in Maryland, first as a county executive and later as Governor. Agnew was also suspected of taking the money even as Vice President, including in his official office in the White House complex.

In January of 1973, just as the second inaugural of Nixon and Agnew was taking place, an ambitious new Republican U.S. Attorney for Maryland, George Beall, was investigating corruption between local and state government officials and contractors. He had blanketed the state with open subpoenas in his fishing expedition.

Among knowledgeable Marylanders, kickbacks for contracts were known to be a common practice. Maryland ranked right up there with New Jersey, Illinois, and Louisiana in its reputation for doing business in this fashion. Beall was not looking to haul in the biggest fish he would eventually land, but Agnew's undoing came nonetheless, when a small-time contractor, Lester Matz, met with his lawyer, Joseph H. H. Kaplan, to solicit advice on his subpoena.

Kaplan advised his client to tell the investigators everything he knew. Matz pressed Kaplan, and his attorney renewed his advice. Matz waffled and suggested he could not cooperate. Now Kaplan pressed his client. Why? "Because," Matz blurted out, "I have been paying off the Vice President."[15]

The *Wall Street Journal* and later the *Washington Post* broke the story in July of 1973, and Agnew vowed to fight the accusations. When the story first appeared, it did not initially have any negative effect on the Vice President. But after several months of an unremitting drumbeat of negative stories coming out of Maryland, it began to take its toll. He had always been the frontrunner for the 1976 GOP nomination, but by the end of August of 1973 Agnew's support among Republicans for the 1976 nomination had fallen to 22 percent, putting him into a virtual tie with Governor Reagan.

Agnew continued to fight the allegations for some months until October 10, 1973, when White House military aide Mike Dunn, whom the Agnew staff detested, gathered them together to inform them that Agnew was at the moment in his limousine on his way to the Baltimore Federal Courthouse to plead *nolo contendere* to one count of tax evasion. Dunn also told them that Agnew would resign as Vice President of the United States.

Agnew's staffers, including Elizabeth Leonard, were stunned, embarrassed, and angry. Keene, then Agnew's political consigliore, slammed his hand down on the table and shouted, "Then the bastard should have told us himself."[16] Rumors swirled around the nation's capital in the days after Agnew resigned as to the reason for his departure—including stories of political blackmail by people wanting him out of the Vice Presidency. Another quiet rumor was that Agnew had a mistress on his staff and fear of disclosure by some of his political enemies in the White House forced him to resign.

Myron Mintz, a young attorney who had worked for Donald Rumsfeld at the Cost of Living Council before joining the firm of Colson & Shapiro, recalled several meetings and phone calls between Agnew and White House Chief of Staff Alexander Haig. At his firm, Mintz had been asked by Chuck Colson to help out on Agnew's case against the Justice Department. He remembered the dark threats leveled at the beleaguered Vice President.[17] Indeed, Agnew recounted in his book, *Go Quietly . . . Or Else* that Haig was, "totally self-centered, ambitious, and ruthless." Further, Haig sent a message via Dunn to Agnew that things could "get nasty—and dirty."[18] Haig turned the screws on Agnew, telling him in September of 1973 that his indictment was imminent and that his resignation must be forthcoming. Haig later threatened that "anything may be in the offing." Agnew feared for his life.[19]

Washington was thunderstruck. Only John C. Calhoun had previously resigned the Vice Presidency in December of 1832. Calhoun had feuded with President Andrew Jackson and cast the tie-breaking vote to defeat Jackson's appointment of Martin Van Buren as Ambassador to Great Britain. After he was elected to the Senate in South Carolina, Calhoun resigned as Vice President to take his seat as his home state debated nullification of federal tariffs.

Agnew's resignation may have been even more earth-shattering in Washington than the resignation of Nixon ten months later. Agnew's resignation inured some people against Nixon's departure. Throughout those ten months, White House staffers dropped like flies as they were subpoenaed, indicted, convicted, and sentenced. Their seemingly daily testimony before Congress and the drumbeat of news stories added to the eventual numbing process occurring in the country over Watergate.

With Agnew gone, the Republican Party was without a frontrunner for the 1976 nomination. But Watergate had not yet set off a public scramble inside the Republican Party. From day one, Agnew had made it clear that he wanted to run for President and had spent five years giving voice to the middle class and the "silent majority," echoing their frustration with the anti-war movement, race riots, the growing unseemliness of the culture, and the discord on American college campuses.

Before Agnew's resignation, the Watergate burglars had pled guilty and the convictions of G. Gordon Liddy and James McCord were just the tip of the iceberg. The nascent investigations had just begun to create a climate of widespread distrust of the government. At this point, Nixon hoped only to survive to 1976. To this end he needed a replacement for Agnew, and not a prospective successor. Congressman Gerald Ford, whom Nixon had known from his days in the House, was not his first choice. But Ford, in meeting with Nixon, assured him that he would not seek the GOP nomination in 1976 and would support the candidacy of John Connally, which satisfied Nixon.

Author Richard Reeves, who had little respect for Gerald Ford and his people, did capture the mindset of Richard Nixon when it came to selecting Ford as his new Vice President. In his book, *A Ford, Not a Lincoln*, he wrote,

> Gerald Ford was not Richard Nixon's first choice. He was his last choice, in more ways than one. In the privacy of his own White House, Nixon had contempt for Ford—to the point, according to one man on the President's staff at the time, that he had Haig deliver the "good news" to Ford because he literally could not bring himself to do it.
>
> The man Nixon wanted to appoint, insisted on appointing, was John Connally, the former Democratic Governor of Texas who had become a Republican and his Secretary of the Treasury. The President insisted while his advisers—particularly Alexander Haig, his Chief of Staff, and Melvin Laird, his most important counselor—argued vehemently that Connally would never be confirmed by Congress. The Texan was too controversial and too dangerous, he was a political turncoat whose extensive business dealings at home and in Washington were too vulnerable to FBI checks and confirmation hearings under the 25th Amendment.[20]

On December 6, 1973, the Senate and House confirmed Nixon's appointment of Gerald Ford by votes of 92-3 and 387-35, and he became the fortieth Vice President of the United States. Ford later expressed his resentment at the votes against him, charging "partisanship."

When Ford was confirmed, some around Reagan believed once again that the White House was not an option for the Californian. While he was not constitutionally limited to two terms, Reagan had earlier ruled out a third term as Governor of California. He was burnt out on Sacramento politics and fighting with the Democrats in the legislature. Frankly, he liked the freedom of the lecture circuit where he could speak his mind instead of dealing with the niggling, day-to-day bargaining with the Democrats in Sacramento.

Some in his camp had urged Reagan to run for the U.S. Senate from

California in the 1974 campaign against the eventual winner, liberal Democrat Alan Cranston. Cranston had been the leader of a "Democratic Truth Squad" in the 1970 campaign, where he literally stalked Reagan from campaign stop to campaign stop. He irritated the hell out of Reagan. But those who knew Reagan knew he was not interested in being a member of a committee and thus would not have been happy in the U.S. Senate, especially in the minority. Reagan had been a leader all his life, in all aspects of his life. He never viewed himself as a follower of the crowd.

Meanwhile, Reagan's men, led in part by Franklyn "Lyn" Nofziger and Edwin Meese, had already begun informal meetings in early 1973, even before Agnew's resignation, to discuss Reagan's political future. Nofziger, a former reporter, had become a political public relations operative who would never have come over from Central Casting. Hard-bitten, tough, and loyal to a fault, he was also a key link for the Reaganites to the conservative movement and to many key offices in Washington, D.C.

Nofziger was widely known and respected in the Republican Party for his political acumen and bad puns, but he was also a peerless quipster. In 1980, at the Republican National Convention in Detroit, a group of senior advisors to Reagan was reviewing the list of his prospective Vice Presidential choices. Nofziger was asked his opinion of Donald "Rummy" Rumsfeld going on the ticket with Reagan. Mindful of Rumsfeld's famous overarching ambition, Nofziger replied, "Rummy would be fine, but you realize we'll have to hire a food taster for Reagan!"[21]

In a memo for his opposition research files at the President Ford Committee, Ford Campaign Manager Howard "Bo" Callaway wrote of Nofziger in July of 1975 that he was "very likeable, but a hard fighter and can be very caustic and divisive in the way that he goes about his business."[22] Once, in frustration, Ford White House Chief of Staff Dick Cheney complained publicly that Nofziger was responsible for all the bad press Gerald Ford was getting. This was at a time when Nofziger was in Sacramento.[23]

While Nofziger's effectiveness and partisanship were legendary, he was also a genuine American hero. On June 6, 1944, Nofziger was an Army Ranger on Omaha Beach as part of the D-Day invasion. It is a testament to his own understated class and style that Nofziger never mentioned his service to his country in his own autobiography, *Nofziger*.

Meese, on the other hand, was a cerebral conservative. A former law professor at San Diego State University and part of the original Reagan inner circle, he helped develop the message and ideological underpinnings of the eventual Reagan campaign in 1976. They offset each other well. Where Nofziger was outspoken,

Meese was soft spoken. Nofziger was the bomb thrower and Meese was the bomb catcher. Where Nofziger rarely wore a tie, Meese was always in a suit. Where Meese was diplomatic, Nofziger was the personification of the famous Winston Churchill quote, "He's a bull who carries around his own china shop." Despite these differences, they worked well together.

The meetings, often over Saturday morning breakfast or Friday night dinner, took place at the Sutter Club in Sacramento. They had no set agenda except the political and business future of Ronald Wilson Reagan. These meetings were fungible and various people came and went. Initially they were referred to as the "Forward Planning Club" or the "Nofziger Group." Eventually they became known as "The National Political Group," later still the "Madison Group," and finally the "M Group."[24]

Other key members of the Reagan "committees" in 1973, 1974, and 1975 were Mike Deaver and Peter Hannaford, two talented young aides in the Governor's office. Also involved were Bob Walker, Reagan's political aide and sometimes eyes and ears in Washington, as well as Jim Lake, who ran the Washington office for the State of California. Some who also occasionally attended included Jim Jenkins of the Governor's office, and David Packard of Hewlett-Packard fame. Packard, ironically, would later become Finance Director for the President Ford Committee.

Although the 1976 GOP nomination was on everybody's mind, the meetings were mostly inconclusive. Therefore, the group retreated into endless discussions and speculations about national politics and Reagan's chances. Reagan's team had gained most of its experience in California politics and was frankly intimidated by Washington and national politics. They viewed the influence of the East Coast as being dominant in the Republican Party. National political reporters were the new "political bosses," as eventual Reagan Campaign Manager John Sears described them.[25] None of the Californians, save Nofziger and Lake, had experience or regular contact with either the national Republicans or the national media. And none really knew any of the state leaders, some whom would become critical to the 1976 Reagan Presidential campaign.

With Agnew out of office and Ford becoming Vice President in the fall of 1973, the Reagan forces were initially crestfallen. They believed that Nixon would tough it out until the end of his term and that Ford would be in a position as Vice President to win the nomination. Reagan's team had hoped both Agnew and Nixon would survive but as political cripples, thus opening the way for a Reagan Presidential bid in 1976.

But when Nixon left the scene, and Ford was firmly in place at the White House, Reagan kept his options open by meeting with prospective supporters and potential staff to help out with a campaign if he decided to pursue the White House. One very early supporter was Senator Jesse Helms of North Carolina, who told Reagan he should run against Ford, and that he would do anything he could to help Reagan win the GOP nomination.

One of those potential staffers Reagan met with was John Sears. In 1974, Sears was with the firm Gadsby & Hanna. He was a young, rational lawyer with a biting wit and little patience for people he believed to be his intellectual inferiors. Originally from Syracuse, New York, he had attended Notre Dame as an undergraduate and received his law degree from Georgetown in the early sixties. He joined the law firm of Nixon, Mudge where he met the former Vice President in 1966. Nixon was immediately impressed with the agility of the young lawyer's mind and turned to him more and more for assisting with advance work, writing and consultation as he hopscotched the country for Republican candidates in 1966, building up political chits for 1968.

Sears became Executive Director of Nixon for President in 1968 and was widely credited with running Nixon's successful delegate operation. As a reward, Nixon brought Sears into the White House in 1969. He served first as a Deputy Counsel and later Counsel to the President. "It was just a title though. I wasn't practicing any law," remembered Sears. "We were just giving away political favors."[26]

Nixon's Attorney General and longtime friend, John Mitchell, was deeply resentful of the close relationship between the new President and the young aide and eventually forced Sears to resign from the White House, but only after ordering the FBI to bug Sears's office. According to Sears, "It was all kind of a look into the mind of Richard Nixon. Mitchell would try to get a meeting or some memo to Nixon, and Nixon would reply, 'send it to Sears,' which just served to antagonize Mitchell even more. It just drove him bananas."[27] When Sears left Nixon, he went to Gadsby & Hanna to replace Charles Colson, who had departed the firm for the White House.

But Sears's thirst for another national campaign was unquenched. Early on, he was cozying up to Agnew, expecting him to be the GOP nominee in 1976 and also expecting to run the campaign. But this plan hit the skids in October of 1973 when Agnew resigned. The Ford people later made overtures to him about 1976, but nothing was ever firm except that it was clear to Sears that he would not be the number one guy.

Also, the prospect of managing a Rockefeller Presidential candidacy intrigued him, but Sears says he told "Rocky" not to accept Ford's offer to become his Vice President in August of 1974, telling him "If you want to be President, then run for President." But Rockefeller didn't take his advice, and Sears was a jockey without a horse.[28]

Ideology was not an issue with Sears. He was from the Republican area of Upstate New York, where being a Republican at that time was like drinking water. It was just something you did. But Sears quickly established himself as someone whose opinions mattered greatly in any political meeting in which he was involved.

Sears's first meeting with the Reagan team in 1974, at the invitation of Walker, did not go according to plan. He flew across the country the day of the planned dinner and on the plane ride had a few drinks too many. By the time he got to the Firehouse Restaurant to huddle with Meese, Nofziger, and company, he was pretty well smashed and, in the words of Hannaford, "just babbled."[29] The Reagan group was unimpressed with Sears's performance and with Walker's recommendation. However, by the time of his appointment the next morning with the Reagans, Sears had sobered up and acquitted himself well. "Sears was seen as the answer to our 'Western inferiority complex,'" said Deaver.[30]

"I realized that they were of the belief that Nixon was going to survive Watergate," Sears recounted.[31] Difficult as it is to believe now, there were people who took Richard Nixon at his word that he was "no quitter" and would tough out the remainder of his Presidency. Sears remembered, "First thing I told them was that Nixon would be out of office one way or the other by fall, and Ford would become President. But while Ford had all the powers of the office, he would not have what was most compelling—a large base of support."[32]

Nixon might have been counting on it. "Nixon hated the idea [of selecting Ford] but he had to go along," said one White House staffer, quoted by Reeves. "There was also the other thing—that so many people thought Ford was too dumb to be President. Impeachment didn't seem possible then, but certainly no one would think of doing it if it was going to put Jerry Ford in the White House. It seemed perfect."[33]

Nonetheless, the events of August 9, 1974, did propel Ford into the Oval Office. Ford proved not to be the buffer against impeachment as Nixon and his people had hoped. Sears advised Reagan and his team that they not give up on running in 1976; however things would not be easy. As longtime Reagan chronicler Lou Cannon wrote in his book, *Reagan*, "What Sears was suggesting was the heretical notion that loyalist Reagan could run for President in 1976 no matter what happened. If Nixon lasted, there would be an open run for the nomination. If Ford inherited the Presidency, then Reagan could seek the Republican nomination against him in the primaries."[34]

It was not that the sunny Reaganites did not envision their man someday in the Oval Office; they certainly did. But no one had articulated how to do it like Sears, no one had made the case like Sears, no one had the national political experience like Sears, no one had the contacts and friendship with the national media like Sears, and no one understood Nixon like Sears. Years later, when asked why he believed Nixon would leave office before the end of his term, Sears said,

> Because I knew him. Because nothing happened around his White House that he didn't know about. And when four days had elapsed after the break-in, and no one was fired, I knew. Nixon fired people for no reason . . . no one had accused him of being involved in the beginning but he was.
>
> He still might have beaten [Watergate] if he'd destroyed the tapes, but he was always postponing things until tomorrow and didn't want to have tomorrow's bad day today. He was a fatalist and [his resignation] was the fulfillment of what he thought would happen.[35]

Sears had met Reagan once or twice before, including when Nixon campaigned for Reagan in 1966, but those encounters were cursory. This was the first time he had spent any real time with Reagan, and he came away impressed. "He was a great piece of horseflesh . . . properly trained, properly working," Sears said somewhat patronizingly.[36]

When Nixon did indeed resign on August 9, 1974, the Reagan team's estimation of Sears—especially Nancy Reagan's—grew by leaps and bounds. Reagan had been one of the last holdouts in the GOP to support Nixon. Shaking his head in private about the Dick Nixon he knew, Governor Reagan always publicly supported the President. Reagan only broke with him after the "smoking gun" tape was released on August 5, 1974. The recording clearly showed Nixon had orchestrated a cover-up of the break-in, including ordering his men to try to block the FBI's investigation of the crime. When Nixon finally resigned, he had the support of only 18 percent of the American people. Articles of impeachment had already been passed by the House Judiciary Committee.

Sears was summoned immediately to Sacramento for a meeting with the Reagan high command "to discuss whether he should run for VP and I said 'no.' 'What do we do if we're offered a Cabinet post?' 'Don't take it.'"[37]

Shortly after Ford became President, Governor Reagan received a phone call from Bob Hartmann, counselor to President Ford, telling him that an informal survey of GOP leaders around the country had emerged with a list of men who would be acceptable as Vice President. Naturally, Reagan's name was on the list.

Although he was not at the top, would Reagan be interested in being Vice President? Reagan's reply was not enthusiastic, but he answered in the affirmative, according to Lake.[38]

Hours after the call ended, rumors began emanating from the Ford White House that were floating back to Sacramento suggesting that Reagan was campaigning to be Vice President. Other whispers said that Ford and his people did not want Reagan for Vice President because he was "too reactionary."[39] Reagan, Mrs. Reagan, and their friends and supporters were furious. They smelled a rat in Hartmann and believed Reagan had been duped. Hartmann was an acidulous man who held Reagan and most conservatives in complete contempt. He also made a habit of making nasty jokes at Reagan's expense in the Ford White House.

The State Chairman of the California Republican Party at the time, Gordon Luce, had sent telegrams to other state party chairmen urging them to contact the White House and voice their support for Reagan. But Reagan never asked for Luce to do this or knew about it until afterwards. Some chairmen did send telegrams, but their endorsements of Reagan were never answered.

"Within hours after Nixon's resignation, Reagan's political operatives were phoning congressional conservatives with sneering asides on Ford's ability and acumen," Hartmann charged in his book, *Palace Politics*. "When the President named Rocky [Nelson Rockefeller] and proposed amnesty for the same kids who razed California campuses, the Reaganite whispering campaign became a shout."[40]

Hartmann never sourced the accusations, the name of the person who called from the Reagan team, or which members of Congress received the calls. But Hartmann's paranoia well summed up the mindset of the Ford White House when it came to Ronald Reagan.

The eventual list of men presented to Ford "boiled down to three possibilities: Rockefeller, Rumsfeld, and George Bush," Cheney said.[41] It was culled from the larger list that included Reagan, Senators Barry Goldwater, Howard Baker, Bill Brock and Chuck Percy, and Ambassador Anne Armstrong. Ford asked the FBI to do background checks on all the men from the short list.

At the time, an allegation surfaced from Hamilton Long, an unsavory conservative lawyer in Philadelphia, that Rockefeller had financed a dirty tricks operation aimed at the Democratic Convention in Miami Beach in 1972. Long's claim, which he relayed to the new Ford legal counsel, Phil Buchen, was that Watergate conspirator E. Howard Hunt had not destroyed all of his files and had the goods on Rockefeller in a bank vault. Although it was second-hand information, Long had enough specific details to force the Ford White House to turn over the matter to Watergate Special Prosecutor Leon Jaworski. Meanwhile, the allegation surfaced in muckraker Jack Anderson's syndicated column.[42] At the same time, a leak to *Newsweek* alleged that George Bush, in his failed Texas Senate campaign in 1970, had accepted over $100,000 from a secret fund controlled by Nixon called "Townhouse Operation."

Both allegations were disproven. Rockefeller had made a $250,000 contribution to the Nixon re-election campaign, but it was entirely above board and legal at the time. Bush was also completely exonerated, but the damage had been done to his desire to become Ford's Vice President.[43]

Meanwhile, the media was engaged in a full-throated, Washington-style guessing game as to whom Ford would select. The *New York Times* suggested that Governor Dan Evans of Washington State, Elliot Richardson, Nixon's former Attorney General, Mel Laird, a former Congressman from Wisconsin, and Rumsfeld all had the inside track.

It was instructive to conservatives at the time that few on any public or private list for the Vice President slot, save possibly George Bush, were conservative—though several were certainly available. "Reagan did not figure in the discussion," Cheney said.[44] According to biographer Lee Edwards, Goldwater was asked if he would accept the veep slot, should Ford offer it. But Goldwater turned Ford down, citing his age and that he "carried too many scars."[45]

Ford announced his selection of former New York Governor Nelson Aldrich Rockefeller, age sixty-six, to fill the vacant Vice President slot on August 20, 1974, in a live 10:04 A.M. speech from the Oval Office. His wife, Betty, who had been lobbying for a female Vice President, and, of course, Rockefeller, accompanied Ford. Rockefeller's wife, Margaretta, known to all as "Happy," was not present.

"He decided to go with Rockefeller because Rockefeller had international stature, everybody knew who he was and Ford felt that he personally needed, in effect as an unknown President, someone of that stature to give weight and heft to his Administration . . . it didn't have much to do with philosophy," Cheney later recalled.[46]

Reagan learned of the news from a White House staffer, instead of the obligatory courtesy call the Governor of California might have expected from the President of the United States. Once again, the Ford people not only misplayed Reagan, they had insulted him. "Reagan got the call at 6 A.M. no less," recalled Jim Lake. "He was furious. All of the Ford White House treated Ronald Reagan badly." In fact, "had Ford and his people treated Reagan better, he might not have run in 1976."[47] Betraying his own disdain for Reagan, Ford later wrote in his autobiography about "Reagan's superficial remedies for all the ills that afflicted America."[48]

George Bush was also mighty angry, but at least he received a phone call from President Ford while vacationing at his summer home in Maine. Bush was serving as the Chairman of the Republican National Committee at the time. He was convinced that Ford would choose him as Vice President, especially since he had the public backing of Goldwater. Bush believed deep down that he was qualified, had earned it, and deserved it. But when Ford passed over Bush and chose Rockefeller, Bush quit as RNC Chairman. "He was pissed," recalled Eddie Mahe, then-Political Director at the Republican National Committee. "It was the second time he had been passed over for veep."[49]

Bush later met with Ford, who offered him a number of Administration posts, which Bush rejected, but he was intrigued by the position of Envoy to China. The Bushes, who had always been popular on the Washington social circuit, found their invitations dwindling as the country and the party sank deeper and deeper into the Watergate morass. Barbara Bush was deeply unhappy and voiced her opinion that her husband should take the China post and get out of town.

The Republican Party, however, had bigger problems than who would become Ford's Vice President. Many of the headaches fell on Mahe. He had been a fixture in New Mexico politics where he gained a reputation as an unassuming, but tough operative, winning local and statewide elections. He caught the attention of national party officials in the early seventies and came to Washington, where he eventually became a trusted aide to Chairman Bush.

In 1974, Mahe had the arduous job of trying to hold together a party to which only 22 percent of the American people claimed allegiance. He had to referee intra-party squabbles and ideological battles between the moderates and the conservatives while also trying to keep the RNC open and functioning. Mahe recalled:

> Money, big money, just dried up. In 1972, Maurice Stans [Nixon's Campaign Finance Director] had vacuumed up every big check for CREEP (the horrible acronym of the Committee to Re-Elect the President) with little left for party operations, party building, candidate donations, etc. . . . We had enough to keep the doors open and finance the convention, but there was little left after that. . . . Rod [Smith] was able to get one piece of direct mail out, but we had to let go 70 employees in December of 1974 and then closed the building for three weeks to save on electricity. The rest of the staff went off payroll for that time too.[50]

There were serious discussions in GOP circles about changing the name of the party, believing it had been so sullied by Nixon, Agnew, and Watergate that the damage was permanent. By the time Watergate began to unfold in the spring of 1973, large "fat cat" contributors and corporations, who had routinely given to the party, had deserted it. The national party limped along on meager contributions and bank loans. In December of 1974, banks were prepared to foreclose on the Capitol Hill Club, the eating, meeting and drinking salon of the national Republican Party and its attendant hangers-on.

It's easy to see why the banks were worried about getting their money back. Republicans, deeply depressed in the fall of 1974, simply decided not to vote. As iconoclastic conservative pollster Arthur Finkelstein pointed out,

> Democratic turnout did not exceed the normal pattern for an off-year election, but Republican turnout was off by ten percent. That was disastrous for the Republicans. In fact, the only two challengers running for U.S. Senate who won that fall as Republicans were Jake Garn of Utah and Paul Laxalt of Nevada.[51]

Republicans in the Senate had fallen below the threshold of forty Senators needed to stop the Democrats from ramming through legislation.

But while the GOP was sinking into oblivion, conservatives were anything but obsequious. They were not going to take from Gerald Ford what they had put up with from Richard Nixon. "Back in August, conservatives, predictably, went ballistic over Ford's choice of Rockefeller," said Stan Evans, then Chairman of the American Conservative Union.[52] In addition to the Rockefeller selection, conservatives became even more angered with Ford when he, only days into his Administration, offered amnesty for Vietnam draft dodgers. In the fall of 1974, he announced he would meet with Soviet Premier Leonid Brezhnev at the Russian port city of Vladivostok, further incensing the Right.

At the time, Washington observers were giving Ford a grace period. If things were a bit bungled or confused, it was argued he had just taken office and deserved a break. But in his first major decision as President, he picked probably the one man who would generate angst, anger, and possibly a primary challenge from within his own party. Rockefeller was the Right's poster child for everything that was wrong with the party.

Further mystifying to conservatives was that Ford had tried to position himself to be Barry Goldwater's running mate in 1964. He was in San Francisco and should have understood what this East Coast liberal meant to the base of the Republican Party.

Richard Viguerie, the well-established "Godfather of the New Right," convened a dinner of leading conservatives the night of the Rockefeller announcement to determine if it was possible to mount a campaign in the Congress to stop the confirmation of Rockefeller. However, the group soon realized they had little influence over the nomination process and their "Stop Rockefeller" effort died a still birth.

At the American Conservative Union board meeting in September of 1974, Phyllis Schlafly, the author of the hugely successful book, *A Choice, Not an Echo,* suggested that since Ford "has no bedrock support which we might offend, we should start speaking out and criticizing him."[53] The organization outlined plans for opposing Rockefeller's confirmation. The ACU had conducted a poll of its membership and it came back showing wide opposition to Rockefeller. The members agreed to form an "ad hoc committee to discredit Rockefeller and show the rank and file Republicans that Rockefeller and Ford are not conservatives." Finally, the idea evolved into a "National Committee Against Rockefeller."[54] Jim Linen, a young board member, made the motion, and the board approved the break with Rockefeller and Ford unanimously. Chairman Stan Evans and other board members present included Keene, author John Chamberlain, Dan Oliver, and *Human Events* editor Tom Winter.

Reagan said nothing publicly about the Rockefeller selection, but he was probably the only conservative in America who did keep his mouth shut. Machiavellians like Pat Buchanan and Keene did believe that a conservative primary challenger to Ford in 1976, such as Ronald Reagan, stood a better chance against a Ford-Rockefeller ticket than a Ford-Bush ticket. Or, if Ford did not run and Rockefeller did, Reaganites saw "Rocky's" selection as getting a head start on their man for 1976.

"In 1974, the prevailing view among the Reagan entourage was that the Rockefeller nomination was designed to stop Reagan. As far back as December 1973, Rockefeller's decision to resign as Governor of New York had been interpreted in Sacramento as an attempt to gain a head start over Reagan in the race for the 1976 Presidential nomination," wrote Lou Cannon in *Governor Reagan.*[55]

Despite the selection of Rockefeller, Ford and his White House made no attempt to reach out to the base of the GOP. This was duly noted as another black mark against his Presidency. Of Ford's own ideology, Cheney would later recall, "Ford was right smack dab in the middle of the pack . . . the Goldwater wing . . . didn't dominate the House the way they came to dominate it in the eighties."[56]

Relations between Ford and Reagan at this point took on a sometimes cool, sometimes cold "sitzkrieg." But it was more complicated than that, as each man had mixed emotions about the other. It was clear, nonetheless, that Reagan was far less hostile towards Ford than the President was towards Governor Reagan.

Upon Ford becoming President, Reagan sent a letter of support congratulating Ford and received a response on August 21, the day after Rockefeller was announced as Vice President. The letter of course made no mention of Rockefeller and certainly not of Reagan having been deceived by Hartmann. The letter was cordial enough, but it could have been written to any one of the thousands of people who sent letters to the White House each day.[57]

When Reagan visited Washington, Ford would complain that Reagan didn't call upon him in the White House. But his complaints just showed how little Ford and his staff understood Ronald Reagan. Reagan would never have the temerity to simply ask to "drop by" and see the President unless he had important business to confer with him. As Hartmann wrote in *Palace Politics*,

> As early as August 24, 1974, a curious comedy of errors occurred in Washington. Reagan, still Governor of California, had come to a meeting with some conservative crusaders in nearby Maryland but stayed a country mile away from the new President's much-touted "open door" at the White House.
>
> Ford felt that Reagan, who'd always found time to call on President Nixon, was showing discourtesy. Reagan, I'm told, was equally miffed that the President didn't invite him over. You don't just barge in on a President as you would a Congressman. Nixon's staff would have set it up before he ever left Sacramento.[58]

In his speculation, Hartmann unknowingly answered his own question. Reagan did not go where he was not invited, and the Nixon people always invited Reagan to the White House.

Reagan received another impersonal letter on September 20, 1974, from Ford. It simply thanked Reagan for a certificate a group of Republican Governors had sent to the President and only stated what Ford intended to do in working with the Governors.[59] Yet another letter from Ford showed up on Reagan's desk in early December of 1974, but this was again a form letter, probably sent out to thousands, which asked for Reagan's support in the President's "Whip Inflation Now!" program.[60]

With few exceptions, Presidents do not draft their own letters. They have staff to handle most of the less important correspondence. But this was sensitive communication with the Governor of the largest state in the Union and a member of his own party. Reagan was also one of the most popular figures in the Republican Party. That should have made such correspondence important to Ford. It wasn't until May of 1975 that Reagan received a letter from Ford that was actually written by Ford and not by a staffer.[61]

The Reagans and the Fords had spent dinner together over the Easter holidays when the Fords were in California. Ford wrote Reagan warmly and personally. But by the spring of 1975, the handwriting was starting to appear on the wall for a Reagan challenge.[62] As Cannon wrote, "Ford had even less respect for Reagan than Reagan had for Ford. The President dismissed warnings from advisers that Reagan would present a difficult challenge."[63] Meanwhile, both camps were growing in their agitation. It seemed as if Ford was determined to write the playbook to force Reagan into the campaign.

Reagan was unafraid to let the President of the United States know of his concerns. Late in 1974, Reagan fired off a telegram to Ford, stating, "Dear Mr. President, I am concerned that press reports indicate you will propose tax increases tomorrow in an effort to curb inflation. The 1972 election mandate was clear: no new taxes for four years, and reduce the size and cost of the federal government. That mandate remains intact today. Any tax increase would be contrary to it." He concluded his telegram by expressing concerns about cuts in the defense budget and advocating cuts in non-defense spending.[64]

Ford had a somewhat different message for the American people and the Republican Party as he delivered his first State of the Union address on January 15, 1975: "The state of the Union is not good." Many of the editorial writers of America agreed with Ford. From the insider's perspective, Casserly wrote, "Gone was the Nixon rhetoric that the American people were the greatest and that the United States was the most powerful. Mr. Ford simply said we were in trouble. Some historians say it was the most downbeat State of the Union message in our two centuries. If only they had seen it in the raw."[65]

Reagan was no Pollyanna but he knew this was exactly what the American people didn't need to hear. He knew the American people realized there were problems, but Reagan would have reminded them that the American experiment had faced many tests in the past two hundred years and had not come up wanting. Nothing illustrated the difference between the two men better than this speech by Ford and any State of the Union speech later given by Reagan after 1980.

While Reagan weighed his options, Ford seemed to have only problems. He was months into his Administration and the wheels were falling off. As a career member of the House of Representatives, Ford was accustomed to and more comfortable with consensus than leadership. He was used to trying to get along, in the admonition made by Tip O'Neill to a young backbencher in the Democratic Party. Through no fault of his own, Ford was not ready to exert leadership, even with his own staff.

The Ford Administration was besieged by leaks to the media, public and private staff infighting, and endless meetings and indecision that seemed to paralyze the Executive Branch. Alan Greenspan, who served Ford as Chairman of the President's Council of Economic Advisers, recounted to a speechwriter that he had been to seventeen meetings in just one day.[66]

Washington observers truly needed a playbook to figure out the factions and players in the Ford Administration. Rumsfeld feuded with Hartmann and had Hartmann's initial office, adjacent to the Oval Office, taken away. Rumsfeld also feuded with Henry Kissinger. Meanwhile, the White House photographer, David Hume Kennerly, by virtue of his close friendship with the Ford children, exerted power and opinion out of proportion for a guy who lugged around a 35mm camera. Foul-mouthed Kennerly was also verbose—as evidenced by a comment Ford once made before the White House News Photographers Association: "There's an old saying that one picture is worth a thousand words. In David Hume Kennerly, I get both."[67]

Another staffer who came with baggage to the Ford White House was Hartmann. Ford depended perilously on him for advice and counsel. He was captured by Casserly as a man "without major ideological or philosophical hangups." He then sourced another opinion of Hartmann: "He's a guy who throws a lot of bulls—, but likes little in return."[68] Fred Barnes, a young reporter for the *Washington Star*, who was assigned by his editor Jack Germond to cover the Ford White House, said, "Hartmann wasn't much use after lunch."[69]

Ford was touring California in April of 1974, the day Watergate Special Prosecutor Leon Jaworski issued subpoenas for sixty-four White House tapes and files. As Richard Reeves wrote acidly of Hartmann, Ford was conducting local television interviews and "at times, while the lights and cameras were being adjusted, the only sound in the huge chilly room was the light snoring of Robert T. Hartmann. . . . It was usually that way in the afternoon after Hartmann had begun drinking."[70]

Ford, determined not to follow in the footsteps of Nixon, decided not to have a Chief of Staff. Although this management model had worked for thousands of businesses and organizations, as well as countless elected officials, Ford confused the title with the character of the person holding that important position. The result was that while Rumsfeld, whom Ford had known from his days in the

House, was nominally in charge, it seemed almost anybody had access to the Oval Office.

Rumsfeld, at age forty-two, had an impressive résumé, which included flying for the Navy and serving as Congressman from Illinois before joining the Nixon Administration, where he served as head of the Office of Economic Opportunity. Later he served as Ambassador to the North Atlantic Treaty Organization (NATO). As John J. Casserly described Rumsfeld in his book *The Ford White House*, "Rumsfeld is articulate, decisive, and handsome. Most who know him well describe Rumsfeld as very ambitious."[71]

Adding to President Ford's misfortunes was the fall of Saigon and South Vietnam on April 30, 1975. Americans and the world saw the sorry spectacle of fleeing Americans and South Vietnamese atop the U.S. Embassy, hanging from U.S. military helicopters in a desperate attempt to escape the Communist onslaught. America's mood sank. Ford attempted to introduce emergency military aid for the South Vietnamese, but the Democratic-controlled Congress would hear none of it, choosing to focus their arguments on the corrupt but pro-Western South Vietnamese regime instead of the brutality of the killing machine of the North Vietnamese.

For the first time, the United States had lost a war, and the failure cut deeply into the psyche of the American people. America had become, as Nixon had warned in a speech several days before the shooting at Kent State, "a pitiful, helpless giant."

While many were counseling Republicans to hide their conservatives in a closet, William Rusher, one of the most astute and respected conservative journalists in America at the time, was urging conservatives to "come out" in his landmark book, *The Making of the New Majority Party*. The book gave aid and comfort to those who were agitating for a new political party.

Citing Ford's policies in making the case, Rusher wrote, "In his proposal for a case-by-case review of the offenses of Vietnam draft-dodgers and deserters, Ford exhibited near-perfect pitch for antagonizing just about everyone; first affronting the Veterans of Foreign Wars before whose convention he called for what must have sounded like 'amnesty' and outraging conservatives generally by designating the ultra-liberal 'dove', Charles Goodell, to administer a part of the new program. . . ." Goodell was a former Republican member of Congress from New York and a close ally of Nelson Rockefeller.

In reviewing the state of the GOP, Rusher observed that while few Americans identified with Republicanism, a large plurality of Americans identified with conservatism over liberalism. The problem was that both parties contained their share of liberals, moderates, and conservatives. Yet the popularity of the Democratic Party had persisted since the New Deal. They continued to have it all over their tired and run-down counterparts. By the 1970s, the iconic John Kennedy was seen as having been the savior of America from Richard Nixon. Rusher also wrote,

> Both major parties have been around so long that they exude the seedy, unmistakable odor of entrenched and callous old age. But in the eye (or nose) of public opinion, thanks to Watergate and various other recent disasters, the GOP has unquestionably forged into a commanding lead in this unhappy respect. No other party in our history has ever had a Vice President resign after pleading *nolo contendere* to a charge of tax evasion—or any other charge. No other party in our history has ever had a President resign to avoid certain impeachment and removal for conspiring to obstruct justice—or any other conspiracy. These disasters may, even will, be forgotten or mossed over in time; but how much time do conservatives—does America—have?[72]

Rusher and others reasoned that a new, vibrant third party built around conservative values and principles would eventually become the new alternative to the Democrats, replacing the Republican Party, which would then be left to wither and die on the vine. He identified four conditions that made the creation of this new conservative party possible. In his fourth point, he cited the cultural differences between the two wings of the party: "The Eastern liberal wing of the Republican Party, drawn from the ranks of upper class WASPs and their fellow-travelers, finds itself acutely uncomfortable . . . under the domination of the GOP by its conservative majority."[73]

In the wake of Jim Buckley's surprising senate win in New York in 1970 running on the conservative ticket and the disastrous condition of the Republican Party, the third party route made sense to a great many people. Rusher gave voice to what many conservatives had speculated about for the previous year or two, and his book sent shockwaves through the Republican Party. Some conservatives had resented the powers-that-be inside the GOP for many years for political and cultural reasons. They weren't members of the GOP's "country club." They were blue collar, Catholic, and they had clear, ideological motives that were unencumbered by the political debate and compromise that represented the shriveled GOP at the time.

Well-liked and respected by conservatives, Reagan would have been a natural to head up a new party. In fact, in October of 1974, the waning months of his

Governorship, Ronald Reagan had been asked at a press conference about the formation of a third party. As Steven F. Hayward wrote in *The Age of Reagan,*

> Reagan appears to have considered the idea briefly. Caught off guard by a reporter's question in the fall of 1974, Reagan said of the third party idea: "There could be one of those moments in time, I don't know. I see statements of disaffection of people in both parties." But by election day of 1974 Reagan had closed the door: "I am not starting a third party. I do not believe the Republican Party is dead. I believe the Republican Party represents basically the thinking of the people across the country, if we can get that message across to the people. I believe that a third party movement has the effect of dividing the people who share the same philosophy and usually winds up, because of that division, electing those they set out to oppose."[74]

Reagan had previously discussed a third party with members of his "Kitchen Cabinet," and they reacted negatively to his initial comments the previous October. One of those, Holmes Tuttle, told the Governor in no uncertain terms, "You're a Republican and you're going to stay one."[75] Also factoring into Reagan's backtracking was the fear of ridicule. He had already left one political party and didn't want to leave another. Nonetheless, he was close to Rusher and respected his thinking.

At the 1975 Conservative Political Action Conference, Stan Evans, Chairman of the American Conservative Union, urged the Republican Party to chart a more conservative course. But he held out the option of a national third party for Presidential campaigns. Reagan also addressed the annual gathering of conservatives at the Mayflower Hotel in Washington, which was sponsored by the ACU, *Human Events, National Review,* and the Young Americans for Freedom. He poured yet another bucket of cold water on the idea, saying, "Is it a third party we need, or is it a new and revitalized second party, raising a banner of no pale pastels, but bold colors which make it unmistakably clear where we stand on all the issues troubling the people? Americans are hungry to feel once again a sense of mission and greatness."[76]

Despite Reagan's sobering comments, the convention of conservatives created a "Committee on Conservative Alternatives," headed by Senator Jesse Helms, "to review and assess the current political situation and to develop future political opportunities." The organization investigated ballot access in each of the states to determine if a third party challenge was feasible. Conservatives proceeded ever further in their wooing of Reagan for the third party bid. As late as June of 1975,

Reagan returned to Washington and attended a private dinner of conservatives at the Madison Hotel to discuss the matter.

Present at the meeting were beer magnate Joseph Coors, Bob Walker, a former Reagan aide who had gone to work for Coors, conservative direct mail fundraiser Richard Viguerie, syndicated columnist Kevin Phillips, Conservative Caucus Chairman and Nixon Administration veteran Howard Phillips, former Nixon speechwriter and syndicated columnist Pat Buchanan, New York newspaper scion Neal Freeman, and two Representatives from the George Wallace camp: Charles Snyder and Bill France. Also attending was Paul Weyrich, a former Senate aide and head of the Committee for the Survival of a Free Congress.[77]

The organizers were fearful of the influence Mike Deaver, who had accompanied him to Washington, had over Reagan. They knew Reagan's young but politically attuned media man was violently opposed to Reagan seeking a third party nomination. After physically barring Deaver from the meeting, the conservatives attempted to persuade Reagan to make a third party bid.[78]

Reagan listened patiently, but he had already decided that if he were to make another Presidential bid, it would not be through a third party and certainly not on a ticket with George Wallace. Reagan admired the populist vein Wallace and Jimmy Carter were working, but found Wallace's racial politics beyond distasteful.

Although Reagan turned them down, the conservatives did not stop. They proceeded to meet with Wallace and then John Connally about a third party bid. Each of these men also turned down the third party advocates, and the idea ended there. Reagan told Deaver later, "Mike, you shouldn't have worried so much. I told them I was a Republican and if I am going to run . . . it will be as a Republican."[79]

Nonetheless, the conservative grassroots were eager for change. The emerging "New Right" was more middle class, more sophisticated politically, and more interested in winning than the old elements of the Republican Party or even the "Old Right." They were as disgusted by Nixon's abandonment of conservatism as by his abandonment of respect for the rule of law. Nixon's resignation from office was not met with joy by the New Rightists, but with the knowledge that they knew Nixon was a fatalist and his ignoble departure was bound to happen sooner or later.

Nixon had won an overwhelming re-election effort in 1972, but it was entirely personal. He rarely campaigned as a Republican and almost never appeared on the same dais with Republican candidates running for lesser offices. As a result, the GOP saw minimal pickups in the House and actually lost ground in the Senate.

"Even more important, he had paid some heavy prices to ensure this victory," penned Michael Barone in *Our Country*. "Lingering controls on energy prices and rents in big cities would distort the workings of the economy and exact heavy costs by the end of the 1970s . . . the Social Security increases and the double cost-of-living adjustment . . . the Soviet wheat deal propped up a rotting Soviet economy and produced a boom-bust cycle in the American Farm Belt."[80]

Wrote Lewis Gould in his landmark book, *Grand Old Party*,

> Of all the Republican Presidents in the twentieth century, Richard Nixon is the most complex and controversial. . . . So activist was his Presidency on environmental matters, welfare reform, and Native American issues of tribal rights that Nixon has been called, with a touch of irony, the last liberal President. In many respects, Nixon was a Republican moderate, to the left of his mentor Dwight D. Eisenhower on a number of social and economic questions.[81]

The party had come a long way since its first nominee, the great explorer John C. Fremont, ran on the platform of "Free men, Free soil, Fremont" in 1856. Unfortunately the Republican Party stood for less, over a hundred years later, than it did at its inception. In fact, no one really was sure what the Republicans represented. Lengthy columns were written and scholarly papers presented predicting the death of the Republican Party, much like their forefathers, the Whigs, who had died out in the 1850s because no one seemed to know what they stood for anymore. Consequently, the party's source of grassroots funding dried up, as its once vibrant list of proved donors to the party—developed from Barry Goldwater's campaign in 1964—had shrunk to nothing.

Regardless of whether they would ultimately form a third party, conservatives realized that they would need to challenge the Republican establishment by fielding a candidate who shared their convictions. Although Reagan continued to deliberate about challenging Ford, plans were already well underway to announce "Citizens for Reagan" in July of 1975. As far as impatient conservatives were concerned, frustrated and furious with the slow pace of his decision, it could not come soon enough.

3

FORD FOLLIES

"I'm damn sick and tired of a ship that has such leaky seams."

In September 1975, what should have been a huge political windfall dropped into Gerald Ford's lap with the bankruptcy of New York City. In the 1970s, the "Big Apple" was rotten to the core with graft, corruption, organized crime, and kickbacks. The city was horribly run, dirty, and dominated by extreme left-wing Democrats. In his 1977 Academy Award winning movie *Annie Hall*, Woody Allen speculated that the rest of America thought New York City was overwhelmed with "left-wing Communist Jewish homosexual pornographers. I think of us like that sometimes, and I live here."

New York City was $4 billion in debt and city fathers appealed to Washington for a bailout to prevent the city from default. Other major cities were also run by corrupt political machines, one example being Richard Daley's Chicago, but he and his fellow Mayors knew that voters would tolerate "honest graft" only as long as essential services like law enforcement, fire protection, trash removal, and public education were efficiently provided. New York City had forgotten this important political lesson, and the city was turning into a cesspool from frequent strikes by garbage men and the growing filth that lined the streets. In 1975, New York's hopelessness was the butt of Johnny Carson's monologues.

Despite reprimands and heavy pressure from Mayor Abe Beame and other supporters of the city, including liberal Republican Senator Jacob Javits and Vice President Nelson Rockefeller, Ford initially said no. The *New York Times* attacked the President's initial refusal to bail the city out as arising from the basest of motives:

> [Ford's] strategy is to exploit New York as the Republican answer to Watergate. When the Democrats bring up Richard Nixon and the

> Watergate scandals, Mr. Ford and his fellow partisans will point to New York as horrible example No. 1 of Democratic misrule.
>
> Only partisan political considerations make Mr. Ford's approach comprehensible. If his real concern were to make sure that New York balanced its budget and followed a prudent fiscal course in the foreseeable future, he would have accepted the Proxmire-Stevenson bill, which would have achieved that objective while extending $4 billion in temporary assistance. But that bill would have prevented default—and default by the nation's largest city is the spectacular event that Mr. Ford needs for his political purposes.
>
> The default scenario has special advantages from the standpoint of the President and his political advisers. It enables him to appeal to the anti-Eastern bias once articulated by Senator Goldwater when he expressed the wish that it might somehow be possible to saw off the eastern seaboard and let it drift out to sea. Mr. Ford can now present himself as the moral avenger who stood up to the big city and told it off.[1]

Ford never told New York to "Drop Dead," as the *New York Daily News* screamed in a headline, but he probably would have been better off if he had done so. "Ford has been wavering all over the lot on the issue of aid to New York City," *Human Events* reported.[2]

While Rockefeller and Javits were pressing Ford from the left to help New York, Ronald Reagan was crowding him on the right. Reagan seized the political opportunity and made it clear that he would have told New York to solve its own problems. Ford missed his chance to exploit the issue and help himself with Republican primary voters. He was two months into his campaign and like comedian Rodney Dangerfield, was not getting much respect.

Ford formally announced his intention of running for the Republican nomination in an Oval Office address to the country on July 8, 1975. Ford was accompanied by a small group of people, including his Campaign Manager, Howard "Bo" Callaway, Finance Director David Packard, Dean Burch, head of Ford's campaign advisory committee, and the campaign's Treasurer, Robert Moot.

The President's candidacy may have been the worst kept secret in Washington, since he had already filed papers with the FEC declaring his intention to run more than two weeks earlier, on June 20, 1975. Offices were opened at 1828 L Street, NW for the President Ford Committee and Callaway began assembling a staff. Once again, Ford was accused in some conservative quarters of completely reversing his position. As Bob Hartmann recounted in his book, *Palace Politics*, "I found Ford voicing the same sort of optimism in a pre-Christmas [1973] interview in

U.S. News and World Report, under the heading 'Why I will not run in 1976.' He was pretty categorical, to the point of saying that even if he succeeded to the Presidency before 1976 he 'would step aside and not run to stay in that office.'"[3]

Ford further explained in this article that he felt he could do a better job as Vice President if he were not perceived as conducting a personal campaign. He named Reagan, Rockefeller, and Connally as the leading GOP prospects for 1976. It is important to note that when Ford spoke these words in December of 1973, he was only leading Reagan by five points in the Harris poll.[4]

While conservatives and Reagan supporters fumed at the slow start of the Reagan campaign, Ford continued to have his own problems, including what to do about Nelson Rockefeller. Callaway was delegated with the unenviable task of explaining to the media why, if he was such a great Vice President, Rockefeller was not running in tandem with Ford for the nomination.

As Witcover recounted in *Marathon*,

> Callaway, meanwhile, determined to get off on the right foot, instead stuffed it in his mouth from the very start. The morning after Ford's announcement of candidacy, he held an open house at the temporary headquarters of the President Ford Committee, an office several blocks from the White House. For more than two hours, he sipped coffee with visiting reporters and conducted what amounted to a floating press conference. A single topic—the future of Nelson Rockefeller—was raised and dealt with repeatedly, until there were as many variations to Callaway's answers as there were reporters, always a dangerous public-relations situation in a political campaign. The committee, Callaway took pains to emphasize, was a vehicle for nominating Ford, not Ford and Rockefeller, and the group's name expressed that fact.[5]

Witcover documented that there were, indeed, historical facts to support Callaway's claims. In 1956, Dwight Eisenhower's campaign committee was designed to get him re-nominated—not him and Dick Nixon. In 1972, Agnew was not named as Nixon's Vice Presidential running mate until just before the Miami Convention in August. Although these were more usual circumstances, the events of the past several years were anything but usual for the GOP or, for that matter, the country.

In Callaway's defense, he had been handed a hot potato that had already been heated by Press Secretary Ron Nessen's comments at a White House press briefing. Nessen had informed the assembled media that the campaign committee would not be a "Ford-Rockefeller" committee, just a Ford committee.

Witcover wrote, "Ford's declaration of candidacy, however, was made against the backdrop of his political agents' effort to keep Reagan out of the race. It was suggested, unofficially, in fact, that Reagan might be Ford's running mate."[6]

Meanwhile, the Washington parlor game of "What to do about Rockefeller?" was the Ford campaign's tar baby. The more they pushed at it, the more the controversy about Rockefeller stuck to them. Ford tried the diplomatic approach saying that it should be left to the delegates at the convention—he was confident the delegates would choose both him and Rockefeller. However, as a conservative mindful of the looming Reagan challenge, Callaway told Witcover, "A lot of Reagan people are not supporters of Rockefeller, and I want it clear to them that we want their support [for Ford] whether they support Rockefeller or not."[7]

Callaway was later accused by some of following Donald Rumsfeld's and others' orders in the Administration to try to push Rockefeller off the ticket. Callaway's heavy-handed handling of the situation was widely criticized when he suggested in a meeting of reporters that Ford might need a younger running mate. But what caused the Georgian the most trouble with the White House was his description of Rockefeller as his "Number-one problem."

In Raleigh, Reagan deplored the "shoddy treatment" of Rockefeller. Going further with reporters, Reagan said "It's embarrassing—it must be—for a man who has served his country in a number of capacities for many years to now be held up as if he were at auction."[8]

The next morning, Rockefeller called Callaway and gave him unshirted hell. Also, Rocky's supporters weren't taking Callaway's criticism without fighting back. In the White House they were using Callaway's performance as a way of getting back at Rumsfeld, who had personally chosen the Georgian to head the campaign. So it came as no surprise that news leaks revealed that Rumsfeld, not Hartmann, would be Ford's liaison with the President Ford Committee. Apparently the news did surprise the White House.

John Casserly wrote of the campaign,

> In the White House, there are "inside" misgivings about President Ford's campaign. Bob Hartmann and others believe Bo Callaway has made some serious tactical bloopers . . . Callaway is blamed for "messing up" the Rockefeller situation. That is shorthand for saying Callaway was to placate conservatives by suggesting that Rocky would have to "prove" himself for a place on the ticket, as the President would have to win the nomination in his own right. [9]

Casserly, and others on the Ford staff, believed that Callaway had gone too far by suggesting that Rocky was a "liability," which set off Rockefeller. He, in turn, badgered Ford for a public vote of confidence, which put Ford right back where he started, and all he had was the public mess to show for it. Ford, for all his efforts to distance himself from Rockefeller, was still held in low esteem by many conservatives in the party.

> The southerners are thus holding out for Reagan. Three recent developments strengthen their unity; the President's "snub" in not seeing Alexander Solzhenitsyn; his trip to Helsinki and suggested "sellout" of Eastern European nations in behalf of a dubious détente; and Mrs. Ford's unfortunate television comments in which she appeared to adopt an easy attitude toward abortion and premarital sex.[10]

Casserly wrote these were chief among Ford's problems with the Right. In fact, it only scratched the surface. Goldwater, thinking he was helping his old adversary, said "I've always thought Nelson Rockefeller would make a good Secretary of State,"[11] but this only served to pour gasoline on the problem.

Throughout 1975, the debate about Rockefeller continued. Ford speechwriter Casserly told a reporter from Mutual Radio, "Jerry Ford does not say one thing in public and something else in private. And he has made it clear he wants Rocky. . . . The President will not drop someone without serious reason. . . . Ford is loyal."[12]

Meanwhile, Hartmann contended that conservatives had nowhere to turn and had to stay with Ford regardless of his policies or personnel decisions. While Reagan was increasingly vocal in his criticisms of Ford, he still was mindful that Ford was the President. Others around Ford, including Dick Cheney, urged him "to pay more attention to conservatives in the party."[13]

But by July of 1975, relations between Ford and Reagan had hit near rock bottom. Ford was still miffed at Reagan for a radio commentary in late 1974 that he believed was a swipe at his foreign policy. But Reagan let Ford have it with both barrels in a column about Ford's slight of Soviet dissident Aleksandr Solzhenitsyn during his visit to Washington in the first week in July. In a column that appeared in many papers on July 15, the former California Governor wrote,

> Press Secretary Ron Nessen gave out a succession of reasons why there wouldn't be a meeting between Solzhenitsyn and the President. First, the President couldn't attend the dinner because he was scheduled to be at a

> party for his daughter. Then, it seems, there wouldn't be a subsequent meeting because Solzhenitsyn hadn't requested one. Next, Nessen said, the President doesn't ordinarily meet with *private* personages (he met that very week with Brazilian soccer star Pele). Then, "for image reasons, the President does like to have some substance in his meetings. It is not clear what he would gain by a meeting with Solzhenitsyn." For substance, the President has met recently with the Strawberry Queen of West Virginia and the Maid of Cotton.
>
> Finally, the real reason for the snub surfaced: a visit with Solzhenitsyn would violate the "spirit of détente."[14]

Solzhenitsyn was the Russian author who had gained fame for his book, *The Gulag Archipelago*, a chronicle of the Soviet Union's treatment of political prisoners, including himself. Solzhenitsyn had too much sunlight for the Kremlin to simply execute, so he was deported and emigrated to America. Jesse Helms and the conservative movement took up his cause and had approached the Ford White House for a meeting between the President and the famous dissident. Coin-cidentally, Reagan's column appeared the day Laxalt announced the formation of Citizens for Reagan.

By this point, Reagan was on a course he probably could not reverse, even if he had wanted to. The personal insults from the Ford White House were more than he could stomach, and he certainly had the ideological reasons to make the race. Hartmann wrote of the tension between the two: "Ford thought Reagan was a phony, and Reagan thought Ford was a lightweight, and neither one felt the other was fit to be President."[15]

Even after the announcement of Citizens for Reagan, the Ford forces were in denial about Reagan's candidacy and could not face the prospect of running against someone they did not understand or respect. Nessen could not understand the rationale for a Reagan campaign, writing in his book, *It Sure Looks Different from the Inside,* that Ford "wasn't doing badly," thus answering his own question.

Nessen went on to write,

> Ronald Reagan—former movie actor, former Governor of California, darling of the conservatives—loomed larger and larger through 1975 as a threat to Ford for the nomination of his own party. At first, the Ford White House refused to believe that Reagan would challenge an incumbent conservative Republican President. When the reality of the threat sank in, various strategies were tried to discourage Reagan from entering the race and to win his constituency over to Ford.

—An indirect effort was made to talk Reagan out of running.

—Ford selected a conservative Southerner as his Campaign Manager, Army Secretary Howard "Bo" Callaway of Georgia.

—Ford did not interfere when Callaway suggested that Vice President Nelson Rockefeller, detested by conservatives, was a hindrance to Ford's nomination, at least in the South.

—The President issued his own arm's-length statement, saying the delegates at the convention would decide whether Rockefeller would be his running mate. And when Rockefeller finally decided he'd had enough humiliation and withdrew from contention for the Vice Presidential nomination, Ford did not try to talk him out of it.

—Published statements of support for the President were solicited from leading Republicans around the country. The Ford campaign organization in California conspicuously included several prominent former Reagan backers.

—The President shifted his policies further to the right.[16]

Nessen was mystified at how Reagan could run. However, Ford's policies did not shift noticeably to the right. They arguably moved left, showcased by the snub of Solzhenitsyn and the equally controversial Helsinki Accords. The Accords were the culmination of years of negotiations between the West and the Soviets dealing with Eastern Europe and mutual respect for borders drawn up at Yalta and Potsdam during World War II. Critics charged it was a one-way agreement favoring the Russians to the detriment to the Warsaw Pact and the "Captive Nations" of the Baltics. Despite the embroilment, Ford traveled to Helsinki, Finland, in August of 1975 to sign the Accords at the urging of Secretary of State Henry Kissinger.

The agreement with the Soviets was yet another stumbling block for Ford and his handling—or mishandling—of the Accords. Congressmen like Republican Ed Derwinski of Illinois, who had large constituencies of Eastern European immigrants and descendants, were furious at what they perceived as the United States "selling out" Eastern Europe to the Soviets. Some even went so far as to refer to Helsinki as "the new Yalta."[17]

Inside the Ford White House, the arguments over Helsinki were just as heated. Kissinger and State Department officials argued for Ford to state publicly that he was signing the Helsinki Accords because they were "balanced," while anti-Soviet hardliners in the Administration wanted Ford to use tougher language. Concern grew between Dick Cheney, Ford's cerebral young Deputy Chief of Staff, and Jerry Jones, another Ford staffer, that Reagan would score political points with the Helsinki Accords.

Casserly described the scene of one of Ford's meetings: "Cheney and Jones zeroed in on Reagan. They insist that Reagan is making mileage in his attacks on détente, that détente is an issue. [They] sound as if they are certain that Reagan [will] formally announce as a candidate." In the meeting, Ford wrongly observed, "A good theme is that détente depends on a strong national defense. If we don't have a strong national defense, we won't need détente. If we don't have détente, defense costs will rise greatly. It seems to me that we have the best of both worlds."[18]

Steven Hayward, in his landmark book, *The Age of Reagan*, explained the controversy well:

> Kissinger's private intellectual pessimism [over the future of the West] might be of little account had it not been perceived as the basis of his enthusiasm for the Helsinki accords of 1975. . . .
>
> The central strategic problem in Europe during the Cold War was the fate of divided Germany, and the nature of any prospective reunification between East and West Germany. A united, "neutral" Germany would favor Soviet interests and complicate the task of defending the rest of western Europe, and hence be unacceptable to the West. But the Soviets were not about to give up East Germany if it meant its incorporation within NATO. . . .
>
> West Germany especially wanted a clause endorsing the "peaceful change of frontiers"—a code phrase not only for reunification with East Germany but also for prudent border adjustments with Poland. The Soviets would only accept the clause if the treaty also included the principle of "inviolability of frontiers"—a code phrase for recognizing existing borders. . . .
>
> The deeper problem with the "inviolability of frontiers" clause is that it represented a *de facto* recognition of Soviet dominance of Eastern Europe. Kissinger saw this as no more than a concession to reality, since there was no prospect of a military liberation of Eastern Bloc nations, and the tradeoff of having the Soviets agree to the principle of de-alignment outweighed the concession to military reality. But especially in the case of Lithuania, Latvia and Estonia—three independent nations the Soviets absorbed by brute force in the 1940s—the acknowledgement of "inviolability of frontiers" ran counter to American policy, especially the annual congressional observance of "Captive Nations Week," which was specifically intended to remind of the three Baltic nations.[19]

Helsinki also ran opposite the staunch anti-Communism of conservatives and the American people. Recognition of the "Captive Nations" had been in the Republican Party platform since 1948. Human rights were also addressed in the Accords. But to critics, it seemed a one-way street. Hayward summarizes conservative sentiment on the issue, saying, "a pledge to observe human rights meant little in regimes without a free press or a judicial process to secure human rights." Reagan was opposed, saying, "I am against it, and I think all Americans should be against it."[20]

At Kissinger's urging, Ford signed the documents. Noted political analyst Michael Barone speculated years later that it may have been the stinging criticism he received over Helsinki that led him in the second debate with Jimmy Carter to misstate American foreign policy, declaring, "There is no Soviet domination of Eastern Europe." Barone thought Ford meant to say that the West and the people of Eastern Europe will never allow the Soviet Union to dominate their desire for freedom and independence.[21]

However, the criticism that Reagan and his conservatives leveled at Ford over Helsinki and détente paled in comparison to the uproar over Betty Ford's interview with Morley Safer on CBS's *60 Minutes* in August of 1975, in which she condoned abortion, marijuana use, and extramarital affairs. Ford, who had trouble enough from the Right over economic and foreign policy issues, now had religious leaders hollering for his scalp. Betty Ford's comments drove them right into Reagan's—and later Carter's—eager arms. Religious leaders across the country denounced the First Lady. Ford himself could only shrug his shoulders, but his more seasoned operatives knew her comments had damaged his campaign.

This was not the way that Ford and his people would have wanted to celebrate his one-year anniversary in the White House. And still, Callaway was attempting to get friends of Reagan's, like Holmes Tuttle, to call Reagan and tell him not to run.

Meanwhile, Ford's angst about Reagan manifested itself in more and more complaints to his staff and anyone who would listen. He complained that Reagan never seemed to be around to meet the President or the Vice President at the airport, or that Reagan charged for political speeches, or that Reagan's public statements were increasingly critical of his Administration. "Reagan is a virtuoso of the political double-entendre, and you never really caught him taking a personal swipe at the President until a good deal later. But Jerry Ford could read his radar, and he didn't like it," Hartmann wrote. "Knowing he wasn't in Reagan's league as an orator or drawing card didn't soften his distaste. Ford usually wasn't one to harbor mean feelings, but Reagan brought out the worst in him."[22]

Cooler heads in the Ford White House—like Cheney and Bill Timmons,

Ford's talented political aide—did not agree with the others around 1600 Pennsylvania Avenue about Reagan's interest in running or his intelligence or his appeal. Mel Laird, an old buddy of Ford's from their days together in the House, never disguised his loathing for Reagan. He thought Reagan was without substance. In this, he and Hartmann agreed. The topic of Reagan was center stage for much of 1975 in the Ford White House. It would have flattered the old actor to know how much people were talking about him.

Adding to Ford's problems, by mid-August 1975, his approval numbers had plummeted to a meager 38 percent in the Harris poll and only a 45 percent approval rating in a Gallup poll. The Harris survey had his disapproval at a Nixon-like 60 percent.[23]

Over the summer of 1975, both the *Washington Post* and the *New York Times* ran lengthy articles on how Ford's looming Presidential campaign would manifest itself. Both articles came to the conclusion that Ford would pursue a campaign of "moderation," proving once again that reporters and editors make lousy Campaign Managers.

The Washington press corps was also closely covering much of the infighting in the White House. The Ford camp was embroiled in such turmoil that Mrs. Ford took it upon herself to take a swipe at Hartmann in the media. Aides were leaking to the media that Ford was "peaking too soon," a favorite political cliché at the time. Moderate Republican Senators were imploring Ford to play down the conservative rhetoric. In a meeting with the President, the Senators advised him that his conservative base inside the GOP was fine, and he should concentrate on the Democratic and Independent vote for the 1976 campaign.

Infighting in Ford's White House was part of the daily routine. Hartmann and Rumsfeld fought over everything—often publicly—including mess privileges and preferred parking for their respective staffs. Rockefeller was a particular sticking point. They managed to agree on the problems posed by Kissinger, though for wildly different reasons. White House speechwriting provided another example of the disarray inside the Ford White House, as a dozen or more people sometimes edited the President's speeches. At one point, Hartmann told his staff not to put their names on drafts for the President's review, a step that struck the writers as absurd since each of them had to meet with Ford to review their respective speech drafts.[24]

Complaints about Ford's White House also ranged from the extent of his travel to the fact that his travels seemed to make no sense. This may have been explained by the fact that the head of his scheduling office, Warren Rustand, played tennis three hours per day according to some inside the Ford White House.[25]

Ford's problems continued into September of 1975, when he ran afoul of Oklahoma farmers and the AFL-CIO as his Administration initially pushed for grain sales to the Soviets. He then reversed course and opposed the sales. Complicating the situation for Ford was George Meany, head of the powerful union and a strong anti-Communist, who ordered his members not to load grain destined for Russia.

Ford also received harsh criticism from the media when he campaigned in New Hampshire extensively for Republican Senate nominee Louis Wyman, who had actually won the election the previous November of 1974 by four votes out of hundreds of thousands cast. The Democratic-controlled Senate refused to seat poor Wyman until a special election had taken place. By the time of the new election in 1975, Big Labor had poured in thousands of workers and hundreds of thousands of dollars into New Hampshire to gain the seat for Democrat John Durkin. Reagan also campaigned for Wyman but escaped any criticism. Ford took the blame for the loss.

The situation became life threatening when, in the span of less than three weeks, two women tried to assassinate Ford during separate forays into California. In September, a woman by the name of Lynette "Squeaky" Fromme, one of the remaining disciples of the Charles Manson Family, pointed a revolver at Ford in Sacramento. Fortunately, the gun did not fire and Ford escaped injury. As she screamed to the Secret Service, "It didn't go off fellas!" Fromme was apprehended while Ford was whisked away.

Later in September, Sarah Jane Moore, whom the media described both as a radical and a former FBI informant, pointed a rifle at Ford as he emerged from a downtown hotel in San Francisco. A Vietnam veteran standing next to Ford hit the barrel downward as the shot fired, and the bullet meant for Ford hit the curb.

The assassination attempts revived harsh criticisms of the Secret Service, renewed Democratic initiatives for federally mandated gun registration and frequent editorials questioning Ford's frenetic gallivanting across the country. Ford courageously refused to curtail his public appearances and opposed the gun control legislation.

At the same time in the conservative challenger's camp, no one had taken a shot at Reagan. That would happen years later. But in the wake of his speech to the Chicago Executives Club, he was accused of shooting himself, and his campaign, in the foot with his proposal to transfer the onus of $90 billion in federal services to the states.

Ford had his own ideas about running a government when he announced a major shakeup of his Cabinet on November 2. In Washington it was widely perceived that conservative hawks were the losers and the moderate supporters of détente were the winners in the Ford Administration. Ford dismissed James R. Schlesinger as Secretary of Defense and installed his forty-three-year-old aide, Donald H. Rumsfeld, in his place. Schlesinger was touted as an effective counterweight to Kissinger and his headlong rush toward more and more arms control agreements with the Soviets. Schlesinger was a favorite of conservatives, but Ford could not personally stand the man, whom he felt talked down to him.

William E. Colby, Director of the Central Intelligence Agency, was also dismissed. He was more hawkish on the Soviet threat than others surrounding Ford. George Bush replaced him after returning from his post as Envoy to China. Bush was not regarded as softer on the Soviets than Colby, but he was seen as loyal to Ford and more of a team player. Colby was offered an Ambassadorship by Ford but politely declined.

It was a Michael Corleone style "hit." Each victim was called individually into the White House to be fired personally by Ford. Schlesinger later became a behind-the-scenes advisor to Reagan on national defense matters.[26]

After the dismissals, Ford departed Washington for a meeting in Florida with Egyptian President Anwar Sadat. During a break in the meetings, Ford went for a swim at a private residence and promptly put a lump on his head when he dove into the shallow end of the pool.

Far more important, however, the shuffling of the Ford Cabinet was a clear-cut victory for Kissinger's policies and his defenders, and a loss for conservatives in the Ford Administration. Kissinger and Schlesinger quarreled often. Although Kissinger was "forced" to give up his dual post of both Secretary of State and National Security Advisor, one of his protégés, Brent Scowcroft, was installed as head of the National Security Council.

A Reagan spokesman assessed the shake-up for the *New York Times*: "It shakes down as a victory for Henry [Kissinger]; it's not going to help Ford very much. A lot of people in the party and the country think Henry has too much power already. A lot have thought of Schlesinger as a ballast against Kissinger in the nuclear arms talks."[27]

Someone else who came out on top in the shakeup was Rumsfeld. Although Rumsfeld had been promoted to Secretary of Defense-designate, he had a bruising year-long battle with the media, especially in Robert Novak and Rowland Evans's nationally syndicated column. Rumsfeld's Deputy, Cheney, also came in for harsh criticism from the feared duo and, according to Nessen, referred to the columnists behind closed doors in the White House as "Errors and No Facts."[28]

Rumsfeld and Cheney had met several years earlier when Cheney was a congressional fellow and Rumsfeld was a Congressman from Illinois. Cheney had interviewed for a position in Rumsfeld office but recalled that "we didn't hit it off. He was arrogant, abrasive, I thought, and he thought I was an air-headed intellectual."

A second meeting occurred later, after Rumsfeld became head of the Office of Economic Opportunity. This meeting went better when Cheney "interviewed" for the congressional relations job. He had been recommended by his boss, Congressman Bill Steiger of Wisconsin, and showed up at the appointed hour. Waiting in a crowded conference room, a secretary called out, "Is there someone named Cheney here?" Cheney replied in the affirmative and she escorted him to Rumsfeld's office: "He looked up for a minute, and then looked back down at his desk and he said, 'You, you're congressional relations . . . now get the hell out of here!'"[29]

In the days following the dismissals of Schlesinger and Colby, rumors floated around Washington that the ambitious Rumsfeld, acting as Ford's consigliore, had been maneuvering to get two rivals for 1976 out of the way. The first was Rockefeller, whom he'd gotten dropped from the ticket. The other contender was George Bush, whose appointment as Director of the CIA would most likely take him out of contention for the ticket in 1976. The rumors claimed that the changes opened the possibility of a Ford-Rumsfeld ticket. Washington, of course, thrived on rumors and the more ridiculous, the more conspiratorial, the better.

Of the shakeup of his Cabinet, Ford's priority seemed to be keeping Kissinger aboard and happy. But he was also interested in forming a team of his own that got along. Nixon enjoyed the squabbling among his Cabinet and White House staff, reasoning that it kept them away from him. But Ford was tired of seeing the details of each staff and Cabinet fight showcased in the pages of the *Washington Post* or the *New York Times*. Ford's White House, in a town where everybody leaked to the media, was the leakiest vessel of them all.

According to Nessen,

> Ford must share some of the responsibility for the staff fighting that went on throughout his Presidency. He was too much Mr. Nice Guy.
>
> Once in awhile, though, Ford did indicate to his staff that he was unhappy about the squabbling and the news leaks about the squabbling . . . Ford appeared at a meeting of his senior aides in the Roosevelt Room and declared, "I'm damn sick and tired of a ship that has such leaky seams. We are being drowned by premature and obvious leaks." During

> one upsurge of stories that Kissinger was losing his power, Ford pounded his desk and told a group of aides, "G—damn it, I don't want any more of this." He threatened "dire consequences" for anyone who leaked stories against Kissinger.[30]

The anti-Kissinger stories died down for a while. But in what would eventually be one of Ford's most significant decisions, Cheney was promoted to Chief of Staff—the first time Ford had allowed the job title to be used in his Administration. Rumsfeld was a moderate Republican in the tradition of the Illinois GOP and did not understand Reagan's appeal. But Cheney, unlike others around Ford, did understand Reagan, for several reasons: "First, I was a Westerner . . . Wyoming was an important part of my upbringing. Second, I was more conservative philosophically than a lot of my colleagues around the Ford Administration. Nelson Rockefeller for example. Rockefeller and I did not get along," Cheney recalled. "He was convinced I was out to get him."[31]

Cheney was also more politically sophisticated than most in the White House, and Ford's fortunes in the executive mansion and his campaign would slowly begin to improve. Not that the press noticed.

The *New York Times* wrote, "Mr. Reagan's staff is superior to the President's, despite the arrival at the President Ford Committee of the highly regarded Stuart Spencer of California as Political Director."[32] Unaware of Cheney's talents, the paper further reported, "A measure of the problems of the Ford enterprise is the fact that the political liaison at the White House is Richard B. Cheney, who has no experience in state or local, let alone national campaigns."[33]

Cheney would eventually assert his control over all aspects of the White House and the campaign, including initiating daily meetings in his office with new hire Stu Spencer, Rog Morton, Callaway, and Bob Teeter, the campaign's pollster.

The turmoil over the Cabinet reshuffling in the Administration was just one more crisis for Ford in an endless stream of problems. Earlier, it was reported that Ford's Director of Campaign Organization, Lee Nunn, had resigned, citing Bo Callaway's inattentiveness to grassroots organizing. In fact, Spencer later said Nunn had been pushed out of the campaign due to his own incompetent work—not Callaway's.[34] Also, David Packard had been let go from the Ford campaign.

In the spring of 1975, the President Ford Committee had trumpeted the arrival of Packard as its National Finance Director. Packard was considered a major acquisition for Ford. Not only was he a Californian and a conservative, but he had also been involved in some early planning of the Reagan campaign. He was also rich and knew a lot of other rich people, but with the passage of the Federal Election Act in 1975, the day of the "fat cat" and $100,000 contributions was over.

Unfortunately for Ford, Packard not only tried to run his operation from California but, upon being named Finance Director, set a public fundraising goal of $10 million by the end of 1975. Several months later, this goal was scaled back to five million. By the time Packard was forced out of the campaign, they had raised less than one million dollars.

Packard was from the old school of campaign fundraising; he tried to raise the money by phone in $1,000 chunks. He eschewed a direct mail program, losing months of precious time needed to develop a national house file of proven Ford contributors. Packard had authorized one small test mailing of 60,000 names, but no effort was undertaken for Ford beyond that. Six precious months essential in building a mail list for an incumbent President were wasted.[35]

Under the newly formed Federal Election Commission, candidates for President were eligible for up to five million dollars in matching funds—courtesy of the American taxpayer—as long as the candidate abided by certain laws.

Attempting to curb the efforts of "fat cats" to buy off candidates, the Commission made corporate contributions illegal and stipulated that all contributions over $250 were ineligible for the federal matching funds program. Candidates also had to agree to spending ceilings in each state primary, which were determined by state population and primary voter turnout in previous elections. After jumping through all these hoops, candidates then had to scrupulously report money raised and spent.

Packard had raised only $950,000 by the time of his dismissal, but even more unfortunate for Ford was that most of this was raised in $1,000 checks from oil executives and old business cronies of Packard's, with only the first $250 of each $1,000 contribution eligible for matching funds. Five members of the Rockefeller family each thoughtfully gave $1,000 to Ford.[36]

The *New York Times* reported, "The departure of Mr. Packard served to underscore the difficulty Mr. Ford appeared to have in getting his campaign under way—an unusual problem for an incumbent President."[37] The *Times* proceeded to summarize Ford's problems in two areas: "Mr. Packard's resignation may prove to be more worrisome than Mr. Nunn's, at least in terms of public perception of how the Ford candidacy is faring, because Mr. Packard had been an ally of Mr. Reagan's before being enlisted in May to head the President's fund-gathering efforts."[38]

Ford would eventually pick Bob Mosbacher of Houston, an ally of George Bush, as his new Finance Director. Mosbacher eventually righted the Ford fundraising operation. Reagan's direct mail guru Bruce Eberle had used the early months to his advantage to begin the process of building a reliable direct mail house file for his financial needs.

As of the September 30 reporting date for the Reagan campaign, it showed income of almost $400,000. Almost 80 percent of Reagan's income was eligible for matching funds, making him competitive with Ford in the money game. Most of this money was coming in the form of direct mail solicitations. Eberle was delighted to see his efforts beginning to succeed. Reagan's house file would eventually grow to over 400,000 names by the time of the Kansas City Convention, according to Eberle.[39]

"Many Republican party officials in Washington and elsewhere believe that former Gov. Ronald Reagan of California, who is not yet an announced candidate, is ahead of the President in terms of organization in several key Republican primary states,"[40] wrote the *New York Times*, echoing the sentiments of political reporters and observers around the country. Reagan was running down the track and Ford was still at the starting gate. Recalled Mahe about the President Ford Committee, it "bumbled along . . . Ford had no control. I wouldn't even go to their meetings. Always they were having meetings."[41]

An additional announcement on November 2 came from Senator Charles Mathias, a Republican from Maryland, who dropped his threat to run in the Presidential primaries as a "liberal." Liberals in the party had become increasingly concerned that Ford, looking over his shoulder at the looming Reagan challenge, was moving too far to the right at the expense of his more moderate and liberal supporters.

But a day later, a liberal Republican of greater stature than Mathias would make an announcement that would once again stun a nation's capital that thought the last three years had made it immune to shock and surprise. Though he retained his office until the end of Ford's first term, Nelson Rockefeller took himself out of contention for the Vice President slot for 1976.

Rockefeller's departure from the ticket also added to the sense of a White House out of control. "One White House source close to the President said that Mr. Rockefeller would have inevitably had to step aside because his presence had become 'detrimental' to Mr. Ford's efforts to win the Republican Party nomination," reported the *New York Times*. "The White House official said that Mr. Rockefeller had been unable to make his peace with the right wing of the Republican Party. He was, therefore, regarded as a liability by the President Ford Committee."[42]

Rockefeller aides did not take the insult lying down and reminded the media of the "cold" nature of Rockefeller's letter to Ford and the fact that he did not make any positive references to either Ford's Presidency or to his nomination. The *New York Times* reported:

> These aides also noted that the letter did not rule out the possibility that Mr. Rockefeller might run himself for President next year. They carefully avoided suggesting that Mr. Rockefeller would seek the Presidency but pictured him as disengaging to wait and watch for new power struggles within the Republican Party,
>
> They also made it clear that Mr. Rockefeller's friends consider the party to be in grave danger. One aide commented that the Vice President had been concerned about the "lurch to the right" and the letter to Mr. Ford was designed for "clearing the air and setting some counter forces in motion."[43]

Peter Hannaford was traveling with Reagan in Florida—a key early state—on November 3. In Boca Raton, where Reagan was speaking at a community college, a reporter approached the Governor and asked him what he thought about Rockefeller's announcement that he would refuse to be on the ticket with President Ford in the 1976 campaign. Would it alter Reagan's plan? Reagan was stunned by the news but gained his composure quickly. Hannaford wrote:

> In retrospect, Rockefeller's move seemed to have been designed to appease conservatives in the Republican Party so that they could get behind Ford. If so, it was a miscalculation. While Rockefeller was unpopular with many grassroots conservatives in the party, they were motivated to support Reagan not so much as a result of Ford's unacceptability, but because in Reagan they had the genuine article, a conservative leader.[44]

Rockefeller's departure finally solved Ford's problem, but the dynamics of who made the decision have never fully been explained. According to President Ford's autobiography, *A Time To Heal*, Ford held his weekly meeting with Rockefeller in the Oval Office on October 28. The conversation inevitably turned to conservatives' angst over Rocky's selection as Vice President and the problem this would pose for Ford in the coming battle with Reagan.[45]

As Ford recounted, though Rockefeller had never officially been on the ticket, he offered to forego a run. Some assumed that Rocky would be on the ticket with Ford in Kansas City once Ford won the nomination. But standing between Ford and that nomination was Reagan and his angry army of conservatives. Ford recounted in his autobiography:

> As we talked, I didn't try to gloss over the fact that conservative opposition to him might jeopardize my own nomination. "There are serious problems," I said, "and to be brutally frank, some of these difficulties might be eliminated if you were to indicate that you didn't want to be on the ticket in 1976. I'm not asking you to do that, I'm just stating the facts."
>
> "I understand," he said. "Well, it's probably better that I withdraw. If I take myself out of the picture, that will clear the air. I'll give you a letter saying that I don't want to be considered as a Vice Presidential nominee."[46]

Over the previous year, Rockefeller had traveled far and wide to meet with conservatives and unsuccessfully attempted to mend fences broken and re-broken since 1964. Conservatives felt Rockefeller had undermined Goldwater in 1964, and they would never forgive or forget his actions.

Both Ford and Rockefeller came to the Presidency and the Vice Presidency via the new Twenty-fifth Amendment to the Constitution, the first time this had ever happened in the history of the United States. Furthermore, neither Ford nor Rockefeller had a strong hold on Republican Party loyalty.

It was a testament to Ford's lack of control over the GOP that he could not force conservatives to accept Rockefeller or his policies in the way Richard Nixon was able to force them to accept his liberal policies and appointments. GOP voters nationwide had invested several votes, starting in 1952, in Richard Nixon but had nothing invested in either Ford or Rockefeller. Thus they were more liberated to disagree with the President. Which explained why Reagan, when pressed by students in Florida on his intentions of challenging Ford, replied, "On a scale of one to ten, I'm at a nine."[47]

John Sears, however, had a different recollection of Rockefeller's abrupt departure than what was stated publicly by Ford and reported in the media. "Rocky was forced off the ticket. He was not the type to offer himself up for slaughter. He was a fighter, and it was Ford who asked him to step down—not the other way around."[48]

During the heat of the upcoming campaign, Rocky would call Sears at his office to cheer him and Reagan on against Ford. To say the Vice President was bitter over his shoddy treatment was an understatement.[49] But in Rockefeller's defense, he never wavered publicly in his support of Ford, nor did his hand-picked lieutenant in New York, the estimable Richard "Rosey" Rosenbaum.

Slowly, Cheney would begin to assert more control over the activities at the White House and the campaign. Problems would continue, but Cheney's placid presence and conservative instincts did much to begin solving Ford's governing and political fortunes in the fall of 1975.

Unfortunately, Cheney's powers couldn't stop the bad personal press Ford continued to receive. The national media gleefully reported each Presidential head bump, errant golf swing or dog leash entanglement. Even worse for Ford, "Physical clumsiness was subtly translated into suggestions of mental ineptitude. Such ridicule in the press and on television undermined public respect for Ford as a leader and damaged his chances in the 1976 election," according to Nessen. "Ford was depicted, literally, as Bozo the Clown in a retouched photo on the cover of *New York* magazine," Nessen wrote. Meanwhile, a young, upcoming comedian named Chevy Chase built a career imitating Ford on NBC's new comic series, *Saturday Night Live.*[50]

As just one example of the media's low opinion of Ford, early in his Administration, Tom Brokaw of *NBC News* asked him, "I have a question that isn't easy to phrase, so I will just bore straight ahead with it. As you know, I'm certain, because I have been told that you have commented on this before, but it has been speculated on in print not only in Washington but elsewhere and it crops up in conversation from time to time in this town—the question of whether or not you are intellectually up to the job of being President of the United States."[51]

Ford dutifully answered Brokaw's insulting question, but the question itself pointed to two problems that continued to plague Ford. First, reporters had the temerity to ask Ford such questions. Second, Ford's continued image problems invited them to do so. And many of Ford's problems stemmed from his own staff, who told the media on background that they had to teach him about governance and foreign policy.

Ford seemed to never catch a break. While on a foreign policy trip to Salzburg, Austria, he slipped on the rain-soaked stairs while descending from Air Force One and fell to his knees and hand in full view of the international community. Later that evening, Ford again slipped, twice this time, while on the balcony of the palace in Salzburg. Typically, the media overreacted and turned the incidents into world-shattering affairs. In fact, while Ford was star-crossed throughout his Administration, these two incidents can be attributed to bad knees from his football days at Michigan.

With all of Ford's bad press and woefully operating White House and campaign until late 1975, it should have followed that his poll numbers would have headed downward. In fact, they were all over the place at any given time, but a memo to Ford from Cheney on October 23 summarized Ford's standing with the electorate at the time. Most of the national polling surprisingly had Ford besting all Democratic comers at the time and he was also beating Reagan in the famous California Field Poll, 54 to 45 percent among all voters.[52] In addition, a Darden poll of the South showed Ford doing better than either Reagan or George Wallace. Ford's national approval ratings had stabilized, for a time, at 47 percent approving and 37 percent disapproving—a dramatic increase since his numbers had tanked in August.[53]

Ford was also presented with a detailed, ninety-page campaign plan in late August and an advisory committee of tough GOP veterans had been assembled, including Dean Burch, Ray Bliss, Kansas Senator Bob Dole, Bryce Harlow and Congressman John Rhodes of Arizona. Moderates who were brought aboard included Senator Hugh Scott of Pennsylvania, Mel Laird, who had left the White House to join *Reader's Digest*, and former Pennsylvania Governor Bill Scranton. The plan was prescient in some areas yet naïve in others. A key phrase throughout the document was "discipline"—a concept previously unknown to the Ford White House. It also said, "In 1976, we find a public which is politically turned off by Watergate and related activities. It seeks a President who is honest, has a high level of integrity and who deals with the American people in a straightforward manner."[54]

Yet Reagan's team had polling data from Dick Wirthlin that showed that honesty and integrity had fallen from the list of the top priorities of the American voter, according to Sears.

> They had been politically battered for years by JFK's assassination, Bobby Kennedy's assassination, Vietnam, Johnson, Watergate, Agnew and a thousand other political scandals that never even made the national news, but they saw and read about in their states and towns. It's no wonder they had little use for politicians and certainly didn't trust them.[55]

The plan was correct, however, in identifying that, "The public is becoming increasingly concerned about bigness—big business, big government, big labor. There exists a perception that with these institutions becoming so large, the identity and needs of individuals will be submerged in the needs of the organization.

Ford's campaign plan did not identify his message, his integrity, or his ideology as his best strengths. It was his incumbency, pure and simple. To be sure, all Presidents use the power of the Presidency to run for re-election—or in Ford's case, for election—but therein was his problem. Republican primary voters saw Ford differently than they would have had they actually voted for him. Indeed, Ford's own polling showed that when he went into a state to campaign, his "numbers" would rise in that particular state, but they would fall nationally. It was a unique paradox that Cheney, Spencer and Callaway would have to reconcile.

But this section in the campaign plan on his incumbency did a commendable job in cataloging most of the advantages Ford would enjoy over Reagan, including command of the national media and his simple "newsworthiness" as President. He was the "automatic frontrunner" and had "at his command all the resources of the federal government to provide him with research on issues, economic analysis, and approximately 2,000 non-career governmental officials who are constantly selling and defending his Administration to the general public."

The documents also listed the disadvantages of incumbency, including the responsibility for decisions made by the President and members of his Administration.

> The President, as the leader of his Administration, shares the responsibility for the acts of his subordinates in the Administration and the campaign. Should one or more of those individuals exercise bad judgment or explicitly commit a wrong, the actions of that individual reflect directly upon the President.[56]

As evident in the campaign plan, many members of the Ford campaign and the White House took little heed of Ronald Reagan's intentions or appeal in 1975. The authors of Ford's campaign plan, to their credit, did. They coolly and crisply reviewed the assets and deficiencies of the Californian.

In the Ford campaign plan,

> Ronald Reagan as a candidate brings to his campaign some significant advantages in terms of attempting to acquire the Republican nomination. He is the strong favorite of the Party's right wing and if not handled correctly, could cause conservative Republicans to unify around him.
>
> His longstanding national visibility in the Republican Party is perhaps his biggest advantage. Reagan has had a national image in the Republican Party since the 1964 election. . . . During that same election, Reagan went on nationwide television advocating Goldwater's candidacy in what has been described as the most effective speech given in the '64 campaign.[57]

In assessing Reagan's other advantages in the campaign, the brief said,

> Since that time, he had twice been elected Governor of the most populous state in the nation and been active across the country as a fundraiser for both state parties and individual candidates. As a result, Reagan is well known to the Party rank and file and has a significant number of outstanding I.O.U.'s.
>
> A second advantage is the flexibility he has as an individual who is not currently holding office and, therefore, not obligated to divide his time between official duties and campaigning. This will allow him to spend much more time in both Primary and Convention states than the President.[58]

Regarding Reagan's drawbacks, the author wrote, "Even among conservatives are many who consider Reagan to have too conservative an image to be a credible candidate in the general election—this may prove to be his greatest negative." The brief continued to note that since Ford was the "Party Candidate," Reagan would be the de facto spoiler in any contest between the two. It concluded this section on a hopeful note by saying, "Finally, many of Reagan's friends consider his candidacy unwise and are privately telling him so. In the end, this may be the deciding factor regarding Reagan's candidacy." It also suggested that some members of Reagan's family opposed his run.

The Ford campaign also looked to an early knockout strategy of Reagan like Sears was planning for Ford. In the case of a long protracted battle, the document naïvely warned, "The 1976 Convention should not give rise to old liberal/conservative splits within the Republican Party."

However, the memo mistakenly suggested that Ford was considered as conservative as Reagan among Republican primary voters. The author imagined that Ford was viewed as a conservative by the rest of the country because he was from the Midwest.

Ford's chances in individual states in the Midwest were explored: "It is important for him [Ford] to do well in Primaries and State Conventions in the various Midwestern states." In fact, Reagan would win five of the eleven Midwest states that the Ford campaign thought it would win.

States were assigned levels of priority, including Georgia. Of course, New Hampshire and Florida were "Priority One," but the addition of Georgia was curious.

> This is the home state of the President Ford Committee Chairman (Callaway) and a place where he has been a statewide candidate and has

many friends. . . . [S]hould the President be able to carry Georgia, this would be the third nail in the coffin of the Reagan campaign.[59]

Reagan apparently had more friends in Georgia than Callaway since he slaughtered Ford there earlier. Nonetheless, the memo correctly identified Reagan's strength in North Carolina, citing his support from Senator Jesse Helms. The document still held out hope for a Ford victory in the Tar Heel State. The balance of the state-by-state analysis was a combination of both the realistic and the surreal. Reagan's chances in some states were accurately portrayed, while others bordered on the ridiculous.

When it came to how the Ford campaign would work at the Kansas City convention in the event that Reagan was still in the campaign, the plan said, "If Governor Reagan remains in the race, much of the President Ford Committee activity at the National Convention will have to surround holding delegations and making sure the President has enough delegates to nominate him on the first ballot."

Despite edicts by some at the Republican National Committee that they take a "neutral" position in the campaign, the Ford campaign clearly saw the RNC as a resource. The memo listed those items it could rely on the national committee to provide in the looming battle with Reagan, including polling and research. Furthermore, "There will, of course, be a relationship between the Campaign Chairman and the Chairman of the RNC, but we would recommend that, in addition, all Division Directors at the PFC also maintain an informal relationship with each of their counterparts at the RNC. A formal liaison between the two should not be designated for purposes other than the transfer of items of value."[60]

A detailed budget allocated nearly $6 million for the primary and convention states, but Ford would actually need to spend over $7 million in those contests before he could beat Reagan at the convention. The budget also broke down staff salaries, with secretaries at the President Ford Committee receiving $10,000. The staff total was projected to number sixty-three.[61] The thoughtful brief could not anticipate all the problems Ford would continue to face, including new challenges from his left.

The President's moderate supporters in the Senate were not thinking about budgets or payrolls. Angered by Ford's drift to the right and his handling of Rockefeller, Senate Republican moderates began to explore the possibility of fielding their own candidate in the Presidential primaries in 1976.

The group of liberal and moderate Republican Senators, members of the

Wednesday Club, met twice in early November to discuss a bid by Howard Baker, a moderate conservative Senator from Tennessee, as reported by Martha Angle in the *Washington Star.*

> "We think [Ford] has been overreacting to the Ronald Reagan threat," said one Western Senator who asked not to be identified.
>
> Although no votes have been taken, and no firm consensus reached, sources said some in the group yesterday expressed interest in urging Sen. Howard H. Baker Jr. . . . to enter the primaries.
>
> Baker is not a member of the Wednesday Club and is generally viewed as a moderately conservative Republican. But as one liberal put it, "we have to recognize that none of our own members could mount a viable campaign in the Republican Party as it exists today. A 'Mac' Mathias or a 'Chuck' Percy could not pull votes in a contest with Ford or Reagan," this Senator said.[62]

Baker was "flattered" at the notion, but still expressed his support for Ford's nomination. The meetings were called by liberal New York Senator Jacob Javits, angry over Ford's treatment of his old friend Rockefeller. It was ironic that the Wednesday Club had opposed Baker's challenge to Senator Hugh Scott of Pennsylvania for the position of Senate Minority Leader several years earlier.

"Javits yesterday said that 'as a senior statesman' with no further political ambitions of his own, 'I feel free to lay before my colleagues all of the options, especially in view of my strong feeling that the President is turning too far right,'" Angle reported.[63]

Percy took a harder line against Ford for his apparent move to the right and an even harder line against Reagan. Percy understood that the party was headed in the direction of Reagan and away from the liberal and moderate elements of the party. Nonetheless, he made it clear that he thought Reaganism was bad for the party and the country.

At one point, Ford raised the possibility of selecting Senator Ed Brooke of Massachusetts, a moderate African American for his running mate, but this gesture did not appease his moderate critics inside the GOP. Meanwhile, the President openly speculated that a third party candidacy by Alabama Governor George C. Wallace, who had previously announced his candidacy for the Democratic Party's nomination, could throw the election into the House of Representatives.

While liberal Republican Senators were pulling Ford in one direction, Barry Goldwater was giving Ford fits from the other side of the ideological divide.

Speaking before the National Press Club, Goldwater, while reiterating his support for Ford's nomination, bluntly assessed Reagan's appeal. He called Reagan "a very strong conservative. . . . I believe my supporters will support Reagan, although some may support Ford. You have to remember that Reagan has a very great following," Goldwater told the assembled media.[64] But he also made clear his opposition to Reagan taking the second position on the ticket with Ford, citing Reagan's age.

A much rougher view of Reagan than Goldwater's was contained in a secret, unsigned White House memo that aggressively reviewed Reagan's record as Governor and found it wanting, citing issues like growth of the California budget under Reagan and his policies on crime ("We are exploring the possibility that we can charge Reagan with being soft on crime, specifically liberal on the parole of felons"). The memo also critiqued Reagan's more recent proposal to transfer $90 billion in federal services to the states.

Reviewing Reagan's energy record, the memo said,

> My plan is to explore the Reagan PUC (Public Utility Commission) appointments and their decisions. I believe that we can build a case for industry favoritism while the consumer got screwed. Politically, this could be used by saying that while Reagan mouthed the line on energy just like everyone else, he was busy screwing the California consumer.
>
> After discreet talks with a number of people ranging from Reagan's former opponents to some of his friends, it appears to me that the anti-Reagan attack with whatever information we eventually produce should be carried on as a second level campaign by those within the campaign structure other than the President himself.

The author concluded to the unknown recipient, "Sorry for the rough typing. I'm being so secretive about all this that I'm scaring myself coming around corners."[65]

One of the darker portions of this Ford White House memo dealt with material obtained from the 1970 Jesse Unruh campaign. Unruh had been the Democratic nominee for Governor of California until the Reagan juggernaut squashed him in the general election. Under the heading "Malibu Ranch Deal," the Ford staffer realized the explosive nature of the material. In his cover memo, which bore no Administration names, they wrote "We have not attempted to review it for accuracy but feel it should be presented as early as possible in order to give the committee the chance to determine whether or not it warrants further checking."[66]

The Unruh memos alleged that the Fox Realty Corporation overpaid Reagan by one million dollars for his former 236-acre ranch in Malibu, initially purchased in 1951 and sold by Reagan to Fox in 1966. Fox Realty was a part of the Fox Studios and the company was looking for additional space for their television and movie productions, having lost their lease. The charge never surfaced in Reagan's 1970 gubernatorial race or the 1976 Presidential primaries, and no allegations came out of the material, but the extent of the Ford campaign's interest in this matter suggested the lengths the Ford campaign was willing to go to defeat Reagan.

The Ford White House was looking for something—anything—to stop the Reagan bandwagon. Meanwhile, frustrated at how he was being treated in the media, the President summoned two *Washington Post* reporters to the White House to try to confront his unfair image.

In an interview with Lou Cannon and David Broder, Ford said, "I think it is an inaccurate depiction. . . . Most of the critics . . . have never played in a ball game, never skied. I don't know whether it is a self-defense mechanism in themselves or what, but I'm kind of amused at that. It doesn't bother me at all."[67]

In fact, Ford was deeply offended at the continued oafish portrayals of him in the media. Ford's former Press Secretary, Jerald terHorst, who had resigned over Ford's pardon of Richard Nixon, became a syndicated columnist and shed light on Ford's plight:

> Creating trouble for President Ford could be easy for Reagan, given the President's penchant for creating trouble for himself in recent months. Republicans of every hue seem disappointed in his performance, faulting Ford for lackluster speeches, his barnstorming around the country, a fumbling Administration shakeup, and a shuffling campaign organization.
>
> Letting Vice President Rockefeller go has displeased the moderates while failing to appease the conservatives—and ditto for Ford's drift to the right on social issues and his zig-zagging line on financial aid for stricken New York City.[68]

TerHorst referred to Ford's situation as a "shambles."

Reagan was also having his problems with his campaign. *The Political Animal*, a widely read tip sheet, reported:

> Sears does not run a tight ship and one result is that practically everybody in the campaign except the receptionist and mailroom staff is talking to the press. This not only undercuts Nofziger, the presumed spokesman,

> but the campaign itself. Unless Sears steps in quickly, supported by RR, and disciplines the campaign staff, including regional directors and local chairmen, further inconsistencies, contradictions and embarrassing stories will continue and escalate. Staff fighting is already public, reminiscent of the disastrous McGovern's '72 campaign.

This particular issue had been circulated to Cheney attached to a handwritten note from Ford.[69]

The newsletter did not detail the staff infighting or embarrassing stories going on inside the Reagan campaign. The story also incorrectly assumed that Sears did not want the staff talking to the press. In fact, he was encouraging Reagan's people to talk to the media without any fear, and to try not to deceive them, Lake later said.[70]

However, the newsletter did (in the minds of some) accurately portray Sears as a "weak administrator." David Keene said, "John was a great strategist and had a fine mind, but the problem in politics is that people [always want] to do the job that they're not good at instead of what they are good at. John should have been head of strategy for Reagan, but not campaign manager."[71]

Even as of the fall of 1975, the Ford White House still could not come to grips with the fact that Reagan was indeed about to jump in the race, despite many staff problems. Cheney asked Lou Cannon if he thought Reagan would run and also asked Spencer. Both men knew Reagan and both were startled that even at that late date the people around Ford could not seem to accept this eventuality.[72]

Reagan's startup problems took place without the glare of the national media that Gerald Ford faced. For Ford, every incident, big and small, seemed to make the front pages and the network news. A United Press International story, dateline Springfield, Massachusetts in November of 1975 seemed almost typical for Ford: "President Ford was rapped on the side of the head today with a 24-inch flag staff by an excited youngster. . . . There was no blood where Ford was struck on the right temple and there was no sign he was injured. . . ."

In Hartford, Connecticut, a street left open by that city's police allowed a pickup truck to barrel into the side of the Presidential limousine. Ford was unhurt, but the Republican State Chairman, Fred Biebel, jammed his thumb in the incident.

Nessen later wrote in his book,

> Also damaging to Ford's image were the news photos of him [taken] at the instant he saw the gun in Sacramento and the instant he heard the

> shot in San Francisco. In both pictures, his eyes were blank, his face white and slack, his expression dazed and frightened. It was not a "Presidential" look to inspire confidence.
>
> In the autumn and winter of 1975, Ford's public standing slumped. Some members of the White House staff blamed this on the assassination attempts and the auto accident, which they felt had created an impression that Ford was an unPresidential klutz forever stumbling into some kind of accident.[73]

Contained in a memorandum prepared for Nessen, Ford staffer Jim Shuman sent along his observations that Reagan's "general ignorance of national affairs—assuming it will continue—will make President Ford look better and better every day." He concluded, however, in what may have been the greatest understatement of 1975 by saying, "Reagan could be a serious threat."[74]

At the end of the year, Ford's pollster, Robert Teeter, presented him with a gloomy assessment of the Republican Party and Ford's standing in the party and as the President. Ford got low ratings from the American people on being a strong leader or intelligent or competent. Teeter also wrote in a memo to Cheney that "détente is a particularly unpopular idea with Republican primary voters and the word is worse."[75]

Teeter also authored a grim memo to Callaway about Reagan's threat. Ford's helplessness was summed up when Teeter wrote, "The Christmas lull may well be the best thing we have going for us in that it should blunt Reagan's momentum."[76]

And when Teeter asked the American people in a poll conducted for the campaign to name one accomplishment of Ford's, 61 percent of the respondents said, "Nothing."[77]

4

CITIZENS FOR REAGAN, TAKE ONE

"We're disgusted with Reagan for not making the commitment. He's our man, but he just won't come on in."

By 1975, conservative Republicans had already decided that Ronald Reagan was their man and that he would run for the party's Presidential nomination against Gerald Ford. They believed that Reagan had waited too long in 1968 before challenging Richard Nixon for the nomination. Lyn Nofziger, who had little use for Gerald Ford and Bob Walker, formerly of the Governor's staff in Sacramento, thought Reagan had already waited long enough—maybe too long.

Peter Hannaford and Mike Deaver, now in business for themselves, arranged with the help of radio producer Harry O'Connor for Reagan to do weekly commentaries on what would eventually total nearly three hundred stations around the country. Although Reagan was keeping his own counsel on a 1976 bid, many grassroots conservatives would not be bothered with anything so frustrating as waiting for Reagan to eventually make up his mind. Shortly after Reagan left office in Sacramento in January, Young America's Foundation initiated the "Reagan Radio Project," directed by YAF Executive Director Frank Donatelli and YAF Chairman Ron Docksai. Donatelli was of the young breed of conservative activists who had been drawn to conservatism by the message of Barry Goldwater in 1964. He had read *Conscience of a Conservative*, Goldwater's clarion call and had been deeply impressed with the Arizonan's clear thinking and message.

The Foundation's affiliated organization, Young Americans for Freedom, had endorsed Reagan for President in 1968 over Nixon and again, in 1972, over Nixon. Of course, Reagan did not run against Nixon in 1972 and in fact had campaigned for his old colleague. But this did not stop YAF from voicing support for their hero. Reagan joined the YAF Board and had spoken at many of their conventions. A long, warm relationship existed between the old actor and the young YAFers.

The project, which consisted of raising money in the mail to independently support Reagan's weekly radio addresses, was undertaken by Bruce Eberle who was just beginning his direct mail firm; becoming yet another competitor to the "King of Conservative Direct Mail," Richard Viguerie. The YAF house file (its list of proven financial donors created through "prospecting" mail) eventually grew to over fourteen thousand names. Contributors had been asked to support the "Reagan Radio Project," and this list became the basis of the direct mail house file for the eventual Reagan campaign.

Furthermore, the house organ of the conservative movement, *Human Events*, underwrote many of Reagan's radio commentaries. The publication was led by two tough-minded conservatives, Tom Winter and Allan Ryskind. Between the efforts of Deaver, Hannaford, O'Connor, YAF, and *Human Events*, Reagan would solidify his position as the conservative with the greatest nationwide name recognition. But one California conservative summed up conservative angst over Reagan's indecision in the spring of 1975 in *Newsweek*: "We're disgusted with him for not making the commitment. He's our man, but he just won't come on in."[1]

Reagan also had support from the Young Republicans. This group was headquartered inside the Republican National Committee. An incumbent President should have been able to count on the institutional support of his party, even in a hotly contested primary. But in the spring of 1975, the Young Republicans elected a new National Chairman, Jack Mueller of Wyoming. The President called Mueller to congratulate him on his election and asked Mueller's support in the upcoming campaign. Mueller, then in his mid-twenties, replied, "Mr. President, I can't support you because I'm waiting for this fellow from California, Ronald Reagan, to get into the race!" When the RNC staff heard of Mueller's impudence, threats were made to cut off the Young Republicans' funding, but nothing came of it.[2]

However, Ford could count on the support of virtually all the elements in the party. RNC Chairman Mary Louise Smith was pulling for Ford's nomination. Still, Eddie Mahe, her astute aide, had made sure the party took an official "hands off" approach to the Presidential contest by getting the Executive Committee of the RNC to agree to a posture of official neutrality in January of 1975.[3] Reagan operatives, especially Nofziger, accused the RNC of a smokescreen—while the top floor of the RNC might have been technically uncommitted, the other floors were a beehive of pro-Ford activity.[4]

Meanwhile, Reagan's own California team worked feverishly to promote him and his views to a broader audience than ever before. Early in 1975, Deaver and Hannaford, through the Copley News Service syndicate, signed up dozens of newspapers to carry Reagan's columns, published twice per week, and recruited hundreds of radio stations to carry his radio commentaries, broadcast every weekday. In 1975, they expected to generate over six hundred thousand dollars in income for "the Governor," as everyone referred to him. He was also fetching five thousand dollars per speech on what Reagan called the "mashed potato circuit."

From some quarters, Hannaford and Deaver had been accused of putting their own interests ahead of Reagan's political future. In Reagan's waning days in Sacramento, they had agreed to form "Deaver and Hannaford," a public relations firm whose major client would be Reagan. They presented their plan to handle Reagan's forthcoming private career, and Ronald and Nancy Reagan quickly agreed.

In fact, Reagan needed the money. He had a home in Pacific Palisades and was in the process of buying a six hundred-acre ranch in Santa Barbara. He had a wife and children to support and, on top of it all, in an incredibly petty and vindictive move, the Democratic-controlled California legislature reduced Reagan's scheduled pension from $49,000 per year to $19,000 per year. Former Governor Brown, whom Reagan had defeated eight years earlier, was receiving a pension thousands above the amount Reagan was to receive.

When possible, Reagan liked to sneak away to his new ranch with his wife, where they were in the process of slowly remodeling the tiny house that was built around the turn of the century. The ranch was located twenty-nine miles outside of Santa Barbara, and he renamed it *Rancho del Cielo*—"Ranch in the Sky."

Ronald Reagan loved the ranch. Owning it was the fulfillment of a lifetime dream, and while Nancy Reagan was less than enthusiastic about the ranch, she knew how her husband loved it and gamely went along.

Mrs. Reagan's taste for the property diminished even further years later. On one occasion, heavy rains had forced snakes out of their lairs and onto the ranch, including under some buildings. Reagan knew his wife's extreme dislike for snakes and proceeded to capture them and bag them to release off the property. Reagan had placed the bag of snakes in the front seat of the vehicle they used to drive to the ranch. As they drove along the harrowing, several miles-long, single lane, dirt and gravel road with sheer drops of several hundred feet, Reagan had forgotten to tell his wife about the bag of snakes until her shriek reminded him of his oversight. She loved the ranch even less after that episode.

Deaver and Hannaford were personally close to the Reagans, and each man brought differing talents to their business. Hannaford, quiet and bespectacled, drafted many of Reagan's speeches. Deaver was shorter, intense, and a shrewd negotiator. They opened offices in Los Angeles to accommodate Reagan's travels. Reagan was living in Pacific Palisades and, according to Hannaford, "wanted our offices fifteen minutes from his home and fifteen minutes from the airport." One or the other would travel with Reagan and they provided him with an office in their eighth floor suite where he would spend a couple of days per week.[5]

Although their hot new public relations firm had other clients, they committed countless hours of work and tireless devotion to Ronald Reagan, their "flagship" client. He represented 60 percent of their business, and his work alone took up the time of seven staff members who did research, answered mail, and scheduled his appointments.

Reagan, for most of his political career, had been dogged by rumors that he was "lazy." In fact, he crisscrossed the country dozens of times in 1975, speaking for candidates, before organizations, doing interviews (including the *Tonight Show),* attending meetings; all in all, a dizzying whirlwind of activity.

Reagan was receiving some fifteen hundred pieces of mail per month including over a hundred speaking invitations. Helene von Damm, his personal secretary, would sort through the invitations and turn them over to the two principals. Reagan was on the road approximately one week out of every month.

The columns—sometimes ghosted by Hannaford, Jeff Bell, and Pat Buchanan—were syndicated by Copley News Service to over eighty newspapers across the country. Many of Reagan's columns were forwarded to the Oval Office by Donald Rumsfeld. Though Ford professed publicly to not be thinking about the 1976 election or Reagan, he was in fact being sent numerous memos and analyses of Reagan, including his record as Governor.

The radio commentaries usually took two full days per month to record. At the height of their popularity, the programs reached twenty to thirty million people each week. Although others took a turn at drafting Reagan's columns, according to Deaver, Reagan himself wrote most of the radio commentaries after reviewing the current events with his staff.[6]

Every three weeks, Reagan would record his commentaries with producer and syndicator Harry O'Connor at his studio at the corner of Hollywood Avenue and Vine Street. O'Connor then distributed the commentaries to subscribing radio stations around the country. Reagan had gotten the idea from his old friend, actor Efrem Zimbalist Jr. who was also doing radio commentaries with O'Connor. Reagan would read fifteen five-minute commentaries that would be put onto record albums for most stations and onto reel tape for others. Since they were taped well in advance of their actual broadcast, Deaver, Hannaford, and Reagan had to choose their issues carefully. Something that was a hot topic of national debate one day might be forgotten by the following week.

Some in Reagan's camp were playing their version of the "Ford won't run" game, aided by the *U.S. News and World Report* article Ford had written in 1973,[7] and a "Periscope" item in *Newsweek* from December 1974 which said much the same. But adding to Reagan's instinct to get into the race was the barrage of messages coming from the Republican National Committee about the need to "broaden the base of the party," which Reagan and his supporters took as a rebuke of conservatism.

In March 1975, *Newsweek* ran a cover story on Reagan titled "Ready on the Right." Still, he was anything but ready to take the plunge.

The Republican Party held a national forum in Washington that month. Seven hundred were expected to attend, but almost three thousand showed up. Leading up to the event, some thought the meeting would resemble the "Last of the Mohicans." Republicans were in scarce supply. But the party needed to do something—anything—to demonstrate it was still viable. "We needed a boost," RNC Executive Director Mahe said with characteristic understatement. "The conference had very little focus on the Presidential [campaign] . . . we were trying to get enough money in the door to save the state parties."[8]

Featured at the conference was speaker after speaker who emphasized the perceived need to "broaden the party." President Ford himself emphasized his belief that the Republican Party needed to expand ideologically in order to be viable. These comments were widely interpreted as the President's defense of Rockefeller. Ford also made it fairly clear at the forum that he had decided to seek the nomination in his own right in 1976.

Only Reagan, who was relegated to a Saturday morning speech in a smaller room, took issue with what the intelligentsia of the party was saying at the time. Predictably, he took a different tack than Ford by reiterating the speech he had given just a month earlier to the annual Conservative Political Action Conference. Reagan challenged the assembled Republican Party regulars to stand for one thing to all people and not try to be all things to all people. Nonetheless, Reagan held back and said nothing about the impending campaign.

Hannaford later said, "He was also holding back because of timing. He always had a good sense of timing. He did not want to appear as a spoiler and said so publicly and privately. He really wanted to give Ford a chance and did not wish Ford any ill whatsoever."[9]

No one can really be sure when Reagan made up his mind to run. But sometime in early 1975, he and Deaver were on a plane that commuted between Los Angeles and San Francisco. Whenever he flew, Reagan would sit in the first row so he could talk to people as they boarded the plane. On one occasion, a woman spotted him, embraced him and said, "Oh Governor, you've just got to run for President!" As they settled into their seats, Reagan turned to Deaver and said, "Well, I guess I'd better do it."[10] Nofziger and others were convinced that Reagan would make the effort. Nofziger "just knew" Reagan was going to jump in.[11]

The mere fact that Reagan had been traveling by plane for the past several years was partially a surrendering to the realities of modern campaigning and his strong sense of God's providence. Reagan had not traveled by plane for nearly thirty years, after a particularly harrowing flight between Catalina and Los Angeles in 1937. In fact, his contract with General Electric that took him across the country through the 1950s specified that he only travel by train and not by plane. But he remained a "white knuckle" flyer for many years after he started flying again.[12]

As Reagan traversed the country, the Ford White House and its allies did little to revive Reagan's sense of loyalty to the incumbent President. According to Lou Cannon, writing in his book, *Reagan,*

> Ford made it easy for Reagan to reach his decision. A traditionalist who accepted the conventional wisdom of Washington, Ford could not really believe that the staid and conservative Republican Party would tear itself to pieces by ousting an incumbent President. Nor, despite Rockefeller, did he believe that many Republicans would accept a portrait of Jerry Ford as a liberal President. Preoccupied with the problems of the Presidency and pulled in different directions by a White House staff divided between old Nixonites and old congressional aides, Ford did not pay consistent attention to the Reagan challenge or treat it seriously enough once he became aware of what was happening. When he acted at all, he did the wrong things. Reagan was especially insulted when Ford had his Chief of Staff, Donald H. Rumsfeld, offer him another Cabinet job, this time Secretary of Commerce. "They're working their way down the scale," a Reagan intimate said incredulously when he heard of this offer.[13]

Cannon also wrote, "Worse than this job offer was the muddle-headed approach devised by Ford's former congressional cronies, notably Melvin R. Laird, who told reporters that Reagan would not actually enter the race once he had weighed his options."[14] Laird, like White House aide Bob Hartmann, was becoming known in

Washington as a chronic Reagan basher, and these stories also made their way to California, where they only served to inflame Reagan followers. Staff apparently used Laird's sharp tongue as a goad for the Governor. Wrote Robert Novak and Rowland Evans in *The Reagan Revolution*, "Laird viewed Reagan as a poseur, straight off the Hollywood sound stages. Consequently, he advised Ford soon after taking office to disregard Reagan. Learning of this, Jeff Bell wrote Reagan a memo on 'Lairdisms' in hopes of pushing the Governor toward a Presidential race."[15]

While Ford usually spoke respectfully of his possible challenger in public, "Reagan was the subject of a lot of wisecracks around the White House in mid-1975." Questions of respect aside, the flippant response to Reagan showed Ford and his advisers didn't consider Reagan a serious threat. Hartmann further recounted,

> There was a personal chemistry between Ford and Reagan that complicated everything. . . . Why would he never butter up Reagan, even a little bit? I had sat in on a number of their meetings over the years—while Ford was Minority Leader, Vice President and President. In these encounters both men were usually uptight, unnatural, pathetically polite and acutely on guard. Betty Ford and Nancy Reagan hit it off even worse.[16]

To pull off a win, Reagan needed allies in Washington. Republicans, by temperament and upbringing, were told to "wait your turn." Only twice in the twentieth-century had a Republican challenger attempted to defeat an incumbent President for the party nomination, and both had failed. Congressman John Ashbrook had attempted a "Hail Mary" insurgent conservative campaign against Nixon three years earlier, but it came to naught. The other exception was in 1912 when Theodore Roosevelt, dismayed with the direction of William Howard Taft's Presidency, emerged from retirement to unsuccessfully challenge the incumbent for the Republican nomination before running on the Progressive ticket in the general election.

In May 1975, Reagan turned to his old friend, Nevada Senator Paul Laxalt. Laxalt had served as Nevada Governor from 1967 to 1971, while Reagan held office in Sacramento. As he was mixing drinks for himself and Laxalt at his suite in the Madison Hotel in Washington, Reagan circumspectly suggested to his fellow Westerner to "keep your powder dry," as he had not yet decided to run. But if Reagan did choose to run, he would want his old friend along for the ride. Laxalt—supported by John Sears, Lyn Nofziger, and Deaver, all of whom were also present at the meeting—strongly encouraged Reagan to make the run.

Sears was also talking to potential vendors. Bruce Eberle, who had been competing with Richard Viguerie for the direct mail contract, fortuitously bumped into Sears one Saturday at Washington National Airport. As they talked, Sears simply told Eberle that he had been awarded the contract. But Sears's haphazard management style was already becoming a problem with individuals inside and outside the campaign. Sears hired the campaign's General Counsel Loren Smith in much the same fashion.[17]

Though Reagan hadn't decided yet, he was intrigued. One Sunday he met with Sears at his office in Washington for four hours. Sears also was learning to appreciate Reagan's strengths. "Nixon was such a squirrel and here was a guy who didn't seem to be a squirrel and wasn't as messed up as the last guy. And, he had a lot of self-confidence. He was smart."[18]

Sears also told Reagan and his team at the meeting that "the primaries made it possible to run. This opened it up for people who didn't have control of the party apparatus. Power can neither be created nor destroyed. And the party didn't have the power anymore. So, if the party didn't have the power . . . someone's got to have it, and it was the press who got it."[19]

As Reagan was moving closer to his decision in the spring of 1975, Senate Minority Leader Hugh Scott of Pennsylvania had circulated a letter supporting Ford and seeking signatures from his Republican colleagues. Laxalt conspicuously refused to sign the letter, signaling his desire to see a debate over the party's direction and future.

In June, Sears and Jim Lake met with Senator Laxalt in his office on Capitol Hill, informing him that they were going forward with a Reagan committee. Laxalt was enthusiastic as they reviewed the list of potential individuals who might be suitable to chair the effort. According to Lake, at the outset of the meeting Laxalt had indicated a preference to stay out of the fray. But after they reviewed the candidates and found all of them wanting for one reason or another, Sears came to one elected official he had deliberately overlooked—"the Senator from Nevada." Laxalt came aboard the campaign shortly thereafter.

Laxalt's decision to publicly support Reagan was important for the campaign because he was a conservative. But more importantly, he was a respected sitting U.S. Senator. He also may have been the most personally popular man in the Senate and the media paid him his due respect. It was just the credibility the nascent Reagan effort needed to prove itself to the skeptical Washington press corps.

The following month, Laxalt stepped before a bank of microphones in the basement of a Washington hotel on July 15, 1975, to announce the formation of Citizens for Reagan, an exploratory committee. His announcement was not a moment too soon for the conservatives who were chomping at the bit to take on Gerald Ford. But it certainly was not the birthday gift Ford would have asked for the previous day, when he turned sixty-two years old. The Chief Executive did, however, receive a clean bill of health from his White House physician.

The choice of the word "citizen" was significant. Reagan never viewed himself as "just another politician." Robert Nakamura wrote in *Political Science Quarterly*, "'Citizen' was selected because he wanted to convey that his beliefs were like those of the ordinary, levelheaded citizens arrived at by reflection rather than political calculation."[20]

Reagan had still not formally announced his candidacy. But the Washington political establishment and the Republican Party, used to the seismic earthquakes of the prior three years, were shaken again at the announcement of Citizens for Reagan. Jim Baker, who would later become Ford's very effective Chief of Delegate Operations said, "It was surprising because we didn't do that in our party. At the Presidential level, you can't find another example." Despite the tradition and history of the GOP, Reagan allowed the formation of Citizens for Reagan to go forward.[21]

Laxalt read from a prepared text which said, in part,

> The purpose of this committee is to build an organization and raise the money necessary to conduct a viable and effective campaign once Governor Reagan decides to become an active candidate.
>
> The decision to take this step has not been an easy one. Mr. Ford came to the Presidency under circumstances unique in American history, amidst problems of confidence, international unrest and domestic instability which are unparalleled. All of us, Democrats and Republicans alike, must give him our support lest others in the world receive the impression that America is too weak or immobile to act.
>
> Yet Mr. Ford's efforts to cope with these problems on a day-to-day basis provide little relief for the vast majority of Americans who yearn for a leader who can communicate a realistic perspective on America's future. . . . We have had far too many instances in our political history where the voters have been left with a choice of deciding between the "lesser of two evils." This country cannot ultimately survive if Presidential elections continue to be decided on the same basis.
>
> The next President must enter office armed with a positive compact between himself and the American people, such that Congress will realize that there is no longer any merit in political expediency. We believe

> that Governor Reagan is a man who stands tall among American politicians in his demonstrated ability to do those things which he promises.

Accompanying Laxalt at the press conference announcing Citizens for Reagan were Sears, former Kentucky Governor Louie Nunn, an ancient conservative Congressman from Iowa named H. R. Gross, and a small band of other supporters. Sears would serve as Reagan's de facto Campaign Manager.

In the question and answer period of the press conference, Laxalt continued to emphasize Reagan's record of governance rather than his ideology, saying, "It's not that we think President Ford is doing a bad job. It's that we think Ronald Reagan can do a better job." Conspicuously absent was any ideological criticism of Ford or of Henry Kissinger's foreign policy. Neither did the committee trumpet Reagan's conservatism. Laxalt's temperament partially explains the low-key style of his statement, but it was also a testament to the powers of persuasion that Sears possessed. David Keene said, "John could talk anyone into doing anything. He was good at that."[22]

Sears and his supporters would argue that Reagan needed to emphasize his experience at governing, rather than highlighting him as a conservative standard-bearer. They reasoned that while voters knew Reagan was a conservative, they were unfamiliar with his success in two terms as Governor of California. Nonetheless, after years of loyal support, many conservatives grumbled that his long-awaited Presidential campaign was starting on the wrong foot. For example, supporters of North Carolina Senator Jesse Helms, like Tom Ellis, found Sears's "résumé strategy" maddening and countered by complaining that if Reagan was going to successfully challenge Ford in the primaries, he needed to make the ideological arguments against Ford that would attract voters.[23] Sears defended his strategy later, explaining, "Voters saw Reagan in 1975 as a Republican version of George Wallace and we had to do something about this."[24]

The grassroots also criticized Reagan's staff, claiming they were not political enough, they were not pushing Reagan hard enough to run and that they didn't understand conservatism. The fight between Sears and his conservative critics continued right up to the Republican National Convention in Kansas City and even after, with Sears arguing that the nomination of a divided party would be meaningless as it had been in 1964 and conservatives arguing that you can't run in the fall unless you win the nomination in the summer.

Ford's forces responded to the Laxalt announcement with a low-key statement that made no mention of Reagan. It said, in part, that Ford's "philosophy in politics has always been to . . . run on his record, and to do his best to convince first the delegates, and then the voters, that they should vote for him. The

President has never based his campaign plans on what somebody else might or might not do."[25]

In order to satisfy the requirements of the new Federal Election Commission, Reagan needed to officially distance himself from his campaign committee as the Presidential effort was announced. In a bizarre kabuki dance, Reagan had to write a letter to Laxalt acknowledging the creation of Citizens for Reagan, without formally endorsing it. But the critical final portion of the letter was all the anxious Reaganites needed to know: "The committee must file with the Federal Election Commission as working on my behalf. I trust this letter will suffice as my consent for purposes of allowing you to do so."

The letter was signed "Ron."[26]

In response to Watergate, the FEC had been created by the Democratic Congress, but the new campaign laws were a mystery to all. "It was the 'Wild, Wild West' when it came to the campaign laws. No one really knew what was legal or illegal," according to Donatelli.[27] But Loren Smith, General Counsel for Reagan's committee, knew one aspect of the law well: if it was clear that Reagan had formally announced his candidacy, the FEC would have ordered him to give up his radio commentaries. Equal time provisions would have required radio stations give the same time to Ford (and maybe all the Democrats running as well), for free, that they were devoting to Reagan's commentaries.

Furthermore, as an officially declared candidate, Reagan would have been forced to forego his lucrative lecture and column fees. But Reagan's disclaimer to Laxalt protected his financial and political interests. Citizens for Reagan could undertake the necessary preparations of developing a direct mail house file for funds, recruiting supporters, hiring staff and beginning to make the case against Ford, Rockefeller, Kissinger and company. Under Smith's guidance, Reagan could have the best of all worlds: while his campaign got underway, he could continue to receive fees as he spoke his mind on public policy issues.

Over the summer and fall of 1975, formal complaints flew back and forth across Washington as both campaigns sought to use the FEC regulations to their advantage. Smith filed a complaint charging that the Republican National Committee should not pay for the travel expenses of President Ford since Ford was, in fact, electioneering and not traveling on official White House business.[28]

The Ford campaign retaliated by filing its own complaint against Citizens for Reagan, charging that Reagan was indeed a candidate for federal office and, therefore, subject to the same laws as any other individual running for a federal office including the "equal time provisions." Smith's counterpart in the Ford campaign was Bob Visser, who argued that "Governor Reagan attempted to distinguish between his becoming an 'active Presidential candidate' from being a technical candidate under the Act, it is now apparent that he has authorized a committee to collect and expend funds on his behalf in connection with his seeking the nomination for the Presidency and is a 'candidate' for purposes of the Act." Also, a complaint was filed by James Horowitz, the president of Burbank Publication Inc., raising questions about the legality of the sponsors of Reagan's radio commentaries.[29]

Even with the announcement in July of 1975 of the organization Laxalt was leading, Reagan continued to proceed cautiously with an actual challenge of President Gerald Ford. It was one thing to oppose or criticize the Administration's policies. It was quite another to actually challenge Ford in the primaries. Reagan had always been ambivalent about challenging a sitting member of his own party.

Reagan's loyalty to the Republican Party had been evident throughout the scandals that it had witnessed in the years immediately prior to his decision to run. When he heard that Agnew had resigned the Vice Presidency after taking kickbacks in the White House, Reagan was furious and threw a ring of keys that actually hit Mike Deaver in the chest. Still, for all his private frustration, Reagan could barely bring himself to criticize Agnew. Furthermore, Reagan was one of the last Republicans to call for Nixon's ouster.[30]

Reagan went through an intense period of soul searching as to whether or not to challenge Ford. In contrast to the enthusiasm both Ronald and Nancy Reagan would show in deciding to run for President in 1980, they were less enthusiastic about making the race against Ford in 1975 than Sears, Nofziger, Walker, and conservatives around the country. In fact, Walker had run afoul of the Reagans earlier in the year when, frustrated at the slow pace, he took it upon himself to announce a forthcoming Reagan Presidential bid. Reagan was furious, partially because Walker's unilateral effort put his fees at risk, and Walker was nearly booted from the entire effort.

On the one hand, Reagan truly wanted Ford to succeed. But he was deeply disturbed about the leftward drift of the Ford Administration, especially when it came to foreign policy. And Reagan was still miffed over the constant barrage of insults and rumors that emanated from Washington and the Ford White House. Further weighing on his decision was the fact that he was beginning to make better money than he had since his salad days with General Electric in the fifties.

While Reagan deliberated, his staff was already several steps ahead of him, securing office space and contacting individuals about their interest in working on the campaign. Initially, the offices of Citizens for Reagan operated out of Sears's law offices, but they eventually established their own headquarters initially at 2021 L Street, NW in Washington, D.C. Becki Black, a tiny Californian and devoted Reagan fan, would eventually be hired as a receptionist for the committee. Sitting before a huge switchboard, she answered hundreds of phone calls each day from eager conservatives around the country wanting to help Reagan. She also supervised the volunteers, including a ninety-three-year-old woman who faithfully came to the office every day.

A skeletal campaign staff began to take shape with Sears, Nofziger, Keene, Lake, Smith, Roger Stone, Charlie Black, Patti O'Connor, Arlene Triplett, Joan Follick, and others. Black (no relation to Becki Black) had cut his teeth in YAF politics in the late sixties and with the successful Helms for Senate campaign in North Carolina in 1972. After the 1972 contest, he had gone to work for the new "Congressional Club," which Senator Helms and Tom Ellis had formed to help other conservatives running for office in North Carolina and beyond.

Andy Carter had also come aboard as Director of Field Operations. He was a "bigfoot" and extended his opinion and advice in many areas. Carter, who had once run for office in New Mexico, was a self-made millionaire in cattle and oil and was a dedicated conservative and Reagan man. He also had a temper. Once, while staying at a Washington hotel, he did not receive the wake-up call he had requested and missed a meeting. Furious, Carter tore up the front desk and the terrified hotel clerk summoned the D.C. police. The Reagan campaign posted the bail money to spring him from jail.

Later, Chuck Tyson and David Fischer joined Dennis LeBlanc and Nancy Reynolds to handle much of the advance work for the campaign. An attractive Mississippian, Neal Peden was brought aboard to assist Keene, Black, and Carter. In an example of the effects of the committee's shoestring budget, Loren Smith remembered that the office furniture was so scarce that he and Stone, the Youth Director, temporarily shared a chair and desk. Nofziger also recruited Pat Nolan, an attorney from Los Angeles to help out with their operations there.

"We worked long hours, but no one complained. We weren't paid much, but we loved Reagan," Peden would later recall. She also remembered getting on the elevator one evening only to have it fall several stories until the emergency brake took hold. And Loren Smith's wife, Kitty, remembered the holes in the wall of the ladies' room.[31]

Over the summer, Sears brought aboard Reagan's gubernatorial pollster, Dr. Richard "Dick" Wirthlin, president of Decision Making Information. Wirthlin had briefly flirted with the idea of going to work for Ford before Reagan had decided to run. However, Ford's Campaign Manager, Howard "Bo" Callaway, could not make a commitment to Wirthlin, who got caught in the crossfire of the ongoing feud between Hartmann and Rumsfeld. But when it was clear to Wirthlin that Reagan was going, he wanted to be along with his old friend.

Another of the first people hired by Sears was Jeff Bell, who had gone to California to work on Reagan's behalf at the Republican State Party headquarters in Sacramento. Bell was a bright, thirty-one-year-old conservative who was as dedicated to Reagan as he was to his principles. After Reagan left office in January of 1975, he went on Reagan's personal payroll, serving as a "utility infielder": acting as Reagan's liaison to the Right, giving political advice, doing advance work, and pitching in to write Reagan's columns. Bell worked on research and speeches, but he also explored—and sometimes advocated—the third party option for Reagan. His third party advocacy was understandable since his patron at the time was Bill Rusher. But the decision had been made by Reagan and the people around him: If he were to run for President, it would be as a Republican—and not some quixotic effort that might leave him as a political joke and footnote in history.

One of Bell's first assignments from Sears in the summer of 1975 was to develop a new stump speech for Reagan. On the lecture circuit, Reagan had been saying much of the same thing—or so critics charged—since 1964. The themes of Reagan's public comments over the preceding twelve years had fallen into a somewhat predictable framework: less government, more freedom, the dignity of the individual, the dangers of the welfare state, the Communist threat, and other conservative ideas. But his speeches, debates, press conferences and public pronouncements were always rich in detail, variety and humor.

"The government in Washington is spending some seven million every minute I talk to you. There's no connection between my talk and their spending, and if they'll stop spending, I'll stop talking," Reagan would like to say in his speeches. Other times, his humor was more pointed: "It's been said that if you put Ford and me together in a dark room, you can't tell us apart philosophically. Well, if you turn on the light, you can."

Sometimes he would quote Cicero or Winston Churchill or Douglas MacArthur or a variety of cultural and spiritual leaders, but the "new political bosses" in the media, as Sears was wont to refer to them, demanded something new out of Reagan. Sears directed Bell to get to work on something original for Reagan to say.

Thus the so-called "$90 billion" speech, as it became infamously known, was born. Bell researched, drafted, and polished the new speech over the summer with help on the side from his friend, Stan Evans, Chairman of the American Conservative Union.

Bell finished the initial draft of the new Reagan speech, titled "Let the People Rule," and shipped it off for review by Reagan and others on staff. It followed

Reagan's standard conservative, federalist themes of reducing the power of the centralized government and returning both that power and its accompanying revenue to the states. Bell's draft was reviewed and vetted by nearly all of Reagan's senior staff including Sears, Keene, Deaver, Hannaford, and Nofziger. All were enthusiastic about the speech and no one objected either to its style or substance.

Reagan delivered the speech in September to the Chicago Executives Club. It caused such little commotion that Reagan gave nearly the identical speech to the thirteenth anniversary dinner of the New York State Conservative Party less than one month later. Reagan's proposals were not all that controversial. Decentralization had been part of conservative orthodoxy over the years, and Presidents Eisenhower and Kennedy had complained privately and publicly about the unwarranted concentration of power in Washington at the expense of the states. Reagan himself was very enthusiastic about the speech and Sears suggested that Bell get to work on a series of "Reagan's vision" speeches. It was the number—$90 billion—and the specific Washington programs Bell and Evans recommended to be returned to the states that would later create so many headaches for the Reagan campaign. Had the transcript of the speech given to the press not included Bell's addendum, it probably would not have been such a contentious issue in the forthcoming New Hampshire primary.

In both versions of the speech, Reagan opened by quoting Thomas Jefferson: "A wise and frugal government which shall restrain men from injuring one another, shall leave them otherwise free to regulate their own pursuits of industry and improvement, and shall not take from the mouth of labor the bread it has earned. This is the sum of good government."

Warming to his topic, Reagan continued,

> Government at all levels will have absorbed 37 percent of the Gross National Product and 44 percent of our total savings. This absorption of revenue by all levels of government, the alarming rate of inflation and the rising toll of unemployment all stem from a single source: the belief that government, particularly the federal government, has the answer to all our ills, and that the proper method of dealing with social problems is to transfer power from the private to the public sector, and within the public sector from state and local governments to the ultimate power center in Washington. This collectivist, centralizing approach, whatever name or party labels it wears, has created our economic problems. By taxing and consuming an ever-greater share of the national wealth, it has imposed an intolerable burden of taxation on American citizens. By spending above and beyond even this level of taxation, it has created the

> horrendous inflation of the past decade. And by saddling our economy with an ever-greater burden of controls and regulations, it has generated countless economic problems—from the raising of consumer prices to the destruction of jobs, to choking off vital supplies of food and energy.
>
> As if that were not enough, the crushing weight of central government has distorted our federal system and altered the relationship between the levels of government, threatening the freedom of individuals and families. The states and local communities have been demeaned into little more than administrative districts, bureaucratic subdivisions of Big Brother government in Washington, with programs, spending priorities, and tax policies badly warped or dictated by federal overseers. . . .
>
> What I propose is nothing less that a systematic transfer of authority and resources to the states—a program of creative federalism for America's third century. Federal authority has clearly failed to do the job. Indeed, it has created more problems in welfare, education, housing, food stamps, Medicaid, community and regional development, and revenue sharing to name a few. The sums involved and the potential savings to the taxpayer are large. Transfer of authority in whole or part in all these areas would reduce the outlay of the federal government by more than ninety billion dollars, using the spending levels of fiscal 1976.

To support the proposals of the speech, Bell had prepared reams of background briefing material for Reagan, including endless sample questions and suggested answers. Bell had done the same for Richard Nixon in 1968. Nixon preferred paper to people and relied heavily on the briefing books his staff had prepared, constantly asking for updates and new information. It followed therefore—at least in the minds of Sears and Bell—that Reagan should behave likewise.

But remembering one occasion, Bell recounted, "Reagan wouldn't read the briefing books. It was the first time I'd seen Reagan and Sears fight because John was constantly on him to read the book. And he'd say, 'Governor, you don't know anything and Stu Spencer is going to kick us in the ass if you don't.' Reagan would say he'd 'get around to it,' but they would go back and forth about it whenever Reagan was in the office."[32]

Bell further explained the reason for the tension between Reagan and Sears: "Sears was concerned that Reagan didn't know enough. And Sears's skepticism is repeated throughout Reagan's career. Nixon had no ideology. . . . Reagan had a worldview. Because he had a framework, everything always came back to his worldview. Nixon needed the briefing book because he wanted the individual answer. But Reagan was a genius at being able to bring everything back to his worldview. He may stumble on a few facts, but you knew he was operating within a framework."[33]

By the 1980s, Republican orthodoxy would become dominated by the federalism he inspired, complete with the mantra of "less government, more freedom." It is unconscionable to think that any modern Republican would aggressively or gleefully embrace the growth of government or oppose the decentralization of power in Washington. But in 1975, Reagan's proposal was nothing short of revolutionary.

Federalism was but one of the new paradigms Reagan was reintroducing to the Republican Party and American political thought. Unfortunately for his campaign, his aides did not know how to manage it to his advantage or the political ramifications of the controversy that would ensue.

The speech received scant attention when it was delivered. Reagan's appearance was only covered by two reporters: a stringer for the *Washington Post* and Martin Schram of *Newsday*, who was writing a "will he or won't he run?" piece for his newspaper. In his book *Marathon,* Jules Witcover would later write of the speech, "Reagan went on, moving now to his favorite culprit. . . . Reagan was humming now, deeply into his view of the world of federal oppression. . . . Now Reagan the clean broom was ready to offer his magic cleansing power."[34]

While this description betrayed Witcover's liberal sensibilities, his newspaper reportage for the *Washington Post* throughout the campaign was professional and unbiased. Reagan and conservatives were sometimes forced to deal with media bias in the 1970s. Ted Kennedy and other Democrats rarely encountered skepticism from a reporter for a major metropolitan newspaper. But for Reagan and company, it happened more frequently—though not as often as they sometimes imagined.

In his book, *The Reagans*, Hannaford observed, "I heard one of Reagan's advisers say with a sigh that he suspected that the news media hold Republicans to a higher standard of conduct than they do Democrats and that they hold Ronald Reagan to a higher standard than other Republicans."[35]

While reporters ignored the speech, it did gain the attention of Stuart Spencer, a California-based Republican political consultant. Spencer and his partner, Bill Roberts, had masterminded the Reagan gubernatorial campaign of 1966 and his re-election of 1970. Spencer was like much of the new breed of professional political consultants in that issues and ideology were a bore for them. The game was the campaign itself. Like a floating poker game, you bet, you bluffed, you won and lost, and you owed your allegiance to no candidate or issue—just yourself and your cronies in the media and the political industry. Politicians were simply vehicles through which to have fun and make profits.

In 1964, Spencer had handled the California primary for Nelson Rockefeller against Barry Goldwater. Goldwater prevailed and won the Republican nomination, but Spencer acquitted himself well enough to gain Reagan's and his team's attention in 1966.

Spencer's "on again, off again" relationship with Reagan was off again by 1975. Spencer complained about being left out of the early planning of the Reagan effort and he blamed some around Reagan for costing him business. Another report at the time quoted Spencer confiding to an associate, "It's one thing to elect that right-winger as Governor, it's another to elect him as President."[36] In any case Spencer arrived "bearing a grudge" according to Cannon:

> Spencer was contemptuous of Reagan's relaxed work habits, saying openly that the former Governor was "lazy." But he was appalled by the underestimation of Reagan he found in the Ford camp. "Hell, they were asking me if he was going to run at a time Sears had organized New Hampshire and Reagan had set an announcement date," Spencer once told me. He knew that Reagan was a far superior political candidate than the President, particularly on television. Savvy and combative, Spencer realized from the outset that Ford's hope of winning the nomination depended on discrediting Reagan.[37]

With Spencer available, Cheney took note of his anger toward the Reagan operation and signed him up for Ford in October of 1975. Spencer arrived with a big ego, but his credentials and ideas backed it up. The Ford forces had also recruited the legendary Cliff White, architect of Goldwater's stunning nomination in 1964. White had also been left out of the Reagan effort despite a long and close friendship with the Governor and Mrs. Reagan. These were but two of many ironies that would occur over the course of the campaign.

Spencer was one of the few around the Ford campaign who knew Reagan, knew his people and knew their weaknesses. He took Reagan's speech and immediately showed it to President Ford Committee staffers, led by Research Director Fred Slight. He also asked economists at the Office of Management and Budget to do a cost analysis of Reagan's proposals. Ford scribbled a note to James T. Lynn, the Director of the OMB, asking "1) Ron R's speech on Federal Budget. Gave it in Chicago about month ago. Q – Have we analyzed it?" Lynn personally authored a detailed three-page memo for Ford, reviewing the Reagan speech. Lynn attached a column critical of the speech by Reagan supporter Pat Buchanan.[38]

Spencer wasn't thinking about what Reagan would eventually call "New

Federalism" or conservative ideology. He was thinking about the upcoming New Hampshire primary, a state where no politician could survive advocating either a state income tax or a state sales tax. Spencer figured, accurately as it would turn out, that he could put Reagan on the defensive in New Hampshire if the Ford campaign could convince the voters there that Reagan's proposal would mean an unheard of tax increase for them. Spencer's plan was to tie the issue around Reagan's neck like a millstone and drown the threat of the Californian.

In the wake of Reagan's eventual loss, Bell would unfairly be hung with the "goat" label as the national media took it upon themselves to pick the winners and losers and heroes and goats of 1976. Bell was following orders and Reagan's later problems in New Hampshire over the speech were less a result of its content than a result of the campaign's inability to handle the controversy. In fact, Dick Wirthlin had polling information showing the Reagan decentralization plan to be politically popular. Ironically, it was the Bell speech that would become the essence of the "New Federalism" proposal Reagan launched during his first year as President in 1981.

Part of the sticky wicket were the conflicting stories and memories about the addendum to the speech in which Bell listed specific targets in the federal budget destined to be returned to the states. While Bell says he had clearance to attach it to the speech, others refuted his claim, saying it was not part of the original speech sent to Los Angeles for review and only showed up attached to the handouts for the media in Chicago. In retrospect, and to his credit, Sears took partial blame for the "$90 billion" speech. "We didn't have our antenna up. We weren't thinking how it would be taken in New Hampshire. It was wrong," he said. "The trouble was not the idea but what it could do to the states."[39] Sears would not worry for long about the speech. He and Jim Lake were busily organizing New Hampshire while Keene was working the South and Black the Midwest.

Eddie Mahe had once quipped that a campaign was "garbage moving in the right direction,"[40] and that harsh but accurate description seemed to summarize both the Reagan and Ford efforts in the summer and fall of 1975. Both were riddled with bad judgment, bad timing, and bad luck. It would take a long shakedown period for each campaign to right itself and start talking to the voters instead of just leaking stories to the media about the infighting. The leaks never stopped entirely, especially in Ford's operation. But the primary season forced both camps to focus on what was most important: winning the nomination.

The animosity between Reagan and Ford and their staffs continued unabated. Most of Ford's White House and campaign staff could not seem to fathom or understand Reagan, but in the wake of Ford's problems and low approval numbers, word was drifting back to Washington from Sacramento in late August that Reagan would indeed challenge the beleaguered Chief Executive.

The Ford White House, which finally came to grips with the fact that Reagan was about to formally enter the race, shifted tactics from mocking or ignoring Reagan and began attempting to minimize the differences between the two men. Ford told CBS's Walter Cronkite "I don't believe there's any serious philosophical differences between Governor Reagan and myself."[41] But while Ford was attempting to narrow the ideological gap between himself and his erstwhile conservative challenger, Citizens for Reagan was humming with activity and the planning for a mid-November announcement. Hannaford wrote,

> In mid-October, Reagan gave his permission for plans to go forward for a late-November Presidential announcement, probably during the week of the seventeenth. Several of us M Group members met October 17 in Washington to review assignments and plans. Meanwhile, Reagan's schedule of radio tapings for his program, his newspaper column, and his speeches continued unchanged.[42]

The news media suggested that a split existed between Reagan's Washington and California supporters about whether or not he should enter the race. In reality, the only disagreement between the two camps was timing. The Washington crowd, led by Sears and Walker, wanted an early announcement and the Californians, led by Hannaford and Deaver, opted for a later announcement.

Finally, in September, the committee sent a nationwide mailing trumpeting, "The Reagan Presidential campaign is underway." Nofziger remembered that Sears wanted to announce on November 22 until Nofziger reminded him that it was the anniversary of the assassination of President Kennedy.

But before Reagan could take center stage, however, there were still several more political bombshells that would drop in Washington: a major shake-up of the Ford Cabinet and, even more stunning, Nelson Rockefeller's announcement that he would take himself out of consideration for Vice President in 1976.

5

SETTING THE STAGE

"Not the candidate of kooks."

Ronald Reagan rated live network television coverage of his Washington press conference announcing his decision to challenge Gerald Ford in the Republican primaries, which spoke volumes about the national media's curiosity about Reagan's appeal. Many did not understand Reagan's allure, most could not explain it, and some did not like it. But they had seen his ability to move adoring audiences since 1964 and knew Ford was in for trouble from the conservative riding in from the West. As R.W. "Johnny" Apple wrote for the *New York Times,*

> Mr. Reagan begins his campaign without having to silence the snickers that greeted the challenges of the late Estes Kefauver in 1952 or Eugene McCarthy in 1968. This is a considerable accomplishment, made possible by the unusual nature of President Ford's ascension to power and by Mr. Reagan's national following and to his sharp sense of timing.[1]

Certainly the addition of John Sears as Campaign Manager to the Reagan team helped increase the media's respect for the former California Governor's bid for the White House. They had known Sears and liked him. They happily wrote stories based on his "leaks." They ate with him, drank with him, and played poker with him. They reasoned that there must be something special about Reagan, or he could have never landed Sears as his manager.

At precisely 9:30 A.M. on November 20, 1975, the sixty-four-year-old Reagan strode to a podium with two microphones wired into dozens of television and radio outlets attached below. That morning, he read from his usual 4x6 cards announcing his candidacy for the Presidency of the United States at the jam-packed press conference at the National Press Club.

Reagan had flown in from Dallas the day before, accompanied by Sears, Mike Deaver, Lyn Nofziger, and several other aides and was later met by Peter

Hannaford at a hotel in Washington. Mrs. Reagan also arrived the day before, accompanied by longtime-aide Nancy Reynolds. Reynolds had previously worked in the Governor's office in Sacramento.

Becki Black sneaked away from her desk and walked the several blocks to watch Reagan's announcement. Waiting in the lobby of the Press Club, she was surprised that only a few aides accompanied Reagan. Black was also from California, which she explained to the Governor when he shook her hand and warmly greeted her. "If only everybody could meet him one on one and see those incredible blue eyes," she recalled.[2]

Hannaford flew into Washington the Sunday before Reagan's announcement to work on the draft of "the Governor's" statement for the press conference that Thursday. Meanwhile, the Reagans took a few days to relax before throwing themselves into the hurly burly of the campaign ahead.

Governor and Mrs. Reagan checked into the Madison Hotel. Reagan made several courtesy phone calls to GOP leaders, including Vice President Nelson Rockefeller and, oddly, Richard Nixon, to advise them of his intention to seek the Republican Presidential nomination and oppose Gerald Ford.

Another one of those leaders Reagan called was President Ford himself. To say the conversation was terse would be an understatement. However, given the previous two years of subtle and not so subtle hostility between Ford's White House and Reagan's conservatives, it is understandable that civility was strained. Ford began the chapter titled "Challenge from the Right" from his autobiography, *A Time To Heal,* with his account of the conversation:

> "Hello, Mr. President," Reagan said, and then he came right to the point. "I am going to make an announcement, and I want to tell you about it ahead of time. I am going to run for President. I trust we can have a good contest, and I hope that it won't be divisive."
>
> "Well, Governor, I'm very disappointed," I replied. "I'm sorry you're getting into this. I believe I've done a good job and that I can be elected. Regardless of your good intentions, your bid is bound to be divisive. It will take a lot of money, a lot of effort, and it will leave a lot of scars. It won't be helpful, no matter which of us wins the nomination."
>
> "I don't think it will be divisive," Reagan repeated. "I don't think it will harm the party."
>
> "Well, I think it will," I said.

Ford wrote of the incident, "Neither of us is the type of person to waste words, and we concluded the conversation quickly. I think he really believed that his candidacy wouldn't be divisive, but I knew he was wrong. How can you challenge an incumbent President of your own party and *not* be divisive?"[3]

Although the call had been formal and correct, Reagan's aides were ever mindful of the previous indignations that had been hurled at him by the Ford White House. Reagan hand Jim Lake later said, "Ford always treated Reagan like a third rate hack."[4]

In his book, Ford worried that while his campaign was in disarray, Reagan's was a well-oiled machine. Ford fretted that he and his people had wasted too much time convincing themselves that Reagan would eventually decide not to run for President. While Reagan's campaign was not as disorganized as Ford's, it had its share of problems, including money management, staff infighting, and clashes over scheduling.

Governor and Mrs. Reagan gathered the night before his announcement for a private dinner with his close aides and advisers, including John Sears, Jeff Bell, Senator Paul Laxalt, Hannaford, Deaver, Lyn Nofziger, Marty Anderson, Dick Wirthlin, and Reynolds. Hannaford arranged for a special bottle of champagne to be served. The Reagans had been in Paris earlier, and although Reagan was not partial to champagne, he and Mrs. Reagan had enjoyed a bottle of Taittinger's while in France. Hannaford arranged for a bottle of the champagne to be served and toasted the forthcoming campaign, noting, "One thing, Governor. You never told us if you are actually running," Hannaford recounted. Reagan laughed with his usual youthful zest.[5]

In November 1975, Reagan was sixty-four, and Ford was sixty-two. Both were twice or thrice as old as many of their key staffers. In fact, what was immediately noticeable about both the Reagan and Ford campaign staffs was their relative youth, contradicting the Hollywood image of the gray-haired, curmudgeonly, back-room, hard-drinking, cigar-chomping, political hack. Among Reagan's campaign staff, Nofziger was the old man of the crew at fifty-one, but of Sears, Deaver, Jim Lake, Hannaford, Keene, Wirthlin, Bell, Anderson, Charlie Black, and Roger Stone, most were in their twenties and thirties.

Virtually all of the senior management of both campaigns and the Ford White House were young for their positions of responsibility. But all had multiple talents, interests, and hobbies, and many were devout in their faith. Most possessed good temperaments, good intentions and college or post-graduate educations. All were patriotic Americans who believed in the American way of life and cherished their children's futures. They were not like their peers in the 1970s—shallow, polyester-clad, disco-hopping yo-yos. These politicos actually read newspapers and books and attended political conferences and would have—had they dared enter a disco—been labeled "squares."

One explanation for the staffers' relative positions of power was that the Watergate scandal had cleared out much of a whole generation of Republican political operatives. This young crop of consultants, Campaign Managers, fundraisers, Press Secretaries, and organizers was left to run things. Their essential decency and moral judgment may have led them to avoid getting too deeply involved with the Nixon White House or the Nixon campaign—which could have led to wreck, ruin and prison. But their honor, temper, and character would be tested, as would Ford's and Reagan's, over the next ten months.

Ford was right when he spoke about disunity. The 1976 campaign would be very divisive, as it would bring forth the culmination of twenty-five years of unremitting hostilities between the moderate and conservative wings of the Republican Party. This time, however, the fight was the *gotterdammerung* for the GOP. One side or another would prevail, and the losing side would either change their ways, their ideology, or leave the party for good.

Reagan, accompanied to the National Press Club by Mrs. Reagan, was dressed handsomely in a gray suit and stylish pinstripe shirt with a pin dot tie and the ever-present folded white handkerchief in his left breast pocket. He easily passed the litmus test of Presidential fashion.

The subject of Reagan's wardrobe had been raised in the Washington office of Citizens for Reagan occasionally. But the Californians who knew the Governor took a decidedly more laissez-faire attitude about his dress. For the Washington crew, used to the dark blue, dark gray, and charcoal suits of the Nixon gang, Reagan's dress could be distinctly more casual than what they were accustomed to.

Reagan wasn't afraid to wear a white sports jacket or a plaid sport coat—or even violate the cardinal sin of politicians and put on funny hats. Few politicians campaigned with such sheer joy at meeting people as Ronald Reagan. Hubert Humphrey's affixed nickname, "The Happy Warrior," could have also easily applied to Reagan. Although Reagan always looked immaculate, he was mostly indifferent to fashion. Deaver said, "People thought Reagan was a clothes horse, but it wasn't true. Clothes just looked good on him."[6]

Years later, during his Presidency and following the assassination attempt, Reagan was aboard Air Force One on a political swing, accompanied by Mrs. Reagan, Deaver, and the usual contingent of Secret Service and White House staff. As was Reagan's habit when he traveled on the plane, he removed his pants, put on sweatpants and hung his suit pants to keep the crease in them.[7]

That day, Reagan was wearing what had become known as the "purple plaid suit," which he loved but no one else did, especially Mrs. Reagan. The suit was, charitably, not what one might expect a President to wear—or even a Senator. It might have worked for a freshman Alderman, but the suit caused comments in Washington. George Will once devoted part of his column to the "purple plaid suit."

Mrs. Reagan sought Deaver out to ask him to tell the President not to wear the suit. Deaver refused, telling her, "I'm tired of talking to him about the suit, I'm sick of the subject." Mrs. Reagan pleaded with Deaver; again and again he refused. Reagan, overhearing the conversation, argued for wearing the suit, insisting how much he liked it. At this point, Mrs. Reagan turned to Deaver and said, "Oh yeah? Mike, tell the President what his staff says about the suit." Reagan, looking at Deaver asked, "Mike, what does the staff say about my suit?"

Deaver replied, "Mr. President, the staff says if you were going to be shot, why couldn't you have been shot wearing that suit!"[8]

Deaver also related the time when President Reagan was due for a new official White House photo. Deaver was waiting in the Oval Office with the photographer when Reagan came in. According to Deaver, the President was wearing a tie that had seen better days. Deaver proudly showed Reagan the new Hermes tie he was wearing and told Reagan he should go out and buy some like his. Reagan leaned into Deaver, looked at his tie, and sniffed, "But, Mike, I don't like your damn tie."[9]

At the press conference, Reagan's wardrobe was one of the last things on the minds of his staff. Here, it was all about his statement announcing his candidacy. An excerpt:

> I have called this press conference to announce that I am a candidate for the Presidency and to ask for the support of all Americans who share my belief that our nation needs to embark on a new, constructive course.
>
> I believe my candidacy will be healthy for the nation and my party. I am running because I have grown increasingly concerned about the course of events in the United States and the world.
>
> In just a few years, three vital measures of economic decay—inflation, unemployment and interest rates—have more that doubled, at times reaching 10 percent and even more.
>
> Government at all levels now absorbs more than 44 percent of our personal income. It has become more intrusive, more coercive, more meddlesome and less effective.
>
> A decade ago, we had military superiority. Today we are in danger of being surpassed by a nation that has never made any effort to hide its hostility to everything we stand for. Through détente, we have sought peace with our adversaries. We should continue to do so but must make

> it plain that we expect a stronger indication that they also seek a lasting peace with us. . . .
>
> In my opinion, the root of these problems lies right here in Washington, D.C. Our nation's capital has become the seat of a "buddy" system that functions for its own benefit—increasingly insensitive to the needs of the American worker who supports it with his taxes.
>
> Today, it is difficult to find leaders who are independent of the forces that have brought us our problems—the Congress, the bureaucracy, the lobbyists, big business and big labor. If America is to survive and go forward, this must change.[10]

Reagan's mostly downbeat statement reflected traditional conservative thought at the time, although the last paragraph of his announcement did take a decidedly different direction from the "doom and gloom" public pronouncements by most of Reagan's contemporary Republicans in the 1970s. It was a foreshadowing of things to come from Reagan:

> We, as a people, aren't happy if we are not moving forward. A nation that is growing and thriving is one that will solve its problems. We must offer progress instead of stagnation; the truth instead of promises; hope and faith instead of defeatism and despair. Then, I am sure, the people will make those decisions which will restore confidence in our way of life and release that energy that is the American people.[11]

Also noteworthy was his open attack specifically on big business. Republicans generally shied away from criticizing big business. Though Reagan had been comfortable being a spokesman for General Electric in the 1950s, he was still a small-town kid from the populist Midwest who was suspicious of the concentration of power, either by government or business. Throughout his political career, Reagan often observed the difficulties that small businesses face—both from government action and from large corporations.

In fact, Wall Street, according to Larry Kudlow, was not very interested in the Reagan campaign in 1976 and only a bit more in 1980. Reagan's appeal was always much stronger with Main Street than Wall Street.[12] Reagan was plowing the same populist field of George Wallace and Jimmy Carter. But his populism appealed to a different set of values—those to the political right of Carter that also disavowed the dark history of racism associated with Wallace.

After Reagan concluded his statement, he took on the National Press Corps, who prided themselves on the ability to nail any politician.

The 1976 political campaign may have been the "golden era" for political reporters. The image of reporters of the era was that they sat at the bars at San Souci or the Class Reunion or the Hay Adams Grill in Washington and drank while they swapped rumors and women. In fact, they did do all of this and more right out of the movie *His Girl Friday,* but they were also consummate professionals, dedicated to their craft. They dearly loved politics in all its forms.

The most widely read were David Broder, Edward Walsh, Jules Witcover, and Lou Cannon of the *Washington Post*; Jack Germond, Fred Barnes, and James Dickenson of the *Washington Star*; R.W. "Johnny" Apple, James Naughton, Tom Wicker, and Jon Nordheimer of the *New York Times*; Bob Shogan of the *Los Angeles Times*; and columnists like Robert Novak and Rowland Evans, George Will, Pat Buchanan, Mary McGrory, Elizabeth Drew, and Bill Safire. The broadcasters, such as Walter Cronkite, Chris Wallace, Charlie Gibson, Sam Donaldson, Tom Brokaw, David Brinkley, Brit Hume, Leslie Stahl, "Cassie" Mackin, and Frank Reynolds were known and respected. These journalists were given wide latitude by their organizations, and friendships often developed between reporters and the politicians they covered.

Reagan got rough treatment from the columnists and editorial writers to be sure but generally received fair treatment from reporters, in part because he knew how to handle them.

For over half an hour, the candidate deftly fielded one question after another and bested the Washington media at their own game. When he was sure of his facts, he answered with great detail and vigor. When he was less sure, he successfully sloughed off the question. After some reporters had danced around the subject, Reagan was asked directly, "Mr. Reagan aren't you out of the mainstream of American life, and do you think the people want an extremist for President?" Smiling, Reagan reminded the reporter that he had been Governor of California for two terms and asked what extremism the reporter could cite that he had been engaged in during those eight years.[13]

Again, the national media had underestimated Reagan and failed to remember that as Governor of California, he held weekly press conferences with the Sacramento media. Reagan became quite agile and able in these settings and left the National Press Club unscathed. He was also immediately assigned a Secret Service contingent that would grow to twenty-one men.[14]

Unlike Carter, Wallace, and Reagan, all of whom had been Governors of their respective states, all of whom had never worked in Washington and all of whom were making their own populist appeal, Ford was a creature of Washington—an unpopular city with the American voter in 1975. But Ford's campaign staff was not concerned with Carter or Wallace's populist appeal in 1975. They were too busy examining what they believed was Reagan's narrow appeal to a minority within the GOP. The statement they issued reflected that sentiment:

> Despite how well Ronald Reagan does or does not do in the early primaries, the simple political fact is that he cannot defeat any candidate the Democrats put up. Reagan's constituency is much too narrow, even within the Republican Party.

The statement concluded:

> Although former Governor Reagan's announcement was not unexpected, it is disappointing to many Republicans. While not unmindful of his ability, he does not have the critical national and international experience that President Ford has gained through 25 years of public service, first in the House of Representatives, then as Vice President and as President.
>
> The President Ford Committee is a broad-based group working for President Ford's nomination. We want a united party going into the General Election. Any motion against unity is counter-productive and damaging to our prospects next November.[15]

Ford and his people, who thought they understood Reagan, the GOP, and the American electorate, were firmly convinced that Reagan's conservative appeal would not fly in the general election. They were positioning Ford to Reagan's left as the defender of the status quo heading into the Republican primaries. This strategy, combined with the mishaps of the Reagan campaign, worked for a time, but it came perilously close to driving Ford out of the race in the later primaries and state conventions. (While most of Ford's campaign staff seemed to be unaware of Reagan's political powers, they also did not seem to know how to spell his name or pronounce it. Memos referred to "Regan" and some would pronounce his name "Ree-gan." The day after Reagan's announcement, Nessen had prepared a summary of the press coverage for President Ford and the cover memo cited "Regan."[16])

Callaway, embellishing on Ford's campaign statement, told the *Chicago Tribune* that Reagan would cherry pick the questions he was willing to answer. Callaway argued that reporters and voters "cannot help but note how he ducked such tough issues as military spending, FBI activities, and federal aid to New York City. A President cannot duck the tough issues, nor should a Presidential candidate."[17]

If there was any way to make Reagan more resolute than he already was naturally, it was to attack his intelligence or manhood. Chuck Percy, a liberal GOP Senator from Reagan's home state of Illinois, took his own apocalyptic line against the conservative: "A Reagan nomination, and the crushing defeat likely to follow, could signal the beginning of the end of our party as an effective force in American life." Percy went on to describe Reagan as "far out of the centrist stream."[18]

But Ford aide Jerry Jones had attended the press conference and came away impressed with Reagan. In a memo he prepared for Cheney, Jones wrote, "Some people around the building thought it was a very poor effort and he showed to be a lightweight. My impression was . . . really quite good. The man had done his homework, he had his answers down pat and he handled the questioners with a sense of candor, humor, and calm. . . . We are in for a real battle."[19] Jones followed the next day with another memo, making clear that another Ford aide, David Gergen, shared Jones and Cheney's opinion about Reagan.[20]

Reporters quizzed Nelson Rockefeller about Percy's overblown statement, and Rocky did not entirely support it. While he downplayed Reagan's chances, Rockefeller told the press that he was not going to be the Administration's point man against Reagan and that he thought the man was qualified to be President. The Goldwater "bloody shirt" was often waved in Reagan's face by moderate Republicans and some in the media during the campaign, as they overlooked the assassination of JFK, Goldwater's mistakes, and Lyndon Johnson's ruthless campaign against the Arizonan in 1964.

When asked about attacks on Ford in the campaign at the press conference, Reagan cited the "11th Commandment": "Thou shalt not speak ill of a fellow Republican." But a White House spokesman snidely told Barry Serafin of *CBS News,* "When you live up to the original Ten Commandments, there is no need to add new ones."[21]

If Percy, the Ford campaign and others in the Republican Party did not understand Reagan's conservative/populist appeal, it was discerned later by a Carter supporter, who demonstrated a prescient insight the Ford campaign lacked. After Carter was elected President, he met with a longtime supporter, Chuck Morgan, who told him he thought Carter could be elected President in 1976 because the most popular show on television at the time was *The Waltons* and because of the near hero status of Senator Sam Ervin of North Carolina, a courtly Southern gentleman who chaired the Senate's investigation into

Watergate. In 1976, Carter had made much of his farmer credentials and as the populist who would clean up Washington.

Morgan, who was originally from Alabama and was head of the Washington office of the ACLU, told his story years later to David Keene. Morgan continued to relate to President Carter that he was in his hotel room one morning late in 1979, shaving and listening to a television show in the background. A guest was to appear who had written and sold 30 million books. "I told Carter any man who could sell 30 million books was worth listening to. The author was Louis L'Amour, but I'd never heard of him. So I went out and I bought a couple of his books and I read them. They were all about good, honest cowboys who always did the right and heroic thing. And damned if you didn't know it—every one of those books was about Ronald Reagan. And that's how I knew he was going to be the next President." Carter and his people looked at Morgan like he had three heads.[22]

Of Reagan's plunge into the campaign, Jack Germond wrote for the *Washington Star*,

> Ronald Reagan opened today a challenge to President Ford that threatens to tear apart a Republican Party already debilitated by the stewardship of Richard M. Nixon and the scandal of Watergate. . . . Reagan is viewed by political professionals in both parties as a genuine possibility for the nomination.
>
> And it is all the more striking because it is being made within a party that in the past has prized political regularity at almost any cost . . . the challenger to an incumbent President . . . can gain imposing momentum simply by making a strong showing in early tests of strength such as those scheduled in New Hampshire . . . and Florida. . . . Indeed, Republicans already are speculating among themselves about whether Ford might abandon his candidacy should he lose either of those primaries.[23]

The same day, the *New York Times* warned in an editorial, "[T]he discrepancy between the Reagan rhetoric and the Reagan record is sure to become well known. As it does, it can only be severely damaging to the challenger's cause."[24] But Tom Pettit of *NBC News,* who at times could be rough on Reagan, reported that the new candidate "can't be dismissed as merely an old actor, ex-sports announcer, and one-time after-dinner speaker. He's a celebrity politician who must now be taken seriously. . . . He was twice elected Governor of California. California survived." Petit also described Reagan's conservative proposals as "simple" and "basic."[25]

Howard K. Smith, in his commentary for *ABC News,* had perhaps the most unusual take of anybody on the Reagan challenge to Ford, charging that Reagan's candidacy would be "damaging to the quality of government for the next year," because it would take Ford away from his duties as President of the United States. Smith's commentary thankfully stopped short of recommending either a monarchy or dictatorship, so that the American people would be able to avoid the distractions of representative government.[26]

After his press conference, Reagan immediately departed on a two-day campaign swing that took him to the first four primary states he was to contest: New Hampshire, Florida, North Carolina, and Illinois. Massachusetts and Vermont fell immediately after New Hampshire, but the Reagan campaign decided to forgo any effort in those states, believing these Republican primary voters would not be susceptible to Reagan's conservative message.

Reagan was paying for his own charter plane, while the Republican National Committee would pay for Ford's travels until January 1, 1976. The Federal Election Commission ruled against a Reagan request that the RNC pay for his travels as well, but said Ford's travels were for "party building."[27] To Reagan and his supporters, it seemed that some were more equal than others.

At the first stop in Florida, Reagan's airport press conference in Miami was marred when a young man named Michael Lance Carvin brandished a gun. Everybody hit the deck, including Nancy Reynolds, who was part of Reagan's permanent traveling entourage. She observed that Reagan never lost his cool, even when the Secret Service was grappling with the gun and the young man. Reagan, in fact, moved forward to catch a little boy who had been pushed down during the mêlée.[28] The gun turned out to be plastic.

It was small wonder that Reagan never flinched. During his tenure as president of the Screen Actors Guild, repeated threats against his life forced him to carry a gun. In 1967, shortly after becoming Governor, the Weathermen firebombed his house in Sacramento. They also bragged that they had a bullet with Reagan's name inscribed on it at their headquarters.

The aftermath of the Miami incident inaugurated the Secret Service's lifelong love affair with Reagan, when he told reporters about preventing assassination attempts, "I don't think there's anything you can do except place your confidence in these guys, and they're awfully good."[29] Asked about its effect on his support for gun rights, Reagan argued that it "would be naïve and foolish to simply disarm the citizen." He reiterated his longstanding support for tougher sentences for anyone using a gun in the commission of a crime. Mindful of the assassinations of some political leaders in America, a Reagan aide told *CBS News,* "If he didn't feel like a candidate before, he does now."[30]

Reagan pushed forward to North Carolina and gave an uneven performance at an airport press conference, where he got into a debate with reporters about desegregation in the U.S. military. The next stop was New Hampshire where things went more smoothly. At one campaign rally in Bedford, Reagan was asked about the "$90 billion" proposal, but he successfully deflected it, and the campaign staff heaved a sigh of relief.

Reagan was also asked in Manchester about Percy's statement, to which he responded, "I think moderation should be taken in moderation." That drew a lot of belly laughs. Reagan then brought down the house when he elaborated, "When you're on the operating table, you hope the doctor has more than just moderate skills. Let's put what we and our party believe on our banner and not water it down."[31]

Almost immediately, the Federal Communications Commission ordered all television stations in the United States to stop airing old Reagan movies or reruns of his television show, *Death Valley Days,* as they would violate the equal time provisions of the FCC Act. Reagan, with tongue firmly planted in his cheek said, "Somebody must have goofed, because I've made some movies that—if they put them on television—I'd demand equal time."[32] When Reagan was sworn in as Governor of California at one minute after midnight on January 2, 1967, he turned to former actor and then U.S. Senator George Murphy and joked, "Well, George, here we are on *The Late Show* again."[33]

Reagan's team had high hopes for a big win in New Hampshire, but they lacked the discipline to keep expectations low. The problem was that they could not stop themselves from telling everyone, it seemed—on and off the record—that Reagan would win in the Granite State.

They reasoned that Reagan's conservative, old-fashioned patriotic message would definitely work with the flinty New Englanders. After all, the state's motto, "Live Free or Die," was proudly proclaimed on every license plate. Liberals and academics complained about the political ramifications of the motto, but that was of no consequence. This was New Hampshire, home of the *Manchester Union-Leader*, its only statewide newspaper, owned and published by the last of the great yellow journalists—William Loeb. Loeb personally authored a front-page editorial each day in his newspaper in *Citizen Kane* fashion, expounding on the dangers of liberalism, collectivism, and Communism, as well as the virtues of America, conservatism, and especially Ronald Reagan.

Loeb loved Ronald Reagan. But no one who offended Loeb escaped his biting pen, including Betty Ford after her *60 Minutes* interview and even President Ford, whom Loeb would often refer to in writing as "Devious Gerald" or, even worse, "Jerry the Jerk."

Loeb, despite his tendency towards what might be charitably called "tough" editorials, had an impressive political pedigree. His father had been the personal assistant to President Theodore Roosevelt when Loeb was a child, and the Old Rough Rider bounced the young Bill Loeb on his knee in the White House many times.

Loeb's editorials were unfortunately much tougher than the old man himself, and they sometimes came across as harsh and even cruel, making some conservatives in the state blush with embarrassment. His support for Reagan came with what was called in later political parlance, "baggage." Loeb had political enemies, including many conservatives in the state. This was unfortunate for Reagan, who might have expected to have broader support with the state's Republicans. In a *Boston Globe* poll, New Hampshire Republicans were asked if Loeb spoke for people like them. Sixty-two percent answered no. Clearly, the man had his critics, including inside the GOP.[34]

Another New Hampshire supporter of Reagan's was Governor Meldrim "Mel" Thomson. Thomson could also be characterized as "controversial." As Jules Witcover observed in *Marathon,* "A man who had once proposed issuing atomic weapons to members of the National Guard was bound to be somewhat controversial."[35] In 1978, when President Carter abrogated the mutual defense treaty between the United States and Taiwan, Thomson flew the American flag upside down at the state capitol, the international sign for distress.

A significant development for Reagan in New Hampshire was the decision by Gerald "Jerry" Carmen, the Republican State Chair, to keep the Granite State GOP neutral. Carmen was an entirely charming small businessman from Manchester who could also be tougher than nails when the situation called for it.

New Hampshire's GOP was one of the very few state parties to take an uncommitted position in 1976, as most were openly for Ford. Carmen scrupulously walked the fine line—from 9 A.M. to 5 P.M. Although he did not endorse Reagan, he made himself available for advice and counsel to Reagan and Lake after hours.

Still, the major coup for Reagan's New Hampshire effort was the acquisition of former Governor Hugh Gregg, who came from the more moderate wing of the state's Republican Party. The suggestion of making Gregg the Chairman of the New Hampshire Campaign came surprisingly from Loeb, Thomson and his people. Thomson was engaged in his own re-election effort. Sears and Jim Lake, who was running the New Hampshire Reagan campaign, could not believe their good fortune. They had thought that Thomson wanted to chair the effort and were trying to figure out how to finesse the problem.

Everyone in New Hampshire and Washington assumed that Gregg would support Ford, but intra-party squabbles between Congressman Jim Cleveland and a mistake by the Ford campaign's Washington office put Gregg on the market.[36]

After some face-saving comments by Ford's people in the wake of the loss ("Let Reagan enjoy him"[37]), Jim Lake had the last word as he told a newspaper, "In getting Hugh Gregg, we were trying to establish we were not the candidate of kooks."[38]

In a curious way, the public problems of the Ford White House and the ongoing problems with his campaign were beginning to dramatically lower Ford's expectations while unnecessarily raising Reagan's expectations heading into the New Hampshire primary. As Elizabeth Drew wrote in *American Journal,* "The President's campaign apparatus is in shaky condition. The opinion polls, to the extent they are known, indicate that the race between the President and his challenger is very close. . . . Ronald Reagan is said to have the more effective organization as the candidates with the more zealous backing often do."[39]

Reagan surely had his own problems as evidenced by the way he was on the defensive for three weeks leading to New Hampshire's February 24 primary. Reagan was trying to handle the fallout from the "$90 billion" speech, but Ford's continued woes in the White House since August of 1974, in the Washington office of the President Ford Committee, and his various problems in the states, were now ironically working to his advantage.

Citizens for Reagan was aggressively moving ahead, and Reagan appeared on the ABC Sunday show, *Issues and Answers,* following his announcement tour. This was the first time the national media bore in on the "$90 billion" speech. The host, Frank Reynolds, pressed Reagan hard on the far-ranging implications of the speech he had given the previous September in Chicago. According to Witcover,

> Reynolds told Reagan that the federal government paid 62 percent of New Hampshire's total outlay for welfare and observed, "That means New Hampshire has to either assume that or cut it down [under your plan]."
>
> Reagan acknowledged that was true: "I think that you would have to have taxes increased at state and local levels to offset this, or to maintain some of these programs."[40]

Correspondent Bob Clark, appearing with Reynolds for ABC, sparred with Governor Reagan asking, "In candor, wouldn't you have to tell the people of New Hampshire that you are going to have to increase your tax burden and that probably means either a sales tax or a state income tax?"

Reagan's retort was direct and to the point: "But isn't this a proper decision for the people of the state to make?"[41] Reagan's answer would have made the Founding Fathers proud, but its direct federalist implications eluded some reporters who saw all problems through the prism of more, not less, centralized power.

Nonetheless, Jeff Bell and his compatriots at the Reagan campaign fretted because Reagan was not reading the sample questions and answers they had prepared for him dealing with controlling the message and any fallout over the "$90 billion" speech.

The issue faded until two weeks later, when nationally syndicated columnists Rowland Evans and Robert Novak wrote that the Reagan campaign was internally concerned about the potential for political trouble because of the speech. Never ones to pull punches, they wrote that concerns were mounting in the Reagan camp and Bell's speech "has become the secret worry of [Reagan's] political managers" with the potential "to be an albatross around his neck."

"The Reagan campaign embraced, needlessly in hindsight, a proposal bearing high political risks. Even if the risks are ultimately avoided, Reagan must begin his campaign partly on the defensive—losing the challenger's greatest advantage," the column said.[42]

With all the previous talk of a divided party, paired with the problems both campaigns had getting to a solid start, a Ford White House staffer authored a memo outlining what they believed were the "four scenarios" of the upcoming Reagan versus Ford campaign. Whoever authored the memo must have been very optimistic about Ford's chances because in none of the four scenarios does Reagan win the nomination and the election. Presciently, however, scenario number two was "Reagan runs strong. President wins nomination. But party split and President loses in November."[43]

Ford's day-to-day operation in New Hampshire was run by a young Vietnam War veteran, John Michels, who told *Newsweek*, "I guess you might say we're trying here to win the hearts and minds of people," paraphrasing the American strategy in Southeast Asia. Using another analogy, he said of the President Ford Committee, "We've found out that, as in Vietnam, the generals aren't always the ones who know the most about local pacification."[44]

In December, the Southern Republican State Chairmen met in Houston. Reagan spoke to them and whacked the ball out of the park. Ford sent Bo Callaway and Nelson Rockefeller, incredibly, who did nothing to bring them into the Ford fold. At a private meeting with the GOP State Chairmen, Rocky was reported to have said, "You got me out, you sons of b—es, now get off your asses and help the President."[45]

On the other hand, the Southern GOP Chairmen felt Ford had snubbed them. To make matters worse, Dave Liggett, a Ford field staffer from California, wrote in his weekly report for the Washington office that "Regarding Bo Callaway's remarks in Houston over the weekend, comments have been generally negative." Liggett's memo also discussed his request for "equal time" from KHJ TV, which had run an old Reagan movie the weekend before.[46]

For the rest of the month of December, Reagan kept a fairly low profile. He met with staff and marshaled his energies for the coming battle by staying close to California. He did not return to New Hampshire until January 5, 1976, where Stu Spencer sprung his trap on Reagan using the "$90 billion" speech. Spencer recalled, "I'd get with Peter Kaye and say, 'we've got to get this guy on the defensive. . . . [H]e'll start stumbling around and it'll take him awhile to get his rhythm back but when he does, we're in trouble.'"[47]

Despite the surprise Spencer had planned for his old boss, both campaigns were working overtime in New Hampshire, Florida, and other early primary states. The Reagan grassroots team was doing a better job of organizing the later state conventions and caucuses in the West. Andy Carter and Frank Whetstone, two of the campaign's most seasoned operatives, were overseeing this aspect of the campaign. Carter was a big man from New Mexico who flew his own plane, wore bolo ties and cowboy boots, and had made a fortune in oil and cattle in that state. Whetstone was also a self-made man from Montana and, like Carter, was an unabashed conservative who spoke his mind.

The Ford team had recruited two veteran Republicans in New Hampshire: State House Speaker George Roberts and State Senate leader Alf Jacobson. They were to be Spencer's point men in New Hampshire, taking on Reagan over the impact his September speech would have on the people of their state. Callaway and Spencer had been presented with a detailed memo in January that dissected the Reagan plan, complete with acerbic asides:

> The single most radical and probably most detrimental aspect of his [Reagan's] proposal is the total elimination of General Revenue Sharing. He is vulnerable on several fronts with this element of the plan. . . . [It] is symptomatic of the thoughtlessness or at best lack of care in projecting budget savings. . . . Reagan's Backgrounder One claimed a $7.2 Billion annual savings. This is just a "careless" $1 Billion dollar error. The program is funded at $6 Billion per annum.[48]

The memo showed a tax shortfall of over $13 million for New Hampshire if the Reagan plan were to be enacted. It also helpfully documented those projects in New Hampshire that would have to be curtailed or cancelled under the Reagan proposal, including a roof for a library and a new fire truck for Manchester and sidewalks and police equipment in Concord.

Press releases were sent from the President Ford Committee to the Washington and New Hampshire media as Reagan was flying into the state. And Roberts and Jacobson held a press conference in Concord where they raised "the specter of new and higher state taxes as the price of Reagan's folly," according to Witcover in *Marathon.* Roberts further assailed Reagan's plan, saying it "would cost the people of New Hampshire tens of millions of dollars just to maintain the existing mandated programs at their present level"; moreover, it would force the state "to eliminate many necessary programs, to add to the local property-tax burden, or to institute a state sales tax, a state income tax, or both."[49]

Lake and Sears were now fully apprised of the Ford offensive and briefed the Governor on his response before his airport press conference. "The people of New Hampshire, I understand, are worried that I have some devious plot to impose the sales or income tax on them. Believe me, I have no such intention and I don't think there is any danger that New Hampshire is getting one," Reagan said.[50] Later that day in Moultonboro, Reagan reiterated his position in a speech at the Lions' Club, saying "I have no intention, with anything I have proposed, that New Hampshire should have either a sales or income tax."[51]

Shortly after Reagan had announced, Terry Drinkwater of *CBS News* reported, "Very shortly, he'll seclude himself here in California again before the real run begins after the first of the year. He'll also rest. There are those who question whether he has the stamina and the stomach for the nonstop campaigning which underdogs usually endure. He's sixty-four and a man who likes to be alone with his family."[52]

Reagan's schedule was crammed with seventeen stops in three days. His campaign knew Spencer was telling the national media that Reagan was lazy and tired easily so they assembled a grueling schedule to banish the whispering campaign against their man. Despite the arduous schedule, Deaver remembered it was, "the most fun I ever had on a campaign. We stored quarts of whiskey and gin in the back of the bus. When we got to a town, the advance guy would run out and get Kentucky Fried Chicken for everyone on the bus."[53]

Reagan was to begin his national campaign with an intense fifteen day, twelve-hundred mile swing through the first five primary states, with the greatest emphasis on New Hampshire, where two, three-day tours were planned for January. The plan was to campaign a total of nine days in New Hampshire in January. However, he was about to be placed on the defensive by Spencer and his personal recruit to the campaign, Peter Kaye, over the "$90 billion" speech, and there he would stay for three more weeks.

Before criticism of the proposal mounted, Reagan's team had sought to defend it. Wirthlin had polling data that showed it was popular with Republican voters. According to a nationwide survey, 59 percent of those surveyed favored transferring federal programs to the states, with only 31 percent opposed.[54] "We're not backing away from the concept at all," Lyn Nofziger, Reagan's campaign spokesman said to the *Boston Globe.* "We think this is a good Republican approach."[55]

While campaigning in New Hampshire, Reagan made the point that in 1955, Senator Hubert Humphrey, no slave to federalism, had been a member of a committee which issued a report questioning the new programs the government was undertaking. The document speculated on "new activities which are susceptible of a larger measure of state and local handling." The unseen hand of Marty Anderson was behind Reagan's counter-offensive.

Reagan's campaign was bounding in high spirits, despite the lingering problems with its poor handling of the "$90 billion" speech as a result of Spencer's offensive against Reagan in New Hampshire. A Harris poll, released in December of 1975, showed the American people in basic agreement with Reagan's conservative philosophy, including clear majorities that believed government meddled too much with private business and strong pluralities that believed Ronald Reagan was no "ordinary politician" and that Reagan's hard-line policies toward the Soviets was appropriate.[56]

Polling in December also showed Reagan surging in national surveys. A January Gallup poll of Republicans nationwide showed Ford and Reagan tied at 45 percent apiece, with the balance undecided. Gallup duly noted that Ford had been in a steady decline against the former California Governor since the previous spring, when he had led Reagan by a nearly two to one margin. Reagan had also moved ahead of Ford among independent voters.[57]

Still, the problems surrounding the speech would not fade, and even Reagan's in-state supporters were backing away. Loeb told the *Boston Globe*, "I think that's probably a program which he will be thinking of taking a second thought on."[58] While defending Reagan, Governor Thomson made it clear that he was against new taxes and would not be supporting Reagan if the candidate was going to increase New Hampshire's taxes.

While Ford's problems were beginning to take a backseat to the Reagan effort in New Hampshire, fresh speculation spread through Washington that former Pennsylvania Governor Bill Scranton, a moderate, would take over his political affairs and oversee Callaway and Spencer. But the rumor proved false. In fact,

Cheney was already quietly at work, stabilizing the Ford campaign operations and meeting each morning with the top management of the committee.

While expectations were building for Reagan in New Hampshire and Florida, Ford wisely told an audience in Boston that he would run in every primary, regardless of the outcome of the first several primaries, effectively lowering perceptions about Ford's chances in the early rounds. However, he later told the Associated Press that he foresaw no "serious obstacles" to winning the nomination, thus contradicting himself and driving Spencer and Cheney crazy.

The *Boston Globe* reported early in January, "Political observers give Reagan the edge over Mr. Ford in New Hampshire, which politically is one of the most conservative states outside the South. Reagan had endorsements from present and past Republican Governors and the state's only statewide newspaper."[59]

The FEC also disbursed the first round of matching funds to the candidates. The President Ford Committee received an initial check of $374,422 and Citizens for Reagan received a check for $100,000. According to Loren Smith, Reagan's Campaign Counsel, the FEC was auditing the Reagan campaign's report. Smith contended that the FEC owed Reagan a great deal more.[60]

Reagan campaigned effectively in New Hampshire, his "star status" clearly an advantage. It was in the Granite State where Reagan unveiled the effective "Citizens Press Conferences" he had used for eight years in California.

Reagan would typically address a roomful of supporters and curious onlookers and afterwards take questions, often lasting well over an hour. He was the master at this and answered all with energy and humor. He would also frequently stand in line, shake hands, pose for photos, and hold babies, without ever losing his poise or charm. Contrary to the opinions of many, Reagan was actually getting a fair ride for the most part from the press. The *Christian Science Monitor*, *ABC News* and NBC's *Today Show* covered the early portion of his campaign favorably.

Many conservative columnists also wrote praiseworthy pieces. Their backing was a given, at least as far as the Reagan forces were concerned. But not all of them were supportive, as *Human Events* complained in their ongoing fight with columnist George Will. The conservative weekly's editors, Tom Winter and Allan Ryskind, had been engaged in a feud of longstanding with Will, the former Washington Bureau Chief of *National Review* who left to become a columnist for the *Washington Post.* Winter and Ryskind thought Will was insufficiently conservative and told their readers so. *Human Events* took delight in reminding their readers that Will was no fan of Reagan's and took occasional shots at the Gipper. One of his columns in 1973 said of Reagan, "around the mouth and neck he looks like an old man." Will also wrote favorably about Rockefeller, before Reagan entered the foray, suggesting that he lead the Republican Party in 1976.[61] But by 1976, Will was often praising Reagan in his column.

Reagan, as might be expected, received favorable coverage from conservative publications like *Human Events* and *National Review.* It was with the editorial pages and the liberal columnists of the major daily newspapers where he sometimes got raked across the coals. When he announced for President in November of 1975, the *Baltimore Sun* wrote acidly, "The Reagan challenge to Mr. Ford comes from the right, the radical right, which cherishes notions that often are too simple, too negative and too risky. Yet, we welcome Mr. Reagan's entry, and if Mr. Ford falters or swings too far right, we would welcome the candidacies of others speaking for the Republican mainstream."[62]

James "Scotty" Reston, one of the deans of the eastern establishment's liberal columnists, wrote that Reagan's challenge to Ford was, "patently ridiculous . . . the astonishing thing is that this amusing but frivolous Reagan fantasy is taken so seriously by the news media and particularly by the President. It makes a lot of news, but it makes no sense."[63]

Garry Wills, a nationally syndicated liberal columnist who had once written for *National Review,* wrote that it is "unfair to expect accuracy or depth" from Reagan, who "seems destined to keep playing second lead, even to a bungler like President Ford." Wills judged the other candidates in relation to Reagan. Fred Harris "offers a more genuine populism." Jimmy Carter "economizes more as Governor." Sergeant Shriver was a better dresser, and George Wallace "is even more ignorant."[64]

Benjamin Taylor, a reporter and columnist for the *Boston Globe,* wrote, "In his political style, Ronald Reagan catered to the fears and anxieties of the great middle class." Reviewing Reagan's political career, he wrote, "His was always a campaign against something."[65] Taylor did come to the conclusion that Reagan had been a fairly effective Governor of California, although he contended Reagan had done so by "compromising" and being more moderate than his rhetoric.

Reagan's media coverage, especially as it related to the "$90 billion" speech and his New Hampshire campaign, was about to take a dramatic turn for the worse. Headlines soon blared about Reagan being confronted at campaign stop after stop about his proposal. All three days of his initial tour were marred with the same questions from the media and the citizenry about his plan. Reagan answered each patiently and never lost his cool, but it must have been maddening. The *Boston Globe* reported,

> At three stops during Reagan's tour of New Hampshire's northern section, he defended his scheme to slash $90 billion from the Federal budget

> by returning various social programs to the states. The plan has been criticized as unsound and potentially disastrous to state and local governments by Ford supporters.[66]

While Ford's forces were effectively injecting the "$90 billion" speech into the national and New Hampshire political debate, the Ford White House showed remarkable discipline for the first time and sent Ron Nessen to tell the media that Ford would not respond to Reagan's attacks.

Reported the *Boston Globe*, "The tack enables the White House to lump Reagan, a potentially strong conservative challenger and the only Republican rival to Mr. Ford, in with the large number of Democrats." The story proceeded to report Ford's new strategy, "We haven't overreacted in the past," said a Ford aide. "For instance, when Reagan made his proposal to cut the Federal budget by $90 billion, the President didn't come out and criticize it directly, he left that to others to do."[67] Others, like syndicated columnist Mary McGrory, officially of the *Washington Star.*

McGrory referred to Reagan's speech as a violation of the Twelfth Commandment (the Eleventh being, "Thou shalt not speak ill of another Republican."), which was, according to her, "Thou shalt not speak of half-baked money schemes in mixed company." McGrory also gleefully quoted Callaway saying that Reagan wanted to "throw old people out in the snow." McGrory opined, "It could be that the people of New Hampshire are as flinty as their reputation and would endorse the idea of throwing old people out in the snow and be glad that Ronald Reagan had made cold-heartedness respectable."[68]

By the end of his first swing in New Hampshire, it seemed all Reagan could talk about was defending his now controversial budget proposal. On the last day, he was asked over twenty times by voters about the "$90 billion" speech, and he patiently gave the same answer each time. The plan would be phased in gradually, there would be no interruption of services, and there would be an identical cut in taxes at the federal level for each additional dollar needed at the state and local levels to offset the loss of federal funds.

The problem was that Reagan was explaining, and the old adage in politics was that if you were explaining, you were losing. Reagan was ahead of Ford in Wirthlin's surveys, and he was hailed as the frontrunner by the press, influenced by the adoring crowds. His own campaign staff was letting expectations get out of control and Reagan was beginning to lose ground in New Hampshire.

6

REAGAN'S REVERSAL

"I hope someone down there lights a candle for me."

Gerald Ford arrived in New Hampshire on January 9, 1976, for his first visit to the state since he stumped unsuccessfully for GOP Senate nominee Louis Wyman in September of 1975. Ford was still carrying the burden of being made sport of by some in the national media, including Mike Barnicle, an iconoclastic liberal columnist for the *Boston Globe.*[1]

Barnicle welcomed Ford to the state, hypothesizing that at one of Ford's first campaign stops someone had asked him about his wife Betty's controversial interview with *60 Minutes* the previous August—in which she made clear she would understand if her daughter, Susan, had an affair. Barnicle spoofed Ford by writing, "Any affair that Susan has while I'm in the White House will be catered. And that's all I have to say on that subject."[2]

Time greeted the New Year by reviewing Ford's ongoing problems in an article titled "The Ridicule Problem." The piece summarized many of Ford's pratfalls and included some favorite lines of comedians: "How can a man who works in an Oval Office paint himself into so many corners." Another was: "The only thing between Nelson Rockefeller and the Presidency is a banana peel." Worse: "The President pierced his left hand with a salad fork at a White House luncheon celebrating Tuna Salad Day. Alert Secret Service agents seized the fork and wrestled it to the ground."[3]

It was all terribly unfair to the President. Some of the political cartoons could be even crueler. But it was the reality his team was forced to deal with, as Bo Callaway addressed in a memo to Stu Spencer: "We run the other risks inherent in travel; slips, falls, accidents, etc. which surely hurt us."[4]

Nonetheless, Ford stolidly carried on with his efforts to forestall Ronald Reagan's challenge. He was getting help from Cabinet officials who were aggressively campaigning for him in New Hampshire. They included Treasury Secretary

Bill Simon; Secretary of Health, Education, and Welfare, David Matthews; and Elliot Richardson, who had recently become Secretary of Commerce, replacing Rogers C.B. "Rog" Morton, who was reassigned to help out with the President Ford Committee. Also campaigning for Ford were Senator John Tower of Texas and former Pennsylvania Governor William Scranton. Tower was a favorite of conservatives in the state.[5]

Some Ford surrogates went too far in their rhetoric for Reagan's supporters. San Diego Mayor Pete Wilson campaigned in New Hampshire, telling voters that Reagan was "the worst Governor in the history of the state." Reagan's Californian supporters like Lyn Nofziger and Peter Hannaford were especially angered at Wilson, and it took some of them years to forgive him.[6]

An important development for Reagan was the decision of the United States Supreme Court to uphold California's "winner take all" primary system. The winner of the state's GOP Presidential primary would carry all 167 delegates with him to the Republican National Convention in Kansas City. Since no one really thought Ford had a shot to beat Reagan in his backyard, these delegates were considered by all to be safely tucked into Reagan's back pocket.[7] However, two additional decisions by the Supreme Court in January of 1976 came in the now-famous *Buckley v. Valeo* case. These decisions dealt with the new federal campaign laws and would have a direct bearing on the Reagan Presidential effort. One would be calamitous, the other beneficial.

While the Supreme Court declared most of the legislation that created the Federal Election Commission constitutional, it ruled that Congress had to reconstitute the FEC. The original act, signed into law in 1975, called for Congress to appoint four Commissioners and for the President to appoint two. However, the Court ruled that because the FEC performed executive functions, Congress had no role in appointing Commissioners, only approving them. Therefore Congress's role was a clear violation of the separation of powers doctrine of the U.S. Constitution.[8]

This decision would hurt the Reagan campaign because of ensuing bureaucratic foot-dragging by Congress and naked politics by the Ford White House. The Court directed Congress to rewrite that portion of the FEC Act, which it did, but in its own sweet time. When the bill arrived at Ford's desk for his signature, it languished there for a time, effectively stopping Reagan from receiving over $1.5 million in matching funds when his campaign desperately needed money. Reagan arguably lost the Wisconsin primary because of the coffer shortfall caused by the Ford White House.

The Court's second decision was more advantageous for Reagan. While it upheld the constitutionality of limiting individual contributions to a single candidate to $1,000 per election cycle and $25,000 per donor for all federal campaigns, it struck down regulations limiting the actions of independent groups of individuals working together to affect the outcome of a federal campaign. Congress had written in the original bill that independent expenditures to support or oppose a candidate for federal office must be limited to $1,000. The Court held that such limits violated parts of the First Amendment and were thus unconstitutional.[9]

This decision would prove vitally important for the Reagan campaign. At critical points in his challenge to Ford, independent conservative groups like the American Conservative Union and the Young Americans for Freedom provided much needed grassroots support when Reagan's campaign was flagging. This was especially the case in North Carolina, where the ACU would eventually spend tens of thousands of dollars helping Reagan.[10]

Democrat Jimmy Carter burst on the national scene with his win in the Iowa Caucuses in January. The importance of the Iowa Caucuses had been growing for the Democrats since George McGovern scored his breakthrough there in 1972, but the Republicans would not put much emphasis on it until 1980. A nonbinding straw poll was held for the GOP, but only in 2.5 percent of all precincts. Ford won by a narrow margin: 45 percent to 42.5 percent for Reagan. It was interpreted as a setback for Ford, since Reagan made no effort in Iowa whatsoever, and Ford had the support of the state GOP and Governor Robert Ray, a popular moderate Republican.[11]

Meanwhile, the Ford campaign made sure that Reagan could not remove the "$90 billion" millstone that hung around his neck in New Hampshire. It continued to drag him down wherever he campaigned. In Bloomington, Illinois, Reagan finally relented. He admitted that "I guess I made a mistake in the speech I made in Chicago last September in trying to point out that if six [programs] that I named [amount to] $90 billion, or one-fourth of what the present government is spending."[12] Marty Anderson was called in to salvage Reagan's position on the issue. Anderson worked well with the Governor. "We worked very closely together. It was my responsibility to give him all the research papers. He would spend a lot of time by himself with papers spread out, glasses on, writing."[13]

In Anderson's modified version, the federal government would spread some tax revenues around to help cushion the impact of transferring some programs to the states.

But in spite of the beating that Ford and the press administered to the Governor on his first campaign swing through New Hampshire, his pollster, Dick Wirthlin, had good news. Wirthlin reported that Reagan had a five percentage point lead over Ford in mid-January.[14]

In his State of the Union address, President Ford ironically proposed transferring over $10 billon of federal revenue to the states so they could administer the Medicaid program. Fred Barnes, writing for the *Washington Star*, noted the probability that the proposal came as a result of the Reagan initiative and the Ford proposal was "put together for its political value in combating Reagan" because the legislation "has yet to be drafted and probably will not be before next month, at the earliest."[15]

Ford also turned sharply right on food stamps, a cap on pay for federal workers, restraint of federal spending, and a proposed 9 percent increase in defense spending after a 7 percent increase the previous year. In contrast, from 1969 to 1975, defense spending had only increased 8 percent over those six years. The *New York Post* told its readers that the Ford speech was in fact, "New Reaganism."[16]

Maybe Ford realized it too late. Unhappy with the speech, the President transferred four of his speechwriters to other government jobs while installing Robert Orben, who had once written jokes for Red Skelton and Jack Paar, as head of his speech writing department.[17]

All the major Presidential candidates released their medical records in January, and both Reagan and Ford were in excellent health. Reagan had mild allergies and wore contact lenses. Ford had undergone surgery twice on his knees for damaged cartilage from his football days at Michigan. While arguably unnecessary for the American people to also know that Ford had hemorrhoid surgery or that Democratic contender Senator Frank Church had a testicle removed, in post-Watergate America "full disclosure" and "candor" had become the watchwords—even if it meant knowing the tiniest, seamiest and most personal details of a politician's life.[18]

Reagan was striving desperately to move into other issues, but three priceless weeks of campaigning had been lost in New Hampshire. Team Reagan knew that there were only three resources in any campaign: time, money and people. Of these, time was the most important because it determined how much money you could raise and how many people you could reach. Once it was lost or squandered, you could not get it back. Still, it would take several more days before he could move on, as he was asked again about the list of specific federal programs Jeff Bell had included at the end of the "$90 billion" speech text.

"I never did pay any attention to that list," the *Boston Globe* reported Reagan saying about Bell's addendum to the now infamous September speech in Chicago. "That was just some stuff the economists gave me. I didn't even agree with all the things on that list."[19] To charges that his plan would result in higher taxes, Reagan replied, "That's the same kind of crap I heard when I proposed welfare reform when I was in Sacramento."[20]

The *Boston Globe* wrapped the story, saying, "But he became particularly angered when he accused the Ford campaigners of preceding him [Reagan] into a state where he is campaigning and feeding some local politicians with figures on what the Reagan plan allegedly would mean in each particular state."[21]

While campaigning in New Hampshire, Ford told Reagan supporters, "By the end of this calendar year some $96 million dollars will have to be paid New Hampshire, to its ten counties, to its thirteen cities and 221 townships."[22]

There was a growing sense in the Ford camp that the Reagan insurgency had been blunted, but they also had difficulty coordinating their own public expectations. After the State of the Union, the *Boston Globe* sniffed that Ford "tried to steer a safe and conservative course for the ship of state last night, slightly to the left of Ronald Reagan's right-wing rhetoric. After the New Frontier, the Great Society . . . his call for a 'new realism' sounded like a low key battle cry. . . . [I]t is doubtful that the 'new reality' will make the kind of mark left by Franklin Delano Roosevelt's New Deal."[23]

Indeed not. Ford was still a mediocre campaigner, and it was not unusual for a crowd to come to see Air Force One or the Presidential motorcade and then listen to the first few minutes of Ford's speech before drifting off, having lost interest in whatever the President was saying.

Nonetheless, a week after the State of the Union, Ford's fortunes were beginning to brighten in Massachusetts. *NBC News* released a survey of 535 registered Republicans in the Bay State, which showed Ford favored by 50 percent, Reagan by 38 percent and the rest undecided. It was a dramatic turnaround for Ford because Reagan, had incredibly led Ford among Massachusetts GOP voters 43 percent to 40 percent in the previous survey. Ford's job approval with Massachusetts Republicans also rose in one month from 51 percent to 56 percent. Reagan's problems in New Hampshire were clearly washing over Massachusetts.[24]

These successes probably fueled the Ford campaign's delusions about Reagan. As *Time* magazine reported earlier in the month, "they insist that the Reagan force is relatively small."[25]

The Ford team rarely seemed to know the full measure of their foe. At one point, White House counselor Bob Hartmann raised the possibility of urging Ford to debate Reagan. The idea fell flat with the cooler heads in the Ford operation. While the Reagan campaign did not pick up on the idea to formally challenge Ford to a debate, Reagan did mention it at one press conference in Concord. It would have been foolish for the often-awkward Ford. With his easygoing charm and quick wit, the Great Communicator would have very likely trounced the

President, and such an opportunity was the last thing the Ford campaign needed to be handing the opposition.

Reagan was getting back on the offensive in New Hampshire, though the rebound was slow. During the second of his three planned tours of the state, he attacked Ford on the budget, charging that the deficit would be much higher than previously announced by the government and would put the country "on the road to re-inflation."[26]

Reagan also handled the hecklers better. Both Ford and Reagan picked up protesters in New Hampshire. A group calling itself the "People's Bicentennial Commission" showed up at Reagan's public appearances, waving signs that read "Fat Cats for Reagan." Given Reagan's continued money woes, his campaign would have probably welcomed a few fat cats if there were any interested in giving him money.

Ford's protesters took a different approach. Perhaps as an allusion to *Bedtime for Bonzo*, at one appearance in New Hampshire during a "town hall" meeting, someone wearing a gorilla costume stood and asked the President of the United States a question, which he dutifully answered.[27]

While most candidates would either ignore protesters or scream at their aides about them, Reagan killed them with kindness. At each stop where there were protesters, Reagan walked right over to chat with them. At one protest site, a girl charged that Reagan was part of a conspiracy between Detroit and government to build roads. Reagan told the young protester that people buy cars and they would not be happy driving over pastures. In his chat with the girl, Reagan gave her a quick and simple lesson about the laws of supply and demand. The leader of the protesters smiled at that one and told a reporter from the *Washington Star*, "He's incredibly good."[28]

When a little girl asked him after a speech in Dumbarton what he would do to improve schools, he said "The first thing I would do would be to get the Federal government out of the business of trying to run the schools and give that responsibility back to state and local government." The crowd went wild.[29]

Reagan was back on his conservative message of limited government, the free market, anti-Communism, and anti-Washington. Often, it would be mixed with humor, as in the case when one voter asked his position on busing, and Reagan replied, "There's only one busing program I'm in favor of, and that's busing the Federal bureaucrats out into the countryside so they can meet the people." He concluded most speeches by saying, "I am not a part of the Washington establishment and I don't consider that a disadvantage."[30]

Reagan enjoyed campaigning in New Hampshire and did not mind the long hours, but Mrs. Reagan was concerned that the campaign was pushing her husband too hard. At one memorable point, Mrs. Reagan called Nancy Reynolds late one evening. Reynolds was traveling in New Hampshire with Governor Reagan and Mrs. Reagan wanted to know that he was in bed and asleep.

In the hotel were Reagan, Reynolds, Deaver, and Sears. Mrs. Reagan insisted that Reynolds go down the hall and knock on the Governor's door to see if he was in his pajamas and in bed. Reynolds protested, but Mrs. Reagan insisted. Reynolds knocked on the door and woke the Governor. When she whispered through the door that Mrs. Reagan wanted to know "Ronnie" was in bed and asleep, the formerly slumbering Reagan yelled back at the door, "Can't I ever escape you two Nancy's!"[31]

The rap on Nancy Reagan in 1976 was that she got involved in campaign strategy and personnel decisions. The whispering was unfair because it was largely untrue. Her concern was the health and well-being of her husband and she mostly confined her concerns to him and him alone in 1976. She too campaigned tirelessly. The Reagans often campaigned separately and tried to avoid flying on the same plane as they sadly remembered a group of parents killed years before in a crash and didn't want to orphan their own children.[32]

Reynolds was an attractive former reporter for CBS's San Francisco affiliate in 1966 when she first met Reagan. Her father had been a Congressman and later a Senator from Idaho. She had seen many politicians over the years and could distinguish the real deal from the frauds. She went to work for the Governor in Sacramento, reporting to Nofziger, and was utterly devoted to the Reagans. As one of the people in charge of Reagan's political advance team, she had many responsibilities—even sometimes just holding the door for the Governor, which proved a problem. Reagan balked at allowing Reynolds to hold the door for him and finally said, "My mother told me ladies go through the door first so we can stand here all day and you let me hold that door for you or we don't go through." Reynolds finally relented and went through first.[33]

She could also be blunt, as when Reagan called her in 1979 to tell her he was running again for President. Reynolds blurted out, "Don't you think you're too old?" Reagan, of course, chuckled. The bond between the two was strong. During a trip to Dallas in 1976, Reynolds took Reagan to the wrong building and an empty auditorium. Meanwhile, "2,000 screaming women" were in the building next door, wondering where their hero was. Sears wanted Reynolds fired for the foul-up, but Reagan would not hear of it.[34]

As is often not the case with politicians, the charming, gracious man that America saw in public did not differ from the private Reagan. Many politicians preferred to eat their meals in their rooms when on the road campaigning, but Deaver, who knew Reagan better than probably any man alive, remarked that

Reagan preferred to eat in public, facing the door of the restaurant so he could see people. He did not mind being interrupted for his autograph and clearly relished his role as a candidate. It was no wonder that his staff was fanatically loyal to him.[35]

Reagan's second tour through New Hampshire since he announced in November was his best yet, and the campaign got high marks for using the candidate to maximum effect. Not much time was devoted to street corner or factory gate handshaking unless it could be developed into a "photo-opportunity" for the media. Reagan was doing his own form of retail politicking through his effective "Citizens Press Conferences." Reagan also got some help from an unexpected quarter in the form of TV commercials starring his old opponent, George Christopher, former Mayor of San Francisco, whom Reagan had defeated in 1966 for the California Republican Party gubernatorial nomination.[36]

Some political observers worried that Reagan was becoming "overexposed," which could dilute his star quality. But the crowds were good, and high expectations for Reagan in New Hampshire were once again creeping out of Pandora's box.

Things were different in Florida. The upcoming Sunshine State primary was slated for March 9 and both candidates were having their share of troubles.

Congressman Lou Frey, head of Ford's operation in Florida, was overly optimistic for some in the Ford camp about the President's chances. He might have even been too optimistic for his own good. A curious story was filed at the end of January by seasoned political reporter Loye Miller Jr. for the Knight News Service on the topic of Florida and the Ford campaign. Frey apparently had told the President "that his chances of beating Republican challenger Ronald Reagan are excellent," but another person talking with Frey heard the opposite—that Frey was "almost entirely negative." Worse, according to the source, Frey thought Reagan's Florida operation was "better organized."[37] Frey denied the story, but the damage was done.

Other problems dogged Ford in Florida. Frey complained about the lack of supplies, Bo Callaway's leadership, and being undercut by the national campaign through leaks to the media.

Things weren't always easy for the Reagan campaign, either. Concerned that the Governor might be misquoted, the campaign had hired Dana Rohrabacher to travel with Reagan and tape all of his interviews and pronouncements. Rohrabacher also took the best "sound bites" and fed them via telephone to radio stations for their news reports.[38] Reagan's son Ron was supposed to help

Rohrabacher, but he didn't like campaign work. Lake later said, "He was a pain in the butt."[39]

Jim Lake, Reagan's New Hampshire Manager, was a Californian with a background steeped in agriculture and had gone to work in the Nixon Administration as Deputy Assistant Secretary of Agriculture after a stint on Capitol Hill. After rejecting two offers from Deaver to go to work for Reagan, he finally agreed to take over the duties of the Washington office of the State of California beginning in February of 1974, after Deaver convinced him that Reagan would run for President in 1976. He signed with the campaign immediately after Reagan left office, and he seemed to be one of the few who got along with both the Washington crew and the Californians. He was unflappable and, as both Becki Black and Nancy Reynolds said, "all the women in the Reagan office had a crush on Jim."

Lake worked from the campaign headquarters at the old New Hampshire Highway Hotel in Concord, a favorite lodging, eating, and drinking establishment of in-state and out-of-state political reporters and politicians. It was just down the street from the state capitol building. The hotel was old, creaky and had a certain rundown charm, like a dowager/aunt whom time had passed by. Lake's unenviable task—trying to build and then hold together the New Hampshire organization for Reagan—required he spend as much time "babysitting" and "handholding" local politicians as he did trying to win the primary.

Few required as much hand-holding as New Hampshire Governor Mel Thomson. Thomson had his following, especially in the blue-collar neighborhoods around Manchester, but he also had his enemies within the more moderate elements of the state's GOP. Lake told Reagan that Thomson should not be allowed to get too close to the campaign, but Reagan genuinely liked the man. Lake did manage to limit joint public campaigning by the two to just one day around Manchester. Any more was too risky; Thomson was an unguided missile. On one occasion, the New Hampshire Governor went on *Meet the Press* two Sundays before the New Hampshire contest and told the world that Reagan would defeat Ford by 5 percent. Lake complained to Thomson that he needed to stop making unrealistic predictions for Reagan, but the damage had been done.

A bigger pain was materializing for Reagan in Florida, however—one that would dog him in New Hampshire as well. Just as he was starting to get beyond the problems of his "$90 billion" speech, Reagan seemed to suggest making Social Security voluntary, the same issue that tripped Barry Goldwater so badly in 1964. The issue incubated for several weeks until it exploded in Reagan's face right before the Florida primary.[40] But before that, the Ford campaign had some toe-stubbing of its own to do.

The President Ford Committee had picked up on Reagan's musings about Social Security, conveniently overlooking the fact that Reagan had qualified his suggestion about privatizing the insolvent retirement plan by saying that all current and future recipients should be protected. The Ford campaign sent out dozens of sample press releases to their supporters in New Hampshire and Florida with blank spaces for people to fill in their names and hometowns. The problem was that some Ford supporters simply wrote in the information rather than retyping the releases or redrafting them so that political reporters would not all receive the same identical press release, which of course, they did.[41]

Reagan seized on the Ford goof and had some fun with the releases, quoting "Blank said this about Reagan, and then another person named blank said that about Reagan." Turning more serious, Reagan then called it "a little bit dishonest" and filed it under the category of "dirty tricks."[42] Ford spokesman Peter Kaye was forced to backtrack, admitting he had prepared the releases. He insisted that their intention was as a guideline for local officials. He denied that the campaign was not trying to put words in their mouths. As it turned out, sending out some common sense to these people would have probably been a better plan for Kaye than filling in the blank press releases.

On the eve of his sixty-fifth birthday, Reagan headed for North Carolina once again with a newfound spring in his step after his third New Hampshire tour de force. He showed his biting wit, such as when a supporter asked him whom he preferred the Democrats to nominate. Reagan quipped, "Bo Callaway." Someone also mistakenly addressed him as "Governor Ford" to which Reagan, grinning with deadpan humor replied, "I didn't stumble when I came in."[43]

Rowland Evans and Bob Novak wrote of Reagan's recovery in New Hampshire, "What Reagan must do now, many advisers feel, is shift attention to what may be the most vulnerable policy and personality in the Ford Administration: détente and Henry Kissinger. In his basic new speech lasting 35 minutes, Reagan devoted 30 seconds to foreign policy, rejecting détente as 'a one way street' for the Soviet Union. Invariably, it gets more applause than anything else. If the $90 billion monster is truly vanquished, Reagan's focus may soon switch from governmental accounting to global strategy."[44]

New Hampshire had no lack of characters, as evidenced by Governor Thomson and *Manchester Union-Leader* editor Bill Loeb, but another Reagan supporter, Stewart Lamprey, the former speaker of the state house stood out. Lamprey ran Richard Nixon's successful campaigns in New Hampshire in 1960 and 1968. But by 1976, his passion was less about politics and more about making a buck. He had developed the first computerized list of 165,000 registered Republicans in the state in 1976. Although he had endorsed Reagan, Lamprey sold the list to both the Reagan and the Ford campaigns, pocketing five thousand dollars from each.[45]

He also had a phone bank contract worth approximately $50,000 with Citizens for Reagan working in Laconia, where paid operators would call the list, asking Republicans for whom they intended to vote and a list of approximately sixty-five thousand Reagan supporters was eventually developed from these calls. Lamprey's callers spent the balance of the month calling undecided voters, about 14 percent, to see if they had made up their minds and for whom.[46]

Ford's campaign was relying on volunteers to man his phone banks. Ford was using about seventy-five phones located all over the state, while Reagan was using just five, all located in one office in Laconia. Lamprey, the ever-present character in New Hampshire Republican politics, did know his state, and as far as three weeks in advance, he said the race between Reagan and Ford was too close to call.[47]

Meanwhile, Ford's campaign hierarchy finally had their fill of Frey in Florida and replaced him with Stu Spencer's longtime business partner, Bill Roberts. Although he was ailing with diabetes, he began to immediately turn the campaign around and thus increase Ford's fortunes in Florida.

A new Harris Survey was released of Republicans nationwide, which showed the President with a razor thin lead over Governor Reagan, 47 percent to 45 percent, a statistical dead heat.

Even better for Reagan, however, was his growing lead over Ford among self-identified conservatives within the GOP, 54 percent to 41 percent.[48] These conservatives constituted the motivated base of the party. They were the volunteers—the small contributors who formed the "hardcore" of the GOP. They would turn out to vote in Republican primaries even if dogs and cats were falling from the sky.

Not surprisingly, Ford was leading among the moderates, the white collar, the more educated, and the higher income individuals within the Republican Party. In an interview with CBS, Ford took on one of the more controversial issues of the day: abortion. The President said that he was against abortion and that he favored returning the issue to the states, but, unlike Reagan, he was against a constitutional amendment to overturn abortion. Ford thought that the Supreme Court was wrong in the case of *Roe v. Wade*, which nationalized and legalized abortion, but he opposed taking effective measures to correct the ruling.[49]

No sooner had Ford completed his interview with Walter Cronkite, than Betty Ford issued a statement of her own from the White House, disagreeing with her husband on abortion. "I am glad to see that abortion had been taken out of the backwoods and put into the hospitals where it belongs," her statement said. The missive also restated her support for the *Roe v. Wade* decision.[50] The editorial pages of the nation's newspapers had a ball, using Mrs. Ford to bash Mr. Ford. The *Boston Globe*, one of America's leading liberal newspapers wrote, "President Ford would be a better man and a better leader if he paid more heed to his wife, Betty, who is consistently demonstrating that she has more sense, honesty and moral courage than the man she married."[51]

In the same interview, Ford awkwardly attempted to criticize Reagan saying, "Some man who is running for office can use words to express how he's going to meet a problem whether it is domestic or foreign and that [is] . . . sometimes totally unreal when you have to deal with the actual problems that come to this desk."[52]

Unlike Ford, Reagan was having no problem putting one word in front of the other, as he charged that the National Education Association wanted a "federal educational system, a national school system. . . . I believe this is the road to disaster." Reagan further made the historical analogy to Hitler's Germany, saying "where they had a nationalized school system . . . when [Hitler] said burn the books, they burned the books."[53] Reagan refused to retreat from these comments.

Sensing the resurgence of the Reagan campaign, the Ford campaign wisely began to tamp down expectations—especially in New Hampshire and Florida where Reagan was drawing big crowds and media attention.

Still hanging around the sidelines was Rockefeller, who once again said publicly that he might jump into the Republican Presidential contest if Reagan knocked Ford out in the early primaries. "I withdrew as Vice President," he said cryptically.[54]

Now it was Ford's turn to hit New Hampshire again, just seventeen days before the primary. Reagan had departed for the sunnier climate in Florida. One Ford insider summarized the closeness of the race for the *Boston Globe*: "The President can't screw up, but neither can Reagan. There's no room for it." According to the same story, only 10 percent of New Hampshire's Republican primary voters were undecided, and when they were "pushed" they split evenly as well.[55]

With the exception of scattered hecklers, Ford was warmly greeted in New Hampshire. He campaigned at the University of New Hampshire in Durham and at a junior high school in Concord, where he presented charts and graphs to 250 invited local officials and took questions from the friendly crowd. Again, Ford had trouble holding a crowd as dozens streamed for the door at an event at the University of New Hampshire before he had finished his address.[56]

At an address to the Nashua Chamber of Commerce, an advanceman's nightmare came true: Ford wound up presenting a civic award to Sam Tamposi, a high-profile Reagan supporter.[57] The awkwardness of the moment did not stop Ford from taking the Reagan challenge head on. Although he claimed Reagan would be acceptable as a Vice President, he also charged Reagan did not have the experience and "hasn't had to make those hard decisions."

Mrs. Ford and their daughter, Susan, also stumped the state. One woman told the *Boston Globe*, "I don't care for her husband, but she's terrific." Unfortunately, Betty Ford was not on the ballot.[58]

Ford was slowly, slowly becoming more comfortable at campaigning. He continued to struggle with a prepared text or a teleprompter speech, but was improving with improvised remarks. At one stop, he relayed a conversation with his daughter Susan about skiing in New Hampshire. She said, "Dad, you do all the falling and I'll do all the skiing," to the delight of the crowd.[59] At another stop, he met a teenage boy, Tommy Boyd, who was wearing a cast on his left arm. Ford asked the boy how it happened, and the boy replied, "I fell." Ford replied, "I fall a lot, too," before signing the boy's cast.[60]

Ford's campaign scrapped previous plans for door-to-door canvassing in favor of the more efficient phone surveys, mailings, advertising, and national media coverage of him doing his job as President, which was key for Ford. However, it was former Senator Norris Cotton, the Honorary Chairman of Ford's New Hampshire effort, who bluntly told reporters that Ford "has a bad organization" in the state. The old man had made a career speaking his mind, and he was not about to change now. Cotton elaborated, "The President is in trouble because he doesn't have a well organized campaign." He blamed the "young kids" who lacked supervision.[61]

Never one to mince his words, Cotton also told reporters that although he supported Ford, he was philosophically more in tune with Reagan. The Ford people grumbled in private over Cotton's frankness. He was an asset at the end of the day, but he also came with headaches, just as Gregg, Loeb, and Thomson did for Reagan.[62]

Both campaigns, however, were reluctant to reveal too many of their tactics. Both were receiving matching funds from the FEC and therefore were required to comply with the ceiling set for New Hampshire of $200,000. It was also the first Presidential campaign where candidates also received Secret Service protection when they qualified for matching funds. By the time of the New Hampshire primary, two Republicans and six Democrats were trudging through the snow, complete with their own personal phalanxes of body guards.

At a GOP conference in Arlington, Virginia, leaders from thirteen states gathered to hear Ford. Reagan could not attend, so Sears went in his stead, still beating the "Reagan can govern better than Ford" drum and then oddly added, "Reagan would go further in that direction [changing the government] than Ford would, but I certainly could endorse them both."[63]

It was a curious thing for such a high-ranking Reagan campaigner to say. Of the differences between the two men, the *Wall Street Journal* editorialized,

> Some months ago, with tongue in cheek, we coined the phrase: Reaganism is extremism in defense of Fordism. We could as easily have said that Fordism is pragmatism in pursuit of Reaganism, for either phrase suggests two men with common philosophies of government, but with differences in their approach to implement the same.
>
> Of the two, President Ford seems by far the more uncertain, appearing to shift back and forth . . . [Voters] are no longer sure they can trust Mr. Ford's pragmatism, which at times becomes extreme.[64]

Rockefeller and Callaway also attended the conference, where Callaway once again proclaimed that Ford would win both New Hampshire and North Carolina. Callaway may have known something that no one else did in the Ford camp because the *Boston Globe* had released the results of its own survey of 849 New Hampshire Republicans. The poll showed that Reagan's team had been far more effective in making contact with their voters. Indeed, of those voters who had heard from one campaign or the other or both, Reagan's team had been in touch with 81 percent while Ford's campaign had only been in touch with 27 percent of New Hampshire's Republicans.

The survey did not ask preferences but did develop some fascinating data:

> On today's important issues . . . agreeing with Ford, 35 percent; agreeing with Reagan 42 percent.
>
> Opinions on the Reagan proposal [to transfer services back to the states] were divided, but tended to be favorable despite the feeling [that it would result in higher taxes.] Overall, Republican voters, by 44 percent to 31 percent, think Reagan's proposal is a good idea, even though 58 percent think it would result in higher local taxes.[65]

Reagan was also seen as a better speaker and more polished than Ford (58 percent to 8 percent), but buttressing Callaway's claim and buried in the data were two critical findings: by a margin of 46 percent to 30 percent, Republican voters thought Ford would win in New Hampshire, and by a margin of 22 percent to 18 percent, the former thought that Reagan could not win in New Hampshire.[66]

In a new nationwide Gallup poll, Ford had fallen into a dead heat with Reagan, 44 percent to 43 percent. Another bit of good news for Reagan came from a straw poll of the statewide convention of the Florida Junior Chamber of Commerce, the "Jaycees," in which Reagan beat Ford by an almost three to one margin.[67]

It was a seesaw battle with each camp claiming a lead as the two candidates squared off in New Hampshire, although never in person. To the delight of the media, most of the tougher barbs came from their surrogates. For example, former New Hampshire Governor Walter Peterson called Reagan nothing but a "trained performer."[68]

Having almost exhausted the political benefits of putting Reagan on the defensive over his "$90 billion" speech, the Ford campaign seized more aggressively on Reagan's statement on Social Security, when he suggested investing the trust fund in the stock market. At a breakfast meeting with reporters at the White House, Ford proceeded to call the idea something that "someone dragged out of the sky." Going further, Ford said Reagan was a "stranger" to Washington.[69]

Also, Ford challenged Reagan to release his recent financial records, hoping to dredge up a scandal like the one that erupted years before, when it was discovered that Governor Reagan had paid no federal or state income taxes in 1970.[70] Reagan capitulated and released his records, which showed over two million dollars in real estate holdings alone, between his home and two ranches. Compared to Reagan, Ford's financial worth was meager. The returns also showed that Reagan had "paid his fair share of taxes" after 1970. In fact, the Ford team's accountants disappointedly noted in a memo that the Reagans probably paid more than necessary in 1975.[71]

But Ford was now forced to deal with the announcement by the government of Communist China inviting former President Richard Nixon to visit Peking. Nixon had decided to go and would arrive in China the morning of the New Hampshire primary. Ford's campaign strategists privately debated what to do, including seizing the plane the Chinese sent to California for Nixon, as reparations for debts owed the United States' citizens for property seized by the Communist government there.[72]

In the end, they decided to take a pass for fear of exacerbating the problem. Yet behind closed doors, more than a few expletives were used to describe Richard Nixon. They accused him of ingratitude and thought he was trying to help Reagan win the nomination and embarrass Ford. Senator Richard Schweiker, a Ford supporter from Pennsylvania, charged Nixon with deliberately trying to sabotage the Ford campaign to grease the skids for John Connally to enter the ring.[73] Also in Pennsylvania, the filing deadline of February 17 came and went without

Reagan's campaign filing one delegate slate in the state, effectively conceding all 103 delegates controlled by Ford's State Chairman Drew Lewis to the President.[74]

More important to the direction of the campaign was a speech, written by wordmeister Peter Hannaford, that Reagan delivered at Phillips Exeter Academy, an exclusive private boarding school for boys. For the first time since announcing his candidacy, Reagan took off the gloves regarding the failures of America's foreign policy under Ford and Secretary of State Henry Kissinger. Although he never mentioned Kissinger by name, Reagan said,

> One wonders if we even have a foreign policy, for it is impossible to detect a coherent view . . . our foreign policy in recent years seems to be a matter of placating potential adversaries. Does our government fear that the American people lack willpower? If it does, that may explain its reluctance to assert our interest in international relations.
>
> [The] Soviet Union has now forged ahead in producing nuclear and conventional weapons, we can afford to be second to no one in military strength, not because we seek war, but because we want to ensure peace.[75]

The media briefly seized on the speech as new material but the audience of fidgety boys was all wrong and the campaign felt this speech had not "taken." Reagan did not pursue this line of attack again until he was campaigning in Florida.

The *Boston Globe*'s Benjamin Taylor, who covered Reagan's New Hampshire foray, concluded, "Reagan finished his campaign swing with an evening appearance at the University of New Hampshire Field House, where President Ford had made an appearance Sunday night. Reagan drew about half as many as the 3,500 people who came to see Mr. Ford, and the President was given a much warmer reception."[76]

The full power of the Presidency would be brought to bear, once again, in the Granite State. Ford's campaign decided to send the President into the state one more time, several days before the February 24 primary. During Ford's previous trip, he had announced he would sign legislation establishing America's coastal fishing boundaries at two hundred miles, thereby rebuffing the Soviets who arrogantly pilfered good fishing grounds up to twenty miles off U.S. shores.[77] Ford's announcement was especially pleasing to the fishing communities of New Hampshire and Massachusetts, both of which just happened to be holding Presidential primaries.

But with the power of the Presidency came the headaches. For instance, in a nakedly crass political move, a Democratic-controlled subcommittee of the House Judiciary Committee announced it would investigate Ford's pardon of Nixon.

For the last ten days of the New Hampshire campaign, the Ford campaign and the national media threw at Reagan everything they could. Elliot Richardson labeled Reagan "gimmicky" and told Ford supporters that a Reagan Presidency made him worry. He also disparagingly referred to Reagan's supporters as "right-wing, ultra-conservatives."[78] California Congressman Pete McCloskey, a liberal Republican stumped for Ford and attacked Reagan with relish in the state. As in the case of Wilson's comments, Reagan's supporters thought McCloskey was hitting below the belt: "When you have the right wing of the Republican Party in charge, they do not just disagree, they tend to see liberal and moderate Republicans as almost traitors to the party."[79] Speaking to the Stratford County Republican Club, McCloskey said Reagan was "not a serious student of government . . . and almost a shame as a Presidential candidate."[80]

Ford's campaign continued to pound Reagan on the "$90 billion" proposal and his comments on Social Security. And Kissinger joyously piled on, suggesting that Reagan was a threat to world peace without mentioning him by name. At a State Department press conference, Kissinger said that negotiations between the three superpowers were "too delicate, too important for world peace to be used for simply partisan sloganeering."[81]

The heat Reagan was taking in the media from the Ford campaign was even too much for Reagan's old appointment secretary, Paul Haerle, who had become Chairman of the California Republican Party courtesy of his appointment by Reagan. Haerle supported Ford in 1976 and also organized fellow Californians Wilson and McCloskey in their opposition to their former Governor.

Ford's team was more effectively controlling expectations than Reagan by playing down their chances while playing up Reagan's. New England Political Director Richard Mastrangelo and others were assuring reporters that Reagan's rock-ribbed supporters would turn out no matter what, but Ford's support was softer. They were conditioning the media for a narrow Ford loss or, even better, an unexpected Ford win. Said one Ford supporter to the *Boston Globe,* "It all depends on the size of the turnout. If people are apathetic and don't vote, Reagan wins because those G—damned Reagan people will vote no matter what."[82]

The President also found time to spend a day and a half stumping in Florida, where his chances were brightening. He campaigned in Orlando, Ft. Lauderdale, Miami, Ft. Myers, and St. Petersburg. At one of Ford's appearances, Frank Cormier reported for the Associated Press, "His speech was marred by a brief scuffle between pro-Ford oldsters and youthful demonstrators . . . the senior citizens, wielding purses and umbrellas, clearly won."[83]

Reagan's local forces were finally backing off landslide predictions they'd been making. His State Chairman, Tommy Thomas, a Panama City auto dealer, had previously told reporters that Reagan would defeat Ford "two to one" in the Sunshine State. Both sides now knew the situation in Florida was so fluid that any stumble or loss in a primary before the Florida March 9 GOP contest could tip the outcome one way or the other.[84]

Reagan's anti-big-government message was starting to sound like a broken record to the reporters covering his campaign. He was also getting hit in the media for accepting contributions from oil executives.[85]

Despite his successes in New Hampshire, Reagan's campaign also appeared in disarray when Loeb and Thomson disagreed publicly over its fate. Loeb said he thought that his man could lose, while Thomson predicted Reagan would prevail over Ford by at least 5 percent.[86]

Working against Reagan's expectations was the growing chorus from the Ford White House, the President Ford Committee and his New Hampshire operation that Ford might pull an upset win. The national media, experienced in such matters, had seen trailing campaigns "puff" their chances, believing wavering voters would want to go with who they perceived was a "winner," and therefore much of the ballyhooing from the Ford camp was dismissed by the media.

It was announced that Ford would make one final swing through New Hampshire the Thursday and Friday before the February 24 primary. But one more attack on Reagan by another one of his opponents must have pleased the candidate. A Soviet commentator, Valentin Zorin, called Reagan a "henchman of the extreme right-wing circles of America" and said that Reagan was "especially zealous" in his attacks on détente between the United States and the Soviet Union.[87]

The Ford White House never seemed to decide whether to label Reagan as an extreme, out-of-the-mainstream, unelectable nuclear cowboy or someone who was in basic philosophical agreement with Ford. They used both stratagems. But when Ford charged once again a mere week before the primary that Reagan was "to the right of me philosophically" and that Reagan could not win the general election, the charge gave Reagan a chance to reach into his bag of tricks.

"I'm a little surprised by this statement about my so-called extremism," Reagan said with a smile. "It does come rather strange because he tried on two different occasions to persuade me to accept any of several Cabinet positions in his Administration, and did appoint me subsequently to his CIA investigating commission." When asked whether he thought Ford offered the positions as a way of dissuading the challenger from running, the Governor chuckled: "No, I just thought he recognized my administrative ability." Embarrassed, the Ford team confirmed the proposed Cabinet offerings.[88]

Just a week before the primary, David Nyhan of the *Boston Globe* summarized the reality of the race: "The President's spear-carriers say a 50.1 percent victory will be received like a victory, and they are probably correct."[89]

Both campaigns were now on high octane, relentlessly driving through the last several days of the campaign. Both candidates were due back in the state just before the primary although they would not directly cross paths. Ford would eventually campaign in Keene and Portsmouth on Thursday and Friday (February 19 and 20) while Reagan would march through a sixth and final swing in Manchester and Nashua on Saturday and Sunday. Reagan would then depart New Hampshire for Illinois until the late afternoon of February 24 when he would return to New Hampshire. This decision to pull Reagan out of New Hampshire would be bitterly debated for years to come.[90]

Meanwhile both camps made phone calls to their committed supporters and the "undecided," made literature drops in Republican strongholds, arranged rides to the polls for the following Tuesday, drank coffee by the gallon, and smoked cigarettes by the carton.

If there was any remaining doubt as to the quirky nature of New Hampshire politics, it should have been put to bed when Ford's Chairman, Senator Cotton, happily introduced Reagan at an event in his hometown of Lebanon. Cotton made clear that he admired Reagan, could work with him and support him if he was the nominee and he was "my kind of fellow."[91]

All parties seemed to agree that it was too close to call, but the low-key style in the final hours of the Ford campaign contrasted sharply with the infectious enthusiasm of their counterparts in the Reagan operation. Many in the media wanted Reagan to win because they wanted a horse race to write about and liked many in the Reagan camp, especially Sears, Lake, Anderson, Nofziger, Black, and Keene. Conversely, they did not like many people in the Ford operation, including Nessen, Morton, and Callaway. Cheney, Spencer, and Peter Kaye were the few exceptions.

Nessen took the "lowballing" of New Hampshire too much to heart, as he told reporters that it was relatively unimportant in the context of thirty other state GOP contests. Ford was forced to do some cleanup when he arrived in the state, telling reporters, "I think New Hampshire is very important. The eyes of the nation are on this state."[92]

Counterintuitively, Ford attacked Reagan from the right, accusing his opponent of being for "back door socialism" because of Reagan public musings about investing the trust fund of Social Security into America's stock market.[93] Reagan was once again forced on the defensive and had to restate his support for Social Security. "It is unconscionable, for whatever political purpose for someone to use people who are dependent on Social Security and frighten them into believing that something may interrupt their payment," the Governor said at senior citizen housing projects in Manchester.[94] Ford also chided Reagan for not running in all thirty Republican Presidential contests that year as he was.

On his final swing through the Granite State, Reagan was accompanied by two of his old Hollywood friends, actors Jimmy Stewart and Lloyd Nolan. They were greeted by large and excited crowds, including the students at St. Anselm's College, before flying out Sunday morning, the 22nd, just two days before the crucial primary.[95]

Inexplicably to many, Reagan jetted off for two days of campaigning in Illinois whose primary was several weeks away. Hannaford said, "There, he spent a day touring boyhood sights and went to Tampico, his birthplace. Nancy Reynolds and I stood outside, talking, when a *New York Times* reporter came up to us and joked, 'Where's the manger, upstairs or down?' We then went to his grammar school and all of his old third grade classmates were there. They all looked twenty years older than Reagan."

"That afternoon, there was a big rally at his Dixon high school," Hannaford said.[96]

After Deaver and Wirthlin boarded a plane in Los Angeles the morning of Sunday the 22nd and found out they were heading for Illinois instead of New Hampshire, Wirthlin said, "I died a little bit when I found that out." Hannaford shared the same concern as Wirthlin.[97]

Years later, Wirthlin wrote that as they were flying into New Hampshire on Monday night, Sears informed Wirthlin that he had not yet shared the latest polling data with Reagan, which warned that he might possibly lose to Ford. Wirthlin was stunned. He had warned Sears in a memo several days before that his data showed Reagan with only a "whisper of a lead."[98]

Even Reagan apparently had misgivings about leaving the state. When he flew back Monday night, he looked out the window at the lights of Manchester and said to no one in particular, "I hope someone down there lights a candle for me."[99]

However, Governor Gregg had insisted that Reagan leave the state for the last two days, and Sears deferred to him.[100] It was Gregg's state and Sears reasoned that he knew it better than the Reagan campaign did. Gregg articulated to them that

Reagan's presence would clog turnout operations and he would be an unnecessary distraction.

The morning of the New Hampshire primary dawned clear and unseasonably warm, atypical for a state famed for its skiing and other winter sports. The national media had descended in the state like a swarm of locusts. The three television networks alone sent over four hundred staffers to the tiny state to cover the two Presidential primaries.

Lake started his morning as he had for the previous three months, with breakfast at 5:30 A.M. He then proceeded to the campaign headquarters where he would usually find Governor Gregg already at work. That morning they reviewed the newspapers, made phone calls to county, town and precinct workers, fielded press calls and exhorted the troops to do their maximum.

Reagan's team gathered at the New Hampshire Highway Hotel that evening. Huddled in a private suite were Reagan, Mrs. Reagan, Lake, Wirthlin, Reynolds, Anderson, Paul Russo, Hannaford, Deaver, Nofziger, and other members of the team. All through the day, Reagan had been clinging to a small lead over Ford, but some worried that the city of Keene would hold its vote results back until all other precincts in the state had reported when the polls closed. Keene's Mayor, the popular Jim Masiello, was a strong Ford supporter and the President Ford Committee had high hopes for a healthy showing in the city.[101]

The day began ominously for Reagan as he lost the midnight vote from Dixville Notch with eleven votes for Ford and only four for Reagan.[102] Dixville Notch citizens liked the bath of national media attention every four years as a result of their bizarre habit of voting just after midnight. It meant little in the larger vote total, but it was the first real news report from New Hampshire and thus was important for both bragging rights and the psychology of the respective campaigns. Overall, Reagan had campaigned in more than one hundred communities, including Dixville Notch.

Jimmy Carter bested the field for the Democrats in Dixville's Democratic vote. Little did anyone know at the time, but the eventual 1976 nominees of the two parties had already been chosen by the few dozen crotchety citizens of Dixville Notch. The story led on the front page of the *Manchester Union-Leader* along with a story in which Reagan not only predicted victory to bolster his troops, but told students in Illinois that his campaign's polling showed he would win. Reagan was usually a better campaigner with a better sense of handling expectations than he showed that day.[103] It was also uncharacteristic because Reagan rarely concerned himself with polls and the happenings of a political campaign, including his own.

Caught in his own apparent inexplicable giddiness, White House political advisor Rogers C.B. Morton told reporters the day before that Ford would win, 52 percent to 48 percent. Nessen was sent out to assure the media that the President, though he expected to win, would not put a number on it like Morton or back it with campaign polling, like Reagan.[104]

On the evening of Tuesday, February 24, Ford's team nervously gathered at his campaign headquarters in Washington and at the White House, taking projections from key precincts across the state and preparing to put the best face on what could only be described as a disaster for Ford if he lost to Reagan. Not since Harry Truman lost to Estes Kefauver in the 1952 New Hampshire primary had a sitting President lost here.[105] Truman withdrew from the race shortly after the loss. Reagan jumped to a 52–48 lead, according to exit polling conducted by the campaign, and he clung to it all day.[106]

Spencer blamed one person for Ford's possible predicament: Richard Nixon. He speculated that the trip to China was a deliberate attempt to cause Ford to lose. At Ford's headquarters, Spencer said loudly enough for reporters to hear him, "The Secret Service better not let me get within thirty feet of the bastard."[107]

Not since Chester A. Arthur in 1884 had a sitting President been denied his own party's re-nomination. Lyndon Johnson had been chased from the White House by Minnesota Senator Eugene McCarthy in New Hampshire in 1968. In 1972, Democratic frontrunner Senator Edward Muskie of Maine had only narrowly won in New Hampshire over peace candidate Senator George McGovern of South Dakota. In both cases, the frontrunners in fact won but failed to meet expectations and thus "lost" New Hampshire.

Ford was staring down the barrel at a devastating defeat like his hero, Truman. His campaign braced for the worst. Manchester and the smaller outlying cities votes came in first, due to more efficient machine tabulations. They showed Reagan winning, but throughout the evening Ford kept creeping up as the small town and rural paper ballots were being slowly counted. At midnight, Reagan was clinging to a 1,500 vote lead and appeared before his crowd of supporters and the media at the New Hampshire Highway Hotel. While he did not claim victory, he was outwardly confident about the outcome. Ford had gone to bed, according to the White House, unsure of the outcome until the next morning.[108]

Lake went looking for a cup of coffee around 12:30 A.M. and bumped into Sears. He asked Sears how things were unfolding, and Sears replied, shaking his head, that "things are closing." Lake then knew it was lost. Along with everything else Lake was handling on Tuesday, he also had to drive to Boston to pick up his wife, Bobbie. She was a tremendous fan of Reagan's, but as they crossed the border from Massachusetts into New Hampshire, an omen came to her. She blurted out, "Reagan's gonna lose today." Lake looked at her and said "nonsense."[109]

Spencer was just as uneasy as Bobbie Lake. "It was not good. We were nervous. I told the guys to hell with it, we'd done all we could so, let's wait and see how it plays out, good or bad."[110]

As it did play out, New Hampshire was good to Gerald Ford. Reagan had lost, even if by the slimmest of margins.

Reagan's aides differed in their view of why Reagan lost in New Hampshire. When Sears was later asked, he observed, "The temperature at 5 P.M. in the afternoon was 60 degrees—in New Hampshire—in February!"[111]

When Lake was asked he said, "That $90 billion speech put us on the defensive for three weeks. We could never make that time up. Rather than coming into the state with the fanfare like from our announcement tour, we were on the defensive . . . it took the wind out of our sails. But another reason was someone told Thomson we were ten points ahead the Sunday before the primary . . . I think it was a leak of a *Time* magazine poll . . . and pulling away from Ford. Thomson went out and told the New Hampshire media . . . it energized the Ford people in the state and unnecessarily relaxed our people."[112]

When Lyn Nofziger was asked, he said, "We never should have pulled Reagan out the weekend before the primary." Reagan's pollster Dick Wirthlin concurred with this opinion.[113] Ford had campaigned in the state four days and Reagan campaigned all or part of nineteen days, but the margin was so narrow that just one or two more days may have made the difference. Spencer would concur years later with Nofziger and Wirthlin.[114]

When Marty Anderson was asked, he said, "It was those three extra Reagan electors, who siphoned off, by many estimates, as many as two thousand votes from Reagan if not even more."[115] Anderson had a critical point. Three people decided, under the antiquated election laws of New Hampshire, to run as Reagan electors, even when they were told the votes they received would not be counted in Reagan's vote total.[116] Thomson estimated that as many as five thousand votes for Reagan were discounted, though the New Hampshire Secretary of State disputed this claim.[117]

Confusing things even more, on the New Hampshire ballot, twenty-one delegates were listed on paper and in machines as "pledged" to Reagan. These were the twenty-one official Reagan delegates selected by the team of Lake,

Sears, Gregg, and Thomson. Confusingly, also listed on the ballot as "favorable" but not "pledged" were these three additional delegates. Reagan's campaign told New Hampshire primary voters to only vote for twenty-one, but as many as two thousand New Hampshire voters did not heed the rules and instead voted for all twenty-four, effectively disenfranchising themselves as their votes were ruled invalid.[118]

No amount of cajoling could convince those three unauthorized Reagan delegates to get off the ballot. All of those votes would have presumably gone to Reagan since each elector was clearly identified in the polling booth and on the voting cards as a Reagan elector. Adding those spoiled ballots to Reagan's total would have meant a narrow win instead of a narrow loss for the conservative, and it would probably have spelled doom for Gerald Ford. Also, over one thousand Democrats had written in Reagan's name, but since the primary was "closed" those votes were not counted in the Reagan total.[119]

When asked why Reagan lost New Hampshire, David Keene said, "The turnout model was all f—ed up. Something over 60 percent of Republican primary voters turned out. In most state Presidential primaries, somewhere between 20 to 40 percent turn out."[120]

Actually, 65.5 percent of New Hampshire's registered Republicans came out to vote, illustrating Keene's point.[121]

All these opinions came from key Reagan staffers who all had differing opinions and they all were right. It was also one of the few times the Gipper had ever lost at anything, going back to his high school days. He didn't like the feeling one bit.

The morning's newspapers, having gone to bed before the counting was over in New Hampshire, all reported that the race was too close to call. But every radio station and every television station in America started the next morning carrying the news of Ford's "upset" win over Reagan. Ford could not help but tweak Reagan the next day, telling a group of small town newspaper editors, "Some of those who didn't do so well yesterday seemed to be satisfied with second. I never knew of any political campaign where running second was very beneficial."[122]

Gerald Ford won the Republican nomination in Kansas City in August 1976 in large part because he won the New Hampshire primary the February before by a scant 1,317 votes out of 108,328 votes cast for the two contenders.[123] Ford had come to the Presidency by way of the Twenty-fifth Amendment to the Constitution, the first President to arrive at this high office without once asking for or receiving the votes of the American people, as a Presidential or Vice Presidential candidate.

Ford said when he became President in August of 1974 that he was beholden to no man and indebted to only one woman. It was a nice line at a terrible time in our nation's history, but it also meant no one, outside of one congressional district in Michigan, had anything invested in Gerald Ford.

But by winning New Hampshire, Ford began the process of forcing Republican voters to make an investment in him and view him through a more legitimate prism than before February 24, 1976. Ford had not simply won, and he had not just beaten anyone; he had beaten one of the most popular Republicans and certainly the most popular conservative in America—no small feat. It was the first time the old football lineman from the University of Michigan had driven back the old football lineman from Eureka College. It would not be the last.

7

AGAINST THE WALL

"Politics is motion."

Ronald Reagan's loss in New Hampshire was devastating. The race was tight, but Washington's political community and those across the country were buzzing with the news of Reagan's unexpected loss. Few thought he would fail to pull it out in the end. "It was probably the first time Reagan had lost anything," said Martin Anderson.[1]

The post-mortems and Wednesday morning quarterbacking started in earnest. Rowland Evans and Robert Novak cited a last-minute campaign poll showing Reagan ahead by 8 percent that was leaked to the media via Governor Mel Thomson and others on the campaign. This information led to the final, unrealistic, and sky-high expectations for Reagan to win big in New Hampshire. "More important," they wrote, "that seemingly comfortable cushion persuaded the Reagan high command not to retaliate in kind against the President's surprisingly cutting anti-Reagan remarks."[2]

More knowledgeable "pols" knew of the power of incumbency and that the race in New Hampshire had tightened considerably, but for those who were not following it so closely, having only seen network footage of Reagan's big crowds while campaigning there or hearing that Reagan had opened with a big lead, Ford's win was shocking, especially to the Gipper himself.

Even *Human Events*, after taking a turn at putting some "editorial English" on the New Hampshire results, said,

> Reagan did not win in a state in which the political environment was favorable toward his candidacy and the polls showed that the people favored his stands on the various issues. . . . There is no question but that this has been a setback to the ex-California Governor's political strategists who were hoping to blow Ford out of the water with two quick, convincing knock-out blows in both New Hampshire and Florida.[3]

The weekly conservative publication, often described as Reagan's favorite, concluded that Florida was now crucial for Reagan and that he needed to take the fight far more aggressively to Ford. Circumstances in 1976 were entirely different from 1958 and 1968, the other elections in which challengers chased incumbents from the political scene by just coming close in New Hampshire.

The narrow loss ate at the former California Governor. Reagan was a man who had made winning a habit. He had already had three successful careers—four if you count his turn as a political commentator. He had been the captain of his swim team in high school, class president at Eureka College, a successful radio broadcaster, five-time elected president of the Screen Actors Guild, a successful movie star, a successful Governor, a multi-millionaire, a loving father, a devoted husband who was deeply religious, and a man with millions of conservative fans. New Hampshire was the first time he had really lost anything since Jane Wyman had filed for divorce from him twenty-eight years earlier.

Worse, a kind of paralysis set in. This was serious trouble, because as John Sears was noted for saying, "Politics is motion."[4] For once, Ford was in motion and Reagan was not.

Reagan was forced to put the best face on the New Hampshire loss, telling reporters that he "couldn't be more pleased" while in Concord, but no one believed him. On the other hand, no one in national politics, save possibly Hubert Humphrey, had as much bounce and resilience as Ronald Reagan. He told a reporter, "One primary doesn't a summer make. It remains to be seen."[5]

At an impromptu press conference before he left New Hampshire, Reagan tried to suggest that it was a virtual tie if the discounted Democratic write-in votes were added to the mix. Frank Reynolds of ABC said to Governor Reagan, "Bo Callaway says they whipped you in one of your best states." Reagan replied by shaking his head and saying, "Oh, Bo Callaway. Sometimes I think I'm running against Bo Callaway."[6]

It fell to Robert Healy of the *Boston Globe* to accurately summarize the results of the New Hampshire primary: "[I]t looks like a long season for the Republicans. No matter who ultimately wins in New Hampshire, the winner can only claim an escape from defeat and the loser can claim he wasn't stomped."[7]

Ron Nessen and Dick Cheney slept on couches in their White House offices waiting for the final returns to report from New Hampshire. President Ford went to bed without knowing the results and learned of the news from a 5:30 A.M. radio broadcast. Later that morning, Ford walked into a staff meeting unannounced, where he was treated to a standing ovation.

At that morning's White House briefing, Nessen was a little worse for wear having been awake nearly all night. He crowed about the Ford victory as he predicted more wins to come, ultimately ending in a first ballot victory for Ford at the convention. Nessen specifically cited the blunder of Governor Mel Thomson, who had predicted a 5 percent win for Reagan, as a key element in the Ford triumph.[8]

Even better for the Ford campaign, Bob Teeter's exit polling in New Hampshire showed the Nixon trip to China had no effect on people's decision to vote for Reagan or against Ford, as Stu Spencer had feared.

The morning after the primary on February 25, all of America's newspapers, having gone to bed hours before, proclaimed the race was "too close to call." But both camps had known hours earlier about the outcome and were doing their best to exploit or explain it. Peter Kaye, the principal spokesman for the Ford campaign, told reporters that Reagan was "now viewed as something of a political opportunist, a vacillator," and that Reagan's downward spiral was a result of the "essentially negative campaign we've been running. We've cast considerable doubt on his competence to campaign and by implication on his ability to govern."[9]

The Ford campaign, looking down the road at the next crucial bout in Florida, did not let up on Reagan. Ford continued his assault on his opponent by implying that he might destroy the "integrity" of the Social Security system. He said, "[Reagan] suggested from time to time" that the system would work better if it were made "voluntary, not mandatory." Ford told reporters, "I believe in the firm integrity of the Social Security program."[10]

Bill Roberts, whom Stu Spencer had asked to take over the Florida Ford operation said that Reagan was "totally unqualified to be President." He told Ford's supporters in Florida, "[Reagan] looks like a President, and he looked like a Governor, but he is a figurehead. He is totally incapable of exerting leadership and is dependent on people bringing programs to him. He is a reactor, not an actor."[11]

Reagan's campaign in Florida was headed by the ever-ebullient Tommy Thomas, the Panama City car dealer. Thomas made New Hampshire's Mel Thomson look like an amateur when it came to putting the candidate in the pickle barrel.

Thomas, a renowned character in Florida politics, was also good copy. Sometime too good, as he told Loye Miller of the *Miami Herald* that Reagan "has got to quit being the nice guy or he's gonna nice-guy himself right out of this race."[12] Referring to the federal government, he also told the paper, "If I was going to give the world an enema, I'd insert the nozzle in Washington."[13]

The campaign had also recruited Al Cardenas, a twenty-two-year-old law student, to run the vitally important operations in Dade County.[14] It wasn't unusual for Reagan's campaigns to be placed in the hands of very young people, as with Rick Reed and Kathy Regan, who were also assisting Reagan in Florida.[15]

They were just three of the "conservative children's crusade" who comprised Reagan's following throughout his political career. Reagan's most passionate supporters always came from young Americans, moved by his message.

For the Ford campaign, the win in New Hampshire was a shot of adrenaline that couldn't have come a moment sooner. It transformed the "gang that couldn't shoot straight" into the "masters of the universe" overnight.

One Reagan supporter tried to put to put a positive spin on it. William Loeb, the acerbic publisher of the *Manchester Union-Leader* wrote two days later that "no incumbent President has ever had a challenger who acquired in a New Hampshire primary 49 percent of the vote." He reminded readers of the odds that Reagan was up against and called down fire on the "professional Republican politicians [who] were breaking their backs in order to keep their positions on the Washington gravy train by putting across their protector, Mr. Ford."[16]

Reagan supporters were smarting all across the country in meetings, conservative circles, at *Human Events, National Review,* and especially at the campaign offices of Citizens for Reagan. Reagan's loss in New Hampshire was "devastating," according to David Keene.[17] The campaign had high hopes for a win in Florida, but New Hampshire made this doubly difficult. Ford had the momentum after his unexpected win.

Before New Hampshire, Reagan had been clinging to a small lead in Florida, according to Dick Wirthlin's polling. The Ford campaign there was in shambles as a result of the incompetence of Congressman Louis Frey, who chaired the President's Florida effort before Stu Spencer bumped Frey and installed Roberts to clean up the mess. The Ford campaign, at least organizationally, had been righted in Florida. After New Hampshire, Reagan had plummeted by seventeen points in the Wirthlin polls in Florida.[18]

Also trying to explain his loss in New Hampshire was former Senator Fred Harris of Oklahoma. A Democrat campaigning in the truest populist fashion, like his hero William Jennings Bryan, Harris lost disappointingly to Jimmy Carter in the Democratic primary. At his post-primary reception, Harris told supporters, "We have not done as well at the polls as we had hoped, perhaps because the little people could not reach them."

While all eyes were now on Florida, Massachusetts and Vermont would hold their state primaries on March 2. The Reagan campaign had already announced it would bypass both, and Ford did not campaign in either state. But the state parties were working hard for Ford in both states.

Not contesting these primaries may have been a mistake. Citizens for Reagan bought into the stereotype of both states being faddishly, hopelessly liberal, while not focusing on the small numbers of primary voters who would be deciding on a decent chunk of delegates. "They argue that Massachusetts, because of its liberal voting patterns of recent years does not represent mainstream Republican thought and will have little bearing on their campaign," wrote the *Boston Globe.*[19]

But the rules of the game were changing. It was no longer just about winning primaries to score psychological wins; it was now also about the all important delegate count. Although Reagan and Ford essentially split the vote in New Hampshire, Ford walked away with eighteen of the twenty-one delegates. However, many Republican state parties had switched to proportional delegate selection. Massachusetts opted for this system in a state committee meeting by a narrow vote of twenty-five to twenty-four the previous September.

The Ford people were learning quickly how to manage their—and Reagan's—expectations. Reagan had announced that he would not make any effort in Massachusetts, would expend no resources, and would not personally campaign there. Indeed, the *Globe* reported, "To say that the Reagan campaign in Massachusetts has been a small scale effort is probably an overstatement—it has been hard to find."[20]

Ford's forces accused the Reagan camp of "playing possum," and charged that Reagan was "trying to sneak up on us in Massachusetts," as reported in the *Globe.* Reagan had spent fifty-eight thousand dollars on Boston television, but that was all aimed at New Hampshire. Reagan had downplayed his non-existent effort in Massachusetts, estimating a return of somewhere around 30 to 35 percent.[21] The Ford people estimated publicly that Reagan could come in as high as 47 percent.[22] But this was simply a case of the Ford campaign boosting Reagan's expectations, knowing that Reagan would most likely lose badly.

The GOP universe in Massachusetts had shrunk from 520,000 to 460,000 registered voters over just two years. The prevailing wisdom was that moderates and liberals were leaving the GOP for the Democratic Party, which was cooler and hipper in Massachusetts in 1976. Still, no one in Reagan's camp thought he could win or even show well in Massachusetts without a concerted effort like Ford's, which spent two hundred thousand dollars in the state.[23]

Reagan's in-state supporters, including Bill Barnstead, who was the GOP's State Chairman, initiated an organic phone effort. It was poorly organized and only reached fifteen thousand primary voters. Meanwhile, Ford's campaign boasted that they had called ten times as many GOP primary voters.[24]

Like Thomas, his Florida Chairman, Reagan had had high hopes for Florida. Even the Ford White House conceded the situation when Nessen told reporters in late January that Ford would get "clobbered" in Florida if the primary had been held the day of his briefing.

Reagan departed Manchester, accompanied by Paul Russo and other aides for a day of campaigning in Illinois. That evening he pushed on to Florida for several days of campaigning. If Reagan was glum about the results, he did not show it to the supporters who showed up to see him off. Reagan looked immaculate in a blue suit and crisp white shirt. He also spoke with reporters before noting a hand-lettered sign to one of his staff that had been taped to the fuselage of his chartered jet, reading, "Air Force One—'77."[25]

Several prominent Republicans believed Reagan was a lightweight and thus saw Ford's win as not impressive, but as a show of weakness, since he could not defeat Reagan decisively in New Hampshire. Nelson Rockefeller, John Connally, and Elliot Richardson all took the measure of Reagan and Ford. Each would bide his time to see if the campaign would produce a divided convention. Or if Ford were to drop out, they would re-evaluate their situation and dive in to pick up the fight against the Californian.

Defying Ford, Rockefeller told the nation's Governors that he supported 100 percent federal financing of welfare and then petulantly went on to say that his views "do not purport to be Administration policy."[26]

Meanwhile, Reagan went to his hometown of Tampico again to campaign and told a crowd of twelve hundred at the high school he attended, "You could get dazed in a warm bath of nostalgia."[27] He was questioned again about the $90 billion speech. Reagan defended it and then said, "Does Ford have a better idea?" playing off the Ford Motor Company's advertising campaign of the moment.

Hours after Ford eked out his win in New Hampshire, Sears "broke out the booze," according to Charlie Black, and his team met to discuss a new rhetorical direction for the candidate. In an all night session, they agreed Reagan needed to start going after Ford on Henry Kissinger, détente, the Panama Canal giveaway, and the relative strength of the U.S. military. Reagan was agreeable.[28]

Ford went into Florida the first weekend after New Hampshire's primary. Although he was soaked campaigning in an open limousine during a six-hour motorcade, he was cheered on by a decent-sized crowd. Ford later dried by the sun, but looking somewhat the worse for wear, said, "I don't look very good, but I think I'm a darn good President," and the crowd of ten thousand at a West Palm Beach shopping center reacted enthusiastically. It was also apparent that Ford was wearing a bulletproof vest under his rain soaked shirt. He told the crowd at many of the fourteen cities he stopped in that America was "on the road to a new prosperity . . . we're not going to be sidetracked now."[29]

While eating barbecue in Sarasota, Ford told a supportive crowd about the differences between himself and Reagan, noting that different recipes are served at different cookouts. "I know some political campaigns have that same approach," Ford said, "but as President, I have to use a political recipe that's consistent. I don't have the luxury of dealing with each of the 50 states one at a time telling each of them what they want to hear. My job is to determine the best recipe for the whole country."[30]

Ford also addressed a group of 1,161 new American citizens and blasted Fidel Castro, calling him an "outlaw." At the naturalization ceremony, Ford told the cheering Cuban Americans, "My Administration will have nothing to do with the Cuba of Fidel Castro."[31]

Once again, as in New Hampshire, all the advantages of Ford's incumbency were on full display and carefully marketed to Florida's Republican voters. A reporter told John Coyne, who was writing an article for the *National Review*, "Ronald Reagan brings a political campaign to town, Gerald Ford brings the White House."[32]

Consensus in the national media was building that the Reagan loss in New Hampshire was costing him his lead in Florida. Reporters assumed he could not continue if he lost in Florida and Illinois. Even Reagan conceded the loss of momentum to reporters when asked, saying, "That may well be."[33]

However, credibility gaps were widening in both camps as Ford told a pleasant crowd in Florida that he had not reversed himself on one issue in the nineteen months he had been President. Reagan's poll numbers in Florida had plummeted, although Sears showed them to no one in fear of the effect it would have on morale. Sears never told Tommy Thomas who continued to tell anybody and everybody that Reagan would win.

In Vermont, where eighteen delegates would fall into Ford's lap without contention or question, and in Massachusetts, voters went to the polls on March 2. As expected, Ford won with 84 percent of the vote. A last minute write-in campaign was organized for Reagan, but it only managed to scare up 4,769 votes compared to Ford's 25,720.[34]

In Massachusetts, Reagan received almost exactly what his campaign predicted: 35.6 percent of the vote—62,951 ballots. Ford received 91,391 votes. Of the forty-three delegates in the state, Ford received twenty-seven and Reagan received fifteen, with one undecided who was eventually convinced to opt for Ford.[35] The cold weather was horrible on March 2, which helped snuff turnout in both states. Nearly a foot of snow fell in Vermont, and three towns were forced to suspend their voting. Ford watched the returns at the White House while Reagan was in California, preparing for his next foray into Florida. An *NBC News-Boston Globe* exit poll showed Ford doing well among liberal, moderate, and even some slightly conservative voters. Reagan was only doing well among those who identified themselves as conservative or very conservative.[36]

The twin victories were yet another psychological win for Ford and his forces. Although Reagan had conceded both states to Ford, two more primary victories under his belt salved a lot of wounds in his campaign, and Ford's stature continued to grow inside the Republican Party. He also began to campaign with more confidence—looking less like a bungler and more like a winner.

During Reagan's initial foray into Florida, his supporters and the media expected him to begin to tear into Ford and his Administration. His Hillsborough County Chairman, Ward Dougherty, introduced Reagan to 600 faithful at a luncheon, telling the crowd, "I wish he would forget all that Eleventh Commandment stuff, but he won't," to the cheers of the Reaganites in attendance. Reagan only gently elbowed Ford as "part of the Washington establishment."[37]

Reagan was holding back because his essential decency and respect for the institution of the Presidency weighed on him. Despite his agreement with Sears and company to boost the specific attacks on Ford, Evans and Novak described Reagan's rhetoric as "wrapped in cotton wadding with scarcely the glint of a sharp edge."[38]

At one point in the Florida effort, David Keene, took it upon himself to less than diplomatically tell the Governor of his concerns about his genteel style of campaigning. Standing in the wings before a speech in Tallahassee with the candidate and Mrs. Reagan, Reagan asked Keene what he should say to the awaiting crowd. Keene replied, "Well, Governor, you have two options: You can go out there and follow the Eleventh Commandment and lose your ass, or you can kick the s— out of Jerry Ford and win this thing."[39] Nancy Reagan was impressed with Keene's combative attitude and told him so. According to Keene, she said, "That's what I like to hear." Reagan did indeed begin to pound on Ford, Kissinger, and company.[40]

Ford was aiming for a knockout blow over Reagan in Florida. The bigger the margin, the more likely it would be that Reagan would be forced to drop out of the race. The Ford campaign began to dream about a 60 percent to 40 percent thumping of the Gipper.

Reagan's strategy had always been the two-state knockout punch of New Hampshire and Florida, expecting Ford to roll over and quit sometime before

Illinois, but Tom Wicker summarized the Reagan campaign's predicament, writing for the *New York Times,*

> Whatever the underlying truth of this psychological warfare, Mr. Reagan did not score a victory in New Hampshire. Now even if he does win in Florida, he cannot project the kind of winner's aura he had hoped to derive from back-to-back triumphs in the first two primaries. Nor will anything other than a landslide defeat here make Mr. Ford look like such a loser that the Republicans should chance the embarrassment of refusing to nominate an incumbent President who has governed in their name for two years.[41]

Wicker pointed out that Reagan had one lone hope: to prove by winning early that he, and not Ford, could win in the fall against the Democratic candidate. Now, the strategy had crumbled. In fact, Ford's exit polls surfaced in Massachusetts showing that GOP voters thought that Ford, not Reagan, was more electable against a Democrat in the fall.[42]

Reagan finally hit paydirt for the first time in several weeks when he sharpened his attacks on the Ford Administration by charging that it had secretly agreed to turning over the Panama Canal to the Panamanian government, which the State Department asserted was untrue. However, Reagan's message was starting to reach the voters, as evidenced by the Ford Administration's denial. Returning to the state on March 4, Reagan assailed the "failures" of the Ford Administration in a press conference in Orlando.

Though he had collapsed in the Florida polls immediately after New Hampshire, he was beginning to recover, yet too slowly for the nerves of Reagan's senior staff. They talked about "Scenario Number Two," where Reagan would lose the early primaries—but not badly enough to force him out of the race—until he came into more favorable terrain in the western and southern primaries in April, May, and June. For Reagan to stay in the campaign, under this back-up plan, the campaign would have to keep the coffers filled with contributions, which proved difficult for a candidate losing one primary after another. Although it was true that the primaries of Texas, Alabama, Arkansas, Nebraska, Montana, Nevada, and California looked like the Promised Land for Reagan and his team, they had to wander through a desert to get there. Reagan would soon discover how hazardous it could be. Sears, bloodied but unbowed, sustained his consistent and unrelenting manipulation of the national media by subtly streaming Reagan's message and story into print and onto the evening news, while keeping the press well-informed of the inner-workings of the Reagan campaign.

The same day Reagan ripped Ford in Orlando, all the campaigns that qualified received their last matching funds from the Federal Election Commission, as Congress was rewriting the act and then would send it to Ford's desk for his signature. Reagan received $175,375, raising his total so far to $1.43 million and eventually the FEC approved $284,000 for Ford, bringing him up to $1.3 million.[43]

Having been alerted by the Reagan campaign to his March 4 press conference in Orlando to challenge Ford directly, the press turnout was heavy, and several local television and radio stations broadcast the conference live. It was essentially the same speech he had given in New Hampshire. But this time, the audience was not a group of squirming young boys but the Florida and national media.

> Reagan unloaded on Ford, saying he and his Secretary of State must be held accountable to history for permitting the United States to slip behind the Russians in terms of military power.
>
> Despite Mr. Ford's evident decency, honor and patriotism, he has shown neither the vision nor the leadership necessary to halt and reverse the diplomatic and military decline of the United States. That is the truth, and even those of us who like Gerald Ford as a person know it is the truth. . . .
>
> All I can see is what other nations the world over see: collapse of the American will and retreat of American power. There is little doubt in my mind that the Soviet Union will not stop taking advantage of détente until it sees that the American people have elected a new President and appointed a new Secretary of State.
>
> Last year and this, the Soviet Union, using Castro's mercenaries, intervened decisively in the Angola civil war and routed the pro-Western forces. Yet, Messrs. Ford and Kissinger continue to tell us that we must not let this interfere with détente.[44]

He also described détente as the Administration's attempt to make "preemptive concessions," elaborating,

> We have given the Soviets our trade and technology. At Kissinger's insistence, Mr. Ford snubbed Aleksandr Solzhenitsyn, one of the great moral leaders of our time. . . . Mr. Ford and Dr. Kissinger ask us to trust their leadership. I confess I find that more and more difficult to do. Henry Kissinger's stewardship of United States foreign policy has coincided precisely with the loss of United States military supremacy.[45]

Reporters asked Reagan if he was violating his "Eleventh Commandment," but Reagan posited that he was attacking Mr. Ford's policies and not his personality. In the question-and-answer session with reporters, Reagan let loose with another hot blast, saying "I fear for my country when I see White House indifference to the decline in our military position."[46]

Ford's camp had a coordinated nonchalant reaction to the Reagan counter-offensive in Orlando on Ford's foreign policy. Both Ron Nessen and Bo Callaway were publicly dismissive. But they, along with Dick Cheney, had known all along that Ford was vulnerable over the foreign policy he had inherited from Richard Nixon in the form of Henry Kissinger. "There's nothing fundamentally new in it. It's the kind of thing you read in every right-wing magazine in the last five years," Callaway scoffed to the *New York Times.* Nessen told reporters, "The President's record and leadership in keeping the national defense second to none is so well known that I really don't think any response is necessary."[47]

But Reagan continued to hold the interest of the White House, as Ford aides in Florida held telephones up to radios and televisions to enable Ford campaign and White House officials at the other end of the line to hear the speech.

Vindicating the distrust with which many regarded the official "ho-hum" reaction of the Ford campaign was the critical fact that Ford had dropped the use of the word "détente" earlier used to describe his foreign policy. This was the most striking concession and proof that Reagan was scoring successful hits on Ford's foreign policy. Ford also pledged to begin to use the phrase, "peace through strength," which was Barry Goldwater's old slogan.

Furthermore, Callaway's comments about "right-wing" magazines missed the point. *National Review, Human Events,* and others were reporting on these foreign policy issues because their readers were troubled about America's position of strength in the world. For the first time in the campaign, Reagan was now speaking directly to those concerns.

The President Ford Committee knew that Reagan's newest attack was dangerous to the health of the Ford Administration. While millions in monthly checks were going out en route to Florida's elderly, the Ford campaign again raised suspicions that Reagan wanted to cancel Social Security.

It all started innocently enough for Reagan, when he said in a speech at an earlier campaign swing through Florida that it was "unfair" for Social Security recipients to have to sacrifice their monthly checks if they were between the ages of sixty-five and seventy-two and earned income of more than $2,700 per year.[48]

A reporter asked Reagan how he would pay for the cost of the "additional" benefits and he replied, "One of the failures of Social Security as a pension program is that the funds do not grow. They are not invested as they could be in the industrial might of America." Reporters pressed Reagan, and he replied, "Some economists have proposed that this kind of investment be made." Reagan had not advocated any fundamental change to the ailing program. He was only musing publicly about solving the system, but it was enough for the Ford campaign to once again make Reagan's life miserable for a couple of weeks, this time leading up to the Florida primary on March 9.[49]

Ford pressed the issue. In a live press conference, Ford had been asked if he thought Reagan was too conservative to be elected President, and he replied in the affirmative. Expanding on his differences with Reagan, Ford said, "Let's take the issue of Social Security. He has suggested from time to time that it ought to be voluntary, not mandatory as it is under the existing law. He has suggested that maybe the funds from the Social Security program ought to be invested in the stock market. I disagree with both of those proposals."[50]

In fact, Reagan had suggested in 1964 that Social Security be made voluntary. But he later switched his position. Reagan was simply expressing his concern for the health of the program. In a state like Florida, with millions of retirees, including many from the Midwest and thus predisposed to support fellow Midwesterner Jerry Ford, the controversy helped to renew their doubts about Reagan. Tommy Thomas conceded his concerns to the *New York Times*, saying, "It hurt Reagan," but he also made it clear that he was "highly distressed over what the Ford campaign has done to distort what Governor Reagan has said about Social Security."[51]

In fact, the Social Security trust fund did grow ever so slowly as it was invested in government bonds. But Congress's constant tinkering with the system and desire to patronize voters by increasing benefits and recipients had removed the system from its sound actuarial basis. Reagan was wrong about the growth of the investments, but he was right about the fundamental problems with the system.

Reagan did not support raising the FICA tax from its 5.85 percent level to 6.15 percent, as Ford did. But he did propose a "blue ribbon" commission to study the plan if he was elected President. Once again, as in New Hampshire, Ford had effectively knocked Reagan off his stride and his message. Reagan had not stepped on the banana peel, per se, but the Ford campaign was doing everything it could trying to throw one under his wingtips.

The elderly vote in Florida in 1976 could not be underestimated. According to surveys, the average age of Republicans in the state was fifty-six, and more than 37 percent were over the age of sixty-five. And the old codgers voted.

A statewide poll conducted in January, long before the New Hampshire primary might have tipped the scales, showed Ford comfortably ahead with older Republican voters. Furthermore, a poll conducted for the *St. Petersburg Times* showed Ford beating Reagan by three-to-one among the elderly voters in

Pinellas County. The previous week in Massachusetts, Ford had smashed Reagan among the elderly, 81 to 15 percent, according to one exit survey.[52] The tricky thing was *why.*

Pro-Ford tallies among seniors baffled pollsters, because, as the *New York Times* reported, "Virtually all surveys taken in recent years show the elderly in Florida to be more conservative than the norm." That should have helped Reagan. Results were similar in New Hampshire where Reagan had just lost. "The *New York Times/CBS News* surveys in New Hampshire found older voters less favorable toward government job guarantees than are those younger, more opposed to détente with the Soviet Union, more against legalized abortion and more likely to believe that the government was giving too much aid to blacks. In other words, on campaign issues, the elderly tend to side with Mr. Reagan." Furthermore, the survey showed significantly more seniors believed Reagan had "the personality a President ought to have" and was better suited to "end the nation's economic difficulties."[53]

Ford's deceptive strength with seniors was due to the fact that seniors were more comfortable with the status quo. Like Ford, many of them were also from the Midwest. Also, much more attention had been given to Reagan's age, though he was only two years Ford's senior. Seniors who felt their age believed Reagan must be feeling his too, and this opened up questions about his vitality to be President.

Campaigning in Venice, Reagan addressed enthusiastic crowds of supporters in shopping malls and retirement communities, rhetorically suggesting that some people thought he should get out of the race. The adoring crowds shouted, "No! No!" The stunt was designed for the media, who were beginning to wonder when Reagan would give it up, especially if he lost in Florida. Reagan and his campaigners were trying to get the media to take the long view on this campaign. Reagan told supporters, "I'm not folding my tent and stealing away. I'll be in Kansas City in August."[54]

Reagan was also not backing away from his contentions about America's waning military strength or that détente had been a one-way street that favored the Soviets. As Steven Hayward recounted in *The Age of Reagan,*

> Just as the controversy over détente was reaching a crescendo in 1976, Admiral Elmo Zumwalt went public with a story that Kissinger had confided his pessimism about America's prospects during a train ride the two had shared to West Point in 1970. Zumwalt's account held that:

> "Dr. Kissinger feels that the U.S. has passed its historic high point like so many earlier civilizations. He believes that the U.S. is on the downhill and cannot be roused by political challenge. He states that his job is to persuade the Russians to give us the best deal we can get, recognizing that historical forces favor them. He says that he realizes that in light of history he will be recognized as one of those who negotiated terms favorable to the Soviets, but that the American people only have themselves to blame because they lack the stamina to stay the course against the Soviets who are 'Sparta to our Athens.'"[55]

Kissinger denied this account in the strongest possible terms, and Zumwalt, who was in the process of running for the U.S. Senate in Virginia, could have been accused of embellishing a story. Yet corroborating evidence existed, as Hayward detailed that Kissinger aides Peter Rodman and Helmut Sonnenfeldt both subsequently confirmed that Zumwalt did not invent the exchange. Furthermore, the editor of *Partisan Review*, William Barrett, said he had essentially the same discussion with Kissinger at Harvard in 1952.[56] Zumwalt's account would become a major topic of conversation in several weeks, and would also become a flashpoint in the campaign.

A flashpoint involving differing recollections occurred between Jim Buckley, the conservative Senator from New York and Vice President Nelson Rockefeller. Both recalled a meeting that took place at Rockefeller's office, ostensibly about the 1976 campaign. The stories diverged when the Vice President said Buckley had offered his support for Ford in exchange for Rockefeller's support for his re-election. Buckley was uncommitted to either Ford or Reagan at the time.

Buckley contends that the real purpose was to pressure him into supporting Ford over Reagan in exchange for their support of Buckley's re-election. Buckley was being challenged in the Republican primary by moderate GOP Congressman Peter Peyser, whom Buckley aides had long suspected had the quiet support of Rockefeller.[57]

Of the Reagan children, the younger two, Patty and Ron, were doing little campaigning for their father, busy with work and school. Maureen and Mike were more involved and they did what they could when they could to pitch in with speeches to young voters, leading rallies and the like. Ron played a small role in Reagan's radio operation in New Hampshire, but it did not last.

The Ford children were also involved in varying degrees. Jack Ford was an aggressive twenty-three-year-old defender of his father who never shied away from speaking his mind. He once told a reporter that Richard Nixon was a "creep." Sons Mike and Steve were away at school and did not do too much campaigning in early 1976.[58] Susan, eighteen at the time, was a hit with the national media because of her wholesome blonde good looks and also because her mother had inadvertently made her the subject of controversy during her *60 Minutes* interview. The Ford family was photogenic, happy and open. After the dark, brooding Richard Nixon, this simple fact alone added to the stability the country needed after the turmoil of Watergate. "Politicians' families are, of course, part of the props; their smiling appearance alongside the candidate may have nothing to do with how they feel about being there, or about him," Elizabeth Drew commented in her book, *American Journal,* "But the Fords do seem a family with real bonds, the President a man with human connections."[59]

Stumping in Champaign, Illinois, just days before the Florida primary, Ford was a study in dispassion, as he never mentioned Reagan by name, simply saying in a veiled way that the country needed "knowledge," leadership, and not the words of "those who would hide behind a blanket denunciation of our national government" and that "rhetoric is no substitute for practical achievement."[60]

James Naughton wrote in the *New York Times,* "The measured response by Mr. Ford, who never once mentioned his Republican rival by name, reflected a decision by the President and his campaign strategists to try to project an air of calm self-confidence in the face of Mr. Reagan's criticism." Turning a nice phrase, Ford told the crowd jammed into a high school auditorium, "We are conducting our foreign policy with our eyes open, our guard up and our powder dry."[61]

Ford noted that his Administration had requested a large increase in defense spending. Directly responding to Reagan's attacks on his foreign policy, but again without mentioning Reagan by name, Ford said, "We know that peace and national security cannot be pursued on a one-way street. But we also know that returning to a collision course in a thermo-nuclear age can leave the human race in ashes." He again described his foreign policy as "peace through strength."[62]

Ford's strategy was simple: stay above the fray, stress experience, use incumbency to its maximum benefit, hit Reagan hard through surrogates, and let the media describe Reagan's flagging campaign in desperate terms. So far, it was working beautifully.

Ford was winning good reviews, and as far as he was concerned, if he never heard a disrespectful question from a reporter or saw another political cartoon, it would not be soon enough. Although he did mispronounce Fidel Castro's name while in Florida, calling him "Fydle" Castro, it went nearly unreported by the media. Winning, as it turned out, paid extra dividends for Ford.[63]

For a time, Ford, often thought of as one of the unluckiest Presidents in American history, was beginning to discover his own luck too, as when headlines across the country trumpeted the drop in unemployment to 7.6 percent the Saturday before the primary in Florida.

Most things were looking up for Ford and his team. Summarizing the now-smoothly running Ford operation, the *New York Times* wrote, "In organizational terms, Mr. [Bill] Roberts hired 24 new staff members in 10 days; developed a direct mail program that included an eight-page tabloid on Social Security designed to appeal to the 70 percent of Republicans over 50; planned two highly successful visits by the President; hired a bagpipe band whose bass drum bore the legend 'President Ford the Budget Saver' to tour shopping centers, and installed hundreds of telephones for a canvass that has reached about 400,000 voters."[64]

Ford's upswing was something to contend with. Just two days before the primary, on Sunday, March 7, Reagan tried to downplay expectations in Florida by telling the panel of journalists on *Meet the Press* that he was engaged in an "uphill battle" against the incumbent President. Reagan analyzed the advantages of incumbency. He said the candidate "can make news and be on the front page of the papers every day without moving out of the Oval Office. An incumbent can go into an area and announce that a shipyard is going to stay open, he can go to another area and say that the highway is going to be built."[65] Ford had done each of these, proclaiming in New Hampshire that the government would keep open the Portsmouth Shipyard. In Florida, he promised to provide the federal funds for a new highway.

Reagan maintained his attacks on Ford's foreign policy during the Sunday morning show, saying that Kissinger had a more "pessimistic view" of the world than he did. Reagan contrasted the Secretary of State's view that "we have to make concessions to the Soviet Union because we are no longer the number one nation in military strength" with his own view: "We will once again become the number one nation."[66]

When the topic shifted to how he would do in Tuesday's Florida primary, Reagan told the panel that he had the lead among committed voters in Florida. He conceded that the pool of uncommitted voters was large enough to swing the results to Ford, but it appeared to some in the media—and was thus reported—as if Reagan was boosting his expectations, rather than playing them down.[67]

On the Ford White House's use of patronage for political gain, Jim Dickenson reported in the *Washington Star*:

> Reagan's advisers [were] outraged that Jerry Thomas, former president of the state Conservative Union is in the Ford camp. Thomas is being considered for an appointment as Undersecretary of the Treasury, which the Reaganites consider a "political bribe." Ford's advisers were unmoved. "The nice thing about the incumbency is that you can use it," says one.[68]

Returning to Florida for a final campaign swing, Reagan stumped in Titusville and extended his attacks on Ford's foreign policy, this time challenging him on Cuba:

> Let us hope there will now be a change in our Government's policy toward Castro. Only last March, Dr. Kissinger said the State Department instructed our delegate to the Organization of American States to vote in favor of lifting the embargo of trade with Cuba. In August, the Administration lifted our prohibition on trade with Cuba by foreign subsidiaries of U.S. firms.[69]

On Monday, March 8, Ford won the endorsement of the influential *Tampa Tribune*, a paper read widely by the senior voters Ford needed. It could not have come at a better time.[70] Ford campaign workers at offices in West Palm Beach, St. Petersburg, Clearwater, and other Florida cities listened to the President as he spoke to them over loudspeakers in each office. "It's going to be a close ballgame, but I think we're going to win," Ford said, telling them not "to quit in the last quarter," perhaps a direct reference to the last-hour faltering in Reagan's New Hampshire campaign that likely led to Ford's victory.[71]

One thing that helped Ford with the Florida voter was that the White House prepared a free audiotape featuring Betty Ford urging the Sunshine State's voters to go to the polls on Tuesday. The White House then sent the cassette to all of Florida's radio stations. With a straight face, Mrs. Ford's Press Secretary, Sheila Weidenfeld, called the recording a "public service announcement" because it did not appeal for votes for her husband.[72]

On the day of the Florida primary, voters turned out beginning at 7 A.M. at 3,405 precincts to choose between Republicans Ford and Reagan or among Democrats Carter, Wallace, Pennsylvania Governor Milton Shapp, Arizona Congressman Morris Udall, and Washington Senator Henry "Scoop" Jackson.

Although a part of the Old Confederacy, Florida had changed much in recent years due to the influx of retirees from other parts of the country. The president of the Florida Poll, Paul Cohen, told the *New York Times* that 95 percent of Florida's Republican voters came from other states, making it "the least Southern state in the South." The population had grown by over 1.6 million in five short years. It had also become a diverse state economically, racially, and religiously.[73]

Ford was now considered a slight favorite, but Reagan was scoring heavy points with his aggressive attacks on the President's foreign policy. He was also still drawing big crowds wherever he went, and this continued to be impressive to the national media covering his campaign. Reagan, once again, vowed to continue the fight, even if he lost in Florida, right to "the final fight on the convention floor." But both camps were also looking ahead to the contests over the next month, including Illinois, North Carolina, Wisconsin, and New York.

Reagan left Florida on Tuesday for Illinois to campaign in his birth state after a final round of campaign appearances while Ford remained in the White House. Laying the groundwork for upcoming expectations, Reagan told reporters,

> I never thought that Illinois was a strong state for me. Illinois was my home state—I know something about Illinois politics and I know the machinery involved. Our case has been taken to the grass roots, but I know the Ford people by reason of the incumbency have had whatever party machine there sewed up from the beginning. I was never optimistic we had it in the bag.[74]

Reagan's aides were now convinced that he would lose in Florida, despite their best efforts, which portended bad things for Illinois. Still, Reagan believed that he and Ford would go to Kansas City with neither having enough delegates for a first ballot nomination.

As if Reagan was not suffering from enough headaches and fatigue from the exhaustive campaigning, the Young Republicans of California failed—by seven votes—to formally endorse his Presidential bid. Their endorsement required a two-thirds ballot win. Reagan received seventy-six votes; forty-one went against him, and seven abstained. The group was from California and conservative and it came as a minor surprise that Reagan did not win.

In Florida, Ford scored his fourth win in a row over Reagan, by 53 percent to 47 percent. Ford received 318,844 votes to Reagan's 282,618. And Ford picked up another forty-three delegates to just twenty-three for Reagan.[75]

Reagan's regular entourage of the national media included correspondents from ABC, NBC, CBS, the *New York Times*, the *Washington Post*, the *Los Angeles Times*, *Time*, and *Newsweek*. Among themselves, they began to wonder where and when the Reagan train wreck would end—and to which campaign they would be assigned next.

The national media took their political coverage seriously. All the networks, newspapers, radio syndicates and wire services had extensive political units which included editors, reporters, and pollsters, along with outside consultants from both parties who would keep them informed on the "inside dope" from both sides of the aisle. It was not unusual for a major daily paper like the *Washington Post* to carry six or more lengthy articles on the national campaign or for the networks to devote four minutes for just one political story.

President Ford told reporters he was "elated" at the outcome, but he refused to speculate on when Reagan would withdraw. All parties agreed Reagan's strategy was in shambles, and the only question was when he would face the obvious and make a graceful exit. Behind the scenes, the White House and the President Ford Committee were devising ways to get Reagan out of the race, despite Reagan's umpteenth proclamation that he was in the race until the bitter end.

Reagan had been enjoying a modest lead prior to his upset in New Hampshire, but that went out the window. Still, in the intervening two weeks, he had climbed back into the race in Florida to lose by "only" six points.[76] But the subtler implications of the effects of his new, more aggressive campaigning were lost on the national media and the political classes. As far as they were concerned, it was probably all over. The *New York Times* wrote, "The Californian's attacks on the Administration's policy of détente with the Soviet Union appeared to avail him little." Spinning anew, the Reagan campaign took a new tack with the media, suggesting that their candidate could lose four or five primaries at the outset of the campaign but still survive by winning caucus states and California.[77]

Reagan was forced again to go before the cameras and supporters to declare himself "delighted" with losing. "I can't act well enough to convince you how delighted I am," he told a group of doubting reporters. "The incumbent in these first couple of primaries has thrown the whole load at us; he has shot all the big artillery there is, used everything in the incumbency he can, and we are still possessing almost half the Republican vote," Reagan said gamely.[78]

The overjoyed Ford staff threw Florida oranges to each other for the benefit of television crews at the Washington headquarters, while letting it be known that Ford would consider Reagan for the number two spot. The Ford campaign was becoming skilled at the "visuals" necessary for campaigns in the media age, having sent hundreds of Michiganders to Florida with thousands of snowballs, to playfully throw at each other—all of which was dutifully recorded by the local Florida media.

Perhaps caught up in the moment, Rogers Morton told the *New York Times*,

"People are not just accepting [Ford], they're falling in love with him as their President."[79] Possibly writing the epitaph for Reagan's campaign, the story also went on to note that the offices of his North Carolina campaign had not been in touch with the Washington office of Citizens for Reagan in over ten days and that television commercials there had been abruptly cancelled.[80] The lead story in the *Miami Herald* began, "President Ford probably ended Ronald Reagan's challenge for the Republican Presidential nomination."[81]

Reagan staggered into Illinois. A "beauty contest" primary would be held in conjunction with the election of delegates and he was trailed by renewed speculation in the national media as to when he would withdraw.

Illinois was the first head to head contest between the two candidates in a state where conservatives did not dominate the Republican Party. It was a moderately liberal party from top to bottom, with the exception of a few, solitary individuals like Congressman Phil Crane and State Rep. Don Totten, who helped lead the Reagan effort in the Land of Lincoln. It was also the place of Reagan's birth, and his strategists hoped this would play well with the voters.

Predictions by both camps showed how the world had changed in just a few short weeks. In the beginning, while most political analysts were forecasting the state as a do or die proposition for Ford, the Reagan people had once again predicted a big showing for Reagan in Illinois. But after earning four big wins, Ford's in-state forces, led by former Governor Dick Ogilvie, were sure of a comfortable win for their man. Reagan was reduced to saying publicly that he would be comfortable with 40 percent. Ninety-six delegates were at stake, with an additional five to be selected at their state convention later in the campaign season. Two hundred fifty grassroots Republicans had filed to run for delegate. Some were for Reagan, the bulk were for Ford, and others were for third party candidates.

In Illinois, Reagan tried a new theme, suggesting for the first time that the events of Watergate would make Ford vulnerable in the fall election against the Democrats if he were to be nominated by the Republican Party. "I don't think we want to go into that battle against the Democrats in November having to defend a part of the past which Republicans would like to be left to history," Reagan told a GOP group in Marion.[82] The new attack not only fell flat; it backfired on Reagan, as he was forced to backtrack from reporters' queries about Ford and his pardon of Richard Nixon. Several days earlier in Florida, Reagan implied that the Chinese government invited Nixon to China because they had no faith in Ford. This attack went largely unreported, but Reagan should have known better. These types of attacks were not part of his natural style.

Furthermore, for the first time in the campaign, Reagan started talking like a Campaign Manager instead of a candidate, telling reporters that he would start winning when the campaign moved to the South and the West. He also analyzed Florida by observing that it was not truly a Southern state because of the high percentage of Midwesterners who had relocated there. The state's high senior citizen population tended to support the status quo.[83]

Reagan was off message and off stride. He was fighting a cold and was depressed. Mike Deaver often asked Totten, when he was traveling with Reagan, to tell him a joke to perk up his spirits. Reagan tried to make the argument that Florida was not such a bad loss because the Ford forces said they would "clobber" him there and they failed to do so. "I was so far behind two weeks ago, and I know there was no celebrating in the White House last night, because they thought they were really going to clobber us in Florida. Anyone who describes their camp as euphoric is out of his mind." He also oddly suggested that before the resignation of Nixon, he and not Ford was on everyone's list of leading Republicans for the 1976 nomination.[84]

Meanwhile, word was leaked to the *New York Times* that Ford was "privately furious over Ronald Reagan's criticism of his policies." According to one official with the President Ford Committee, "He's got the blood coursing through his veins right now. He's unhappy with Reagan and determined as a result." The story devolved into patronizing Reagan, as Senator Chuck Percy told the *Times*, "Ronald Reagan has sharpened up the Ford organization. His campaign has helped us. It would have been a very poor organization. We wouldn't have been prepared without the Reagan challenge."[85]

Resentment was also boiling in the Ford White House over Reagan's earlier comments about Ford and Watergate. Reportedly, Ford was incensed by the comments, and aides were urging Ford to destroy the Reagan challenge, once and for all.[86]

The Reagan campaign's frustrations were also running high with the inability of Congress to rewrite the section of the federal election law pertaining to the appointment of the FEC Commissioners. While the Supreme Court previously ruled that the joint naming of Commissioners by Congress and the Executive Branch constituted a violation of the separation of powers, the FEC continued to operate, disbursing up to eleven million dollars to qualifying candidates. But even this function would cease on the March 22 deadline set for Congress by the Court. Then the bill would go to Ford for his signature and the disbursements would presumably keep flowing. The FEC was also budgeted approximately forty-eight million dollars for both parties' conventions and their fall campaigns. This was the first time in American history that the taxpayer would subsidize political parties.[87]

Ford was also forced to "subsidize" Henry Kissinger while campaigning in

Chicago, defending his Secretary of State from Reagan's attacks. Ford's defense, while low key, came on the heels of a vigorous speech Kissinger had made in Boston defending his stewardship of American foreign policy. Kissinger, while not mentioning names, charged those who were criticizing the Ford Administration's foreign policy with "erroneous and reckless allegations." Ford had initially defended Kissinger to an inquisitor at Wheaton College. Later, speaking before the Council on Foreign Relations, he expanded, telling listeners, "I do regret that foreign policy has been injected into both the primary as well as potentially in the Presidential election. Our policy of peace through strength is not something I recently invented."[88]

As possibly an omen of things to come for Gerald Ford after Illinois, a storm of tornados marched across the Midwest, including Chicago, where one barely missed the President's motorcade including the limousine that was carrying him. But four people were killed and one hundred injured.

Storming against Ford's ongoing use of political patronage, Don Totten told a group of Republicans that the President was trying to buy the primary. Totten charged, "It's actual buying of votes by outright bribery. The President says he has honesty and integrity, but I question the use."[89] Reagan did not disavow Totten's tough charges and leveled a couple of his own, accusing the Ford operation of "lying through their teeth" and of "the cheapest kind of politics" when the topic of Ford's campaign's tactics was raised.

To Reagan and Totten's point about the uses of incumbency, Ford had invited the anchormen for the top four Chicago television stations to interview the President on the eve of the Illinois primary. Reagan had complained that the White House was now even manipulating the news.

Reagan appeared on an obscure local Chicago television show hosted by the little known Phil Donahue and the challenger was asked about the interviews with Ford. Did Reagan intend to appeal to the stations under the new, equal time provisions of the Federal Election Commission? Reagan paused for a moment, brightened, and said to Donahue, "That's a good idea!" Within minutes, Reagan aides were on the phone to the managers at all four Chicago stations, and all assured them that, yes, Reagan would indeed be granted the same amount of broadcast time as Ford.[90]

While the former Governor of California was flailing, another Governor, Milton Shapp, dropped out of the campaign for the Democratic nomination. Shapp had been a successful businessman and was equally accomplished as Governor of Pennsylvania, but the media never took him seriously. Shapp was the first Jewish candidate to campaign actively for a party nomination. He joined four others, including former North Carolina Governor Terry Sanford, Texas Senator

Lloyd Bentsen, and Indiana Senator Birch Bayh in folding their tents and withdrawing from the race.

Reagan's successor as Governor of California, Jerry Brown, also casually threw his love beads into the ring by announcing to one reporter in the Sacramento State House that he too would run for President. Mike Royko, one of the toughest political columnists in the country, later hung Brown with the moniker, "Governor Moonbeam" because of Brown's devotion to yoga, yogurt, Zen Buddhism and sleeping on a mattress in the Governor's office. The nickname stuck, and Brown never quite escaped ridicule again.

Meanwhile, the former Governor of Texas and former Democrat, John Connally, let it be known that he would not consider accepting a Vice Presidential selection. When he appeared before a group of reporters and Republican Party officials at his ranch, he was asked about being Vice President and replied, "I've never known a happy one yet." Connally had one of the best, most ribald senses of humor in either parties, as when he told the gathering, "I know you all came here expecting an announcement of some kind and you're going to get one. We have a new herd bull here and we're going to start selling semen this fall at $10 an ampule."[91] He declined to endorse either Ford or Reagan, preferring to see if his chances would open should the nomination be deadlocked, and the party be looking for a compromise candidate.

Three days before the Illinois primary, Citizens for Reagan filed an FEC complaint charging Secretary of State Kissinger with abusing his office by overtly campaigning for Ford in the primaries. Loren Smith, General Counsel for Reagan, filed a petition that stated Kissinger "is using his high office for the express purpose of a campaign platform to promote the Ford candidacy."[92] Smith alleged that Kissinger's travel and speeches defending Ford's foreign policy should be charged against the Ford campaign's expenditures and not paid for by the U.S. Treasury. Reagan finished campaigning in Illinois and headed for California for a few days of rest to watch the returns from Illinois. He departed saying once again that he did not expect to win Illinois. His campaign would continue to other states in the South and the West where he felt his message would resonate better. The message was about all Reagan had at this point. While Ford now had an operating surplus of almost $1.5 million, Citizens for Reagan was showing a deficit of $688,000, according to FEC reports.[93]

On March 16, 11,321 voting machines opened at 6 A.M. to allow the 5.8 million voters of Illinois the opportunity to vote for their choice for President from a narrowing field of Democrats and an already narrow field of Republicans. Crossover voting was allowed in both primaries. Reagan actually did slightly better than the 40 percent he had predicted—he gained 40.9 percent of the vote. However, Reagan's low-balling of his chances in Illinois afforded him no bounce with the media or political prognosticators. It was a smashing win for Ford, his biggest yet.

Ford clobbered Reagan 450,812 to 307,305. Reagan eventually came away with only fourteen delegates, fewer than the modest twenty his campaign had publicly said they hoped he would win. Ford took eighty-six delegates from Illinois.[94] Ford won across the board among GOP primary voters, regardless of income, ideology, or region. He also benefited from the belief that the economy was improving.

Another of Reagan's supporters in the state, Phil Crane, had not helped things when he had told the *Washington Post* back in January that Illinois would be "pivotal" for Reagan.[95] Crane inadvertently made sure that Reagan would lose the expectations game. The *New York Times* wrote, "[T]he former California Governor has actually made an impressive showing in the two primaries in which he has actively campaigned. Running against a President who is personally well-liked and at a time when the economy is improving and the country is at peace, Mr. Reagan polled 49 percent in New Hampshire and 47 percent in Florida."[96]

Almost immediately, the White House increased the drumbeat for Reagan to leave the race for the good of the party. Ford, Rockefeller, Morton, Callaway, and others issued statements or spoke to reporters. They also began backdoor communication to the Reagan camp, suggesting help with Reagan's debt if he got out soon. A more heavy-handed effort was also initiated, involving elected Republican Party officials including the National Conference of Republican Mayors, to publicly call on Reagan to get out of the race. Others in the GOP would join in to pressure Reagan, but to no avail. Reagan issued a statement from California, saying,

> We appear to have met our goal with something over 40 percent of the vote. I have never been under any illusion that our grassroots campaign could successfully buck both the Illinois Republican organization and the promises being issued so bountifully by the White House.
>
> However, the fact that I have won something over 40 percent of the vote in this organization-dominated state once again indicates there is major dissatisfaction in our party with the kind of leadership it has been receiving.
>
> I look forward to the North Carolina primary next week.[97]

So did Gerald Ford.

As a small consolation, Reagan would have expectations working to his benefit because he could not do any worse in North Carolina than he had in Illinois. It was the only silver lining he could take comfort from as he left behind the state of his birth. As Sears was fond of saying, "The times you get in trouble are when you're not moving. Motion is what you need in politics and when you don't have it, you have a problem."[98] And Reagan had a problem.

8

NORTH CAROLINA

"I'm not going to quit!
I'm going to stay in this until the end!"

Ronald Reagan had been beaten in five successive primaries. Morale in the conservative challenger's camp could not have been lower. The losses in Massachusetts and Vermont were expected since Reagan had not campaigned there, but John Sears's front-loaded strategy was being heavily second-guessed in the media and conservative circles—and by Reagan.

Sears's plan had always been to "upset" Gerald Ford in New Hampshire and then finish strong in Florida. Sears believed that Reagan's conservative appeal would work well in these early states. If Reagan won these states, Ford would withdraw from the race. Unfortunately for Reagan, his campaign was not unfolding as Sears planned.

Reporting for *ABC News* while traveling with Reagan in North Carolina, Frank Reynolds said, "The odds against him are very long now and because he is not a dreamer, Ronald Reagan must know he is on the edge of defeat. . . ."[1]

In his landmark book, *The Conservative Revolution*, Lee Edwards wrote, "Reagan's showing [in New Hampshire] against a sitting President was undoubtedly impressive but it could not erase the fact that he had been expected to win."[2] Even Stuart Spencer later confided to James M. Naughton of the *New York Times*, "If we didn't win those two, we were going to be out of the ballgame."[3] But now it was Reagan who appeared to be headed for the showers, not Ford.

William Safire, Nixon's old speechwriter and by 1976 a columnist for the *New York Times*, penned, "Most Democratic strategists and most political analysts wish Ronald Reagan would pull out of the race for the Republican nomination. They attribute this wish to 'most Republicans' who are supposed to see the Reagan campaign—after five defeats—as 'pointless.'" Safire's column was somewhat of a backhanded compliment to Reagan, making the point that the Reagan challenge had shaped a flaccid Ford campaign and transformed Ford from a loser into a winner. However, Safire also correctly illustrated that it was Reagan who forced the Administration into a tougher stance against the Soviets. He forced Ford to stop using the phrase "détente" during the Florida primary, and he forced the Ford Administration to cancel the planned normalization of relations with Fidel Castro and Communist Cuba.[4]

Meanwhile, media reports from the Federal Election Commission showed that one week before the North Carolina primary, Ford had raised over two and one half times more money than Reagan for the month of February. Ford began March with nearly one million dollars cash on hand while Reagan had an overall debt of $250,000. Complicating Reagan's financial woes was a recent one million dollar loan his campaign had taken from the National Bank of Washington. Reagan's matching funds operation—mistakenly internalized—was not processing the incoming contributions fast enough to keep up with the campaign's demands.

Reagan had the worst of both political worlds. He was seen, on the one hand, as Ford's credible challenger. On the other hand, he was getting no credit for near wins in New Hampshire and Florida against the incumbent. He was an underdog who was not perceived as an underdog. The campaign had allowed expectations to get out of control and was now paying a heavy price.

By March of 1976, staffers were either laid off or working for no pay. Reagan would eventually lose his charter plane and was forced to fly commercial and the Reagan campaign offices in North Carolina had been closed to save funds. Prior to losing the plane, Peter Hannaford remembered waiting with Reagan on a chartered flight in Los Angeles that was headed for Salisbury, North Carolina. Hours passed and Hannaford asked what was the holdup. The reply was that the direct mail checks were being counted at the campaign headquarters to see if there was enough funds to pay for the plane.[5] Laxalt later wrote in his memoirs:

> Very early in the morning the Reagans were to fly to North Carolina for their final campaign swing in the Tar Heel State, their charter plane sat on the tarmac at Los Angeles airport, filled with the campaign team and reporters.
>
> Time dragged on. The delay, it turns out, was necessary for the Reagan campaign staff in Washington to open the mail to see if there would be enough money to pay United Airlines for the flight. There was—barely.[6]

Nancy Reagan was deeply concerned that her husband would be made to look "foolish" if he did not get out of the campaign, and there were serious discussions in his camp about him quitting before the North Carolina primary. At one such "meeting," she took Lyn Nofziger aside and pleaded with him to tell the Governor to drop out of the race. Nofziger was of no such mind and told Nancy that there were enough resources to continue through March 23, the day of the North Carolina primary.

Reagan walked into the room, overheard part of the conversation, and assumed that it was Nofziger telling Mrs. Reagan that he should get out instead of the other way around. Reagan yelled, "Lynwood, I'm not going to quit! I'm going to stay in this until the end!" Nofziger recalled, "Reagan was angry, but he could also feel something out there that we couldn't. Finally, it seemed to him that his message was getting through."[7]

Next to Reagan and perhaps Paul Laxalt, the two men who probably deserve the most credit for breathing life into the dying Reagan campaign were Tom Ellis, a controversial, but hugely effective political operative from Raleigh, and Senator Jesse Helms. Ellis was not a native North Carolinian, but you would never know it. He was born in California and attended Dartmouth College, where he played football in 1939. He once watched some classmates make an ice sculpture on the campus and later related to *North Carolina* magazine, "That darn thing was still there the next May, hadn't melted a bit. I wasn't really satisfied at Dartmouth anyway, and when I saw that block of ice hanging around for so long I knew it was time for me to get out."[8]

By 1940, Ellis had transferred to the University of North Carolina and remained there. He liked the weather, the people and the politics. He became a shrewd trial lawyer, setting up shop in Raleigh and in 1972 had engineered Helms's surprising victory for the U.S. Senate in a campaign that no one had given the conservative a chance of winning. Ellis knew his adopted state and his adopted people. He was no stranger to the "bourbon and branch water" hardball politics of North Carolina. He knew the voters would be susceptible to Reagan's "no pale pastels" message.

What Ellis did not know—and what no one in the Reagan camp knew—was that John Sears had been in ongoing discussions with Rogers "Rog" Morton, Ford's Campaign Manager, about engineering a graceful exit from the race for Reagan. According to some sources, including Ford campaign staffers, Sears initiated the conversations. But Jim Lake and Sears both agreed that it was the Ford camp that was hounding the Californian's Campaign Manager for Reagan to get out of the race.[9] It is unclear who really introduced these discussions, which were ultimately inconclusive. But all agree Reagan would have been furious had he known about them.

Sears said, "Morton was calling me at least once a week. Just before the North Carolina primary, I told him, 'Look, this public humiliation of Reagan is backfiring. Get off his back and leave us alone until Texas. If we lose Texas, we'll get out.'" Sears later chuckled that, in fact, the President Ford Committee did indeed call off the dogs where Reagan was concerned, which helped him get off the mat. He also recalled having bluffed Morton, since the Reagan forces did not have the resources then to contest anything as big as Texas.[10]

Initially, the Ford campaign thought it would be a good idea to have surrogates publicly pressure Reagan to get out of the race. At one memorable press conference in North Carolina, reporters badgered Reagan with questions about how much longer he would stay in the race, citing statements and press releases from leading Republicans, including a handful of his fellow Governors.

Reagan was usually slow to anger. In fact, for a national politician, he was unusually cool under pressure. Some might ascribe it to his actor's polish, but many would say that he just had it. But this time, he barely concealed his temper in front of the assembled media saying, "For heaven's sake fellas, let's not be naïve. That pressure to quit the race is being engineered from the same place that engineered pressure for me not to run in the first place—the White House! I'm not getting out! I'm not going to pay any attention to them now when they suggest that I should quit. Why doesn't he quit?" After yet another question on the same topic, Reagan replied, grimly, "I'm not talking about this subject anymore."[11] After several uncomfortable seconds passed, Reagan walked away from the microphones.[12]

Any chance that Reagan would get out of the race before the North Carolina primary—and with it any semblance of the Eleventh Commandment—went out the window because of the heavy-handedness of the Ford campaign. At the end of a hard day on the campaign trail, Reagan and Laxalt were surprised when a messenger delivered a telegram to the motel that was signed by GOP elected officials telling Reagan to get out of the race. Laxalt recalled in his memoirs, "Instead of intimidating him, the message had just the opposite effect. In profane terms, which he rarely used, he told us what the Republican politicians could do to themselves."[13]

Once again, the Ford forces had misunderstood and misplayed Reagan. They had insulted him and virtually all political observers agree that had Reagan withdrawn or lost in North Carolina, his political future would have been over. By provoking him again, the Ford forces awoke the more aggressive Reagan, who, up until Florida, had only begun to gain some traction on his message—especially when it came to the Panama Canal, Henry Kissinger, the Soviets, and America's national defense posture.

"The people in the White House seem to think I should be withdrawing," Reagan told a crowd of some three to four hundred people gathered at the Raleigh airport. Answered by shouts of "no" and "stay in," Reagan said, "You took the words right out of my mouth. . . . I'm not walking away from this."[14]

"Reagan was never more energized than when confronting opposition," Dick Wirthlin would later write. "His enthusiasm would soar, his sights would focus and his passion would stir. He was one of the few leaders I've ever known who actually derived pleasure from confrontation."[15]

Ellis and Helms also relished confrontation and were aided by Carter Wrenn, a large man whose huge appetites included bonded whiskey and cheap cigars. Together, they did not wait for permission from Sears as to what to do with the ailing Reagan campaign in North Carolina. They simply went to work.

Wrenn was a young conservative who became a confirmed "Reaganite" in 1975 after hearing Reagan deliver a speech at Chapel Hill. He had been scheduled to graduate one year earlier, but he took a volunteer job at Helms's Congressional Club in 1974 stuffing envelopes and licking stamps. He became hooked on politics. When Charlie Black offered him a job making eight hundred dollars a month at the Club, Wrenn jumped at the chance and never went back to get his college degree.

Ellis thought Sears was a "genius" but he also made no secret of his disdain for him—even though the men had only met several times.[16] He simply did not like Sears, his politics, his secretive manner, or his perceived apostasy when it came to the "red meat" conservatism that got the blood pumping of "True Believers" like Ellis. Wrenn would later say,

> It would be an understatement to suggest that Ellis didn't have time for Sears and the D.C. people. They wanted to run a character campaign versus an issue campaign. Ellis and Helms wanted to talk about the gospel and the message. It got very contentious, lots of arguing and fighting back and forth.
>
> It culminated at a meeting in Helms's office in D.C. Ellis basically laid out his strategy and Sears kept quiet, nodding his head. This took place before the New Hampshire primary. Ads had already started in New Hampshire and Ellis said, "You can't say Ronald Reagan is more

> qualified than Gerald Ford." Sears pointed out that Reagan was ahead in the New Hampshire polls.
>
> And Ellis would say, "If you're not going to do what I want you to do, will you at least make up some issue ads and keep them in the can in case you need them?" Eventually, they all weren't speaking to each other.
>
> David [Keene] was in a hard spot and [as] conservative as Ellis, but he had to argue the party line. Both he and Charlie [Black] got in the middle of it. Eventually, Ellis just told them he didn't want to talk to them, didn't want them around, [and not] to call.[17]

One of the first things Ellis did was kick out of the state or simply ignore all the Reagan campaign people from the national headquarters—including Charlie Black and David Keene. But this occurred after a powder keg that Keene had warned Ellis about had exploded. Ellis's efforts for Reagan in North Carolina stipulated that he operate with complete autonomy. He really had no use for most of the Reagan staffers, even though Black and Keene were personal friends.

Ellis had concluded that while the two young operatives were just as conservative as he was, it was Sears who signed their paychecks. Although he knew they would plead their case in North Carolina to Sears, they were getting nowhere. It was best they just get out from underfoot and let Ellis and his people do their jobs.

One close confidant of Ellis's observed, "He had a remarkable talent for getting under people's skin. He was intuitively a very smart man, not without his flaws . . . but his ability for single-mindedness was extraordinary."[18]

Ellis did make one major mistake when his forces in North Carolina reprinted an article from a local newspaper speculating that Ford might pick Senator Edward Brooke of Massachusetts as his running mate. Brooke was a respected moderate liberal who had been elected in 1966. Brooke also was black and this was North Carolina in 1976. Keene told Ellis to destroy the flyers or, he warned, "Reagan will denounce them and you publicly." Ellis complied and Mike Deaver ordered several boxes of the offending flyers put on the plane. In one town this message was not communicated and some of the copies made their way into the hands of the media. As Keene predicted, Reagan blew the whistle on Ellis and the flyers at a press conference. But when Keene was proven right, Ellis threatened him and furiously ordered him out of the state.[19]

Reagan was especially sensitive to the "racist" label many liberals tried to hang on him and other conservatives during this era. Years earlier, while playing football for Eureka College, the team was making a road trip and several black members of the team could not stay at the local "whites only" hotel. The coach scrambled to make alternative plans for the players, but Reagan took his black teammates to his home to stay.[20]

It must have touched Reagan deeply when the recently-appointed black Democratic Mayor of Gastonia, North Carolina, Theboud Jeffers, introduced Reagan at an event as "our distinguished next President." When a reporter asked the new Mayor about his introduction of Reagan, Jeffers said, "I think he's tremendous. I've always been an admirer of his."[21] Reagan had also been especially proud of his record in California of appointing more than 250 black public servants to office, "more than any other Governor in California's history."[22]

Another thing Ellis did was call in Arthur Finkelstein. A polling and tactical genius who did not always play well with others, Finkelstein was a man of enormous talent and ego whose libertarian roots dated to years before at Columbia, where he once shared a college radio show with philosopher, novelist, and libertarian iconoclast Ayn Rand.

Finkelstein had cut his teeth working for the legendary Bud Lewis, head of survey research for *NBC News.* In 1969, he wrote a long letter to Jim Buckley, brother of William F. Buckley Jr., telling him how he could win the U.S. Senate election in New York in 1970, running only on the Conservative Party line. Buckley had run for and lost the seat in 1968. He was intrigued, so he invited the brash young man to lunch. Although Finkelstein could not read the menu at the French restaurant, after some follow-up meetings and phone calls, he acquitted himself well with Buckley. Buckley entered the race and hired the legendary F. Clifton White and his protégé, Finkelstein, to do polling and campaign strategy.[23]

White and Finkelstein were among the growing breed of fulltime political consultants. The political consulting industry had come far, and many people earned a good living by consulting, polling, fundraising, and working the media. Previously, most Campaign Managers and campaign staffers worked other "real jobs" and would take leaves of absence to work on political campaigns. But politics had changed as races became longer, more expensive, and more sophisticated. The consulting industry changed along with it. White had guided the Goldwater campaign in 1964 and helped organize Reagan's late-starting drive for the GOP nomination in 1968.

Buckley won in 1970, defeating the Republican candidate, Charles Goodell, a moderate who had been appointed to fulfill the unfinished term of Robert Kennedy, as well as the Democratic nominee, Congressman Dick Ottinger. After Buckley's stunning victory, Ellis reached out to Finkelstein to seek his help with Helms's campaign in 1972. Shortly after Helms's big victory, they created the Congressional Club, which became Helms's vehicle to conduct permanent campaign activities, including helping Reagan. Ellis brought Finkelstein in to help in

1976, and his efforts for Reagan in North Carolina and Texas would prove crucial to the campaign.[24] By 1976, White had been shunted aside by Sears and the Reagan folks, and he ended up working for Ford.

Reagan threw himself into the desperate effort of North Carolina. Laxalt was now traveling with Reagan fulltime and told the old performer to get rid of the now famous "4x6" cards, which Reagan used for his stump speech, and just speak from the heart. The response from the crowds in North Carolina immediately improved. "He was like a little kid when he got rid of those cards," Laxalt said later. "He told Nancy he was so excited when he gave speeches for a whole day without his cards."[25] He was also sick with a cold. Judy Sarasohn of the *Raleigh Times* remembers interviewing Reagan, hunched over in the backseat of a tiny car, "sucking on smelly lozenges."[26]

Furthermore, the campaign had eschewed any mention of Reagan's Hollywood career, fearing it would make voters think Reagan was "play acting." Nonetheless, the grave condition of Reagan's campaign before the North Carolina primary called for a change in tactics. Laxalt remembered, "So we go down to North Carolina and we're at the edge of the precipice waiting to be pushed off and I forgot who thought about it . . . maybe Nancy . . . she didn't often offer suggestions but when she did they were very good. She said we were trying everything else and nothing's working. Maybe it's time to call some of our Hollywood friends and we, very tenderly, had an event with Jimmy Stewart and had many more show up later."[27]

But there was little time or money to bring in the big Hollywood guns. Sometimes they were invited for an occasional appearance with or for Reagan. Other times they were asked to stop by the campaign offices in Washington and around the country to boost staff morale. But for the most part they were kept at arm's length until later in the primary season.

Laxalt also suggested to Reagan that he bring in his "Hollywood buddies" to help the campaign in North Carolina and beyond. For months, Jimmy Stewart, Pat Boone, John Wayne, Efrem Zimbalist Jr., Lloyd Nolan, Jack Webb, Ken Curtis (who portrayed "Festus" on the popular show, *Gunsmoke*), and other actors had offered to assist their old friend, who had led them as president of the Screen Actors Guild and befriended all of them at trying times in their lives.

Wayne was especially difficult, not because he was hard on the staff or demanded too much of Reagan, but because he hated the media and made his disdain clear anytime a reporter came near him. Wayne had hosted a fundraiser for Reagan at his home in California and proceeded to have a few cocktails. When a reporter for *NBC News* approached him and asked why he would support Reagan over Ford, Wayne replied, "Because Jerry Ford is too f—ing dumb to be President."[28] Reagan's Hollywood friends would be very prominent later in the campaign as they traveled with him, met with wavering delegates, and talked to the media in Kansas City.

Three important factors would come into play in the crucial North Carolina primary. The first was that Stan Evans, Chairman of the American Conservative Union, persuaded the organization's board to approve an independent expenditure campaign on Reagan's behalf in Illinois, North Carolina, and Texas. The ACU spent tens of thousands of dollars in North Carolina alone on newspaper and radio advertising that touted Reagan's conservatism and hammered Gerald Ford.

The ACU effort itself stirred up a small controversy after the North Carolina primary when Ron Nessen, in a daily White House briefing, incorrectly charged that while independent groups like the ACU could raise or spend as much as they liked to support Reagan's bid, they were not required to report to the Federal Election Commission. "Perhaps some places 80 percent of the advertising for former Governor Reagan is paid for by groups which say they are unauthorized or unofficial and, therefore, they don't have to report their spending," Nessen said.[29]

Nessen was rebuffed shortly thereafter in a memo from President Ford Committee General Counsel Bob Visser, who explained that all independent groups must report all expenditures to the FEC. "First, any 'unauthorized' groups . . . would be required to file quarterly reports with the FEC," Visser wrote. But he also went on to charge in his memo that such independent groups were, in fact, coordinating with the official Reagan campaign. "The fundamental basis of our objection to such so-called unauthorized activities is that such expenditures which were actually conducted with the advice, consent and/or cooperation, direct or indirect, of the Citizens for Reagan Committee would not be reported by the *Reagan Committee* as campaign expenditures, and, therefore, directly chargeable to its expenditure limitations."[30]

Visser also reiterated that he had urged Ford Campaign Manager "Rog" Morton to file a complaint with the FEC against the Reagan campaign and the ACU. Visser sent a copy of his memo to Morton, perhaps to stir the pot one more time. Visser kept up the drumbeat against the ACU, as he sent another detailed memo to Ford strategist Stu Spencer, this time complaining about a letter sent by Evans to ACU contributors asking them to send "earmarked" contributions to the organization's "Reagan Project."[31]

But the President Ford Committee never acted upon the memos. The damage that the ACU did to the Ford campaign in North Carolina and later in Texas would be done. Stan Evans later asserted that it was impossible for the ACU to coordinate with Sears because, "Sears wasn't doing it right."[32] There was a minor FEC investigation of the ACU after the election, but the organization was cleared.

The ACU's effort in North Carolina for Reagan, organized by Jim Roberts, included running 882 radio commercials on major stations and thirty-three newspaper advertisements. The activity could not have done anything but help Reagan and hurt Ford. The ACU's newspaper ad was a detailed, side-by-side comparison of Ford and Reagan on the issues, including Nelson Rockefeller, Henry Kissinger, the Panama Canal, and busing. The accompanying photos showed a smiling, jovial Reagan and a less-than-flattering shot of Ford.[33]

The radio ad was equally hard hitting:

> Gerald Ford appointed Nelson Rockefeller as Vice President of the United States. He appointed Henry Kissinger as Secretary of State, and fired a Secretary of Defense who disagreed with Kissinger's "détente." . . . Ronald Reagan, by way of contrast, says he would fire Henry Kissinger and is committed to a balanced budget. Ronald Reagan would not cave in to Castro, and says American sovereignty in Panama must be maintained. The choice for North Carolina Republicans is clear: continued deficits and the weakness of "détente" or Ronald Reagan's new initiatives in freedom.[34]

Although the ACU had started its activities in Illinois one week before the North Carolina primary, it was not until North Carolina that the organization's effort began in earnest. Helms noticed the ACU campaign and praised the group's contributions in a letter to Evans two days after the primary. Helms wrote, "the ACU's efforts were crucial in putting the Reagan campaign over the top."[35]

The second development before the North Carolina primary was that Ford, for a time, had moved past the "buffoon" representation that had plagued him throughout his Presidency. But the long-loathed image came back to haunt him in North Carolina where he gave what may have been one of the most insipid speeches in the history of the Presidency to a national convention of homemakers. He was then photographed in a Rockettes-like chorus line, kicking his leg up with a group of dancers in Spruce Pine. Ford's Campaign Press Secretary at the time, the too-often-quotable Peter Kaye, later told Jules Witcover, "It was in North Carolina where Ford became a crashing bore."[36]

Ford's campaign in North Carolina led by Governor Jim Holshouser, who had also won in 1972, albeit by a much narrower margin than Helms, never got its act together. Complicating things at the time was a bitter ideological, regional, and cultural fight between the Helms faction and the Holshouser forces. There was no love lost between the two, and, according to Jim Burnley, a Republican activist, "There were serious intra-party conflicts in the state."[37]

The third key factor in Reagan's effort in North Carolina was turnout. Keene cited the turnout model in New Hampshire as what cost Reagan that primary. Indeed, over 65 percent of Republican primary voters turned out in New Hampshire. "It was in North Carolina that the turnout model returned to its normal pattern. About thirty percent of registered Republicans turned out."[38] Actually, the turnout was closer to 40 percent, but Keene's point was well taken.

Ellis took control. He personally supervised the Reagan speaking and campaign schedule, raised the money, and bought the television and radio time. Finkelstein wrote radio scripts and advised Ellis on tactics and strategy on a daily basis. Helms stumped daily for Reagan, sometimes together, sometimes alone.

Ellis left no stone unturned. Earlier in the year, he had attempted a statewide effort to encourage Democrats to reregister Republican so they could vote for Reagan. When that didn't work, Ellis turned his attention to registering new voters, including many young people, and at this he was more successful.

But money was a major problem for the Reagan campaign from beginning to end. It was not that Reagan couldn't raise it; he was a better fundraiser than anyone in the Republican Party at the time. The problem for Citizens for Reagan was not cash flow as much as money management. One major cause of this problem was a decision by Darrell Trent, the campaign's new Comptroller, whom Sears had brought in to get the situation under control. Sears had hired Trent to replace John Magnotti, whom everybody agreed was a nice guy—too nice because he said yes to everything. This, coupled with Sears's undisciplined spending, made for a financial mess.

Trent and Sears had met during the 1968 Nixon campaign. Trent insisted that the campaign not hire a "caging and batching" operation to handle the incoming flood of direct mail. As part of the growth of the political industry, such operations became invaluable to political direct mail fundraising. They could process the checks much more quickly and reliably than volunteers were able to. But Trent wanted to save money and use campaign volunteers who were unschooled in how to handle the mail. Trent's decision slowed dramatically the process of depositing the checks and applying for the matching funds from the FEC.[39]

Consequently, unopened bags of mail, filled with thousands of checks totaling hundreds of thousands of dollars littered the Washington offices of Citizens for Reagan. "We had fifty to sixty bags of cash and checks. We were trying out how to protect them. Initially we used guards. We used a taxi service to transport the money. Eventually, we set up a revolving line of credit with a bank that weighed the bags and estimated the amount in each around $55,000 per," Smith said.[40]

Ellis made a deal with Sears that whatever was raised in North Carolina was to be used in North Carolina, but Sears insisted that the national campaigns receive the matching funds. Ellis agreed to this condition. Each day in the weeks before the primary, Mark Stephens or Alex Castellanos, two youthful Reaganites recruited by Ellis, would board a plane from Raleigh and fly to Washington National Airport, where they would go to the Citizens for Reagan campaign headquarters and hand over the daily checks and cash to Angela "Bay" Buchanan, the campaign's Treasurer. After the money was processed, Buchanan would cut a check for the young men and they would then fly back to North Carolina and give the check to Ellis for the day's media and other costs associated with the campaign—minus the matching funds, however, that came from the money raised in North Carolina.

In another critical move for Reagan in North Carolina, Ellis had been pleading with the campaign for months to give him footage of Reagan speaking to air on the state's thirteen television stations. Just as Reagan's staff had hesitated to involve Reagan's Hollywood friends in the campaign without reminding voters of his acting career, for months they debated over how to put Reagan on television. Nonetheless, Dick Wirthlin claimed his polling showed Reagan's celluloid career was an asset to the campaign rather than a detriment. Sears even went so far as to hire Harry Treleven, who had produced effective commercials for Nixon in 1968, to actually make "bad commercials" for Reagan's early effort. The lighting was poor and the film quality was intentionally kept mediocre to prevent voters from remembering Reagan's career in film. But the commercials themselves were ineffectual and Treleven quietly left the campaign.

Reagan used to plead with the campaign hierarchy to air him. Typically, the response was, "Governor, that stuff worked for you back in 1964, but this is different." Nofziger later told Witcover in *Marathon,* "Everybody wants to do something their own way with Ronald Reagan. And the best way is to just let him talk. Nobody ever figures it out. Each time, you have to go through this whole hassle."[41]

Ellis threatened to broadcast Reagan's 1964 speech on behalf of Goldwater. The campaign had been ignoring Ellis, and he called Laxalt in frustration and made a last ditch effort to get something—anything—to air. Miraculously, a thirty-minute speech by Reagan appeared. During the Florida primary, a television station in Palm Beach had offered thirty minutes to both Ford and Reagan. Ford had declined the opportunity but Reagan grabbed it. The film was of poor quality, and the set was a simple desk with a threadbare curtain behind Reagan. The lighting was terrible. And there were palm trees in the background. But it did not matter. References to Florida were deleted as were the palm trees, and the response was overwhelming and enthusiastic among North Carolina's Republican primary voters.

Ellis, to this day, believes the unseen hand of Nancy Reagan was behind his finally getting the thirty-minute speech. He believes that Laxalt and Helms mentioned the problem to Nancy and she, in turn, told the campaign staff to get Ellis what he wanted.[42]

And Reagan ripped into Ford on the stump. The Ford White House pulled all the stops when it came to announcing federal pork projects in the primary states, including the Tar Heel state. Attacking the federal largess Ford was handing out state by state, primary by primary, Reagan said, "When Ford comes to North Carolina, the band won't know whether to play 'Hail to the Chief' or 'Santa Claus is Coming to Town,'" recounted Black, who had run afoul of "Emperor Ellis."[43]

Reagan went after Ford on the Panama Canal especially hard. The canal, it was rumored at the time, was going to be turned over to the military dictator of Panama, Omar Torrijos. Although the Ford White House and Kissinger's State Department denied it, the "giveaway" came to symbolize the frustration Americans felt in 1976 in the aftermath of losing the Vietnam War. Reagan, in speech after speech, would make his case for keeping the Canal, usually thundering, "It's ours! We built it! We paid for it! And we should keep it!" Reagan was once again in motion, following the Sears maxim that "politics is motion."

Ford and his campaign, meanwhile, were going nowhere. The President's young Chief of Staff, Dick Cheney, worried that the campaign was making a serious mistake by backing away from Reagan, per the agreement between Sears and Morton. In retrospect, Cheney was right. Reagan's comeback allowed him to continue the fight, refreshed with an upset win, that brought in new funds for his depleted campaign coffers.

Ford's campaign still had its ongoing difficulties. Although he had announced back in July of 1975 that he would indeed run for President in his own right, the President Ford Committee had been often times a bumbling operation, riddled with inexperience, factions, power struggles and missed opportunities.

Much of the controversy centered on the eminently likable Howard "Bo" Callaway. Callaway had been a member of Congress from Georgia who literally had the Governorship stolen from him in 1966 when he won a plurality of the vote, but the matter was sent to the Georgia legislature as prescribed by the Georgia state constitution. The legislature was dominated by "yellow dog" Democrats who would "rather vote for a yellow dog" than allow a hated Republican, albeit a conservative Republican, to occupy the Governor's mansion.

Callaway always had his problems with the press simply because he trusted people. And he sometimes had a problem organizing his thoughts before he spoke publicly. During the 1968 campaign, he caused a minor brouhaha when he suggested publicly that George Wallace and his supporters be encouraged to join the Nixon forces. More sophisticated political observers knew what Callaway meant, but the media jumped on it with glee in an attempt to smear the Nixon campaign as appealing to Southern racists.[44]

Callaway's judgment was also sometimes called into question, as when he paid a courtesy call to John Sears at his law office in Washington in June of 1975, trying to encourage him to join the Ford campaign. Sears had already signed on for the forthcoming Reagan campaign and was hard at work, along with Jim Lake and Lyn Nofziger, organizing the Citizens for Reagan press conference which would be held the following month.

On March 12, 1976, the *Denver Post* and *NBC News* carried a bogus report that charged Callaway with using his position as Secretary of the Army to meddle in Forest Service affairs, arranging for the expansion of a ski resort investment in Colorado that he and his brother-in-law referred to as "Crested Butte." As President Ford recounted in his autobiography, *A Time To Heal,*

> As soon as he heard the allegations, Cheney spoke to Bo, who insisted that the charges were untrue, that he had done nothing illegal. Yet the appearance of impropriety seemed to be there: Bo had met in his Pentagon office with two officials of the Department of the Interior (the parent agency of the Forest Service) and discussed Crested Butte's expansion plans; in the post-Watergate atmosphere, such an appearance could be very damaging to my campaign.[45]

To Ford's credit, he asked for Callaway's side of the story in person. On Air Force One the next day, Callaway explained that he had spoken to the Interior officials two days after he had resigned as Secretary of the Army. And both of the officials were old friends. Callaway's story was the story of all businessmen who had to deal with governmental red tape and petty bureaucrats. He and his brother had applied five years earlier for an approval or rejection of their expansion plans. They simply wanted an answer, one way or the other. He had exerted no pressure and the two Interior officials confirmed Callaway's story.

But this was the era of the crusading investigative reporter, and every reporter was a wannabe Bob Woodward or Carl Bernstein. This was the era in which ink-stained wretches were heroically portrayed by Robert Redford and Dustin Hoffman on the silver screen. It created an atmosphere of report first, ask questions later. Woodward and Bernstein were the toast of every liberal in America at the time for using a single, unnamed source ("Deep Throat") in bringing down the odious "Tricky Dick" Nixon.

In Callaway's case, his "Deep Throat" was the liberal Senator from Colorado, Floyd Haskell, who hated Republicans with a passion. Using sources that would later be discredited and trumped up congressional hearings, Haskell completely abused his power in trying to undermine Callaway and, by extension, the Ford campaign. Callaway was later exonerated in an article in *Harper's* in 1977, "The Persecution and Character Assassination of Howard 'Bo' Callaway as Performed by Inmates of the U.S. Senate Under the Auspices of the Democratic Party."[46]

But it was no use. This was the post-Watergate hothouse of Washington, and some of the Ford forces saw the silver lining in forcing Callaway out of the campaign. For months, his management style had been the subject of criticism inside the White House, and his memos were the butt of jokes. Overlooked in all this, of course, was the fact that under Callaway's management, Ford had defeated Reagan in the first five primaries of 1976, and the Ford campaign was financially much better off than the Reagan campaign. For all of the media's love affair with Sears and its open disdain for Callaway, the courtly Georgian had pasted the smooth New Yorker five times in the kisser.

Meanwhile, Nofziger had been sending the beleaguered Campaign Manager little missives over the course of the campaign. He took the opportunity to once more needle Callaway by sending him a note stating that his career with the Ford campaign had "crested." But Callaway was in no mood at the time for Nofziger's jokes. As Nofziger later recounted in his autobiography,

> [Callaway] didn't think that was funny. In fact, as I discovered eventually, he didn't find humor in any of my notes. During the summer [1975] when he was looking for a Campaign Press Secretary, he told one reporter, who later told me, "I want someone to do to them what Nofziger is doing to me."[47]

Nonetheless, Callaway would have to take a "leave of absence," which was widely interpreted as his dismissal from the campaign. All that was left was the actual execution. At Callaway's last meeting with Ford, Cheney, and Campaign Press Secretary Peter Kaye, Kaye had a written statement announcing Callaway's departure in hand. Callaway was gone shortly thereafter.[48] The powers that be would not even let him write his own statement of defense.

Callaway had his detractors and second guessers, but he was the only manager for Ford to go undefeated against Reagan in 1976. Overlooked in all the sniping, backbiting, and second-guessing of Callaway's performance was the fact that he won all five of the primaries against Reagan he was responsible for. He was eventually replaced by "Rog" Morton, who had been at the White House as a Presidential political advisor to Ford. The position of Campaign Manager for Ford had been offered to Spencer, but he wisely turned it down.[49]

Ellis continued to shape the North Carolina effort, despite the fact that all polls showed Ford with a comfortable lead over Reagan. At one point, in frustration, Ellis threatened to Sears that he would quit unless he got total control in North Carolina. Sears acquiesced.

For the last two weeks before the primary, unbeknownst to the national media and the President Ford Committee and the White House, Ellis's efforts in North Carolina were hitting on all cylinders. Mail was going out, phone calls were being made, volunteers were doing "lit" drops and Reagan was aggressively campaigning anywhere and everywhere. Helms also dropped everything and hit the road on his own—sometimes with Reagan, but often times alone—tearing into Ford, Kissinger, and company, with even more zest than Reagan himself. Reagan devoted the last week of the primary to campaigning exclusively in North Carolina, traveling with Laxalt, Mrs. Reagan and his old friend, Jimmy Stewart. Jim Burnley, who was trying to build the GOP in Gilford County, could only watch with amazement as Ellis and his forces mobilized for Reagan at every level in the state.[50]

Ellis and Finkelstein directed Wrenn to produce a list of Republican primary voters in the state, a tactic unheard of at the time. With no records computerized, volunteers were sent out to county courthouses and other offices, in order to dig through old files and attics to gather a list that would eventually be used for mailings and phone calls. The final list of approximately eighty thousand names would be key to the Californian's last-ditch effort.[51]

According to Black, the fundraising efforts in North Carolina were going well and Ellis was raising anywhere between ten and twenty thousand dollars per day. More important, the "résumé" strategy favored by Sears had been thrown out the window. The North Carolinians were running the ideological holy war that Sears had wanted to avoid.

The day of March 23 dawned warm and clear—perfect for an incumbent with a soft base of support, and terrible for a challenger with a small, but more determined group of supporters. A higher than expected turnout could spell defeat for Reagan, just as it did in New Hampshire several weeks earlier. Ellis, Wrenn, and Helms were nervous, thinking even one day before the election that they might very well lose. But they were satisfied they had done everything necessary they could to secure a much needed win for Reagan.

Reagan departed North Carolina that day for Wisconsin. Ellis, mindful of the way Reagan had left New Hampshire too soon at the behest of Hugh Gregg, kept Reagan in the state until the last minute, in order to squeeze out as much media coverage of him as possible. Ford had only made one stop in the state and it had not gone well.

That night Reagan and his team were in La Crosse, Wisconsin, as he delivered a speech to Ducks Unlimited. Frank Reynolds, covering the campaign for ABC, approached Hannaford and Marty Anderson and asked if they had heard any of the results of North Carolina. The answer from the two depressed aides was "no."

"Well I have," Reynolds said, "and your man is winning." The Reagan staffers were dumbfounded.[52] They huddled with Reagan and Nofziger and decided not to meet the press. They remembered the egg Reagan got on his face in New Hampshire when he materialized too soon at the ballroom in the old New Hampshire Highway Hotel before his supporters and the media, appearing to claim victory.

After the speech, team Reagan boarded a plane for Los Angeles and learned in the air of their man's eventual win. "We all had vanilla ice cream and champagne on the plane when he'd accepted that we'd won," said Anderson.[53] Late in the evening, Reagan called Ellis and Helms at their hotel suite in Raleigh and once again, Black, whom Ellis had only recently let back in the state, ran afoul of the Helmsite. "I had told Charlie not to make any phone calls or take any phone calls, but when Reagan called, Black answered the phone and congratulated Reagan on his win. I was fit to be tied," Ellis said. Black had a different take, saying he had been asked to call Reagan and inform him of the win. But this disagreement was not important. Reagan had his first victory in hand over the incumbent Ford, and everybody could claim a piece of the credit.[54]

Also partying that night in Washington was a group of conservatives, aligned with the American Conservative Union and the Washington office of Citizens for Reagan. They gathered at the home of Becky Norton, a stalwart, take-no-prisoners activist. Evans was there as well and the good cheer, booze, and conversation flowed freely.

The final results in North Carolina were 53.4 percent for Reagan and 46.6 percent for Ford. Reagan received 100,984 votes to Ford's 88,249.[55] The next day, Reagan called the headquarters and spoke to each staffer personally to thank them for their hard work. Helms, Ellis, Wrenn, and the staff were deeply moved by Reagan's gesture.

Winning North Carolina paid many dividends for Reagan, including some that were not immediately obvious. Prior to New Hampshire, Republicans had nothing invested in Ford, according to Sears, because they had never voted him into office in the first place. But when Ford won the first five primaries, Republicans nationwide took a closer look at him, and his stature began to rise. By losing North Carolina to Reagan, Ford hit the bottom again, and, even worse, it now became permissible and acceptable to vote against the incumbent President and leader of the Republican Party. According to Gerald Pomper in *The Election of 1976*,

> The most vital asset of the Presidency, however, had already been lost: its aura of invincibility. When Ford began to move down in polls, primaries, and committed delegates, the majesty of the office was debilitated. . . . Once Ford began to slip, the Republican delegates no longer needed to fear the power of his office. Thus the President almost learned Machiavelli's truth: "Any prince, trusting only in [men's] words and having no other preparations made, will fall to his ruin."[56]

The week between the Illinois and North Carolina primary, no one knew this. Though few Republican Party operatives or voters knew who Machiavelli was and even fewer could quote him, all knew from experience about the psychological advantages of winning, especially against all odds.

Both Ford and Reagan had played college football in the 1930s and both knew a few tricks. Reagan's contest against Ford in North Carolina in March of 1976 was no less shocking to the political world than say, if tiny Eureka College where Reagan played football, had beaten the much vaunted, much bigger, more powerful Michigan where Ford played college ball. Winning North Carolina for Reagan was not the entire ballgame, but it was like scoring a touchdown just before halftime. He was still behind, especially in the delegate count, but it was just the boost he and his conservative followers needed for the second half. Reagan was back in the game.

Going into North Carolina, Reagan's campaign had been $2 million in debt and every day more and more Republican officials and political columnists were calling on him to retire from the field.

Had Reagan lost North Carolina, despite his public pronouncements, his revolutionary challenge to Ford, along with his political career, would have ended unceremoniously. He would have made a gracious exit speech, cut a deal with the Ford forces to eliminate his campaign debt, made a minor speech at the Kansas City Convention later that year, and returned to his ranch in Santa Barbara. He would probably have only reemerged to make speeches and cut radio commentaries to supplement his income.

And Reagan would have faded into political oblivion.

Conservative author and leader Stan Evans has asserted that the two most important primary victories in the history of the conservative movement were the 1964 California primary—when Barry Goldwater defeated Nelson Rockefeller, which propelled him to the GOP nomination—and Reagan's victory over Gerald Ford in North Carolina in 1976. Given Reagan's unexpected win over Ford in the Tar Heel state and the history that would eventually follow, few would dispute Evans's assertion.

Cannon observed, "North Carolina was the turning point of Reagan's political career. It kept him in the race to Kansas City, and it made him the presumptive Presidential nominee in 1980. At all times after North Carolina, Reagan was a legitimate, full-fledged candidate."[57]

In North Carolina, expectations were finally working for Reagan. He was making his comeback and would score more than a few upsets in the second half of the contest before the August convention in Kansas City.

9

CITIZENS FOR REAGAN, TAKE TWO

"I'm not going to rearrange the furniture on the deck of the Titanic!"

Buoyed by his upset win over President Ford in North Carolina, Ronald Reagan began to find his stride and his swing. Finally, he was neither on the defensive nor explaining himself. Reagan was in motion, having stumped for twelve aggressive days in the Tar Heel State compared to Ford's two passive days.[1] Senator Paul Laxalt told people it was the best he had ever seen Reagan as a campaigner. Elizabeth Drew wrote at the time, "Reagan looks good. His cheeks are rosier than when I saw him earlier in the year. He is successful now and it shows in his looks and his demeanor." She attributed the shift to two things. Reagan "got more confident and he got angry."[2]

Mike Deaver told Drew that he could cite the exact day when Reagan's demeanor and self-assuredness changed. "The real turning point in his mind was the day the Ford people had the Mayors calling him to get out, the Governors calling him to get out, and then the President suggesting he should get out. That was it for him. . . . He became more aggressive, more confident."[3] James Dickenson of the *Washington Star* wrote the morning after the North Carolina primary,

> All the experts laughed every time Ronald Reagan sat down to bravely argue that his early primary losses to President Ford were not fatal because he would do much better in the later primaries in the South, Southwest and Far West, more favorable political turf for him.[4]

No one was laughing now. "There are very few candidates who have that kind of utter belief in themselves and that would have hung in there," Reagan biographer Lou Cannon said.[5] Even more forebodingly for Ford, Dickinson noted, "Ford's defeat marks the first time an incumbent President has been beaten in a primary in which he campaigned."[6]

Dickenson was right. Harry Truman had lost in New Hampshire to Senator Estes Kefauver in 1952, but Truman never put one wet foot in the state. In 1912, ex-President Theodore Roosevelt beat President William Howard Taft in twelve Republican primaries, but as in the case of Truman, Taft never campaigned in any of those states. Virtually everybody in Ford's camp, Washington's political circles, and the national media had expected him to win in North Carolina. Many in Reagan's own camp had expected Ford to win—including Reagan himself. Tom Ellis, who along with Senator Jesse Helms had engineered the come-from-behind win for Reagan, told Mary McGrory of the *Washington Star* that although he knew Reagan was moving up in the polls over the last week he "wouldn't have bet a dollar" on victory.[7]

The Reagan haymaker had flattened Ford and his campaign. Ford's staff was stunned. They had beaten Reagan in five successive primaries, and they were expecting Reagan to throw in the towel as soon as the President chalked up another win in North Carolina. Little did Ford and his supporters suspect that California's "Comeback Kid" would do just that. Stu Spencer worried about North Carolina and that the Ford campaign did not understand Reagan's toughness and resolve. "I said this guy's for real . . . he's here to stay . . . he ain't getting out."[8]

Reagan's rhetoric on the stump was getting sharper too, as he lacerated Ford on the Panama Canal, détente, Angola, government regulations, and spending. Liberals did not escape his attention either as he attacked Ted Kennedy's national health insurance plan. Reagan warned,

> What the nation does not need is another workout of a collectivist formula based on an illusion promoting a delusion and delivering a boondoggle. It is up to the private sector to provide answers in the onrushing health care political battle. If not, nationalized medicine will represent one more instance of surrendering a freedom by default.[9]

Many in the East among the intelligentsia of the academy, the media, and the elites of the Republican and Democratic parties had an extremely low opinion of Reagan's intelligence. They were unaware of how extensively he read, wrote, and listened. Yet his speeches were laced with vivid prose, historical facts, and intellectual humor—all designed to get his point of view across to his audience. Their persuasiveness always mesmerized his listeners. No politician in 1976 could paint the verbal picture that Ronald Reagan could. Of the failures of the U.S. Postal Service, Reagan said,

> Thirty-five years ago you could make a telephone call long distance from San Francisco to New York and it cost you $20 and 70 odd cents. And for that amount of money, you could send through the Post Office from San Francisco to New York 1,036 letters. Today, you can make the same phone call for 56 cents. And for that amount of money you can only send five letters. So the government is suing the phone company.[10]

To illustrate the failures of collectivism practiced by the Soviet Union, Reagan said,

> They have had more than half a century without hindrance or interference to fully implement and put into operation socialism in that country. And we could be just like them. We'd start by cutting our paychecks 80 percent, moving 33 million workers back to the farm, destroy 59 million television sets, tear up 14 out of 15 miles of highway, junk 15 out of 20 of our automobiles, tear up two-thirds of our railroad tracks, knock down 70 percent of our houses, rip out nine-tenths of our telephones, and then all we'd have to do is find a capitalist country that would sell us wheat on credit so we wouldn't starve.[11]

Hubert Humphrey called Reagan's criticism of government a "disguised new form of racism." Although Jimmy Carter was also campaigning on the same anti-Washington theme as Reagan, Humphrey said his comments did not apply to Carter but only to Ford and Reagan.[12]

Next in line for the Ford-Reagan contest was Wisconsin. Reagan had expected to do well there, especially because it was a crossover state with a heavy Catholic population. Before the term was coined, these "Reagan Democrats," in states like Wisconsin felt a cultural and social affinity for Reagan. Charlie Black, Reagan's Midwest Political Director, was directing the grassroots effort in the state but he bumped up against the Reagan campaign's financial troubles. Black said that "without money, there were no radio or television commercials, there was no money for phone banks, for mailings, or most importantly, for polling. It was just maddening because you knew Reagan could do well there."[13]

Exacerbating the Reagan campaign's money problem was the new matching fund system set by the Federal Election Commission. For a time, these regulations doomed the role of the fat cats in national politics. Now, money had to be raised in small chunks from a variety of states if a Presidential campaign decided to take the matching funds from the federal Treasury. It was a Rube Goldberg operation to say the least, as campaigns spent untold dollars copying checks and producing report after report, giving rise to a growing cottage industry of accountants and lawyers, all working to protect their new "Full Employment Act." More than one political operative over the years has speculated about the aching irony of the hard-earned twenty-five dollars some pensioner had sent to their favorite candidate, only to have it pay for a lawyer's lunch at The Palm in downtown Washington. Aggravating the financial problems of the Reagan campaign was that many of their small donors sent cash and money orders along with checks. These donations had to be "qualified" by the campaign before they could be submitted for matching funds to the FEC.[14]

Volunteers worked long hours calling donors all across the country to verify their contributions and to obtain their addresses and information about their employment.[15] Phil Alexander, David Bufkin, and Maiselle Shortley were three young conservatives working long hours for little pay, qualifying checks under Angela "Bay" Buchanan's and Paul Russo's supervision. They would open envelopes and make copies of the checks. If money came in the form of cash or money orders, they had to track down the donor and get the required information, including occupation, to satisfy the FEC. It was a grueling process, and the teams worked around the clock in twelve-hour shifts.[16]

Complicating Reagan's money problems was the fact that Sears spent willy nilly and there was never a budget. Bruce Eberle had assiduously built a house file for the campaign that at the time included over eighty-five thousand names. After Reagan won in North Carolina, a mailing went out that netted an astonishing $778,000, almost a hundred dollars per name. This success rate was unheard of then and since in direct mail fundraising. Reagan had that much drawing power among the conservative base.[17]

Eberle, like others in the campaign, butted heads with Darrell Trent, the campaign's Comptroller. Trent was brought in to bring order, but he immediately called in Eberle, whom the campaign hadn't paid in months, and accused him of double billing. Eberle was widely known and universally liked and respected in the conservative movement. He was genuinely shocked when someone questioned his integrity. Eberle was eventually paid, but not without a fight with Trent. Eberle raised millions in the mail for Reagan, and Sears would later confide to Jim Lake that while the campaign made a lot of mistakes, they had at least hired the right direct mail fundraiser.

Despite the Reagan campaign's fundraising efforts and mistakes in money management, many of the financial difficulties were beyond their control.

Because of congressional foot-dragging, the FEC went temporarily out of business on March 22, 1976. This was at a time when Citizens for Reagan was owed well over a million dollars in matching funds.[18]

Congress eventually passed and sent a bill reconstituting the FEC to the White House. On May 5 the legislation arrived on the President's desk for his signature, which Ford did provide—six days later. Compounding their money problem was the campaign's inability to manage its own internal fundraising. This, combined with the Ford White House's delays in signing a bill that would allow Reagan and the other candidates to receive matching funds, made any real budgetary planning for the campaign impossible.[19]

Government bureaucrats and political shenanigans had denied Reagan's campaign the matching funds it deserved for over a month and a half. The consequences were disastrous for Reagan. Ron Nessen denied that the White House was playing politics with the new FEC bill and instead blamed the Democrats in Congress. "Clearly he's not trying to 'starve out' Reagan," he told the *Washington Post*.[20] When asked later about the suspected hardball tactics by the Ford White House, John Sears simply shrugged his shoulders and said, "That's politics."[21]

The campaign tried to obtain additional bank loans against the soon-to-becoming money from the FEC. "The bank just wouldn't loan us any more money," Sears said. "I think they were afraid of repercussions from the White House."[22] In the wake of the Supreme Court's decision in *Buckley v. Valeo*, political action committees, or "PACs," became the rage. Through the seventies and eighties, the ruling and favorable postage rates allowed groups to effectively raise money through the mail. Had the Court upheld the limitations affecting these groups, the American Conservative Union and the Young Americans for Freedom could not have spent unlimited funds to run their independent campaigns in support of Reagan. These campaigns provided the vital support Reagan needed in North Carolina, Texas, and other states.

Shortly before the North Carolina primary, Sears flew to Wisconsin to meet with Reagan, Peter Hannaford, and others.[23] Sears's recommendation was to scrap any future efforts in Wisconsin, including Reagan's three scheduled days of campaigning. Many in Wisconsin, including Black, fought Sears bitterly. They believed that Reagan could win the primary, or at least some delegates there, with some additional campaigning, but Sears prevailed.

Instead, Reagan would make a thirty-minute nationally televised broadcast to take his message to the American people and appeal directly to his supporters for contributions.[24] The campaign issued a press release announcing this decision and restated Reagan's intention to stay in the race until the convention in Kansas City. Nonetheless, the announcement led to some speculation in the media and political circles that Reagan might use the speech to withdraw from the race—or would scale back his operations to become a regional candidate.

The new strategy was to focus on the speech by Reagan. There was one small problem, however. All three networks declined the campaign's request to purchase the time. Reagan was all for the speech and had been pressing Sears and others to put him on television. Following the surprising success of Reagan's taped address in North Carolina, Sears had now become a convert. Conventional wisdom in 1976 was that the American people just would not want to watch a politician speak for half an hour on television. But then again, Ronald Reagan was not just another politician.

One aide said to the *Washington Star* of the planned speech, "He'll talk about what America is all about, why there is reason for hope, how things can get better, and how we can fight apathy." The story continued,

> He will talk about what he hoped to accomplish when he decided to make his Presidential race. . . . Reagan doesn't feel he got a chance to discuss the campaign in a broader, loftier sense in New Hampshire and Florida. "He didn't get to talk uplift and hope for tomorrow because he got all wrapped up with the $90 billion thing and Social Security and the Loebs and Thomsons," says one aide.[25]

The campaign announced that Reagan would go to California for one week to prepare for the thirty-minute speech, but the skeptical national press did not buy this explanation. In fact, the campaign was in such poor shape financially, the decision was made to take Reagan off the road for a week to save money.[26]

As in virtually every other state, Ford had the strong backing of the Republican state party in Wisconsin, and the campaign made plans for two appearances by the President before the primary. Reagan had made four previous stops there but would not commit more time to campaigning there. The Reagan budget in Wisconsin was to total only $100,000, less than one-third of what the campaign spent to win the North Carolina primary.[27]

Reagan did make one appearance in the week prior to the Wisconsin primary at a campaign rally in Richmond, Virginia. He appeared tanned and in good spirits, despite telling the crowd he was having trouble getting any of the three networks to agree to sell him a half hour of broadcast time. He speculated that if the networks' final decision was "no," then his campaign would put together a string of independent stations to carry the broadcast. "This is part and parcel of a whole ridiculous situation where the incumbent can pre-empt time . . . and I can't have a thirty-five-year-old movie run on the late, late show without them having to offer equal time," Reagan complained to a reporter.[28]

If Reagan had been Robert E. Lee incarnate, he could not have been more welcomed in Richmond that evening, March 27. When it was announced that Reagan would attend the event, a fundraiser for the Virginia GOP's annual "Commonwealth Dinner" sold hundreds more of the fifty-dollar-per-plate tickets than it did the previous year.[29]

Governor Mills Godwin, a Ford supporter and one of the state executives who had signed the letter sent to Reagan the week before the North Carolina primary urging him to leave the race, was forced to eat a big plate of crow, which was definitely not on the menu that night for the other attendees. Introducing Reagan, Godwin said he had signed that letter "B.C.—Before Carolina." He added that Reagan's resurgence "simply proves that even Republican Governors do not always assess accurately the realities of politics."[30] Reagan, for his part, was hitting on all cylinders, telling the crowd one pleasing political joke after another. The *Washington Star* detailed how Reagan told an old standby about a Social Security foul-up and effortlessly transitioned into his own campaign situation:

> A pensioner allegedly received a letter informing him his payments were stopping because he was dead, Reagan explained.
>
> When the recipient of the letter went to his downtown Social Security office to demonstrate that he was not deceased, Reagan continued, he was told no immediate change could be made in the retirement system's computer banks for restoring his normal payments. But officials offered their client $700 in "funeral expenses" to "tide him over," Reagan said.
>
> "North Carolina kind of gave me my $700, but I never had any intention of using it for a funeral," the former California Governor told [the] crowd.[31]

Reagan was well known for his sense of humor, especially in zapping his opponents. While Governor, he once encountered a young hippie holding a sign that read, "Make Love Not War." Reagan later told reporters that "from the looks of him, I don't think he could do either!"[32]

Reagan finally scored a breakthrough in his negotiations with the networks when NBC announced that it had decided to sell Reagan one half hour of media time for a national broadcast. The speech would take place on Wednesday, March

31 at 10:30 P.M. Eastern Standard Time. The address would take place the night before April Fool's Day, but no one for a second, especially Ford, thought Reagan was fooling. Reagan would go up against two "cop shows." CBS was broadcasting *Blue Knight*, and ABC was airing its top-rated *Starsky and Hutch*.[33] Initially, all three networks had turned down Reagan's request. They cited various reasons, but Reagan objected and responded by firing off telegrams to the chairmen of each, protesting the fact that while he was shut out, President Ford had easy access. Such an arrangement was not "in the interest of fairness and justice" or "the people's right to know. . . ."[34] "Reagan aides have complained that Ford, through Presidential press conferences and other devices, can obtain massive free media exposure unavailable to his GOP challenger," recorded the *Washington Star's* Martha Angle.[35] Smith and Mark Fowler, who was doing pro bono legal work for Reagan, went to New York and walked between the offices of the three networks, lobbying for Reagan. CBS flatly turned them down. ABC said they would consider it, but an executive at NBC seemed moved by Smith's "fairness" argument. He told Smith to come back in half an hour and when he did, the General Counsel for NBC, Corey Dunham, told the elated attorneys that NBC would sell Reagan one half hour of time.[36] In changing their mind, NBC issued a statement, which read,

> Ordinarily, NBC would not sell national network time to a candidate this early while the state primaries are still in progress. However, in view of the unique situation of the campaign for the Republican Presidential nomination, where Governor Reagan is one of two major candidates and opposes an incumbent President, NBC feels that an exception to its general policy is warranted.[37]

But the other two networks stuck by their original decisions. Two Democratic Congressmen from Massachusetts, including a Kennedy family ally, Torbert MacDonald, complained to the FEC about the decision by NBC to sell time to Reagan.

In the background, another fight developed in the Reagan campaign, this time over how to pay for the national broadcast. Although the campaign had won North Carolina, it was still in dire financial straights and in debt by over $1.5 million.[38] Hundreds of thousands of dollars were stuck in the direct mail pipeline, and the FEC owed the campaign another $1.5 million. Loans had already been taken against the projected income and spent. No more bank loans were available to Citizens for Reagan.

Jimmy Lyons, a dedicated conservative, longtime Reagan supporter, and president of the River Oaks Bank in Houston, Texas, was approached about making a $100,000 loan to the campaign to pay for the national speech.[39] The first lawyer to review this loan was Reagan's personal attorney, William French Smith in Los Angeles, who reviewed FEC law and said the loan was illegal. Sears then took the matter to the General Counsel for Citizens for Reagan, Loren Smith, who pronounced the loan legal.[40]

Lyons sent the money, and a check was cut to the National Broadcasting Company, which understandably wanted the money up front, for a little over $104,000.[41] But first, Lyons called Bruce Eberle, who was handling the direct mail for the campaign, to see if he would be able to raise the money to repay Lyons for his loan. Eberle assured the banker he could do it.[42]

In the meantime, *Washington Post* reporters Bob Woodward and Carl Bernstein, who had uncovered much of the Watergate conspiracy, released their much-anticipated second book on the Nixon Administration. Entitled *The Final Days*, it became an immediate bestseller. A few remaining Nixon defenders charged the duo with reporting things differently than they remembered them, but the book held up under scrutiny.[43] Regarding differing recollections in 1976, a Reagan staffer recounted for an editorial writer at the *Washington Star* that one of the networks refused to sell Reagan the time for a nationally broadcast speech, saying that Reagan was not a national candidate. "If such an argument was in fact made, it ranks among the dumber statements to come out of televisionland," opined the paper.[44]

Reagan taped the speech the afternoon of March 31. The setting was tasteful and understated, but the message and the messenger were anything but subdued. That night, Reagan ripped into the "wandering" foreign policy of President Ford and the looming national deficits. Reagan charged that although Ford had previously dropped the use of the word "détente" and replaced it with "peace through strength," the policies of the United States towards the Soviets had not changed. Reagan charged that "peace does not come from weakness or from retreat. It comes from the restoration of American military superiority."[45]

Reagan's speech was nothing new for the media that had been covering him for the past several years. But for the American people it was electrifying and it galvanized Reagan's campaign. Lou Cannon wrote for the *Washington Post*:

> Earlier in the day, at a breakfast meeting with reporters, Reagan National Campaign Chairman John P. Sears had said that the former California Governor would use his speech to "redefine his candidacy."

> While Reagan did not do that last night, he did bring to millions of Americans for the first time the basic message he had been using since March 4 in Orlando—a message that his strategists believed helped him score an upset victory over Mr. Ford in the March 23rd North Carolina primary.[46]

Peter Hannaford drafted the speech, and Reagan spent several days fine-tuning it. Mike Deaver supervised the building of the "set" in Los Angeles where Reagan would tape the speech.[47]

That night, Reagan tore into his opponent. Referring to the account in a newly released book by former Chief of Naval Operations Elmo Zumwalt, Reagan hit Ford on signing the Helsinki Accords, saying they

> put an American stamp of approval on Russia's enslavement of the captive nations. Now we must ask if someone is giving away our freedom. . . . Dr. Kissinger is quoted as saying he thinks of the U.S. as Athens and the Soviet Union as Sparta. The day of the U.S. is past and today is the day of the Soviet Union.[48]

Reagan also seized on a quote attributed to Kissinger aide Helmut Sonnenfeldt that "the captive nations should give up any claims of national sovereignty and simply become a part of the Soviet Union." Columnists Rowland Evans and Robert Novak reported that Sonnenfeldt had made this remark to U.S. Ambassadors in Europe.[49] On the issue of foreign aid, Reagan assailed the Administration over a provision in a bill that would have allowed the United States to initiate a lifting of the complete embargo against Vietnam that Ford himself had signed into law the previous year after the fall of Saigon. The issue was tied to the POW/MIA argument, but few felt that Vietnam would show any good faith in helping to recover the remains or secure the whereabouts of missing Americans servicemen.[50] The response to Reagan was overwhelming. The offices of Citizens for Reagan were flooded with phone calls, according to receptionist Becki Black.[51] Eventually, over $1.5 million would cascade into the Californian's campaign as a result of his speech. Nationally, Reagan received approximately a 20 percent "share," meaning one out of every five television sets in America was tuned in to Reagan. The rating was considered excellent for a purely political show.[52] Viewers were encouraged to make a contribution to Reagan's campaign by calling the phone number listed on the screen. Individuals who called eventually received a Western Union Mailgram restating the request for money that told the recipient when to send their checks to help Reagan.[53] The response to Reagan's speech at Kissinger's State Department was also overwhelming. Kissinger's spokesman, Robert Funseth, denounced Reagan's accusations, calling them "false" and "irresponsible." The State Department issued a ten-page refutation of the Reagan speech titled, "The Reagan Speech and the Facts."[54]

It was all a tempest in a teapot, since few Americans had ever studied Greek history, much less remembered the wars between the two city-states, or that Athens has actually survived Sparta by several centuries. But the American people understood Reagan's point. More importantly, Reagan had achieved a major hit against Ford, and now it was the Ford campaign's turn to explain.

Campaigning in Wisconsin the next day, the President attempted a counter-offensive against Reagan's speech, saying, "It's a distortion; it's a misleading statement for people to quote numbers without quoting what the military capability is. . . . It could alarm the American people, it could have an adverse effect on our allies and it could encourage our enemies."[55]

Initially, Ford called Reagan's charges against Kissinger "a fabrication." Ford attacked Reagan by name, saying his charges were a "rerun" of earlier statements by his opponent. Ford's own script had been to stay above the fray and let surrogates attack Reagan, but that strategy was dismissed after their loss in North Carolina and Reagan's nationally televised speech. Reagan did not want to alarm the American people, but he did want them to know his opinion about America's foreign policy, which is exactly what he did. The trouble for Ford was that many in the GOP shared Reagan's opinion and not Ford's.

Reagan did not need a script to seize the political advantage, despite the "rerun" innuendo by Ford. In a Saturday morning press conference, he jumped right back at Ford, saying the President was "speaking rather loosely and in an unjustified way" when Ford attacked the Reagan speech. Then Reagan challenged Ford to a debate. He told reporters, his eyes twinkling, "It would seem we have touched a nerve."[56]

Six days after Reagan's speech, on Tuesday, April 6, both Jimmy Carter and Gerald Ford won their respective primaries in Wisconsin, as expected. Reagan won 45 percent of the popular vote in Wisconsin, but he did not take a single delegate. Ford swept the forty-five delegates at stake, both in congressional districts and at-large. But Ford received little credit from the national media, who saw his 55-45 percent win over Reagan as unimpressive.[57] The Reagan campaign issued a statement from Mike Deaver, saying that Citizens for Reagan was temporarily forced to give up its charter plane. But even this setback did not deter the now reenergized Reaganites. Said Deaver, "This decision, while it may inconvenience the campaign and the news media and force some schedule revision, in no way means Governor Reagan's campaign effort is being reduced." Wisely, the campaign released the announcement the day before the primary, knowing the media would be swamped with other political news.[58] Reagan was fortunate not to be forced to stand in line and wait for a boarding pass like every other traveler as he flew on commercial flights. His campaign ensured that he would have some privacy at an office in a given terminal before boarding the plane ahead of everybody else.[59]

Despite this minor embarrassment, the campaign was looking forward to future contests. On the Monday before the Wisconsin primary, Reagan departed for Texas by commercial plane to barnstorm the state, aiming to win the GOP primary there three weeks hence. Sears conveyed to the *Washington Post*, "In a sense, Texas is like New Hampshire all over again. It gives us an opportunity for a new beginning and for the momentum which any campaign needs." One hundred delegates were up for grabs in the Lone Star State.[60] On April 6, the New York primary also took place, and again Reagan forces had only filed a few delegate slates in the state. All the delegates would be technically "uncommitted." But New York State Party Chairman Richard "Rosey" Rosenbaum, a Rockefeller protégé, would do everything in his power to ensure that Ford would eventually receive most of the Empire State's delegates. Rosenbaum was impossible to miss in a crowd. He was a large man with broad shoulders but also had an unexpectedly high-pitched voice. Most noticeably, was he was completely bald and wore oversized horn-rimmed glasses. Rosenbaum had several nicknames, including "Dick" and "Rosey" to his friends and "The Iron Chancellor" to his adversaries. Rosenbaum was a liberal Republican and a fierce competitor, but if he was on your side, he would walk through fire for you.[61]

Rosenbaum said publicly that he estimated as many as thirty to thirty-five of the 154 uncommitted delegates might be for Reagan. But he worried privately that Ford's support could crumble, especially if he lost to Reagan in Michigan.[62] Rosenbaum would have preferred to switch to Rockefeller if Ford faltered, but the rest of the New York delegation was another matter.

New York's Republican delegates in 1976 ran on the primary ballot with their name only, and they were not identified as aligned with any candidate. Running was logistically difficult, especially if a delegate/candidate did not have the organizational support or funding from the state. Local parties were, with few exceptions, all supporters of Ford. One of the exceptions was Brooklyn, which was controlled by George Clark, a staunch conservative and foe of Rockefeller's machine in New York.

Reagan, however, received some good news in mid-April when Ohio's Secretary of State reversed a previous decision, which allowed Reagan to appear on the statewide ballot in the Ohio primary on June 8. As a result, he was entitled to vie for twenty-eight at-large delegates, in addition to the sixty-nine delegates selected by congressional districts. Black once again pushed Sears to commit more money and effort by the candidate to the Buckeye State. But most of their meager resources were being thrown into the fights against Ford in Texas, Indiana, Georgia, and Alabama.[63]

Another individual being second-guessed at the time was White House Press Secretary Ron Nessen, for his controversial decision to host *Saturday Night Live.* In 1976, campaign consultants and White House staff were not the "celebrities" they would later become. The rule more than the exception at the time was that staff should be seen and rarely heard from. The only star of the show should be the candidate. Nessen not only broke with the old tradition, but smashed it into a million pieces. Nessen was booed by the liberal audience, despite taking part in several skits that made fun of Ford's intelligence and physical prowess and convincing Ford to tape three self-deprecating pieces for the show. It wasn't just the audience; people everywhere—even in the Ford campaign—were scandalized. And on the heels of renewed questions about Ford in the wake of his defeat at the hands of Reagan in North Carolina, Nessen's appearance could not have come at a worse time for Ford.[64]

Hoping to prevent another loss like North Carolina, the Ford campaign started playing hardball in Texas, as hundreds of letters went to individuals running as Reagan delegates, stating, "Your activities raise serious questions under the law and may expose you and others involved to possible criminal violations."[65] No one is less susceptible to intimidation than a conservative from Texas, and many fired white hot telegrams back to the Ford campaign, threatening lawsuits for "malicious slander" and accusing the campaign of "dirty tricks."[66]

On April 24, the state conventions for the Arizona and South Carolina Republican parties took place, and Reagan, as expected, did well in these two states. In South Carolina, Reagan prevailed, seizing twenty-seven of the thirty-six delegates at stake. Reagan was helped there by one of the two Governors in the country to endorse him—Jim Edwards. The only minor disappointment was Edwards's failure to gain his convention's support for a "unit rule" whereby all delegates had to vote with the majority. Reagan did even better in the Grand Canyon State, taking twenty-seven of the twenty-nine delegates selected, despite a speech by Goldwater lauding President Ford.[67]

The Pennsylvania primary took place on April 27, but the Reagan forces, as decided by Sears, had decided to forego any effort there. They reasoned that the state party had such an iron grip that any effort there would be futile. The Republican Party in Pennsylvania was controlled by Ford's supporters including

Drew Lewis, who had lost for Governor two years before, as well as Senators Hugh Scott and Richard Schweiker. Lewis had spent months combing the state for delegates who would be certainly loyal to him and at least marginally loyal to Ford.[68]

Pennsylvania's delegates, like New York's, were technically listed as "uncommitted," but the vast majority would eventually go for Ford—a total of 257 between the two states.[69] Again, Sears's decision was disputed, but his side had one simple answer on the matter of bypassing these big industrial states: power. The GOP machines were all on record for Ford and used their own financial resources to help him. Any startup grassroots organizational effort on behalf of Reagan would have cost more than what was available to the Reagan campaign. Sears's reasoning was sound in the eyes of many but not all: win impressively in other states, impress these uncommitted delegates with the victories Reagan was rolling up, and bargain with them in the days leading to the convention.

Others, like Paul Weyrich, then an up-and-coming conservative activist, had met with Sears and pleaded to let them organize conservative groups that could assemble their own delegate operations for Reagan. But according to Weyrich, Sears demurred.[70] Of Reagan's new strategy, Lou Cannon wrote in the *Washington Post*,

> Both the South and West will be disproportionately represented at the Republican convention, largely because of the success of conservatives at the last two conventions in turning back effort to increase the representation of the most populous states.
>
> As a result, there are nearly 1,000 delegates in the Southern and Western states, and [John] Sears estimates that Reagan needs about 700 of them to have a realistic chance of securing the Presidential nomination. The other 430 delegates needed for the nomination would come from a scattering of Reagan delegates in other regions and from uncommitted delegates.[71]

Rowland Evans and Robert Novak also spotted a new trend in Reagan's appeal in Texas:

> The remarkable gathering of over 3,000 lacked the sleek, chic look of Texas Republicans and seemed much more like a typical Wallace rally—women in housedresses, sport-shirted men, lots of small American flags. If the virtual collapse of Wallace's candidacy is sending right-wing populist Democrats across party lines to Reagan, President Ford is in deepening trouble here.[72]

They also observed that Reagan was now "far more combative and assured" than he had been in New Hampshire.

A newly released poll showed the largely unknown Jimmy Carter beating Gerald Ford.[73] Adding to Ford's headaches, another issue was emerging in Texas that would eventually serve Reagan's purposes. Back in December, Ford had signed an energy bill that was strongly opposed by Texas's oilmen. Reagan attacked the bill, saying it discouraged domestic production. The "oil depletion allowance," which Ford and Congress had all but eliminated in the bill, was as sacred in Texas as the Alamo.[74]

Texas was also another open primary state, and although Bob Teeter's polling of Republican voters showed Ford competitive, his calculations could not factor in the flagging campaign of George Wallace and the thousands of conservative Democrats his demise would cut loose in Texas on May 1. Making Teeter's job virtually impossible was that voters did not register by party in Texas, so there was no realistic way in which to measure support or turnout. Furthermore, this would be the first contested Presidential primary in Texas Republican history, leaving no way to "guesstimate" turnout.

The Texas high command for Reagan—Ron Dear, Ernie Angelo, and Ray Barnhart—had been impressed with the win their old conservative friends Tom Ellis and Jesse Helms had achieved for Reagan in North Carolina. Ellis and Helms gladly accepted the Texans' invitation to the Lone Star State to help. Ellis also brought along pollster Arthur Finkelstein, who scripted much of the North Carolina effort, hoping he could be of use in Texas as well. Establishment Republicans had long ago dismissed the trio of Dear, Angelo, and Barnhart as "extremists." Indeed, the Texas Republican Party "held a press conference in which they said they weren't worried about the Reagan operation in Texas because they didn't have anyone of 'substance' working for them," Angelo recalled.[75]

Jeff Bell, who had been in the campaign's doghouse since the "$90 billion" speech, had been keeping a low profile in the headquarters. But he finally pleaded with Sears to let him go to Texas to help his friend Ron Dear, and Sears agreed.[76] While in Texas, Bell discovered a lifetime Democrat in Fort Worth, Rollie Millirons, who was planning to cross over and vote for Reagan.

Finkelstein was alerted to Millirons and immediately wrote a radio script that was broadcasted repeatedly across the state. In the commercials, Millirons told his listeners that he had been a Democrat all of his life, and he was planning on voting for George Wallace, but Wallace could not win. Reagan could, and that was why Millirons would be voting for Reagan. The commercial was a revelation to many Democrats in Texas, who had been "yellow dog" Democrats all their lives, following in their parents and grandparents and great-grandparents' footsteps. The Reagan campaign also handed out fliers, stating, "Democrats: You will not be committing a major indiscretion if you vote, this year, in the Republican primary." The fliers had drawings of a Republican elephant saying "I'm for Reagan!" and a Democratic donkey saying "Me too!"[77]

Ford was scheduled to make two trips to Texas, but his campaign was reassessing its strategy. Incumbency, it was determined, was no longer enough to win primaries. The campaign believed Ford would have to get more specific about where he stood and where he disagreed with Reagan, and how he and not Reagan was in basic agreement with Republican primary voters.

On the day of the Wisconsin primary, Reagan was campaigning in Texas while his campaign was going through a reorganization of sorts. Reagan's Press Secretary, Lyn Nofziger, was detailed back to California to run the Reagan effort there for the June 8 primary and was replaced by Jim Lake. Nofziger was battling with Sears over strategy and ideology but had never been a favorite of Nancy Reagan's. Lake was popular with both.[78] The campaign was still strapped for cash, and one of Reagan's Texas Chairmen, Ray Barnhart, told the media that his plans for a phone bank would have to be scrapped. Barnhart said that Reagan would win two-thirds of the one hundred delegates to be chosen on May 1, thus raising the bar for Reagan at a time when Ford had financial resources, and Reagan did not. Furthermore, Ford had the support of the state GOP and Texas Senator John Tower, a favorite of conservatives there.

However, the Ford campaign had also forgotten how to manage its expectations. They were consistently telling the media that although they thought Reagan would win, it was possible for Ford to win or at least stay competitive with Reagan, especially when it came to delegates.

In primary after primary, it was the same story. A small group of dedicated conservatives were backing Reagan, while the state GOP and local party apparatchiks were supporting Ford. These grassroots conservatives did not know that "it could not be done," so they simply did it. Some were middle-aged white males, but not all. For example, Chris Lay, a young movement conservative and staffer for Congressman Steven Symms of Idaho, traveled to Texas at his own expense to volunteer for the campaign. Symms also went into Texas to campaign for Reagan.[79] But all of them were hardworking and dedicated and refused to back down. They also shared a joy at beating the GOP country club establishment.

Regarding the shift of cultural attitudes, the Democrats' frontrunner,

Carter, suddenly found himself on the defensive over a comment he made about the "ethnic purity" of neighborhoods. Carter backtracked and issued a statement that suggested he had been forced to make the comment. The media jumped on him for that, but it died fairly quickly. However, the other two contenders for the coveted Democratic nomination, Fred Harris and "Scoop" Jackson dropped out of the race, bringing the total to seven Democrats whom the diminutive peanut farmer from Georgia had banished from the field.[80]

The Ford operation announced that sixty former Reagan officials from California and "friends" had endorsed Ford for President. Lou Cannon interviewed several of them for the *Washington Post* including David James, a Los Angeles businessman who said of Reagan, "His talents are not suited to the management of great enterprises." Another, Norman "Skip" Watts said that a Reagan Presidency "would be dangerous to the country and dangerous to the party." Later in the story, Watts was identified as the Director of Primary States for the Ford campaign. He had no further direct relation to Reagan and only a very thin indirect relation. Yet another, on background, told Cannon of Reagan, "He is a fine decent man who did a good job in California. But he lacks the wide intellect necessary for the Presidency. Not that Ford has all that much intelligence, either."[81]

Shadowboxing continued between the two Presidential contenders over the next several weeks. Ford bizarrely interpreted the results of Wisconsin as a referendum on Kissinger.

In a Rose Garden ceremony, he told a group of visiting businessmen, "As far as I am concerned, my full support for Secretary Kissinger is fortified by the decision in Wisconsin."[82]

Campaigning in Texas, Reagan's take on Wisconsin was different. Noting that in Texas, like Wisconsin, Democrats were allowed to cross over and could vote in Republican primaries, Reagan said before a morning rally, "Let us ask them if they can't see their way to join us in what I see as a crusade to save this country before it is too late."[83]

Reagan was also getting help in Texas from some of his old Hollywood friends, including Efrem Zimbalist Jr., Jimmy Stewart, and Ken Curtis.[84] It was not unusual for these celebrities, along with Chuck Connors, Jack Webb, and Mike Conner, to also stop by the Reagan headquarters in Washington and boost morale. All of Reagan's operations, including Texas and Washington, were putting in long hours, but before the offices in Washington were closed for the evening—and they often weren't—someone had to send the final baseball scores to Reagan whenever he was on the road.

At one point, Reagan aide David Bufkin found himself working in the lobby of the campaign's headquarters because so many volunteers had shown up for Reagan. On the phone with a friend, he complained about the national media, unaware that Leslie Stahl of CBS could hear his conversation. When Sears appeared for his interview with Stahl, she pointed at Bufkin and barked at Sears, "I want that man fired on the spot!" Despite Stahl's demand, Bufkin stayed.

The volunteers for Reagan, according to Bufkin, ran the gamut from "Ivy Leaguers to hippies to cowboys, all types." Sometimes the young staffers for Reagan and Ford would run into each other at a Washington watering hole where the Ford kids would refer to the Reagan kids as "right-wing nut jobs" and young Reaganites would call the Ford kids "geeks."[85]

Ford arrived in Irvington, Texas, stressing the need for tougher sentencing on convicted drug dealers. His campaign reasoned that he had not talked enough about "law and order" issues.[86] Ford was off stride and the "Bozo the President" suspicions began to creep back into the race when he was photographed at a Texas event eating a tamale without first removing the corn husk.[87] Clearly, Reagan's win in North Carolina, his national speech, and his victories in South Carolina and Arizona had unnerved Ford. He was also spending virtually all of his time answering Reagan's charges. Edward Walsh wrote of the President's predicament in the *Washington Post*:

> At airport press conferences, local TV interviews and open question-and-answer sessions, Mr. Ford was asked about the future of the Panama Canal, U.S. relations with Hanoi and Secretary of State Henry A. Kissinger's diplomacy.
>
> The President and his advisers are unable to move their campaign toward issues they would prefer—notably, the signs of improvement in the nation's economy. As a result, Mr. Ford was forced into a defensive posture.[88]

Even more frustrating for Ford, the national economic picture was brightening, yet he was getting little credit from Republican primary voters. The gross domestic product was up, and unemployment was falling. Ford's mantra on the stump was, "Everything that should be going up is going up and everything that should be coming down is coming down." But Reagan's issues, not Ford's, were holding the interest of voters.

Back in Washington, Muhammad Ali defeated Jimmy Young at the Capital Centre in fifteen rounds. In Texas, Reagan and Ford were engaged in their own title fight, and Ford was desperately trying to keep his crown from his California

The Reagans in New Hampshire. Reagan aide Martin Anderson is at Reagan's right. Note hand holding between Reagan and Mrs. Reagan.

Reagan speechifying in New Hampshire.

photo courtesy of Nancy Reynolds

Reagan's Revolutionaries, the night before his announcement. Clockwise: Reagan, John Sears, Nancy Reynolds, Jeff Bell, Paul Laxalt, Peter Hannaford, Martin Anderson, Franklin Nofziger, Mike Deaver, Richard Wirthlin, Mrs. Reagan.

Reagan announces, November 20, 1975.

Reagan stumping in New Hampshire. Reagan aide Paul Russo is in background in white rain coat.

Paul Laxalt in New Hampshire. Reagan's tireless corner man.

Unless otherwise noted, all photos courtesy of Dennis Warren

Reagan at senior citizens home,
New Hampshire.

Reagan on the ropes in North Carolina.

Supporters greet the Reagans. Youthful voters were always his most devoted fans.

The Reagans always enjoyed campaigning.

Reagan, local television interview, Oregon.

Reagan, Mrs. Reagan, greet Senator Schweiker in Kansas City.

Mrs. Reagan and Ron "Skipper" at Kemper Arena.

Reagan greets supporters at airport in Kansas City.

Reagan and trusted aide Michael Deaver.

Reagan and Mrs. Reagan greet supporters at airport.

John Sears (with cigarette), Anderson, and Deaver on the road.

1976 Republican National Convention.

Pat Boone, actor, singer, and Reagan delegate from California.

Columnists Robert Novak and Jack Anderson.

Rogers C.B. Morton, Ford's second Campaign Manager.

Congressman Bob Michel and Sam Donaldson.

Ford Floor Manager, Senator Robert Griffin in hat, confers with aides while Tom Brokaw of NBC listens in.

Lyn Nofziger.

A Reagan delegate sends a message to Nelson Rockefeller.

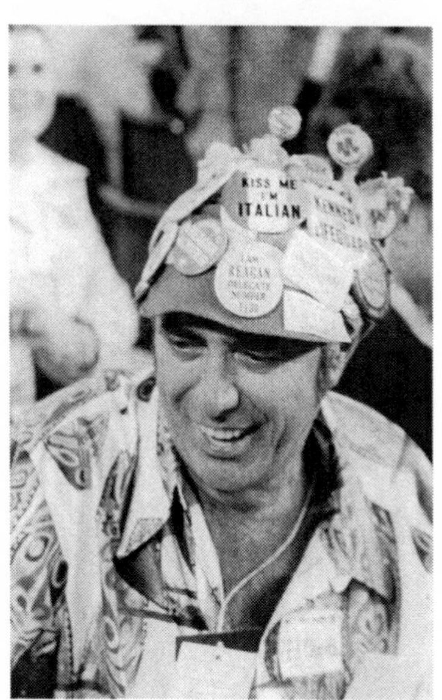

Reagan's delegates were passionate.

Ford had passionate supporters too.

A young and sweaty Fred Barnes at right attempts to interview Mississippi delegates.

Ford Library credit

No love lost, Reagan and Ford confer.

Reagan and Ford delegates compete for attention.

With Ford's nomination all but confirmed, Reagan's supporters staged a last gasp, noisy demonstration for their man.

Ford Library credit

The battle over. Ford pays a visit to Reagan as agreed upon by John Sears and Dick Cheney.

The fight over, Ford's supporters exalt.

Ford and family beckon Reagan to come to the podium.

Reagan and Mrs. Reagan, August 19. Many thought this would be the last time they would see Reagan.

"Unity" press conference the morning of August 19.

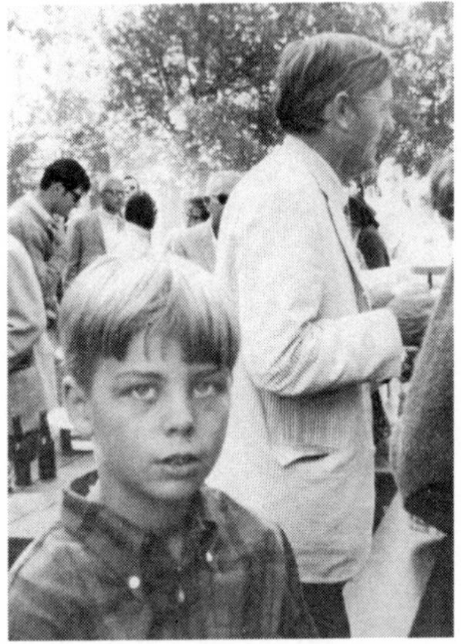

Craig Shirley Collection

Author just finished lecturing William F. Buckley Jr. on the philosophy of conservatism, 1966 Onondaga County Conservative Party fundraiser.

Ford Library

Reagan electrifies the convention. "This is our challenge."

Ford Library

Bob Dole, Mrs. Reagan, Reagan, Ford, Rockefeller, and Ford family. August 19, 1976.

Reagan White House photo

Author and Reagan, 1984.

photo courtesy of Andi Hedberg

Andi Hedberg, Vice President Dick Cheney, and author.

conservative challenger. Fred Barnes, who was traveling with Ford through Texas as he stumped for votes, wrote in the *Washington Star* of the fresh problems for the President on the eve of the big Lone Star State primary:

> During a stem-winding speech in Dallas on Thursday, President Ford boasted loudly that he would win. . . . By yesterday, however, he was not so bold, choosing for the most part to talk about "momentum" instead of victory over Ronald Reagan in Texas.
>
> At an appearance Wednesday night in Houston, about 6,000 people showed up to see Ford. They listened to his brief speech, but then half of them streamed out of the auditorium as Ford went on for another 30 minutes answering questions."[89]

Ford also lost an audience in Lubbock. As he spoke at an indoor mall, many people chatted loudly, ignoring the President until he introduced Dallas Cowboys' football coach, Tom Landry, who was supporting him.[90]

Ford spent more time and money campaigning in Texas than any primary to date. It was also in Texas where he adopted his harshest tones against his opponent and attacked him by name. "When it comes to the life and death decisions of our national security, the decision made must be the right one. There are no retakes in the Oval Office."[91] This newest slight of Reagan's previous career was duly noted by the candidate. Reagan had been asked by a reporter of he would be interested in being Ford's running mate to which Reagan retorted, "Well, maybe he would like to have a Vice President that makes retakes and who is irresponsible," reported the *Dallas Morning News.* Ford also called Reagan's positions "simplistic" and "rash."[92]

Nelson Rockefeller piled on, when he told the Associated Press that Reagan was "deceptive" and "misleading."[93]

Reagan got a bonus when Henry Kissinger responded to Reagan's attacks on his Africa policy, calling the Californian, "totally irresponsible."[94] The Ford campaign and his Administration were completely on the defensive. Wherever Ford went, he was forced to answer reporters' questions about Reagan's charges over détente, Soviet missile strength, Africa, Kissinger and, of course, the Panama Canal.

Nonetheless, reporters got "spun" badly by Ford's people leading up to the May 1 Texas primary. For example, Barnes wrote a story that appeared on the day of the primary that Ford might have a chance to do well in Texas. The *New York Times* reported the day before the primary, "Political leaders here believe that heavy, last minute campaigning by President Ford has cut substantially into

Ronald Reagan's early lead in Texas, turning tomorrow's Presidential primary into a cliff hanger that they said was too close to call."[95]

On primary day, Reagan won a crushing victory over Ford in Texas, taking all ninety-six delegates at stake and winning most of the twenty-four congressional districts by better than two to one.[96] Reagan later took the four at-large delegates, making it a clean sweep of the state—an even hundred. The Reagan forces even denied a delegate slot to Senator Tower. Later in Kansas City, the Texas trio of Dear, Angelo, and Barnhart, who had engineered the Texas win, would attempt to prevent poor Tower from even getting a floor pass at Kemper Arena.

Turnout was extraordinarily heavy in both primaries, and long lines were announced at GOP polling places in Houston, Dallas, Longview, and elsewhere across the state. "'They're swamping us,' said R. Douglas Lewis, state Republican Executive Director," to the *New York Times.* The paper also reported that turnout in one Republican precinct in Waco was around eight hundred, as opposed to the last GOP primary when eighty-four people had showed up to vote.[97] "Nancy Reagan called that afternoon and wondered how we were going to do. I told her we were going to win them all . . . all the delegates. And she said, 'Oh no, I don't want to get my hopes up,'" Angelo said.[98]

It was the worst primary defeat ever inflicted on an incumbent President.[99] Ford had attended the annual White House Correspondents dinner that Saturday evening. Although he was braced for a loss to Reagan, he had been hopeful of salvaging as many as forty of the hundred possible delegates. Ford had invited Dick Cheney, Ron Nessen, and David Kennerly to the White House residence after the dinner to watch the returns. Ford won in Maine's caucuses, as expected. But all eyes were on Texas.

As Nessen described the scene in his book *It Sure Looks Different from the Inside*, "It was clear from the 11:30 P.M. TV specials that the Texas primary was a disaster for Ford. . . .The President was alternatively glum, silent, angry and profane. 'G—damn it!' he exploded periodically."[100] Nessen dejectedly told reporters that Ford had hoped to do better in Texas. Peter Kaye, the Ford campaign's spokesman was even more forthright as he told the *New York Times,* "We were prepared to lose. We didn't expect to lose this big . . . nothing is going to be easy from now on—anywhere."[101]

The mood at the Reagan headquarters in Houston was unvarnished joy. Reagan called from Indianapolis and sang a few lines of "The Eyes of Texas Are Upon You" over a speakerphone to the cheers and delight of his supporters.[102]

The *Washington Star* called Ford's defeat in Texas, "astonishing." Reagan was so clearly controlling the agenda that each time he mentioned the Panama Canal, voters would inundate Ford's campaign offices with phone calls, wanting to know why the President was giving it away.[103] The Ford Administration denied it was going to "give away" the Panama Canal, but a congressional committee revealed at a particularly bad time for Ford that Ambassador Ellsworth Bunker was, indeed, working on that very issue. According to Witcover, a report released just before the Texas primary said that Bunker

> was acting directly on orders from Ford to negotiate a turnover of the control of the Canal Zone to Panama "after a period of time" and the canal itself "over a longer period of time." The testimony seemed to contradict what Ford had declared a few days earlier in a Dallas press conference, "I can simply say, and say it emphatically, that the United States will never give up its defense right to the Panama Canal and will never give up its operational rights as far as Panama is concerned."[104]

The Ford campaign presented Barry Goldwater to criticize Reagan on the Panama Canal after Reagan's big win, telling reporters that Reagan should stop talking about the issue since he did not understand it.[105] However, Reagan was not about to give up on something about which he cared deeply and that was helping his campaign. Rockefeller also joined in the public criticism of Reagan over the canal, but he was the last person to whom conservatives would listen.

Reagan's refrain was now all too familiar to the Ford team: "We built it! We paid for it! It's ours, and we're going to keep it!" Reagan's reference to Panamanian strongman, General Omar Torrijos as a "tinhorn dictator" was another crowd pleaser. Torrijos did not help his cause when he hinted at a "Ho Chi Minh" strategy against the United States if it did not turn over the Canal to him. But the threat only illustrated Reagan's point. He was not alone, however, as thirty-seven Senators also took tough public positions against any new treaty that would hand over control of the Canal Zone to Torrijos—enough to stop it from being ratified.[106]

In 1976, Reagan could have been talking about the Panama Canal, the Love Canal, or the Erie Canal. In some ways it did not matter. He was tapping into a deep-seated anger that had been building in the country over the losses in Vietnam and Southeast Asia, the national embarrassment over Watergate, Soviet advances, and a general feeling that America's day was over. "Vietnam was a great disillusionment to most Americans . . . the failure to win militarily in Vietnam was a failure of the national will which they desperately want redressed. Reagan is making a potent appeal to these people," Dickenson wrote in the *Washington Star*.[107]

An unsigned memo was generated in the Ford White House, analyzing the Texas results. It came to the conclusion that of the primary voters, "the people coming to vote . . . are unknown and have not been involved in the Republican political system before; they vote overwhelmingly for Reagan." It also went on to lay the "blame" for Ford's defeats at the feet of Richard Viguerie, Joseph Coors, the National Rifle Association, and a plethora of conservative groups that were spending money outside the FEC limits. The memo concluded, "We are in real danger of being out-organized by a small number of highly motivated right-wing nuts."[108]

The two candidates were now facing a faster and more furious primary and state convention schedule over the next two months. Four days after Texas would come three state primaries in Georgia, Alabama, and Indiana. The President Ford Committee once had high hopes for Georgia, as it was the home state of Bo Callaway. But he was long gone and Spencer and Morton harbored no illusions about either Southern state. Consequently, only one day of campaigning was devoted to Alabama for the President in the hope of drafting some delegates there.

In Indiana, they felt they would win, and so did the national media. After all, a statewide poll taken months earlier had shown Ford leading by twenty-five points over Reagan in the Hoosier State.[109] In fact, two days before the Indiana primary, a headline in the *New York Times* blared, "Ford and Carter Favored in Indiana Race Tuesday." Indiana state GOP Chairman Thomas Milligan told the paper that he thought Ford would receive 55 percent of the vote. Ford's own State Chair, Donald Cox, hinted that Ford's margin of victory might go even higher. Now it was Reagan's turn to manage his own expectations—and Ford's—as he told a local reporter, "This is a very uphill fight because I think the party establishment here is with the incumbent."[110]

In Indiana, three delegates were selected from each of the eleven congressional districts, and twenty-one were at-large.[111] Again, Ford had the support of the entire party infrastructure, including Governor Otis Bowen. Ford had campaigned in the state, but another glitch seemed to summarize the renewed problems of his campaign. A large balloon drop at a rally in Ft. Wayne failed to happen, and Ford was furious, threatening to drop his lead advanceman, Red Cavaney, from a ceiling the next time balloons did not drop when they should. Ford also encountered some unusually nasty questions from the crowd, and Nessen suspected they were Reagan plants. One questioner asked the President,

"Do you plan to continue to lead this country to full socialism?"[112]

One bright spot for Ford happened while campaigning in Indianapolis. In an advanceman's dream, Ford was asked by a little girl to sign her excuse from school since she was attending his rally, which he gladly did. The local and national media loved it. However, at another campaign stop before what was supposed to be a friendly crowd, Ford was booed when he reiterated his support for his beleaguered Secretary of State.[113]

Under Dave Keene's guidance, Reagan won big in two of the three contested primaries, taking all of Alabama's thirty-seven delegates and all of Georgia's eighty-five delegates. Reagan received an astonishing 71 percent of the vote in Alabama and 68 percent of the vote in Georgia. But the sweetest victory of the evening, orchestrated by Charlie Black, was Reagan's upset win in Indiana, winning with 51 percent and taking forty-five of the fifty-four delegates at stake there. The win in Indiana was particularly welcome for the Reagan team, since it was the first non-Southern state in which he won.[114]

Sears had introduced Black to Keith Bulen, an influential GOP leader in Indiana. Bulen had been somewhat tarnished by Watergate, so he opted to help Reagan behind the scenes despite having told Sears and Black—over cognac at four o'clock in the morning—that he thought Reagan was "a right-wing nut." But Bulen recruited the Indiana Chairman for Reagan, Dr. Denny Nicholas, a county coroner who thought he was really for Rockefeller until Bulen told him he was now for "that actor" Reagan.[115]

On May 4, the night of the three primaries, the President Ford Committee invited reporters to its D.C. headquarters to watch and report on the results and ply them with alcohol. As the results came in, the Ford staff became more and more despondent. When the returns were final and reporters were clamoring Morton for a comment about the Ford campaign, he blurted out, "I'm not going to rearrange the furniture on the deck of the *Titanic*!" It may have been the most unfortunate comment in the history of American politics.[116]

Morton was also photographed looking askew in front of a table filled with half-empty bottles of liquor, which was sent on all the wires and published in both the *Washington Post* and the *Washington Star*.[117] The photo was unfair, as the media, according to Jules Witcover, had consumed most of the booze.[118]

Black, with his ever-present Winston cigarettes, was a tall, lanky North Carolinian whose quiet manner belied a tough and agile political mind. Only Sears surpassed Black in his persuasive abilities, but Black could also do it without making unnecessary enemies. Although Black was as conservative as the rest of the Reaganites and a disciple of Jesse Helms, he was liked by everybody in the GOP. He considered himself a "soldier in the conservative movement."[119]

By the next day, Ford's campaign was in shambles. The President told reporters he was, "disappointed," but aides reported that he was much more than just "disappointed" and used some colorful language to denounce his campaign, Reagan, crossover states, and the media. Again, reporters at the daily White House briefing hounded Nessen. Morton and Spencer were summoned to the White House for a meeting with Ford and Cheney to discuss campaign strategy, and a conference call was arranged with GOP leaders from around the country to solicit their advice. Walter Mears of the AP wrote, "Reagan's victories put the President's political future in jeopardy."[120]

A meeting of Ford cronies and GOP "muckety-mucks" that included Senators Dole and Goldwater was also hastily arranged at the Mayflower Hotel in Washington for an all-around rant session. Cheney and Nessen did not attend, so naturally they received most of the criticism as leaked to the media. The President Ford Committee announced that sixty staffers would be laid off so that money could be devoted to other operations in the campaign. The staff would eventually be reduced from 207 to 145.[121]

It was generally agreed at this point that the Ford campaign was taking too strident a tone against Reagan, but apparently Morton did not get the memo. He told the *Washington Star*, "Mr. Reagan's demagogic statements may have gained him a temporary advantage. But every national poll shows the President to be far more popular than Mr. Reagan."[122]

Another small but nagging problem for Nessen to handle was an embarrassing story that surfaced involving White House photographer David Kennerly and Elizabeth Ray, the secretary who could not type but had other talents she had performed for Congressman Wayne Hays of Ohio, as it was later revealed. Kennerly had taken nude photos of Miss Ray and sent them to the Navy photo labs for developing. The story was leaked to *Newsweek*, and Kennerly was forced to send a check for $4.50 to cover the cost of developing.[123]

With his fourth win in a row, Reagan went ahead in the national delegate count over Ford, according to the *Washington Star's* tabulations, 381-372 with 328 uncommitted.[124]

Many of the uncommitted delegates were from "machine states" like Pennsylvania and New York and thus were believed to be pro-Ford. But in a fluid situation, anything could happen.[125] Many state party rules did not bind delegates to vote for the candidate in whose name they were chosen, and while some states did have such rules, they were virtually unenforceable. It was rare for delegates to break with their candidate, but anything was possible in 1976. Besides, no one had ever gone to jail for voting for someone other than whom they were pledged at a national convention.

It was the "jail break" of Democratic crossover voters that deeply worried Morton, Cheney, Spencer, and others at the Ford White House and campaign. On the Democratic side, opposition to Carter had largely collapsed, which gave further credence to the notion that even more Democrats might cross over to vote for Reagan. Four of the next six primaries would be held in states that permitted Democrats to vote in Republican primaries, including Ford's home state of Michigan.

Michigan had a sizable quantity of Democrats who fit the profile of what would eventually become known as the "Reagan Democrat." They included blue-collar laborers, Catholics, pro-life advocates, NRA enthusiasts, and union members. If Ford lost in his own backyard, it would be the end of his bid. And in a new poll by the *New York Times*, Reagan was running strongest against Ford among Catholics, garnering a majority of their vote. Senator Bob Griffin of Michigan, a close Ford ally, told the *Star* that no longer could Michigan "be taken for granted."[126]

One week after Ford's triple loss were the primaries in West Virginia and Nebraska, The President was still expected to do well in both. But over a period of only eleven days, beginning with the Arizona and South Carolina state conventions, Reagan had won 282 delegates to Ford's twenty-seven.[127]

On his way to campaign in Nebraska, Ford first made a brief appearance in President Harry Truman's hometown of Independence, Missouri, where he attended the unveiling of a statue of the former President, whom Ford considered his role model.

Ford also unveiled a new tone when he told the ten thousand people in attendance, "President Truman, like Abraham Lincoln, had a great faith in the ultimate good sense of the people."[128] Ford continued, "He liked them, he liked their language—and in 1948 they went to the polls and proved that his faith was fully justified." One several occasions, Ford became emotional when talking about Truman's travails. Indeed, the *New York Times*, covering the event, wrote, "Some observers said they sensed that Mr. Ford's emotion might bespeak an awareness that his Presidency could be of a brief duration."[129]

But Truman was driven from the race in 1952, and this was the historical analogy on the Reaganites' minds, not 1948. Ford's campaign was consoling itself with a new poll from the *New York Times* that showed him far ahead of Reagan nationally. But the poll could not measure the intensity of support in individual states. The "natives" were Reagan people, coming out of both parties, and they would continue to give Ford fits. Meanwhile, the *Washington Star's* political cartoonist, Pat Oliphant, who possessed a dagger for an ink pen, depicted Reagan as an aging tortoise running over and then away from Ford, the hare. *Newsweek's* cover headline was "A President in Jeopardy."[130]

Under fire from all quarters, Ford now found someone in his backyard taking aim. New York GOP Chairman Richard Rosenbaum led a coalition of ten northeast states that included all of New England, Pennsylvania, and several others. Taking full advantage of Ford's predicament, they were threatening to withhold their 300 uncommitted delegates unless those delegates played a large role in writing the Republican Party's platform and had a major voice in Ford's choice for his running mate.

To place the Ford White House on notice, Rosenbaum invited John Sears to a highly publicized two-hour meeting at the Hotel Roosevelt in New York. Cheney, Spencer, and Morton were not amused at Rosenbaum's strong-arm tactics. They sensed the unseen hand of Rockefeller behind Rosenbaum's actions.[131] Rosenbaum hinted that if Ford lost his home state of Michigan, a third candidate might come into the race. No one needed to guess who that third candidate might be, since the man in question had harbored Presidential aspirations since he had first been elected Governor of New York in 1958.

Regarding the Texas victory, the Ford campaign had filed yet another complaint against the Reagan campaign, charging potential illegal coordination between Citizens for Reagan and independent groups supporting him there, as well as overlapping contributors. The groups named included the Texas-based Delegates for Reagan, the American Conservative Union, Conservative Victory Fund, and the National Conservative Political Action Committee.[132]

Becky Norton, a talented and strong-willed conservative from Ohio, had initially worked for the ACU, but later went to Texas to help out with the Reagan campaign. Having pitched in to help with the New Hampshire and Florida campaigns, Texas was her second tour with Reagan. She served as an effective Press Secretary for Reagan's operations there. Although no laws were broken, Loren Smith, the General Counsel for Citizens for Reagan, thought it best that Norton remain with the ACU for the duration of the campaign after the Texas primary. Her work was not the focus of the Ford's campaign's complaint.[133]

Smith brushed off the complaint in a letter to the President Ford Committee saying, "Your quarrel is not with our committee but with Mr. Ford who signed a confusing and poorly drafted bill."[134] Since the FEC was at that time in limbo, awaiting action by the Congress and the Ford White House, it had no enforcement powers to investigate the charges. Sauce for the goose, since all the campaigns—including both Carter's and Reagan's—suspected politics was involved in the Ford White House's unwillingness to sign a new FEC bill that would allow the matching funds to be disbursed to the campaigns.

Reagan staffers also marveled at the ability of the Ford campaign to outspend Reagan in the primaries and still remain in the black. Ford had a unique advantage over Reagan and over prospective Democratic opponents because the commercial airlines would grant credit to his campaign. Conversely, all the challengers had to pay up front.[135] In fact, the commercial airlines' credit to Ford had been extended to sixty and—in some cases—ninety days, effectively granting the President's campaign interest-free loans worth hundreds of thousands of dollars. In addition, Ford could use White House employees, whose salaries were paid for by the taxpayers, to plan his travel and handle many of his political issues. He also could use Air Force One and government limousines when his travel was classified as "non-political."[136]

Still, these advantages did not dissuade Nessen from complaining to reporters about independent groups supporting Reagan who were using "loopholes" in the laws. "Perhaps in some places, 80 percent of the advertising for former Governor Reagan is paid for by groups which say they are unauthorized or unofficial and therefore don't have to report their spending," he told the *New York Times*.[137]

Ford arrived in Omaha, Nebraska, via Air Force One for two days of campaigning. Following the shellacking they had been taking over the previous several weeks, his campaign hoped to rebound in the primaries in Nebraska and in West Virginia the following Tuesday. Also, the state Republican parties began their delegate selection process in Oklahoma, Louisiana, and Missouri, on Saturday, May 8, while Wyoming and Kansas would host state conventions.

Ford continued with the new strategy of projecting an upbeat tone. He emphasized the accomplishments of his Administration, his plans for a second Ford Administration, and a fresh start in the primaries against Reagan. Several days before, the Ford campaign had floated a trial balloon in the media portraying Reagan as "dangerous." But Cheney killed that idea. He was nearly unique in the Ford White House and among the campaign staffers. He never made fun of Reagan and had always taken him much more seriously than anyone else around Ford. "I was a conservative and a Westerner, so I understood Reagan better," he said.[138]

"The fight for the Presidency begins again here in Nebraska on Tuesday,"

Ford told reporters on Air Force One.[139] Ford also backed off on his attacks on Reagan and never mentioned his name or inferred his presence in the race. No longer was he telling crowds that Reagan's credibility was "severely at stake," as he had done in Texas.

While the "local boy makes good" argument did not work for Reagan in Illinois, Ford had higher hopes for Nebraska. In his first day of campaigning in the Cornhusker State, Ford stopped by the home where he was born and told the crowd of supporters there that he was "the first native of Nebraska to serve as President of the United States."[140] Later that day, he delivered the commencement address at the University of Nebraska and kept to the high road.

The high command of the Ford campaign had concluded that while some in the GOP were not enthralled with Reagan's conservatism, Republicans almost universally liked him. Ford's attacks in Texas and elsewhere were seen as beneath the dignity of the President and personally unfair to Reagan. It would remain to be seen if the new strategy would work.

Reagan had yet another good Saturday and began to extend his delegate lead over Ford, starting on May 8. Several states were beginning their caucus and convention delegate selection processes. In Wyoming's GOP state convention, Reagan would prevail by ten to seven. In Oklahoma's first round of delegate selection, Reagan first took eighteen and would eventually win all of the thirty-six delegates that were to be selected. In Louisiana, Reagan seized nine delegates initially, and he eventually won thirty-six delegates to Ford's five at the state convention on May 15.[141]

At Missouri's state convention, held on June 11, guerilla tactics combined with skillful legerdemain by Reagan's ground forces seized victory from the jaws of defeat for Reagan. Delegates had been elected to the state convention on May 8, and it appeared at the time that most, if not all, of the delegates selected in the Show Me State for the national convention would go to Ford. The Ford forces were hoping to win big in both Kansas and Missouri, to begin the process of blunting the Reagan recovery and claim that the President's campaign itself was recovering. Sears and Keene had made a brief trip to Missouri to scout the situation but quickly concluded that Reagan's chances there were questionable. They eventually dispatched Don Devine and Morton Blackwell, two seasoned and savvy conservative infighters who specialized in convention politics, to handle the Missourians.[142] Earlier, on April 25 at district caucuses, 1,439 delegates had been elected to attend Missouri's GOP state convention.[143]

The unguided missile of the GOP, Barry Goldwater, appeared in fresh radio ads attacking Reagan in Nebraska and telling listeners, "I know Ronald Reagan's public statements concerning the Panama Canal contained gross factual errors. . . .

He has clearly represented himself in an irresponsible manner on an issue which could affect the nation's security."[144] In an interview with the *New York Times*, Goldwater professed his "love and affection" for Reagan, but the paper reported that the Senator's behavior had left many conservatives puzzled and hurt.[145] Several days later, Goldwater rebuked the commercials he appeared in, saying he had never authorized them. Stu Spencer's answer to Goldwater's claim was short, simple, and impossible to misinterpret: "bulls—." Even so, the ads were pulled.[146]

Reagan won in Nebraska by a surprisingly comfortable margin of 55 percent to 45 percent and took the majority of delegates eighteen to seven.[147] Statewide polls taken for the two of major newspapers, the *Omaha World-Tribune* and the *Lincoln Journal*, had shown Ford with a large lead over Reagan just one month before.[148] It was Reagan's first win in a closed primary state and this fact was not lost on the President Ford Committee. Over the previous several weeks, they had begun a drumbeat of public complaints about Democrats being able to help pick the Presidential nominee of the Republican Party. The argument met with hostility in the press when the Reagan forces pointed out that the eventual nominee had to appeal to more than just Republicans. Since Reagan was doing so much better with Democrats, wasn't he the better nominee for the fall campaign?

This was not overlooked by Reagan, either, as he had been stung by charges over the previous several weeks that he was making an appeal similar to George Wallace, telling reporters that his win would "answer some of the charges that have been made in the last few primaries. This kind of confirms it wasn't a Wallace vote or anything of that kind. It was a legitimate test within the Republican Party."[149]

Despite his new nice guy strategy, Ford got poor reviews in Nebraska. Another major factor in his loss was the "off again—on again" grain embargo against the Soviets and the lingering resentment in this farm state. Ford was also handicapped because of disorganization by his campaign on the ground and its inability to tell primary voters which delegates running were for Ford. The Reagan forces in Nebraska had out-hustled their opponents in the weeks leading to the primary.

Nebraska was disheartening for Carter too, as he lost to a late entry into the Democratic field, Senator Frank Church of Idaho. But it was the Reagan victory that was on everybody's lips, not the Carter loss. "Frankly, the Ford campaign wasn't very good," said his media man, Doug Bailey.[150] R. W. "Johnny" Apple of the *New York Times* wrote that "many influential Republicans" were telling him that "they now consider it possible, if not probable, that Mr. Ford could become the first Republican President denied the nomination since Chester A. Arthur in 1886."[151]

A young Reagan aide, Pat Pizzella, was dispatched to Charleston to see if he could "jumpstart" the local Reagan effort. Pizzella found to his chagrin that the two women in charge did not believe in using direct mail or telephones to organize a campaign. As he recalled, "they mostly sat around smoking cigarettes and b—ed about everything."[152] One of the women, State Senator Judith Herndon, was publicly rebuked for not allowing a list of the pro-Reagan delegates to be published or circulated. She was fearful of offending the GOP powers-that-were in West Virginia who wanted to be elected as uncommitted delegates.[153]

Ford could take some solace over his win in West Virginia, 57 percent of the vote to Reagan's 43 percent, especially since Reagan had campaigned there, and Ford had not.[154] While the Ford campaign had expected this good news, it had gone three weeks without a win anywhere, so it was welcome.

But the *New York Times*, along with most of the national media, was focused on Nebraska, not West Virginia, and wrote in an editorial, "The Nebraska defeat transforms Mr. Ford's political condition from serious to critical. If he loses in Michigan next week, it may well become terminal."[155] And it was Reagan whom the media was now calling the "frontrunner."

10

FORD STORMS BACK

"That damned Stu Spencer!"

As the new leader for the Republican Presidential nomination, Ronald Reagan now looked to press the advantage over his wounded opponent. Campaigning in Idaho before heading to Ford's adopted home state of Michigan, Reagan told a crowd, "With Jimmy Carter the possible, or even probable, Democratic nominee, Republicans are faced with some important questions. Will we, as a party, be offering new solutions to old problems or defending old policies against the attacks of a Democrat who is not part of the Washington establishment?" Reagan continued, "The results of the last several primaries—in both parties—reveal a great desire on the part of the people for a change, an end to politics as usual."[1]

Looking down the road, Reagan told conservatives and the media that it was he, and not Ford, who could successfully challenge Carter in the South in the fall campaign. He said of his eventual choice for a Vice Presidential candidate that he would, "look to the same Republican mainstream for a running mate whose principles are strong and whose practices are sensible."[2]

Media coverage in the weeks leading up to the May 18 Michigan primary included apocalyptic phrases like "crucial," "critical," "embarrassment," "vital," "embattled" and "last chance," when describing Ford's campaign in his home state primary, which would be held two weeks after his disastrous triple loss to Reagan in Indiana, Georgia and Alabama.

The *New York Times* editorialized, "A second unfavorable omen for Mr. Ford is the geographic location of most of the remaining primaries. The Northeast and the industrialized Middle West, the two regions where the President is strongest, have already chosen most of their delegates." Besides Michigan, only primaries in Ohio, New Jersey and Rhode Island remained. "Otherwise, the candidates fight it out in a dozen Southern, border, and Western states where Mr. Reagan can be expected to do well."[3]

The Reagan campaign weighed a more aggressive effort in Michigan, since it, like Texas, provided for crossover voting. In 1972, hundreds of thousands of

Republicans had crossed over to join the other 800,000 who voted in the Democratic primary for George Wallace, helping him win.[4] Now there was a very real threat to Ford that the same might happen in reverse, to Reagan's benefit. As always, however, money was a major problem for the Reagan campaign.

Adding to Ford's worries was the fact that Wallace had nearly disappeared from the field and, in Michigan as in Texas, his supporters could be cut adrift to potentially land on Reagan's shore. Wallace's political support was fading before the new, ascending son of the South, Jimmy Carter. Wallace would be on the ballot in Michigan but would be doing little active campaigning.

The *New York Times* took a look at the "typical" Wallace/Reagan voters and, in turn at cultural stereotyping, described them as, "nursing their frustrations about government giveaways, welfare cheaters, featherbedding bureaucrats who loaf, and politicians who are tax-squeezing the middle class to pay for social programs that do not work." A sociologist told the Times they were, "middle class radicals."[5]

Michigan, of course, was the President's backyard. Though he had been born Leslie Lynch King Jr. in Omaha in 1913, his parents had divorced at an early age. After moving to Michigan, his mother remarried a man named Gerald Rudolph Ford. At an early age, his adoptive father, whom he adored, changed Leslie's name to Gerald R. Ford Jr.[6]

President Ford had grown up in Michigan and was voted most valuable player by his teammates when he played center in the 1930s for the Wolverines.[7] Though he'd gone to Yale School of Law and had served heroically in the Navy during WWII, his plan had always been to return to Grand Rapids.

Ford was elected to the Congress after a primary victory over the incumbent conservative Republican, Bartel Jonkman, in 1948. He served for twenty-five years until being tapped by Richard Nixon to become his Vice President.[8] Ford had intended to retire in 1976 after the added burdens of serving as House Minority Leader for eight years and promised his wife as much. They planned on returning to Grand Rapids, where Ford would add his name to a law firm, teach, lecture, play golf, and enjoy his retirement years.

Watergate changed all that.

He had suffered great embarrassment, much of it undeserved, in serving his country as President. Now he was faced with the real possibility of his greatest embarrassment: losing his own home state primary to Reagan and with it, the nomination of the Republican Party. As important as winning the North Carolina primary was to Ronald Reagan, Michigan was even more important to Ford.

He had the usual lineup of elected GOP officials and the Republican state party supporting him in Michigan, but their assistance had been less than decisive in other states and he could not count on their support bringing him to victory now. Typical was Governor William Milliken, yet another of the moderate to liberal Republican Governors supporting Ford. Milliken held little sway over the conservative primary voters in Michigan, and virtually none over the conservative Democrats who were expected to turn out in droves for Reagan.[9]

Ford was also taking more flak from the national media, as when one reporter asked him if he would be interested in serving as Ronald Reagan's Vice President.[10] Even better for Reagan, it was now he, not Ford, whom Carter was attacking. Carter labeled the Californian, "divisive." But Carter also noted that Reagan "has much more fervent support" than Ford.[11]

Widespread discontent in America with "politics as usual" had propelled both Reagan and Carter to the forefront of their parties' attention. H. L. Mencken once wrote, "The only way to look at a politician is down," and though politicians had always been the butt of jokes and the focus of derision, in 1976 they were especially despised. Good news for Reagan and Carter, because of all the major candidates running for President, they had never served in office in Washington, worked in a government agency, or lived in the nation's capital. They were unique outsiders, and each honed a populist message of reform that he would bring to Washington if elected.

Reagan heard more good news out of Indiana when a *New York Times/CBS News* post-election poll found that GOP voters in the Hoosier State thought Reagan had a better chance of winning in the fall than Ford.[12] Reagan had also benefited in Indiana from radio commercials and print advertisements produced and placed by the American Conservative Union, just as the organization had done in North Carolina and Texas.[13] Stan Evans, a former editor of the *Indianapolis Star* who had become Chairman of the ACU, told the *New York Times* that Ford was, "operationally a liberal, whatever his subjective opinions."[14] The group hit Ford hard, including linking him with feminist Congresswoman Bella Abzug of New York City.[15]

Panic deepened at the Ford White House as aides continued to try to solve the mystery of Ronald Reagan, his message, and Ford's lack of appeal. Ford had always been baffled at why, exactly, Reagan had taken him on in the first place. Ford believed that he was just as conservative as Reagan and had earned the right to the nomination. Ford further could not understand why conservatives in the Republican Party could not see that campaign rhetoric was one thing, but ideology should be subdued when it came to governance. Conventional wisdom at the time inside the Republican Party was that if they were to succeed, Republicans had to be "pragmatic," they had to "broaden the base," and they had to "compromise." Otherwise, they would always be in the minority.

Another sign of fear emerged when it was discovered that in a meeting between Ford and Republican elected officials, one Senator suggested that Ford ask for Kissinger's resignation as a response to Reagan's attacks. Ford rejected the idea, knowing that to do so would inevitably lead to the conclusion that Reagan had been right all along about the Administration's foreign policy.[16]

At the same time, the League of Women Voters announced that they were planning to host Presidential debates in the fall between the nominees of the two parties.[17] Kennedy and Nixon had participated in four debates in 1960, but Johnson refused to debate Goldwater in 1964, as did Nixon in 1968 with Humphrey and again in 1972 against McGovern. The prevailing thinking in 1976 was that no debates would take place, because one camp or another would feel the risks weren't worth it.

Bookies in London also now saw Reagan as the favorite. Playboy Bookmakers, a division of Hugh Hefner's empire, offered odds on Reagan's nomination at six to four. One month before, his campaign was going off at ten to one against. Ford had been the favorite at eleven to ten, but had fallen to seven to four against him becoming the GOP nominee.[18]

Campaigning in Baton Rouge, Reagan predicted a first ballot nomination. District delegates had been chosen in the state, but the delegates to go to the Republican National Convention would be chosen on June 5 at Louisiana's state convention. Telling the crowd about campaigning earlier in the day in Shreveport, Reagan said, "This morning, I arrived at the airport at Shreveport and saw a crowd I had not anticipated, complete with a high school band. Suddenly it dawned on me: We're way ahead of where our projections were for this point. So, for the first time, standing there, I said to these people what I discovered suddenly I believe in my own heart, that I can go to the convention with enough delegates to win on the first ballot."[19]

Indeed, Reagan was ahead in the delegate count. Most of New York's 154 previously uncommitted delegates were about to be thrown into Ford's pot to help the beleaguered President. But Brooklyn's Chairman, George Clark, was a conservative who detested liberal Republicans in New York. Clark controlled eighteen delegates and John Sears was hoping to bargain for these and a few more from Upstate New York in the next few months leading up to the convention.[20]

Sears faced an uphill battle for the bulk of New York's delegates. Many of the uncommitted delegates were ready to switch their status, but they were presumed to support either Ford or Nelson Rockefeller, rather than Reagan. The *New York*

Times asked Rockefeller if he might yet become a candidate. Instead of offering a flat "no," the cagey old pol simply said, "I don't see that scenario."[21]

Some good news for Ford came in a poll conducted for conservative Senator Jim Buckley by Arthur Finkelstein which showed the President to be more popular with the New York Republicans than either Reagan or Rockefeller.[22]

New Jersey's Republicans were also anxiously awaiting a better effort from Ford in the primaries. Early on, Reagan's campaign had written off its chances there, as New Jersey had a long tradition of electing moderate to liberal Republicans. The entire lineup of elected GOP officials was supporting Ford. A handful of moderates and liberals including Assembly Speaker Thomas Kean, U.S. Senator Clifford Case, and three Congressmen—including pipe-smoking Millicent Fenwick—had climbed aboard the Ford bandwagon in early March.[23] Although the delegates would technically run as uncommitted, the GOP machine in New Jersey would control whom they voted for in Kansas City.[24]

A small, disorganized group of New Jersey conservatives was attempting to file slates for Reagan in some of the more favorable areas. But they had little money and no support or direction from the Washington office of Citizens for Reagan. Sixty-seven delegates were at stake. Of the four big industrial states where the Reagan campaign would make only a half-hearted effort—New York, Pennsylvania, Ohio, and New Jersey—Sears reasoned that Reagan had the least chance of winning or bargaining for delegates in New Jersey. "Despite Mr. Ford's recent losses to the former California Governor in Indiana and the South and the political trouble the President is believed to be in in his home state of Michigan, New Jersey is regarded as a strong Ford state. 'What we anticipate is that New Jersey will be the President's trump card,' a Republican leader said this afternoon," wrote the *New York Times*.[25]

Internal strife within Ford's operation deepened. One side believed he was squandering the advantages of incumbency and called for pulling him back from too much campaigning. Yet the other side argued just as vociferously that he needed to take to the road and fight by calling Reagan an "extremist," a "demagogue," and a "zealot."

Eventually, a hybrid emerged, with Ford campaigning aggressively on the road. Instead of talking down Reagan, he would talk up his and his Administration's accomplishments. It would be a departure from the barbs the two were leveling at each other. Ford had told one audience, "Reagan and I both played football. I played for Michigan and he played for Warner Brothers."[26] Reagan said, "Well at least when I played football, I played with my helmet on."[27]

According to all media reports, Reagan was comfortably ahead of Ford in the delegate count, but the "x-factor" was the uncommitted delegates and whether or not state party bosses could control them. Further, most believed at the time that neither man would have enough delegates for a first ballot nomination. The Republican Party faced the real possibility of its first brokered convention in years.

Despite enacting their "Scenario Number Two" strategy to replace the failed quick knockout strategy, poor planning by the Reagan campaign would come back to haunt them in the delegate rich states of New York, Pennsylvania, Ohio, and New Jersey. An earlier effort to target congressional districts in conservative areas within those states might have yielded the campaign more delegates than they eventually received. By not organizing in these states, the campaign also overlooked the effect some Reagan delegates may have had as "inside" lobbyists within their individual delegations prior to and at the convention.

But the Reagan campaign was encouraged in states like Colorado and Missouri, which appeared to have uncommitted delegates who were open to persuasion. Reports from these states indicated that Reagan's recent surge was giving delegates pause, as they considered seriously the candidacy of the Californian. The White House and President Ford Committee heard these reports too and found them disquieting. "There is a developing trend for people we had counted on in the caucus states to move to an uncommitted posture," said one worried Ford official.[28]

Ford had decided to continue his high road strategy by "acting Presidential" and would only refer to Reagan obliquely, for the most part. However, each time a White House aide would announce to the media that Ford was "acting Presidential" or "being Presidential," this would only serve to undermine his credibility further with the American people as being somehow phony.[29]

The Ford high command also decided that Reagan had been given the upper hand for too long in the campaign, especially on matters of foreign policy and national defense. They decided that Ford needed to start making his own headlines on these issues. Reagan had been dominating the debate ever since North Carolina. As Senator Bob Dole of Kansas told Elizabeth Drew, "Reagan has been running both campaigns, his and Ford's. He lays out the issues, and Ford responds."[30]

Ford kicked off his new offensive with a speech in which he promised to keep the military "not strong for the sake of war, but strong for the sake of peace."[31] To help jump-start his flagging campaign, a resolution was prepared by Republican members of Congress that praised Ford for striving "effectively for a strong national defense." Every member of the Republican leadership on Capitol Hill save one, Congressman John Rhodes of Arizona, signed it.[32] The President headed to Michigan for several days of intensive campaigning, with quick side trips to Tennessee and Kentucky, where later primaries were to be held.

Meanwhile, an interesting story broke when it was learned that Soviet agents had made overtures to the Carter campaign, expressing outright opposition to the prospect of the nomination of Senator Henry "Scoop" Jackson on the Democratic side and dismay over Ford's recent retreat from détente. The Soviets also suggested to Carter's aides that they could possibly pursue policies that could affect the outcome of the election so as to favor Carter.[33] The Soviets blamed Reagan for publicly embarrassing Ford into a new, tougher stance against them.

It wasn't the first time the Soviets had attempted to influence the outcome of an American Presidential election. In 1960, it was generally assumed that the Soviets delayed the release of American U-2 pilot Gary Powers until after the election to help John F. Kennedy defeat Richard Nixon. The Soviets had also tried to affect the outcome in 1968 to help Hubert Humphrey defeat Richard Nixon. But by 1972, the Soviets had developed a taste for Nixon's policies and, as the *New York Times* wrote, "showered attention and friendship on Mr. Nixon in his race against McGovern."[34]

The Ford White House was also taking a tougher stance against Reagan and any Democratic candidates for that matter, since a bill reconstituting the Federal Election Commission had yet to be signed by the President. Reagan's campaign estimated that the FEC owed them approximately $2.2 million dollars in matching funds. Reagan's debts, around $1.2 million, were mounting daily.[35]

Charlie Black again was faced with running a threadbare effort, this time in Michigan, as he had been in Wisconsin, Illinois, and the other states in his region. He was doubly unfortunate because in most of his states, there were no homegrown grassroots organizations—like those that had emerged in North Carolina and Texas—to carry the load for the cash-strapped national campaign of Ronald Reagan. Spirits were high in the Reagan campaign, but if some money didn't loosen up quickly, they would be facing a fresh set of problems.[36]

Despite his string of losses, Ford still could marshal all the powers of his office and the party while Reagan had only his conservative message, which jibed with the attitudes of the American people. According to a poll conducted by the *Washington Post*, a majority, 54 percent, favored a smaller government with fewer services, as opposed to 46 percent who favored a larger government and more services. But it remained to be seen if Reagan could continue to win the upcoming primaries without the array of resources the President had at his command.[37]

Ford's message was simple and direct: "Peace, prosperity and trust are my record of performance in the nearly two years since I became President." For all concerned, however, Michigan might well be Ford's last stand. "But the President, opening an intensified, last-ditch campaign effort in the state, seemed in a somber mood, reflecting the fact that his quest for the Republican Presidential nomination was in trouble," the *Times* wrote. "Members of his campaign staff . . . have conceded that a loss here in his home state, coming on top of other sharp setbacks at Mr. Reagan's hands, would be an extremely damaging blow to his chances of winning the nomination."[38]

At one stop, a speech before the Economic Club of Detroit, Ford asked rhetorically why he was asking Americans and Michiganders for their vote. Then he answered himself in a woeful manner, saying, "Because I've done a good job. Because I've turned a lot of things around and we're going in the right direction. Because I want a mandate from Michigan and the American people to finish the job."[39]

Ford was introduced by Milliken, who could not conceal his contempt for Reagan. "Narrow concepts and shallow rhetoric," was how he described the Californian's agenda in his presentation.[40] He had also cut a radio commercial attacking Reagan on his "box office diplomacy," calling Michigan "the state where the celluloid candidacy of Ronald Reagan will be exposed."[41]

While Ford was tied down in Michigan, the Reagan campaign again trumped the Ford campaign when it was announced by Sears in Washington that George Clark, the leader of the Brooklyn Republican Party, would endorse Reagan. Clark predicted he could deliver fourteen of his eighteen delegates, plus himself, for Reagan in Kansas City. Richard Rosenbaum, the State Chairman, was not pleased.[42]

Ford finally signed a bill reconstituting the FEC several days before the Michigan primary, but then declined to appoint the six Commissioners necessary to reactivate the agency, thus effectively delaying the millions owed all the candidates running for President.[43] The Senate would have to confirm the six Commissioners, though it had adjourned the Friday before the Michigan and Maryland primaries and would not return to session until the following week. But since Ford had actually never sent six nominees to the Senate for its consideration, the finer point of the Congress being out of session was moot.

The Administration had been put on the defensive by Reagan's charges over the Panama Canal. But by May, Henry Kissinger engaged in a counter-offensive, attacking Reagan for interfering with the negotiations, telling the *Boston Herald American* that Reagan's public pronouncements on the canal "have certainly not helped the negotiations." He also told the newspaper that Reagan's position on the Panama Canal was a "disaster."[44]

Yet another example where Reagan was certainly having an impact on the Ford Administration's foreign policy was the abrupt delay of a long planned signing ceremony with the Soviet Union to limit the megatonnage of underground nuclear blasts.[45] Speculation was rampant that the White House wanted to avoid handing Reagan yet another contentious foreign policy issue to use against Ford.

Pressure was increasing for Ford. A supporter who was running as one of his delegates from New Jersey, former Congressman Charles Sandman, told the *New York Times*, "The President should withdraw as a candidate if he loses to former Governor Ronald Reagan . . . in next week's Presidential primary election in Michigan." Sandman went even further, saying a close race there could "finish the President" and that Ford was "already terribly weakened." Sandman also said that he would assist in organizing a meeting of New Jersey's Republicans to determine their next move.

Though he was a conservative who personally liked Reagan, Sandman opposed Reagan for either position on the national ticket, likening his nomination to Goldwater's in 1964. Sandman preferred Rockefeller as the party's standard-bearer should Ford falter in the face of the Reagan challenge.[46]

Clark had more confidence in Reagan than Sandman did. At a press conference at the Biltmore Hotel with Paul Laxalt, Clark announced that fifteen New York delegates, all from Brooklyn, had endorsed Ronald Reagan. "It illustrates Mr. Reagan's strength in the New York delegation and it comes at a significant time for us in relation to the momentum we have developed in other states," Laxalt told the assembled reporters. Rosenbaum would have much more to worry about in the days and weeks ahead. The Reagan camel had its nose under his tent, and Rosenbaum didn't like the lobbying that was going on inside one bit.[47]

Two more FEC complaints were filed against the Ford campaign, one by Citizens for Reagan and another from the Democratic National Committee. The DNC asked for the FEC to review its earlier decision to allow the Republican National Committee to pay for Ford's political travels in late 1975. While the Reagan complaint was that all the expenditures by the Ford committee were not being reported, it also asked again that Kissinger's travels be charged to the Ford campaign, rather than the U.S. taxpayers. In his letter to the Commission, Reagan General Counsel Loren Smith wrote, "It is clear to everybody that Dr. Kissinger is using his high office for the express purpose of a campaign platform to promote the Ford candidacy."[48] Both complaints were harassing actions, designed to distract the President Ford Committee from the more immediate task of winning in Michigan.

Reagan arrived in Detroit on May 14 and delivered a speech of his own to the Economic Club, sharply criticizing the regulations Washington was placing on the long-suffering auto industry. The two thousand attendees greeted him warmly. Reagan said, "The automobile and the men and women who make it are under constant attack from Washington . . . from the elitists, some of whom feel guilty because Americans have built such a prosperous nation, and some of whom seem obsessed with the need to substitute government control in place of individual decision making."

Continuing his remarks, Reagan blamed Ford for the plights of the auto industry. He cited the energy bill the President had signed the previous December, because it contained mandates to the industry and "regulates the marketplace, dictates to the consumer and, in the process, will make Detroit's unemployment problem worse than it already is." Reagan also charged that Ford's signing of the legislation could cost Detroit over two hundred thousand jobs.[49]

At a press conference before the speech, Reagan downplayed his chances for a victory in the Wolverine State and gave himself little chance of an upset, telling reporters he could not be expected to win against "even an appointed incumbent in his home state." Reagan avoided calling on Ford to get out of the race if he lost in Michigan, saying, "That's his decision, not mine." He then elaborated, noting that he'd been in much the same position as Ford less than two months before, in the weeks leading up to the North Carolina primary. As pressure had mounted for Reagan to get out of the race, he explained, "Somebody tried to make decisions for me and I didn't like it."[50]

Reagan would only devote a little over twenty-four hours to campaigning in the state, with airport rallies in Flint, Battle Creek, and Kalamazoo.[51] Several other speeches and receptions were thrown into the schedule. There was little money for television, radio, newspaper ads, phone banks, or even an official office for Citizens for Reagan.

But the Reagan forces also knew that cross-pressuring conservative voters' desire to cast their ballots for Reagan was their pride in a home state hero. Even if the Reagan campaign would have had the necessary financial resources, it would have been difficult to defeat the President in his hometown. In fact, Ford finally found a solution to the mystery of combating the crossover votes Reagan was receiving in one primary after another: if you can't beat 'em, join 'em. Ford decided to make open appeals to Michigan's Democrats to vote for him in the primary, playing on their sympathies and their desire to not embarrass one of their own.[52]

Party affiliation was declining at the time, especially among Republicans. The cliché, "I vote for the man and not the party," had a great deal of basis in fact. In 1972, nine of the twenty-three primary states allowed for crossover voting. But by 1976, fourteen of the thirty primaries, or almost half, allowed for crossover voting.[53] Political analysts at the time misinterpreted Reagan's appeal to conservative voters as unrepresentative of the majority of voters. In fact, both parties had vocal conservative elements and conservatives constituted the majority of the Republican Party. Liberal Republicans described conservatives in the GOP as a "minority of a minority." But in fact, the opposite was true. The leadership of the Republican Party was unrepresentative of the grassroots of the party, though Reagan's leadership was supplanting the old guard with his new, bold, conservative ideas. Reagan was accelerating the process of redefining the two parties that Goldwater had begun twelve years earlier. America was, in fact, a majority conservative country. Reagan knew this better than anyone else at the time. How?

Jeff Bell once recounted how Reagan spent so much time reading and answering his mail, which Bell thought was a waste of time: "Reagan would spend endless hours reading and answering his personal mail. I now believe it was at the heart of his populism. It gave him a vivid window on how voters think."[54]

A new distraction developed for Reagan as he headed into the Michigan primary. The *New York Times* published an analysis of the income statements his campaign had released several months earlier. In a front-page story, on May 16, two days before the primary, the paper charged that Reagan, "almost certainly paid no Federal income tax in 1970."[55] Speaking for the campaign, Peter Hannaford denied the charge, but the damage had been done.[56] The allegations were heavily reported in Michigan and were seen by millions of taxpaying citizens who resided there. Hannaford's denial was in a much shorter article and was buried on page nineteen of the paper two days later on May 18, the day of the Michigan primary.

Meanwhile, Senator Jacob Javits of New York, a liberal and supporter of Ford, blasted Reagan in a speech before the Ripon Society in New York. The Ripon Society was named after Ripon, Wisconsin—one of the locations where the Republican Party was believed to have been founded. The organization was decidedly liberal, and Javits's speech was met with great fanfare and support. Javits charged Reagan would take the Republican Party, "on the way to extinction as a national governing alternative before the year is out." Javits argued that Ford could lose "to a candidate who has adopted positions so extreme that they would alter our country's very economic and social structure and our place in the world to such a degree as to make our country's policy at home and abroad, as we know it, a thing of the past."[57]

Reagan's response was more measured than Javits's hyperbole. At an airport press conference in Los Angeles, he said, "Senator Javits has talked about the

Republican Party being destroyed for years and years and, so far, it hasn't been destroyed. I would like to have Senator Javits's support if I'm a nominee, but I would also match my record of service to the Republican Party and my devotion to not destroying the party against that of Senator Javits any time." Javits also broke with the agreement of the New York Republicans and declared his intention to vote for Ford at the convention.[58]

Javits's intemperate remarks about Reagan were in fact tame. Harsher rhetoric was often used when liberals were describing conservatives. For all the rhetoric stating that conservatives were the haters, in fact, the crueler, more baseless charges came far more often from the Left rather than the Right.

The Saturday before the Michigan primary, which would be held on Tuesday, May 18, Ford stumped the state, from Flint to Niles, via a train called the "Presidential Express."[59] Ford campaigned for three of the final five days in Michigan leading up to its primary, much of it by this train, which included six stainless steel Amtrak cars and an observation car. The *New York Times* speculated that it might have been the first time a President had campaigned by train since Harry Truman in 1948. Stops included Lansing, Kalamazoo, and Battle Creek. Large and friendly crowds turned out, and Ford appealed to their sense of pride in having a fellow Michigander in the White House. "Help us on Tuesday," was Ford's oft-used phrase.[60]

The President took stock of his two years in office, saying, "When I was sworn in, I said our long national nightmare was over. And it is. . . . My Administration has been as honest, as open and as candid as I can make it and so is my campaign for the high office I hold." Ford may have been getting more comfortable campaigning on the stump, but no one ever called him "electrifying."[61] Ford also cited the improving economy. But in Michigan, unemployment remained at 12 percent.[62] Still, the reaction was good and the media coverage positive. But with Wallace's campaign on life support, no one could really know what would happen on Tuesday.

Reagan's campaign had decided that their candidate should only spend one day in the state, reasoning that if he campaigned heavily and Ford won big, the result would be interpreted as a major setback for Reagan. But if Reagan campaigned only a little and did well, or even won, then Ford would be finished.

Also, the Reagan campaign was eyeing the delegates at stake in Michigan, since they would be apportioned proportionally. So a limited grassroots effort was mounted, but nothing compared to the campaign Ford was waging. Reagan's campaign was still financially strapped. Mailings from Reagan's campaign in Michigan were sent to National Rifle Association members that stated, "This will be the best opportunity you'll have this year to send our message to the Washington politicians who want to take away our guns."[63] Some limited radio ads also ran and the ACU spent a small sum on radio spots as well.

Ford's staff did let it leak out that if he lost or, in the worst case, lost badly in Michigan, he would in all likelihood curtail campaigning in the remaining primary states and instead reassess the wisdom of pursuing the nomination any further.[64]

Over the weekend, Reagan won additional delegates in convention and caucus states. He picked up the final eighteen delegates available in Oklahoma and several more in Louisiana, Virginia, and Missouri, bringing his total to forty-six for the weekend, according to the *New York Times*. Cumulatively, according to the paper, Reagan had extended his delegate lead over Ford by a margin of 476 to 333. Additionally, Reagan was in good shape in the state of Washington, as he won 61 percent of the state delegates for the statewide convention that would be held in Spokane; his ground forces would control the agenda and the selection of Washington's delegates to the national convention in August.[65]

In the meantime, the Federal Election Commission released the first filing made to the government agency on the financial contributions of corporate political action committees to the various candidates. The agency was only performing some of its functions. For the Presidential candidates, distributing their matching funds—not reporting disbursement—would have been far more important. Some outside of the Republican Party were mildly surprised when it was learned that Ford was receiving far more in corporate contributions than Reagan.[66] It had been widely assumed that Reagan's free-market message was more appealing to corporate America.

More importantly, Ford had finally signed the bill reconstituting the FEC, but only after it sat on his desk for six days. He then waited another six days before re-nominating five Commissioners, whom the Senate confirmed. But Ford then refused to swear them in until a sixth was confirmed, using a specious argument about "political balance" at the FEC. So Reagan and the Democratic candidates were still being denied millions in matching funds, just as they had been for weeks. An editorial in the *New York Times* concluded, "If there is not a deliberate design at work here, then Candidate Gerald Ford is needlessly and foolishly letting the country suspect that there is."[67]

Both Maryland and Michigan held Presidential primaries on May 18, and Ford won a landslide victory in Maryland. Reagan had not contested the Maryland GOP primary, and Ford took all the forty-three delegates there.[68] But in Michigan, Ford swamped Reagan with 64 percent of the vote. He also won most of the delegates at stake, by a margin of fifty-five to twenty-nine. Wallace was not a factor, as he took only 7 percent of the vote in the Democratic primary. For all intents and purposes, the Democrats who crossed over to the Republican primary voted not for Reagan, as once expected, but for Ford.[69] Pat Caddell, Carter's pollster in 1976, had conducted a survey of Michigan's voters that showed Ford with a solid three to two lead over Reagan among Republicans. It was harder to measure the crossover intensity for Reagan among Democrats, which did show Reagan leading two to one.[70]

Initially, Reagan was caught off guard by Ford's margin, telling reporters it was "our worst day in May." He then got more on message saying, "The thing that had them so uptight was that they had to win by substantial amounts in that state. Even a close race with him on the winning side would be considered a defeat. This was vital to him, but I don't think anyone can say it was crucial to us."[71]

Reagan was right. The President had lost five of the previous six primaries, had thrown everything into the fight against Reagan, and had still come up short. This win was crucial for Ford. Evans and Novak revealed after Ford's win in the Wolverine State that a knock-down, drag-out fight had occurred between Ford's White House staff and his in-state supporters over how to conduct the campaign there. Ford's staff opposed the whistle-stop campaign tour, which ultimately proved effective. But far more importantly, Senator Bob Griffin and others urged Ford to stop complaining about crossover voters and instead appeal to Michigan Democrats. The stratagem worked. The columnists fingered Head of Advance "Red" Cavaney, scheduler Jerry Jones, and Chief of Staff Cheney as those opposed to the change in tactics and strategy.[72]

For the "bantam rooster," of the Democratic Party, George Wallace, Maryland and Michigan represented the end of the line.[73] Four years earlier, he had won both. Wallace may have been well on his way to winning the Democratic Party's nomination before Arthur Bremer shot him as he campaigned in Maryland on the day of his twin victories. With Wallace's political demise, many expected Democrats to cross over and cast votes for Reagan in Michigan in 1976.

Carter won Michigan narrowly over Mo Udall, and lost Maryland surprisingly to Governor Jerry Brown of California.[74] The loss in Maryland and the close win in Michigan were interpreted as setbacks for the Georgian. Brown confidently told his supporters, "I'll see you in the general election and I'll see you in January."[75] Carter admitted his surprise at the margin of Brown's win, but pledged no essential changes in his campaign's message or strategy.[76]

Ford had been at a reception at the French Embassy the night of the primaries, but notes were passed to him all evening keeping him informed of the events in both states. While the delegate count remained close and Reagan was by no means out of the race, Ford had once again found renewed life. A thrilled President told his supporters, "This is going to play very well all over the United States," and described the win as "fantastic."[77]

"Before yesterday, the President looked weak, on the ropes, beleaguered. Today, he is the victor, successful, in charge. . . . But there are still questions about the strength of his candidacy, the nature of the race he has run, and the prospects for the Republican Party," wrote Elizabeth Drew in *American Journal*.[78] The see-saw battle had "seesawed" again. One Ford aide, mindful of Rog Morton's disastrous comment about rearranging deck chairs on the *Titanic* several weeks before, told the *New York Times* they'd "re-floated the *Titanic*."[79]

Still, according to the *Times*, Reagan led in the delegate count, 506-432, with 392 still uncommitted from New York, Pennsylvania, Wyoming, Mississippi, and elsewhere. The paper had done an informal survey of uncommitted delegates and speculated that the bulk leaned towards Ford, but in such a fluid situation, no one could know with certainty.[80] Other media organizations had slight variations in their numbers, but all agreed that Reagan was ahead.

R.W. Apple Jr. in the *Times* summed up the situation writing, "Mr. Ford thus revived a sickly campaign, but he remains a sorely beleaguered incumbent who has already lost six primaries. He is expected to lose more next Tuesday, possibly as many as five out of six on the schedule—Tennessee, Kentucky, Arkansas, Idaho, Oregon, and Nevada—as attention shifts back to the South and West, Mr. Reagan's strongest areas."[81] The key phrase in the *Times* account, for both Ford and Reagan was, "expected to lose."

Ford's campaign hierarchy had decided to stay positive. Ford would stress the accomplishments of his Administration and what he planned to do in a new term, and let his surrogates take it to Reagan. Still, Reagan was dictating some White House decisions as planned speeches in California by Kissinger were abruptly cancelled.[82] They also had a rare double advantage working for Ford for once. The President had certainly regained some momentum with his wins in Michigan and Maryland. But six primaries were ahead where he could lose all, thus effectively lowering his expectations.

Two days after the Michigan primary, Reagan pressed on to Nevada, the home state of his Campaign Chairman, Paul Laxalt. At an airport press conference, he was asked if he could have put Ford away had he won in Michigan. Reagan, accompanied by Jim Lake, Marty Anderson, and others, replied, "I don't know whether we would have wrapped it up or not. Certainly that race was a crucial one for him, and not for me. It was a make-or-break for him. . . . If there had been some kind of miracle there, it would have been quite a blow to him."[83]

Privately, Sears and company had hoped to get 40 percent in Michigan, but that was water over the dam. They were looking to the next six primaries, only several days away.[84] Most observers believed all six were in what was "Reagan Country" in the South and the West, and that Reagan would extend his delegate lead over Ford while also recapturing the psychological edge. Only Oregon was seen as possibly going for Ford.[85] Still, Reagan's campaign was not going to give up Oregon without a fight, as Reagan would campaign there for some of its thirty apportioned delegates. He would also stump in Arkansas and Tennessee.

Reagan's campaign in Nevada included stops in Reno, Elko, and Las Vegas. He was well received by large crowds in all three cities.[86] As it turned out, Reagan and Ford both campaigned in Oregon the Saturday before the primary. Reagan spoke at a long planned forum at a Masonic Hall in Portland, while Ford gave a "major policy address" at Lewis and Clark College near Portland.[87]

The primary would be closed and, as in the case of virtually every other battleground state, the Republican hierarchy in Oregon was fully supporting Ford, along with elected officials, including moderate Republican Senators Bob Packwood and Mark Hatfield. The state GOP had a moderate tradition, and there was a built-in cultural resentment in the state towards anything Californian. Still, a recent poll conducted by the *Oregonian* had Ford with 48 percent, Reagan with 35 percent, and 17 percent undecided. Reagan had run against Richard Nixon in 1968 in Oregon, but Nixon smashed him, 67 percent to 21 percent, with Rockefeller getting 12 percent in a write-in effort. And Reagan's foreign policy issues, including the Panama Canal and détente, were not uppermost in Oregon Republican primary voters' minds, as they were in other more conservative states.[88]

Carter was having problems too. Labor leaders were growing suspicious of him and renewed their effort to draft Hubert Humphrey into the race.[89] They were hoping to win a brokered convention if Carter fell short of the 1,505 delegates needed for the nomination. Also, he was caught in a problem of his own making, when he denied ever offering support for Lt. William Calley, who had been convicted for his conduct at My Lai during the Vietnam War. Carter, as Governor, had expressed support for Calley, calling him a "scapegoat."[90]

Meanwhile, rumors began to emerge from New York that State Republican Chairman Richard "Rosey" Rosenbaum was planning to discard his previous plan to keep his delegation officially "uncommitted." It was learned that he had invited all 154 GOP delegates to Albany for a meeting on the Monday before the next round of primaries. Vice President Nelson Rockefeller would also attend. Rosenbaum was also rumored to be mulling an outright personal endorsement of Ford as well.[91]

One hundred and seventy-six delegates would be decided in the May 25 primaries, most of whom were presumed to be for Reagan. If Rosenbaum, who controlled approximately 125 of New York's 154 delegates, threw them toward Ford, he would create a huge psychological and numerical advantage for the President and deal a serious blow to Reagan. Sears had hoped to pick off a healthy number of the New York delegates, and he thought a big Tuesday by Reagan would aid him in making his case. Nineteen delegates from throughout New York State, led by Brooklyn Chairman George Clark, had already broken with the uncommitted agreement and endorsed Reagan. Ford's campaign was fearful of further erosion of his expected delegate base towards Ronald Reagan, especially if he scored a big win on Tuesday.

In a press conference with reporters from Tennessee, the President said he was not currently considering Reagan as a running mate. Ford explained, "I have read that Mr. Reagan does not want to be considered for Vice President and I have taken him at his word. Under those circumstances he is not being considered." He did share with the reporters that both of the state's Senators, Bill Brock and Howard Baker, were under consideration.[92]

Several months before, Sears had decided that Reagan would not campaign in New Jersey, no money would be spent there and sixty-seven delegates would thus be surrendered to President Ford without a fight. Ford, with the support of the state's Republican Party, including virtually all its elected Republicans such as liberal Senator Clifford Case, was able to then devote additional resources to states like California and other places where Reagan was actively campaigning. Ford hoped to score a breakthrough in these states anyway.[93] Once again, a decision by Reagan's high command would be bitterly debated.

Nonetheless, Reagan's New Jersey supporters decided to move forward on their own. They filed a statewide slate, as well as slates in eight of the state's fifteen congressional districts just minutes before the deadline, on April 29. But Ford's forces played hardball, as the ballots for the primary buried the Reagan delegates' names, making them difficult to find on primary day.[94]

The *New York Times* described the Gipper's forces in the Garden State as "political nobodies." The leader of Reagan's team was a little-known phone installer, Robert Davis, forty-one, who had been active in conservative politics in the state for a decade and had been a leader in Young Americans for Freedom. The paper did note that what they lacked in resources, they made up in energy, which was lacking in the Ford campaign.[95]

Reagan's New Jersey supporters opened up a headquarters, and at their first meeting a typical cross-section showed up: small businessmen, retirees, housewives, and college students. They all were estranged from the Republican Party's status quo, and they all were dedicated to conservatism and its messenger, Ronald Reagan. Their angst was best summed up in a quote given to the *Times* by Mrs. Eleanor Day Winmill: "A vote for Ford is a vote for Kissinger and I'm not going to let the Republican Party sell our country down the river or down the Panama Canal either."[96]

Meanwhile, hearing the rumors from New York about supporting Ford before the national convention, the previously uncommitted delegates in Pennsylvania also switched their decision and voted, eighty-nine to nine, to adopt a resolution supporting Ford's nomination. The resolution had been drafted by Congressman "Bud" Shuster and was immediately endorsed by Senators Hugh Scott and Richard Schweiker. While holding the delegates technically "uncommitted," the resolution was in fact another major boost for Ford.[97] Still, Reagan, Sears, and their supporters held out hope that some in the Pennsylvania delegation might change their minds about the conservative candidate.

The weekend before the May 25 primaries, Reagan campaigned in Tennessee, where he spoke to thirty-five hundred cheering supporters at Tennessee Temple College on his opposition to limited war: "Never again should this country send its young men to die in a war unless this country is totally committed to winning it as quickly as possible."[98]

But in a press conference, he ran afoul of the zealous supporters of the long controversial Tennessee Valley Authority.[99] The TVA had been a New Deal project and was a source of consternation to supporters of the free market in the rest of the country for many years. It had been intended to supply low-cost electricity to the poor of Tennessee during the Great Depression and pay for itself. But its size and scope had grown over four decades. And American taxpayers subsidized it all.

Even the most conservative politician in Tennessee bowed down before the subsidized god of TVA . But Reagan told the assembled reporters, "I still believe in free enterprise, and the government doesn't have any place in it." Reporters pressed him: would he sell TVA? Reagan replied, "We'd have to look at it."[100]

The Ford campaign jumped on this statement as did Senator Baker and virtually every Republican official in Tennessee. Baker, one of the classiest men on either side of the aisle, went easy on Reagan in his statement. After all, Governor and Mrs. Reagan had been his houseguests several nights before. Baker had invited the Reagans, even as he was supporting Ford's nomination. He told the *Washington Post* that he did not "allow my politics to interfere with my friendships."[101] Baker also appeared on *Face the Nation* and speculated that Reagan's comments could "cost him dearly in Tennessee, Kentucky and possibly Arkansas."[102]

Reagan tried to backtrack, telling the media that while he had no plans to sell the TVA, he was "philosophically opposed" to it. But he had difficulty shaking the issue. Ford immediately criticized Reagan's comments, telling a hastily arranged group of Tennessee reporters in the White House, "I think it's been a very, very important energy producer in that great part of our country, and I believe it's continuing to perform a very important responsibility."[103]

Rog Morton, Ford's Campaign Chairman, issued a statement, piling on: "Mr. Reagan's statements will be weighed carefully next Tuesday by thousands of voters in Kentucky and Tennessee who depend on TVA for jobs and lower power rates." In addition to lining up these critical comments, the President Ford Committee also attempted to persuade Republicans in Kentucky, who would also be holding a primary on May 25 and where voters also enjoyed the subsidized electricity generated by TVA, to vote against Reagan.[104]

Goldwater was also experiencing his own problems as he whined to Sally Quinn of the *Washington Post.* In the aftermath of criticizing Reagan over the Panama Canal, conservatives had deluged the curmudgeonly Senator's office with letters, telegrams, and phone calls denouncing him. "I didn't realize Western Union would send telegrams like that," he told Quinn.[105]

While Reagan was on the defensive, Ford embarked on a five-day swing through California, Nevada, Oregon, and Ohio. But he stuck to the plan his campaign had re-introduced in Michigan to avoid confronting Reagan directly. The movement towards Ford in New York and Pennsylvania, along with the chance of winning Oregon, had visions of a first ballot nomination dancing in the heads of Morton, Cheney, Spencer, and the President. Now, with Reagan in trouble in Tennessee, their spirits were brightening even more. And all six of the forthcoming primaries would send proportional delegates to Kansas City, so Ford was assured of getting his share from each. Still, most observers believed—or hoped—that neither Reagan nor Ford would win the necessary delegates needed for a first ballot nomination and the Republicans would have a good, old-fashioned donnybrook on their hands in Kansas City.[106]

For Ford, this meant that to take Reagan on directly would be tactically foolish. So he stuck to the plan and defended his foreign policy, while mixing in a generous portion of pro-American and anti-Soviet rhetoric.[107] In California, Ford campaigned in Orange County, the home base for the state's conservatives. He attracted a large and pleasant crowd, except for one protester who held aloft a sign that read, "I Want President Nixon Back."[108]

The direct attacks on Reagan were again left to his spokesmen and surrogates including Carla Hills, a Californian who was Ford's Secretary of Housing and Urban Development and had been a longtime liberal critic of Reagan. Peter Kaye, Ford's acerbic campaign spokesman and also a Californian, told the *New York Times*, "This is one state where Reagan can't fake it."[109]

Reagan, in his swing through Oregon before returning to California for two days to recharge, spoke optimistically about a first ballot nomination. According to newspaper accounts, Ford had pulled slightly ahead of Reagan in the delegate count, when some uncommitted votes were factored in. Reagan was not dissuaded, except when he charged the White House with heavy-handed pressure on New York's and Pennsylvania's uncommitted delegations, saying their approach "smacks of bossism." He also flashed anger at the Kansas GOP for attempting to bar his supporters who were not delegates from attending the state convention in Topeka to hear him deliver the keynote address.[110]

At one rally at Oregon State University before 2,500 supporters, several protesters heckled him and held up signs that read, "Reagan is Rancid," "Stop Rotten Ronnie," and "Curb Ronnie's Ray Gun." Reagan dispatched them with his typical, self-deprecating humor when he said, "Perhaps some time before the morning's over I can convince somebody that I don't eat my young."[111]

Over the weekend, Reagan continued to speak positively about the "probability" he would nab the nomination on the first ballot—for good reason.[112] After all, the Gallup organization released the results of a national survey that showed Americans decidedly right of center 47 percent, with 29 percent leaning left and 12 percent claiming the middle. Even better, within the GOP, an overwhelming 61 percent called themselves "right," while only 21 percent of Republicans called themselves "left."[113] A few days later, a national Gallup poll showed the race between the two contenders tightening considerably. Ford only led Reagan 53-40 percent, the closest the contest had been since just before the New Hampshire primary.[114] Virginia was about to wrap up its drawn-out selection process, with fifty-one delegates to be decided upon. Kenny Klinge, one of the toughest and nicest GOP operatives around at the time, led Reagan's forces there.[115]

Against Sears's best efforts, New York's GOP made it official on May 24, when 119 of their 154 delegates pledged their votes to Ford. Ford then zoomed ahead of Reagan by more than 100 delegates. In fact, Rosenbaum and Rockefeller had hoped for more from New York and were a bit disappointed that a handful had decided to stick to the original agreement and stay uncommitted. According to the *New York Times*, an argument broke out between Clark and Rosenbaum over the strong-arm tactics being used on behalf of Ford. Clark charged him with a "fast shuffle," to which Rosenbaum responded, "I make the rules here!"[116]

Pennsylvania's delegates had also broken with their previous decision to stay uncommitted and went for Ford, putting yet another eighty-eight delegates in the President's hip pocket. The *Washington Post* estimated that Ford now had approximately 675 delegates to around 550 for Reagan. It was the first time the President had the delegate lead in over three weeks.[117] Over that weekend, Ford also won the low-key contest in Alaska and took most of the delegates at the Kansas convention, which had concluded an extended selection process.

Ford's team had caught a lot of wind in its sails over the previous week. But they were still nervous. With the decisions in New York and Pennsylvania, they wondered if momentum would hold. After all, in three of the six primaries on May 25, Democrats were allowed to cross over and vote for a Republican candidate, a tactic that had frustrated Ford throughout the campaign. He had written off two of the crossover states, Arkansas and Idaho. But Cheney tacked, and said that a victory in Tennessee, once considered unlikely, was now "do-able." Ford also had a chance to win Kentucky.[118]

May 25 turned out to be more that just "do-able" for Ford. The day exceeded anything he and his team had entertained. Ford won in Oregon as he had hoped. But most importantly and surprisingly, Ford defeated Reagan in Kentucky and Tennessee, both of which had long been considered "Reagan Country." Reagan won Arkansas, Nevada, and Idaho, as expected. Although the six combined contests produced a relatively small amount of delegates and, in fact, Reagan won one more delegate in Tennessee than Ford, twenty-two to twenty-one, Ford scored a huge psychological victory by winning these two state primaries and thus won the day.[119]

In Tennessee, Ford's margin was about 2,000 votes out of approximately 240,000 cast. Pundits and Reagan officials pointed to the eleventh hour controversy over Reagan's comments on the TVA as the reason for his narrow loss. In Kentucky, Ford defeated Reagan by a little over 5,000 votes in a contest that saw approximately 130,000 voters turn out.[120] Ford was also helped by his Administration's announcement that it would seek a new way to review the Supreme Court's ruling on forced busing. The issue had been contentious in both states, with conservatives strongly opposing the meddling by federal courts.[121]

The result in Kentucky was especially bizarre because the state GOP had already selected its delegates at a state convention in April. Reagan's forces overwhelmed this convention, and he prevailed with twenty-seven delegates to only eight for Ford, with two uncommitted.[122] However, the results of the primary would trump the decision of the state convention. So by winning the Kentucky primary, delegates initially chosen for Reagan would in fact have to vote for Ford on the first ballot in Kansas City, according to state party rules. By winning the primary, Ford prevailed on the final go-around, seizing nineteen out of thirty-seven delegates, even though the vast majority of Kentucky's delegation was rabidly pro-Reagan.[123]

Reagan enjoyed the support of former Governor Louie Nunn and was also helped in Kentucky by the American Conservative Union, which ran radio ads that highlighted his opposition to forced busing.[124] Ironically, Governor Nunn's brother Lee, whom the Ford campaign had fired in the fall of 1975, had just been elected State Chairman of the GOP. Although virtually every state party was supporting Ford, it was unknown whether Lee Nunn was holding a grudge against Ford and would undermine his campaign there.

Winning in two Southern states was a major breakthrough for Ford. Reagan's camp had been claiming that the South and West were their province since his victory in North Carolina, and that Ford was the regional candidate. No more. For the day, Reagan won seventeen of twenty-seven delegates in Arkansas, thirteen of eighteen in Nevada and seventeen of twenty-one in Idaho. In Oregon, Kentucky, and Tennessee, he won a total of fifty-four delegates to Ford's fifty-six for a total of one hundred and one to seventy-five.[125] Although Reagan had added handsomely to his delegate total, it was Ford who won the day in the minds of the national media.

The events of May 25 proved once again Sears's maxim: "Politics is motion." Reagan's message had lost some of its steam, and the controversy over his comments on TVA threw his campaign into reverse gear in Tennessee and, to some extent, in Kentucky. Ford was in motion as he aggressively defended his two years in office, pointed to the recovering economy, and seized on any mistakes by Reagan. In fact, Ford was beginning to sound more and more like Reagan on the stump. While he could never compete with the Gipper in terms of style and presentation, his rhetoric became more about limited government, freedom and the free enterprise system, capital punishment, and other issues important to conservatives. Nonetheless, Reagan could always craft a line better than anyone, especially Ford, as he would tell audiences on the stump, "If we get the federal government out of the classroom, maybe we'll get God back in."[126]

Reagan's counterpart on the Democratic side, Jimmy Carter, was also faltering, as Jerry Brown was winning a couple of primaries, Frank Church had scored a win over Carter in the Oregon primary, and Mo Udall was still hanging around. Still, because all the Democratic primaries were proportional, Carter was moving out in front inexorably, towards a first ballot nomination at their convention in New York.[127]

Reagan and Ford now focused on the biggest primary day of the year, June 8. California's 167 delegates, winner-take-all, would be the grand prize of the day. Ohio and New Jersey would also hold their primaries.

Reagan's forces were surprisingly cocky. As one staffer told the *Washington Post's* David Broder, "Reagan's going to win that last and biggest battle in California. When was the last time they didn't give the decision to the guy who hammered his opponent in the last round?"[128] Actually, in the popular new movie just released in 1976, *Rocky*, the hero did batter his opponent and defending champion Apollo Creed in the final round. But the decision still went to the champion.

According to the *Washington Post*, Ford had moved ahead of Reagan in the delegate count, 796 to 616. But many were left to be decided, and Ford was still well off the 1,130 needed for the nomination.[129] Most observers felt Reagan was in excellent shape on his home turf in California, despite an attempt by some of Ford's California supporters to change the rules from "winner-take-all" to a proportional vote but the move was crushed by Reagan's forces.[130] Ford's supporters at the Ripon Society had earlier attempted to have the U.S. Supreme Court intervene, but the Court threw the lawsuit out.[131]

Ford's chances in California were bleak, as documented in polling done by Pat Caddell for Evans and Novak. An astronomical 87 percent of Republicans in California approved of Reagan's stewardship as Governor, while only 48 percent approved of Ford's Presidency. In one particular column, the two reporters detailed how ill the voters thought of Ford. They seemed to go out of their way to find reasons to dislike him. One said, "The Fords are too liberal with their children," while still others complained about First Lady Betty Ford and son Jack Ford. Even the President's support seemed lukewarm. One Ford backer could only sum up this praise for Ford: "A man of average intelligence, down to earth just like the rest of us."[132]

The Young Americans for Freedom enlisted Efrem Zimbalist Jr. to appear in radio ads supporting Reagan on his home turf while lambasting Ford. The organization had sent out hundreds of thousands of letters to conservatives, signed by Ron Robinson, who was heading the California effort for the YAF.[133]

California was an odd assortment of hard-core conservatives and ultra-leftists, of traditionalists and malcontents, communes and suburbs. The state had great weather, scenery, beaches, and mountains. But it also had smog and some of the worst traffic in the country. It had Patty Hearst and Charles Manson, Disneyland and oil spills, Haight-Ashbury and San Diego. California was impossible to categorize or generalize. As Reagan had pointed out many times, it truly was a country unto itself in many ways.

Ford stumped in California and Ohio on May 26 and proclaimed himself the only Republican who was a "national candidate" and who could beat the Democratic nominee in the fall election. He told reporters, "I am not a regional candidate, I am a national candidate and I know I can win. I have some reservations about any other Republican candidate being able to win in November." Ford also dismissed Reagan as a "Sun Belt" candidate.[134]

Ford had directed Attorney General Edward Levi to ask the Supreme Court to clarify its decisions on school busing. At a news conference in Ohio, the President brushed off questions from reporters who were pressing him and implying that this request was politically motivated.[135]

New Jersey would decide on sixty-seven delegates. Sears had decided to not only bypass New Jersey, but also to avoid antagonizing the state party leadership there by aiding the in-state Reagan operation. Consequently, the bulk of New Jersey's delegates were already being counted for Ford.[136] Ohio would have ninety-seven delegates at stake. This state would be difficult for Reagan since its Governor, Jim Rhodes, who always seemed to be under an ethical cloud, controlled the GOP machinery from top to bottom. Reagan's campaign was late starting and Black's efforts for Reagan were again woefully under-funded.

Ford's strategy was to make a play for California and keep Reagan pinned down there, minimizing the time the challenger could spend campaigning in Ohio. Reagan, in fact, was forced to campaign heavily and spend resources in his own state that might have been better aimed at picking up some additional delegates in the Buckeye State.

Speaking to a convention of California peace officers, Reagan reiterated his strong views on law enforcement and justice, telling the police group, "We do have a problem with lenient judges, but far worse is the problem that laws, precedents, procedures and rules of prosecution are stacked in behalf of the criminal defendant—and hence against the society he threatens." He received a tumultuous ovation from the convention. Ford had earlier addressed the group, but did not receive nearly the warm reception that Reagan did.[137]

While Ellis Island was opening up for tourism and Northern Virginia was looking into banning the SST Concorde from landing at Dulles Airport, Nelson

Rockefeller was making some noise of his own, when he told a breakfast group of reporters that Ford's move to the right was "very dangerous" for his prospects in the general election. He also told the media that he felt it was "inconceivable" that Ford would pick Reagan. Reagan's forces, of course, shared that sentiment—but for different reasons than Rocky's. Rockefeller also said he would not accept a request from Ford at the convention to run with him. But this would have been highly unlikely; Rockefeller had been a loose cannonball rolling on the decks of the *USS Ford* for nearly two years. Everybody in the White House and the Ford campaign was sick and tired of his antics, despite his help with the New York delegation.[138]

Washington was starting to settle into yet another long, humid and hot summer. Polyester leisure suits were selling at Raleigh's Department store for $55 and three custom-made shirts for men could be purchased at a tailor in Alexandria for $40.[139] Delegates to the conventions would be wearing their "finest," including the Ohio-labor special, "Full Cleveland" at the Democratic convention. The ensemble consisted of a white leisure suit, white shirt, white socks, and white patent leather belt and shoes. Though Democrats tended to dress more proletarian, both conventions were nonetheless braced for the worst their sartorially challenged delegates could throw at them.

And Washington was atwitter at the revelation that Congressman Wayne Hays, one of the meanest and most powerful men in Congress, was keeping a mistress, Elizabeth Ray, on his payroll, and paying her fourteen thousand dollars a year, courtesy of the American taxpayer. Ford's photographer, David Hume Kennerly, worried that his mini scandal might come back to haunt him again, now that she'd become "famous."[140]

The FEC finally began to release matching funds to the Presidential candidates. Citizens for Reagan received $349,138, but it was far below the nearly two million the government agency owed the campaign.[141] The commission also fired a warning shot across the bow of conservative groups supporting Reagan in the primaries, especially the American Conservative Union. Jim Roberts, who headed the ACU's efforts to support Reagan in the primaries, told the Commission that the ACU had spent over $230,000 in thirteen states to support Reagan, but no laws against coordination had been violated.[142]

A charge had been made against the ACU that it was soliciting contributions in excess of the five thousand dollar federal limit for an individual giver to the group, but no evidence against the organization was presented to the FEC. Roberts denied any wrongdoing. Still, the admonition against the conservative group was seen once again by Reagan's forces as an attempt by the Ford White House to play politics with the FEC.[143]

Cheney had attempted to better coordinate the White House and the Ford campaign, but he was not always successful. Reagan's effort also was somewhat disorganized—but nothing like Ford's. While Ford went through three Campaign Managers, Reagan kept Sears the entire time. The President Ford Committee went through two Press Secretaries, two Finance Directors, and made other innumerable staff changes. With little exception, Reagan had the same team in 1976 that he had started with in 1975 and earlier. Morale was also higher at Citizens for Reagan than at the President Ford Committee, where staff came and went and campaign tactics seemed to shift from day to day.

On the subject of the vagaries of two campaigns, the *New York Times* opined, "Another factor favoring Mr. Reagan is his superior political staff. Even when events were going badly for their candidate in March and early April, the Reagan staff remained united. President Ford's much larger and less cohesive amalgam of White House aides, election committee staff, and 'Kitchen Cabinet' had displayed inexperience and confusion."[144]

The discord in Ford's ranks continued when he fired his advertising man, Peter Dailey, and hired, for a time, James Jordan, a Madison Avenue type. Jordan was president of a run of the mill New York City firm that cranked out tasteless commercials featuring little men in people's toilets or actors complaining about the merits of various shampoo products and which did a better job of getting rid of dandruff. Jordan came at the recommendation of his old crony, Don Penny, one of the two joke writers on the White House payroll.[145]

Jordan tried to "sell" Ford to the American people using actors portraying housewives, one named "Ellie," doing a comparison shopping routine of Ford, as if they were noting the price difference of frozen peas in a supermarket. The commercials bombed, and Jordan was sent packing back to New York. Dailey, a talented and politically savvy ad man, was restored to the campaign.[146]

The good news for Ford was that around the same time, a more talented and thoughtful individual than Jordan joined the President Ford Committee: James A. Baker III. He would prove to be an extraordinarily effective political operative, despite the admonitions of his grandfather to stay away from politics if he was going to build the family law firm. Baker had been a close friend of George H.W. Bush since the early 1960s. The young attorney, only in his thirties, was mourning the tragic loss of his wife due to cancer. His tennis partner, Bush, suggested he needed a distraction in his life to take his mind off his sorrow and got him involved in Texas Republican politics.

Baker eventually became Chairman of the Republican Party in Harris

County and turned a moribund organization into one of the most powerful in Texas. Politics was now fully injected in his bloodstream, and he headed for Washington. He served first at the Commerce Department and later, as head of the Ford delegate operations. An old Ford crony, Jack Styles, was supposed to have run the Ford delegate operation. But Styles wrapped his car around a tree one snowy night in Michigan and the job fell to Baker.[147]

The Ford campaign had other personnel issues to attend. Henry Kissinger, for instance, was forced to distance himself from a *Parade* magazine article in which he suggested he would be willing to debate Reagan over America's foreign policy. Kissinger also took the opportunity to counter rumors surrounding the abrupt cancellation of two long-planned speeches he was to give in California. Kissinger claimed that he had cancelled the speeches himself because of the nearness of the California primary. But most believed the White House was keeping Kissinger under wraps since he was such a lightning rod for conservative criticism.[148]

Kissinger may have been effectively muzzled, but Nelson Rockefeller, in the commencement address at the Air Force Academy, said America needed "détente" and "a better working relationship between the two superpowers."[149] At the time, a correspondent for Agence France Presse, Louis Foy, asked plaintively, of the discredited word, "Has this become a dirty French word?"[150]

Reagan's campaign was confident of safely winning California. As a result, on the first weekend of June, Reagan went to Ohio to stump there, hoping his last minute effort might yield some of the ninety-seven delegates at stake.[151] Unfortunately, his campaign had only filed in two-thirds of the twenty-three congressional districts. Three delegates would be selected from each of the districts and the balance at-large according to who won the primary.[152]

Before leaving California, however, the Gipper saddled up for a high profile media event and rode along with a group of cowboys and ranchers before attending a campaign event in Newport Beach, where he was introduced by John Wayne and Andy Devine. Reagan had some fun with the crowd, telling them, "May the all-seeing eye dwelling in the treetop of infinite knowledge bring its light of peace upon the tranquil meadows of the turbulent night of your hours of darkness." The befuddled crowd looked at Reagan, wondering if the months of grueling campaigning had taken their toll until Reagan said, "You may wonder what this has to do with this barbecue. The answer is nothing. It's just a bumper sticker I saw for Jerry Brown!"[153] The crowd roared, accustomed by then to reading stories each day detailing new oddities about their Governor.

Determined not to be embarrassed in California, Reagan's campaign spent over eight hundred thousand dollars (compared to Ford's six hundred thousand). Furthermore, Reagan devoted considerable time to a state where he had run and won two times and where he had been a successful and popular Governor.[154] Some thought his effort in California in 1976 was overkill and that his time and money would have better devoted to Ohio and possibly picking off a couple of delegates in New Jersey.[155]

But Nofziger, who had returned to California to run the primary, would not leave anything to chance. Reagan and Mrs. Reagan were bound and determined to not be embarrassed in their home state primary, which Reagan called "the big casino."[156] Even their offices were open all Memorial Day weekend, while the Ford offices in California were closed.[157]

In California, Reagan received a Father of the Year Award, but the *Washington Post* could not resist a taking a gratuitous shot by reporting that he would miss his son's high school graduation, because he would be campaigning in Ohio.[158] Reagan also speculated about losing the nomination for the first time since announcing his candidacy, as he suggested he would want concessions from Ford on the Republican platform in exchange for his full support in the fall campaign.[159]

Reagan also, for the first time, mused that either Senator Bill Brock or Senator Howard Baker, both of Tennessee, would be an acceptable running mate should he win the nomination. Reagan told the small group of reporters, "Neither one has ever taken philosophical positions different from mine. I've thought of them as philosophically similar to me." Jon Nordheimer of the *New York Times* insightfully wrote, "There has been speculation throughout the campaign on the problems Mr. Reagan might encounter as nominee in the selection of a running mate since he has insisted that he would not want someone who did not share his conservative philosophy."[160]

On Tuesday, June 1, Ford took all of the nineteen Republican delegates in Rhode Island's primary. Although the state allowed crossover voting, the Reagan campaign had made only the most minimal effort there. While the delegates would be apportioned according to percentage, Reagan only received 31 percent of the vote, two percentage points under the threshold for proportional representation. Consequently, all the delegates went to Ford. The turnout was so small, less than twenty thousand voters, that even one mailing into the state for Reagan would probably have yielded him some of the delegates at stake there.[161]

Also on the first, the South Dakota and Montana Republican Parties held their primaries. Reagan was confident about both. Neither of the candidates had campaigned for the twenty delegates in South Dakota. But Ford's brother, Tom—a Michigan businessman—and Mrs. Ford had both stumped there.[162]

Montana's GOP primary was the first to be held in twenty years and although the results would be non-binding until their state convention on June 26, the delegates it sent to Kansas City were Reagan supporters.[163] In fact, all twenty voted for Reagan's nomination.[164] South Dakota was a bit of a setback for Reagan, however, as he only took eleven of the twenty delegates available. Reagan had won two of the three primary contests, but the day came out as pretty much a wash between the two contenders.[165] Unfortunately, this meant Reagan was not gaining on Ford. The *Post* tally had Ford with 802 delegates and Reagan with 650.[166] Still, there were more than 800 delegates yet to be selected.

Reagan was also keeping his stump speech fresh, much to the joy of the traveling press. Reagan was never shy about speaking his mind and taking risks—sometimes to the dismay of his staff. But the candidate embraced the free exchange of ideas more than any other candidate running in 1976, and possibly in a generation. He wasn't afraid to take on the established order, as when he spoke out forcefully against busing. But he also offered a solution for poor and inner-city parents when he advanced the idea of offering vouchers as a means of creating more competition in schools, thereby improving public schools right in the children's neighborhoods.[167]

Vouchers were not a new idea. What was new was the presence on the national scene of a candidate who had the courage to embrace them openly, risking the ire of the status quo, as represented by the liberal media and the National Education Association. The federal government, Reagan said, "has injected itself increasingly into the local schools, interfering in their conduct, prodding, harassing, molding them according to bureaucratic ideas."[168]

Reagan had been asked a hypothetical question about Rhodesia, where Soviet-backed revolutionaries were battling the white minority government. When pressed, Reagan speculated that possibly the United States and Great Britain might mediate a peaceful transfer of power to avoid a bloodbath there and possibly, possibly, both countries would send troops to preserve the peace and insure a democratic government in Rhodesia.[169] The *San Francisco Chronicle* blared a headline that inaccurately stated, "Reagan Would Send GI's To Avert Rhodesian War." In fact, Reagan had said, "But I believe in the interest of peace and avoiding bloodshed, and to achieve democratic majority rule which we all, I think, subscribe to." But his reasonable comments were all lost in the ensuing uproar, as Ford denounced Reagan as "irresponsible." The new controversy dredged up other comments by Reagan over the course of the campaign that the national media deemed questionable.[170]

Later, at an airport press conference in Santa Barbara, Reagan attempted to quell the situation, telling reporters, "Let's get one thing straight. I'm not talking about sending troops to Rhodesia. I'm talking about a plan to hopefully preserve the peace and I don't think it calls for any troops."[171]

While Ford made a quick dash to New Jersey the weekend before the June 8 primaries, and Rockefeller was sent to a meaningless meeting of Maryland's GOP, Stu Spencer produced a commercial that widened the chasm between Ford and Reagan and helped to create a permanent rift that never really healed between the two men.[172]

Reagan landed in Columbus on Saturday, June 5, where Charlie Black awaited his arrival. Upon landing, Black rushed aboard and handed Reagan a piece of paper and said, "Governor, before you get off, I think you'd better read this."[173] Reagan did, and Black saw the anger rise in his face. Reagan slammed his fist against the bulkhead of the plane and yelled, "That damned Stu Spencer!" Reagan cut his hand from hitting it so hard.[174]

The paper Black had handed Reagan was the script for a new Ford commercial that read,

> Last Wednesday, Ronald Reagan said that he would send American troops to Rhodesia. On Thursday, he clarified that. He said they could be observers or advisers. What does he think happened in Vietnam? When you vote Tuesday, remember, Governor Reagan couldn't start a war. President Ronald Reagan could.

The radio and television commercial was airing heavily in California and there was little Reagan could do, except to attack it. Angrily, he told the media the commercial was an "absolute fabrication and misstatement of fact." The *New York Times* said, when talking to the media, "the words poured out of him in angry snapping tones." Reagan gained his composure and then shook his head sadly and said of Ford's campaign, "I wished they had chosen to campaign on a higher plane."[175]

Reagan could, however, take some comfort in winning nineteen of the remaining twenty-one delegates up for grabs in Virginia. In all, Reagan took thirty-five of the Commonwealth's fifty-one delegates. Reagan's leadership in Virginia had charitably offered to give two more delegate slots to Ford supporters in the interest of party unity but when it went out for a vote, the Reagan rank and file voted against the move. [176]

Reagan also won fifteen delegates in caucuses in Louisiana and picked up an additional three delegates in Colorado, for a total of thirty-seven for the weekend.

Once again, Reagan was slowly closing the gap with Ford. The count now was 803 for Ford and 687 for Reagan, according to the *Washington Post*.[177]

Massachusetts Democrats also met over the weekend and elected Birch Bayh's only delegate in the country, Thomas P. O'Neill III, the state's Lieutenant Governor and son of the powerful House Speaker. He was known as the "million dollar delegate" because of the amount Bayh had spent on the primaries, all for naught.[178]

Reagan had opened up a 24 percent lead over Ford in California according to the respected Field Poll, and his victory was not in doubt. Three hundred thirty-one delegates were available on June 8—by far the largest amount contested in one day of voting.[179]

In the end, Spencer's commercial backfired badly on Ford. Although Ford defended the advertisement vociferously, Reagan crushed him in California, 66 percent to 34 percent.[180] Years later, Spencer would laugh and say, "I probably added eight points to Reagan's margin in California!" Spencer was one of the most talented and toughest operatives around in 1976, but that year his judgment about how to stop Reagan was sometimes clouded by his anger at Reagan and others in the campaign he blamed for real or imagined slights.[181] As previously stated, he also was reported to have remarked to another political operative in early 1975, "It's one thing to elect that right-winger as Governor, it's another to elect him President!" Spencer was no conservative, and most observers in 1976 thought he was much more in tune philosophically with Ford than with Reagan.[182]

Spencer reconciled with Governor and Mrs. Reagan several years later, but not before a memo had been prepared for President Ford with talking points for a conversation with Reagan in September of 1976, one month after the Republican convention. The memo detailed items the President should review with Reagan regarding fundraising, campaigning that Reagan could undertake to help the ticket and the like. Handwritten at the bottom of the page by Dick Cheney, after seven typewritten points, was an extra line: "Don't mention Stu Spencer."[183]

Reagan had been invited on Sunday, June 6 to appear on the ABC program, *Issues and Answers.* While most candidates welcomed an opportunity to appear on national television, Reagan declined so he could make the most of the few remaining hours in Ohio before the primary. Ford meanwhile appeared on the CBS program, *Face the Nation*.[184]

The Republican candidates could barely conceal their contempt for each other. Ford returned to his earlier strategy of attacking Reagan head on, as he told the Associated Press that Reagan's opposition to the Panama Canal Treaties could lead to "guerrilla warfare" and also warned of a Republican "debacle" if Reagan were nominated.[185] Reagan was a bit more reserved when he told the AP of Ford, "He places his faith and confidence in his longtime buddies in the Congress and they turn him down. I have said that leadership today, I believe, calls for going to the American people and telling them the truth."[186]

Reagan was realistic about the chances of his delayed campaign in Ohio and set a very low goal of winning ten of the ninety-seven delegates available. Just seventy-two hours before the filing deadline, Reagan had only filed slates in two-thirds of the congressional districts.[187] Sears had called Loren Smith at the Reagan campaign headquarters to ask him how many petitions Reagan would have to sign. The total, as Smith recalled, was somewhere around three hundred. Sears then asked him how long would it take Reagan to sign that many petitions? Smith had his secretary time himself with a watch while he signed his name over and over and then gave Sears his answer.[188]

Reagan's self-appointed chair in Ohio was Peter Voss, another conservative who had upset the Republican Party establishment, as was the case of Reagan activists in various states.[189] Voss was running the campaign out of his living room and was being assisted by Jim Kuhn, a young volunteer. Both were working at Charlie Black's direction, along with a small, ragtag group of committed Reagan supporters including State Senator Buzz Lukens, Congressman John Ashbrook, and another youngster named John Kasich.[190] Black only had about $100,000 to devote to television advertising in the last days of the primary. But even that was an improvement—originally, the campaign had only planned to spend $50,000 in Ohio. Sears was feeling confident about California, so some money was shifted to Black's operation.[191]

Once again, Reagan was behind the eight ball. By not filing in eight districts, Reagan handed twenty-four uncontested delegates over to Ford. Reagan concentrated on the more conservative districts in the southern portion of the state, rather than the outside chance of beating Ford in the statewide primary, which would award twenty-eight at-large delegates to the winner. Black frankly told David Broder at the *Post,* "It's a real longshot for him to win statewide."[192]

Ford campaigned in Ohio the Monday before the primary, beginning his day in Cincinnati after an event in Cleveland the previous night. Accompanying him were Governor Rhodes and Senator Robert Taft Jr., son of the conservative Senator who inspired so many—including Reagan. Rhodes crassly reminded the audience that Ford had promised the construction of a uranium enrichment plant for Portsmouth and that Ohio had been given more latitude in the

Highway Fund by the Ford Administration than any other state. Rhodes strongly implied that with such tributes to the state, the least they could do was vote for Ford.[193]

Ford was a bit subtler, as he told the crowd, "In 1976 I don't want to see a reliable Ford turned in for a flashier model." He also made reference to "the tragedy of 1964," drawing an allusion between Goldwater and Reagan yet again.[194] Ironically, Reagan had nothing but kind words to say about Goldwater. But Goldwater criticized Reagan hard in private, Ford called Goldwater a disaster in public, and Goldwater was supporting Ford over Reagan.

But Reagan still hadn't cooled off over the ads Spencer had produced, and he startled some of his supporters when he suggested he might not support Ford if he were the nominee. He attacked Ford anew and charged him with "taking the low road." Reagan had always said he would support Ford if he were unable to defeat him for the nomination, until now. Reagan told reporters when pressed on whether he really meant to withhold support for Ford, "Just say you caught me at a moment when I didn't want to answer that question."[195]

Ford tsked-tsked Reagan, telling reporters, "I am very disappointed that someone would put a personal view above a party view."[196] On the other hand, Reagan had never called Ford a warmonger as the Rhodesia commercial had implied Reagan was. The *Washington Post* reported, "When the President personally endorsed the commercials, Reagan flew into a rage."[197] Reagan's campaign was deeply concerned that although the commercial was backfiring on Ford in California, it might cause damage in Ohio and New Jersey, where voters did not know him as well as those in his adopted home state.

During a two-hundred-mile motorcade, Ford handed out more federal largess, as in Middletown, where he announced a limitation on the importation of stainless steel pots and pans, surely pleasing to the workers at the Armco plant there. He also announced thirty-six million dollars in new construction for Wright-Patterson Air Force Base when he was in Dayton, which was considered a Reagan stronghold.[198]

Carter was about to close the sale with the Democratic Party, despite Brown's late entrance into the race and the fact that Hubert Humphrey was once again making noises about accepting a draft at the convention. Carter was ahead in Ohio and was assured a large share of proportional delegates from California and New Jersey.[199]

On June 8, Reagan won big in California, as expected, and swept all 167 delegates. But he only won six of the ninety-seven delegates in Ohio and only four of the sixty-seven delegates in New Jersey. His total for the day to 177, far less than the 200 his campaign had once hoped for.[200] "We put too much money into

California. That money could have been spent in Ohio and elsewhere," Bell bitterly recalled.[201]

The primaries had concluded, but eleven state Republican conventions remained where the selection of delegates would be decided. Ford was ahead uncomfortably in the delegate count, 961 to 856. But many of these conventions were in the West, "Reagan Country."[202] In fact, one cover of *Time* in June featured photos of Jimmy Carter, Gerald Ford, and Ronald Reagan with the caption, "Our Next President (Pick One)." The story led off, "Now the choice is down to three—and they are among the most unusual politicians in the nation's history. The next President of the United States will be either Jimmy Carter, the one-term Georgia Governor who has had the most spectacular political rise since Wendell Wilkie in 1940; or Ronald Reagan, the two-term California Governor who staged the most successful challenge against an incumbent since Theodore Roosevelt took on William Howard Taft in 1912; or Gerald Ford, the longtime Michigan Congressman whom fate, Watergate and the 25th Amendment propelled into the Oval Office."[203]

It was still, as Reagan reminded his crowds, "Anybody's ballgame."

11

CONTENTIOUS CONVENTIONS

"There's no room for charity now."

After thirty Republican primaries in which over nine million people voted during a six month period, after thousands of workers and volunteers dedicated hundreds of thousands of hours, and after millions of dollars spent by the two campaigns, the party was no closer to deciding who would lead the GOP than it had been at the beginning of 1976. The contest between Gerald Ford and Ronald Reagan was tied like a wet shoelace.

Although the primaries had concluded without a nominee selected, the battle might finally be decided in the eleven remaining state GOP conventions to take place prior to the Republican National Convention in August.[1] But conventional wisdom had been wrong all year, so it was anybody's guess whether Reagan or Ford could formulate a breakthrough in these state GOP meetings and lock up the 1,130 delegates needed for a first ballot nomination.

Some in the party hoped to avoid a protracted fight in Kansas City, to avoid airing the GOP's dirty laundry in public yet again. But after Nixon, Watergate, Agnew, and the woes of the Ford Administration there was little chance that anything was left to further damage the Republican Party. In fact, the protracted fight was happening whether or not the party elders wanted it. "What some Republican professionals feared was a nasty summer, a bloody convention—and a party split so badly that only a shotgun pairing of Ford and Reagan on the same ticket could heal it," wrote *Newsweek*.[2]

In the remaining state conventions to occur over June and July of 1976, the fate of several hundred delegates would be decided. Of the conventions, some would be the culmination of weeks and sometimes months of extended selection processes. Others would be more isolated events, where all the delegates to the national convention would be selected at a given state Republican Party convention over a one or two day period.

The fight would be furious and the future of the GOP was at stake. State and local activists were accustomed to getting along despite their ideological differences. But this time, activists at all levels would be at each other's throats. Finding common ground was the least of their worries, and the tactic of offering a delegate slot or two to the losing side was rarely an option. This time, every single delegate mattered. As one Virginia GOP activist told the *Washington Post* after the Old Dominion's state convention, "There's no room for charity now."[3]

Also, there was the matter of around 150 uncommitted delegates.[4] It is easy to understand why they stayed uncommitted for so long; they loved being wooed. Many had achieved a measure of success in their own chosen fields of endeavor: homemakers, small businessmen, elected officials, or community leaders. They paid their bills, worked hard at their jobs, worshiped each Sunday, participated in local Republican Party politics, and tried to raise their children to be upright, moral, contributing members of society. But it was quite another thing when these delegates received personal phone calls from the President of the United States, inviting them to breakfast, lunch, or to a private meeting in the Oval Office where their advice would be solicited on relations with the Soviets. It tended to turn one's head. And when Ronald Reagan sent them personal notes and called them on the phone, inviting them to have dinner with him and "Nancy" and "By the way, do you mind if I bring along John Wayne and Jimmy Stewart?" Well, that can be a real head-turner too.

To top it all off, Walter Cronkite was calling, trying to find out who they were leaning towards today, Ford or Reagan? And so was Tom Brokaw from NBC, Frank Reynolds from ABC, and other reporters from all the networks, and the *New York Times*, the *Washington Post*, the *Wall Street Journal*, and the Associated Press. And then, at the backdoor, there was a photographer from UPI who wanted to take their picture. These reporters wanted their advice too. They wanted to know what they thought of Ford's speech, or Reagan's newest announcement, how the Ford campaign was being run, and did Reagan make a mistake by not going into Ohio more aggressively?

And then, there they were, quoted on the evening news, and in the big newspapers. Someone on the radio mentioned their names because they were "uncommitted" delegates. And then the neighbors and friends called them, squealing with delight that they also saw them on television, being interviewed by John Chancellor of NBC. So after months of being wined and dined, of being sought after by the biggest politicians, the biggest movie stars and the biggest people in media, what have they finally decided to do?

They decided that this was a tough decision, one that would require a lot more thought.

The upshot was that all the attention and wooing had gone to many of their heads, and both the Ford and the Reagan campaign came to regard many of these uncommitted delegates as royal pains in the ass. "Some of these delegates probably have learned it's romantic to be an uncommitted delegate," James Baker wryly noted for the *Washington Post*.[5]

"The words, 'The President is calling,' dazzled many of the uncommitted. Missouri's Marlene Zinzel, who with four other delegates had been flown to Chicago at the Reagan campaign's expense to meet the Californian for an hour was nevertheless 'shocked' when Ford tracked her down by phone at a beauty shop in Oakville, MO. 'I couldn't believe it,' she recalls. 'I can hardly remember it. He told me he could win over Carter. He asked me if I would consider him and I said that I would,'" reported *Time*.[6]

One of the best political cartoonists at the time, Jeff MacNelly, summarized the situation by drawing a huge Marine One helicopter hovering over a small country store bearing the name "Merle R. Spruggins Groceries." Two women were sitting on the front porch and one said to the other, "That must be President Ford again . . . Merle's an uncommitted delegate, y'know."[7]

Of those approximately 150 uncommitted delegates, thirty were from Mississippi. All parties and everybody in the media had long ago counted those delegates for Reagan. Nonetheless, the fight for Mississippi ended up as a collision involving the animosities between the two campaigns and the over-feted, self-patronizing uncommitted delegates of 1976. Long friendships would end and some people would never speak to each other again. Political careers were wrecked in the wake of this bitter intra-state fight that occurred on the national stage under the full glare of the national media.

"In its final days, the Ford-Reagan contest was marked by a bitterness that reflected the effects of four grueling months of campaigning that was still likely to leave the GOP nomination out of the grasp of either man. And, at the end as in the beginning, the dominant issues in the Republican race were foreign policy and military power," wrote Ed Walsh for the *Washington Post*, the day after the June 8 primaries.[8]

Only ten weeks remained before the gathering in Kansas City, and there was plenty of work to go around. Both sides conceded that Reagan's campaign had done a better job of organizing the state conventions and that he had an additional advantage since many were in the West and South. But Ford had a delegate lead of around ninety votes, and it was open to question whether Reagan could close the gap in time.[9]

In late June 1976, *Time* reported, "As the struggle for the nomination moves toward what looks like a close brawling finish, Reagan's superior organization shows, especially in the remaining Western convention states that still are electing delegates. For months Reagan's men burrowed into the bedrock, taking control of the local parties at the ward and precinct levels. While Ford built his organization from the top down, Reagan built from the bottom up." In the same story, a Ford spokesman bemoaned the situation, saying of Ford's local supporters, "We let them go. We didn't even have any pros to guide us. . . . [O]ur poor dumb people."[10] Betty Ford, who was never at a loss for words, told *Women's Wear Daily* of her husband's campaign staff, "I can tell you that they just sat back complacently, thinking that the President would be nominated, that it was some sort of shoe-in."[11]

If Ford was nervous, Jimmy Carter was supremely confident, as his totals for June 8 put him at 1,514 delegates, nine more than needed for a first ballot nomination. At this point, the "stop Carter" movement collapsed, and the Democrats began to fall in line behind their improbable nominee.[12]

While Carter was soaring, an old and legendary political aide to Franklin Roosevelt, James Farley, passed away at age eighty-eight. He was the architect of FDR's political career until 1940, when Roosevelt decided to break the "No third term" rule of all previous Presidents. Farley broke with FDR and ran for President himself in fit of pique.[13] In many ways, Farley was the political architect of the modern Democratic Party and his efforts led to the party's forty-year dominance.

With George Wallace thoroughly trounced by Carter, Myra MacPherson of the *Washington Post* did an interesting profile of the Alabamian, which perceptively covered how Carter, Reagan, and Scoop Jackson had superseded his populist appeal. The reporter wrote, "He was an old face selling old wares, wares that had been picked up and polished and improved upon by new faces that lent them a new respectability. Busing and law and order became issues for everyone from President Ford and Ronald Reagan to Jimmy Carter and Scoop Jackson. 'All of them done stole my water. They're drinking out of my dipper,' he complained."[14]

Wallace was by and large right. But he had always been just an "aginner" and never really proposed solutions to the problems he identified in America. Reagan and Carter not only identified the problems, albeit it in softer tones than Wallace, but they also proposed concrete solutions. Still, Carter flew to Alabama to express his appreciation when Wallace released his delegates to the former Governor of Georgia.[15]

Illinois and Texas had to go through pro forma state conventions, but since Reagan had destroyed Ford in Texas and Ford had routed Reagan in Illinois, the selection of their final delegates was a *fait accompli.* Missouri, Minnesota, Idaho, and Colorado had to complete their selection processes at their respective state conventions. And Utah, Montana, Connecticut, North Dakota, Iowa, Delaware,

New Mexico, and Washington still had to host conventions where all their respective delegates would be chosen.

Ford met with his strategists at the White House to map out his plans for winning the delegates that would be allocated at the state conventions. Reagan met with his team at Lake Tahoe for two days. Both predicted first ballot nominations, naturally, but virtually all of the national media reported that neither side would have enough committed delegates before the national convention. Yet Reagan was feeling a bit more confident, as five of the conventions would be in his stronghold areas in the South and the West. Part of Ford's strategy to win delegates was to continue to raise the specter of Goldwater's landslide defeat in 1964 in order to scare GOP activists into turning away from Reagan.

Although Reagan had not backed away from his earlier statement that he might not support Ford in the fall if he lost the nomination, Sears was telling reporters that yes, Reagan would support the President. But he did go so far as to say that he questioned whether or not Reagan would be doing any campaigning for the Ford ticket or if Reagan's supporters would be backing Ford.[16]

Some in the Ford camp were seriously debating the wisdom of the Stu Spencer commercials suggesting Reagan could start a war, fearing that they enraged Reagan's supporters too much. There was deep concern over their interest in supporting Ford if he were the nominee. "The issue was working for us, but we couldn't let it alone. Instead, we tried overkill and drove away the very people we'll need to win in November," one campaign insider complained.[17] Many felt that Spencer was engaged in a vendetta against Reagan that affected his judgment.

Reagan's forces attempted to strike back on their own. At a Reagan event in California, a helicopter trailed a sign that read, "Reagan's ahead because Ford bumped his." Of the deteriorating relations between the two campaigns, the *Washington Post* referred to the GOP's Eleventh Commandment as a "dead letter."[18]

The first major post-primary contest between Ford and Reagan was the Missouri state convention over the weekend of June 12-13. Ford arrived on Friday to speak to and meet with delegates. His in-state leader, Governor Kit Bond, kept up the "Reagan can't win" drumbeat by telling a crowd about a poll that showed Ford running better against Jimmy Carter than Reagan.[19] The entire hierarchy of Republican officials was supporting Ford, including Attorney General John Danforth and his Deputy John Ashcroft.[20] Reagan also arrived Friday evening and met with delegates, but he would speak to the convention on Saturday, while Ford would depart for Washington Friday evening after a brief stay in Springfield.

Missouri would send a total of forty-nine delegates to the national convention. Of those, thirty had already been selected by balloting in congressional districts. As the state convention began, where the final nineteen delegates would be chosen, Ford had a slight lead over Reagan, fifteen to twelve with three uncommitted.[21]

Once again, the Reagan and Ford forces did not even attempt to put on a show of harmony or good humor. Ford's team filed challenges to 395 of Reagan's delegates to the state convention and included language that would have prevented those challenged Reagan delegates any voice in deciding their own fate.[22]

Sears had sent Don Devine and Morton Blackwell to handle things for Reagan at the convention. When the Ford forces attempted to disenfranchise the Reagan state delegates, Devine immediately held a press conference in which he announced the Reagan campaign's determination to hold a competing convention, elect its slate of delegates and send them to Kansas City.[23] Signs which read, "Thou Shalt Not Steal," a brainstorm of Blackwell's, also appeared on the floor of the Shrine Mosque, the convention's venue. Blackwell and Devine successfully used intimidation tactics to bluff the Ford camp, including a harsh draft of a newsletter that Blackwell taped on the door of the Ford offices. After a night of intense negotiations, the challenges to the Reagan delegates were withdrawn.[24]

While Ford was slightly ahead in the count of Missouri delegates already elected for the national convention, he was behind in delegates for the Missouri state Republican convention in Springfield that weekend. A total of 1,439 state delegates attending this event would determine the final nineteen national delegates who would join the other thirty in Kansas City.[25] Reagan's forces rammed through a slate of nineteen individuals and would have won all nineteen had Governor Bond's wife not made a tearful plea for her husband to be included as a delegate so that he would not be embarrassed.[26]

Devine and Blackwell were of no mind to give up even one slot. Their job was to win as many as possible for Reagan. Bond was up for re-election and only moderately conservative, but he was personally popular with the Missouri Republicans. Devine and Blackwell relented, and Bond was awarded the last delegate position.[27] It was one of the few examples of charity by either side. Danforth was denied a delegate slot.[28]

Ford was wiped out at the Missouri convention and embarrassed himself by attending. His aides had erred and assumed they had a tighter control of the event than they really did. Once again, finger pointing was going on inside of the President Ford Committee. But Reagan's forces were elated. Andy Carter, Reagan's

Political Director told the *Washington Post*, "This was the first convention since the primaries ended, and we won it big."[29]

The results also opened up new worries for Ford—that he could never match Reagan as a public speaker at the state conventions, and that his followers lacked the passion of the Reaganites. Ford's people were being "out hustled" by Reagan's passionate supporters. "These Reagan people don't care: they're absolutely ruthless. They want all of it. Our people just aren't used to this uncompromising hardball stuff," Jim Baker—misidentified as "Fred" Baker—told *Time*. Baker's complaint was uncharacteristic for the normally cool Texan.[30]

Reagan's speech in Springfield had electrified the hall and may have moved some soft Ford supporters or uncommitted delegates over to his side. Reagan would speak to the Iowa state convention the following weekend, and Baker, Spencer, Rogers Morton, and Dick Cheney worried that Reagan might do there what he and his team had done in Missouri.

The President expressed his own concerns about his ability to match Reagan's fierce oratory in an interview with *Time* columnist Hugh Sidey, telling the respected journalist, "I'm the first to admit that I'm not an accomplished speaker. My own speechmaking ability from a text is not first class. . . . I have developed a bad reputation both as to speeches and presentation." He also betrayed his concerns about his campaign's abilities compared to Reagan's.[31]

After the weekend, Reagan had closed the gap once again and trailed Ford by only approximately seventy delegates. The *Washington Post* estimated that Ford had 958 delegates and Reagan had 887. There remained another 259 delegates to be selected.[32]

Iowa's state convention took place on June 19 and culminated a six-month delegate selection process that had begun with the January caucuses. Texas's state GOP convention was also to be held that weekend, but since Reagan had earlier won all 96 delegates, there was no doubt as to who would get the last four.[33]

Republicans in Washington State would also be holding their convention. Reagan had near total control and was assured of getting nearly all the delegates available.[34] On the other hand, Ford had almost complete sway over the upcoming Delaware state GOP convention and hoped to win all of the 17 delegates they would send to the national convention.[35]

The Federal Election Commission issued the June reports of all the candidates. Reagan had whittled his debt down to around $150,000 from the million-dollar debt he'd been carrying. The surge in funds was a direct result of his nationally televised address, his direct mail and the recent release of FEC funds. If there was any doubt as to the closeness of the race between Ford and Reagan, it was shown in the filings with the federal agency. Since the beginning of the campaign, Ford had raised and spent $11.4 million while Reagan had raised and spent $11.3 million.[36]

Ford had planned to campaign in Iowa where both he and Reagan were to appear on the same dais for a dinner honoring RNC Chairman Mary Louise Smith, who was from the state. But Ford ducked out at the last minute and some Reaganites speculated he just wasn't up to a personal confrontation with Reagan.[37] In fact, a crisis was developing in Lebanon and hundreds of Americans were at risk from Arab terrorists. Ford decided to forgo campaigning to monitor and oversee the Americans' evacuation.[38] Mrs. Ford was sent in his place and, as the *Washington Post* reported, aimed "an apparent barb at Reagan: 'This is a very delicate time and issues have to be handled with great delicacy. You cannot be forceful in a way that would get our country in trouble.'"[39]

At the Iowa convention Ford won nineteen delegates and Reagan won seventeen. Still, the Reagan forces were pleased, as they had won more than originally expected. The results came after many protracted late night and early morning discussions, as well as stubbornness on the part of one pro-Ford state delegate, who at the last minute switched his vote to support a friend who was running as a pro-Reagan delegate to Kansas City.[40]

Ford, in fact, should have done much better in Iowa. His Campaign Chairman, Governor Robert Ray, had confidently predicted that Ford would win twenty-three delegates and Reagan only thirteen.[41] Once again, Evans and Novak had the inside dope on how the Ford forces flubbed their chance: "Adding to Reagan's skill in selling himself here as Goldwater never could was a continuing stream of mistakes by Ford's managers. Lack of nerve, poor timing and a simple ignorance of known political facts by Ford operatives all took their toll."[42]

Simply put, the Reagan forces, led by Sears, bluffed the Ford forces into surrendering a stronger position when it came to control of six at-large delegates.[43] Sears had not made a lot of money playing poker for nothing. Conservatives had lodged numerous complaints against Sears during the previous year over the Campaign Manager's tactics and decisions. Some of the complaints were justified, but Sears also possessed a "creative conceit" that allowed him to pivot and focus the campaign's and the media's attention in new directions. He also excelled at the "inside baseball" aspects of hardball convention negotiations and strategies. Through June, July, and August of 1976, Sears performed one magic act after another to keep Reagan's chances alive and moving forward.

Unlike in Iowa, Reagan's forces in Washington state had the strength to seize all the delegates available. But a threatened walkout, this time by Ford's supporters, forced a settlement.[44] Nonetheless, Governor Dan Evans, a Ford supporter, was refused a delegate position—as was another Ford supporter, North Carolina Governor Jim Holshouser, at his state's convention the same weekend.[45]

That Washington's Reaganites denied Evans a slot was understandable. He had spoken out loudly against Reagan, as he told the *New York Times* several weeks before that a Ford-Reagan ticket would be a "sure ticket to disaster. It would reinforce all the President's weaknesses."[46] Of course, Evans was also promoting himself for the second spot if Ford won the nomination.

Reagan had addressed the Washington convention and later summed up his feelings to reporters, saying, "All in all, a good weekend."[47] Reagan's coordinator in the Evergreen State was Dale Duvall, who had started out working with the Ford campaign, but concluded that Ford could not be elected President. Duvall had been courted by Andy Carter and Frank Whetstone from the national office of Citizens for Reagan, but had made it clear that if he were to make the switch, then he would have to be in charge. They agreed, and Reagan's fortunes in the Evergreen State improved immediately under Duvall's decisive leadership.[48]

When Reagan spoke in Washington, he turned the "electability" argument on its head, telling the delegates, "Look at the record in California, where I was elected in a state where Democrats outnumber Republicans almost 2-to-1 and I won the Governorship by nearly a million vote margin." As the *New York Times* reported, "'This electability thing' is now the first subject Mr. Reagan brings up when he talks to undecided Republicans in the last 10 states choosing national convention delegates." For some months prior, Ford had tried to make this his issue.

At the North Carolina GOP convention, delegates were selected in accordance with party rules, and so were apportioned, twenty-eight to twenty-five, according to the primary vote back in March which Reagan had won, 53 percent to 47 percent.[49] But Tom Ellis, mindful of the possibility that neither candidate might win on the first ballot in Kansas City, loaded the delegation with pro-Reagan supporters at his state convention.[50] Although bound on a first ballot at the national convention, they would be freed to vote their individual preference on any subsequent ballots.

In Colorado, which was also beginning its selection process that weekend,

Reagan won the first three slots available. Reagan eventually took twenty-six delegates to only five for Ford.[51]

Ford was being outgunned in the early state conventions, but he was not without resources. He invited the uncommitted delegates from West Virginia to lunch, presumably not to talk about how the Mountaineers would do in football that fall. But six declined the invitation, and Governor Arch Moore told reporters it was because they were for Reagan.[52] The invitation to the West Virginians was just the beginning of the pampering uncommitted delegates would receive from the White House.

Ford also invited the New Jersey delegates and alternates over for cocktails in the East Room of the White House and fielded questions for forty minutes. Vice President Nelson Rockefeller had traveled to the state in June to plead with the delegates to change their stance.[53] Sometime after meeting with Rockefeller, Tom Kean, the speaker of the New Jersey Assembly and head of Ford's campaign in the state, went on television to pronounce the Reagan nomination a "disaster" for the GOP.[54] The Pennsylvania and Maryland GOP delegates would also receive a much-coveted invitation to the White House.[55]

Reagan was inching up on Ford, and the *Washington Post* blared the headline: "Republican Race Grows Tighter Still." Under the byline of the estimable David Broder, a story detailed how Reagan had closed the gap with Ford. He was now only down fifty-five delegates.[56]

"According to the estimates of the rival camps, the scorecard when the final state conventions are finished on July 17 will show Mr. Ford no more than 25 votes ahead of Reagan and could conceivably put the former California Governor a handful of votes in front. In either case, the balance of power will lie with the bloc of uncommitted delegates, now numbering 159," Broder wrote. The paper's freshest estimate of the race for delegates between the two put Ford at 997 and Reagan at 942. And Reagan was expected to do well in the next three state conventions in Montana, Idaho, and New Mexico on the weekend of June 26.[57]

Ominously for Ford, Broder continued, "If the Reagan estimates prove right, the Californian could regain the lead in the delegate count . . . for the first time since early May."[58] The key phrase in Broder's piece was "estimates." In fact, media tabulations fluctuated enough to keep people guessing. The Ford forces accused Sears of floating phony counts, and Sears accused Morton and Baker of doing likewise. Both sides were heavily engaged in this psychological warfare for good reason: supporters, volunteers, the media, and all involved had a common interest in keeping the race lively and interesting. And it was important for Sears to motivate the Reagan forces while simultaneously attempting to demoralize Ford's supporters by boasting about Reagan's delegate counts.

Reagan was once again on offense, telling crowds and supporters that it was Ford, and not he, who was a regional candidate. Reagan explained that he had been doing very well in the primaries and conventions in the South and the West, and that these states would be needed in the fall campaign against Carter.[59]

America's attention was turned momentarily from the nail biter between Reagan and Ford to two breaking stories about conspiracies. The Senate Intelligence Committee released a report that charged the members of the FBI and CIA with conspiring to cover up evidence in the days after the assassination of President John F. Kennedy.[60] Also, Anthony Provenzano, "Tony Pro," a "Goodfella" of longstanding who had been rumored to have been involved with the disappearance of Teamster boss Jimmy Hoffa, was indicted in connection to a 1961 murder of another Teamster official.[61]

Although the weekend of the twenty-sixth was another good one for Reagan, he came up short in Minnesota and did not pick up a proportional amount of delegates as some reformers had proposed at the state convention.[62] In the end, he received only ten of the forty-two delegates. Reagan made a speech to the convention and was only politely received. Mrs. Ford campaigned there and wore a button that said, "Betty's Husband for President," never suspecting how much this message was undermining Ford's authority as President.[63]

The previous day, Mrs. Ford had experienced a horrific event in New York. Dr. Maurice Sage, president of the Jewish National Fund of America, was about to present Mrs. Ford with a Bible when he collapsed and died of a heart attack. While Secret Service agents tried to revive him, Mrs. Ford coolly and kindly led the crowd in a silent prayer for the man.[64]

Minnesota's GOP had changed its name the previous fall to the Independent-Republican Party in an attempt to burnish its image after the battering Republicans had taken throughout the previous several years.[65] Sears and David Keene had negotiated an agreement with the local GOP forces that would not give Reagan a proportional number of delegates, but more than what they had expected until the national Ford staff moved in and terminated the entire agreement.[66]

Reagan's forces threatened a "rump" convention, and Keene staged a frenzied scene in front of Rudy Boschwitz, an excitable Ford supporter, knowing he would fall for the ruse. Nancy Reagan walked in and, not realizing what was happening, thought Keene and his people were "crazy." The fight finally came down to one delegate, which Reagan's forces won by choosing a nineteen-year-old activist, sensing the convention would view this as sending a good message to young voters across Minnesota. As Keene said, "They thought it would be 'cute' to send this kid to Kansas City."[67] One dark cloud occurred for Ford when the 1,985 state delegates voted to formally endorse Ford, but fell short of the required 60 percent.[68]

Good news for Reagan came from New Mexico, Idaho, and Montana where he completed a near sweep of the delegates available at the three state GOP conventions that same weekend. In New Mexico, Ford's forces had proposed the very same proportional proposal they had shot down in Minnesota. But it didn't work. Reagan was awarded all twenty-one delegates available. "They didn't give us anything in Minnesota," Sears told the *Washington Post* as justification for killing the Ford proposal.[69] Andy Carter had dispatched Kenny Klinge to New Mexico, Carter's home state, with a blunt message for the conservatives there: "Get off your asses or I'm coming back." They did.[70]

And in a surprise to absolutely nobody, Reagan took all twenty delegates in Montana.[71] He had already won the state primary on June 1 over Ford, 65 percent to 35 percent, so the convention was a pro forma affair. Still, Reagan paid a quick visit to the state to speak to the convention and meet with delegates. Once again, the "fairness" issue came up, but Reagan told the assembled Big Sky Republicans, "Every vote counts. Now if we're going to suddenly be told at this late day in the game we should in the sprit of fairness start dividing up delegates, I will agree to that if we go all the way back to New Hampshire. . . . Because if the delegates had been distributed proportionally to vote in every contest so far, I'm the winner."[72]

A Ford supporter who was also a notorious Reagan-basher, Skip Watts, told the *Post* his take on the fight in Montana: "The Reagan people in the state were willing to compromise but Sears and [Frank] Whetstone have insisted on a political bloodbath." Whetstone was a tough conservative operative from Montana, where he published a newspaper in the town of Cut Bank.[73] He had opposed all "fairness" initiatives and would not allow even one uncommitted individual in the delegation.

The *Post* forecasted yet another dramatic reduction in Ford's delegate lead over Reagan after the weekend. Its tabulations showed Ford with a razor thin lead of only 49 delegates, 1,037 to 988.[74] But the *New York Times* had the race even closer, with Ford at 1,052 and Reagan at 1,018, a margin of only 34 delegates.[75]

Following the weekend's conventions, at a Republican National Committee meeting in Washington (in the name of "reform"), a proposal was put forward and approved that would require delegates in Kansas City to vote according to the will of the primary voters in their state and prevent "Trojan horse" delegates.[76] The move was a clear attempt by the pro-Ford Republican National Committee to keep conservative delegates who were pledged to Ford from breaking with the President to vote for Reagan in Kansas City. Republicans traditionally eschewed mandates to the states, unless they served their own purposes.

The gathering of the national committee also selected Senators Bob Dole and Howard Baker as the Chairman and keynoter of the Kansas City convention. Only Texas GOP Chairman Ray Hutchinson objected, noting they were both Ford supporters. Given the closeness of the race, Hutchinson argued the party should have picked two uncommitted individuals.[77] Dole and Baker, along with Senators Bob Griffin and John Tower, had been involved in lengthy secret meetings with Gerald Ford to try to find a way to revive his flagging campaign, as reported by Evans and Novak. They told the President that his campaign was "dangerously outclassed by Ronald Reagan's superior organization at the delegate-selecting state conventions."

Some of the blame centered on Donald Rumsfeld, for not taking Reagan's challenge to Ford more seriously beginning in the summer of 1975. A proposed solution to Ford's problem-plagued campaign was to replace Morton with Republican Congressman John Anderson, according to the two columnists. But Anderson had no national political experience and his outspoken liberal attitudes offended many conservatives in the party. The columnists also took a shot at Dick Cheney, calling him a "neophyte."[78]

Then there was the basic question of whose machine worked better. One Ford insider wryly told the *New York Times*, "politically, we're not very ept."[79] The Reagan campaign leaked less often, possibly due to the fact that most in the media got along well with the Reagan campaign's leadership. Nor did the campaign view the media as adversaries. Morale, too, was almost always higher in the Reagan office, than at the President Ford Committee.

These underpaid and overworked conservatives arrived early, worked late, and socialized after hours with each other. They were an ideological band of brothers and sisters engaged in a cause they believed in and working for a man they adored. To a person, they all would have walked through fire for Ronald Reagan.

However, the camp was not without its moments. One example was when Sears brought in a new Comptroller, Darrell Trent, to get a handle on the money management at Citizens for Reagan.[80] Trent often offended the hard-working staff, sometimes suggesting that workers and vendors were not being truthful in their expense vouchers and billings. He gained an unpopular reputation as a result. In one legendary confrontation, Trent questioned the expenses of a full time volunteer, Peter Monk, whom Dave Keene had recruited to the campaign to help with advance work in the South.

Monk wanted his money. Trent wouldn't give it to him. Monk told Trent that if he didn't get his money by the same time tomorrow, he would punch Trent out. The next day, Monk walked into Trent's office and demanded payment, but Trent still said no. Monk calmly took off his watch, reached over the desk, and punched Trent right in the nose, sending him sprawling. "I didn't mean to hit him as hard as I did. I busted his nose open and he fell to the ground. The whole time, Keene was standing there, packing his pipe." Monk received a standing ovation from the staff when he walked out of Trent's office. He was paid the next day, and despite the rocky start, the two men became close friends years later.[81]

Monk was "Indiana Jones" before the movie. He worked in Africa, South America, and other far-flung regions. It was not unusual for Monk to disappear for months or even years, traversing the world in search of adventure and fortune. He was also handed the unenviable task of producing a radio commercial with John Wayne, at Wayne's insistence. Wayne was out on his yacht, which was a converted PT boat. Monk waited two days for Wayne to return. When he did, Wayne spent another considerable length of time, "drinking and bashing Bill Roberts and Stu Spencer. 'That son of a b— betrayed my friend Ronnie Reagan. I'll get him some day,'" Monk recalled The Duke saying. "The radio commercials were worthless."[82]

The final round of state conventions would be held in Utah, Connecticut, North Dakota, and Colorado. On paper, Reagan was assumed to be strong in three of the four, with only Connecticut seen as a sure bet for Ford.

One bit of bad news that would eventually bode ill for Ronald Reagan was a rumor coming out of Mississippi that its delegation was not as solidly in support of him as everybody had assumed. Ford campaign officials at first dismissed the gossip. After all, Mississippi had long been known to be a hothouse of conservative sentiment. Reagan had visited the state many times for the Republican Party, and had campaigned there just the year before for "Gil" Carmichael, who had run for Governor and lost, albeit narrowly.

At the center of the brewing controversy was Clarke Reed, the GOP's National Committeeman and State Chairman. Reed was a through and through conservative, but as Keene said, "He was weak and he was sloppy."[83] In fact, Reed was never the head of the Reagan operation in Mississippi; Billy Mounger, a successful banker from Jackson was. But the Reagan operatives often deferred to Reed rather than Mounger when it came to in-state politics. Mounger sometimes bristled at being bypassed. The incoming State Chairman, Charles Pickering, a dedicated Reaganite, shared Mounger's sentiments.[84]

In an attempt to mollify the moderates in the Mississippi GOP, Reed had put many of them in the delegation as delegates or alternates at the state convention in April. Mississippi had a "unit rule" (which ironically was prohibited by the rule of the national party at the time) that called for the delegation to vote as a bloc.

There were thirty delegates and thirty alternates, and each had one-half of a vote. The rumors from the state centered on some Ford supporters who were intent on breaking the unit rule and casting their votes for the President. The idea behind the unit rule was the notion that it gave the Mississippi delegation more leveraging power. In 1976, this is precisely what happened. Reagan had recently paid a visit to the state to meet with the delegation, but this was widely interpreted as a "watering the garden" visit, and not some sort of salvage operation.[85]

As yet another example of the image problems of the Republican Party, Senator Henry Bellmon of Oklahoma, a nice man of indistinct ideology, proposed that the federal government begin to collect a 15 percent withholding tax monthly, as it already did with paychecks, from dividend checks, stock bonuses, interest on saving accounts, and the like.

No wonder only 20 percent of Americans thought Republicans were worth a damn in 1976.

As plans for the convention in Kansas City were proceeding, a new controversy emerged when it was learned that the Republican National Committee planned to allocate 388 rooms in the city to the Ford campaign, but only 100 for Reagan. The convention was also planned to give Ford 650 gallery passes, and only 300 to Reagan.[86] Similar actions over the course of the previous year by the national committee had been a source of consternation to Citizens for Reagan, especially their hard-charging General Counsel, Loren Smith, and Senior Aide Lyn Nofziger.

Smith fired off a letter to the party's Chairman, Mary Louise Smith, charging the committee with violating the Federal Election Committee laws in treating the two candidates differently and, in the opinion of Smith, unfairly.[87] The actions by the RNC and Smith's swift response only served to underscore the animosity between the warring camps.

Ford's problems in the state conventions were beginning to spill into New York and Pennsylvania. The Associated Press had previously reported that 119 delegates from the Empire State were supporting Ford. But a later count had eight delegates moving back to an uncommitted status. And in Pennsylvania, AP had reported that eighty-eight delegates had gone from uncommitted to supporting Ford. But the later AP assessment had eighteen now moving back to uncommitted.[88] Ford's frontrunner position was becoming increasingly tenuous.

Baker, Ford's delegate headhunter, had his hands full with the possibility of Ford delegates slipping away due to Sears's "raiding parties." And he still had to contend with wooing 159 uncommitted delegates in the meantime.[89] But he was prepared. Baker had a large staff of fulltime workers and volunteers. Each was assigned a state and the delegates from that state.[90]

According to one Baker aide, Peter McPherson, detailed profiles of each delegate were developed. These profiles included ideologies, jobs, spouse's names, ages, hobbies, religions, and people who influenced the delegate. Baker then assigned a priority to each, as solidly Reagan, soft Reagan, uncommitted, soft Ford, or solidly Ford.

All files were updated almost daily, and Baker sent phone logs daily to the White House for Ford to personally make calls.[91] Also, some delegates were supporters of Ford but were bound under their state party rules (if they had been elected as Reagan delegates) to vote for Reagan on the first ballot. Nonetheless, these delegates would be free to vote their personal preference after that.[92] Baker needed to track these delegates as well. All parties were rapidly concluding that, in all probability, neither contestant would have enough delegates in August for a first ballot nomination.

Baker and his staff, including one young volunteer, Brad Minnick, spent countless hours on the phone staying in touch with delegates, listening to their gripes, doing favors for them, and on and on. Minnick said years later, "We were, in effect, political babysitters."[93] Even the shift of one delegate, as in the case of Salvatore Tortorici of Brooklyn, from Reagan to Ford, earned national news coverage.[94]

Holding on to delegates was but one problem facing both candidates. The GOP faced an even greater problem in holding onto what was left of their voters. Carter's anti-Washington themes were striking a chord with conservatives, especially in the South.

Additionally, the Ford camp revived a new strategy for stalling Reagan's drive for the nomination. Although Ford had wavered over the previous six months over whether or not he considered Reagan to be qualified for Vice President, his staff was now leaking that Reagan was, in fact, under consideration.[95] The obvious goal was to undermine Reagan with the remaining delegates, as Ford's team reasoned the conservatives would settle for a Ford-Reagan ticket. *New York Times* columnist James "Scotty" Reston took his usual shot at Reagan writing, "In fact, the Vice Presidency, if it weren't for the possibility of its leading to the Presidency, is almost perfect for Ronald Reagan: decorative, theatrical and not too much work."[96]

Several days earlier, Reagan had asserted to the Mississippi delegation that there was "no way" he would accept the number two slot with Ford, but the speculation continued to dog him right up until the convention in Kansas City.[97]

On the eve of the nation's bicentennial, a minor scandal erupted in the nation's capital when Bob Woodward and Carl Bernstein reported in the *Washington Post* that Senator Clifford P. Hansen of Wyoming had attempted to trade the votes of seven delegates from his state for an agreement from the Ford White House to sign a bill that would enhance the state's mineral and oil revenue.

At first, Hansen confirmed he had struck a deal with Ford. The White House, however, said that while there had been conversations about the bill with the Senator, no deal had been made. Wyoming's delegation had long been assumed to be safely in the Reagan camp, but it was technically uncommitted. With the contest so close, a shift of even a handful of delegates could tip the balance. Under tough questioning, Hansen at one point told one of the reporters "Well, maybe I did. Okay, I did. G—damn you." Hansen was but one of many politicians to be nailed by the assertive investigative reporters.[98]

One day later, both Hansen and the White House denied there had been any quid pro quo. Nessen shot down the story, asking reporters rhetorically that if the President had been using his signature pen to help him politically, then why had he signed the energy bill that hurt him in Texas, and why had he favored an increase in Social Security taxes? With that, fortunately for the President, the issue faded.[99]

On the Wednesday before the final round of state conventions, Reagan took to the airwaves again, this time on ABC, for a half-hour address to the nation. The cost was less than that of the speech on NBC, according to Jim Lake. But ABC's market share was substantially smaller than the older network. The cost for the airtime was $58,000 and the production cost another $25,000.[100]

This time, however, Reagan never mentioned President Ford's name—or Henry Kissinger's or Jimmy Carter's for that matter. But he directed some criticism towards the Georgian. Reagan mainly called for a "New Coalition" of politically conservative minded people from the two parties and from independents. Alluding to Carter, Reagan said, "You can't get to the heart of an issue by being vague about it. I'm not asking you to help me because I say, 'Trust me, don't ask questions, and everything will be fine.' I ask you to trust yourself. Trust your own knowledge of what's happening in America."[101]

Clearly, Sears wanted the uncommitted delegates going to Kansas City to see Reagan in another light: more Presidential, more visionary, and more upbeat. Sears always had his eye on the fall election and not only the convention. He had always resisted the ideological holy war Reagan's conservative supporters had wanted to wage against Ford. Although Reagan's campaign had only taken off after he moved right in his message, Sears wanted to now bring him back to the center ever so gently. This action too by Sears was the subject of much debate for years after.

Sears and his defenders believed that Reagan's winning the nomination of the Republican Party would only be worthwhile if the nomination was worth something. Sears knew Catholics were uncomfortable with the overtly "born again" Carter.[102] And that strategy was evident in the newest speech, when Reagan made open appeals to ethnic voters in the Northeast, especially Catholics. The *coup de grace* was when Reagan closed by quoting Pope Pius XII: "The American people have a genius for great and unselfish deeds. Into the hands of America, God has placed the destiny of an afflicted mankind."[103]

The next state convention began on July 8, when Ford shocked Reagan and took the majority of North Dakota's eighteen delegates.[104] It had been widely assumed that this upper plains state would be receptive to Reagan's populist message. Reagan's supporters had told the media that their man, and not Ford, would receive ten or eleven of the delegates.[105] Reagan spoke to the five hundred delegates assembled in Fargo and was greeted with only polite applause until he warmed up the crowd with his regular stump speech. It was then that he was interrupted by hearty applause several times.

In fact, the state GOP machine, firmly under Ford's lieutenants' control, muscled out two likely Reagan delegates at a nominating committee meeting (which the Reagan people had not attended) the morning of Reagan's speech. When their move was learned, Reagan's supporters threatened a floor fight and so were eventually granted four delegates in an effort to prevent a whole scale range war inside the state party. The agreement was not made for charity's sake but for survival.[106] At the national convention, Reagan actually received seven votes for his nomination from North Dakota.[107] But at the time, the result was better than expected for Ford.

Baker later released a new list of Ford's committed delegates, including the twelve from North Dakota, which showed Ford extending his count to 1,067. Reagan was hovering just below a thousand, according to most sources.[108] But Reagan wasn't out of the race by any means. He had been slowly closing the gap throughout the conventions, but he was also running out of Western and Southern states.

Ford regained the rhetorical offensive when, in an Oval Office press conference, he came out four square for Reagan joining him on the ticket. The President Ford Committee finally concluded that it was better to love thy conservative brother for the time being. Ford sloughed off questions about the sharp rhetoric between the two that might keep them from working together. "I exclude nobody," Ford said. Once the Ford campaign settled on the "how to handle Reagan" issue, it became an effective tactic.[109] Reagan was once again forced to refute his interest in being number two, this time in Colorado.

Ford told the media he believed the delegates should be aware of his potential running mates and, curiously, even suggested it be left to them to decide. "A Presidential nominee ought to make his wishes known to the delegates." His nomination would rise or fall in Kansas City on this issue.[110]

In the meantime, while both camps were attempting raids on the other's delegates, the Israelis, to the applause of many and the denunciation of others, staged a daring raid on Entebbe, Uganda, where they successfully rescued hostages from a hijacked airliner.[111]

While Baker was strongly asserting control over the delegate hunt and Ford was wisely romancing Reagan, doubts remained about much of the President's campaign operation, just as they had dogged him for two years. "President Ford's fractious campaign is lurching toward his increasing probable nomination in an atmosphere contaminated by recriminations, backstabbing and personal power plays which have brought the campaign to the brink of anarchy," reported Evans and Novak. They quoted one insider as saying, "I'd say there's a lot more gossip than work going on here."[112]

Ford operatives who came in for the most barbs from the acerbic columnists were Morton, Spencer, Cheney, Nessen, and Bob Hartmann.[113] In fact, several days later, Hartmann had his stripes yanked when his authority over issuing Presidential statements was taken away from him. And another media adviser to Ford, Robert Mead, resigned under heavy criticism, mostly due to complaints lodged against him by PBS and Robert MacNeill for providing poor assistance during a state dinner that featured Queen Elizabeth.[114]

Also attending that dinner were several delegates being wooed by the Ford campaign. In fact, sitting next to the Queen of England was the loquacious Clarke Reed.[115] When it came to handing out the goodies and perks, Reagan could not match the allure of the Ford White House, and people like Reed were especially susceptible to such courting.

Colorado began its convention process and Ford scored a small, but important psychological advantage over Reagan when he won three and Reagan only five of the delegates initially selected. But on Saturday, July 10, Reagan scored a comeback and won fifteen out of sixteen at-large delegates, despite being rudely cut off by the pro-Ford Convention Chairman, Carl Williams, while speaking.[116] Jack Ford was also in Colorado, campaigning for his father, who had been warned that he could suffer another embarrassment like Missouri and did not attend. The younger Ford gave an impressive speech on his father's behalf. He spoke for sixteen minutes, thus also violating the ten-minute speaking rule, but he was not silenced.[117] The hall roared its disapproval of Williams's childish actions against Reagan.

Reagan had spoken for twenty-six minutes, but he was thrilling both his and Ford's delegates. Reagan was clearly miffed at the slight, but Williams would not back down and even slashed his hand across his throat to give the sign to technicians to turn off Reagan's microphone. Four years later, in New Hampshire, Reagan would declare he was "paying for this microphone" insuring a place in American political history. As they left the convention hall at Colorado State University, Reagan and the young Ford encountered each other. They shook hands, and in a classy move, Jack Ford told Reagan, "Good luck."[118]

Following the Colorado results, according to most news agencies, Reagan once again cut Ford's lead to around forty delegates. He was closing the gap, but not fast enough.[119] Colorado proved another disappointment coming on the heels of the surprise in North Dakota.[120] Reagan's forces had hoped to capture all thirty-one Colorado delegates.

On Monday, July 12, Democrats gathered at a unity and harmony convention in New York City to nominate James Earl Carter of Georgia for President and Senator Walter Mondale of Minnesota for Vice President. Post-convention polling showed Carter trouncing both Reagan and Ford by 30 percent, and the Democrats were confident, especially in light of the fierce contest still going on inside the GOP.

Most of the speakers in New York at the Democratic Convention aimed their fire not at Reagan, but at Ford. They attacked the "Nixon-Ford Administration."[121] Many of the Democrats in New York bought into the false image of Reagan, but one who did not was Senator Edmund Muskie of Maine. Several days before his party's convention, Muskie told reporters that he thought Carter viewed Reagan as a "potentially tougher campaigner" than Ford.[122]

Both the Ford and Reagan camps slammed the ticket as "liberal." But Henry Kissinger didn't help Ford's cause when he told reporters that Carter's foreign policy would be "fairly consistent" with the Ford foreign policy.[123] Reagan issued a statement regarding Carter and Mondale that said, in part, "They're going to go forward on the same big government idea in seeking solutions in Washington programs for our problems."[124] Mondale was not nominated unanimously, as several minor candidates received a smattering of votes, including one for gonzo journalist Hunter S. Thompson.[125]

Two of the three networks would provide "gavel to gavel" coverage of the Democrats, as they would of the Republican meeting one month later. Only ABC began later than the other two, because of their broadcast of the annual All-Star Game during the Democrats' convention.

Network coverage typically began at 8:00 P.M. and concluded around midnight, but the coverage would continue even if the conventions did not run on time. And they rarely did. Correspondents like Tom Brokaw and Katherine Mackin of *NBC News* and Charlie Gibson of *ABC News* prowled the floor, interviewing dignitaries and delegates but rarely each other. High above the floor were the anchormen, and all involved had a ball. The networks devoted millions of dollars to convention coverage every four years.[126]

The last state conventions remained in Utah and Connecticut, on the weekend of July 18, but not before President Ford took a break to attend the All-Star Game in Philadelphia, where he threw out the first ball. Ernie Banks, the great former shortstop for the Chicago Cubs joined Ford in his box, along with America's catcher, Joe Garagiola. Banks was famous for once saying, "It's a nice day, let's play two."[127] Ford himself had two more to play before the Republican World Series at the Kemper Arena in August.

New FEC reports were issued. For the first time in the campaign, Reagan had actually raised more money overall than Ford.[128]

Reagan made his first foray into "Ford Country" to meet with "uncommitted" delegates from New Jersey, Delaware, and Pennsylvania. He was warmly received, but nonetheless came away empty handed. Reagan's old friend, actor Efrem Zimbalist Jr., introduced him.[129] In an interview, Paul Laxalt later remembered this phase of the campaign and recalled that Reagan was never very good with names. "I remember flying to New Jersey and I practically had to hold his hand, point people out to him. He said to me, 'There's some guy in New Jersey I'm supposed to be mad at. Can you tell me who?'"[130]

However, Stephen Isaacs, reporting for the *Washington Post,* told of a meeting in Harrisburg between Reagan and a twenty-one-year-old college student and Republican delegate, James Stein, who had been leaning towards Ford. But after meeting privately with Reagan, he "emerged from the meeting . . . to announce that he was now 'unleaned.'"[131]

In the meantime, Ford met with two hundred leaders from the American

Indian community, but the event was considered a farce as the leaders charged it was all a publicity stunt; they were requested to wear their Indian outfits though few did.[132] It was not known if they were asked to also put on "war paint."

Before the weekend's final contests, the *New York Times'* count of the delegate race put Ford at 1,067 and Reagan at 1,043, a difference of only 24 delegates.[133] Yet a somber mood was overtaking the Reagan campaign, as the fight for the uncommitted delegates was not proving fruitful.

Ford was also concerned, as he confided in his autobiography, *A Time To Heal*, "The uncommitteds weren't the only delegates about whom we had to be concerned. My advisers warned that some of my support was 'soft,' that anywhere between 50 and 100 delegates already pledged to me might waver and capitulate to pressure from the other side."[134]

Reagan lassoed the twenty delegates in Utah, as expected, and Ford took all thirty-five in Connecticut. According to most media tabulations, which included some uncommitted delegates who had declared for Ford over the weekend, the President had just over 1,100 delegates and Reagan around 1,063.[135] Both were within striking distance of the number needed for nomination, but Ford was now far closer. Reagan had won two of every three delegates available in the eleven state conventions and had won the majority of the total popular vote in the thirty primaries. But he would still need to win two of every three of the remaining uncommitted delegates.[136] And that was the fly in the buttermilk.

Charlie Black had the unhappy duty of trying to pry a few delegates out of the Nutmeg State. Ford's in-state supporters at the convention passed a motion to allow only votes for full slates, not individuals.[137] Had the convention proceeded under the old rules, Reagan probably would have received five delegates.

Connecticut's GOP had a reputation for moderation and reform, but not this time. Black told the *Post*, "It was an awfully heavy handed means of adopting rules. They've rigged it about as tightly as they could."[138] Ford's aides, knowing they had total control of the process, sent the President there to meet with delegates and address the convention in Hartford. Fred Biebel, the GOP State Chairman, had previously promised to grant some delegates to Reagan in exchange for fundraising help, but recanted and said that he'd "see to it that Connecticut sends not one Reagan delegate to Kansas City."[139]

Reagan meanwhile addressed Utah's state delegates, assembled in Salt Lake City, where an attempt was made to gavel him down by the convention's Chairman, as had occurred the previous week in Colorado. This time, however, Reagan had asked ahead of time about a time limit and was told he had thirty minutes to address the delegates. So he was startled when a note was passed to him indicating that he only had two minutes left to speak when he had only reached the thirteen-minute mark.

After upbraiding the note passer to the crowd, Reagan swung into an abbreviated speech, much to the disappointment of the rabidly pro-Reagan delegates in the Salt Palace. Still, Reagan managed to get in a couple of swipes at Carter, telling the delegates that Jimmy Carter was "standing tall in the straddle."[140] Christopher Lydon for the *New York Times* wrote, "Mr. Reagan illustrated his view of government as an alien force with a new anecdote about his days in the California Governor's office. The motto of his inner circle in Sacramento, he said, was: 'When we begin to talk of government as "we" instead of "they," we've been here too long.'"[141] Once again, as had happened in so many other states, a popular elected official was left off the delegate list because he had made the mistake of supporting Ford instead of Reagan. This time it was Utah Senator Jake Garn.[142]

Despite the Utah sweep, Reagan had lost precious ground to Ford over the weekend, and many in the media were beginning to smell defeat in the air. Lou Cannon flew back to California with Reagan and wrote a story that enraged the Reaganites. A banner headline in the *Post* the following Monday screamed, "Reagan's Camp: Air of Resignation." The story led, "Ronald Reagan has returned home to his ranch from the last Republican state convention, with some of his top aides and supporters acknowledging privately that he may have reached the end of the Presidential political trail."

Cannon proceeded to describe Reagan as "subdued." Reagan spoke as if his candidacy was over when he told the journalist, "I think my candidacy has been worthwhile." Reagan visited the press section of the plane to thank the journalists who had been covering him for many months and told them, "I don't have a complaint in the world. I think you've all been fair as hell." Reagan also worried how he would be treated at the convention, and Cannon concluded his piece by writing, "They were the words of a seemingly defeated candidate who was going back to his ranch content, believing that he had done his best even if that best proved to be not quite enough for victory."[143]

In fact, Reagan was exhausted. When he was exhausted, he became more reflective—but never defeatist. Reagan just needed to get his batteries recharged. Anybody who knew the man knew that that word "quit" was not a part of his vocabulary.

At that point, the *Washington Post's* tabulators had 1,093 delegates for Ford and 1,030 delegates for Reagan, with 136 uncommitted.[144] According to Cannon, Sears and Deaver were so mad at the journalist over the story that the pair refused to speak to him for a year.[145] *Time*, like other media publications, had the race much closer than the *Post.* According to their count, it was 1,104 for Ford and 1,090 for Reagan.[146]

All hell broke loose the next day when the Reagan campaign held a press conference. Senator Paul Laxalt, Reagan's Campaign Chair, assailed the *Washington Post* and an unnamed network. "What we are seeing on the part of the *Washington Post* and at least one television network is an effort to psych out Ronald Reagan's delegates, potential delegates and supporters. It won't work. They are not about to be fooled into forfeiting that chance by liberals in the media who . . . are fearful that Reagan will win," Laxalt told the reporters.[147]

Sears also participated in the press conference and announced that, in fact, Reagan had enough delegates to win a first ballot nomination. As part of his tactic, Sears released the names of three previously uncommitted delegates from North Dakota, Virginia, and Delaware who were declaring their allegiance to Reagan.[148] Baker scoffed to *Time* that "He's blowing smoke."[149] Of course, in making the charge, Baker himself was blowing smoke back at Sears by casting doubt on his claims.

The situation was so fluid that the media had to take both Laxalt's charges and Sears's claims seriously. They had seen Reagan's team pull more than a few rabbits out of the hat over the past year. But they had yet to witness the biggest, most shocking, most impressive and most controversial magic trick ever performed by John Sears, a.k.a. "Mandrake the Magician" to his supporters and things unquotable to his detractors.

12

THE SCHWEIKER STRATAGEM

"Do you think he'd do it?"

At the conclusion of the last round of Republican state conventions in the middle of July 1976, neither Ronald Reagan nor Gerald Ford had the delegates necessary for a first ballot nomination in Kansas City. Virtually all media organizations calculated that Ford was short of his goal by between thirty and forty delegates, while Reagan needed somewhere between fifty and seventy to reach the magic number of 1,130. Reagan had pulled closer due to superior work by his field staff in the state conventions, but not close enough. William Shannon, in a column for the *New York Times* wrote, "The prolonged competition between President Ford and former Governor Reagan had the quality of a death struggle."[1]

Still in play were the last remaining uncommitted delegates who would decide which of the two candidates would lead the Republican Party against Jimmy Carter in the fall campaign. And when many of the uncommitted delegates were pressed and asked whom they were leaning towards, Ford was moving even closer to his goal.

Citizens for Reagan put up a brave front, but the situation was getting worse. The former Governor of California, though persuasive and popular, could simply not match the perks that Ford could offer including invitations to state dinners, private meetings in the Oval Office, lunches in the East Room with the President and personal phone calls from Cabinet officials. Several were also invited to sit on the deck of an aircraft carrier, the *USS Forrestal*, in New York Harbor with Ford to celebrate the country's bicentennial.[2] Ron Nessen recounted in his book a joke that was circulating around the White House: An uncommitted delegate from New Jersey received a phone call from the President asking him to a state dinner with Queen Elizabeth. After a long pause, the delegate said to Ford, "What's for dinner?"[3]

Such jokes weren't far from the bizarre truth. In a survey of uncommitted delegates, the *Washington Post* reported that one, James White of Rochester, New York, told the paper, "I hope they're sending Air Force One for me, because I won't settle for anything else."[4] *Newsweek* reported, "By day, he was the President of the United States . . . but at night, Gerald Ford was a candidate running just slightly scared, retreating to the White House family quarters to call uncommitted delegates around the U.S. and earnestly seek their support in what was an increasingly tight and tense race for the Republican Presidential nomination."[5]

The Reagan campaign was also having its candidate call all the uncommitted delegates. He spent hours on the phone soliciting their support, guided by detailed memos written for him by Buzz Lukens, David Keene, and others. For hours on end, Mrs. Reagan would place the phone calls for Reagan, hand the phone to him, and he would discuss world events and the progress of the campaign, make small jokes, and remind them to call if they had any questions.[6]

During each call, Reagan would make notations on the memos, such as after his conversation with Mrs. Gail Healy, a delegate from Mississippi: "A good talk. She had many questions—I think she was pleased with the answers. Still says she is waiting to make her decision but I think the call was worthwhile."[7]

But Reagan, like everybody else, was also getting the runaround from some, as in the case of Bill Patrick, another Mississippi delegate: "He's for me . . . but then says he won't make a decision until the other side has had a chance to tell it's side. . . . Then he adds he hopes he won't hear anything to change."[8]

Next to a phone call he made to Joe Margiotta, the GOP Chairman for Nassau County, New York, Reagan wrote, "I don't know whether this call was useful at all. . . . I tried to get into a discussion of who had the best chance nationally . . . to sum it up, he terminated the conversation."[9] Keene had written in his memo that although Margiotta was a machine politician and committed to Ford, Reagan's charm might keep him from working overtime for Ford. It didn't. Next to some names were neat, small cursive notes by Mrs. Reagan that said, "No ans. We'll keep trying."[10]

Reagan wasn't converting anybody, but he was helping to hold most of them in an uncommitted posture in the face of the Ford White House and Jim Baker's full court pressure campaign. But it was only a matter of time before they began to buckle. Sears feared that the trickle could become a stampede long before the convention and that Reagan's long campaign would arrive in Kansas City "dead on arrival." *Newsweek* referred to the efforts by Ford and Reagan as "vote grubbing."[11]

Baker and Stu Spencer hit the road to "chat up" uncommitted delegates on their home turf. Baker went to Louisiana, and—in what appeared to many as a fool's errand—Spencer headed for Oklahoma. Still, the mere fact that Spencer was headed into the heart of "Reagan Country" must have sent chills through the Reagan campaign. Sears told author John Robert Green in *The Presidency of Gerald R. Ford*, "The incumbent could offer them anything. And he could do it.

So we were in a position where if we just stayed and did nothing, we were gonna be beaten."[12] Reagan confided to author Lee Edwards later, "There are still machines with that kind of power. . . . In those areas where people are told how to vote, we lost."[13] To make matters worse for Reagan, some delegates previously committed to him, or still uncommitted—including a few in Virginia and Louisiana, like David Treen—were moving to Ford, having been persuaded that he had a better chance against Carter than Reagan.[14]

The dynamics of the contest needed to be changed quickly, and John Sears thought he had the solution that would keep the campaign alive until August and possibly deliver the nomination to Reagan at Kemper Arena by shaking loose some uncommitted delegates.

After Paul Laxalt and Sears's press conference, during which Sears claimed that Reagan had the nomination in hand, Jim Baker jumped right back at them, releasing the names of sixteen formerly uncommitted delegates who he claimed had come around to Ford.[15] David Broder wrote in the *Washington Post* of Baker's announcement that "The accelerating psychological warfare between the contending Republican rivals had reporters scurrying between headquarters in downtown Washington to keep abreast of the latest claims."[16]

Sears responded to Baker by releasing the names of four previously uncommitted delegates who had declared their allegiance to Reagan, including Senator Strom Thurmond of South Carolina.[17] But Elizabeth Drew, in *American Journal*, calmly pointed out that of the claims of both camps were totaled, it would exceed the number of delegates available.[18] The *Post* account of the entire mess put Ford at 1,099 delegates and Reagan at 1,038 with 122 uncommitted.[19] Again, the *New York Times* had the contest closer—1,102 to 1,063—but all agreed that Reagan was behind and Ford was within striking distance.[20]

Sears could keep Reagan's hopes alive for a time by keeping the situation murky, but he would not be able to sustain Reagan's candidacy until the convention. The simple fact was Reagan lacked the firepower that Ford had at his disposal to whittle down the number of uncommitted delegates and put himself over the top.

Sears stuck to the claim that Reagan had 1,140 delegates. He also told reporters the campaign would give them a state-by-state list of Reagan delegates but then increased the smokescreen by telling reporters that they had hidden delegate strength. According to Sears, "closet" Reagan supporters, perhaps as many as forty to fifty, had told the media tracking the delegates that they were supporting Ford.[21]

Something needed to be done. Something that was, in the opinion of all, then and since, either brilliant, controversial, or both. Sears's newest tactic would be defended for years by his supporters and criticized just as virulently by his detractors, including many conservatives.

Sears decided that Reagan should pick a running mate well ahead of the convention. He reasoned that this tactic would put pressure on Ford to name his own running mate before the convention, as well as give Reagan's campaign maneuvering room until the convention. If they could keep the President Ford Committee off balance and the media in a holding pattern until August 18, they might find something else in Kansas City that could be used to help get Reagan the nomination.

Sears sat down with Andy Carter, Dave Keene, and Charlie Black to discuss the situation. All were confidants, and all knew how to count. Sears reviewed the bleak situation and offered up the idea of shaking things up with selecting a Vice Presidential candidate well ahead of the convention. The three saw the merits in Sears's arguments and agreed immediately with the revolutionary concept.[22] Keene later wrote, "At the very least, we would be off the defensive and that would in itself be worthwhile."[23]

In fact, Northeastern delegates had already attended a "stop Connally" meeting organized by Nelson Rockefeller in Maine. Liberals were paranoid that Ford might pick John Connally to placate conservatives if Reagan failed to get the nomination. For Sears, the questions were who would do it, and who would bring the most to the table? Whoever it was, the move needed to be made quickly. Time was running out.

With the primaries and the conventions over, Ford now had time to spend with uncommitted delegates using the most potent lobbying tool available to him: 1600 Pennsylvania Avenue. However, it's safe to say Ford wished he hadn't spent time with one particular delegate from New York.

State Senator Fred Eckert of Rochester was technically an uncommitted delegate who had previously been listed as a Ford supporter, but he was in fact a committed conservative and closet Reagan supporter who spent much of his time in Albany tweaking the liberal leadership of both parties. Eckert had been invited to the White House as part of the entire delegation from New York of "uncommitted" delegates to meet with the President. Ford had been briefed beforehand that Eckert was influential and so was invited into the Oval Office for a private meeting with Ford as Baker and Dick Cheney looked on. Ford went into his standard pitch, as Eckert appeared respectful and interested. That is, until Ford asked Eckert if he had any questions. Eckert replied in the affirmative.

"Well, Mr. President, I am just so honored to be here in the White House and so in awe that I am sitting here in the Oval Office with the President of the United States. But I do have just one question for you Mr. President." Ford, sitting behind his desk and smoking his pipe, nodded for Eckert to go ahead with his question.

Eckert said, "Mr. President, if Aleksandr Solzhenitsyn was an uncommitted delegate from New York, would he have been invited here today?" After an uncomfortable pause, Ford nearly choked on his pipe while Cheney and Baker stared at the ceiling, wishing with all their might that they were someplace, anyplace other than there in the Oval Office. Suffice to say, the meeting ended quickly.[24]

The *New York Times* had reported on the invitation to the New Yorkers, referring to the White House's wooing of those still uncommitted delegates and "rewooing" of those who were committed to him.[25]

Prior to the meeting with Eckert, Ford had been given a rough time by two delegates from Brooklyn who assailed him over the closing of Ft. Harrison. Broder wrote after the session, "He could be excused for concluding that there has got to be an easier way to get nominated." Broder described the delegates as complaining about the White House oeuvres while questioning Ford about why he never aspired to anything other than a seat in the U.S. House of Representatives. One of the delegates, Vito Battista, told Broder he preferred Italian food to what had been served in the White House.[26]

Other meetings with individual delegates went better. But one local official from Long Island expressed concern over a sewer project, which the President of the United States agreed to look into. Another individual delegate Ford was powerless to do anything about was his own Secretary of Agriculture, Earl Butz. Butz was a delegate from Indiana, but Indiana had gone for Reagan, so he would be compelled to vote for Reagan on the first ballot.

Still, the retail wooing effort was paying off for Ford, as delegates declared for the President came from Reagan's strongholds—including several from South Carolina, where Governor Jim Edwards was supporting Reagan and from Virginia, where Governor Mills Godwin was not, but the bulk of the party was.

In Virginia, Lt. Governor John Dalton expressed support for Ford, but the Reagan forces had never considered him a possible ally. Dalton would be running for Governor in 1977 and could not go against Godwin and hope to have his support the following year. Dalton's choice was offset by the Old Dominion's

GOP Chairman, Dick Obenshain, a strong conservative supporter of Reagan. Obenshain would die tragically in a plane crash just two years later, while running for the U.S. Senate in Virginia.[27]

Tempers were running high in Virginia, as several Reagan delegates switched to Ford. Several uncommitted delegates, whom the Reagan people thought were theirs, also declared for Ford. Kenny Klinge, Reagan's Virginia coordinator, was obviously not happy. Yet he assertively told the *Post*, "This was clearly not one of our better days, but we will be back."[28]

Ford's campaign also scored in the case of an assumed Reagan delegate from South Carolina. As reported in the *Washington Post*,

> The lists of converts to the Ford candidacy also included a South Carolina delegate who earlier had become a classic example of an obscure party figure whose uncommitted status earned him the ear of high level Administration officials. He is Bobby Shelton, Cherokee County Republican Chairman and a small businessman embittered by the cancellation of a $30,000 Small Business Administration loan two years ago and his inability to get any sympathy for the last several years from Washington officials. In an interview last month, Shelton told how his uncommitted status had produced a solicitous hour-long phone call from Secretary of Commerce Elliot L. Richardson and a personal letter from the President.[29]

Shelton and his wife were later treated to a meeting in the Oval Office with the President and he finally committed after that. Unfortunately, Reagan called just one day after Shelton had made his decision, though Shelton had been leaning his way.[30]

The uses—or abuses, depending on one's point of view—of the White House and the perks it could offer uncommitted delegates were drawing increased unfavorable scrutiny from the media, so a fig leaf memo was distributed to the White House staff from Cabinet Secretary James Connor warning that such "considerations, favors or rewards" were verboten.[31] Still, there were no charges of outright illegal behavior by the Ford White House. They had walked the line closely in several situations, but never actually crossed it. Green wrote in his book on Ford that "patronage jobs were dangled everywhere." But in fact there was never any evidence of outright abuse of power.[32]

Nonetheless, while it was 1976, some delegates apparently confused the White House with Tammany Hall. Several of the delegates being targeted by Baker had crassly raised the possibility of receiving federal jobs or contracts in exchange for their support of Ford. But Baker diplomatically stopped them short, reminding them it was against federal law to promise a federal contract in exchange for political favors. Baker told the *New York Times*, "We don't entertain those kind of suggestions."[33]

Reagan had his own unpleasant experiences with delegates. In one meeting, Reagan, accompanied by Dave Keene, was startled to hear an uncommitted delegate from Illinois explain that his law firm was failing. In exchange for Reagan arranging for $250,000 in business for him, his vote could be had. Reagan departed quickly with Keene, turned to him, and said sourly, "I feel like I need to take a shower."[34]

It was important to keep Reagan in the news and for him to keep making news. At one point, he went on the *Today* show to reiterate his challenge to debate Ford at the convention, which the President brushed aside. He also charged the Administration with trading favors for delegate votes and using "heavy handed" tactics, but Ron Nessen quickly denied the charge.[35]

Events were moving faster now, too fast for Sears's liking, between the two campaigns. On Friday, July 23, Baker released the names of fifteen previously uncommitted delegates from Hawaii and claimed that this announcement now put Ford over the top, with a total of 1,135 delegates. The *Washington Post's* numbers at the time showed Ford at 1,101 and Reagan at 1,027.[36] While the Associated Press and United Press International also put Ford under the magic figure, things were now getting just a little too dicey for Reagan.[37] Buttressing the skepticism in the media was Baker's initial refusal to release a complete list of pro-Ford delegates, despite having promised to do so several days before. Shortly thereafter, however, the names, addresses, and phone numbers of 1,119 delegates pledged to Ford were released to the media.[38] Still, some in the media were dubious.

The problem lay in delegates themselves telling the media one thing and the Reagan and Ford camps another, serving only to prolong the guessing game. Sears and Baker may not have agreed on much in 1976, but they did agree that most delegates were almost more trouble than they were worth. In three weeks, only a handful of delegates had made a commitment to one candidate or another. It was courting season, and the love of attention was in the air for any uncommitted Republican delegate in July and August 1976.

Pennsylvania was a perfect example. The Ford campaign had tallied more delegates than media tabulations. This discrepancy was typical. Concerning the East Coast delegates, the *Washington Post* wrote, "Reagan has had tough sledding in these eastern delegations, where he feels his record is much misunderstood and where some people feel he is some kind of kook."[39]

Also, freezing some of the more conservative uncommitted delegates was the rumor that Ford really did want Reagan for the ticket and that Reagan would accept the Vice Presidential slot. Reagan had to keep beating down the idea, but it hung around. In the minds of Reagan's men, the rumor was wholly impractical, for one reason: the two candidates could not get along. Something no one could have predicted was the second reason: Sears was about to drop his bombshell.

Citizens for Reagan sent a press release to the media touting a "major statement" on Monday, July 26, in Washington and Los Angeles. Reagan would be in Los Angeles and speak first.[40] Another press conference in the Senate would follow, but the release only listed Sears and Laxalt as participants. Some speculation centered on whether or not Reagan was announcing his withdrawal from the campaign.

Eight days prior to the distribution of the press release, Laxalt had placed a phone call to Senator Richard S. Schweiker of Pennsylvania, who was vacationing in Ocean City, New Jersey.[41] Schweiker was not only a member in good standing of the liberal Wednesday Club, he was also a Ford delegate.

Previously, Sears had reviewed the situation with Laxalt after talking it over with Black and Keene. All parties agreed that something needed to be done, but the pickings in the GOP were pretty slim. Choices for a running mate came down to Governor Jim Rhodes of Ohio and Schweiker—although some conservatives felt a case could have been made for Senator Jim Buckley of New York.[42]

Rhodes controlled the ninety-seven Ohio delegates and most likely could have delivered them while not antagonizing Reagan's conservative delegates. All parties agreed that if winning the convention were the only goal, Rhodes would have made sense. But no one wanted to run a general election with the curmudgeonly and controversial Rhodes. Jules Witcover described him as "slightly unsavory" in *Marathon* and Sears dryly told Witcover his feeling about the choice of Rhodes: "You've got to have some responsibility in this business."[43]

Laxalt was intrigued by Sears's idea and personally liked Schweiker. They sat next to each other in the Senate. History has written that Schweiker was a liberal. In fact, he was from a heavily unionized state, and if his pro-union votes were removed from his record, Schweiker was fairly conservative. Schweiker was not a movement conservative. Still, he was solid on anti-Communism, solid on national defense, solid on the Second Amendment, anti-abortion, opposed to forced busing, and a leader in the Captive Nations issue surrounding the Soviet imprisoned Baltic countries, unlike many other GOP Senators of his era.[44]

He was also a Navy veteran of World War II, personable, pleasant, and had never come down with "Potomac Fever." The *New York Times* noted that the Schweikers "are not part of the Washington political party set."[45] He was devout in his faith and was married to an attractive and articulate woman, Claire, who had once hosted her own television show in Philadelphia. Together they had five telegenic children. He was also a team player and, like Laxalt, Sears, and Reagan, was a gambler. Never in the history of American politics, had a non-incumbent candidate for a major party nomination ever named his running mate ahead of his nominating convention. *Time* magazine wrote, "In Washington, Schweiker enjoys a reputation as a diligent and amiable Senator with clever political instincts."[46]

Sears previously had made a brief, aborted run at William Ruckelshaus, the former Deputy Attorney General, who refused to fire Special Prosecutor Archibald Cox during the Watergate scandal. Ruckelshaus was a Catholic and a moderate from Indiana, but Reagan already controlled the Indiana delegation, at least on the first ballot. Ruckelshaus later told Witcover that Sears had indeed made the offer, but Sears denied it at the time.[47]

Actually, Sears did not reveal his first choice to the group: Nelson Rockefeller! When asked what would have been the reaction of Jesse Helms and the other conservatives to selecting Rockefeller, Sears calmly replied, "They would have come off the ceiling in a day or two." Further, Sears said, "I thought very strongly that he [Rockefeller] would have liked the irony of it, and he had firm control of his delegates. And, Mrs. Reagan liked him a lot. But you couldn't trust that others wouldn't talk him out of it, and you couldn't take that chance."[48]

Although Rockefeller controlled Dick Rosenbaum and Rosenbaum controlled the vast majority of the New York delegation, it is unknown whether delegates would have gone along with them and supported Reagan had Rockefeller joined the ticket. Still, it was no secret that Rockefeller and Rosenbaum were angry and dismayed over the treatment afforded Rockefeller by Ford and the President Ford Committee. The question would have been whether Reagan could hold his conservative delegates in the face of such a selection.

Another factor was involved in Sears's daring strategy. He had learned that CBS was working on a story scheduled for broadcast the evening of July 26 that would announce, according to the detailed count conducted of delegates nationwide by the network's political unit, that Gerald Ford had clinched the nomination—meaning Reagan's campaign would have been dead in the water.[49] Lou Cannon later wrote that Lyn Nofziger knew Reagan staffers were already casting about for other jobs, themselves thinking it was over for Reagan.[50]

A meeting was hastily arranged between Schweiker, Laxalt, and Sears in Laxalt's office on Capitol Hill on the Tuesday following Laxalt's phone conversation with Schweiker. At the time, Schweiker thought that the two wanted to review a list of potential running mates for Reagan—not his own possible interest in the position. In fact, they wanted to talk with Schweiker about him joining the ticket. "It really threw me for a loop," he recalled. Sears laid out the logic. "[F]rom a political standpoint it would change the dynamic of the campaign; people would stop saying how many delegates went for Ford that day."[51]

That Friday, Sears flew to California to make the case to Reagan for picking a running mate ahead of the convention. Sears laid out the current status to Reagan and Mrs. Reagan regarding the hemorrhaging delegate situation. Reagan knew his situation was tenuous. After narrowing the field of available Republican officials, Sears came to Schweiker, whom Reagan had once met at a dinner party at Walter Annenberg's home in Philadelphia. Schweiker had always been an admirer of Reagan. While he was supporting Ford—and was, indeed, a Ford delegate—he was never a Reagan basher like so many other Republicans. Sears listed the pros and cons of choosing Schweiker. At the conclusion of Sears's presentation, Reagan's first question was, "Do you think he'd do it?" Sears replied in the affirmative. "As a matter of fact, he's coming out here tomorrow to see you. Paul and I have discussed it with him, and he'll do it."[52]

Sure enough, on Saturday Schweiker flew to Los Angeles under the name of his Press Secretary, Troy Gustavson, and met with Reagan and Mrs. Reagan for over six hours at their home. Mrs. Reagan served lunch, and the two men gradually warmed up to each other. Also attending were Laxalt and Dave Newhall, Schweiker's Chief of Staff.[53]

As Witcover recounted in *Marathon*, "The first serious question on Reagan's mind was whether Schweiker would support his positions in the campaign and later in office. . . . 'As long as I'm on the plane on the take-off, I'll be the first one out defending it after the crash,' he told Reagan, who liked what he heard."[54]

Toward the end of the meeting, Reagan asked Schweiker if he would join him on the ticket. Schweiker had already discussed the offer with his wife several days before and she was all for it. The Senator agreed and returned to Washington with Laxalt and Sears to prepare for the Monday press conference.[55] The Schweikers told their children only the night before and they were ordered to stay off the phones until the next day. Over the weekend, the belief that Ford was just inches away from the nomination was confirmed in a *New York Times* account that had the President just six votes short of the nomination. This story appeared to support Baker's earlier claims.[56]

Sears ordered the staff to begin calling conservatives and supporters around the country on Sunday and Monday, in order to prepare them for the announcement the next day. Reagan made calls also, including to Senator Jesse Helms, who was not pleased. Nonetheless, Helms kept his objections private.

"Reagan personally telephoned Helms at 9:05 P.M. Sunday. Helms noted the hour because, 'I wanted to record for posterity the exact time I received the shock of my life.' Shocked though he was, Helms went along and stood beside Schweiker at Monday's news conference," according to syndicated columnists Rowland Evans and Robert Novak.[57]

Other conservatives did not stay quiet, including Congressman John Ashbrook of Ohio, who called it "the dumbest thing I ever heard."[58] Another Reagan supporter, Congressman Steve Symms of Idaho, told his colleague, Pennsylvania Congressman E.G. "Bud" Shuster, he was "deeply shaken by the . . . announcement . . . and is seriously considering changing his allegiance from Reagan" to Ford, according to a memo prepared for Cheney by his assistant Jim Connor.[59]

Jeff Bell had been deputized earlier to call Ashbrook and inform him of the choice. Ashbrook, stunned, told Bell, "You can tell him that he [Reagan] can go plumb f— himself."[60] And then he hung up on Bell. Ashbrook's office was flooded with letters from conservatives across the country, appalled at the Schweiker announcement.[61] Ashbrook stood by Reagan, but wrote back that he could not support Schweiker on the ticket with Reagan.

"Ticket splitting" had been an issue with conservatives for many years and indeed, Reagan had railed against it himself on several occasions, including an interview that very month in *Time* magazine, when he said, "Ford would lose the South . . . the balance of the country is in the Sun Belt and that's where the future of our party is."[62]

Reagan was, of course, right. Ford could not get away with choosing a moderate from the Northeast. But Ford was not Reagan and did not have over twenty years of political chits built up with conservatives across the country as Reagan did. The question was, "Could Reagan get away with it?"

Schweiker did not make any calls to the Pennsylvania delegates before the announcement. In fact, he was surprised when Sears and Laxalt specifically said they did not want him to make any calls. They did not want anyone to suggest a quid pro quo. All parties had to come to the agreement with clean hands. And he and Claire read the Bible and prayed over their decision.[63]

One phone call in particular after Reagan's press conference in Los Angeles is in dispute. Drew Lewis was the de facto head of the Republican Party in Pennsylvania and one of Schweiker's oldest friends. They had practically grown up together. Although Lewis had been the nominee for Governor in 1974 and lost in the wake of Watergate, he still earned high marks for his campaign and was eyeing another run for public office. In 1975 and 1976, he had traveled the length and breath of the Keystone State to personally recruit nearly every delegate who ran in the April primary. As a result, they were loyal to Lewis, even before Ford or Schweiker.[64]

Schweiker had tried to reach Lewis and in fact did—according to Schweiker—two hours after Reagan's press conference.[65] But Lewis had a different recollection, claiming years later they never spoke until after he had heard about the announcement at a restaurant, where a reporter tracked him down for his reaction.[66] Still, Lewis did not hear the news first from his old friend and was deeply upset. Lewis was having his ups and downs with the White House and Baker, partially because he refused to give them a hard count of delegates committed for Ford. It may have been a missed opportunity for Schweiker to bring his friend and some in the Pennsylvania delegation over to Reagan.

Schweiker recalled that the conversation was pleasant, although Lewis "was in a state of shock. I asked him if he'd at least think about it and he promised me that he'd give it some thought."[67]

Reagan went first at his press conference, at 9 A.M. Pacific Time in Los Angeles. He read a short statement but did not take any questions from reporters. Reagan spelled out his reasons and laid out the arguments for his unprecedented decision. Elaborating, he said that Schweiker had "the same basic values" as he did, including beliefs in American strength, compassion, morality, and decency—and "in an America governed by the rule of law, not by men."[68]

Reagan also stated, "The convention delegates should know well in advance who I would select as my running mate." He reiterated, "Since I now feel that the people and the delegates have a right to know in advance of the convention who a nominee's Vice Presidential choice would be, I am today departing from tradition and announcing my selection."[69] Ford could not help but notice the shot fired across his bow. Reagan, the old thespian, always knew how to hold a crowd. Thus, after laying out his reasoning, he did not mention Schweiker's name until the next to last paragraph of his statement.

Schweiker, Laxalt, and Sears went immediately after Reagan in Washington. In a jam packed Senate Caucus Room, flanked by his beaming family, Schweiker read a statement that said, in part, "Governor Reagan's decisive stroke in one fell swoop united the Republican Party for November by bringing together the conservative and moderate wings of our party . . . It instantly gives our party across-the-board appeal." Schweiker continued, "I am proud of the leadership Governor Reagan has shown in this striking departure from the old-style politics and I am especially proud to have been Governor Reagan's first choice."[70]

The press conference sometimes devolved into a debate over conservatism and liberalism, but Schweiker acquitted himself well. On differences between he and Reagan over past policies, Schweiker frankly told the reporters, "We make no apologies. We think it's the only way to win in November."[71] Poker faced, Sears told the media that Schweiker "was a very compatible running mate for Governor Reagan."[72] Afterwards, Schweiker was immediately assigned a Secret Service detail.

Washington was stunned and reaction to the announcement ranged from dismay to anger to praise to mockery. The media extensively reported on Schweiker's voting record, especially reviewing his favorable ratings by labor organizations including the AFL-CIO.[73] But Sears expected this. He was further braced for a loss of several delegates in the South and the West, as his staff had warned him. The *Washington Post* did a quick survey of nine uncommitted Pennsylvania delegates and found only two who thought the selection would lean them towards Reagan. Still, the Reagan team took that movement as a positive sign. One who moved from "unleaned" back towards leaning for Ford was James Stein, the young man Reagan had charmed back to a neutral position after meeting with him in Harrisburg several weeks before.[74]

The hope was that those losses would be offset by "soft" Ford and uncommitted delegates coming over, especially in Pennsylvania around Philadelphia, New Jersey, New York, and West Virginia. Reagan's forces also reasoned that the reaction would settle after the first forty-eight hours, after the shock had subsided and things had stabilized with Reagan's passionate supporters in the South and the West—especially in Mississippi, where things were becoming more and more fluid for Reagan.[75]

One disgruntled conservative suggested to Leslie Stahl of CBS, "The reason Reagan chose Schweiker was because Mondale was already taken."[76] And Mel Thomson, the Governor of New Hampshire told the *New York Times* in a flight of hyperbole, "It is a sad day in American history when a public leader of Reagan's stature would abandon all that he stood for." Other conservatives who complained included junior Congressman Phil Crane of Illinois, who reaffirmed his support for Reagan yet pledged to work against Schweiker at the convention if Reagan won.[77]

But one in the Ford camp who was impressed by Reagan and Schweiker's decision was Baker. He issued a statement calling the move, "obviously significant." He also recalled that his operation, "had to go to battle stations to keep Pennsylvania."[78] Schweiker told the press conference he would begin immediately to attempt to round up delegates in Pennsylvania and elsewhere for the "Reagan-Schweiker" ticket. He expected heavy resistance, and Shuster told the *New York Times*, "I think Governor Reagan is going to be disappointed, because it's much too late for that."[79]

Young Americans for Freedom, closely allied with the Reagan campaign, issued a press release "reluctantly" praising the selection of Schweiker. The organization had been close to Reagan since the 1960s, but it was one of the few conservative groups or individuals to praise Reagan's decision.[80] Others, like Ashbrook, described himself to the *New York Times* as a "former" supporter of Reagan.[81] Still another, Richard Viguerie, publisher of the *Conservative Digest*, told the paper that the decision by Governor Reagan was, "a coalition built on expediency and hypocrisy."[82]

But the most important and immediate benefit was that Walter Cronkite of CBS tore up the lead story for that night, which was to announce Ford had clinched the nomination.[83]

Other media organizations were forced to go back to counting and recounting delegates, which was exactly what the Reagan campaign wanted. They had bought the time needed to get to Kansas City. And all the participants were forced to play from a new deck; no one knew what cards they would be dealt. The next day, the *Washington Post* led with an editorial entitled, "Gov. Reagan's Gamble" and opined,

> Ronald Reagan has done a rather dazzling thing in announcing his choice of Pennsylvania Senator Richard S. Schweiker to be his running mate, should he win the Republican Presidential nomination. Given the tightness of the race between him and Mr. Ford, the finely honed sense of opportunity any number of delegates have perceived in it and the ideological passions of some of Mr. Reagan's supporters, it is all but impossible to guess whether the move will hurt or help him. . . . But that is the definition of a gamble, and you must say this for Mr. Reagan's move: It was bold. We will go farther: It may even have been wise.[84]

Lyn Nofziger was quoted in the *New York Times* as saying the choice of Schweiker proved that Reagan was "not so far right he's falling over the edge."[85]

Nofziger and other conservatives had been battling Sears off and on over the past year over the direction and tone of the campaign, but no conservative staffer inside the campaign ever thought the choice of Schweiker was a bad idea.[86] It was only with outside conservative supporters and delegates where Reagan ran into opposition. This was another testament to Sears's persuasive abilities.

Another key element in Sears's strategy was to pressure Ford to do likewise. Even if names were only floated tentatively, Sears believed that someone, somewhere in the Republican Party would be offended by any of Ford's choices. The conclusion of the *Post* editorial must have been music to the ears of Reagan strategists: "President Ford, on the other hand, has only told the nation whom he will *not* have. It remains to be seen whether he feels confident enough to respond to Mr. Reagan's gambit by offering the country an advance look."[87] Sears also hoped the move would quash Ford's speculation that, in the end, Reagan would accept the second spot on the ticket.

In praising the choice of Schweiker, the *Post* added to his credentials that he had once been on the Nixon White House's "Enemies List." Schweiker had never been a favorite of Nixon's. He had been a critic of the Vietnam War, had voted against several of Nixon's judicial nominees, and was among the first of the GOP to call for Nixon's resignation.[88]

Ford's White House held back from any comment and only focused on its intention to chose a running mate who could take the fight to Jimmy Carter in the South. There was some cackling to the media on and off the record by some Ford operatives about Schweiker's liberal voting record and Reagan's seemingly desperate ploy. According to Ron Nessen in *It Sure Looks Different From the Inside*, Ford's staff was gleeful at the Reagan move, seeing it as a sure sign he was floundering. But Dick Cheney threw cold water on their premature cheer, telling them, "Look, we have to keep up the same posture we have had. . . .We don't have the nomination. Let's not go overboard. Let's not get euphoric. Let's just stick to the same hard work we have been doing." He added, "Remember North Carolina."[89]

Still, extensive memos flew around the White House measuring the response to Reagan's announcement inside the Pennsylvania delegation and around the GOP.[90] Jack Marsh, in a memo for Ford, said the "view seems to be disbelief, incredulous. . . ."[91]

The next day, July 27, John Connally, who was exceeded by no one when it came to spotting a political opportunity, endorsed Ford for President.[92] Clearly, Connally was maneuvering to get on the ticket with Ford. But his move only served Sears's purposes by antagonizing some of Ford's liberal supporters in the North. Sears brushed off the endorsement, telling the *New York Times*, "The truth of the matter is John Connally is a phenomenon of the press and his own wits and he had no constituency outside of a few friends in Texas." Sears also noted that Connally "still has Watergate all over him."[93]

The same day, Senator Laxalt succinctly summed up the situation for Jules Witcover in the *Washington Post*, "Yesterday was the reaction we anticipated—shock and dismay. But around the country today, it has generally dissipated." Sears added, "We won't take a lot more heat over who this guy [Schweiker] is. You were going to get some of it no matter who was picked. The rest is whether this is a good political move."[94]

With a few notable exceptions, such as that of Bill Buckley, who praised Reagan's move, virtually all conservative and liberal columnists denounced it. George Will compared it to "slapstick" and wrote, "Reagan and Schweiker have not exactly contributed to the public stock of harmless pleasure. Their caper is another subtraction from the dignity of the political vocation."[95] Another conservative supporter of Sears's bold strategy was Jude Wanniski, associate editor of the *Wall Street Journal*. "It was clear a week ago that Mr. Reagan had to do something, that his pat hand was a losing one. . . . The conventional wisdom is saying that the Schweiker move will fail. But not making a move at all would have certainly failed," he wrote.[96]

The *New York Times* initially ridiculed the selection, but later reversed field and praised Reagan's and Schweiker's decision, writing, "He [Reagan] has probably eliminated the possibility that he will lose the Presidential nomination to Gerald Ford before the convention. . . . In doing so, the former California Governor has also increased the possibility—still not a probability—that he can defeat Mr. Ford on the floor of the convention."[97]

At the same time, according to author John Green, "Congressman John Heinz of Pennsylvania, a Ford supporter, told [Ford White House aide] Jack Marsh not to worry too much about Schweiker 'because he is not too much with the hard core, regular Republicans in Pennsylvania.'"[98] How the blue-blooded inheritor of a vast fortune would know anything about "regular Republicans" was a question without an answer. John Heinz hadn't shaken the hand of a common man since the last time he had tipped the attendant at the Philadelphia Club.

Contributing to the initial negative reaction to the announcement of Schweiker was that many Reagan supporters around the country confused him with Senator Lowell Weicker, a very liberal Republican from Connecticut who despised conservatives and joyously rubbed their noses in his liberal voting record. Weicker's ego defied description, especially after he served on the televised Senate committee investigating Richard Nixon. For example, *Time* reported, "Similarly confusing Schweiker with Connecticut's Senator Lowell Weicker, a table of lunching Chicago businessmen wondered why 'that Watergate Senator' would join Reagan."[99]

Due to Reagan's assiduous damage-control phone calls to his supporters around the country, almost none of the previously pledged Reagan delegates switched to Ford after the surprise of the announcement began to wear off. For instance, while one Reagan delegate from Virginia switched to Ford after the Schweiker decision, others were more resolute. "I'd rather commit adultery than commit my vote before the convention," one Virginia delegate told UPI.[100]

Schweiker began calling individuals in the Pennsylvania delegation immediately after the press conference and continued all day on the following day. As a result, his spokesman told the *New York Times*, "A number of them were moving from Mr. Ford to an uncommitted stance." This was confirmed by Baker in a quick survey of Pennsylvania's delegation that showed several possible defections to Reagan and Schweiker. Ford's campaign had immediately reached ninety-five of the 103-member delegation, and only eighty-two were reaffirming their commitment to the President.[101]

Meanwhile, Schweiker made an initial foray into South Carolina to meet with Republican delegates at the official residence of Governor Jim Edwards. Twenty-three of the state's delegates attended. Edwards later told reporters he had not backed away from supporting Reagan and that Schweiker, "had no horns growing out of his head." He explained that, in fact, he found much in common with the Pennsylvanian.[102]

Also, *Human Events* editorially supported Reagan and made a compelling case for conservatives to not flee his cause.[103] The paper's support helped hold the Right in place behind Reagan in the days before the convention in Kansas City. Still, there was carping, criticizing, and second-guessing from conservatives outside the campaign. But most, like Jimmy Lyons of Texas, decided to stay put with the Californian.[104] They had a lot invested in him and were not about to walk away now. Guy Hunt, Co-Chairman of the Reagan campaign in Alabama, summarized well how conservatives thought of the Reagan gambit: "The church ain't just for the righteous. Sinners can come in too."[105]

Years later, Laxalt recounted, "We would have been dead in the water. . . . All the undecideds were being marched into the Oval Office . . . that's when Sears suggested Schweiker. He laid it on me and my first reaction was 'holy God,' but the more we discussed it . . . as only Sears can do . . . the more it made sense. Unfortunately, a lot of conservatives gagged. But we went into the convention alive."[106]

In a letter to supporter Jim Lacy in 1979, Reagan made clear his belief that picking Schweiker was the right thing to do. Reagan, ever the loyalist, went much further than simply defending his pragmatism. He really liked Schweiker and wrote, "He is a deeply religious man with a fine family and great integrity."[107]

According to Molly Ivins, writing in the *New York Times*, one prominent conservative who had a rather rough take on Reagan's choice was Howard Phillips. At the annual meeting of the Young Americans for Freedom, Phillips made an analogy between Reagan and a Republican Congressman who had recently been arrested for soliciting a prostitute, but gave "credit" to the Congressman since at least he had been approached, and not the other way around.[108]

Some of those initially put off by the decision did see the light. "A classic Reagan bitter-ender is Malcom Mabry, a 43-year-old state legislator and small farmer from Dublin, in the Mississippi Delta. An ardent Reaganite, he was stunned by Schweiker's selection and instantly decided to abandon Reagan. But after a sleepless night, Mabry changed his mind while working in the pea patch the next morning and determined that Vice President Schweiker was a lot easier to take than Secretary of State Kissinger," reported columnists Rowland Evans and Robert Novak.[109]

However, one passionate conservative from Mississippi, Clarke Reed, was about to make the biggest leap of any delegate anywhere and anytime. Reed had professed his admiration and devotion to Reagan countless times over the years. In summer of 1976, he was unofficially for Reagan, yet officially uncommitted. But through his apostasy he would write himself deeply into the 1976 Reagan campaign and the history of American politics. Reed was about to become, according to Ford political aide Harry Dent, "the most wooed delegate in the GOP."[110]

13

BLOODY MISSISSIPPI

"Well, screw them, not me!"

Don't worry about Clarke." Dave Keene must have said that a thousand times to dozens of people over the spring and summer of 1976 about the mercurial, slightly unstable, voluble, and certainly excitable Chairman of the Mississippi Republican Party, Clarke E. Reed.[1] Unfortunately for Ronald Reagan, Keene, and company, it would turn out they did have Reed to worry about.

"Reed was right out of some Hollywood casting director's dream of the political operator. He was slick and so fast talking as to be almost incomprehensible. On top of that he was a whisperer; he liked to pull people aside and exchange confidences mouth-to-ear. He was Byzantine in style, and consumed with the intricacies of politics. He was consumed also, to his ultimate misfortune, with a desire to always be on the winning side, to hold onto power and influence," wrote Jules Witcover in *Marathon*.[2] Keene thought he had good cause not be concerned about his old friend. They had waged many ideological battles together over the years, despite Keene's relative youth.

Elizabeth Drew described Keene in her insightful book about the campaign, *American Journal: The Events of 1976*, as "a blue eyed, somewhat chunky, and utterly pleasant young man."[3] At thirty-one years of age, Reagan's Southern Political Director had already fought liberals at the University of Wisconsin, had worked on the Goldwater 1964 campaign, had been elected National Chairman of the Young Americans for Freedom, and had been a top political adviser to Vice President Spiro Agnew and later Senator Jim Buckley of New York before joining Reagan's challenge to Ford.

Keene had three weaknesses. First, he was a self-proclaimed "wiseass." The second was that he lacked the tact that most other men in Washington attempted to exhibit and live by. He said what was on his mind, didn't give a damn, and if you didn't like it you could go pound salt. Years later, in 1989, Keene was leading a coalition of conservatives opposed to a nomination made by President George H. W. Bush. Bush's Chief of Staff, John Sununu, asked Keene to come over to the

White House for a meeting to discuss the matter. Sununu told Keene the offending nominee was being withdrawn and then pleaded with him to be more cooperative and try to work with Bush to help the next nominee. Keene responded to Sununu's olive branch by saying, "That's fine, Governor, but you have to realize that I'm better at destroying things than I am at creating them." In 1986, when he was advising Lee Atwater on how to deal with then Vice President Bush's Ivy League friends, Keene pointed out to the drawling South Carolinian, a self-described "cracker," that there were certain things that simply could not be overcome, including culture. "Lee, those people think you talk funny, and their problem with me was I went to a land grant college." Keene's third weakness was an unrequited love for the hapless Chicago White Sox.[4]

But he took his politics and his libertarian/conservative philosophy seriously and was an effective member of the Reagan team. When Keene joined the campaign in 1975, his reputation had preceded him. But with a blue-collar background with roots in Illinois and Wisconsin, he did not opt for that region. Instead, he traded regions with Charlie Black. "You shouldn't do politics in your own backyard," Keene said. "You gotta say 'no' to too many friends, and who needs that s—?" Black concurred, but in more diplomatic terms. So Black, the wily Confederate, took the industrial belt from New Jersey to Illinois. Keene, the Yankee, took the South.[5]

Keene was also tapped because of his experience working with conservative activists in the South, which was expected to be a bulwark for the forthcoming Reagan insurgency. One key reason Sears recruited him to join the campaign was his longstanding relationship with the South's "Mr. Republican," Clarke Reed.[6]

Reed came from a wealthy family and proceeded to make even more money, mostly in agriculture. He also owned a Mississippi River barge company. In his late twenties, Reed decided he needed to get involved in politics. But Mississippi, from the time of Reconstruction until the 1960s, was a "yellow dog" Democratic state. There was a long line ahead of Reed in the Democratic Party, so he decided to become a Republican. In the GOP, the hunting would be easier and the chances better for ascending quickly in the party ranks.

"For a Southern gentleman, Reed looked the part but didn't act the part," Keene said. "He was one high-strung character. And he called everybody 'cat' like 'Man, this cat is good' or 'Man, that cat is smart.'"[7] Witcover also wrote that Reed talked like a "Motown hipster."[8] Although he was only forty-eight years old, Reed, with his mane of silver hair, exuded the "white shoe" linen-jacketed image of the Southern gentleman, except for one thing: unlike the stereotype and to Reagan's eventual dismay, Reed could not keep his word.[9]

In every story, there is an antagonist and there is a protagonist. There is the introduction, conflict, and resolution. There is the bitter fight, the acrimony, the retribution, and the finger pointing. And history, as judged by political scribes and especially Reagan's revolutionaries, recorded that Clarke Reed would become their "Benedict Arnold."

In fairness to Reed, he had done a commendable job building the Mississippi Republican Party over the years. The party had actually begun to elect Republicans to office, including state legislators, as well as the youthful Trent Lott and Thad Cochran to the U.S. Congress in 1972.

Reed had been a critical backer of Richard Nixon eight years earlier in Miami, when Reagan made his eleventh hour bid for the nomination. In 1972, he had been a valuable ally of Keene's when they stopped an attempt by liberals to rewrite the party rules and instead wrote their own rules. These new party bylaws included, ironically for Reagan in 1976, the reapportionment of delegates to future conventions that recognized the growing power of the West and the South and the waning influence of the North in the Republican Party.

By 1975, however, Reed had had enough of the "split ticket" mentality of the Republican Party, as practiced to perfection by Ford when he had picked Nelson Rockefeller. The Reaganites thought they had nothing to be concerned about when it came to Clarke Reed or Mississippi. Although he was officially neutral, he was known by all to be a Reagan man. Reagan's State Chairman, Billy Mounger, another successful businessman, was a lifelong friend of Reed. In Mississippi, they had become known as the "Gold Dust Twins."

Reed told Elizabeth Drew, in reviewing the situation in his state, "What Ford needs right now is to show that he's going to pick a running mate that will be compatible to his philosophy. The split ticket is a nightmare and a horror." He then added, coldly, "With the so-called balanced ticket between a liberal and a conservative, you vote for a conservative and if he dies you get a liberal."[10]

Mounger had been recruited out of high school to play football for the legendary Red Blaik at West Point in the 1940s. Afterward, he was in the first class out of the "Point" to join the new Air Force. Mounger flew B-29s and B-50s and delivered nuclear bombs to post-war Europe. After his tour, he eventually settled back in Jackson and made a fortune in banking, especially financing for oil and gas companies. At only 5'7" and 175 pounds, what Mounger lacked in size, he made up in toughness. And discretion. And loyalty. While Reed was constantly talking to the media, Mounger was quietly doing his job for Reagan.

Furthermore, the incoming Chairman of the Party, State Senator Charles Pickering, was also a solid Reagan man, and this was added insurance.[11] Mississippi seemed the least of the Reagan campaign's worries in 1976. Both Mounger and Pickering were too gentlemanly and too discreet to complain at the time about their oft-quoted colleague. They may have resented the national media and national politicians who ignored them in favor of talking with Reed, but they never said anything publicly. Still, it must have rankled, and Keene and others occasionally urged Reagan to call Mounger and Pickering, seek their advice, and keep their spirits up.

"Billy is also our Chairman in Mississippi and should be singled out for some kind remarks," Keene wrote in one memo to Reagan. In another, he said of Pickering, "He is with us . . . however, he should not be taken for granted. Pickering is a good man and may slightly resent the fact that he is often by-passed by people dealing in Mississippi who are more likely to call Clarke Reed."[12]

In the early stages of the Republican primaries, columnist John Lofton had interviewed Reed and Barry Goldwater. *Human Events* excerpted portions of the article, which was about the nasty tone the Ford campaign was taking against Reagan. Goldwater described the treatment of Reagan as a "very poor tactic." The conservative weekly wrote,

> In a similar vein, Clarke Reed, the highly influential Chairman of the Mississippi Republican Party who is officially neutral but believed leaning toward Reagan, told Lofton that the President's charges against Reagan "turn me off bad. When he says Ronald Reagan is an extremist, he is calling me one, too." Reed called the President's attacks on Reagan "irresponsible," "divisive," and "damaging to the party."
>
> "This kind of stuff is kamikaze," said Reed. "I was very disappointed to see the President join with people like Rockefeller and Scranton, who have made careers out of attacking conservatives who make up a majority of the Republican party."
>
> "If the President really thinks Reagan is too far right to be elected," said the Southern GOP leader, "then why has he been moving so rapidly in Reagan's direction lately?"[13]

Still, Clarke's wobbly reputation preceded him. Early in January of 1976, Tom Anderson, Congressman Trent Lott's Administrative Assistant, met with John Sears and Jim Lake and implored them to overrule Reed's plans for a state convention and tell him that Mississippi should hold a statewide primary between Reagan and Gerald Ford, instead. "You can't trust Clarke Reed. He's a slippery, no good son of a b—," Anderson told Sears and Lake. He informed them that there was enough time to pull together a primary to replace the planned April state convention. "You will win all thirty delegates and not have to worry about them," Anderson told them.[14]

Sears told Anderson he would get back to him after huddling with Keene and others at Citizens for Reagan. Sears asked Keene, "Can we trust Reed?" Keene replied in the affirmative, and Sears decided to ignore Anderson's suggestion.[15] Because Citizens for Reagan was strapped for cash, a state convention that was paid for by the state party was certainly preferable to a primary—which might require several hundred thousand precious dollars that could go elsewhere for Reagan.

At the Mississippi state GOP convention, Reed cobbled together a group of thirty delegates and thirty alternates who would go to Kansas City. Each had one half vote on all matters. Mississippi Republicans had used the "unit rule" as a means of leveraging their position in national politics. Although this practice was against the bylaws of the national party, it was ignored. Ominously, not all of the sixty chosen were the "true believers" who would follow Reagan to the ends of the earth.

In late 1975, Keene and Reed had discussed a commitment to Reagan, and Keene extracted a solemn promise from Reed that he would support Reagan publicly at the right time and deliver thirty delegates to Reagan when needed. Reed had stipulated that if Reagan's campaign failed seriously and became a joke before the Republican National Convention, then he would be off the hook and free to support Ford. Mounger had also extracted the same promise from Reed. "So when the time came, I simply asked him to keep up his work—and keep his pledge to Reagan," Mounger recalled.[16]

In the fall of 1976, Keene wrote an article on the "Battle for Mississippi" in *The Alternative: An American Spectator*. He explained, "Early in the campaign, Reed had personally indicated that he was with us, but refused to endorse Reagan publicly or deliver his delegation to us before the convention." Reed told Keene he wanted to do it his way, and that his way would ensure that Reagan would receive twenty-eight and possibly all thirty delegates. Consulting with Sears, Keene went ahead and allowed Reed to handle the situation as he saw fit. Keene contacted Reed again and told him "that we were both on the line. He because he had given his word and me because I had backed him up. He told me that he understood and that I had nothing to worry about."[17]

Yet rather than selecting sixty solid Reagan supporters, Reed attempted to placate all elements in the party by picking liberals, moderates, and conservatives. Of course, no one at Citizens for Reagan was paying any attention to the Mississippi convention in April of 1976. At that time, they were desperately trying to keep Reagan's campaign alive.

In a May story about the uncommitted delegates from New York, Pennsylvania, and other states including Mississippi, the *New York Times* reported,

"In Mississippi, for example, the challenger [Reagan] is thought to have overwhelming support among 30 delegates who have not yet declared their preferences. Clarke E. Reed, the State Party Chairman, said it was 'very likely' that Mississippi would adopt an informal unit rule, as it had in the past, and thus give all of its convention votes to Mr. Reagan."[18]

Both camps saw the story and drew their own conclusions. The Reagan campaign took comfort from the story. They could work on uncommitted and wavering delegates from other states. For Ford's forces, the report meant that trying to pry anything loose from Mississippi, especially since it would abide by the unit rule, would be a waste of time. Still, as Ford inched up on the nomination, Reed was inching away from Reagan.

In the first week in July, *Time* magazine wrote, "Reagan is . . . confident of winning all of Mississippi's 30 seats since the delegates have adopted the unit rule (whoever wins a majority, however narrow, gets all thirty). Ford is pondering a last-minute trip to Mississippi. 'The delegation is probably 2 to 1 for Reagan now,' says GOP National Committeeman Clarke Reed. 'But who knows? Hard work could push it either way.'"[19]

Later in the month, Reed told the same publication he would urge the delegation to switch if "it appears Ford is the man."[20] Reed was also telling other publications inferentially that Mississippi was not locked up for Reagan as previously thought. Comments like these made the Reagan forces want to strangle Reed. They had enough on their plates with attempting to win some uncommitted delegates, preparing for the looming convention, and continuing to put up a brave front that would keep all their forces in line until they could figure something out in Kansas City to win the damn thing. But Reed was telegraphing invitations to Harry Dent, Jim Baker, and Dick Cheney to come into the state for Ford and play havoc.

And play havoc they did.

Dent had been brought aboard the Ford campaign to help the President in the South. A charming, roguish, and eminently knowledgeable South Carolinian, Dent had been slightly brushed by the Watergate scandal while working on Nixon's White House Staff, so he kept a low profile and had resisted pressures to join Ford's campaign until May. Dent had been the Nixon Administration's liaison to the South to "hold the hand of the South while the Nixon Justice Department enforced busing to achieve school integration."[21] Although he had not been implicated in any wrongdoing, his unpleasant experience with the special prosecutor made him sensitive to the political atmosphere of the day. He thought his formal presence on the campaign might prove an embarrassment to President Ford and his effort.

Dent knew Clarke Reed and understood his strengths and weaknesses. So too did Mounger. "Clarke is one of the weakest individuals," he said in an interview years later.[22] "Mississippi was to account for most of my waking hours for the next three months, through the end of the GOP convention on August 19," Dent wrote in his book, *The Prodigal South Returns to Power*.[23]

Dent, Jerry Jones, and Cheney were among the few who had understood the changing nature of the conservative opposition to Ford within the GOP, and Dent was frustrated in his inability to educate others in the White House, the Republican National Committee, and later the President Ford Committee of that alarming development.

"For Ford, however," Dent wrote, "there were two problems: Ronald Reagan's frustrated desires left over from his abortive 1968 nomination try and Ford's political advisers who seemingly refused to understand the Reagan threat and the difference between a primary season and the general election."

"The essence of the Ford problem," Dent continued, "was the failure to see the Republican Party realistically as the conservative party it is."[24] Yet Dent also had a blind spot about Reagan. He constantly described Reagan's followers as "Birchers," a derisive reference to the John Birch Society, a group founded in the late 1940s and named after what was believed to be the first victim of the Cold War, an American Army officer who had been captured, tortured, and killed by the Communist Chinese.

Reed started receiving phone calls from Dent, Cheney, Ford aide Bill Timmons, as well as Cabinet Secretaries Earl Butz and Bill Simon, all of whom pressured him to support the President. But he was also getting calls from Reagan, Keene, and Sears, reminding him of his promise.

Dent slowly kept badgering Reed to announce his support for Ford, in private and public, otherwise he would be on the losing end by staying with Reagan, the prospect of which drove Reed crazy. Dent was also working inside the Mississippi delegation courtesy of Gil Carmichael, a car dealer and Doug Shanks, a Jackson city commissioner. Both were active Ford supporters. Another key to Dent's strategy was John Davis, who had been working in Ford's Southern office until it was closed in the spring and he was laid off to save money. It was Davis, according to Dent, who initially alerted him to the notion that opportunities existed in Mississippi for Ford. "There's gold to be mined in that Mississippi delegation. I think we can turn the Reagan tide in Mississippi around and win all thirty votes under Clarke Reed's unit rule," Dent recalled Davis telling him. Shanks had already stated publicly that he might not abide by the unit rule and break precedent to vote for Ford at the convention.[25]

In the meantime, as the situation developed in Mississippi, Dent was calling uncommitted delegates in other Southern states, including his home state. He told them that Mississippi was crumbling and that when it switched to Ford, Reagan's challenge would be finished. Other Ford operatives were calling delegates in the North to hold them in line, telling them that Reagan was not even holding his base. This tactic was especially effective in Pennsylvania, where Sears was making a strong pitch for a group from the Philadelphia area.

Reed, like many others, thought the campaign would be over shortly, as both Citizens for Reagan and the President Ford Committee were attempting to implement early knockout strategies. No one, especially Clarke Reed, could foresee the extended trench warfare of the campaign. He also told *American Journal* author Drew, "the delegation's not deliverable," in complete contradiction to his promises months before to Keene.[26]

"The worst thing that happened to Clarke Reed in his entire career was the fact that it wasn't over early. Because he then discovered that he put his delegation together in the sloppiest manner imaginable, that he had trouble on both sides, that he couldn't deliver it—at least to the extent that he thought he could. That was not a result of deviousness. That was a result of weakness, and a result of trying to please everybody," Keene told Witcover.[27]

From Shanks and Carmichael to Davis and Dent, the message of "don't give up on Mississippi" finally caught the attention of Cheney in June. Rog Morton, like others at the Ford campaign, was still assuming Mississippi's delegation would support Reagan. But when Morton learned that Dent was dealing directly with Cheney on the matter, Morton got hot and told Dent as much. Later, Cheney intervened and "advised Morton that he was taking a special interest in Mississippi," according to Witcover.[28]

Reed and Pickering were in Washington for a GOP meeting on June 25 and were invited to the White House by Cheney. By design, each was escorted into a private meeting with Ford in the Oval Office. Pickering went in first. He then exited with the President, in full view of Reed, which only served to fuel his paranoia. As Dent recounted, "When we got into the East Room, the military aide announced, 'Ladies and Gentlemen, the President of the United States!' Walking in with the President was Pickering. When Reed saw this he was astonished, and his startled reaction showed. Reed needed to know we might win Mississippi without him. Now he saw that potential for the first time."[29]

Reed was then taken into the Oval Office for his own meeting with the President. Although he did not yet break his promise there and then, he was weakening. But Reed did invite Ford to Mississippi to meet with the delegates, and the President accepted. The Mississippi bloc was the largest group of undecided voters, and Ford's nomination was on the line.[30]

But after working over Reed for two months, Dent was getting tired of waiting for him to switch. So, together with Shanks and Carmichael, Dent began calling and sending telegrams to the other Mississippi delegates, telling them that others in the delegation were wavering or had already gone over to Ford, and their vote could put him over the top. They obviously had not consulted Mounger, who was busy organizing a tennis tournament, or Pickering. When Reed found out about these calls and telegrams, he hit the ceiling and the pro-Ford effort was halted. Mounger also was furious. Mounger had told Reed for months that he had been planning this tournament and not to schedule anything for that time period. In between managing 256 kids from all over the world, Mounger made desperate phone calls to hold the line for Reagan after being chided by Reed to do something. Mounger shot back, "You are just as committed to Reagan as I am . . . it's your turn to do something for a change!"[31]

The fight boiled over when Reed scheduled a meeting with all sixty delegates and alternates to plead with them to stay uncommitted, in accordance with their original plan. Nonetheless, Dent invited Cheney to attend and speak on Ford's behalf, and Keene and Andy Carter were there to represent the Reagan camp. Cheney only attended reluctantly. The feeling around the Ford campaign was that if Cheney was rebuffed, the situation would reflect badly on Ford.

Reed's intention may have been an attempt to keep his promise to Keene or to simply protect his position heading to Kansas City. But on the eve of the meeting, the *New York Times* carried a major story that was headlined, "Shift of Mississippi G.O.P. To Ford Termed Imminent." James Naughton reported, "Such a reversal would represent a severe, and perhaps final, blow to Mr. Reagan's effort to wrest the nomination from Mr. Ford. Until the President's agents moved into Mississippi it had been expected that the Californian would have the support of at least 25 of the 30 members."[32]

The meeting took place on Sunday, July 25 in Jackson, the state capital. According to Witcover, Dent told the assembled crowd, "Now my good friend Clarke is probably a little peeved with us because we've been down here trying to lobby you good folks. But I told Clarke that you can't dress sixty beautiful women up in bikinis and put them on Broadway, and not expect Gerald Ford and Ronald Reagan to turn their heads and look at 'em." Playing on their resentment of the northern liberals in the party, Dent said, "It's a question of whether Clarke's gonna be the kingmaker or Rosey Rosenbaum's gonna be the kingmaker. That is, New York, or Mississippi."[33]

Cheney followed Dent. Keene wrapped up the meeting, making an abbreviated pitch for Reagan. Both took a few questions. The meeting ended with the delegates having decided, thirty-six to seven, not to break the unit rule. Several abstentions and missing delegates accounted for the deficient seventeen votes. This decision represented a victory for Reagan and a defeat for Ford. The delegation did, however, reaffirm Reed's invitation for Ford to come to Mississippi.[34]

Reed momentarily went with the Reagan program by forcing the vote on the unit rule and embarrassing Shanks and Carmichael. Reed accurately summed up the real position of the Ford supporters in Mississippi in the *New York Times*, "They can't have it both ways that 'we're for the unit rule if we win but if we lose we're going to break it.'" And the young Shanks sanctimoniously told the paper, "I'm going to do what I consider morally right. I'm going to put Presidential politics above state politics. I'm going to exercise my conscience."[35]

While everyone milled around the lobby of the Ramada Inn, talking with the national reporters who had come to cover the meeting, Keene took Reed, but not Mounger, aside and reviewed the national situation for Reagan and his precarious position. Keene told Reed that Reagan's chances were slipping away, and that there was only one thing to do to try to salvage the campaign: select a running mate. Then Keene confided to his old friend Reed the name of the man who would be announced the very next day: Senator Richard Schweiker of Pennsylvania. His selection represented the very "ticket-splitting" that Reed, Reagan, and other conservatives in the party had criticized for years.

Keene recalled that Reed was not terribly upset about the decision and thought the choice of Schweiker might be better received by the Mississippi delegation than previously thought. After meeting with Reed, Keene flew back to Washington to begin calling Reagan supporters around the country to prepare them for the bombshell that was about to be dropped the next day. Mounger told Keene that Reed was preparing to double-cross Reagan, but Keene didn't believe him. "David believed Reed was a man of his word," Mounger said.[36]

Washington was abuzz the next day at the Schweiker announcement, and Reed—in contrast to his calm response to Keene—decided to go ballistic. Reagan's supporters in Mississippi and across the South called Reed to complain about Schweiker, which only added to his easily agitated state. Cheney and Dent consulted and knew that Reed would be highly persuadable at this point. Dent called Reed to cajole him once again to switch to Ford. Mounger too was agitated about the choice of Schweiker, but he got over it: "I jumped straight up in the air and out of my shoes but I landed back in them. The only man in the U.S. that didn't end up back where he started was Clarke."[37] Mounger was right. Despite the complaints by Reagan's conservative supporters, most stayed in Reagan's camp. Reed was the only prominent delegate to change his support to Ford.

What Keene hadn't counted on was that Reed was just waiting for an excuse to do so.[38]

Reagan called Reed to try to convince him that Schweiker wasn't all that bad. But Reed didn't buy it and brushed off Reagan's arguments.[39] Sears believed that once the announcement had settled in and the initial shock had worn off, he could move ahead with his plans to capture uncommitted or wavering Ford delegates, mostly in the North. He had expected to lose between ten and twenty delegates, mostly from the South, but had hoped to pick up even more from Pennsylvania and New York.[40] Reagan also called Mounger, who colorfully told Reagan about the choice of Schweiker, "Governor . . . you gave me the biggest dose of Ex-Lax and you got all my insides . . . that is what this is like." But Mounger assured Reagan he would stay put.[41]

On Monday evening—just hours after announcing Schwieker—the leadership of the Mississippi Republican Party met at Mounger's house to try to sort things out. Present were Mounger, Reed, Pickering, Executive Director Haley Barbour, and several others. None was happy about the pick of Schweiker, but none was about to bolt from Reagan, except Reed.[42]

Reed informed the group he was switching, using Schweiker as his excuse, and they argued with him to hold off. After much haranguing, Reed promised the group he would wait one week before taking any public action. The very next morning, Dent started in on Reed again, badgering him to endorse Ford. Yet Reed resisted again because of his promise the night before and because of his commitment to Keene and Mounger months earlier.

On Tuesday evening, in yet another phone call, Reed told Keene that all the Mississippi delegates were switching, and he would too. But Keene had already made other calls to Mississippi and knew Reed was exaggerating. As Sears predicted, the initial shock over Schweiker was wearing off with the other delegates. They spoke one last time, late in the evening.[43] The conversation did not go well. When Keene held Reed to his promise of backing Reagan, Reed told him he'd made other promises, too. "Well, screw them, not me!" Keene told him.[44]

Years later, Keene would say, "Look, Clarke was going one way or the other. He's been making noises about going long before we picked Schweiker. If it hadn't been the excuse of Schweiker, he would have found another."[45] Reed, weary of the corner he was backing himself into, promised Keene that he would wait another twenty-four hours before taking any action. That is, until the very next morning, when the pressure came from another source: the President of the United States.[46] Dent wrote,

> I called Cheney and gave him the solution to the Reed reluctance: "You've got to play the big card—get the President on the phone to tell Clarke to come and come now, today. Tell the President not to be his nice self—to push for a certain time and not to hang up till he gets it. Clarke won't back up on his word to the President." . . . So on Wednesday morning the President made his call to Reed. Every time previously when I took a delegate or delegates in to see the President he had not asked them directly for their vote. However, this call was different. He pressed for a Reed commitment and got it. Then he insisted Reed come over that day—Wednesday. And again, Reed agreed.[47]

Ford was close, very close to the nomination. The hope was that Reed would declare for the President and thereby bring other Mississippi delegates, as well as undermine Reagan's position in other states. As rumors swirled around Reed, Ford's men were calling uncommitted delegates in other parts of the country, telling them that Reagan could not even hold on to his base in the South. Dent's bluffs were working.

Reed finally capitulated to Dent's orchestrated pressure and began writing a statement announcing his decision to endorse Ford. Dent called Reed repeatedly, asking for the statement. In the meantime, Reagan, Mounger, Keene, and Barbour all were calling Reed, trying to bring him back into the fold.

"Finally, Reed read me the statement about 5 P.M. He said he was calling it to Barbour to be released through state headquarters. I was anxious to get the announcement on the network news that evening—under strong pressure from Cheney. However, I ran into difficulty with Barbour, who was for Reagan and knew what I did not: His boss was breaking a Reagan commitment," recalled Dent.[48]

Dent leaked word to CBS's Walter Cronkite, who reported it that evening. Reed, who had broken yet another promise to Keene, rationalized that while he had not waited the full twenty-four hours he had pledged to Keene, he had at least waited until the end of the day.[49]

"The influential Chairman of the Mississippi Republican Party endorsed

President Ford last night with a jab at the 'cynicism' of Ronald Reagan's selection of Sen. Richard S. Schweiker of Pennsylvania as his running mate," wrote Lou Cannon in a front page, above-the-fold story in the *Washington Post*.[50] Reed made it clear that his endorsement of Ford was "personal" and not on behalf of the state party or the delegation, but the damage was done.

Reed also attempted to justify his actions by complaining to reporters about Reagan's selection of Schweiker, calling it "wrong and dumb. It was an act of desperation. It was a double sin inasmuch as it didn't work." This last sentence by Reed should have spoken volumes to Reagan's campaign.[51]

Even worse for Reagan, the paper reported, "Confirmation that Reagan has slipped badly in Mississippi came from a *Washington Post* survey of 58 of the 60 delegates, each of whom has half a vote. The survey, taken before Reed's statement, showed 25 for Mr. Ford, 14 for Reagan, and 19 uncommitted. This was a change of 13 Reagan delegates to uncommitted and a gain of two for Mr. Ford, one from Reagan and one from the uncommitted category."[52]

A *New York Times* survey found that twenty-eight were supporting Reagan and twenty-six were for Ford. Keene himself estimated that even with some slippage, Reagan still had the support of thirty to forty of the sixty delegates and alternates.[53] As with other uncommitted delegates around the country, their answers depended on what time they were called and what mood they were in. Sometimes their hearts told them to be for Reagan. Sometimes, their heads told them to be for Ford. Sometimes, their egos told them to stay uncommitted.

In any event, Dent felt it now was safe to bring Ford to Jackson, Mississippi, to meet with the delegation. While some at the President Ford Committee expressed reservations over the trip, Ford and Cheney overruled them. Ford met with the delegates that Friday for over two hours and fielded, according to Dent, many "Birch-type questions." Most of the questions surrounded Henry Kissinger, détente, forced busing, and his choice for Vice President. They were pointed, but respectful.[54]

By all accounts, Ford acquitted himself well. He told the gathering he would poll all the delegates to the convention to seek their ideas on a running mate. And Ford was aided further in Mississippi when its two Republican Congressmen, Trent Lott and Thad Cochran, also endorsed the President the day of the meeting. Although they were not delegates, Lott and Cochran were influential among their fellow Mississippi Republicans.

Another Reagan supporter who flipped to Ford was Tommy Giordano, whom Mounger had recruited to run a congressional district in Mississippi for Reagan. Although Reed's duplicity angered many, Giordano's behavior was just as infuriating. After the convention he drifted out of politics, largely because he had been ostracized, according to Mounger. Years earlier, Senator Gene McCarthy of Minnesota described a particular off-again, on-again political associate as, "the type of person who in a war would go out onto the battlefield and shoot our own wounded." That description well summarized the Reagan team's sentiments over Reed and Giordano.

Reagan and Schweiker flew in the next week and met with the delegation. Reagan, not known for rudeness, greeted Reed with an icy smile. Schweiker and Reagan took some tough questions, and some found their performance wanting. But despite the surveys conducted by the media, this meeting and Reagan's relentless phone calls to individual delegates in the state had isolated the defection to only Reed. The rest, besides Shanks and Carmichael, would abide by their decision to go to the convention uncommitted.

Reagan and Schweiker also met with some nervous Alabama delegates to hold them in line. Still, their blunt talk to Reagan appalled Schweiker and his wife, who had accompanied them on the Southern swing. Keene remembered one Alabama delegate, Wallace Stanfield, who bluntly told Claire Schweiker that when he had heard of her husband's selection, "I drank a pitcher of whiskey sours—and I'm not a drinker. I'd rather have the doctor call and tell me my wife had the clap."

Of Ford's tenuous position, James Baker told *Time*, "We're a hundred votes ahead of them, and we're still confident of victory, but there hasn't been any spectacular development to resolve the thing once and for all."[55]

Drew spoke to Reed several days later and described him as "uncharacteristically glum." Second guessing himself, he remorsefully told the journalist, "More Mississippi delegates accepted this Schweiker thing than I thought would. The people who normally agree with me are sticking by Reagan, and the people that approve of what I did are not the people I'm normally comfortable with. Maybe I jumped too quickly . . . so I'm kind of lonely."[56] Reed would still have to go to Kansas City, where he would be condemned and courted, feted and frozen out, before he would really begin to feel truly lonely.

As the days counted down to the convention and the possibility for discord was on the rise in Kansas City, Reed told the *New York Times*, "I'm a lot more worried about the possibility of chaos than I am about who the nominee will be." History would show that it was Reed himself, who was the principal cause of the "chaos" in Kansas City.[57]

14

KANSAS CITY

"We come with our heads high and our hearts full.
We're going to come here and do what we have to do."

The word "convention" is derived from the Latin word *venio,* which means "to come." When it is further linked to the word "convene," combined they mean "to come together." "Convention," according to Mr. Roget, is alternately defined as "agreement," "assembly," and "treaty of peace." The 1976 Republican National Convention was anything but a treaty of peace, as it forever altered the direction of the Republican Party.

The prevailing wisdom in 1976 about political conventions was echoed in a white paper issued by the Brookings Institution:

> To the extent that conventions do have power, their capabilities for damaging their respective parties may be greater than for repairing or rebuilding them. Any convention has the power to degrade its party image even in victory or to lessen its popular appeal and make victory impossible for the time being; on the other hand, when the party has already been severely damaged by the preconvention campaigns, the convention has only limited capability to heal the breach.[1]

Kansas City prepared for the invasion of the Republicans and hoped for a peaceful gathering. The city's brand spanking new Kemper Arena would host the GOP convention and glistened white in the hot summer sun of 1976. Kansas City had spent millions to roll out the red carpet for the Grand Old Party. Even its "red light" district was festooned with red, white, and blue bunting, as dancing elephants were placed in the windows of several smut peddlers. The city's Mayor even planned to cut up the mahogany gavel post from the podium following the convention, in order to sell pieces to souvenir collectors and generate even more revenue for the municipal treasury.

City fathers had also planned to float a giant gas-filled elephant named "Biggie" over the arena for the week of the convention. But plans went awry. According to one account, "Biggie, a 50-foot-long plastic elephant weighing three-quarters of a ton . . . didn't work. Biggie became entangled in some nylon haulage wires, tore out its stomach, and never got off the ground."[2]

Sophisticates from New York and Los Angeles referred to the middle part of the country that divides the liberal salons in Manhattan from the liberal salons in Beverly Hills as "flyover country." Kansas City was probably one of the last places in America they would ever contemplate visiting or vacationing in. Shows what they knew.

As a matter of fact, other than Biggie, everything was "up to date" in Kansas City. Its stockyards, which had made it famous as a "cow town" were mostly closed or were closing. Situated on the Missouri River, Kansas City was well run and clean. It had an excellent municipal services sector, libraries, parks, museums, healthy white-collar businesses, and a new airport that was the hub of a major airline, TWA. Direct flights were available to the city from Washington, D.C., New York, and other American cities. Farm trade was still a large part of the local economy, but it was far from the only source of revenue or jobs.

Its population of over five hundred thousand made it one of the larger cities in America[3] and its citizens cheered the fortunes of the Kansas City Chiefs, the Kansas City Royals, and the Kansas City Kings while enjoying plays coming in from New York. With St. Louis and Chicago, Kansas City had some of the finest restaurants in the Midwest. It was still the best place in America to get a steak.

One of the leaders of the Pennsylvania delegation complained that his accommodations, at a hotel near the airport were "like getting stuck in the middle of a corn field—you can't walk to a bar or get a suit pressed." Not so, as *Time* explained. "Though the Hilton plaza is eleven miles away from Kemper Arena, it is not in a cornfield, had four bars, swimming pool, tennis courts and one-day valet service," reported the magazine. The hotel's manager, Maurice Bluhm, threatened to cancel the reservations of the state's entire delegation until the man apologized.[4]

Kemper Arena was an ultra-modern structure that had cost over twenty-three million dollars to build and seated seventeen thousand. Unbeknownst to anyone, its silent concrete, steel girders, and glass would behold history in the making. Less than three years later, the arena's roof collapsed during a thunderstorm in 1979. Perhaps the boisterous and noisy GOP delegates of 1976—through four passionate days and nights of exhorting their candidates, yelling at speakers at the podium, cheering for Nancy Reagan and Betty Ford, stomping their feet, blowing horns, and leading demonstrations for Gerald Ford and Ronald Reagan into the wee hours of the morning—contributed to weakening the arena's superstructure and thereby hastened its eventual collapse.

Over thirty thousand people descended on the city, including 4,515 delegates and alternates—more than double the number that had gone to Miami Beach four years earlier. Nine thousand members of the media were also present. Others included campaign staffs, foreign dignitaries, White House staff, Secret Service personnel, vendors, and the like.

The city had not hosted a national political convention since 1928, when the Republican Party nominated Herbert Hoover. Some wags tried to draw a correlation between 1928 and 1976, but time would prove that, as far as the GOP was concerned, they had nothing in common. In fact, 1976 joined 1856, 1860, and 1964 as the most important Republican conventions in the party's history, and one of the most important in American history.

But none of these convention years was uppermost in the mind of President Ford. He was thinking about the convention of 1884, when incumbent President Chester A. Arthur was turned aside by his own party. Ford did not want to become only the second President to be rejected by the GOP.

Pro-Ford forces had near total control of the entire convention apparatus—even down to the details of the official program, which featured twenty-three photos of Ford and only one of Reagan. Also, Ford's delegates were awarded the choicest and closest hotels, while Reagan's delegates were relegated to motels as far away as seventy miles from the convention center. One Reagan delegate told Robert Nakamura in the *Political Science Quarterly*, "The tactics used by the people in power—the Republican National Committee—were ruthless, cold-blooded and bordering on the fringe of being unethical."[5]

Before heading to Kansas City, John Sears held a press conference in Washington and claimed a pickup of another twelve uncommitted delegates for Ronald Reagan. He attempted once again to cast as much doubt on the delegate count as possible.

Jim Baker disputed Sears's claim, telling reporters that eleven of the twelve had already been counted in the Ford campaign's tabulations as committed Reagan supporters. Only one, State Senator Fred Eckert of New York, was a new, public supporter of Reagan. But after his private meeting with Ford several weeks earlier, it was evident to Baker that Eckert had been a Reagan fanatic all along.[6] Reagan himself noted Eckert's eccentricity. Memos had been prepared by David Keene with lists of uncommitted delegates for the Governor to call. After speaking with Eckert, Reagan scribbled next to his name, "He is very conservative. Agrees with my every position. He (and this must be a secret) is going to K.C. to vote for me."[7]

Sears was also floating the media-inspired "Trojan Horse delegate" argument; that many of Ford's delegates really preferred to vote for Reagan. This was true enough in North Carolina, Florida, and other states. But it was also offset by some of Ford's own Trojan Horse delegates. For example, Indiana delegates were legally required to vote for Reagan on the first ballot, though most clearly favored Ford. Still, Sears's fog machine was working, and most observers, save possibly the estimable Baker and his team of delegate hunters, believed that neither man had the delegates locked up for a first ballot nomination in Kansas City.

Several months earlier, Baker had righted the delegate operation of the President Ford Committee. He had assembled a top-notch team including his key assistant, Peter McPherson, to count, cajole, and coddle GOP delegates. And Dick Cheney was asserting increased discipline over the Ford White House. Each morning Cheney, Stu Spencer, Bill Timmons, Rog Morton, and Bob Teeter would meet at the White House to review the day's events, including Ford's travels and public activities, the campaign's activities, and how to coordinate the day between the two.[8] Yet some elements of the campaign still creaked along, especially the areas under Campaign Chairman Morton's control. Morton was ailing at the time, but he was still under heavy criticism, especially for his too-frank comments to the media. "Maybe some new leadership over here would be stimulating," he told the *Washington Post*.[9] Ford himself had upbraided Morton several times for his intemperate statements.

Ford's problems aside, Reagan was having his own trouble in spades with his own delegates and those who had, previous to the Dick Schweiker announcement, wanted to be his delegates. Many of these Reagan delegates in Ford clothing were still bristling over the selection of Senator Richard Schweiker. One real Trojan Horse delegate from North Carolina told *Time*, "Nobody's going to break the law for Reagan now."[10]

The delegate was referring to one stratagem under consideration by the Reagan operation: that delegates simply violate the directives from their state leaders and vote for Reagan rather than Ford at the convention. Another tactic under consideration was for these Trojan Horse delegates to abstain on the first ballot, possibly denying Ford the nomination. Then they would be free to vote their individual consciences in the balloting that would follow.

To prevent this possibility, the Ford-dominated Republican National Committee passed the so-called "Justice Amendment" that would mandate that all delegates abide by their state laws as they pertained to procedural matters. Still, the RNC had no jurisdiction over the convention, and the matter would have to be taken up by the Rules Committee and the Platform Committee in Kansas City.

The Reagan team, led by Paul Laxalt, fought the proposal. The issue was but one more part of the delicate balancing act the campaign was attempting to perform. On the one hand, they wanted to win the nomination, but not in a way that would enrage the Ford forces and cause them sit on their hands in the fall, as moderates and liberals did in 1964. As Jim Lake said, "You are talking about a strategy that would make the Ford people mad. We want to get the nomination, but we also want to win in November."[11] *Time* magazine reported,

> In addition, many Ford-bound delegates really preferred Reagan. They are Republican right-wingers who had been assigned by local party leaders to vote for the President because he won a proportion of their state's popular vote in the primaries. If the voting at the Kansas City convention goes to a second ballot, a number of Ford's 18 Vermont delegates would shift, and all but two of his 25 North Carolina delegates would jump to Reagan.
>
> The finish would be so tight that John Sears, Reagan's campaign manager, predicts that his man will be ahead, but perhaps by three votes—1,031 to 1,028. Ford's aides forecast a squeaker victory for the President.[12]

Minor delegate movement between the camps and between committed and uncommitted status was greeted by the media with the fanfare usually reserved for visiting heads of state. A headline blared over a story in the *Washington Post* by Margot Hornblower, "Reagan, Schweiker Pick Up 6 Delegates in Northeast."

> The series of personal delegate meetings, which began. . . in Mississippi and will continue this week in Pennsylvania and West Virginia, is part of the final frantic scramble for votes before the Kansas City convention 10 days away. Although Mr. Ford is 72 votes ahead of Reagan, by the Washington Post count, the character of the race could still change with 119 delegates remaining uncommitted and others changing their minds daily.[13]

Baker and his delegate honchos must have dreaded picking up the newspapers every morning.

In another story on August 6, the *Post* also reported, "Reagan picked up two delegates in New York and two in New Jersey, while in Minnesota a Reagan delegate and a Ford delegate announced that they are now uncommitted." The newspaper's count had Ford at 1,106 and Reagan at 1,034 with 119 uncommitted delegates.[14]

From early on both campaigns had assumed that delegates would decide which candidate to support by considering ideology, who could most likely win in the fall campaign, or what was in the national interest. They were sorely mistaken. One New Jersey delegate, Joseph Yglesias, told Hornblower he had decided to support Reagan because, "Mr. Ford failed to show concern about the loss of jobs at a Bayonne military base."[15] Yglesias had replaced a Ford delegate who had died one month earlier, and a credentialing fight was looming over whether or not to seat the stand-in delegate.

As both campaigns, the White House, the media, the interminably infuriating delegates, party staffers, and hangers-on were all preparing to descend upon Kansas City, the Ford and Reagan camps were confronted with fresh problems. For Ford, the economy was cooling and unemployment had gone up for the second month in a row. This was in contrast to the primary season, when Ford had complained about how he had not received any credit from Republican voters for the turnaround in the economy. His point was well taken.

From 1975 to 1976, the GNP had turned around, from negative growth to a sharp spike in positive growth. And, just as importantly, inflation had been halved, from over 12 percent to 6 percent. The Ford campaign hoped the slowdown in the economy would not adversely affect the President's ability to gather the last remaining delegates needed for the nomination. But it was another headache they did not need.

Reagan's problem was more immediate and threatening. Several disgruntled conservatives made a clandestine effort to oust Schweiker from the ticket. Led by Senators Jesse Helms and Strom Thurmond, they made clear their unqualified support for Reagan, but their qualified support for a Reagan-Schweiker ticket. Since the stunning announcement of Schweiker, conservatives—especially those independent of Citizens for Reagan, had fumed privately and publicly. But the attempt by Helms and Thurmond was the first real effort to dump Schweiker.

While Reagan was favored by most conservatives, these purists did not shy away from criticizing him. Still, their anger was not aimed directly at Reagan so much as Sears and Schweiker, whom they felt free to criticize. Conservative circles hummed with talk of an "open convention" to select another running mate for Reagan, should the Californian gain the nomination. Escaping their attention was the obvious fact that if Reagan did win the nomination in Kansas City, it might very well be due to both Mr. Sears and Mr. Schweiker.

Reagan and Schweiker also struggled to gain support among uncommitted delegates. They made a foray into the Senator's home state and found the pickings thin. A luncheon in Philadelphia was attended by about half of the state delegation. While the event was cordial and both Reagan and Schweiker were well received, it did nothing to turn around any more delegates for the ticket.

Reagan and Schweiker both noted to the media the continuing pressure being placed on delegates by the Ford operation. Reagan said that Ford operatives were, "virtually breaking down the door" to keep delegates in line. Reagan and Schweiker told the media that the five Pennsylvania delegates who had previously announced support for Reagan were now being harassed and ostracized for doing so by the President's campaign. Ford's Chairman, Drew Lewis, denied their charges.[16]

Schweiker took an unusually hard hit from columnists Rowland Evans and Robert Novak, two of the few political journalists immune to the charms of Sears. The duo charged, "Whereas poisonous erosion of Reagan strength in the South can be blamed on Schweiker, he cannot take credit for modest Reagan advances in the Northeast."[17]

They were also continuing to have problems with the national media, who kept hammering Reagan and Schweiker on their philosophical differences. Things were somewhat better in West Virginia, where Schweiker spoke to the GOP state convention and received a standing ovation. They also managed to pick up one previously uncommitted delegate there.

Suffering from buyer's remorse, Clarke Reed told the reporters he "may have overreacted" when he endorsed Ford over Reagan several weeks earlier. Reed did throw the Reagan camp a bone when he expressed the sentiment that many delegates would like to know Ford's choice ahead of time. The incoming State Chairman in Mississippi, Charles Pickering, had also moved from supporting Reagan to undecided like others. But Keene felt he did so cunningly, in order to maneuver with the uncommitted delegates and turn them back toward Reagan.[18]

Outside the glare of the national media, John Sears and Dick Cheney discussed how to minimize friction between the two warring camps in Kansas City once the nomination was decided. They initially agreed that the winner would call upon the loser immediately after the roll call vote. Also, they were to meet in private, without staff or family in attendance. Later, once the convention was underway, Sears added the proviso that Ford not offer the Vice Presidency to Reagan, which Cheney said he would carry to the President for his consideration.[19]

Staff assignments had been handed out for the two camps. Nofziger was to manage the convention operations for Citizens for Reagan. His counterpart would be Bill Timmons, a veteran of convention politics who managed the 1968 and 1972 conventions for Richard Nixon. Timmons was a well-regarded player in GOP politics who, like Nofziger, was fiercely loyal.

The week before the actual convention, many delegates began to arrive in Kansas City for a week of often-heated meetings, hearings, and discussions, as the party's platform was drafted. "Platform Week" was, for many, the more enjoyable week at a convention. Delegates were able to catch up with old friends, relax at the end of the day, and still get a table at a good restaurant without a reservation. Yet if anyone thought the fights during Platform Week between the Reagan forces and the Ford forces would be any less contentious than the battles of the previous two years, he thought wrong.

Originally, Governor Robert Ray of Iowa, a moderate and a supporter of Ford's, planned to choose the seven platform subcommittee chairmen. Ray had been appointed as Chairman of the overall platform committee, and his candidates all were supporters of Ford. Wielding those eight gavels would have given Ford effective control of the entire drafting and rules process.

But Charles Coy, a Reagan delegate and member of the platform committee, objected and offered an amendment that passed forty-two to thirty-nine. This measure allowed each subcommittee to chose its own Chairman. It was a significant victory for Reagan and only passed because so many Ford Representatives to the platform committee had failed to show up for the Sunday evening meeting. Ford spokesman Peter Kaye told the *Washington Post*, "The right-wingers always come early and stay late."[20]

Another important advance for Reagan came when a delegate from North Carolina offered a resolution that provided for all the subcommittee hearings to be open to the public and the press. The Reaganites were convinced that the moderates would ramrod amendments through to support the President and undermine Reagan. Although this resolution did not pass in its original form, Congressman John Anderson offered a substitute amendment that provided for the hearings to be open until mid-week, when the entire platform committee would revisit the issue. Anderson's amendment eventually passed. Reagan's supporters believed he would get a fairer deal if the processes were open to scrutiny.

Reagan's campaign was moving ahead with two direct challenges to President Ford's authority. One was made under the guise of reasonableness, while the other was a more direct and harsh challenge to Ford's foreign policy. Senator Jesse Helms and his able Director of the Congressional Club, Tom Ellis, would lead this second effort. They would coordinate with Peter Hannaford and Marty Anderson on the drafting of this plank.[21] These two initiatives were the essence of the yearlong debate between those aligned with Sears's "pragmatic" strategy and those aligned with Reagan's conservative supporters.

Since the Schweiker announcement, Sears had been beating the drums daily, claiming that the only fair thing for the Republican Party and for the country would be for Ford to announce his choice for Vice President in advance of the convention. Initially, the media did not give Sears's line much credence. But slowly, as names began to emerge and the Washington guessing game took off, his story line began to appear more frequently in news reports and political columns. Sears and Baker held dueling press conferences daily, as each tried to gain the psychological advantage over whose candidate had enough delegates for the nomination.

A particularly effective point Sears made was that since Ford was an unelected incumbent, he was in a unique, more tenuous position than past GOP incumbents. Since he had little grip on the party, Ford owed it to the delegates to let them judge for themselves his choice of a running mate. Indeed, Ford had personally paid to send letters to all the GOP delegates and party leaders soliciting their advice on his running mate. Initially, this tactic was part of the counteroffensive against the Schweiker announcement. But the Reagan campaign began to use it against Ford, reasoning that since he wanted their advice, it was simply the logical next step to tell them his choice.

Sears's plans came together during the first day of the platform hearings when he announced that Reagan proposed an amendment to the platform known as "Rule16-C." Simply stated, the new rule would mandate that Ford, or any candidate, name his running mate before the actual nomination process began. If 16-C passed and a candidate did not name his choice ten hours before the Presidential roll call, he would forfeit all his pledged delegates.

Sears testified before the rules committee and presented 16-C as a "simple notice rule that says 'trust the delegates.'"[22] He expected the committee, loaded with Ford supporters, to reject the amendment. But he knew the rules of the party allowed for a "minority report" to be filed before the full convention, provided that the amendment received 25 percent of the votes in the full committee of 106 members.

The rules committee for the convention immediately rejected the proposed 16-C. Paul Haerle, the California GOP Chairman and a Ford supporter, charged the proposal was a "misery loves company" gambit. But Sears brushed criticism aside, saying of the rule, "All it does is put the delegates and the people in the candidate's confidence before he is the irrevocable choice of the party."[23]

The committee also voted down another proposed rules change inspired by Governor Jim Edwards of South Carolina. Edwards's proposal would have compelled both candidates to address the convention before the nomination process began. An amendment proposed by the Ford campaign that would force delegates to vote according to state law rather than their personal choices was set aside for a day to be revisited.

Insight on Reagan's strategy came from one unexpected quarter, as Vice President Rockefeller told Witcover and Cannon, "They really are interested in winning and not just in ideological concepts." He also said it represented "a fundamental and interesting shift."[24] Another Ford strategist, Dean Burch, expressed concern that the proposal could draw sufficient votes from Ford delegates to insure its passage.[25]

Another fight came over Governor Ray's selection of Congressman Silvio Conte of Massachusetts to head the subcommittee handling abortion and women's issues. The dispute was not orchestrated by the Reagan forces, but was simply an organic effort by conservatives on the committee who felt Conte was too liberal and would not arrive in Kansas City until later in the week. In his place, they elected Pickering. Still, the remaining six subcommittees voted to approve those chairmen originally proposed by Ray, although Ford's control of the executive committee narrowed to only eight to six. The executive committee was comprised of Ray and the subcommittee chairmen and co-chairmen.

The full committee heard testimony from a variety of Republican leaders, including Nelson Rockefeller. When questioned, Rockefeller surprised the committee when he said that he felt Ford had made a mistake the year before by not meeting with Soviet dissident Aleksandr Solzhenitsyn. The Vice President then elaborated, telling them he had dined in secret with the writer and with AFL-CIO President George Meany.

The committee moved on to the Ford proposal to bind delegates to vote according to their state laws rather than their personal preferences. Ford's supporters were clearly worried and cited a quote several weeks earlier from Reagan Chairman Paul Laxalt suggesting delegates might vote their personal preferences. The proposed amendment passed the rules committee easily, despite the arguments offered by Reagan's attorneys, Loren Smith and Roger Allan Moore that the amendment was "insulting" to the delegates.

Passage of the Ford proposal effectively locked up 939 total delegates who came from states that had existing state laws to mandate that delegates vote according to the wishes of the primary voters in their respective states. This was a significant victory for the Ford campaign. "Officials in both . . . campaigns estimate that if the primary results were ignored . . . and they simply voted their preferences,

Reagan might gain 25 to 35 votes and Mr. Ford lose an equivalent number," wrote David Broder.[26] The President Ford Committee ultimately won an important final battle in the full platform committee, as the Justice Amendment was approved.

Platform Week was half over, and proposed amendments flew all over the subcommittees. John East and Tom Curtis, two Reagan backers, were working on as many as twenty-two plank proposals, all designed to make the GOP more conservative. East and Curtis drafted amendments pertaining to issues including the Panama Canal, détente, busing, gun control, and trade. On the other side, GOP women's groups, who supported Ford, were pushing proposals to encourage more women to become delegates.

The national media covered every aspect of the process. Lengthy reports were filed in all the major newspapers and on all three networks. In a long commentary, CBS's Eric Sevareid pronounced the death of the Republican Party, due in large part to demands of conservatives. Sevareid derided Reagan's campaign as "a revival tent across the road where the orthodox could kneel and touch the remnant of their true cross."[27]

Leslie Stahl, also of CBS, speculated that "Republicans will go the way of the Whigs." She interviewed Kevin Phillips to make her point and further reported that the party "lacks the critical mass just to stay alive." She also interviewed both Richard Viguerie and Senator Charles Mathias, both of whom forecast the demise of the GOP.[28]

Social conservatives achieved a significant victory when a pro-life plank passed Pickering's subcommittee overwhelmingly. Despite a *Washington Post* survey of a handful of delegates showing a majority favored "a woman's right to choose," the party was moving towards the pro-life position Reagan advocated.[29]

A proposal to reject the Equal Rights Amendment, which had been part of the 1972 platform, was in limbo on a vote that deadlocked seven to seven, despite the plea from Ford to keep it.[30] The ERA was a special favorite of Betty Ford. Before the full committee, support for the ERA would eventually be kept in the platform. But this plank won by only by a vote of fifty-one to forty-seven. The mere fact that the ERA was open to question, and the pro-life plank added, was a victory for Phyllis Schlafly, a leader of the social conservatives. At the 1980 GOP convention, the ERA plank would be rejected.[31]

Since the announcement of Dick Schweiker, Sears had hammered away at the challenge to Ford to name his running mate well in advance of the convention, as

Reagan had already done. This tactic began to pay some dividends. Names were beginning to be floated in Washington, from HUD Secretary Carla Hills and Commerce Secretary Elliott Richardson (two liberal nemeses of Reagan) to CIA Director George Bush to Ford's Ambassador to Great Britain, Anne Armstrong.

The President was beginning to get advice from all quarters, and one of his aides indelicately suggested to *Time*, when Treasury Secretary Bill Simon's name was floated, "Simon's perfect: he's a Catholic with a Jewish name."[32]

Despite the fact that White House Press Secretary Ron Nessen told reporters that Ford would not name his running mate prior to the convention, "in the traditional manner,"[33] the Washington guessing game would not stop. Neither did the ever-present leaks and speculations coming out of the executive mansion or the President Ford Committee.

John Connally's name was also being test-driven, but a group of ten Northeastern GOP state chairmen considered issuing a public objection to the Texan. Conservative supporters of Ford were equally chagrined about the names of liberals under consideration. These included including Congressman John Anderson of Illinois, former Pennsylvania Governor Bill Scranton (whose name was second only to Nelson Rockefeller's when it came to raising the hackles of conservatives who were mindful of 1964), and Washington Governor Dan Evans. Senators Howard Baker and Bill Brock of Tennessee were also on Ford's list. Brock was one of the few real conservatives on this list. Baker gave himself low chances for being picked when he told *Time*, "In Washington I'm thought of as a conservative, but in Tennessee I'm thought of as a Bolshevik."[34] Beyond ideology, Baker stood little chance of getting the nod from Ford. He was well qualified, but media reports surfaced that his wife Joy had once struggled with a drinking problem, and speculation cast a pall over his name.

But rumors about Ford's choices and rumors about opposition to supposed candidates for Vice President all served Sears's attempts to put Ford on the hot seat prior to the convention. Still, the White House, despite the leaks and speculation, was exhibiting unusually good discipline. On making a final choice, Rockefeller told the *Washington Post*, "You've got one person who is happy for a period and you've lost sixteen friends."[35]

To counter Sears's pressure tactics, the White House implemented a plan to consult with anybody and everybody—including mailing questionnaires to delegates, alternates, and elected GOP officials, soliciting their advice on whom Ford should pick. In effect, Ford was countering Reagan with his own fog machine, and the list grew daily. The search was on for the "perfect" running mate.

The White House released a culled-down list of sixteen possible choices for Ford, and asked many of the prospective running mates to provide detailed information about their backgrounds, including health and finances. Some who immediately declined were Senators Bill Brock, Ed Brooke, and Lowell Weicker. Others who were on the list, but were not asked for the information, included Reagan and Rockefeller.[36]

Meanwhile, a party that thought itself immune to surprises was surprised once again when Senator Jim Buckley of New York floated his name as a "compromise" presidential nominee. Despite charges then and since from Ford operatives, the move was never orchestrated by Sears or the Reagan team or even revealed to them before the announcement. The move was shrewd, as up to 150 delegates were only pledged to Ford and not committed.

Senator Helms, Tom Ellis, Arthur Finkelstein, and Congressman Phil Crane, impatient with Sears's tactics, decided that Buckley could conceivably "run" for President to provide delegates an additional option on the first ballot. But some in the media speculated that the move was designed to take enough conservative delegates away from Ford to deny him a first ballot nomination. Some of these delegates might include those pledged to Ford in the New York delegation of 154, courtesy of Rockefeller and Rosenbaum. Buckley understood the strategy clearly as he told *Newsweek*, "My only purpose would be to deadlock the convention on the first ballot and thus give all the delegates the chance later to vote the way they want."[37]

In fact, beyond the New York delegates, Finkelstein, who had developed the brainstorm of Buckley running after talking with David Keene, was thinking about the uncommitted conservative and Catholic delegates from many states who were pledged to vote for Ford on the first ballot, but not mandated to do so. Ellis once said of Finkelstein, "Just knock on his head and he'll give you an idea."[38]

ABC's Harry Reasoner reported, "The possible entry of New York's conservative Senator James Buckley into the Presidential race had added to the confusion and the infighting already underway. With the nomination still undecided, the jockeying for position becomes more complex every day."[39]

Reasoner's colleague, ABC correspondent Frank Reynolds, nailed the story and the ingenious strategy behind it: "Its aim is not to win over Ford delegates in Buckley's home state of New York, but to offer southern delegates, particularly those in Mississippi, a face-saving device that will also gain time for Reagan. The goal is an inconclusive first ballot that will free southerners bound to Mr. Ford of their obligation to vote for him at least once. Then, so the plan goes, they will follow their hearts to Reagan. The Buckley ploy will also give the uncommitted delegates . . . and there are still probably at least 100 of them . . . chance to stay uncommitted through the first ballot . . . but the true target is Mississippi."[40]

Laxalt and Helms, on a separate matter, did agree to work together on the platform. It also meant they could keep an eye on each other. They created a six-member committee to work with them. This committee included Anderson, Ed Meese (who had recently joined the campaign), Curtis, East, Dick Obenshain, and Jimmy Lyons. Lyons was the Houston banker who had loaned the campaign the critical $100,000 it had needed to put Reagan on national television several months earlier.

Actually a tentative agreement to work together had been hammered out the previous weekend in Atlanta, at a meeting between Helms and his forces and Nofziger, Andy Carter, Lake, and David Keene. Helms, Ellis, Keene, and Black had not exactly patched up their differences since the North Carolina primary, but they were at least talking again. Helms called the meeting and asked delegates from a number of Southern states to attend. The four Reaganites also showed up to keep a wary eye on Helms's forces.

But the focus for several days was on the Buckley announcement and what its ramifications might be for both Ford and Reagan. Rosenbaum called Buckley directly and threatened to withhold support for his Senate re-election campaign, but Buckley refused to back down to Rosenbaum's threat. At a press conference, Buckley would not commit to a full blown announcement but told reporters he would not "slam the door" on a possible candidacy.[41]

Sears gave the Ellis plan a wide berth, but he told the *Washington Post*, "All I know is, this would hurt Mr. Ford more than it would us." Some of Ford's strategists discounted the Buckley initiative, but Baker knew better, and he was worried.[42]

The White House announced that Ford would travel to Kansas City the Sunday before the convention opened on August 16. The President's schedule was an unmistakable sign of his tenuous hold on the convention, as incumbent Presidents traditionally arrived in their convention city on the eve of the balloting for the nomination. Ford would be needed there to meet with nervous supporters and to attempt to sway uncommitted delegates. It was an awful sign of weakness, but he had little choice.

Reagan also would arrive on Sunday, but this was to be expected. He was the challenger and was behind in the delegate count. Schweiker and his wife, Claire, would arrive on Saturday to an enthusiastic reception. Rockefeller also was greeted on Saturday by a large and supportive crowd, while Ford aides, including Mel Laird, talked up the possibility of Ford deciding in the end to stay with his beleaguered Vice President. Such talk only helped Reagan's case with the convention to force Ford to name his running mate before he could gain the nomination.

Once again the tiresome Clarke Reed shifted when he warned Ford publicly that the Mississippi delegation might not support him if several of the names floated for Vice President were not removed from the list. These included Senators Chuck Percy of Illinois, Mark Hatfield of Oregon, and other liberals. He further hinted that he might support 16-C when it came to the floor for a vote the following week.[43] Rumors also floated around that in addition to the possibility of a Buckley eleventh hour candidacy, Helms himself might run for the nomination. A sense was taking hold that the situation was spinning out of control in Kansas City for both Ford and Reagan. Lake had to knock down a rumor, published in the *Pittsburgh Post*, that Reagan was going to ask Schweiker to step aside. Schweiker blamed the Ford campaign for spreading the rumor to create mischief in the Reagan camp.[44]

Still, Sears pointed to the Reed threat and another from the Maine delegation, concerned that Ford might pick Connally, as evidence that Ford would be forced to name his running mate in advance of the balloting the following Wednesday.

The conservatives, led by Helms and his ideological soul mate, John East, a professor from East Carolina University, suffered a setback when their platform challenge, a proposed foreign policy initiative that became known as the "Morality in Foreign Policy" plank, was voted down by the Foreign Policy subcommittee. Senator Roman Hruska of Nebraska chaired this subcommittee. Anderson and Hannaford helped draft the language of the plank. While the Helms forces were suspicious of the Reagan team, especially Sears, they were on good terms with Anderson and Hannaford, despite their being part of Citizens for Reagan. Helms aides Jim Lucier and John Carbaugh also wrote some of the plank challenging Ford's foreign policy.

The initial draft was a tough Cold War denunciation of the Soviets as well as Henry Kissinger, arms control, détente, the Panama Canal, Ford's treatment of Solzhenitsyn, the Helsinki Accords, and trade with Communist countries. It also included strong language reaffirming support for Taiwan. The entire amendment was culled from Reagan's public positions over the last several years, and it was simply too much for the Ford operatives to accept. It amounted to a complete refutation of Ford's foreign policy over the prior two years.

The proposal was voted down by the committee by a vote of nine to seven. Watered down substitute language was offered and accepted instead. East had attempted some parliamentary maneuvers to get the committee to vote on individual pieces of the plank, but heavy-handed tactics by Hruska gaveled him down. Still, the process, which began at 6:30 P.M., did not finish until 3 A.M.

The week of platform hearings was winding down, and the previously watered-down foreign policy plank was rejected by the full committee, fifty-five to forty-three. Before final passage, it was gutted even more as support for maintaining "sovereign rights over control and operation of the Panama Canal Zone" was also eliminated.

One delegate offered in the full committee an amendment called "Morality in Government" to the platform that would condemn all the elected officials in Washington who were involved in sex scandals (there were at least three going on at the time) and also condemned all involved in Watergate. The assembled members regarded the proposal in the same way they would a dead skunk on the table and quickly and overwhelmingly defeated it.

A final platform was approved. But Helms, East, Tom Curtis of Missouri and other conservative supporters of Reagan were furious and vowed floor fights the following week, where planks could be voted on by the full convention, provided they had the support of enough states. Nonetheless, the final document did end up with more conservative language, and this was a partial victory for the Helmsites. The final preamble of the Republican Party's 1976 Platform read:

> The Democrats' platform repeats the same thing on every page: more government, more spending, more inflation. This Republican platform says exactly the opposite—less government, less spending, less inflation. In other words, we want you to retain more of your own money, money that represents the worth of your labors.[45]

While Ellis, Helms, Terry Boyle (another key Helms aide), Carter Wrenn, and others were strategizing on how to introduce their planks to the full convention, they were also working behind the scenes to move the Buckley candidacy forward.

Sears, meanwhile, was planning to bring his 16-C amendment before the full platform committee and was disregarding other proposed planks, including one that would have forced the two candidates to address the convention before the balloting started. As far as Sears was concerned, he regarded 16-C as the "silver bullet" for Reagan. The rules change that allowed for a minority report to be presented to the full convention, provided the amendment had 25 percent backing of the full platform committee, eventually aided him in this effort.

A *Washington Post* survey found that 63 percent of the delegates going to Kansas City described themselves as "conservative," an increase of 10 percent from four years earlier. Also, those calling themselves liberal had dropped from 12 percent to 6 percent. The parties were slowly, inexorably become more polarized.[46]

The previous day, Reagan received a rousing sendoff in Los Angeles from "Youth for Reagan," at which his son Michael introduced him. Reagan told the young crowd that the idea of picking Schweiker had not occurred to him, but that Paul Laxalt had encouraged the choice and Reagan heartily agreed after meeting the Pennsylvanian.[47] After the breakfast, Reagan saw a bus caravan of the young people off for Kansas City, where they would produce pro-Reagan demonstrations. Reagan had spent the week at his home in Pacific Palisades, calling delegates and supporters and monitoring the developments in Kansas City.

On Sunday, August 15, Sears put his 16-C proposal before the full platform committee while Reagan and Ford were both receiving tumultuous welcomes—Ford at the Crown Center Hotel and Reagan at the airport and again at the Alameda Plaza Hotel, where he and Nancy joined up with Dick and Claire Schweiker. To the laughter of the crowd, Schweiker tweaked Ford when he said, "What's his name can't even find a Vice President yet."[48] Reagan had come east from California with Nancy, his daughter Maureen, his two sons Michael and Ron, and Ken Curtis, the actor who portrayed "Festus" in the hit television show *Gunsmoke.*

During the week of the platform hearings, James Baker held a press conference to announce that Ford had 1,135 "firm" delegate votes, only 5 more than what was needed to win the nomination. Sears immediately shot back that Reagan had 1,140. But all newspapers' accounts, including the *Post,* had both candidates short of the required 1,130.

The *Kansas City Times* found a wide discrepancy in the count performed by all the major newspapers, magazines and wire services. The Associated Press tallied Ford 1,104 and Reagan 1,023, while *Time* totaled 1,121 for the President and 1,078 for his conservative challenger. *Human Events* counted 1,127 for Ford and 1,132 for Reagan. *Newsweek* and the *Washington Star* both reported Ford tantalizingly close, but not over the top. Also, two previously uncommitted delegates from Missouri declared for Reagan, and this development only added to a surreal sense in the days leading up to the convention.[49]

The *Washington Post* wistfully wrote: "President Ford is to leave Washington today on the most important political journey of his life."[50] In a sendoff interview with Ford before he departed for Kansas City, the paper reported, "The spectacle of a President enduring such blatant pressure tactics from the party rank and file is mind-boggling to anyone who recalls the manner in which Mr. Ford's two most immediate predecessors, Lyndon B. Johnson and Richard M. Nixon, lorded over their party conventions."[51]

Reagan restated his support for his choice of a running mate and pointed out that he had given the party three weeks to consider his decision. Ford, if nominated, would only give them a half a day. He also told the crowd, "We come here with our heads high and our hearts full. We're going to come here and do what we have to do."[52]

Ford had arrived three hours later on Air Force One with Betty and his photogenic children in tow. Joining them were Senator Jacob Javits and several staff members. Most Ford staff, especially from the President Ford Committee, had arrived earlier in the week on a chartered jet.

Both Reagan's and Ford's arrivals in Kansas City were covered live by the networks. "The Republican affair has taken on all the appearances of a horse race . . . and that is exactly the type of story television seems to appreciate best. Early commercials for the coverage were stressing the G.O.P.'s new element of drama," reported the *New York Times*.[53]

Sears was greeted with less fanfare than the candidates, as the Platform Committee shot down his proposed 16-C amendment, fifty-nine to forty-four. The Ford forces, for a moment, thought they were out of the woods. Said Presidential confidant Dean Burch to the *Washington Post*, "We're out of the procedural minefield now." Another Ford supporter mocked Sears: "It's not a right to know amendment. It's a right to save a campaign manager amendment."[54] Sears had known all along that the Ford supporters had enough votes to defeat 16-C. But unlike Burch, he also knew he had more than the 25 percent necessary to bring his proposal before the full convention the following Tuesday.

Several more uncommitted delegates from Pennsylvania, West Virginia, and Illinois had announced for Ford. Reagan similarly had also picked up a couple more from Pennsylvania over the weekend. For the first time since 1952, Republicans would gather at a national convention not knowing who their nominee would be.

And while some merely smiled when Schweiker asserted on the ABC Sunday news show *Issues and Answers* that he and Reagan had hidden delegate strength and might pull in as many as fifty from Pennsylvania, no one could be sure.[55] Of those states whose delegates were now frozen, Reagan actually had more delegates than Ford.

The contentious Mississippians caucused Sunday evening and came away without a decision on whether to support 16-C when it came to the floor Tuesday evening. The only thing they agreed upon was to support the eventual nominee, whoever that might be. They would also caucus again on Tuesday afternoon to decide whether or not to dissolve the unit rule. Also, Dent passed along a rumor to Reed that Sears was considering pulling a fast one by introducing 16-C first thing Monday morning, while there would be few delegates in the hall and while the convention was still being governed by temporary rules.[56] Reed naturally overreacted, which was Dent's intention in the first place. Sears was considering nothing of the sort, but Dent was playing Reed like a Stradivarius. Keeping Reed agitated against Sears meant keeping him on Ford's side.

Although the rules and platform initiatives of both Sears and Helms lost in committee, they received sufficient support for 16-C and the nearly two-dozen separate ideological planks would be brought before the convention on Tuesday evening, but not sooner. Temporary rules would govern the convention on Monday, and the permanent rules and the platform would be adopted Tuesday evening.

Helms despised the proposed 16-C rule and thought it was ridiculous. Ellis told the *Washington Post*, "There's not a whole lot of enthusiasm for it . . . it's not such a great deal."[57] But Sears feared that the Helms-inspired ideological planks, while partially useful, could only lead to a Reagan nomination in a "runaway" convention scenario, which he believed would lead to a divided party and a disaster in November.

Years later, Baker would agree with Ellis and Helms that the tougher ideological planks might have been more effective. The more Ford was humiliated, the more likely it would have been that he would have had to fight the platform proposals, maybe lose those fights, and with them lose the nomination. When the argument of Sears's strategy of winning without bloodletting was pointed out to Baker, he replied, "But to win in the fall, you have to win the nomination first."[58]

Still, Sears brought most of the conservative grassroots supporters in line to support 16-C. "However gimmicky John Sears's politics may be, it at least is giving a case of convention jitters to the President's managers," wrote Rowland Evans and Robert Novak.[59] The Reagan campaign had put the finishing touches on its version of the "Morality in Foreign Policy" plank that was also to be offered Tuesday evening. Although it was tougher than the one adopted by the Platform Committee, it was not as tough as the one Ellis was holding in the wings, just in case.

Sears won a tactical victory when, sensing the problems 16-C posed for Ford, the President's supporters attempted to amend the procedural rules to only allow such amendments if they had the support of two-thirds of the rules committee, instead of the previously agreed 25 percent. Having failed at this attempt, the Ford campaign reverted to the argument that 16-C, if passed, would prevent Ford from choosing Reagan. Still, Sears could safely proceed with his plan.

Reagan's Campaign Manager was operating as he had for the last year. He hated meetings, hated writing memos, and kept information to himself. He would plot the strategy without input from the rest of the staff and then meet with them to persuade them of the merits of his newest initiative. No one besides Sears knew what the next steps would be after introducing 16-C and the foreign policy plank. It was sometimes maddening to the rest of the campaign, even to those who defended his decisions. Dick Wirthlin later wrote, "Sears is one of the most complex persons I've ever met. He is at once one of the most talented, undisciplined, manipulative, creative and insecure people I've ever met."[60]

Monday, August 16 dawned early for the warring camps. Outside the Kemper Arena, two trailers had been set up as the command posts for Citizens for Reagan and the President Ford Committee. Each was similar in having televisions to monitor local and network coverage and telephones connected to each of the delegations on the floor of the convention. From here, Sears and Nofziger would direct their floor lieutenants, as would Timmons and Baker. Ford's floor team was better organized and wore yellow or red baseball caps so they could be easily spotted. They also had walkie-talkies, runners, and assorted other accoutrements. The Reagan people gloated that while the Ford trailer only had one air conditioner, they had two. By week's end, the trailers were littered with overflowing ashtrays, food wrapping, and other assorted trash.

After their inconclusive meeting over the weekend, Dent had suggested a compromise to the Mississippi delegation: to dissolve the unit rule and split the delegation down the middle, with each side getting fifteen votes, thus changing their vow to stick to the previous agreement.[61] Some of the delegates, weary of the protracted and unresolved fight, were listening to Dent. Others were not. Meeting under the Mississippi placard, Mounger and Dent got into a heated discussion, and reporters started squeezing in trying to catch a few choice words for a story.[62] Humorously, the Executive Director of the party, Haley Barbour, began to loudly recite the Mississippi counties backwards to interfere with reporters' ability to record the brouhaha.[63]

As the convention opened, Buckley withdrew his nascent campaign. It had become clear that no delegates had expressed any interest in supporting him over Ford. He had also been subjected to a flood of phone calls and enormous pressure to end speculation about running for President before he hurt his own re-election chances in New York.

A nasty situation developed when Ford's Chairman in Illinois, former Governor Dick Ogilvie, charged that the Reagan campaign had attempted to bribe two of his delegates. He offered no evidence, and Reagan promptly denounced the charge. Reagan accused the Ford campaign of dirty tricks and was personally insulted, especially since he and Ogilvie had become friends while serving as the Governors of their respective states. Reagan's Illinois point man, Don Totten, was forced after the convention by local law enforcement officials to take a lie detector test over the altercation. The officer who administered the test told Totten he was the only politician he had ever tested who passed.[64]

Reagan and Ford both spent Monday meeting with delegates and groups of delegates, cajoling them to either support or oppose 16-C the next night. Meanwhile, delegates, in minute spurts, were declaring and undeclaring their preferences. Only the Ford campaign claimed the President had enough votes for a win Wednesday evening. In addition to the delegates, Ford also spoke to a group of boisterous young supporters, including a pretty brunette from Arizona named Zorine Bhappu, called "The Presidentials." They were the Ford campaign's answer to "Youth for Reagan," and they would "spontaneously" appear at every Ford public appearance to cheer the President. Still, when Reagan encountered the group on several occasions, they were respectful.[65]

Reagan had lunch at the Alameda Plaza Hotel, the headquarters for his campaign, with a dozen conservative leaders, including Helms and beer magnate Joe Coors. The group was cautiously optimistic about Reagan's chances for the nomination. Hollywood celebrities showed up for the convention, as Pat Boone, Efrem Zimbalist Jr., and others stumped for Reagan. Cary Grant also showed and spoke out for Ford.

The high point of the first evening, before the proceedings got down to business, were the competing welcome demonstrations for Nancy Reagan and Betty Ford. An agreement between the two camps to minimize any embarrassing competition had melted under the television networks' watchful eyes, and long, prolonged cheers greeted Mrs. Reagan, whose welcome topped Mrs. Ford's.

Mrs. Reagan arrived first, and the band struck up "California Here I Come." The noisy demonstration lasted well into the time of Mrs. Ford's scheduled arrival. When she did arrive, there was no song to greet her for several minutes, and the Ford campaign was furious with the band director, Manny Harmon. They took steps to ensure this embarrassment would not be repeated Tuesday evening. "The Ford people were extremely upset," according to Brad Minnick, who was an aide to Senator Griffin, Ford's Floor Manager.[66]

The temporary Chairman of the convention, Senator Robert Dole of nearby Kansas, opened the proceedings, and two old antagonists spoke that evening: Nelson Rockefeller and Barry Goldwater. Both were greeted warmly by the crowd. All three excoriated the Democratic nominee, but Dole had the best line, citing Jimmy Carter's flip flop on an important part of the Taft-Hartley bill that permitted states to have right to work laws, known as 14-b. Dole said that first Carter supported 14-b, then he opposed it, and "now Carter thinks 14-b is his shoe size." Also speaking that night was Senator Baker, who had been introduced by Senator Buckley who had been reinstated as a speaker after dropping his threatened candidacy. He got his own zinger in when he parodied the Democratic nominee by telling the delegates, "My name is Jimmy Buckley, I'm running for Senator."[67]

Unmentioned and unnoted in Kansas City was former President Nixon. His name had been completely deleted from the platform, and his photos appeared nowhere. It was as if he had been a Soviet official who had fallen out of favor and was then erased from a photograph atop Lenin's Tomb. However, present at the convention but also unnoticed by a party that had left him behind years before was another once "boy wonder" of the GOP, former Minnesota Governor Harold Stassen. At one time Stassen had been a real hope of the party.

Some GOP leaders tried to gloss over the differences between the Ford delegates and the Reagan delegates. In many respects, they were right. But unlike the Ford supporters, the Reagan delegates were more ideological and more optimistic about their candidate. The *Washington Post* measured this interesting phenomenon, showing that of Reagan's supporters, 86 percent thought he had a good chance of beating Carter. Only 67 percent of Ford's followers thought the same of their man.[68]

"It was a day of madness in the news media, as the thousands of reporters in Kansas City scrambled to record the erosion of the uncommitted delegates. For the first time in the memory of long-time convention-goers, obscure individual delegates held news conferences for national reporters to disclose their first ballot votes," wrote the *New York Times*.[69]

If there was any doubt as to the competing makeup of the Ford and Reagan delegates, it was confirmed Tuesday afternoon in the showdown over Mississippi. Once again, Clarke Reed would be at the center of a controversy that was entirely of his own making. The Reagan forces needed the Mississippi delegation to keep its unit rule intact, if they were to have any hope of winning that night on 16-C. But several days before, Baker had become more confident of Ford's delegate strength. At this point, he was content to add to his counts going into Wednesday night's nomination balloting with several of the Mississippi delegates, providing the unit rule was dissolved, rather than none of them. That day, the *New York Times* finally projected Ford as having barely enough delegates for the nomination, but the *Washington Post* still had him short by four votes. And Ford still had to negotiate the thicket of 16-C and what would follow if the amendment were to pass.[70]

Reed was being pulled in every direction—by David Keene, Billy Mounger, and Charles Pickering for Reagan and by Harry Dent, Doug Shanks, and Dick Cheney for Ford. He kept telling both sides what they wanted to hear on 16-C and the unit rule, and neither side trusted him.

The Mississippians finally got together in a room at the Ramada East Hotel to decide once and for all whether or not to support the unit rule and 16-C. Dent had previously arranged for some of the uncommitted delegates, including Reed, to meet privately with Ford. But Dent clearly remained worried about his flip-flopping friend, who had gone on national television earlier to say he would support 16-C only shortly after assuring Dent he would oppose it. After meeting with Ford, John Hart of *NBC News* reported that Reed would now oppose 16-C. Reed called Cheney to upbraid him for the audacity of trying to keep him to his word, but Cheney did not back down, telling Reed, "Look, Clarke, we expect you to do what you told us."[71]

The Reagan people were putting renewed pressure on Reed after they heard the NBC report, telling him that he could partially make it up to Reagan for his previous betrayal by sticking with them on 16-C and delivering his thirty votes to support the proposal.

Reed was once again flopping around like a large mouth bass in the bottom of a fishing boat. Dent was unrelenting in his drumbeat to him about being a "kingmaker" and had told Witcover at the time, "There was a battle going on to retake Clarke Reed. We had Clarke's body but we didn't have his soul."[72] Complicating Dent's task were his new orders from Baker. Previously, the Ford campaign wanted to dissolve the unit rule and split the vote. But now Baker could only count 1,130 votes for that evening against 16-C: just enough to win but far too close for comfort. He now told Dent all 30 of Mississippi's votes were needed for Ford.[73] The margin for the nomination was, according to his counts, more comfortable for the next evening. But for Baker, those twenty-four hours were an eternity away. How many other Clarke Reeds might be out there, telling him one thing and then doing another?

Both campaigns had surrogates address the assembled Mississippi delegates and Reagan himself came by to answer questions. Also, Reagan's friend, Efrem Zimbalist Jr. spoke to the Mississippians. Finally, Dent and Dave Keene were asked to leave the room and even when John Connally showed up to speak on Ford's behalf, he was rebuffed by Barbour.

Keene had made it clear to Mounger that 16-C was the last chance for Reagan. "You lose this thing and it's over; that's it. If Mississippi goes down the chute on 16-C, we lose it on the floor, we lose the nomination."[74] Both sides now needed all thirty of Mississippi's votes. After a good deal of deliberations and recriminations, the delegation finally voted.

Haley Barbour left the room after the vote and bumped into Dent, who anxiously wanted to know the outcome.

"Y'all won," said Barbour, glumly.[75]

One delegate missed the vote, but no matter, as Ford prevailed thirty-one to twenty-eight. Thirty votes had been taken out of the Reagan column for 16-C and placed in the Ford column against 16-C. Baker had the cushion he needed for the President. Reed deliberately cast his vote at the end, when the outcome was clear, for Reagan—even as he knew it would do no good for the Californian.

Word spread quickly throughout Kansas City of the Mississippi delegation's switch to Ford. The psychological impact for Ford and against Reagan was resounding. Sears had commitments from individual delegates in New Jersey and Pennsylvania to support 16-C, but when they found out about Reagan's collapse with the Magnolia State GOP, they ran for the tall grass. Gil Carmichael and Doug Shanks were exultant while Mounger and Pickering were crestfallen. Most of the rest were simply glad it was finally over and went to have some beer, courtesy of Coors.

While the Mississippians were shuffling off for beer, increasing numbers of uncommitted delegates were shuffling off into the Ford column. No point holding back now, and they might as well go with an apparent winner.[76] Adding to Reagan's woes was the *CBS News* report that had, for the first time in the network's tabulations, placed Ford over the top with 1,132 "firm or committed" delegates.[77]

The highlight of Tuesday evening was the keynote address by Connally. He did not disappoint the delegates, as he ripped into Carter and the Democratic Party. But eyes in the Reagan and Ford camps were not on Connally's speech. They were anticipating the showdown over 16-C.

After Connally spoke, the convention heard from a number of delegates arguing from the podium supporting and opposing 16-C. One who argued against it was a pretty blonde form South Carolina, Sherry Martschink, who had driven both camps to distraction over the preceding several months as an uncommitted delegate. She clearly relished the attention from all, including the media. Martschink was booed heavily during and after her speech.

Speaking in favor of 16-C was Reagan's old friend from Missouri, Tom Curtis, who had been a Congressman and Chairman of the Federal Election

Commission. Leading the pro-Ford group against 16-C was Michigan Senator Bob Griffin, who was also Ford's Floor Manager.

But again, before the convention could get down to business, round two began of the battle of the candidates' wives. Mrs. Ford entered the arena first and was greeted with loud applause, followed by Mrs. Reagan a few minutes later. The Reaganites on the floor went wild, engaging in a long and loud welcoming ceremony for the pretty former actress. She stood in the VIP skybox designated for Reagan and his close friends, high above the floor. For minutes on end, she waved and the crowd cheered. And each time the band struck up "California Here I Come," the cheers grew even louder and longer. Disco singer Tony Orlando, sitting with Mrs. Ford, would dance with her when the band played his song, "Tie a Yellow Ribbon," giving the cue to Ford supporters to cheer more loudly than the Reagan supporters.

Dole tried but failed to bring the convention under control from the podium. At one point, he quipped to the milling Republicans, "Will the delegates please take their seats . . . or any seat." Still, the famous Dole temper was visible several times that evening as the proceedings fell further and further behind schedule.

Morton blundered again when his interview with the *Birmingham News* appeared in a story headlined: "Ford Would Write Off Cotton South?" In this story, which circulated among the Mississippi delegates, Morton had speculated to the paper that Carter was too strong in the South and that Ford might bypass the region. This caused renewed angst among many in the delegation.[78]

On the floor, under heavy questioning by CBS correspondent Dan Rather, Morton backtracked from the story, and Rather invited Morton to go over to the Mississippi delegation to explain himself. A quick-thinking Ford operative, watching this unfold, arranged for an order via walkie-talkie to Morton to leave the floor—immediately.[79] Bringing Reed back into line required a phone call from Ford himself to Reed on the floor to calm him down and assure him he would not bypass the South.

Reed received a new request via phone from Sears in the Reagan trailer. Sears sought to salvage some votes for Reagan by having Reed hold a quick caucus and dissolve the unit rule. Reed was simultaneously boiling mad at Morton for his comments, was under a crush of reporters at the back of the hall, and was being interviewed live by Tom Pettit of NBC and other journalists. So he could not have moved to hold the caucus Sears had asked for, even if he had wanted to. Pettit reported that the Mississippi delegation was "coming apart at the seams."[80]

Mounger, Keene, and Pickering also tried to get the delegation to re-caucus, given this development—knowing it would stiffen the spines of the Reagan delegates. But the Ford supporters in the delegation refused to leave their seats on the floor. They knew that as long as they remained on the floor and did not leave to meet with the alternate delegates, a quorum would be impossible, and the unit rule would hold for Ford. The last hope of retaking Mississippi for Reagan collapsed.

"In a convention hall aboil with emotion, the former Governor's partisans demanded a rules change requiring Mr. Ford to disclose his running mate and 'tell us who is on the team before asking us to join it,'" wrote the R.W. Apple Jr. in the *New York Times.*[81]

About the only person in Kansas City who was keeping his cool was Reagan himself, who would be seen periodically throughout the evening watching the proceedings on television and laughing at some of the charges leveled at him and Schweiker from some speakers at the podium.

Tempers were running high. A confrontation involving Nelson Rockefeller took place on the floor before the vote, when a Utah delegate ripped out the white phone that connected the New York delegation to the Ford command post after he saw Rocky had taken a Reagan placard from a delegate in the North Carolina contingent. Perspiring heavily through his shirt, the Vice President held up the phone and attached cord for all to see, but many saw the image as a metaphor of his inability to communicate with his own party. Rockefeller finally relented and gave the Reagan sign to a delegate, but not before ripping it in half. Security had escorted the Utah delegate, Doug Bishoff, out of the hall. Later, the Secret Service arrived to escort Rockefeller off the floor as well, fearing the altercation might lead to a more threatening situation.

Rosenbaum was using the phone at the time and was surrounded by a crush of reporters. Dole, visibly angry, gaveled and asked repeatedly for the hall to come to order, for the aisles to be cleared, and for the vote to proceed. But it was to no avail. The famous incident ended on a light moment when Tom Brokaw of NBC interviewed an extraordinarily large delegate from North Carolina, who had taken it upon himself to break up the scuffle over the sign that now involved Rockefeller and the delegations of Utah, South Carolina, and North Carolina. Brokaw told the man, "Well, given the dimensions of you, I doubt anyone is going to take it away." Reagan, watching on television, dissolved in laughter.[82] The next night, handmade signs held up by Reagan delegates appeared on the floor saying, "Rocky don't steal this sign."

"Whistles, catcalls and a scuffle on the floor delayed the debate and drowned out the voices of the speakers on both sides," wrote the *Times.*[83] Earlier in the day, anticipating the pent up anger of the Reagan delegates, the Ford campaign had announced it would not fight Reagan's "Morality in Foreign Policy" plank. Sears's only card to play was 16-C. Secretary of State Kissinger had arrived quietly in

Kansas City and had urged the Ford campaign to fight the foreign policy plank, but they wisely demurred. Knowing how he antagonized the conservatives in Kansas City, the campaign had kept him under virtual house arrest.

Time had expired for debate, and Dole directed a roll call vote on 16-C after the Chairman of the Idaho delegation, Wayne Kidwell, asked to be recognized. Dole did, and Kidwell notified the podium that he had the support of a majority of the delegations from his state, New Mexico, Texas, California, Alabama, and Arizona to ask the convention for an up-or-down roll call vote on 16-C. According to the rules, delegations from six states were required in order to make this motion.[84]

The states voted alphabetically. During the previous week, in the rules committee hearings, some Ford supporters worried about the possibilities of ballot momentum for Reagan as many of the early states favored him. Ford's Representatives to the rules committee attempted to have the states vote randomly, but this was shot down as a ridiculous idea.

As the convention got down to business, a blue cloud materialized over the hall. The tense delegates lit cigarettes, cigars, and pipes. Ashtrays were plentiful, but when they overflowed, delegates simply stubbed their cigarettes on the floor.

After Dole confirmed that the six states indeed wanted a vote, the balloting began. Reagan pulled out to an early and healthy lead with the votes of Alabama, Arizona, and California's big bloc of 167. Colorado extended his lead, as did Georgia and Idaho. It was not until Illinois that a big state went overwhelmingly for Ford. Still, as the states moved along, Reagan had the lead until the voting came to New York, when Ford moved into the lead. Mississippi had taken a pass at Keene's request, as he hoped for a miracle to bring their thirty delegates back into the Reagan fold.

When the vote came to New Jersey, Senator Clifford Case announced his state's vote as sixty-two to four against 16-C. But when one delegate, Thomas Bruinoog, moved to have the delegation polled individually, a groan went up from the hall. Sears had called Bruinoog and asked for the vote, believing he had been betrayed by several of the delegates after they learned of Reagan's loss of Mississippi earlier in the day. Sears wanted their duplicity on record. When Texas voted all hundred delegates for 16-C, a prolonged cheer went up from the Reaganites in the hall.

The issue was still in doubt at the end of the alphabetical role call of states. Two states had passed and would be asked to now announce their votes. Florida had passed, as Mississippi had done, so it followed Wyoming. Wyoming surprisingly had only voted nine to eight for Reagan. "We did a masterful of peeling delegates out," Cheney remembered.[85] Although the delegation had been heavily pro-Reagan, they had been invited to the White House dinner for Queen Elizabeth and successfully swayed to support Ford. Florida proceeded to cast thirty-eight votes against 16-C and twenty-eight in favor. Only at that point did Ford top the 1,130 votes needed to stop 16-C.

When all the votes had been tallied, Ford defeated Reagan 1,180 to 1,069 on Sears's Rule 16-C.[86] A handful of delegates abstained or did not bother to show up, but the hall went wild with pro-Ford cheers, as all knew this test vote meant Ford would be most likely nominated the next evening.

Mississippi's thirty delegates voted against 16-C. As it turned out for Ford, their votes were not necessary. But the impact of their announced switch to Ford could not be underestimated. And Reed had lost his chance to clinch the nomination for Ford and make himself a "kingmaker."

The convention next had to consider the Reagan campaign's foreign policy plank. It was well after midnight, and the delegates were streaming for the doors. The Ford campaign debated once again whether to fight it or to take a pass. Baker and Cheney worried that opposing the amendment and possibly losing might stop the ballot momentum they had gained from the defeat of 16-C.

Reagan's foreign policy plank "did everything but strip Henry bare of every piece of clothing on his body," Cheney recalled. "And Rockefeller and Kissinger were pushing to have the fight to defeat the platform plank. I was arguing this is not the time to have the fight on the platform. And Kissinger said at one point, 'If you don't take on this fight, I'm going to resign. I'm going to quit here and now. [Tom] Korologos piped up and said, 'Well Henry, if you're going to quit, do it now. We need the votes.'"[87]

Rockefeller was especially angry with Cheney. "Rockefeller had spoken to the convention. And in the middle of the speech, the sound system went dead, and he accused me of pulling the plug. It was that kind of relationship," Cheney said.[88] Baker and Cheney won the argument, and Ford grudgingly decided not to fight the Helms foreign policy plank. Witcover wrote,

> Jim Baker never was able to understand why Reagan's foreign-policy plank was written in language that was so easy to swallow. "I could see a two-word plank: 'Fire Kissinger,'" he said later, "and we would have had to fight it. And if we had been beaten, we could have lost the whole thing. We had eleven hundred and forty-five commitments and they were as strong as we could make them. But until that first vote was taken,

> how could we know we had them? Minds change. If there was going to be some ballot momentum for Reagan, it would have had to come on some emotional issue." But Sears insisted such heavy-handedness would never have worked. "If we had won on 16-C," he said afterward, "we would have moved immediately to have both tickets come before the convention and address the convention. That would have passed easily, and it would have raised the anxiety level on the other side. They were always afraid that if Reagan got before the convention, all hell would break loose."[89]

Baker also speculated to the author that had Ford selected a running mate at that point, some delegates would have withdrawn their support.

As the bitter loss over 16-C settled in among Reagan's team, Ellis was on the floor desperately trying to get the attention of the permanent Convention Chairman, Congressman John Rhodes, in order to force a roll call vote on the foreign policy plank in a last ditch effort to embarrass Ford and possibly stop his nomination. Pat Nolan, a Reagan aide from California, had assured Ellis that his state would support a roll call vote, as did Governor Mills Godwin of Virginia. Along with these and several others, Ellis had more than enough required states needed to force a roll call vote on Helms's tough denunciation of Henry Kissinger and Ford's foreign policy, but Rhodes ignored him. Ellis needed to be recognized by Rhodes in order to force the vote. Hoarse from long days and nights for Reagan, Ellis croaked, "Railroad! Railroad! You have broken the rules!" to Rhodes.[90]

Hannaford quickly consulted with Ellis on the floor and called Sears in the trailer to propose the last-gasp maneuver. Sears okayed it, but Hannaford could tell the fire had gone out of Reagan's Campaign Manager.[91]

Mysteriously, Ellis's microphone went dead, ensuring that Rhodes could not recognize him even had he wanted to do so. Hannaford remembered speaking later with a friend who was in the trailer with Sears. The friend recounted that over the direct phone line from the trailer to the podium, someone had told Rhodes to "shut him off"—referring to Ellis's microphone. Rhodes declared that the convention had approved the platform, without discussion, including Helms's plank, and gaveled the evening proceedings over. Ellis thereafter believed that Sears had ordered his microphone to be turned off.[92]

Wednesday morning and afternoon, Reagan and Schweiker put up a brave front and met with numerous delegations, but their hearts were not in it. It was evident to all now that Reagan's long quest for the Presidency was nearing its end. Sears and other staffers from Citizens for Reagan also spoke, usually in desultory terms, to the media and delegations. But they too were just going through the motions. An eleventh hour effort was orchestrated by Lyn Nofziger to oust Sears as Campaign Manager, but most felt that there would be no point.

By now, Sears was number one on Nofziger's enemies list. "Sears always thought he was the smartest guy in the world . . . and didn't know why he was stuck with this dumb actor."[93] The day was filled with bitter second guessing and recriminations by Reagan supporters over Sears's 16-C scheme as well as his earlier decisions to pick Schweiker, bypass the Wisconsin primary, and pull out of New Hampshire the weekend before the critical votes, among other transgressions. Sears was angry too, but at Clarke Reed. As he told reporters, "When Mississippi bailed on us, most of the others did, too."[94]

Some Reagan supporters were mounting a campaign to persuade Ford to add Reagan to the ticket. But Reagan himself had made clear that he was not interested. When delegates he met with raised the issue, Reagan reiterated that the differences between the two men were too stark.

Or was he interested? In 1982,White House Chief of Staff Jim Baker was in the Oval Office with President Reagan. While reminiscing about the 1976 campaign, Baker asked Reagan if he would have accepted the offer, if it had come from Ford. Seconds passed, and Reagan finally said, "Yes, Jim, I probably would have."[95]

Between meetings on Wednesday, Hannaford was buttonholed by Jude Wanniski, who told him that if Reagan embraced a plan of tax cuts—what would later be known as "supply side economics"—they might be able to persuade Congressman Jack Kemp, a Ford delegate from Buffalo, to switch to Reagan. But Hannaford looked at him dismissively and then brushed him off.[96] Early in the Ford Administration, Arthur Laffer, the father of "supply side economics," and Wanniski had met with Cheney and Donald Rumsfeld at the Two Continents Bar to urge the Ford White House to embrace the radical notion that cutting taxes would increase government revenue. "This was the first time he'd [Laffer] ever drawn the curve. With a magic marker, he drew the first version of the 'Laffer Curve,'" Cheney recounted.[97] Both camps rejected this policy—which was to become the fundamental basis of Reaganomics—after 1976.

Once again, an effort was made by some conservatives to oust Schweiker from the ticket, thinking this might free up some delegates for the nomination vote that evening. When Schweiker learned this news, he met with Reagan to make an offer to withdraw his name. Without a pause, Reagan told the Senator, "Dick, we came to Kansas City together and we're going to leave together."[98]

Around 5:00 Wednesday morning, "some of us went to see Reagan to see if he'd dump Schweiker. We met at the Reagans' suite. Governor Reagan came out and before we could even get started, he shut us down real quick. 'If you could . . . guarantee me the nomination, I still wouldn't do it,'" Ernie Angelo recalled. "And that made us all feel really small for even suggesting it."[99] Meanwhile, Ford was keeping a close counsel on who his choice would be, and the *New York Times* speculated that the list had narrowed to Senator Baker and William D. Ruckelshaus.[100]

Wednesday evening, Paul Laxalt spoke to the convention and placed Reagan's name in nomination. Governor Bill Milliken of Michigan, Ford's friend, did likewise for the President. Reagan's supporters launched a prolonged demonstration for their man. When the demonstration would begin to fade out, the California and Texas delegates would revive the cheers by chanting "Viva!" to which the other would reply "Ole!" Ford's Floor Manager, Senator Bob Griffin, and his staff were helpless to stop the fracas that lasted almost an hour and it pushed the balloting out of prime time for television viewers across much of the country. The din was so loud that their walkie-talkies were ineffectual.[101]

Reagan asked Chuck Tyson to make the demonstrators stop, but Tyson replied that there was nothing he could do. "Again and again, they blew on two-foot-long plastic horns, filling the hall with a sound uncannily reminiscent of the ululations of Arab women," reported the *New York Times* about the Reaganites.[102] The band played "California Here I Come" again and added "The Pennsylvania Polka" for Schweiker. "The floor, as usual, was a madding, milling jumble of bodies, posters, banners, standards, flags, and delegates," the paper reported.[103] One sign read, "Send Ford to Helsinki, Send Reagan to Washington." Some Ford supporters in the balcony dumped trash on the Texas delegation.[104]

The nomination voting finally got underway, but it was not until West Virginia cast twenty votes for Ford that he passed the magic number of 1,130 delegates and won his party's nomination.

Washington state delegates, who had cast most of their votes for Reagan just a few moments before the West Virginia delegates clinched the nomination for Ford, went through a minor flap when Reagan's figurehead Chairman, Warren McPhearson, offered his delegates the opportunity to switch their votes to Ford. This way they, rather than the West Virginia delegates, could be seen on national television putting Ford over the top. The real power for Reagan in the state, Dale Duvall, was appalled and disappointed in McPhearson. Apparently, so was the rest of the delegation. They were polled, and not one wanted to switch to Ford. As Duvall expected, Reagan kept thirty-one of the thirty-eight delegates.[105]

The final tally was 1,187 for Ford and 1,070 for Reagan. One delegate from Illinois abstained, and one delegate was unaccounted for.[106] Ford received just fifty-seven votes more than the minimum number required to win the nomination. It was over.

Mississippi's delegation, barely on speaking terms with each other, cast sixteen of its thirty votes for Ford. John Hart of NBC described the delegation as being in "intensive care."[107] They had finally dissolved their unit rule, but Mounger wanted everybody's apostasy on record as having voted against Reagan so they could face the music when they went home. He was exhausted and only acquiesced when Pickering and Keene asked him to do so.

Later, after the vote that made Ford's nomination official, Claire Schweiker tearfully told Reagan in his suite at the Alameda Plaza Hotel, "Oh Governor, I'm so sorry!" Reagan immediately embraced her and said, "Claire, you really shouldn't be upset about the outcome because it wasn't part of God's plan."[108] Mike Reagan remembered his father telling him, "God chooses his own time."[109]

The Schweikers and the Reagans had become close, and the Schweikers later remembered Reagan's many kindnesses, such as when one of their daughters was elected class President. She got a note telling her "at least one of us will get to be President."

Late in the evening, the family dined together, and Nancy Reagan lifted a glass, her eyes glistening and "in her toast she apologized to him for the loss."[110]

In accordance with the prior agreement, the winner would call upon the loser. So Ford arrived at Reagan's suite in the Alameda Plaza Hotel around 1:30 in the morning. It was reported that the two met alone. But unbeknownst to anybody, Nancy Reynolds and Reagan's son Ron, in the hubbub, got stuck in a small kitchenette in the suite, where they could overhear the conversation between the two. They debated whether or not to excuse themselves politely but decided to simply wait unobtrusively. Reynolds said years later there was no animosity between Ford and Reagan and that they talked politely.[111]

Ford had a short list of choices for Vice President and asked Reagan's opinion. Reagan's name was not on the list despite heavy lobbying of Ford by the Californian's staff. "A couple of weeks before the convention, we went up to Camp David to try to persuade him [Ford] that the right answer for a running mate was Reagan. . . . He really didn't want to hear it. It had been by that time a pretty bitter, knock-down drag out between the two of them," Cheney remembered.[112]

At their meeting, Reagan spoke favorably to the President about Bob Dole, whom he admired.[113] Ford also asked Reagan if he would like to take part in the

Thursday night proceeding, and Reagan declined. Earlier in the day, Dole had asked Nofziger, who was an old friend, to put in a good word for him with Reagan if Ford was to ask the Governor his opinion about the war hero.[114] Nofziger had worked for Dole at the Republican National Committee, and they shared a ribald sense of humor. Furthermore, as two veterans of World War II, there was a special sense of fraternity between the two men.

On Thursday morning, Reagan met with his campaign staff one last time to thank them and spoke to them movingly about their commitment. He started with a joke: "Backstage politics is like looking at civilization with its pants down."

The networks televised the remarks live, and Mrs. Reagan, with tears in her eyes, had to turn her back to the cameras. Reagan told his mostly young and utterly devoted followers, "The cause goes on. . . . Nancy and I aren't going back to sit on a rocking chair and say that's all there is for us. . . . We're going to stay in there and you stay in there with me. . . . The cause is still there. Don't give up your ideals, don't compromise, don't turn to expediency, don't get cynical. It's just one battle in a long war. The cause will prevail because it is right." Of course, he then reminded them of "the shining city on a hill."

And then Reagan himself wiped a tear away. The *Times* speculated that "At 65 years of age," Reagan was "too old to consider seriously another run at the Presidency." This opinion was nearly universal among the media and indeed the political world.[115] About 200 crying staffers filled the room, including Neal Peden, who had worked so long and so hard for Reagan at the campaign. The Schweikers joined Governor and Mrs. Reagan on stage, and Mounger recalled that he has never cried as hard as he did then.

Along with Mrs. Reagan, everybody else in the room was now crying including Clarke Reed, who audaciously joined the gathering, though he was greeted with icy glares and cold shoulders from all—including Reagan himself.

Several members of the staff had tried to bar Reed from the room, but finally relented because they didn't want to cause a scene in front of the media. As Reagan departed and walked towards an elevator with Mrs. Reagan, Mike Deaver, Peter Hannaford, Jim Lake, Nancy Reynolds, and his Secret Service contingent, Reed rushed up to him and exclaimed, "Oh Governor, I've made the worst mistake of my life." Sources vary on Reagan's retort to Reed, but all agreed it was anything but warm. Lake remembered distinctly Reagan telling Reed, "It's a little late now, Clarke."[116] Billy Mounger, Reed's lifelong friend, would never speak to him again.

Reagan had attended a unity press conference with Ford Thursday morning and spoke warmly about his chance against Carter in the fall campaign. Later that morning, Ford announced his choice of Bob Dole as his running mate. Dole and Ford had served together in the Congress and had worked together for many years. The delegates voted overwhelmingly for Dole as Vice President, with 1,921 going to the Kansan and 338 to others, including Reagan, Bill Buckley, and a smattering of Congressman and Senators. David Keene and John Sears also received votes for Vice President, and 102 delegates abstained.[117]

Ford delivered his acceptance speech forcefully, and it was widely praised. His address was made memorable by his direct challenge to Carter to debate the issues. Dole had spoken previously, and he too was well received. Ford's family joined them at the rostrum along with Dole's wife Elizabeth and daughter Robin. Nelson Rockefeller also arrived, along with the rest of the meager leadership of the GOP. But one very important person was missing.

In their crowded skybox, Ronald and Nancy Reagan were joined by their family and some close friends, the Schweiker children, and campaign staff. Reagan was being interviewed by Brokaw and, in the melee, Mrs. Reagan was almost poked in the eye by Brokaw's antenna. Brokaw asked Reagan if he was going to address the hall, and once again Reagan said, "No."[118] Previously, after concluding an interview with Reagan outside his skybox, Frank Reynolds broke down crying. A deep affection existed between Reynolds and the Reagans. But he would not be the only person in tears before the night was over.[119]

Reagan was utterly content to watch the proceedings with Nancy, sign a few autographs, and savor the rousing reception he had received earlier from the convention. Since their father would have no further role that evening, Michael and Maureen Reagan had left the arena earlier and returned to the hotel, where they planned to meet him for dinner. And the Secret Service wanted Reagan out of the building before the end of the proceedings. Nofziger had not even gone to the hall that night. He had gone to bed early at the Alameda Plaza.

Mike Reagan remembered that, before he and Maureen left, a very intoxicated RNC aide had come to Reagan's skybox and asked Mike Deaver to please ask Reagan once again to reconsider the invitation to speak to the convention. But the aide was summarily dismissed. Later, Jim Lake received several phone calls from Deaver, who was furiously negotiating on Reagan's behalf with Ford's staff, who were pressing hard for Reagan to make an appearance at the podium. Minutes passed.

Ford then asked, before a national television audience and in front of the assembled hall, for "my good friend, Ron Reagan to come down and bring Nancy." Reagan initially rebuffed Ford's entrees. Waving and shaking his head "no," he smiled and gave Ford the "thumbs up" sign.

Then Ford's family joined the President, and they too waved for Reagan to come down to the podium. And then the convention hall weighed in, as the delegates began cheering and applauding and chanting "We Want Ron! We Want Ron! We Want Ron!" The delegates created an ever louder and louder din that rolled up to Reagan, urging him, pleading with him to go to the podium. Kemper Arena was shaking, as the delegates were stomping their feet and yelling for Reagan.

Reagan reflected for a moment.

Finally, a more senior and sober convention official, Bryce Harlow, showed up to once again ask for Reagan's presence at the podium. But Reagan had already decided. He didn't want to disappoint the Republican faithful. Reagan truly wanted to help his party. And he hated letting anyone down. And so, somewhat reluctantly, Ronald Reagan stepped out of his skybox.

And into the future.

15

REAGAN'S REMARKS

"There is no substitute for victory."

Thank you very much.

Mr. President, Mrs. Ford, Mr. Vice President, Mr. Vice President to be, the distinguished guests here and you ladies and gentlemen:

I am going to say fellow Republicans here, but those who are watching from a distance—all of those millions of Democrats and independents who I know are looking for a cause around which to rally and which I believe we can give them.

Mr. President, before you arrived tonight, these wonderful people here, when we came in, gave Nancy and myself a welcome. And that, plus this, plus your kindness and generosity in honoring us by bringing us down here, will give us a memory that will live in our hearts forever.

Watching on television these last few nights, and I've seen you also with the warmth that you greeted Nancy, and you also filled my heart with joy when you did that.

May I just say some words? There are cynics who say that a party platform is something that no one bothers to read and it doesn't very often amount to much.

Whether it is different this time than it has ever been before, I believe the Republican Party has a platform that is a banner of bold, unmistakable colors with no pastel shades.

We have just heard a call to arms based on that platform. And a call to arms to really be successful in communicating and reveal to the American people the difference between this platform and the platform of the opposing party, which is nothing but a revamped and a reissue and a running of a late, late show of the things that we've been hearing from them for the last 40 years.

If I could just take a moment—I had an assignment the other day.

Someone asked me to write a letter for a time capsule that is going to be opened in Los Angeles a hundred years from now, on our Tricentennial.

It sounded like an easy assignment. They suggested I write something about the problems and issues of the day. And I said I could do so, riding down the coast in an automobile, looking at the blue Pacific out on one side and the Santa Ines Mountains on the other, and I couldn't help but wonder if it was going to be that beautiful a hundred years from now as it was on that summer day.

Then, as I tried to write—let your own minds turn to that task. You're going to write for people a hundred years from now who know all about us. We know nothing about them. We don't know what kind of a world they'll be living in.

And suddenly, I thought to myself as I wrote of the problems, they'll be the domestic problems of which the President spoke here tonight; the challenges confronting us; the erosion of freedom that has taken place under Democrat rule in this country; the invasion of private rights; the controls and restrictions on the vitality of the great free economy that we enjoy. These are our challenges that we must meet.

And then again there is that challenge of which he spoke, that we live in a world in which the great powers have poised and aimed at each other horrible missiles of destruction, nuclear weapons that can in a matter of minutes arrive in each other's country and destroy virtually the civilized world we live in.

And suddenly it dawned on me, those who would read this letter a hundred years from now will know whether those missiles were fired. They will know whether we met our challenge.

Whether they had the freedom that we have known up until now will depend on what we do here. Will they look back with appreciation and say, thank God for those people in 1976 who headed off that loss of freedom; who kept us now a hundred years later free; who kept our world from nuclear destruction? And if we fail, they probably won't get to read the letter at all because it spoke of individual freedom and they won't be allowed to talk of that or read of it.

This is our challenge. And this is why we are here in this hall tonight. Better than we've ever done before, we've got to quit talking to each other and about each other and go out and communicate to the world that we may be fewer in numbers than we've ever been. But we carry the message they're waiting for.

We must go forth from here united, determined, that what a

great general said a few years ago is true: There is no substitute for victory.[1]

Every conservative who was old enough remembers where he or she was on the night of August 19, 1976, when Reagan gave his speech at Kemper Arena.

Lou Cannon said, "In a sense, it wasn't a great political speech saying to vote one way or the other . . . it wasn't political in the sense of dealing with strategy . . . but it was Reagan's heart . . . it set him apart from other politicians and political figures at the time."[2]

"From that day forward, I think American politics changed," said Al Cardenas, Reagan's Dade County Chairman, who had driven from Florida to Kansas City to volunteer for the campaign. He was so poor at he time that he had to borrow cash from some of the Reagan staff just to pay for the gas to drive back home.[3]

Jack Germond of the *Washington Star* made the analogy between Reagan in 1976 and John Kennedy in 1956, when Kennedy lost the nomination for Vice President. "He'd made a strong showing at the convention and you could see right then that he'd be a hell of a player in 1960."[4]

All across America, men and women, most of them decades younger than Reagan, were moved and motivated to "get involved."

At a seafood restaurant on Cape Cod, a nineteen-year-old waiter and bartender was mesmerized as he watched Reagan's speech on the television in the cocktail lounge and vowed to "get involved" when he got back to college.

Two thousand miles away on a wheat farm in eastern Colorado, a fair, red headed twelve year-old girl, who had spent the day helping her father in the fields, came in for the evening. After supper, together she and her family watched Reagan's speech. She too was moved to "get involved."

Literally thousands of other young men and women across the country were compelled by Reagan's speech, and they too decided to "get involved." They would descend on campaigns and Capitol Hill, work in the state parties and state houses, intern for conservative organizations and publications, or start their own companies and organizations. Some would become writers while others would run political campaigns. Whatever form their efforts took, these young men and women would become the soldiers and captains and generals in Reagan's Revolution.

16

THE END OF THE BEGINNING

"One of ours."

There is a well-known phrase among conservatives that serves as a treasured pass or a secret handshake, as in any fraternity. Beginning with the 1976 Reagan campaign and ever after, when one conservative is talking to another while discussing or introducing a third, he or she is referred to as "one of ours."

Although the phrase was originally the title of a book about World War I—*One of Ours*, written in 1922 by Willa Cather, for which she won a Pulitzer Prize—Michelle Laxalt says it was the Reagan people who started to use the phrase in 1976. To be referred to as "one of ours" was better than any endorsement inside the conservative movement. And the "ours" were growing and extending their influence, as things began to move very quickly inside the conservative movement and the Republican Party by early 1977.

The conservative movement was pouring its new ideas and energies into the empty vessel that was the Republican Party. "Above all, more than a few Republicans were beginning to wonder out loud whether their party had any long term future. 'We're staging a political dance macabre,' muttered one middle-of-the-road delegate during the pre-convention maneuverings. 'It's the dance of death for the Republican Party.'"[1] That was true enough in August of 1976. But out of the ashes of the old Republican Party would arise a new political movement.

Groups like Terry Dolan's National Conservative Political Action Committee (NCPAC) and Bob Heckman's Fund for a Conservative Majority (FCM) sprung up and would go on to run vitally important multi-million dollar independent expenditure campaigns in House and Senate races in 1978 and 1980, as well as for Reagan in 1980. Several years earlier, Dolan had battled it out for Chairman of the College Republicans with Karl Rove and had lost. Both went on to make significant contributions to American politics.

Reagan had signed a direct mail letter for NCPAC in 1977, and the contributions poured in. Similarly, Stan Evans founded the National Journalism Center in 1977 to train a new generation of conservative writers and editors.

Heckman had worked on the 1976 Reagan campaign before starting his new organization. FCM alone spent over $750,000 in the first six primaries on radio and print ads in 1980, lending critical help to Reagan at a time when his campaign was nearly broke. At his and John Gizzi's direction, this author produced the pro-Reagan radio spots and bought the time on the stations.

Paul Weyrich began hosting important weekly meetings of conservatives at his offices at "Library Court," which became the name of the meeting. Senators, Congressmen, and conservative leaders all attended to listen, learn, coordinate and plot strategy. Howard Phillips's Conservative Caucus also was part of the vanguard of the Conservative Movement. Phillips was yet another who had traveled the ideological road from liberal Republican to conservative activist. He was a large man with a booming voice whose organization helped train candidates for office while also lobbying against liberal initiatives.

Many of these conservative organizations were aided in their important fundraising by the Richard A. Viguerie Co., known as "RAVCO," and Bruce Eberle and Associates. But other conservative direct mail firms would also spring up shortly.

Republicans, at the national level, were slow to grasp the exponentially growing power of the conservative movement. For example, in 1977, conservatives mounted an effective, though ultimately losing, effort, to stop Jimmy Carter's Panama Canal Treaties. Ford was supporting the treaties, and although the conservatives inside the party were routing the liberals, they were not gone. The treaties only passed the Senate by one vote, but became a litmus test for Republicans and conservatives everywhere.

Reagan had been approached and had agreed to sign direct mail fundraising letters for the Republican National Committee. But when he asked for some of the money to be used to organize a "Panama Canal Truth Squad" to travel the nation to organize grassroots opposition to the treaties, he was rebuffed by the new National Chairman of the RNC, Bill Brock, a former Senator from Tennessee. In one memorable moment, Reagan was speaking to Brock via speakerphone at the offices of Senator Paul Laxalt. Terry Wade, a journalist with the *Las Vegas Journal,* was seated in the lobby outside of Laxalt's offices, overhead one side of the conversation, and described Reagan's mood as "quite heated." Reagan debated Bill Buckley on PBS, in a most friendly fashion, over the treaties. Reagan's able second in the debate was Admiral John McCain II (ret.).

In 1978, three "New Right" Senate candidates won in New Hampshire, Iowa, and Colorado. The candidates—Gordon Humphrey in New Hampshire, Roger Jepsen in Iowa, and Bill Armstrong in Colorado—had been largely shunned by establishment Republicans, and their wins were purely the result of the efforts of the conservative movement. Walter Cronkite reported on CBS that these "kamikaze" candidates, who normally lost, were winning that evening.

A handful of conservatives also won in the House in the late 1970s. In 1977, conservative Bob Livingston won a House seat in Louisiana that Republicans had not held since Reconstruction, again due to the efforts of the "New Right." Reagan campaigned extensively for GOP nominees in 1978, but did not endorse primary candidates, save one: George W. Bush's opponent in the congressional primary for a race in Midland, Texas. Ambassador Bush was decidedly unhappy and called Reagan in California and gave him hell for supporting his son's opponent.

In 1979, the conservatives stopped Jimmy Carter's SALT II treaty dead in its tracks. A movement that five years earlier could do nothing to stop the confirmation of Nelson Rockefeller had blocked a major initative by the Carter Administration from ratification by the Senate. It was a signal moment for conservatives.

Conservative think tanks began to flex their muscles—from the Heritage Foundation, led by Ed Feulner, to the libertarian Cato Institute and many others, including new state-based policy think tanks. A veritable flood of new ideas and white papers cascaded out of each institution, dealing with economic, social, political, and national defense matters. Elected officials eagerly read these papers. Their authors, in speeches in Washington and around the country, often addressed overflow crowds. Books too, like Milton Friedman's *Free to Choose* and George Gilder's *Wealth and Poverty*, became important contributions to the shaping of conservative thought.

The early conservatives relied upon a few publications for information. These included *Human Events* and *National Review. Human Events* was founded in 1946, and Tom Winter and Allan Ryskind acquired the publication by the early 1960s. Reagan had been a loyal subscriber since 1961 and would occasionally write notes to Winter and Ryskind or call them. After he became President, Reagan wrote that he was reading *Human Events* more but enjoying it less. Once, when Reagan called Ryskind at home, his daughter answered the phone, and Ryskind—thinking it was his friend Bill Schulz playing a joke—picked up the phone and said, "Hello Ronnie Baby."

But now other conservative publications, including *Conservative Digest*, were springing forth. And the number of conservative columnists was growing exponentially as well. The original unholy four of George Will, Pat Buchanan, William Safire, and William F. Buckley—hired by the mainstream media to give conservatives some sort of voice on the editorial pages of the leading newspapers—would soon be joined by Bob Tyrrell and others.

By 1981, even Harvard was paying attention to the conservative movement.

Richard Viguerie, Howard Phillips, Morton Blackwell, Paul Weyrich, and others were invited to conduct nine seminars for the students there. The conservative movement had arrived.

Still, the conservatives needed a leader to bring it all together. Would Reagan, at age sixty-nine by 1980, try one more time? Although some conservatives flirted with other Presidential campaigns beginning in 1978, for the larger majority of the Right, Ronald Reagan was still their man.

Reagan too, like the conservatives, was evolving in his thinking and beliefs, constantly reading and meeting with scholars and intellectuals of the Right. Hannaford wrote that in September of 1976, he met with Reagan to discuss some ideas for columns and radio commentaries. One of those presented to Reagan was Jude Wanniski's and Art Laffer's "supply side concept" which had manifested itself in a jobs creation bill, introduced by Congressman Jack Kemp of New York. Reagan immediately embraced the idea. He wrote a column and recorded a commentary touting the revolutionary concept.

At the invitation of Jerry Falwell, Reagan journeyed to Dallas to address thousands of religious leaders who would form the core of the Moral Majority. Reagan told his audience, "I know you can't endorse me, but I endorse you."[2] With that simple line, Reagan was assembling the third leg of his new party.

Larry Kudlow credited Reagan with taking the GOP from Wall Street to Main Street, explaining that Reagan's message "was a call to arms for conservatives." He "redefined modern Republicanism. But Wall Street never cared for Reagan, even after he became President." But what we've learned, through his writings, is that Reagan was a one man think tank."[3]

Some people wrote to Reagan and urged that he become the Chairman of the Republican Party, but he had bigger things on his mind. He was frankly assessing the role of John Sears in a future campaign, writing one supporter in 1979, "We are very much aware that there were shortcomings and criticism, particularly of John Sears, as a result of the last campaign. On the other hand, we feel that he does have talents and something to offer. . . . Our organization was hastily put together . . . John went off on his own many times, and, in so doing, upset a number of people. That will not be true this time."[4]

Before parting company in Kansas City, Sears told Reagan, with eyes brimming with tears, "I wish I had done better for you, Governor." Later he said, "History is made while you're doing things. And I was trying to win. We felt we changed things for the better."[5] Paul Laxalt reflected and said,

> Had Reagan not come on the scene at the '76 convention, I don't know where we'd be right now. It emboldened the conservatives and allowed

> them to run the party—and Reagan's departure [at the convention] was unbelievable. Though we lost we really won.
>
> After '76 was over and the Reagans felt their time was past, I went to see Jimmy Carter to discuss water regulation with thirty or forty Senators. . . . And he plainly didn't know his ass from first base and thought we were somewhat of a nuisance. I could hardly wait to get back to the office to call Ron. And I called and told him that I had just met with a one-term President.[6]

Marty Anderson remembered the flight back to Los Angeles from Kansas City after the narrow loss. "On the plane after the convention, he was one of the few who wasn't down . . . and within a few days, he's written fifteen of his commentaries and was back on the radio."[7] As always, Reagan was not looking backwards but forward.

One month after the convention, Ronald Reagan hosted a lunch in Los Angeles with many of his former staff and conservative friends. Over sandwiches, he made it pretty clear that he was not ruling out running again in 1980. But in the meantime, he had directed the remaining $1.5 million dollars left over from Citizens for Reagan go to create a new organization to help conservative candidates running for office around the country. Reagan could have pocketed the money as allowed under the laws of the Federal Election Commission, but this never, ever crossed his mind. It would be used to advance the cause of conservative candidates on Reagan's behalf.

Lyn Nofziger was placed in charge of the organization, which was named "Citizens for the Republic." There was some initial consternation over the acronym, "CFR," as it was the same as the acronym of the hated Council on Foreign Relations, an international organization of industrialists, philanthropists, academics and scholars. The organization was decidedly liberal and thus clearly in the enemy camp. So Reagan's new entity would become known as "CFTR."

Reagan was also honing his message, sharpening it, and proving that an old dog can learn new tricks. "Reagan invariably gravitated toward the aspects of American conservatism that were optimistic not cynical, populist not elitist, egalitarian not hierarchical, moral not relativistic—in short, what is distinctively American in American conservatism," Jeff Bell wrote years later for the *Weekly Standard*.[8]

Four years later, conservatives, led by Reagan, took over the GOP. And all the gathering energy, all the gathering wisdom, all the gathering ideas, all the camaraderie, all of the devotion to their ideology would combine to produce the revolutionary election of Ronald Reagan as the fortieth President of the United

States in November of 1980. The effects of this election are still being felt a generation later. As Ed Meese said, "We came to change the government and ended up changing the world."[9]

"Saying you are a Reagan Republican is redundant. Nobody says they are a 'Nixon Republican,'" said longtime scribe Ralph Hallow to me years later. To which this author replied to his old friend, "We're all Reaganites now."[10]

EPILOGUE

"The last great lion of the twentieth century."

It should come as no surprise that John F. Kennedy and Ronald Reagan are the last two American Presidents who could go to college campuses across the country and speak without fear of massive protests or reprisals. After all, both were young at heart, and both spoke to the hearts of young people. Both exuded a hope, a message, and a challenge for the future to the young men and women of America. Indeed, in his landside re-election in 1984, Reagan received his highest level of support from voters under thirty years of age.

Reagan was always mindful of the young citizens of his country, as evidenced by a note he sent the Schweikers' daughter, Lani, shortly after the convention. "Lani, we didn't achieve our goal but the race was worth the effort. We influenced the platform, we are listened to more than we were before and I'm sure we have caused the people to think about issues and problems more than they did before. . . . Regards from all of us to your parents and brothers and sisters. We hope we'll see you again soon. Sincerely, Ronald Reagan"[1]

A wise man once said that a leader has a "physical, moral and intellectual presence." These public qualities certainly applied to JFK and RWR. An old friend of mine, Paul Corbin, who had worked for Kennedy, told me that when he walked into a room, electricity flowed through the setting and the people there. Kennedy's very presence changed the room and the individuals in it. Having been in the same room with Reagan many times, I know exactly what he meant.

A favorite pastime in politics is speculating on "What would have happened if?" or "If only such and such had happened" or "If we had the money at the time." As baseball fans forever debate the merits of Babe Ruth versus Barry Bonds or the 1961 Yankees versus the 1998 Yankees or Mark McGwire versus Roger Maris, so too do politicos and journalists like to debate the merits of various political campaigns and candidates. Probably no political Presidential contest in recent memory invites more speculation and "what ifs" than the titanic struggle between

Gerald Rudolph Ford and Ronald Wilson Reagan in 1975 and 1976 for the Republican Party's Presidential nomination.

"What if Reagan had won New Hampshire?" or "What if Ford had won North Carolina?" or "What would have happened had the Reagan campaign filed enough delegate slates in Ohio or New York or New Jersey?" or "What did the surprise selection of Schweiker do to help or hurt Reagan?" or "Would Reagan have run had Ford not selected Nelson Rockefeller?" or "If the Ford people had only treated Reagan better . . ." The questions and speculations will continue endlessly.

Of course, there is no answer to any of these questions except that had Reagan received the nomination instead of Ford, he would not have run the type of campaign that he ran in 1980. In fact, Reagan was "somewhat incomplete" in 1976, according to Paul Weyrich, an astute observer of national political trends and a longtime leader in the conservative movement.

"Reagan had introduced the new paradigm of defeating Soviet Communism, but had not yet acquired fully the hopeful message of supply side economics or the social message that was so important in the creation of the 'Reagan Democrat'; the urban and suburban Catholic and socially conservative voter who would become part of his eventual winning coalition. True, he did well in crossover states in 1976 with these types of voters, but it is unclear whether his appeal would have worked with them in the fall election of 1976," Weyrich said.[2]

Chris Matthews echoed this sentiment: "Had Reagan won the nomination in 1976, he would have campaigned as a traditional balance-the-budget conservative. Had he won the election, he would have governed that way. Running in 1980, Reagan adopted the supply-side, tax cutting doctrine of Jack Kemp."[3]

Of course, we will never know. What we do know is that Reagan, in 1976, helped complete a process of redefining the Republican Party by turning it from elitist to populist. Reagan took the GOP from a Tory style conservatism in which power flows downward to an American brand of conservatism, where power flows upwards. "The Reagan campaign has been a struggle against the seedy Republican establishment by spirited outsiders, nourished by belief in their more elevated devotion to principle," wrote Rowland Evans and Robert Novak in July of 1976.[4]

The *New York Times* also grasped this phenomenon the day after the Kansas City convention ended, writing, "For the Republican Party, after the catastrophe of Watergate, the candidacy of Ronald Reagan was an understandable response. . . . Governor Reagan responded . . . by mounting a campaign based on the most fundamental interpretations of the party's creed."[5]

A letter to *Time* magazine on August 30, 1976, summed it up: "The Republican Party, from national to county level, supported an unelected

President. How on earth Governor Reagan did so well with all the odds against him is a tribute to the man."[6]

Through no fault of his own, the GOP was evolving away from Ford and his brand of Republicanism.

Ford was a good man who served his country well in World War II, in the Congress, the Vice Presidency and, finally, the Presidency. In August of 1974, there were thinking people who truly believed that America might not survive the Watergate crisis—that our great experiment in self-rule, wisely created by our founding fathers, was teetering on the brink of oblivion. Ford's calming presence in the moments after Richard Nixon departed Washington did much to restore Americans' belief in their system of government. "Mr. Ford is a decent man. His White House aides, whatever their merits, are free of arrogance. His Cabinet includes persons of the highest quality who would clearly resign if asked to undertake anything improper. At best, Jimmy Carter's jibe at the 'Nixon-Ford' Administration is campaign sophistry," wrote columnist Joe Kraft on the eve of the Republican National Convention.[7]

Ford served America well in a time of great national crisis. But he was not a visionary, he was not a leader, and he was not Ronald Reagan. Ford was a transitional figure and was a product of the past. Reagan was a transactional figure who was a product of the future.

Ford was made by the times he lived in; Reagan made the times he lived in.

Reagan always saw the best in his fellow Americans. And they, in turn, always saw the best of America in him. Reagan knew what the sophisticates and elites did not—that the American people were thirsting for leadership and to be told that it was okay to cherish their children's future. Indeed, Reagan knew it was the responsibility of all Americans to believe that the fundamental values he articulated were timeless, and that Americans had an obligation to pass them along to their children and grandchildren. This was America's—and Reagan's—"rendezvous with destiny."

Leadership was no mystery to Reagan. One observer in 1980 said that if you asked Carter what time it was, "He'd tell you how to build a watch." And if you asked Reagan what time it was, "He'd tell you it's time to get this country moving again." Reagan always knew where he was going and where he wanted to lead the American people.

Peter J. Rusthoven, writing for the *The Alternative: An American Spectator* in October of 1976 summed up well what Reagan meant to America, to conservatism, to our collective past and, most importantly, to our collective futures in the 1976 campaign. Rusthoven's words are nearly prescient and totally eloquent. This author blushes at his prose. He reached into the hearts and minds of conservatives everywhere in his piece.

> Purely as a political story, it was a fascinating tale, and the most suspenseful in many years. Not since Robert A. Taft and Dwight D. Eisenhower fought it out over delegate seating credentials in 1952 has a convention begun without one candidate having enough firmly committed delegates to ensure a first ballot nomination. . . . Out of a total of 2,259 delegates, he fell only 60 short of victory. . . .
>
> The closeness of the final outcome led many to speculate that only slightly greater effort in the industrial Northeast might have pushed Reagan over the top. The defeated candidate himself wondered out loud whether a few more days in Ohio—which went 91-6 for Ford at the convention after a primary in which Reagan, with almost no campaigning, polled well over 40% of the vote—might have made the difference. . . .
>
> What impresses me the most in reflecting on his bid for the White House is that he spoke to the American people, with an eloquence and passion unmatched in our generation, about matters which go to the core of our being and our survival as a free Republic. . . . But now that Ronald Reagan has ceased—probably forever—to be a candidate for this nation's highest office, I hope you will indulge me a few words on what in my view set his candidacy apart. . . .
>
> He alone addressed a set of concerns that involve the fundamental role of this nation as a free Republic and as a constitutional moral order—in a world where Republics are few, freedom is scarce, constitutions are ignored, and morality is rarely seriously considered. Those who cherish the label "intellectual" are wont to dismiss conservatives as simplistic, unsophisticated, and decidedly unintelligent souls; and there can be no doubt that Ronald Reagan has, over the last nine months, borne the full brunt of this subtle and not-so-subtle scorn from most of the media and almost all of academe. . . .
>
> We have witnessed in our lifetimes a steady erosion of those systems of government and philosophy which cherish the ideals of human dignity on which this Republic was founded; and today, governments which have slaughtered more human beings than Adolf Hitler ever dreamed of are thriving over half the globe.
>
> Yet it was only Ronald Reagan—among a chorus of candidates seeking in various ways either to ignore this fact or assure us that it entailed

> no discomfiting possibilities for our own welfare—only Reagan who echoed the warnings of Solzhenitsyn, only Reagan who made it a point to impress upon his audience that the survival of human freedom involves burdensome global responsibilities for this nation. We have also witnessed in our lifetimes a steady erosion within this country of those institutions such as church and family which form the foundations of our own freedom and prosperity; and today, our perceptions on so basic an issue as the dignity of human life are sufficiently skewed that a hundred thousand unborn babies are tossed into the Hudson each year under the aegis of a newly discovered and supposedly Constitutional "right," while we debate in language of subtle sophistication whether and to what extent that same Constitution permits the "barbarity" of executing convicted murderers. Yet it was Reagan alone—amid a score of Presidential aspirants who in vague and halting tones spoke at the periphery of such issues—Reagan alone who emphasized that such issues involved the center of our continued existence as a moral people. Reagan alone who made such issues a focal point of his campaign. And finally, though I deplore the present indulgence in apocalyptic rhetoric, I believe it is no exaggeration to state that the next quarter-century may well determine whether this nation in fact survives; yet it was Reagan alone, speaking just a few moments after Gerald Ford had just accepted the Republican nomination, who reminded the nation in the most graceful and elegant language of the campaign that the question of survival is precisely what confronts it. . . .
>
> Richard Schweiker may well have been right in saying on the morning following Gerald Ford's nomination, that Americans had lost their chance to have the best leader ever presented to this generation; and I confess to a certain wistful regret that Ronald Reagan will not be on the ballot this November. For Ronald Reagan spoke to this nation, with an eloquence that springs only from the deepest and most serious conviction, about those issues which I believe should be the first concern of civilized and responsible men. It is this which I hope to remember of the 1976 campaign; and it is this for which I personally wish to express my gratitude to the man my party chose not to nominate.[8]

Virtually everybody who left Kansas City was convinced that Reagan's political future was over—his senior aides, maybe he himself, and certainly the political elites and the national media. The *New York Times* editorialized that "Mr. Reagan presumably grows too old to run again, the battle will have to be carried on with new leadership."[9] Fortunately for all Americans, Rusthoven, Schweiker, and most everybody else was wrong about Reagan's political future after his 1976 Presidential campaign.

One who did know of Reagan's smoldering ambition was his old friend and counselor, Ed Meese. He said, "It [the 1976 campaign] made him a credible candidate. When he left Kansas City in 1976, he was still unsure about running again. But when the 1980 campaign began in 1978, he was ready to go. He learned more about other parts of the country, and Reagan was a person who learned from every experience he had. He learned the intricacies of national politics. He learned what his followers were looking for. He had a spiritual side to him that it was up to God whether it happened or it didn't and was 'OK' with it either way."[10]

When the caisson bearing Ronald Reagan's body arrived at the U.S. Capitol on June 9, 2004, Vice President Richard Cheney was there to greet him and Mrs. Reagan. In a moving speech, Cheney said that Reagan's Presidency was "providential." Perhaps it was.

Reagan did go on to win the Presidency over Jimmy Carter in a landslide in 1980 and won re-election over Walter Mondale by another landslide in 1984. In 1980, the Soviet Union was winning the Cold War. To many, it seemed only a matter of time before all was lost. America was in retrenchment at home and across the globe, but most of the elites continued to deride Reagan's "simplistic" notions about freedom, restoring America's morale, defeating Soviet Communism, and exporting democratic rule around the world as absurd. Yet Reagan knew something his critics did not: the future was not for the timid but for the brave.

Ronald Reagan left office in January of 1989 with a love and affection from the American people not seen since President Kennedy. Years later, Jack Kemp would movingly say of Reagan that he was "the last great lion of the twentieth century."

Upon becoming President in 1981, Reagan changed the Republican Party, Reagan changed America, and Reagan changed the world—all because he came within an eyelash of winning his party's Presidential nomination in 1976.

And the rest, as they say, is history.

AUTHOR'S NOTE

Before I began to research and write *Reagan's Revolution: The Untold Story of the Campaign that Started It All*, I had come to the project with several preconceived notions and biases about some of the people involved in the momentous political events inside the Republican Party from 1974 to 1976.

I was wrong.

One of the people I interviewed, Jim Baker, Reagan's first White House Chief of Staff in 1981 and Ford's Campaign Manager in 1976, turned the tables on me and asked what I had learned in the course of writing this book. I told him I had discovered, with few exceptions, that there were no bad guys in this story. Everybody was pretty much a good guy, trying to honestly do his job. And I detected, again with only a couple of exceptions, little venality on the part of people in the Ford and Reagan camps. Baker agreed with this assessment.

Vice President Cheney said as much, except when I pointed out that one person who really did seem to have it in for Reagan was Ford's aide Robert Hartmann. Cheney dryly said, "Hartmann didn't like anybody."

When I interviewed my old friend Phyllis Schlafly for this book, she said, "Now Craig, I hope you're going to write what a disaster John Sears was!" Actually, some of my conservative friends will be disappointed, but I don't think Sears was a disaster. He made mistakes and showed some bad judgment. But I also think some of his actions were brilliant, or could at least be justified. Sears was no manager, that is for sure. He would have been better suited to be the campaign's chief strategist, which he was—but he should not have run the campaign. Other more ably suited people could have performed the mundane, but vitally important tasks of making the trains run on time for the 1976 Reagan campaign.

Even Sears's friend Jim Lake said, "He had no management skills. He never pretended he had management skills." Still, Sears had his unvarnished admirers, like Paul Laxalt who said, "Even his mistakes were brilliant."

Of one fact there can be no doubt: had Sears not appeared on the scene in

1974, Reagan would not have run. Sears was the only person who explained to Ronald and Nancy Reagan how they could run a successful campaign. Both of them were deeply impressed with his grasp of politics.

Early in the interview process, I gave up on asking key Reagan campaign staffers to diagram an "organizational chart" for the campaign. Most simply rolled their eyes or let out a derisive laugh. As Peter Hannaford said, "There was no campaign chart. Everybody simply gravitated to what they liked to do best." More important than any management chart, they were caught up in the swirl of history. The events they were involved in were bigger and more consequential than anyone knew at the time, save the principal character at the center of this maelstrom: Ronald Wilson Reagan.

Not everyone agreed to be interviewed, including Bob Hartmann and Al Haig. Not everyone could be interviewed, and some I decided not to interview, including Clarke Reed. I came to this conclusion after speaking to many about his actions in Mississippi and concluded that all I would get out of Reed would be "spin." Reed broke his word to Reagan's people, and no amount of discussion can change this.

The Republican Party was undergoing dramatic changes, some of which would have happened without Reagan. Nonetheless, he brought to the fore issues and a direction that would eventually change the party, the country, and the world. The GOP was being reborn as a political movement based on, as Reagan said in 1964, "maximum freedom consistent with law and order." This was the essence of the "constitutional libertarian" philosophy.

Like thousands of others, Reagan's speech inspired me. Not to say that I didn't have a lifelong commitment to conservatism. My parents were charter members of the New York State Conservative Party, beginning in 1962. They were foot soldiers in Upstate New York, and they dragged my brother and me to every political event you could imagine. They attended every Conservative state convention as delegates. Fundraisers for Barbara Keating, Paul Adams, John Jaquith, Jim Buckley, and others became a rite of passage for New York conservatives at the Shirleys' modest suburban home in Syracuse.

In 1965, my father arrived home with a record album and made my brother and me sit down and listen to it. When it was over, Dad exclaimed, "This man Reagan himself should be President!" The recording was of Reagan's speech the previous October for Barry Goldwater entitled *Rendezvous With Destiny*. My father was also the first registered Conservative in the state of New York, having gone to the Board of Elections the night its status had been granted and waited for hours until the office opened.

As the head of the Onondaga County Conservative Party, he organized an annual summer outdoor fundraiser, which both Bill and Jim Buckley often attended. It was in 1966 when Bill showed up in a seersucker sport jacket. It was the first time I had ever seen such a jacket, and I thought it was the coolest thing I'd ever beheld.

Every night over dinner our family had extended political debates and discussions ranging from the Vietnam War to the environment to race relations to unions. They went on and on. Here, my brother and I developed our conservative philosophies through argument and discussion. In 1970, my mother ran for the county legislature against the incumbent liberal Republican and a run-of-the-mill Democrat. Although she did not win, she took enough votes away from the Republican to deny him re-election—and that was the point. The GOP could not take conservatives for granted any longer. Also, she was the first Conservative running for office in all of New York to be endorsed over her opponents by a major daily newspaper, the *Syracuse Herald Journal.* When my father passed away in 1977, he was running for the school board on the Conservative *and* Republican lines. By 1977, Republicans were finally beginning to understand.

When I got back to college in the fall of 1976, I volunteered on the Ford campaign in Springfield, Massachusetts, where we did lit drops, registered voters, and did whatever we could with the meager resources provided to Massachusetts by the national campaign. As one can imagine, since the Bay State was the only state George McGovern carried against Richard Nixon four years earlier, it was not a top priority for Ford.

Twenty-eight years later, I am still involved in politics. And I am just one of the thousands of young Americans who heard the Reagan message, felt the magic, and decided to do something about it.

Many of the two hundred people I interviewed have asked me about the behaviors and varying pathologies of some of the people involved—on the Ford side, on the Reagan side, at the White House, in the media, and at the Republican National Committee. Some involved women, others mild drug use, others gambling, and, with many, drinking. In fact, part of the backdrop of politics in 1976 was that everybody drank—sometimes a lot. Even Gerald Ford was known to enjoy a couple of high balls after 5 P.M. or while relaxing with reporters on Air Force One. It was completely normal for most men in politics—and some women—to have two or three drinks at lunch and then meet up for cocktails after work.

But I chose to write this book because it is a missing part of the history of Ronald Reagan's rise from a former Governor to World Leader, and how he transformed American politics—not to trash people for their foibles and personal misbehavior.

I concluded that I would only address those problems that had a direct bearing on the ability of these people to do their jobs. In the case of Bob Hartmann, Ford's key aide, after speaking to many people, I came to the conclusion that his heavy drinking affected his ability to perform his tasks. In the case of John Sears, while he clearly liked to drink at the time, I concluded after talking with the people who knew him best that his drinking did not affect his ability to do his job. Jack Germond, for example, told me that John Sears would drink martinis all through dinner, "but it didn't stop him from being smarter than hell . . . it didn't affect his performance."

Reagan also enjoyed a glass of wine or a cocktail, but he would usually stick to just one or two drinks—he could mix a martini with the best of them. It was also a different time in that politicians, politicos, and reporters would often drink and dine together without fear of what was said showing up in the newspaper the next morning.

On the subject of women, one senior member of one of the two campaigns parked a Winnebago in the parking lot of the Kemper Arena and stashed his girlfriend there for the week of the convention—even though this man was "happily" married. But this indiscretion did not adversely impact his ability to perform his job, so there is no need to name him, his wife, or the woman involved. The details are simply not important.

I also found the media coverage of the 1976 campaign—especially of Ronald Reagan—to be professional and for the most part fair. Reagan did experience the occasional pot shot from the mainstream media and certainly from the editorial writers and liberal columnists. But the newspaper reporters were generally fair to Reagan. However, the networks and the weeklies—especially CBS and *Time*—would sometimes take gratuitous shots at Reagan.

Still, the material I gathered from all these sources was invaluable. I don't know how many hours I put in working on this book, but I never looked at it as anything other than a labor of love. Writing this book has been one of the most enjoyable experiences of my life.

Perhaps as much as having had the chance to work for Reagan himself.

ACKNOWLEDGMENTS

My deepest appreciation and gratitude goes to my colleague, Andi Hedberg, for all of her hard work reviewing drafts, researching, fact checking, transcribing interviews, watching endless hours of video, traveling to the Reagan and Ford Presidential Libraries, her advice and counsel, and especially for putting up with the author's quirkiness. This book would have not been possible without her tireless work and steadfast leadership of the "blonde mafia" of researchers and interns.

Special kudos go to Brittany Moore, Max Courington, Stephen Saunders, and Dan Szy for their outstanding work in research and editing. Without them, this book would have remained just a dream. Also thanks to Kyle Vander Meulen, Jamie Curtis, Karol Sheinin, Jenise Snyder, and Laura Russell for their help with this book as well. Dennis Warren, former UPI photographer who covered the 1976 Reagan campaign, was most generous in allowing us access to his library of photos, and to him we are also indebted.

And special thanks to Mrs. Ronald Reagan and President Reagan's Chief of Staff, Ms. Joanne Drake, for generously granting us unprecedented access to previously unopened files on the 1976 campaign stored at the Reagan Library.

Also thanks to Vice President Richard Cheney for granting me so much interview time despite the pressures of his position. This interview took place on the day the Vice President was to greet Mrs. Reagan and the caisson bearing the body of President Reagan on June 9, 2004, at the U.S. Capitol. It was an emotional day for both of us.

I am also deeply indebted to my friend and business partner, Diana Banister, on whose shoulders I placed so much in the many months I was working on this book. The staff also at Shirley and Banister Public Affairs had to put up with a lot, and I thank them for their patience and understanding.

I am deeply grateful to my friend Fred Barnes for agreeing to write the foreword to this book. As he has covered American politics for over thirty years, including the 1976 campaign, Fred has a unique perspective on Reagan's challenge to Ford.

Special mention must be made of Jules Witcover, Lou Cannon, and Peter Hannaford, whose many fine books and writings that covered much of this period provided so much critical research for *Reagan's Revolution.* They all also graciously granted me extensive interview time for which I am indebted to each of them.

Finally, many thanks are owed to David Dunham and Joel Miller with Nelson Current for having the faith and confidence in this book. Their support has been invaluable.

Also, thanks to:

American Conservative Union
Brigham Young University
Human Events
John M. Ashbrook Center for Public Affairs
Library of Congress
Republican National Committee
The Smithsonian Institution

And:

Rick Ahern
Phil Alexander
Richard Allen
Marty Anderson
Ernie Angelo
Katheryn Ashbrook
Doug Bailey
James Baker III
Jeff Bell
Charlie Black
Morton Blackwell
Duke Blackwood
Terry Boyle
Steve Branch
Bill Brock
Floyd Brown
David Bufkin
Jim Burnley
Howard "Bo" Callaway
Lou Cannon
Al Cardenas
Jerry Carmen
Maria Cino
Brooke Clement
Madeline Cohen
Muriel Coleman
Phil Crane
Stacy Davis
Michael Deaver
Don Devine
Eric Dezenhall
Stacey Disterhof
Marci Dobal
Ron Docksai
Becki Donatelli
Frank Donatelli
Becky Norton Dunlop
George Dunlop

Dale Duvall
Bruce Eberle
Fred Eckert
Tom Edmonds
Lee Edwards
Tom Ellis
Stan Evans
Jerry Falwell
Ed Feulner
Howard Fineman
Arthur Finkelstein
Tom Finnigan
Jack Germond
Charlie Gerow
Ed Gillespie
Mike Goldfarb
Mike Grebe
Robert Griffin
Kenneth Hafeli
Mike Hallow
Ralph Hallow
Steph Halper
Peter Hannaford
Kelly Hedberg
Jesse Helms
J. Curtis Herge
Jim Hooley
Brit Hume
Christian Josi
David Keene
Craig Keith
Kevin Kellems
Kenny Klinge
Larry Kudlow
Jim Kuhn
Carole Kuhn
Cara Kresge
Marvin J. Krinsky
Bill Lacey
James V. Lacy
Jim Lake
Art Laffer
Frank Lavin
Michelle Laxalt
Paul Laxalt
Chris Lay
Ladonna Lee
Elizabeth Leonard
Richard Lessner
Drew Lewis
Carrie Anne Liipfert
Mike Long
Tom Loringer
Eddie Mahe
Jason Maloni
William H. McNitt
Peter McPherson
Michael McShane
Ed Meese
Matt Messina
Jim Miller
Zell Miller
Brad Minnick
Nancy Mirshah
Peter Monk
Steve Moore
Billy Mounger
Ed Nichols
Lyn Nofziger
Pat Nolan
Grover Norquist
Bob Novak
Brad O'Leary
Neal Peden-Jones
Benjamin Pezzillo
Kristine Phillips
Charles Pickering
Pat Pizzella

Pam Pryor
Mike Reagan
Rick Reed
Kathy Regan
Nancy Reynolds
Bill Rhatican
Anna Roberts
Jim Roberts
Patti Roberts
Steve Roberts
Ron Robinson
Dana Rohrbacher
Marc Rotterman
Paul Russo
Allan Ryskind
Phyllis Schlafly
Wayne Schley
Bill Schulz
John Sears
Bob Shuster
Claire Schweiker
Richard Schweiker
Kittie Smith
Loren Smith
Tony Snyder
Stuart Spencer
Scott Stanley
Jennifer Sternaman
Roger Stone
Don Totten
Aldo Tutino
Bob Tyrrell
Chuck Tyson
Mary Frances Varner
Richard Viguerie
Terry Wade
Bill Walsh
Victoria Walton
Paul Weyrich
George Will
Tom Winter
Dick Wirthlin
Jules Witcover
Ann Wixon
Bob Woodward
Carter Wrenn
David Yepsen

NOTES

PREFACE

1. Gerald Pomper, *The Election of 1976: Reports and Interpretations* (New York: Longman, 1977), 25.
2. Robert Ajemian, "Reagan: I Don't Want Another 1964," *Time*, August 2, 1976, 10-11.
3. *Des Moines Register*, "264-248 Edge for President Over Reagan: Preference Poll at GOP Caucuses," January 20, 1976.
4. *Des Moines Register*, January 20, 1976.
5. *Des Moines Register*, January 20, 1976.
6. Brad Minnick, in discussion with the author, March 4, 2004.
7. Dick Wirthlin, in discussion with the author, March 11, 2004.
8. Terry Wade, in discussion with the author, June 22, 2004.
9. Frank Donatelli, in discussion with the author, April 2, 2004.
10. Paul Laxalt and Michelle Laxalt, in discussion with the author, April 21. 2004.
11. Paul Laxalt, *Nevada's Paul Laxalt: A Memoir* (Reno, NV: Jack Bacon and Company, 2000), 307.
12. Steven F. Hayward, *The Age of Reagan: The Fall of the Old Liberal Order* (Roseville, CA: Forum, 2001), 479-480.
13. Sam Donaldson, *ABC Evening News*, ABC, Videotape, August 19, 1976, White House Communications Agency Collection, Gerald Ford Presidential Library, Ann Arbor, MI.
14. Kenny Klinge, in discussion with the author, May 24, 2004.
15. Doug Bailey, in discussion with the author, June 16, 2004.
16. Lou Cannon, in discussion with the author, June 28, 2004.
17. Robert T. Hartmann, *Palace Politics: An Inside Account of the Ford Years* (New York: McGraw-Hill, 1980), 180.

INTRODUCTION

1. Robert T. Hartmann, *Palace Politics: An Inside Account of the Ford Years* (New York: McGraw-Hill, 1980), 113.
2. Donald J. Devine, in discussion with the author, 2004.
3. Michael Barone, in discussion with the author, January 9, 2004.
4. Nancy Gibbs and Matthew Cooper, "Living In Bill's Shadow," *Time*, January 26, 2004, 22+.
5. Roger Stone, in discussion with the author, April 5, 2004.

6. Doug Bailey, in discussion with the author, June 16, 2004.
7. *The American Experience: Reagan*, producers Austin Hoyt and Adriana Bosch (Boston: WGBH, 1998).
8. George F. Gilder and Bruce K. Chapman, *The Party That Lost Its Head* (New York: Alfred A. Knopf, 1966), 5.
9. David S. Broder, "Ford and Reagan Gear for Fight on Convention Rules," *Washington Post*, August 15, 1976.

CHAPTER ONE — The Beginning of the End

1. Gary Bauer, in discussion with the author, April 2004.
2. Ralph Hallow, in discussion with the author, January 9, 2004.
3. Herbert S. Parmet, *George Bush: The Life of a Lone Star Yankee* (New York: Scribner, 1997), 197.
4. Nelson W. Polsby and Aaron Wildavsky, *Presidential Elections: Strategies of American Electoral Politics, 6th ed.* (New York: Charles Scribner's Sons, 1984), 149.
5. Doug Bailey, in discussion with the author, June 16, 2004.
6. Lewis L. Gould, *Grand Old Party: A History of the Republicans* (New York: Random House, 2003), 403.
7. *New York Times*, "Now the Republicans," July 19, 1976.
8. Eddie Mahe and Ladonna Lee, in discussion with the author, March 5, 2004.
9. Gould, *Grand Old Party*, 321.
10. Gould, *Grand Old Party*, 345.
11. Gould, *Grand Old Party*, 343.
12. Gould, *Grand Old Party*, 345.
13. Gould, *Grand Old Party*, 346.
14. Bill Schulz, in discussion with the author, February 23, 2004.
15. Tom Edmonds, in discussion with the author, 1998.
16. Lyn Nofziger, in discussion with the author, February 12, 2004.
17. Richard Viguerie, in discussion with the author, February 2, 2004.
18. Richard Nixon, *RN: The Memoirs of Richard Nixon: Volume 1* (New York: Warner Books, 1978), 325.
19. Roger Stone, in discussion with the author, April 5, 2004.
20. David Keene, in discussion with the author, December 16, 2003.
21. Jules Witcover, *Crapshoot: Rolling the Dice on the Vice Presidency* (New York: Crown Publishers, 1992), 218.

CHAPTER TWO — Awakening Ambitions

1. *Human Events*, "Leading Conservatives 'Suspend Support' of Nixon," August 7, 1971; Jeff Bell, in discussion with the author, May 5, 2004.
2. Richard Reeves, *A Ford, Not a Lincoln* (New York: Harcourt Brace Jovanovich, 1975), 13.
3. Bill Schulz, in discussion with the author, February 23, 2004.
4. Jules Witcover, *Crapshoot*, (New York: Crown, 1992), 236, 242.
5. Roger Stone, in discussion with the author, April 5, 2004.
6. David Keene, in discussion with the author, December 16, 2003.
7. Confidential interview with bar owner, 2004.
8. Confidential interview with bar owner, 2004.

9. Alfred E. Lewis, "Five Held in Plot to Bug Democrats' Office," *Washington Post*, June 18, 1972.
10. Confidential interview with bar owner, 2004.
11. Lewis, *Washington Post*, June 18, 1972.
12. Lewis, *Washington Post*, June 18, 1972.
13. Michael McShane, in discussion with the author, 2004.
14. McShane, in discussion with the author.
15. Richard M. Cohen and Jules Witcover, *A Heartbeat Away: The Investigation and Resignation of Vice President Spiro T. Agnew* (New York: Viking, 1974), 5.
16. Tish Leonard, in discussion with the author, 2004; Myron Mintz, in discussion with the author, 2004. Keene, discussion.
17. Myron Mintz, in discussion with the author.
18. Spiro T. Agnew, *Go Quietly . . . or Else* (New York: William Morrow and Company, 1980), 190-191.
19. Agnew, *Go Quietly . . . or Else*, 190.
20. Reeves, 39.
21. Lyn Nofziger, in discussion with the author, 2004.
22. Memorandum by Bo Callaway, "Opposition Research," Robert Hartmann Papers, Box 164, Gerald Ford Presidential Library, Ann Arbor, MI.
23. Ron Nessen, *It Sure Looks Different From the Inside* (Chicago: Playboy Press, 1978), 154.
24. Nofziger, discussion.
25. John Sears, in discussion with the author, March 18, 2004.
26. Sears, discussion.
27. Sears, discussion.
28. Sears, discussion
29. Peter Hannaford, *The Reagan's: A Political Portrait* (New York: Coward-McCann, 1983), 30; Nofziger, discussion.
30. Michael Deaver, in discussion with the author, December 23, 2003.
31. Sears, discussion.
32. Sears, discussion.
33. Reeves, *A Ford*, 40.
34. Lou Cannon, *Reagan* (New York: G.P. Putnam's Sons, 1982), 192.
35. Sears, discussion.
36. Sears, discussion.
37. Sears, in discussion.
38. Jim Lake, in discussion with the author, January 16, 2004.
39. John J. Casserly, *The Ford White House: The Diary of a Speechwriter* (Lincoln, NE: iUniverse.com, 1977), 194.
40. Robert T. Hartmann, *Palace Politics: An Inside Account of the Ford Years* (New York: McGraw-Hill, 1980), 336.
41. Richard Cheney, in discussion with the author, June 9, 2004.
42. Hartmann, *Palace Politics*, 224.
43. Hartmann, 225.
44. Cheney, discussion.
45. Lee Edwards, *Goldwater: The Man Who Made a Revolution* (Washington DC: Regnery, 1995), 402.

46. Cheney, discussion.
47. Lake, discussion.
48. Gerald R Ford, *A Time To Heal* (New York: Harper & Row, 1979), 363.
49. Eddie Mahe, in discussion with the author, March 5, 2004.
50. Mahe, discussion.
51. Arthur Finkelstein, in discussion with the author, 2004.
52. M. Stanton Evans, in discussion with the author, February 25, 2004.
53. Minutes of the American Conservative Union, 1974-1976, M. Stanton Evans, personal collection, Alexandria, Virginia.
54. Minutes of the American Conservative Union, 1974-1976.
55. Lou Cannon, *Governor Reagan*, (New York: PublicAffairs, 2003), 396-397.
56. Cheney, discussion.
57. Gerald Ford to Ronald Reagan, August 21, 1974, White House Central Files, Box 2608, Gerald Ford Presidential Library, Ann Arbor, MI.
58. Hartmann, *Palace Politics*, 335.
59. Gerald Ford to Ronald Reagan, September 20, 1974, White House Central Files, Box 2608, Ford Presidential Library.
60. Gerald Ford to Ronald Reagan, December 4, 1974, White House Central Files, Box 2608, Ford Presidential Library, Ann Arbor, MI.
61. Gerald R. Ford to Ronald Reagan, May 13, 1975, White House Central Files, Box 2608, Ford Presidential Library, Ann Arbor, MI.
62. Gerald Ford to Ronald Reagan, May 13, 1975.
63. Cannon, *Governor Reagan*, 398.
64. Telegram, Ronald Reagan to Gerald Ford, October 7, 1974, White House Central Files, Box 2608, Ford Presidential Library, Ann Arbor, MI.
65. Casserly, 31.
66. Casserly, *The Ford White House*, 117.
67. David Hume Kennerly, *Shooter* (New York: Newsweek Books, 1979), 192.
68. Kennerly, *Shooter*, 21.
69. Fred Barnes, in discussion with the author, February 2, 2004.
70. Reeves, *A Ford, Not a Lincoln*, 43.
71. Casserly, *The Ford White House*, 20.
72. William A. Rusher, *The Making of the New Majority Party* (Ottawa, IL: Green Hill Publishers, 1975), 13.
73. Rusher, *The Making of the New Majority Party*, 83.
74. Steven F. Hayward, *The Age of Reagan: The Fall of the Old Liberal Order* (Roseville, CA: Forum, 2001), 449.
75. Lou Cannon, *Governor Reagan* (New York: PublicAffairs, 2003), 401.
76. Frank van der Linden, *The Real Reagan: What He Believes, What He Accomplished, What We Can Expect From Him* (New York: William Morrow and Company, 1981), 112-113; James C. Roberts, ed., *A City Upon A Hill: Speeches by Ronald Reagan Before the Conservative Political Action Conference, 1947-1988* (Washington DC: American Studies Center, 1989), 20.
77. van der Linden, *The Real Reagan*, 112-113.
78. Michael Deaver, in discussion with the author, December 23, 2003.

79. Michael Deaver, discussion.
80. Michael Barone, *Our Country: The Shaping of America from Roosevelt to Reagan* (New York: Free Press, 1990), 511.
81. Lewis L. Gould, *Grand Old Party: A History of the Republicans* (New York: Random House, 2003), 382.

CHAPTER THREE — Ford Follies

1. *New York Times*, "Bankruptcy Politics," November 2, 1975.
2. *Human Events*, "Ford Continues to 'Reaganize' Campaign," November 8, 1975.
3. Robert T. Hartmann, *Palace Politics: An Inside Account of the Ford Years* (New York: McGraw-Hill, 1980), 101.
4. Hartmann, *Palace Politics*, 101.
5. Jules Witcover, *Marathon: The Pursuit of the Presidency, 1972-1976* (New York: Viking Press, 1972), 53.
6. Witcover, *Marathon*, 53-54.
7. Witcover, *Marathon*, 56.
8. Witcover, *Marathon*, 55.
9. John J. Casserly, *The Ford White House: The Diary of a Speechwriter* (Lincoln, NE: iUniverse.com, 1977), 120.
10. Casserly, *The Ford White House,* 148.
11. Witcover, *Marathon*, 51.
12. Casserly, *The Ford White House*, 123.
13. Don Bonafede, "Presidential Focus: Ford's Advisers Push Him to Campaign," *National Journal*, April 19, 1975, 600.
14. Rowland Evans and Robert Novak, *The Reagan Revolution: An Inside Look at the Transformation of the U.S.* (New York: E.P. Dutton, 1981), 48.
15. Hartmann, *Palace Politics*, 336.
16. Ron Nessen, *It Sure Looks Different from the Inside* (Chicago: Playboy Press, 1978), 195.
17. Casserly, *The Ford White House*, 131.
18. Casserly, *The Ford White House*, 135.
19. Steven F. Hayward, *The Age of Reagan: The Fall of the Liberal Order* (Roseville, CA: Forum, 2001) 435-436.
20. Hayward, *The Age of Reagan,* 436.
21. Michael Barone, *Our Country: The Shaping of America from Roosevelt to Reagan* (New York: Free Press, 1990) 555-556.
22. Hartmann, *Palace Politics*, 336.
23. Casserly, *The Ford White House*, 139.
24. Casserly, *The Ford White House,* 172.
25. Casserly, *The Ford White House*, 164-165.
26. Peter Hannaford, in discussion with the author, January 8, 2004.
27. Leslie H. Gelb, "Moves a Surprise," *New York Times*, sec. 1, November 3, 1975.
28. Nessen, *It Sure Looks Different*, 150-151.
29. Richard Cheney, in discussion with the author, June 9, 2004.
30. Nessen, *It Sure Looks Different*, 161-162.
31. Cheney, discussion.

32. R.W. Apple Jr., "Reagan's Challenge for Leadership of Republican Party: Assets and Liabilities," *New York Times*, November 21, 1975.
33. R.W. Apple Jr., *New York Times*, November 21, 1975.
34. Stuart Spencer, in discussion with the author, June 21, 2004.
35. Warren Weaver Jr., "New Law Balked Ford Fund-Raiser," *New York Times*, November 2, 1975.
36. Weaver, *New York Times*, November 2, 1975.
37. James M. Naughton, "Head Fund-Raiser for Ford Resigns," *New York Times*, November 1, 1975.
38. Naughton, *New York Times*, November 1, 1975.
39. Bruce Eberle, in discussion with the author, April 28, 2004.
40. Naughton, *New York Times*, November 1, 1975.
41. Eddie Mahe and Ladonna Lee, in discussion with the author, March 5, 2004.
42. Philip Shabecoff, "Mutual Decision: Vice President's Letter Gives No Reason for Withdrawal," *New York Times*, November 3, 1975.
43. Philip Shabecoff, "Mutual Decision: Vice President's Letter Gives No Reason for Withdrawal," *New York Times*, November 3, 1975.
44. Peter Hannaford, *The Reagans: A Political Portrait* (New York: Coward-McCann, 1983), 77.
45. Gerald R. Ford, *A Time To Heal* (New York: Harper & Row, 1979), 327.
46. Ford, *A Time To Heal*, 328.
47. Hannaford, discussion.
48. John Sears, in discussion with the author, March 18, 2004.
49. Sears, discussion.
50. Nessen, *It Sure Looks Different*, 163.
51. Nessen, *It Sure Looks Different*, 164.
52. Memorandum by Dick Cheney, October 23, 1975, White House Operations, Richard Cheney Files, Box 17, Gerald Ford Presidential Library, Ann Arbor, MI.
53. Memorandum by Dick Cheney, October 23, 1975.
54. Brief, "The President Ford Committee Campaign Plan," August 29, 1975, Howard Callaway Files, Box 1, Gerald Ford Presidential Library, Ann Arbor, MI.
55. Brief, "The President Ford Committee Campaign Plan."
56. Brief, "The President Ford Committee Campaign Plan."
57. Brief, "The President Ford Committee Campaign Plan."
58. Brief, "The President Ford Committee Campaign Plan."
59. Brief, "The President Ford Committee Campaign Plan."
60. Brief, "The President Ford Committee Campaign Plan."
61. Brief, "The President Ford Committee Campaign Plan."
62. Martha Angle, "GOP Liberals Look to Baker to Counter Moves to Right," *Washington Star*, November 13, 1975.
63. Martha Angle, "GOP Liberals Look to Baker to Counter Moves to Right," *Washington Star*, November 13, 1975.
64. Martha Angle, "Goldwater Leaves Door Open on Support For Reagan," *Washington Star*, November 15, 1975.
65. Memorandum, unsigned, November 3, 1975, White House Operations, Foster Chanock Files, Box 4, Gerald Ford Presidential Library, Ann Arbor, MI.

66. Memorandum, unsigned, November 3, 1975.
67. Lou Cannon and David Broder, "Ford Hopes for Last Laugh," *Washington Post*, January 4, 1976.
68. Jerald terHorst, "Ronald Reagan Places His Bet," *Chicago Tribune*, November 21, 1975, as quoted in a memorandum by Ron Nessen, November 21, 1975, White House Central Files, Box 16, Gerald Ford Presidential Library, Ann Arbor, MI.
69. Memorandum by Peter Kaye, White House Operations, Richard Cheney Files, Box 19, January 21, 1976, Ford Presidential Library, Ann Arbor, MI.
70. Jim Lake, in discussion with the author, January 16, 2004.
71. David Keene, in discussion with the author, March 3, 2004.
72. Lou Cannon, in discussion with the author, June 28, 2004; Stuart Spencer, in discussion with the author, June 21, 2004.
73. Nessen, *It Sure Looks Different*, 190.
74. Memorandum by Jim Shuman, November 21, 1975, White House Central Files, Box 16, Gerald Ford Presidential Library, Ann Arbor, MI.
75. Memorandum by Robert Teeter, November 12, 1975, "Analysis of Early Research," Robert Teeter Papers, 67-77, Box 63, Gerald Ford Presidential Library, Ann Arbor, MI.
76. Memorandum by Robert Teeter, December 11, 1975, "Momentum," Robert Teeter Papers, 67-77, Box 63, Gerald Ford Presidential Library, Ann Arbor, MI.
77. Memorandum by Robert Teeter, November 12, 1975, "Analysis of Early Research."

CHAPTER FOUR — Citizens for Reagan, Take One

1. Steven F. Hayward, *The Age of Reagan: The Fall of the Old Liberal Order, 1964-1980* (Roseville, CA: Forum, 2001), 450.
2. Roger Stone, in discussion with the author, April 5, 2004.
3. Eddie Mahe and Ladonna Lee, in discussion with the author, March 5, 2004.
4. Lyn Nofziger, in discussion with the author, 2004.
5. Peter Hannaford, in discussion with the author, January 8, 2004.
6. Michael Deaver, in discussion with the author, December 23, 2003. Reagan scrawled most of these in longhand on yellow legal pads. To see many of these reproduced, see *Reagan, in His Own Hand: The Writings of Ronald Reagan That Reveal His Revolutionary Vision for America*, Skinner et al, eds., (New York: Free Press, 2001).
7. Richard Reeves, *A Ford, Not a Lincoln* (New York: Harcourt Brace Jovanovich, 1975), 47.
8. Mahe and Lee, discussion.
9. Hannaford, discussion.
10. Deaver, discussion.
11. Nofziger, discussion.
12. Deaver, discussion; Hannaford, discussion.
13. Lou Cannon, *Reagan* (New York: G.P. Putnam's Sons, 1982), 199.
14. Cannon, *Reagan,* 199.
15. Rowland Evans and Robert Novak, *The Reagan Revolution* (New York: E.P. Dutton, 1981), 45.
16. Robert T. Hartmann, *Palace Politics: An Inside Account of the Ford Years* (New York: McGraw-Hill, 1980), 334-335.
17. Loren Smith, in discussion with the author, July 29, 2004; Bruce Eberle, in discussion with the author, April 28, 2004.

18. John Sears, in discussion with the author, March 18, 2004.
19. Sears, discussion.
20. Robert T. Nakamura, "Impressions of Ford and Reagan," *Political Science Quarterly*, vol. 92, no. 4: 647-654.
21. James A. Baker, in discussion with the author, March 25, 2004.
22. David Keene, in discussion with the author, December 16, 2003.
23. Tom Ellis, in discussion with the author, May 10, 2004.
24. Sears, discussion.
25. "Reaction to Reagan Announcement (If asked)," July 15, 1975, Ron Nessen Papers, 74-77, Box 39, Gerald Ford Presidential Library, Ann Arbor, MI.
26. Ronald Reagan to Paul Laxalt, July 14, 1975, Reagan Candidacy, President Ford Committee Records, 75-76, Box D13, Gerald Ford Presidential Library, Ann Arbor, MI.
27. Frank Donatelli, in discussion with the author, April 2, 2004.
28. Loren Smith to Federal Election Commission, October 14, 1975, Reagan Candidacy, President Ford Committee Records, 75-76, Box D13, Gerald Ford Presidential Library, Ann Arbor, MI.
29. Bob Visser to Peter Kaye, November 16, 1975, "Ronald Reagan Candidacy," Reagan Candidacy, President Ford Committee Records, 75-76, Box D13, Gerald Ford Presidential Library, Ann Arbor, MI.
30. Deaver, discussion.
31. Neal Peden, in discussion with the author, 2004.
32. Jeff Bell, in discussion with the author, May 5, 2004.
33. Bell, discussion.
34. Jules Witcover, *Marathon: The Pursuit of the Presidency, 1972-1976* (New York: Viking Press, 1977), 375-376.
35. Peter Hannaford, *The Reagans: A Political Portrait* (New York: Coward-McCann, 1983), 30.
36. Confidential interview, March 2004.
37. Cannon, *Reagan,* 204.
38. Memorandum by Gerald Ford to James T. Lynn, October 18, 1975, White House Operations, Richard Cheney Files, 1974-77, Box 19, Gerald Ford Library, Ann Arbor, MI.
39. Sears, discussion.
40. Mahe and Lee, discussion.
41. David Nyhan, "Ford Wants Abortion Left Up to States," *Boston Globe*, February 4, 1976.
42. Hannaford, *The Reagans,* 75.

CHAPTER FIVE — Setting the Stage

1. R.W. Apple, "Reagan's Challenge for Leadership of Republican Party: Assets and Liabilities," *New York Times*, November 21, 1975.
2. Becki Black Donatelli, in discussion with the author, January 15, 2004.
3. Gerald R. Ford, *A Time To Heal* (New York: Harper & Row, 1979), 333.
4. Jim Lake, in discussion with the author, January 16, 2004.
5. Peter Hannaford, in discussion with the author, January 8, 2004.
6. Michael Deaver, in discussion with the author, December 23, 2003.
7. Deaver, discussion.
8. Deaver, discussion.

9. Deaver, discussion.
10. "Reaction to the Reagan Announcement," November 20, 1975, Ron Nessen Papers, Box 39, Gerald Ford Presidential Library, Ann Arbor, MI.
11. "Reaction to the Reagan Announcement," November 20, 1975.
12. Larry Kudlow, in discussion with the author, March 8, 2004.
13. William F. Buckley, "Reagan's Performance is Exhilarating," *Washington Star*, November 25, 1975.
14. "Manifest For UAL 5776: LAX to MAN," January 5, 1976, California Office Scheduling, Dec. 11, 1975 – Jan. 1976, Box 80, Campaign, Ronald Reagan Presidential Library, Simi Valley, CA.
15. "The President Ford Committee's Reaction to R. Reagan Announcement," November 20, 1975, President Ford Committee Records, A4, Gerald Ford Presidential Library, Ann Arbor, MI.
16. Memorandum by Ron Nessen, November 21, 1975, White House Central Files, Box 16, Gerald Ford Presidential Library, Ann Arbor, MI.
17. Jim Squires, "'U.S. Needs New Course;' Reagan to oppose Ford," *Chicago Tribune*, November 21, 1975, as quoted in Ron Nessen's memorandum, November 21, 1975.
18. Apple, *New York Times*, November 21, 1975.
19. Jerry H. Jones to Dick Cheney, November 20, 1975, Jerry Jones Files, 74-77, Box 25, Gerald Ford Presidential Library, Ann Arbor, MI.
20. Jerry H. Jones to Dick Cheney, November 21, 1975, Jerry Jones Files, 74-77, Box 25, Gerald Ford Presidential Library, Ann Arbor, MI.
21. Barry Serafin, *CBS Evening News,* November 20, 1975, CBS, White House Communications Collection, Gerald Ford Presidential Library, Ann Arbor, MI
22. David Keene, in discussion with the author, March 3, 2004.
23. Jack W. Germond, "Reagan Challenges Right of Ford to GOP Nomination," *Washington Star*, November 20, 1975.
24. *New York Times*, "Enter Reagan," November 20, 1975.
25. Tom Pettit, *NBC Nightly News*, November 20, 1975, NBC, White House Communications Agency Collection, Gerald Ford Presidential Library, Ann Arbor, MI.
26. Howard K. Smith, *ABC News*, November 20, 1976, ABC, White House Communications Agency Collection, Gerald Ford Presidential Library, Ann Arbor, MI.
27. Jules Witcover, *Marathon: The Pursuit of the Presidency, 1972-1976* (New York: Viking Press, 1977), 56.
28. Nancy Reynolds, in discussion with the author, February 25, 2004.
29. James R. Dickenson, "Presidential Hopefuls Share a Dreadful Bond," *Washington Star*, November 21, 1975.
30. Dickenson, *Washington Star*, November 21, 1975.
31. James R. Dickenson, "Reagan's Opening Salvos Unmuffled By Toy Gun Scare," *Washington Star*, November 21, 1975.
32. Associated Press, "Reagan's Old Films Off TV for a While," *Washington Star*, November 23, 1975.
33. Paul E. Boller Jr., *Presidential Anecdotes* (New York: Penguin, 1981), 349.
34. Benjamin Taylor, "GOP Contest Lead Seesaws Into Morning," *Boston Globe*, February 25, 1976.

35. Witcover, *Marathon*, 73.
36. Witcover, *Marathon*, 74.
37. Memorandum by Bo Callaway, President Ford Committee Records, Box A7, 22 September 1975, Gerald Ford Presidential Library, Ann Arbor, MI.
38. Benjamin Taylor, "The Power of Ford Incumbency is Reagan's Biggest Problem," *Boston Globe*, February 12, 1976.
39. Elizabeth Drew, *American Journal: The Events of 1976* (New York: Vintage Books, 1976), 26.
40. Witcover, *Marathon*, 378.
41. Ronald Reagan, interview by Bob Clark and Frank Reynolds, *Issues and Answers*, ABC, November 30, 1975, as quoted in a memorandum by Ron Nessen, Ron Nessen Files, Box 67, Gerald Ford Presidential Library, Ann Arbor, MI.
42. Rowland Evans and Robert Novak, "Ronald Reagan's '$90-Billion Scheme,'" December 9, 1975, as quoted in Jerry Jones Files, Box 25, Ford Presidential Library.
43. Memorandum, unsigned, "Four Scenarios," White House Operations, Richard Cheney Files, Box 17, Gerald Ford Presidential Library, Ann Arbor, MI.
44. *Newsweek*, "The Candidates' Men," February 23, 1976, 22.
45. Ford, *A Time To Heal*, 345.
46. Memorandum by Dave Liggett, December 15, 1975, President Ford Committee Records, Box D13, Gerald Ford Presidential Library, Ann Arbor, MI.
47. Stuart Spencer, in discussion with the author, June 21, 2004.
48. Memorandum by Jim Falk, 9 January 1976, President Ford Committee Records, Box D13, President Ford Committee.
49. Witcover, *Marathon*, 380.
50. Witcover, *Marathon*, 380.
51. Witcover, *Marathon*, 380.
52. Terry Drinkwater, news commentary, *Reagan is Seasoned for '76*, CBS, November 20, 1975 as quoted in a memorandum by Ron Nessen, White House Central Files, Box 16, November 21, 1975, Gerald Ford Presidential Library, Ann Arbor, MI.
53. Deaver, discussion.
54. *Human Events*, January 17, 1976.
55. H. Josef Hebert, "Reagan Spending Cut Plan Stirs N.H. Fears of State Taxes," *Boston Globe*, January 2, 1976.
56. *Human Events*, January 17, 1976.
57. *Boston Globe*, "Ford Reagan Tied in Gallup GOP Poll," January 11, 1976.
58. Hebert, *Boston Globe*, January 2, 1976.
59. *Boston Globe*, "Reagan Zeroes in on N.H.," January 4, 1976.
60. *New York Times*, "11 Presidential Contenders Get First U.S. Funds for Campaigns," January 3, 1976.
61. *Human Events*, "When George Will Writes, Should Conservatives Heed?" January 24, 1976.
62. *Baltimore Sun*, "Reagan is Not Acting," November 21, 1975.
63. James Reston, "Presidential Script is Best Reagan's Ever Had," *Washington Star*, November 20, 1975.
64. Gary Wills, "Being Fair to Reagan," *Boston Globe*, January 21, 1976.
65. Benjamin Taylor, "Ronald Reagan: The Rhetoric Vs. the Record," *Boston Globe*, January 4, 1976.

66. Benjamin Taylor, "Reagan Tries to Calm N.H. State Tax Fears," *Boston Globe,* January 6, 1976.
67. Taylor, *Boston Globe,* January 6, 1976.
68. Mary McGrory, "Reagan Ford's Big Asset in N.H.," *Boston Globe*, January 10, 1976.

CHAPTER SIX — Reagan's Reversal

1. Jules Witcover, *Marathon: The Pursuit of the Presidency, 1972-1976* (New York: Viking Press, 1977), 61.
2. John J. Casserly, *The Ford White House: The Diary of a Speechwriter* (Lincoln, NE: iUniverse.com, 2000), p.138; Mike Barnicle, "Granite State Hails the Chief," *Boston Globe*, January 19, 1976.
3. *Time*, "The Ridicule Problem," January 5, 1976, 33.
4. "New Hampshire Strategy," President Ford Committee Records, Callaway NH, Box A7, Gerald Ford Presidential Library, Ann Arbor, MI.
5. David Nyhan, "Ford: Growing Optimism of an Incumbent." *Boston Globe,* January 18, 1976.
6. Peter Hannaford, *The Reagans: A Political Portrait* (New York: Coward-McCann, 1983), 92; Peter Hannaford, in discussion with the author, January 8, 2004.
7. Lesley Oelsner, "Supreme Court Upholds Winner-Take-All Rule for California's Republican Presidential Primary." *New York Times*, January 20, 1976.
8. Warren Weaver Jr., "Election Board Loses Most of Power," *New York Times*, March 23, 1976.
9. Witcover, *Marathon,* 219-220.
10. M. Stanton Evans, in discussion with the author, February 25, 2004.
11. R.W. Apple Jr., "Carter Defeats Bayh by 2-1 in Iowa," *New York Times*, January 20, 1976.
12. Associated Press, "Reagan, Conceding 'Mistake,' Attempts to Clarify Program," *New York Times*, January 13, 1976.
13. Martin Anderson, in discussion with the author, June 23, 2004.
14. Benjamin Taylor, "Ford Backers Prepare for Reagan's Return to N.H. Today," *Boston Globe*, January 15, 1976.
15. Fred Barnes, "Budget Tailored to Conservatives," *Washington Star*, January 21, 1976.
16. *Human Events*, "Reagan Threat Reflected In Ford's 1977 Budget," January 31, 1976.
17. Fred Barnes, "4 of Ford's Speech Writers Get Ax," *Washington* Star, January 22, 1976.
18. Lawrence K. Altman, "Presidential Rivals Found in Good Health," *New York Times*, January 28, 1976.
19. Richard Bergholz, "Governor Reagan Disavows List of Program Costs," *Boston Globe*, January 28, 1976.
20. Bergholz, *Boston Globe*, January 28, 1976.
21. Bergholz, *Boston Globe*, January 28, 1976.
22. Gerald R. Ford, *A Time To Heal* (New York: Harper and Row, 1979), 361.
23. David Nyhan, "Ford's Political Map: To the Left of Reagan, Right of Democrats," *Boston Globe,* January 20, 1976.
24. *Boston Globe*, "Bay State to Host 8 Presidential Candidates This Week," January 27, 1976.
25. *Time*, "The White House: Hoping to Win by Working on the Job," January 12, 1976, 12.
26. *Boston Globe*, "Aide May Urge Ford to Debate Reagan," January 28, 1976.
27. Ford, *A Time To Heal,* 361-362.

28. John Fialka, "Reagan Seems a Natural to Challenge a President," *Washington Star*, January 18, 1976.
29. Benjamin Taylor, "Reagan Assails Big Government," *Boston Globe*, January 30, 1976.
30. Taylor, *Boston Globe*, January 30, 1976.
31. Reynolds, discussion.
32. Reynolds, discussion.
33. Reynolds, discussion.
34. Reynolds, discussion
35. Michael Deaver, in discussion with the author, December 23, 2003.
36. Lyn Nofziger, *Nofziger* (Washington DC: Regnery Gateway, 1992), 185.
37. Loye Miller, "Ford's Political Advisers Differ on Health of His Florida Campaign," *Boston Globe*, January 29, 1976.
38. Dana Rohrabacher, in discussion with the author, June 10, 2004.
39. Jim Lake, in discussion with the author, January 16, 2004.
40. Witcover, *Marathon,* 386.
41. Dave Riley, "No 'Dirty Tricks' Says Ford Aide," *Boston Globe,* January 29, 1976.
42. David S. Broder, "Reagan Scores Ford Backers' 'Dirty Tricks,'" *Washington Post,* January 29, 1976.
43. Rowland Evans and Bob Novak, "Reagan Slays One Monster, But Runs Into Another," *Boston Globe,* editorial, January 30, 1976.
44. Evans and Novak, *Boston Globe,* January 30, 1976.
45. Benjamin Taylor, "Technocrat Works Both Sides of GOP Race in N.H.," *Boston Globe*, February 2, 1976.
46. Taylor, *Boston Globe*, February 2, 1976.
47. Taylor, *Boston Globe*, February 2, 1976.
48. *Boston Globe*, "Ford Holds Narrow Lead as Reagan Gains Steadily," February 2, 1976.
49. David Nyhan, "Ford Wants Abortion Left Up to States," *Boston Globe*, February 4, 1976.
50. *Boston Globe*, "From the Ford's: 2 Abortion Views," February 4, 1976.
51. *Boston Globe*, "Mr. Ford Vs. Mrs. Ford," editorial, February 5, 1976.
52. Nyhan, *Boston Globe*, February 4, 1976.
53. *Boston Globe*, "Reagan Fears NEA Impact on Schools," February 5, 1976.
54. *Boston Globe*, "Rockefeller's Situation is Fluid," February 6, 1976.
55. Richard Stewart, "Ford Seeks Primary Votes Today in N.H.," *Boston Globe,* February 7, 1976.
56. David Nyhan, "Reagan Untested, Ford Tells Newsmen in N.H.," *Boston Globe,* February 9, 1976.
57. Witcover, *Marathon*, 385.
58. Maria Karagianis, "Stumping for Husband, Mrs. Ford Wins Votes Herself," *Boston Globe*, February 8, 1976.
59. Nyhan, *Boston Globe,* February 9, 1976.
60. *Boston Globe*, "Sidelights of Ford's New Hampshire Campaign," February 9, 1976.
61. Nyhan, *Boston Globe,* February 9, 1976.
62. Nyhan, *Boston Globe,* February 9, 1976.
63. Rachelle Patterson, "Ford Takes Credit For Jobless-rate Dip," *Boston Globe*, February 7, 1976.

64. *Wall Street Journal*, "Fordism, Reaganism and Extremism," January 5, 1976.
65. *Boston Globe*, "How N.H. Voters Size Up Ford, Reagan," February 8, 1976.
66. *Boston Globe*, "How N.H. Voters Size Up Ford, Reagan," February 8, 1976.
67. *Boston Globe*, "Gallup Poll: Ford, Reagan in Dead Heat in Latest Test," February 9, 1976; *Boston Globe,* "Brooke Could Swing Votes, Black Caucus Leader Says," February 9, 1976.
68. Benjamin Taylor, "Political Styles of Ford and Reagan," *Boston Globe,* February 9, 1976.
69. Jack Nelson, "Republicans Take Gloves Off," *Boston Globe*, February 11, 1976.
70. Nelson, *Boston Globe*, February 11, 1976.
71. Memorandum by Tim Ryan, President Ford Committee Records, Box D13, February 27, 1976, Gerald Ford Presidential Library, Ann Arbor, MI.
72. Witcover, *Marathon,* 391.
73. *Boston Globe*, "Ford People Say Nixon Hurt Them," February 25, 1976.
74. Martin F. Nolan, "Reagan vs. the Calendar," *Boston Globe*, February 29, 1976.
75. Taylor, *Boston Globe*, February 11, 1976.
76. Taylor, *Boston Globe*, February 11, 1976.
77. Nyhan, *Boston Globe*, February 9, 1976.
78. Robert Healy, "Ford Hitting Reagan Hard," *Boston Globe*, February 13, 1976.
79. Benjamin Taylor, "McCloskey Stumps N.H. for Ford, Says Reagan Spells Disaster for Party," *Boston Globe*, February 15, 1976.
80. *Human Events*, "Ford Shatters '11th Commandment,'" February 28, 1976.
81. Associated Press, "Kissinger Says Reagan Hurting World Peace," *Boston Globe*, February 13, 1976.
82. Taylor, *Boston Globe*, February 15, 1976.
83. Frank Cormier, "Ford For Death Penalty," *Boston Globe*, February 15, 1976.
84. Nofziger, *Nofziger*, 177.
85. Rachelle Patterson, "Oil, Gas Donations Flowing to Reagan," *Boston Globe*, February 15, 1976.
86. *Boston Globe*, "Loeb Says Reagan Loss Possible in N.H. Primary," February 16, 1976.
87. *Boston Globe*, "Ford to Miss Boston on N.H. Trip," February 17, 1976.
88. Witcover, *Marathon*, 391.
89. David Nyhan, "The Races," *Boston Globe*, February 17, 1976.
90. Benjamin Taylor, "Ford and Reagan play out hands in New Hampshire," *Boston Globe*, February 19, 1976.
91. Robert Healy, "Ford's Hopes: Two Opinions," Political Circuit, *Boston Globe*, February 20, 1976.
92. David Nyhan, "Ford, Back in N.H., Attacks Reagan on Social Security," *Boston Globe*, February 20, 1976.
93. Nyhan, *Boston Globe*, February 20, 1976.
94. Richard Stewart, "Reagan, in N.H., Says He Supports Social Security," *Boston Globe*, February 22, 1976.
95. Stewart, *Boston Globe*, February 22, 1976.
96. Peter Hannaford, in discussion with the author, January 8, 2004.
97. Dick Wirthlin, in discussion with the author, March 11, 2004; Hannaford, discussion; Witcover, *Marathon*, 394.

98. Dick Wirthlin, *The Greatest Communicator: What Ronald Reagan Taught Me about Politics, Leadership, and Life* (Hoboken: John Wiley & Sons, 2004), 20-22.
99. Lou Cannon, *Reagan* (New York: G.P. Putnam's Sons, 1982), 209.
100. Witcover, *Marathon*, 394.
101. Lake, discussion.
102. *Manchester Union-Leader*, "Polls Show Reagan Ahead in Tight Race," February 24, 1976.
103. *Manchester Union-Leader*, "Polls Show Reagan Ahead in Tight Race."
104. Martin F. Nolan, "Reagan vs. the Calendar," *Boston Globe*, February 29, 2004.
105. Witcover, *Marathon*, 28.
106. Witcover, *Marathon*, 395.
107. Witcover, *Marathon*, 395.
108. Witcover, *Marathon*, 395.
109. Lake, discussion.
110. Stuart Spencer, in discussion with the author, June 21, 2004.
111. Sears, discussion.
112. Lake, discussion.
113. Lyn Nofziger, in discussion with the author, 2004; Wirthlin, discussion.
114. Spencer, discussion.
115. Marty Anderson, in discussion with the author, June 23, 2004.
116. Witcover, *Marathon*, 397.
117. Stephen F. Hayward, *The Age of Reagan: The Fall of the Old Liberal Order* (Roseville, CA: Forum, 2001), 462.
118. Sears, discussion; Anderson, discussion; Lee Edwards, *Ronald Reagan: A Political Biography* (Houston: Norland Publishing International, 1981), 180.
119. Donn Tibbetts, "City Votes Called Decisive," *Manchester-Union Leader*, February 26, 1976.
120. David Keene, in discussion with the author, December 16, 2003.
121. Witcover, *Marathon*, 75; 1976 New Hampshire Presidential Primary, February 24, 1976: Republican Results, http://www.politicallibrary.org/TallState/1976rep.html.
122. Witcover, *Marathon*, 397.
123. Witcover, *Marathon*, 396.

CHAPTER SEVEN — Against the Wall

1. Martin Anderson, in discussion with the author, June 23, 2004.
2. Rowland Evans and Robert Novak, "Reagan Put on Offensive," Boston *Globe*, February 26, 1976.
3. *Human Events*, "Florida Primary Now Crucial for Reagan," March 6, 1976.
4. Elizabeth Drew, *American Journal: The Events of 1976* (New York: Vintage Books, 1976), 353.
5. Richard H. Stewart, "Reagan," *Boston Globe*, February 25, 1976.
6. Frank Reynolds, *ABC News*, February 25, 1976, White House Communications Agency Collection, Gerald Ford Presidential Library, Ann Arbor, MI.
7. Robert Healy, "Long, Hot Road for GOP Rivals," *Boston Globe*, February 25, 1976.
8. Ron Nessen, *It Sure Looks Different From the Inside* (Chicago: Playboy Press, 1978), 199.
9. Lou Cannon, "Reagan Hurt, Ford Aide Believes," Washington *Post*, February 8, 1976.
10. Edward Walsh, "Ford Says Reagan Can't Win," Washington *Post*, February 18, 1976; Fred Barnes, "Prime Time and the Price is Right," *Washington Star*, February 18, 1976.

11. Walsh, *Washington Post*, February 18, 1976; Barnes, *Washington Star*, February 18, 1976.
12. Loye Miller, "Reagan Camp Seeking Some Way to Stop Ford," *Miami Herald*, March 2, 1976.
13. James Nolan, "State Aides Urge Reagan to Openly Attack Ford," *Miami Herald*, March 3, 1976.
14. Al Cardenas, in discussion with the author, July 13, 2004.
15. Rick Reed, in discussion with the author, March 18, 2004; Kathy Regan, in discussion with the author, March 21, 2004.
16. William Loeb, "President Ford is in Trouble," *Manchester Union-Leader*, February 26, 1976.
17. David Keene, in discussion with the author, December 16, 2003.
18. Dick Wirthlin, in discussion with the author, March 11, 2004.
19. Benjamin Taylor, "Ford Got His Support Where Aides Expected," *Boston Globe*, February 26, 1976.
20. *Boston Globe*, "Ronald Reagan Wants Spending Cuts," February 29, 1976.
21. Benjamin Taylor, "Reagan and Ford Play Numbers Game With Bay State Primary Predictions," *Boston Globe*, February 27, 1976; David Nyhan, "Ford Aide Fears Trick by Reagan," *Boston Globe*, March 1, 1976.
22. Taylor, *Boston Globe*, February 27, 1976.
23. Taylor, *Boston Globe*, February 27, 1976.
24. Benjamin Taylor, "GOP Voters Turn Down Reagan by Nearly 2 to 1," *Boston Globe*, March 3, 1976.
25. *Boston Globe*, "Ford's Narrow N.H. Win Leaves Reagan Smiling," February 25, 1976.
26. Benjamin Taylor, "GOP Contest Lead Seesaws Into Morning," *Boston Globe*, February 25, 1976.
27. Peter Hannaford, in discussion with the author, January 8, 2004.
28. John Sears, in discussion with the author, March 18, 2004.
29. *Washington Post*, "Ford taking Advantage of Incumbency," March 2, 1976.
30. James M. Naughton, "Ford Stresses His on the Job Experience," *New York Times*, March 1, 1976.
31. Drew, *American Journal*, 64.
32. John R. Coyne Jr., "Slipping Landslide," *National Review*, April 2, 1976.
33. David Nyhan, "Reagan Florida Lead Slipping," *Boston Globe*, February 29, 1976.
34. Richard Stewart, "Vermont Gives Carter, Ford Easy Victories," *Boston Globe*, March 3, 1976.
35. Drew, *American Journal*, 24.
36. Robert Cooke, "Ford Voters Span Spectrum, Polls Show," *Boston Globe*, March 3, 1976.
37. Rowland Evans and Robert Novak, "In Florida, Reagan Swings Dull Blade," *Boston Globe*, March 3, 1976.
38. Evans and Novak, *Boston Globe*, March 3, 1976.
39. Keene, discussion.
40. Keene, discussion.
41. Tom Wicker, "Florida: Decisive Battles?" *New York Times*, March 2, 1976.
42. John Kifner, "Ford Tops Reagan," *New York Times*, March 3, 1976.
43. *New York Times*, "Biggest Allocation Goes to Jackson," March 4, 1976.
44. Jon Nordheimer, "Reagan, in Direct Attack, Assails Ford on Defense," *New York Times*, March 5, 1976.

45. Nordheimer, *New York Times*, March 5, 1976.
46. James Nolan, "Reagan Changes Strategy, Attacks Ford on Military," *Miami Herald*, March 5, 1976
47. James M. Naughton, "Ford's Reaction," *New York Times*, March 5, 1976.
48. David Rosenbaum, "Social Security a Major Issue in Florida as Primary Day Nears," *New York Times,* March 5, 1976.
49. Rosenbaum, *New York Times,* March 5, 1976.
50. Rosenbaum, *New York Times,* March 5, 1976.
51. Rosenbaum, *New York Times*, March 5, 1976.
52. David Rosenbaum, "Florida's Elderly Raise Hopes of Ford and Jackson," *New York Times,* March 6, 1976.
53. Rosenbaum, *New York Times,* March 6, 1976.
54. Jon Nordheimer, "Reagan Declares He's in Race to the End," *New York Times*, March 6, 1976.
55. Steven F. Hayward, *Age of Reagan: The Fall of the Old Liberal Order* (Roseville, CA: Forum, 2001), 434.
56. Hayward, *Age of Reagan*, 434.
57. Martin Tolchin, "Buckley Differs With Rockefeller," *New York Times*, March 7, 1976.
58. Nick Thimmesch, "Fords for Ford," *New York Times*, Sunday Magazine, March 7, 1976.
59. Drew, *American Journal,* 27.
60. James M. Naughton, "Ford, Stumping in Illinois Cites 'Proven Leadership,'" *New York Times*, March 7, 1976.
61. Naughton, *New York Times*, March 7, 1976.
62. Naughton, *New York Times*, March 7, 1976.
63. James Wooten, "A Significant but Eccentric Race," *New York Times*, March 8, 1976.
64. R.W. Apple Jr., "Ford, in Turnabout, Now Seems to Lead Reagan in Florida Vote," *New York Times*, March 8, 1976.
65. Jon Nordheimer, "Reagan Says Committed Voters Favor Him in Florida Primary," *New York Times*, March 8, 1976.
66. Nordheimer, *New York Times*, March 8, 1976.
67. Nordheimer, *New York Times*, March 8, 1976.
68. Jim Dickenson, "Is Reagan a Sprinter in Long-Distance Race?," *Washington Star*, March 7, 1976.
69. Nordheimer, *New York Times*, March 8, 1976.
70. *New York Times*, "Tampa Tribune Backs Ford," March 8, 1976.
71. Philip Shabecoff, "Ford Says 'We're Going to Win' Today," *New York Times*, March 9, 1976.
72. Shabecoff, *New York Times*, March 9, 1976.
73. Roy Reed, "Political Rivals Find Economic Worry is Now Dominate in a Changed Florida," *New York Times*, March 9, 1976.
74. Jon Nordheimer, "Reagan Doubtful on Florida Voting," *New York Times*, March 9, 1976.
75. Gerald Pomper, *The Election of 1976* (New York: Longman, 1977), 21, 24.
76. Pomper, *The Election of 1976*, 24.
77. Roy Reed, "Ford Defeats Reagan in Florida; Carter is Winner Over Wallace in Democratic Vote, Jackson 3d," *New York Times*, March 10, 1976.
78. Jon Nordheimer, "Reagan Voices 'Delight' on Florida Vote," *New York Times*, March 10, 1976.

79. James M. Naughton, "Ford's Aides Send Signal to Reagan," *New York Times*, March 10, 1976.
80. Reed, *New York Times*, March 10, 1976.
81. Loye Miller, "Ford Blitz Near Fatal to Reagan," *Miami Herald*, March 10, 1976.
82. Nordheimer, *New York Times*, March 10, 1976
83. Nordheimer, *New York Times*, March 10, 1976.
84. Jon Nordheimer, "Reagan Will Stay in Race; Denies Ford Won Triumph," *New York Times*, March 11, 1976.
85. James M. Naughton, "Reagan Criticism is Seen Spurring Ford," *New York Times*, March 12, 1976.
86. Naughton, March 12, 1976.
87. Drew, *American Journal*, 355; Warren Weaver Jr., "Republicans Denounce Campaign Bill," *New York Times*, March 12, 1976.
88. James M. Naughton, "Ford Upholds Kissinger Against Reagan's Attacks," *New York Times*, March 13, 1976.
89. Jon Nordheimer, "Reagan and Aide in Illinois Denounce Ford Campaign," *New York Times*, March 13, 1976.
90. Nordheimer, *New York Times*, March 13, 1976.
91. James P. Sterba, "Connally Declines to Bar a Vice-Presidential Race," *New York Times*, March 14, 1976.
92. Jon Nordheimer, "Kissinger Scored on Campaign Role," *New York Times*, March 16, 1976.
93. *New York Times*, "Ford is Far Ahead of Reagan on Funds," March 16, 1976.
94. Pomper, *The Election of 1976*, 24.
95. Joel D. Weisman, "Ill. Primary Said Pivotal for Reagan," *Washington Post*, January 1, 1976.
96. *New York Times*, " . . . Stronger Ford," March 11, 1976.
97. William E. Farrell, "Ford Decisively Defeats Reagan in Illinois Voting; Carter is a Solid Winner," *New York Times*, March 17, 1976.
98. Lou Cannon, "Tight Reagan Team," *Washington Post*, August 9, 1976.

CHAPTER EIGHT — North Carolina

1. Frank Reynolds, *ABC News*, August 17, 1976, White House Communications Agency Collection, Gerald Ford Presidential Library, Ann Arbor, MI.
2. Lee Edwards, *The Conservative Revolution: The Movement that Remade America* (New York: Free Press, 1999), 201.
3. James M. Naughton, "Campaign Without a Knockout Punch," *New York Times*, Sunday Magazine, June 6, 1976.
4. William Safire, "Life of the Party," *New York Times*, March 16, 1976.
5. Peter Hannaford, in discussion with the author, January 8, 2004.
6. Paul Laxalt, *Nevada's Paul Laxalt: A Memoir* (Reno, NV: Jack Bacon and Company, 2000), 291-292.
7. Lyn Nofziger, *Nofziger* (Washington DC: Regnery Gateway, 1992), 179-180; Lyn Nofziger, in discussion with the author, February 25, 2004.
8. Ned Cline, "True Believer," *North Carolina*, April 2004, 50-51.
9. John Sears, in discussion with the author, March 18, 2004; Jim Lake, in discussion with the author, January 16, 2004.
10. Sears, discussion.

11. Lou Cannon, in discussion with the author, June 28, 2004.
12. Daniel C. Hoover, "Three Presidential Hopefuls Woo Tar Heels: Reagan," *Raleigh News and Observer*, March 19, 1976.
13. Laxalt, *Nevada's Paul Laxalt*, 292.
14. Daniel C. Hoover, "Three Presidential Hopefuls Woo Tar Heels: Reagan," *(Raleigh, N.C.) News and Observer*, March 19, 1976.
15. Dick Wirthlin, *The Greatest Communicator: What Ronald Reagan Taught Me about Politics, Leadership, and Life* (Hoboken: John Wiley & Sons, 2004), 21.
16. Tom Ellis, in discussion with the author, May 10, 2004.
17. Carter Wrenn, in discussion with the author, May 12, 2004.
18. Confidential interview with the author, May 2004.
19. David Keene, in discussion with the author, December 16, 2003.
20. Edmund Morris, *Dutch: A Memoir of Ronald Reagan* (New York: Random House, 1999), 89.
21. Hannaford, discussion.
22. "The Reagan Record in California," Positions 1976, Box 447-446, Ronald Reagan Presidential Library, Simi Valley, CA.
23. Arthur Finkelstein, in discussion with the author, 2004.
24. Ellis, discussion.
25. Paul Laxalt, in discussion with the author, April 21, 2004.
26. Judy Sarasohn, in discussion with the author, July 9, 2004.
27. Laxalt, discussion.
28. Brad O'Leary, in discussion with the author, 2001.
29. Memorandum by Bob Visser, May 20, 1976, Robert Hartmann Papers, Box 164, Gerald Ford Presidential Library, Ann Arbor, MI.
30. Memorandum by Bob Visser, May 20, 1976.
31. Memorandum by Bob Visser and Tim Ryan, April 27, 1976.
32. M. Stanton Evans, in discussion with the author, February 25, 2004.
33. Memorandum by Bob Visser and Tim Ryan, April 27, 1976.
34. Memorandum by Bob Visser and Tim Ryan, April 27, 1976.
35. Jesse Helms to M. Stanton Evans, March 25, 1976, Robert Hartmann Papers, Box 164, Gerald Ford Presidential Library, Ann Arbor, MI.
36. Jules Witcover, *Marathon: The Pursuit of the Presidency, 1972-1976* (New York: Viking Press, 1977), 412.
37. Jim Burnley, in discussion with the author, July 28, 2004.
38. Keene, discussion.
39. Bruce Eberle, in discussion with the author, April 28, 2004.
40. Loren Smith, in discussion with the author, 2004.
41. Witcover, *Marathon*, 414.
42. Ellis, discussion.
43. Charlie Black, in discussion with the author, 2004; Witcover, *Marathon,* 411.
44. Witcover, *Marathon*, 52.
45. Gerald R. Ford, *A Time To Heal* (New York: Harper & Row, 1979), 361.
46. Ford, *A Time To Heal*, 372.
47. Nofziger, *Nofziger*, 167.

48 Witcover, *Marathon*, 406.
49. Stuart Spencer, in discussion with the author, June 21, 2004.
50. Burnley, discussion.
51. Ellis, discussion; Wrenn, discussion; Finkelstein, discussion.
52. Martin Anderson, *Revolution* (New York: Harcourt Brace Jovanovich, 1988), 44-45.
53. Martin Anderson, in discussion with the author, June 23, 2004.
54. Ellis, discussion; Wrenn, discussion.
55. Gerald M. Pomper, et al, *The Election of 1976: Reports and Interpretations* (New York: Longman, 1977), 24.
56. Pomper, *The Election of 1976*, 25-26.
57. Lou Cannon, *Reagan* (New York: G.P. Putnam's Sons, 1982), 218.

CHAPTER NINE — Citizens for Reagan, Take Two

1. Paul Laxalt, *Nevada's Paul Laxalt: A Memoir* (Reno: Jack Bacon & Company, 2000), p. 292.
2. Elizabeth Drew, *American Journal: The Events of 1976* (New York: Vintage Books, 1978), 237.
3. Drew, *American Journal*, 237.
4. James R. Dickenson, "Stunning Ford Loss Gives Renewed Life To Reagan Candidacy," *Washington Star*, March 24, 1976.
5. Lou Cannon, in discussion with the author, June 2, 2004.
6. James R. Dickenson, "Stunning Ford Loss Gives Renewed Life To Reagan Candidacy," *Washington Star*, March 24, 1976.
7. Mary McGrory, "Reagan an Enigma In Moment of Victory," *Washington Star*, March 26, 1976.
8. Stuart Spencer, in discussion with the author, June 21, 2004.
9. M. Stanton Evans, "The Ronald Reagan Story," *Human Events*, January 24, 1976.
10. Evans, *Human Events*, January 24, 1976.
11. Evans, *Human Events*, January 24, 1976.
12. *New York Times*, "Campaigns Against Washington Termed 'Racism' by Humphrey," March 25, 1976.
13. Charles Black, in discussion with the author, 2004.
14. David Bufkin, in discussion with the author, March 5, 2004.
15. Bufkin, discussion.
16. Bufkin, discussion.
17. Bruce Eberle, in discussion with the author, April 28, 2004.
18. Warren Weaver Jr., "Election Board Loses Most of Power," *New York Times*, March 23, 1976.
19. *Federal Election Campaign Act Amendments*, S.3065, 94th Congress; *New York Times*, "A Little Late, Agreement on A Campaign Law," April 18, 1976; Warren Weaver Jr., "President Considers Veto Of Campaign Funding Bill," April 21, 1976; Richard D. Lyons, "Six Ford Rivals Filing Fund Suit," April 22, 1976; *New York Times*, "Freeing Campaign Funds," May 6, 1976; Warren Weaver Jr., "Election Funding Delayed Further," *New York Times*, May 14, 1976.
20. John P. MacKenzie, "7 Candidates Ask Freeing of Funds," *Washington Post*, April 23, 1976.
21. John Sears, in discussion with the author, March 18, 2004.
22. Sears, discussion.

23. Jules Witcover, *Marathon: The Pursuit of the Presidency, 1972-1976* (New York: Viking Press, 1977), p. 414.
24. Witcover, *Marathon*, 414.
25. James R. Dickenson, "Reagan Now Can Put More Punch in Debate," Politics Today, *Washington Star*, March 25, 1976.
26. Jack W. Germond, "Reagan's Eye On Texas and Later Voting," *Washington Star*, March 26, 1976.
27. Germond, *Washington Star*, March 26, 1976.
28. Brian Kelly, "Reagan's Network Problems," *Washington Star*, March 28, 1976.
29. Kelly, *Washington Star*, March 28, 1976.
30. Kelly, *Washington Star*, March 28, 1976.
31. Kelly, *Washington Star*, March 28, 1976.
32. Peter Hannaford, in discussion with the author, January 8, 2004.
33. Lou Cannon and John Carmody, "Reagan Gets Half Hour for Speech on TV," *Washington Post*, March 30, 1976.
34. Martha Angle, "Reagan to Speak On Prime-Time Tomorrow Night," *Washington Star*, March 30, 1976.
35. Angle, *Washington Star*, March 30, 1976.
36. Loren Smith, in discussion with the author, 2004.
37. Angle, *Washington Star*, March 30, 1976.
38. Smith, discussion.
39. Jim Lake, in discussion with the author, January 16, 2004.
40. Lyn Nofziger, *Nofziger*, (Washington DC: Regnery, 1992), p. 183-4.
41. Smith, discussion.
42. Eberle, discussion.
43. Associated Press, "Book Disputed By Sons-in-Law," *Washington Star*, April 3, 1976.
44. *Washington Star*, "TV Time for Candidates," March 31, 1976.
45. Lou Cannon, "Reagan, in National TV Talk, Attacks Ford Foreign Policy," *Washington Post*, April 1, 1976.
46. Cannon, *Washington Post*, April 1, 1976.
47. Hannaford, discussion; Michael Deaver, in discussion with the author, December 23, 2003.
48. Cannon, *Washington Post*, April 1, 1976.
49. Cannon, *Washington Post*, April 1, 1976.
50. Spencer Rich, "Ford May Be Vulnerable on Aid," *Washington Post*, April 2, 1976.
51. Becki Black-Donatelli, in discussion with the author, January 15, 2004.
52. Lou Cannon, *Reagan* (New York: G.P. Putnam's Sons, 1982), p. 219; Lou Cannon, "Speech Buoys Reagan Aides," *Washington Post*, April 2, 1976.
53. Cannon, *Washington Post*, April 1, 1976.
54. Lou Cannon, "Speech Buoys Reagan Aides," *Washington Post*, April 2, 1976.
55. Edward Walsh, "Ford Scores Reagan For 'Political Attack,'" *Washington Post*, April 3, 1976.
56. Bill Richards, "Reagan Firm On Kissinger," *Washington Post*, April 3, 1976.
57. *New York Times*, "'I Wish, I Wish,'" April 9, 1976.
58. William Claiborne, "HHH Is Factor," *Washington Post*, April 7, 1976.
59. Lake, discussion.
60. Lou Cannon, "Reagan Seeking New Start in Texas," *Washington Post*, April 5, 1976.

61. Witcover, *Marathon*, 439, 448, and 495.
62. Thomas P. Ronan, "G.O.P. Leader in Brooklyn Gives Support to Reagan," *New York Times*, May 13, 1976.
63. *Washington Post*, "Reagan, Wallace Win Ruling," April 17, 1976.
64. Ron Nessen, *It Sure Looks Different Form The Inside* (Chicago: Playboy Press, 1978), 175.
65. Text for Mailgram from President Ford Committee to Reagan Delegates in Texas, April 21, 1976, Reagan Texas Activity Complaint, President Ford Committee Records, 75-76, Box D 14, Gerald Ford Presidential Library, Ann Arbor, MI.
66. Mailgram from Dr. Richard R. Moore to President Gerald Ford, April 23, 1976, Reagan Texas Activity Complaint, President Ford Committee Records, 75-76, Box D 14, Gerald Ford Presidential Library, Ann Arbor, MI; Mailgram from Mary Martin Jackson to Rogers Morton, April 25, 1976, Reagan Texas Activity Complaint, President Ford Committee Records, 75-76, Box D 14, Gerald Ford Presidential Library, Ann Arbor, MI.
67. Gerald M. Pomper, et al, *The Election of 1976: Reports and Interpretations* (New York: Longman, 1977), Table 1.3, p. 20-23.
68. Drew Lewis, in discussion with the author, April 7, 2004.
69. Pomper, *The Election of 1976*, Table 1.3, p. 20-23.
70. Paul Weyrich, in discussion with the author, March 4, 2004.
71. Cannon, *Washington Post*, April 5, 1976.
72. Rowland Evans and Robert Novak, "In Texas, a Wallace-to-Reagan Switch," *Washington Post*, April 21, 1976.
73. Cannon, *Washington Post*, April 5, 1976.
74. Lou Cannon, "Reagan Asks Oil Depletion Be Renewed," *Washington Post*, April 7, 1976.
75. Ernie Angelo, in discussion with the author, May 4, 2004.
76. Jeff Bell, in discussion with the author, May 5, 2004.
77. Witcover, *Marathon,* 419.
78. Nofziger, *Nofziger*, 182.
79. Chris Lay, in discussion with the author, June 25, 2004.
80. Christopher Lydon, "Carter Defends All-White Areas," *New York Times*, April 7, 1976.
81. Lou Cannon, "60 Reagan Allies Back Ford," *Washington Post*, April 20, 1976.
82. James M. Naughton, "Ford Sees Wisconsin Vote As Kissinger Endorsement," *New York Times*, April 8, 1976.
83. Edward Walsh, "Ford, Reagan Disagree On Kissinger Standing," *Washington Post*, April 8, 1976.
84. Angelo, discussion.
85. Bufkin, discussion.
86. Lou Cannon, "Ford, on Stump in Texas, Urges Long Terms for Drug Dealers" *Washington Post*, April 10, 1976.
87. Drew, *American Journal*, 172.
88. Edward Walsh, "Reagan Charges Denied," *Washington Post*, April 24, 1976.
89. Fred Barnes, "Ford Isn't So Quick to Brag Anymore," *Washington Star*, May 1, 1976.
90. Barnes, *Washington Star*, May 1, 1976.
91. James R. Dickenson, "Ford Walloped As Challenger Gains New Life," *Washington Star*, May 2, 1976.
92. Stewart Davis, "Reagan Rejects Casting in Running Mate's Role," *Dallas Morning News*, April 29, 1976.

93. Associated Press, "Reagan Can't Win, Rocky Says," *Dallas Morning News*, May 1, 1976.
94. Jon Nordheimer, "Reagan Attacks Kissinger For His Stand on Rhodesia," *New York Times*, May 1, 1976.
95. Barnes, *Washington Star*, May 1, 1976; James P. Sterba, "Ford Believed to Have Cut Reagan Strength in Texas," *New York Times*, May 1, 1976.
96. James P. Sterba, "A Heavy Turnout," *New York Times*, May 2, 1976.
97. Sterba, *New York Times*, May 2, 1976.
98. Angelo, discussion.
99. R.W. Apple Jr., "Reagan's Big Need Now," *New York Times*, May 3, 1976.
100. Nessen, *It Sure Looks Different*, 209.
101. James M. Naughton, "Ford Prepares for a Difficult Fight For Nomination After Texas Defeat," *New York Times*, May 3, 1976.
102. Jon Nordheimer, "Reagan Says Texas Shows He IS the Best Candidate," *New York Times*, May 3, 1976.
103. Dickenson, *Washington Star*, May 2, 1976.
104. Witcover, *Marathon*, 418.
105. Robert D. Hershey, "Goldwater Calls Reagan In Error," *New York Times*, May 3, 1976.
106. *Washington Star*, "Much ado about Panama," May 2, 1976.
107. James R. Dickenson, "Reagan's Foreign Policy Attack Is Working," *Washington Star*, May 3, 1976.
108. Memorandum, "An Explanation of the Reagan Victories in Texas and the Caucus States," Reagan Campaign Material, Jerry Jones Files, 74-77, Box 25, Gerald Ford Presidential Library, Ann Arbor, MI.
109. Apple, *New York Times*, May 3, 1976.
110. William E. Farrell, "Ford and Carter Favored In Indiana Race Tuesday," *New York Times*, May 2, 1976.
111. William E. Ferrell, "Reagan Defeats Ford In Indiana And Also Wins Georgia Primary; Carter Is Victor In Both States," *New York Times*, May 5, 1976.
112. Nessen, *It Sure Looks Different*, 420.
113. James M. Naughton, "Ford Says Carter Does A 'Flip-Flop,'" *New York Times*, May 4, 1976.
114. Black, discussion.
115. Black, discussion.
116. Witcover, *Marathon*, 420.
117. *Washington Post*, photo, May 13, 1976; *Washington Star*, photo, May 12, 1976.
118. Witcover, *Marathon*, 420.
119. Black, discussion.
120. Walter R. Mears, "New Reagan Victories Put Ford in Jeopardy," *Dallas Morning News*, May 5, 1976.
121. Philip Shabecoff, "Ford Aides Reported Critical of White House Staff," *New York Times*, May 11, 1976.
122. Fred Barnes and Martha Angle, "Stung by New Loss, Ford Will Review Campaign Strategy," *Washington Star*, May 5, 1976.
123. Nessen, *It Sure Looks Different*, 210.
124. *Washington Times*, Chart: "Counting The 1976 Delegates," May 5, 1976.
125. Sears, discussion.
126. Barnes and Angle, *Washington Post*, May 5, 1976.

127. James J. Kirkpatrick, "Still Ford over Reagan," *Washington Star*, May 11, 1976.
128. James M. Naughton, "Ford Praises Truman as Man of the People," *New York Times*, May 9, 1976.
129. Naughton, *New York Times*, May 9, 1976.
130. Pat Oliphant, political cartoon, *Washington Star*, May 6, 1976.
131. Frank Lynn, "Rockefeller Seen Gaining Support," *New York Times*, May 7, 1976.
132. Letter from Robert P. Visser to Loren Smith, April 14, 1976, Reagan Texas Activity Complaint, President Ford Committee Records, 75-76, Box D 14, Gerald Ford Presidential Library, Ann Arbor, MI.
133. Becky Norton Dunlop, in discussion with the author, July 2004.
134. Letter from Loren Smith to Robert P. Visser, April 20, 1976, Reagan Texas Activity Complaint, President Ford Committee Records, 75-76, Box D 14, Gerald Ford Presidential Library, Ann Arbor, MI.
135. David E. Rosenbaum, "Incumbency Helping Ford On Campaign Travel Cost," *New York Times*, May 5, 1976.
136. Smith, discussion.
137. David E. Rosenbaum, "Incumbency Helping Ford On Campaign Travel Cost," *New York Times*, May 5, 1976.
138. Richard Cheney, in discussion with the author, June 9, 2004.
139. Lyle Denniston, "Ford Projects 'New' Presidential Look," *Washington Star*, May 8, 1976.
140. Denniston, *Washington Star*, May 8, 1976.
141. Pomper, *The Election of 1976*, Table 1.3, p. 20-23.
142. Donald J. Devine, in discussion with the author, 2004; Morton Blackwell, in discussion with the author, 2004.
143. Devine, discussion; Blackwell, discussion.
144. R.W. Apple, Jr., "Goldwater States Ford Case in Nebraska," *New York Times*, May 10, 1976.
145. Apple, *New York Times*, May 10, 1976.
146. Spencer, discussion.
147. Pomper, *The Election of 1976*, Table 1.3, p. 20-23; Table 1.4, p. 24.
148. Seth S. King, "Nebraska to Test Candidates With Midwestern Farm Vote," *New York Times*, May 9, 1976.
149. Douglas E. Kneeland, "Reagan Declines to Call Himself Winner Over Ford in Nebraska," *New York Times*, May 12, 1976.
150. Doug Bailey, in discussion with the author, June 16, 2004.
151. R.W. Apple Jr., "Ford Is Reviewing Strategy In Light Of Reagan's Gains," *New York Times*, May 6, 1976.
152. Pat Pizzella, in discussion with the author, January 30, 2004.
153. *New York Times*, "Ford Favored in West Virginia," May 11, 1976.
154. Pomper, et al, *The Election of 1976*, Table 1.4, p. 24.
155. *New York Times*, "The Long March: G.O.P.," May 13, 1976.

CHAPTER TEN — Ford Storms Back

1. Walter Taylor, "Victorious Reagan Heads East," *Washington Star*, May 12, 1976.
2. Douglas E. Kneeland, "Reagan Declines to Call Himself Winner Over Ford in Nebraska," *New York Times*, May 12, 1976.

3. *New York Times*, "Indiana's Verdict," May 6, 1976.
4. William K. Stevens, "'72 Wallace Voters Lean To Reagan in Michigan." *New York Times*, May 11, 1976.
5. Stevens, *New York Times*, May 11, 1976.
6. Gerald R. Ford, *A Time To Heal* (New York: Harper & Row, 1979), 43.
7. Ford, *A Time To Heal*, 53.
8. Ford, *A Time To Heal*, 64.
9. James Reston, "The Republican Dilemma," *New York Times*, May 9, 1976.
10. James M. Naughton, "Ford Says Carter Does A 'Flip-Flop,'" *New York Times*, May 4, 1976.
11. Charles Mohr, "Carter Says Reagan Would Be 'A Divisive Figure' for G.O.P.," *New York Times*, May 5, 1976.
12. Robert Reinhold, "Indiana Indicates Growing G.O.P. Rift," *New York Times*, May 6, 1976; "1,440 Voters Polled In Indiana Survey," *New York Times*, May 6, 1976.
13. "ACU Reagan Project," March 26, 1976, Robert Hartmann Papers, Box 164, Gerald Ford Presidential Library, Ann Arbor, MI.
14. Joseph Lelyveld, "Reagan Aided by Ads Conservative Group Paid For," *New York Times*, May 6, 1976.
15. M. Stanton Evans, in discussion with the author, February 25, 2004.
16. Bernard Gwertzman, "G.O.P. Leaders Tell Ford He's Harmed As Criticism of Kissinger's Moves Rises," *New York Times*, May 7, 1976.
17. Les Brown, "Presidential Debates on TV Are Planned," *New York Times*, May 7, 1976.
18. *New York Times*, "Reagan Now Favored By London Bookmaker," May 7, 1976.
19. Wayne King, "Reagan Predicts First-Ballot Victory," *New York Times*, May 7, 1976.
20. Frank Lynn, "Rockefeller Seen Gaining Support," *New York Times*, May 7, 1976.
21. Lynn, *New York Times*, May 7, 1976.
22. Arthur Finkelstein, in discussion with the author, 2004.
23. Associated Press, "7 Jersey G.O.P. Leaders Form Special Unit for Ford," *New York Times*, March 9, 1976.
24. Ronald Sullivan, "Ford Urged To Bid For Jersey Votes," *New York Times*, May 8, 1976.
25. Sullivan, *New York Times*, May 8, 1976.
26. Ford, *A Time To Heal*, 377.
27. David Bufkin, in discussion with the author, March 5, 2004.
28. R.W. Apple Jr., "Unpledged Votes Could Determine G.O.P. Candidate," *New York Times*, May 9, 1976.
29. Philip Shabecoff, "Ford Aides Reported Critical of White House Staff," *New York Times*, May 11, 1976.
30. Elizabeth Drew, *American Journal: The Events of 1976* (New York: Vintage Books, 1978), p. 181.
31. John W. Finney, "Ford-Reagan Race Focusing on Arms Issue," *New York Times*, May 11, 1976.
32. Richard L. Madden, "President Backed By G.O.P. Leaders," *New York Times*, May 12, 1976.
33. Leslie H. Gelb, "Aides Say Carter Is Courted by Russians," *New York Times*, May 13, 1976.
34. Gelb, *New York Times*, May 13, 1976.
35. Douglas E. Kneeland, "An Absence of Crossover Voting In Nebraska Is Cited by Reagan," *New York Times*, May 13, 1976.

36. Charles Black, in discussion with the author, 2004.
37. William Chapman and Barry Sussman, "And the Voters," *Washington Post,* May 16, 1976.
38. Philip Shabecoff, "Ford Opens Urgent Drive For Victory in Home State," *New York Times,* May 13, 1976.
39. Shabecoff, *New York Times,* May 13, 1976.
40. Shabecoff, *New York Times,* May 13, 1976.
41. Jules Witcover, *Marathon: The Pursuit of the Presidency, 1972-1976* (New York: Viking Press, 1977), p. 423.
42. Thomas P. Ronan, "G.O.P. Leader in Brooklyn Gives Support to Reagan," *New York Times,* May 13, 1976.
43. Warren Weaver Jr., "Election Funding Delayed Further," *New York Times,* May 14, 1976.
44. Associated Press, "Kissinger Scores Reagan On Canal," *New York Times,* May 14, 1976.
45. *New York Times,* "Mr. Reagan's Veto," May 14, 1976.
46. Ronald Sullivan, "Sandman Unsure Of Ford Strength," *New York Times,* May 14, 1976.
47. Thomas P. Ronan, "15 Brooklyn G.O.P. Delegates Shift From Neutral to Reagan," *New York Times,* May 14, 1976.
48. Weaver, *New York Times,* May 15, 1976.
49. Douglas E. Kneeland, "Reagan, in Detroit, Asserts U.S. Curbs Auto Industry," *New York Times,* May 15, 1976.
50. Kneeland, *New York Times,* May 15, 1976.
51. Kneeland, *New York Times,* May 15, 1976.
52. Kneeland, *New York Times,* May 15, 1976.
53. John Herbers, "Crossover Voting Makes Primaries More General" *New York Times,* May 16, 1976.
54. Jeff Bell, in discussion with the author, May 5, 2004.
55. Eileen Shanahan, "Data on Reagan Indicate He Paid No U.S. Tax in '70," *New York Times,* May 16, 1976.
56. Associated Press, "Aide Denies Report That Reagan Paid No '70 Income Tax," *New York Times,* May 18, 1976.
57. Thomas P. Ronan, "Javits Sees G.O.P. Hurt By Reagan," *New York Times,* May 16, 1976.
58. Ronan, *New York Times,* May 16, 1976.
59. Richard L. Madden, "President Backed By G.O.P. Leaders," *New York Times,* May 12, 1976.
60. Philip Shabecoff, "President Stumps Michigan By Train," *New York Times,* May 16, 1976.
61. Philip Shabecoff, "Ford Ends 3-Day Appeal For Support in Michigan," *New York Times,* May 17, 1976.
62. Shabecoff, *New York Times,* May 16, 1976.
63. William Safire, "Conventional Foolishness," *New York Times,* May 20, 1976, National Rifle Association archivist, 2004.
64. Shabecoff, *New York Times,* May 17, 1976.
65. Associated Press, "Reagan Gets 46 Delegates in Five States," *New York Times,* May 17, 1976.
66. Warren Weaver Jr., "Companies Aid Ford," *New York Times,* May 18, 1976
67. *New York Times,* "It Looks Like Dirty Pool," May 20, 1976.
68. Ben A. Franklin, "Brown's Victory Sets Back Georgian's Presidency Bid," *New York Times,* May 19, 1976.
69. William K. Stevens, "Ford Beats Reagan In Michigan And Maryland; Carter Defeated By

Brown, Challenged By Udall," *New York Times*, May 19, 1976; R.W. Apple Jr., "Candidates Seem In Vote Standoff For Next 3 Weeks," *New York Times*, May 20, 1976.

70. Rowland Evans and Robert Novak, "Crossovers in Ford Country," *Washington Post*, May 15, 1976.
71. Jules Witcover and Joel D. Weisman, "Ford Wins in Michigan; Brown Is Victor in Md.; Carter, Udall Neck and Neck," *Washington Post*, May 19, 1976.
72. Rowland Evans and Robert Novak, "Campaign Trail: 'The Mother's Day Massacre,'" *Washington Post*, May 29, 1976.
73. R.W. Apple Jr., "Candidates Seem In Vote Standoff For Next 3 Weeks," *New York Times*, May 20, 1976.
74. Charles Mohr, "Carter Plans No Change," *New York Times*, May 19, 1976; William K. Stevens, "Ford Beats Reagan In Michigan And Maryland; Carter Defeated By Brown, Challenged By Udall," *New York Times*, May 19, 1976.
75. Richard D. Lyons, "'Campaign Just Beginning,' Brown Says," *New York Times*, May 19, 1976.
76. Charles Mohr, "Carter Plans No Change," *New York Times*, May 19, 1976.
77. James M. Naughton, "President Hails 2 Comeback Victories as 'Fantastic,'" *New York Times*, May 19, 1976.
78. Drew, *American Journal*, 179.
79. James M. Naughton, "Ford Elated by Victories; Sees First-Ballot Sweep," *New York Times*, May 20, 1976.
80. R.W. Apple Jr., "Candidates Seem In Vote Standoff For Next 3 Weeks," *New York Times*, May 20, 1976.
81. Apple, *New York Times*, May 20, 1976.
82. Naughton, *New York Times*, May 19, 1976.
83. Douglas E. Kneeland, "Reagan Is in Nevada to Change His Luck," *New York Times*, May 20, 1976.
84. Kneeland, *New York Times*, May 20, 1976.
85. Apple, *New York Times*, May 20, 1976.
86. Kneeland, *New York Times*, May 20, 1976.
87. Wallace Turner, "Candidates in Both Parties Campaign Hard in Oregon," *New York Times*, May 21, 1976.
88. Turner, *New York Times*, May 21, 1976.
89. Warren Weaver Jr., "Committee to Draft Humphrey Is Set Up," *New York Times*, May 21, 1976.
90. Charles Mohr, "Carter Credibility Issue: Calley and Vietnam War," *New York Times*, May 21, 1976.
91. Frank Lynn, "New York's G.O.P. Reported Moving To Endorse Ford," *New York Times*, May 21, 1976.
92. *New York Times*, "Ford Bars Reagan As A Running Mate," May 22, 1976.
93. Ronald Sullivan, "'Grass-Roots' Drive in Jersey Backs Reagan," *New York Times*, May 22, 1976.
94. Sullivan, *New York Times*, May 22, 1976.
95. Sullivan, *New York Times*, May 22, 1976.
96. Sullivan, *New York Times*, May 22, 1976.

97. *New York Times*, "Ford Gets Support In Pennsylvania," May 23, 1976.
98. Douglas E. Kneeland, "Reagan Says He Opposes Limited War," *New York Times*, May 22, 1976.
99. Kneeland, *New York Times*, May 22, 1976.
100. Kneeland, *New York Times*, May 22, 1976.
101. Edward Walsh, "Ford Backer Hosts Reagan," *Washington Post*, May 21, 1976.
102. Jules Witcover, "Political Past Shadows GOP Race in Tenn.," *Washington Post*, May 24, 1976.
103. Kneeland, *New York Times*, May 22, 1976.
104. Kneeland, *New York Times*, May 22, 1976.
105. Sally Quinn, "Goldwater Assailed As Critic of Reagan," *Washington Post*, May 21, 1976.
106. Philip Shabecoff, "Ford Aides Seek Standoff With Reagan in 6 Contests," *New York Times*, May 22, 1976.
107. Shabecoff, *New York Times*, May 22, 1976.
108. *New York Times*, "Ford Asks Return To Moral Quality," May 24, 1976.
109. Philip Shabecoff, "Ford and His 'Advocates' Seek Votes in California," *New York Times*, May 25, 1976.
110. Douglas E. Kneeland, "Reagan, Now Trailing Ford, Renews First-Ballot Hopes in Tour of Oregon," *New York Times*, May 24, 1976.
111. Kneeland, *New York Times*, May 24, 1976.
112. Edward Walsh, "In Western Swing, Reagan Predicts 1st Ballot Victory," *Washington Post*, May 23, 1976.
113. George Gallup, "'76 Voters Tilted to The Right," *Washington Post*, May 23, 1976.
114. George Gallup, "Ford's Lead Falls Despite Latest Wins," *Washington Post*, May 25, 1976.
115. Donnel Nunes, "88 Delegates in Pennsylvania," *Washington Post*, May 23, 1976.
116. Frank Lynn, "119 New York Delegates, In Switch, Endorse Ford," *New York Times*, May 25, 1976.
117. Nunes, *Washington Post*, May 23, 1976.
118. Richard Cheney, in discussion with the author, June 9, 2004.
119. Lou Cannon, "1-Ballot Win Seen By Reagan," *Washington Post*, May 27, 1976.
120. *New York Times*, "Ford Rallies . . . ," May 27, 1976; Gerald M. Pomper, et al., *The Election of 1976: Reports and Interpretations* (New York: Longman, 1977), Table 1.4, p. 24-25.
121. R.W. Apple Jr., "Ford Defeats Reagan In Kentucky, Loses Arkansas; Tennessee Close: Carter Is Winner In the 3 States," *New York Times*, May 26, 1976.
122. Jules Witcover, "Ford Asking Ky. Voters to Reverse Party Pros' Decision," *Washington Post*, May 23, 1976.
123. Pomper, *The Election of 1976*, Table 1.3, p. 20-3.
124. William Chapman, "Ford Is Winning 3 States; Church Leads in Oregon: Republicans," *Washington Post*, May 26, 1976; Fred Masck, "GOP Race About Even," *Washington Post*, May 31, 1976.
125. Pomper, *The Election of 1976*, Table 1.3, p. 20-3.
126. Edward Walsh, "'The Speech' Is Reagan's Major Asset," *Washington Post*, May 24, 1976.
127. Warren Brown, "Udall Is Hanging In There," *Washington Post*, May 24, 1976.
128. David S. Broder, "The Oregon Primary: A Pause for Reflection?" *Washington Post*, May 26, 1976.
129. *Washington Post*, "Delegate Totals," Chart, May 27, 1976.

130. *Washington Post,* "California Primary Bill Gains," May 26, 1976.
131. Lou Cannon, "Winner-Take-All Haunts Ford Camp in California," *Washington Post,* May 29, 1976.
132. Rowland Evans and Robert Novak, "Ronald Reagan On Home Turf," *Washington Post,* May 26, 1976.
133. "Reagan California Fund," Reagan Campaign Material, Jerry Jones Files, 74-77, Box 25, Gerald Ford Presidential Library, Ann Arbor, MI.
134. Edward Walsh, "Ford Calls Self Only GOP Hope," *Washington Post,* May 27, 1976.
135. Walsh, *Washington Post,* May 27, 1976.
136. Walsh, *Washington Post,* May 27, 1976.
137. Lou Cannon, "1st Ballot Win Seen By Reagan, *Washington Post,* May 27, 1976; Lou Cannon, "A Question of Style," *Washington Post,* June 1, 1976.
138. Margot Hornblower, "'Isle of Tears' to Reopen as U.S. Monument," *Washington Post,* May 28, 1976; Thomas Grubisich, "Fairfax Eyes Legal Action On SST Noise," Washington *Post,* May 20, 1976; Stephen Isaacs, "Rockefeller Worried by Ford's Move to the Right," *Washington Post,* May 28, 1976.
139. *Washington Post,* advertisements, May 28, 1976.
140. John M. Goshko, "Repayments Sought From Hays and Ray," *Washington Post,* June 17, 1976; David Hume Kennerly, *Shooter* (New York: Newsweek Books, 1979), p. 194.
141. Associated Press, "FEC to Stop Funding of Former Candidates," *Washington Post,* May 29, 1976.
142. Stephen Isaacs, "Independent Spenders are Warned by FEC," *Washington Post,* May 29, 1976.
143. Isaacs, *Washington Post,* May 29, 1976.
144. *New York Times,* "The Reagan Challenge . . ." May 30, 1976.
145. *Washington Post,* "Ford Election Group Fires Ad Director," May 30, 1976.
146. Joseph Lelyveld, "Ford Ads on TV Get A New Sales Pitch," *New York Times,* June 3, 1976; John Robert Greene, *The Presidency of Gerald R. Ford* (Lawrence: University Press of Kansas, 1995), 167-8.
147. James A. Baker, in discussion with the author, March 25, 2004; Witcover, *Marathon,* 434.
148. *Washington Post,* "Kissinger Hits 'Parade' Article," May 30, 1976.
149. *New York Times,* "Nation Needs Détente, Rockefeller Declares," June 3, 1976.
150. James M. Naughton, "Campaign Without A Knockout Punch," *New York Times,* June 6, 1976.
151. Lou Cannon, "Reagan Confident," *Washington Post,* May 31, 1976.
152. David S. Broder, "Ford, Reagan Scrambling For a Few Ohio Delegates," *Washington Post,* June 6, 1976.
153. Cannon, *Washington Post,* May 31, 1976.
154. Cannon, *Washington Post,* May 31, 1976.
155. Bell, discussion.
156. Jules Witcover, "Reagan Previews Races Against Humphrey, Carter," *Washington Post,* June 2, 1976.
157. Cannon, *Washington Post,* May 31, 1976.
158. Cannon, *Washington Post,* May 31, 1976.
159. Jon Nordheimer, "Reagan Wants Concessions if He Is Loser," *New York Times,* May 29, 1976.

160. Nordheimer, *New York Times*, May 29, 1976.
161. Edward Walsh, "Carter and Ford Win One, Lose Two," *Washington Post*, June 2, 1976.
162. Fred Masck, "GOP Race About Even," *Washington Post*, May 31, 1976.
163. Walsh, *Washington Post*, June 2, 1976.
164. Pomper, *The Election of 1976*, Table 1.3, p. 20-3.
165. *Washington Post*, "Tuesday Primary Results," June 3, 1976.
166. *Washington Post*, "Delegate Totals." Chart, June 3, 1976.
167. Lou Cannon, "Reagan Takes Aim at 'Forced Busing'," *Washington Post*, June 3, 1976.
168. Cannon, *Washington Post*, June 3, 1976.
169. Lou Cannon, "Reagan Clarifies His Stance on U.S. Troops in Rhodesia," *Washington Post*, June 4, 1976.
170. Cannon, *Washington Post*, June 4, 1976.
171. Cannon, *Washington Post*, June 4, 1976.
172. William Claiborne, "Ford to Visit N.J., in Effort To Spur Vote," *Washington Post*, June 5, 1976; Harold J. Logan, "Rockefeller Visits Md. GOP Session," *Washington Post*, June 5, 1976.
173. Black, discussion.
174. Black, discussion.
175. Jon Nordheimer, "Ford, In Ad Shift, Describes Reagan As Peace Threat," *New York Times*, June 6, 1976.
176. Donnel Nunes and Thomas Grubisich, "Reagan Sweeps Virginia," *Washington Post*, June 6, 1976; Pomper, *The Election of 1976*, Table 1.3, p. 20-23.
177. *Washington Post*, "Reagan Gains 37 Delegates," June 7, 1976.
178. *Washington Post*, June 7, 1976.
179. *New York Times*, "Poll Shows Reagan and Brown Gaining," June 4, 1976.
180. *Washington Post*, "State-by-State Voting in Tuesday's Primaries," June 10, 1976.
181. Stuart Spencer, in discussion with the author, June 21, 2004.
182. Spencer, discussion.
183. Memorandum, "Talking Points for Phone Call to Governor Reagan," September, 1976, Presidential Telephone Calls, 9/76 – 11/76, Box 18, Gerald Ford Presidential Library, Ann Arbor, MI.
184. Lou Cannon, "Reagan's Rhodesian 'Lapse,'" *Washington Post*, June 6, 1976.
185. Associated Press, "Ford, Reagan Talk of Panama, Rhodesia, Angola, Defense," *Washington Post*, June 6, 1976; James M. Naughton, "Ford, Stumping in Ohio, Warns G.O.P. Of a 'Debacle' if Reagan Is Nominated," *New York Times*, June 8, 1976.
186. Associated Press, "Ford, Reagan Talk of Panama, Rhodesia, Angola, Defense," *Washington Post*, June 6, 1976.
187. Broder, *Washington Post*, June 6, 1976.
188. John Sears, in discussion with the author, March 18, 2004.
189. Broder, *Washington Post*, June 6, 1976.
190. Black, discussion.
191. Broder, *Washington Post*, June 6, 1976.
192. Broder, *Washington Post*, June 6, 1976.
193. Drew, *American Journal*, 241.
194. Drew, *American Journal*, 242.

195. Jon Nordheimer, "Reagan Attacks Ford TV Tactics," *New York Times*, June 8, 1976.
196. Lou Cannon and Edward Walsh, "Reagan Assails Ford," *Washington Post*, June 8, 1976.
197. Lou Cannon, "GOP Scarred By California Dissension," *Washington Post*, June 10, 1976.
198. Cannon and Walsh, *Washington Post*, June 8, 1976.
199. David S. Broder, "Georgian Loses in N.J., Brown Wins Calif.," *Washington Post*, June 9, 1976.
200. Pomper, *The Election of 1976*, Table 1.3, p. 20-3.
201. Bell, discussion.
202. *New York Times*, "Effects of Tuesday Voting," June 10, 1976.
203. *Time*, "Stanpede to Carter," June 21, 1976, Vol. 107, No. 26.

CHAPTER ELEVEN — Contentious Conventions

1. Edward Walsh, "Reagan Scores Decisively in California," *Washington Post*, June 9, 1976.
2. "How Tight Can It Get?" *Newsweek*, July 12, 1976.
3. Donnel Nunes and Thomas Grubisich, "Reagan Sweeps Virginia," *Washington Post*, June 6, 1976.
4. Walsh, "Reagan Scores Decisively . . . ," *Washington Post*, June 9, 1976.
5. Edward Walsh, "North Dakota Gives Ford 12 Delegates," *Washington Post*, July 9, 1976.
6. *Time*, "Ford is Close, but Watch Those Trojan Horses," August 2, 1976.
7. Jeff MacNelly, political cartoon, *Time*, July 6, 1976.
8. Walsh, "Reagan Scores Decisively . . . ," *Washington Post*, June 9, 1976.
9. *Washington Post*, "Delegate Totals," June 10, 1976.
10. *Time*, "How Reagan Plays G.O.P. Hardball," June 28, 1976.
11. *Time*, June 28, 1976.
12. David S. Broder, "Endorsements Clinch Carter Victory: His Delegates Put at 1,514, Indicating A First-Ballot Win," *Washington Post*, June 10, 1976.
13. Kenneth Crawford, "James Farley Dies, FDR Political Aide," *Washington Post*, June 10, 1976.
14. Cannon, *Washington Post*, June 10, 1976.
15. Warren Brown, "A Farewell to the Old South," *Washington Post*, June 13, 1976.
16. John Sears, in discussion with the author, March 18, 2004.
17. Cannon, *Washington Post*, June 10, 1976.
18. Cannon, *Washington Post*, June 10, 1976.
19. Edward Walsh, "Ford-Reagan Race Enters New Phase," *Washington Post*, June 12, 1976.
20. Don Devine, in discussion with the author, January 29, 2004; Morton Blackwell, in discussion with the author, February 9, 2004.
21. Walsh, *Washington Post*, June 12, 1976.
22. Edward Walsh, "Reagan Takes 18 Delegates In Missouri," *Washington Post*, June 13, 1976.
23. Blackwell, discussion.
24. Devine, discussion.
25. Walsh, *Washington Post*, June 13, 1976.
26. Blackwell, discussion.
27. Devine, discussion.
28. Walsh, *Washington Post*, June 13, 1976.
29. David S. Broder, "Reagan Aiming Oratory At Iowa Delegates Next," June 15, 1976.

30. *Time*, June 28, 1976.
31. Hugh Sidey, "'This Is the Toughest,'" *Time*, June 28, 1976.
32. Broder, *Washington Post*, June 15, 1976.
33. Broder, *Washington Post*, June 15, 1976.
34. David S. Broder, "Iowa: Ford 19, Reagan 17," *Washington Post*, June 20, 1976.
35. Edward Walsh, "Ford, Reagan To Woo Iowa Delegates," *Washington Post*, June 16, 1976.
36. "Jimmy Carter Debt Put at $1.2 Million," *Washington Post*, June 17, 1976.
37. David S. Broder, "Exuberant Reagan Leader Forecasts November Win," *Washington Post*, June 17, 1976.
38. *Washington Post*, "U.S. Navy to Evacuate Beirut Foreigners," June 20, 1976.
39. David S. Broder, "Ford Wins 8 Delegates in Iowa," *Washington Post*, June 19, 1976.
40. Broder, *Washington Post*, June 20, 1976.
41. Broder, *Washington Post*, June 19, 1976.
42. Rowland Evans and Robert Novak, " . . . And Growing Credibility for Ronald Reagan," *Washington Post,* June 22, 1976.
43. Kenny Klinge, in discussion with the author, May 24, 2004
44. Dale Duvall, in discussion with the author, July 6, 2004
45. R.W. Apple Jr., "G.O.P. Governors find Role Limited," *New York Times*, July 6, 1976.
46. Apple, *New York Times*, July 6, 1976.
47. *Washington Post*, "Reagan Has 'Good Weekend,'" June 20, 1976.
48. Duvall, discussion.
49. Pomper, *The Election of 1976,* Table 1.4, p. 24.
50. Jim Burnley, in discussion with the author, July 28, 2004.
51. *Washington Post*, June 20, 1976.
52. *Washington Post*, June 20, 1976.
53. Ronald Sullivan, "State G.O.P. And Reagan," *New York Times*, July 4, 1976.
54. Sullivan, *New York Times*, July 4, 1976.
55. *New York Times*, "Ford Drives for First-Ballot Victory," July 25, 1976.
56. David S. Broder, "Republican Race Grows Tighter Still," *Washington Post*, June 21, 1976.
57. Broder, *Washington Post*, June 21, 1976.
58. Broder, *Washington Post*, June 21, 1976.
59. Christopher Lydon, "Reagan Aide Borrowing Ford's 'Electability' Issue," *New York Times*, June 20, 1976.
60. George Lardner Jr., "Panel Says CIA, FBI Covered Up JFK Killing Data," *Washington Post*, June 24, 1976.
61. John M. Goshko, "Teamster Provenzano Indicted in 1961 Murder," *Washington Post*, June 24, 1976
62. Sears, discussion.
63. Edward Walsh, "Ford Gains Edge in Minn. Contest," *Washington Post*, June 26, 1976.
64. Photograph and caption, "Moment of Prayer," *Washington Post*, June 24, 1976.
65. Eric Pianin, "Rule Shift Key To Ford Sweep Of Minn.Votes," *Washington Post*, June 24, 1976.
66. David Keene, in discussion with the author, March 3, 2004; Sears, discussion.
67. Keene, discussion.
68. Walsh, *Washington Post*, June 26, 1976.

69. Lou Cannon, "Reagan Scores Heavily in West," *Washington Post*, June 27, 1976.
70. Kenny Klinge, in discussion with the author, May 24, 2004.
71. Gerald Pomper, ed., *The Election of 1976: Reports and Interpretations* (New York: Longman, 1977), Table 1.3, p. 20-21.
72. Cannon, *Washington Post*, June 27, 1976.
73. Cannon, *Washington Post*, June 27, 1976.
74. Edward Walsh, "Ford Edges Toward Nomination, but Reagan Closes Gap," *Washington Post*, June 28, 1976.
75. R.W. Apple Jr., "Ford's Delegate Lead Is Put at Only 34," *New York Times*, July 1, 1976.
76. David S. Broder, "GOP Committee Eyes Change In Delegate Binding Rules," *Washington Post*, June 26, 1976.
77. Broder, *Washington Post*, June 26, 1976.
78. Rowland Evans and Robert Novak, "A Campaign Warning," *Washington Post*, June 26, 1976.
79. James M. Naughton, "Campaign Without A Knockout Punch," *New York Times*, June 6, 1976.
80. Neal Peden, in discussion with the author, August 1, 2004.
81. Peter Monk, in discussion with the author; Becki Black Donatelli, in discussion with the author, January 15, 2004.
82. Monk, discussion.
83. Keene, discussion.
84. Billy Mounger, in discussion with the author, April 19, 2004.
85. Keene, discussion.
86. Warren Weaver Jr., "Reagan's Lawyers Call Ford Unfair," *New York Times*, July 9, 1976.
87. Lou Cannon, "GOP Panel Assailed by Reagan," *Washington Post*, July 1, 1976.
88. Joseph Kraft, "If Ford is No. 1 Reagan Won't Be No. 2," *Washington Post*, July 1, 1976.
89. James Baker, in discussion with the author, March 25, 2004.
90. Peter McPherson, in discussion with the author, March 7, 2004.
91. McPherson, discussion.
92. Baker, discussion.
93. Brad Minnick, in discussion with the author, March 4, 2004.
94. *New York Times*, "White House Hails Shift of a Delegate In Brooklyn to Ford," July 10, 1976.
95. Joseph Kraft, "If Ford is No. 1 Reagan Won't Be No. 2," *Washington Post*, July 1, 1976.
96. James Reston, "Ford *and* Reagan," *New York Times*, June 13, 1976.
97. Christopher Lydon, "Reagan, in Mississippi, Rejects Plea That He Accept No. 2 Spot," *New York Times*, June 25, 1976.
98. Bob Woodward and Carl Bernstein, "Sen. Hansen Offers Deal On Support," *Washington Post*, July 2, 1976.
99. Edward Walsh, "Ford, Hansen Deny Vote Deal," *Washington Post*, July 3, 1976.
100. Lou Cannon, "Reagan Calls for 'New Coalition,' Takes Aim at Carter," *Washington Post*, July 7, 1976.
101. Jon Nordheimer, "Reagan Attacks Carter As Vague," *New York Times*, July 7, 1976.
102. Sears, discussion.
103. Cannon, *Washington Post*, July 7, 1976.

104. Jon Nordheimer, "Ford Picks Up 12 In North Dakota," *New York Times*, July 9, 1976.
105. Edward Walsh, "North Dakota Gives Ford 12 Delegates," *Washington Post*, July 9, 1976.
106. Walsh, *Washington Post*, July 9, 1976.
107. Pomper, *The Election of 1976*, Table 1.3, p. 22-23.
108. Edward Walsh, "North Dakota Gives Ford 12 Delegates," *Washington Post*, July 9, 1976.
109. James M. Naughton, "Ford Now Finds Reagan Qualified To Be President," *New York Times*, July 10, 1976.
110. Cynthia Kadonaga and Edward Walsh, "Reagan as 2d Not Excluded," *Washington Post*, July 10, 1976.
111. John Nordheimer, "Bold Reagan tactician," *New York Times*, August 2, 1976.
112. Rowland Evans and Robert Novak, "Chaos and Bitterness Inside the Ford Camp," *Washington Post*, July 10, 1976.
113. Evans and Novak, *Washington Post*, July 10, 1976.
114. *Washington Post*, "White House Adviser for Television Resigns," July 12, 1976.
115. *Time*, "They're So Close—And Yet So Far," July 19, 1976.
116. *Time*, "Reagan: 'I Don't Want Another 1964'," August 2, 1976.
117. Christopher Lydon, "President Gains 3 Colorado Votes," *New York Times*, July 10, 1976.
118. Lou Cannon, "Reagan Wins 15 At-Large Delegates in Colorado," *Washington Post*, July 11, 1976.
119. Edward Walsh, "Ford Gain: Small, Significant," *Washington Post*, July 12, 1976.
120. Cannon, *Washington Post*, July 11, 1976.
121. Lou Cannon, "Democrats Fix Sights on Ford," *Washington Post*, July 16, 1976.
122. *New York Times*, "Muskie Says Reagan May Defeat Ford," July 7, 1976.
123. Bernard Gwertzman, "Kissinger Says Position of Carter Is 'Compatible,'" *Washington Post*, July 11, 1976.
124. Spencer Rich, "Democrats' Slate Hit By GOP as 'Liberal,'" *Washington Post*, July 16, 1976.
125. *New York Times*, "The Vote for Mondale," July 16, 1976.
126. Les Brown, "25% of Adults Saw Carter Speech on TV," *New York Times*, July 17, 1976
127. Stephen Isaacs, "Ford Teams With 'the Bird' In Bid for TV Spotlight," *Washington Post*, July 14, 1976.
128. Associated Press, "Candidate Ford Outspent By Reagan Campaigners," *Washington Post*, July 14, 1976.
129. Stephen Isaacs, "Reagan Courts Delegates," *Washington Post*, July 15, 1976.
130. Paul Laxalt, in discussion with the author, April 21, 2004.
131. Stephen Isaacs, "A Year Later, Reagan's Goal Is Still Elusive," *Washington Post*, July 16, 1976.
132. Cynthia Kadonaga, "Indians Meet With Ford, Charge Publicity Pitch," *Washington Post*, July 17, 1976.
133. *New York Times*, "Ford Is Pressing Drive for Delegates," July 17, 1976.
134. Gerald R. Ford, *A Time To Heal* (New York: Harper & Row, 1979), 393.
135. Philip Shabecoff, "Democratic Slate Assailed by Ford; G.O.P. Unity Urged," *New York Times*, July 18, 1976.
136. Christopher Lydon, "Reagan Easy Utah Victor, Captures All 20 Delegates," *New York Times*, July 18, 1976.
137. Jules Witcover and Suzanne Dean, "Ford, Reagan Trade Sweeps in Delegate Bids," *Washington Post*, July 18, 1976.
138. Witcover and Dean, *Washington Post*, July 18, 1976.

139. "The Right Report," July 2, 1976, Ron Nessen Papers, 74-77, Box 39, Gerald Ford Presidential Library, Ann Arbor, MI.
140. Witcover and Dean, *Washington Post*, July 18, 1976.
141. Christopher Lydon, "Reagan Easy Utah Victor, Captures All 20 Delegates," *New York Times*, July 18, 1976.
142. Lydon, *New York Times*, July 18, 1976.
143. Lou Cannon, "Reagan's Camp: Air of Resignation," *Washington Post*, July 19, 1976.
144. Cannon, *Washington Post*, July 19, 1976.
145. Lou Cannon, in discussion with the author, June 28, 2004.
146. *Time*, "They're So Close—And Yet So Far," July 19, 1976.
147. Jules Witcover, "Reagan Camp Claims Enough Delegates to Win," *Washington Post*, July 20, 1976.
148. Witcover, *Washington Post*, July 20, 1976.
149. *Time*, "Ford is Close, but Watch Those Trojan Horses," August 2, 1976.

CHAPTER TWELVE — The Schweiker Stratagem

1. William V. Shannon, "The Last Republican," *New York Times*, June 21, 1976.
2. Jules Witcover, *Marathon: The Pursuit of the Presidency 1972-1976* (New York: Viking Press, 1977), 441.
3. Ron Nessen, *It Sure Looks Different From the Inside* (Chicago: Playboy, 1978), 222.
4. Stephen Isaacs, "Most Uncommitted GOP Delegates Are Just That," *Washington Post*, July 25, 1976.
5. David Alpern with Tom Joyce and Gerald C. Lubenow, "A Game of GOP Hardball," *Newsweek*, July 4, 1976.
6. David Keene, in discussion with the author, March 3, 2004.
7. Memorandum by Ronald Reagan, (RR Campaign) Delegate Themes Files, Box 447-446, Ronald Reagan Presidential Library, Simi Valley, CA.
8. Memorandum by David A. Keene, July 1, 1976, (RR Campaign) Delegate Themes Files, Box 447-446, Ronald Reagan Presidential Library, Simi Valley, CA.
9. Memorandum by David A. Keene, July 2, 1976.
10. Memorandum by David A. Keene, July 2, 1976.
11. *Newsweek*, "How Tight Can It Get?," July 12, 1976.
12. John Robert Greene, *The Presidency of Gerald R. Ford* (Lawrence, Kansas: University Press of Kansas, 1995), 170.
13. Lee Edwards, *Ronald Reagan: A Political Biography* (Houston: Nordland, 1981), 181.
14. David Keene, "Why Reagan Chose Schweiker: An Insider's Account," *The Alternative: An American Spectator*, November, 1976.
15. Jules Witcover, "Reagan Camp Claims Enough Delegates to Win," *Washington Post*, July 20, 1976.
16. David S. Broder, "Ford's Forces Claim to Add 16 Delegates," *Washington Post*, July 21, 1976.
17. Broder, *Washington Post*, July 21, 1976.
18. Elizabeth Drew, *American Journal*, (New York, Vintage, 1976), 330-332.
19. Broder, *Washington Post*, July 21, 1976.
20. *New York Times*, "Tally on G.O.P. Delegates," July 20, 1976.

21. Broder, *Washington Post,* July 21, 1976.
22. Keene, discussion; Charlie Black, in discussion with the author, January 27, 2004.
23. Keene, *The Alternative,* November 1976.
24. Fred Eckert, in discussion with the author, August 4, 2004; Bill Schulz, in discussion with the author, February 23, 2004.
25. Frank Lynn, "Most of State's Republican Delegates to Meet With Ford Today," *New York Times,* July 21, 1976.
26. David Broder, "Working the Delegates, White House Style," *Washington Post,* July 23, 1976
27. Paul G. Edwards and Austin Scott, "Chats Win Va. Votes For Ford," *Washington Post,* July 21, 1976.
28. Edwards and Scott, *Washington Post,* July 21, 1976.
29. Edwards and Scott, *Washington Post,* July 21, 1976.
30. Stephen Isaacs, "Dial D for Delegate—But Reagan Delayed," *Washington Post,* July 23, 1976.
31. *Washington Post,* "Ford Bars Inducements For Support," July 23, 1976.
32. Greene, *The Presidency of Gerald R. Ford,* 170.
33. James M. Naughton, "White House Denies Reagan Accusation On Bid to Delegates," *New York Times,* July 23, 1976.
34. Keene, discussion.
35. Naughton, *New York Times,* July 23, 1976.
36. Lou Cannon, "Delegates for Ford Increase," *Washington Post,* July 24, 1976.
37. *Washington Star,* "Counting the 1976 Delegates," July 25, 1976.
38. David S. Broder, "Ford's Forces Claim to Add 16 Delegates," *Washington Post,* July 21, 1976.
39. Stephen Isaacs, "Most Uncommitted GOP Delegates Are Just That," *Washington Post,* July 25, 1976.
40. Peter Hannaford, in discussion with the author, January 8, 2004.
41. Jon Nordheimer, "Reagan, Says a Strategist, Had to Make Move to Left," *New York Times,* July 28, 1976.
42. Keene, discussion; Paul Laxalt, in discussion with the author, April 21, 2004.
43. Witcover, *Marathon,* 460.
44. Witcover, *Marathon,* 460.
45. Nicholas M. Horrock, "Reagan's 'Coalition' Running Mate," *New York Times,* July 27, 1976.
46. *Time,* "The Road from Slippery Rock," August 9, 1976.
47. Witcover, *Marathon,* 457.
48. John Sears, in discussion with the author, March 18, 2004
49. Sears, discussion.
50. Lou Cannon, *Reagan* (New York: G.P. Putnam's Sons, 1982), 221.
51. Witcover, *Marathon,* 459; Richard Schweiker, in discussion with the author, April 1, 2004.
52. Witcover, *Marathon,* 461.
53. *Time,* "A Gamble Gone Wrong," August 9, 1976.
54. Witcover, *Marathon,* 461.
55. Schweiker, discussion.
56. James M. Naughton, "Tally Indicates That Ford Is Close to Delegate Goal," *New York Times,* July 24, 1976.

57. Rowland Evans and Robert Novak, "Reagan's Gamble," *Washington Post*, July 28, 1976.
58. Drew, *American Journal*, 334.
59. Memorandum by Jim Connor, 26 July 1976, Presidential Handwriting Files, Box 39, Gerald Ford Presidential Library, Ann Arbor, MI.
60. Jeffrey Bell, in discussion with the author, May 5, 2004.
61. Reagan Correspondence, John M. Ashbrook Center for Public Affairs, Ashland, Ohio; Ashland University.
62. Robert Ajemian, "Reagan: 'I Don't Want Another 1964,'" *Time*, August 2, 1976.
63. Schweiker, discussion.
64. Schweiker, discussion; Drew Lewis, in discussion with the author, March 7, 2004.
65. Schweiker, discussion.
66. Lewis, discussion.
67. Schweiker, discussion.
68. Lou Cannon, "Bid for Wider Base," *Washington Post*, July 27, 1976.
69. *New York Times*, "Text of Reagan Statement," July 27, 1976.
70. *NBC Nightly News*, 26 July 1976, NBC, White House Communications Agency Collection, Gerald Ford Presidential Library, Ann Arbor, MI.
71. David E. Rosenbaum, "Schweiker Says He Can Help on Unity," *New York Times*, July 27, 1976.
72. Cannon, *Washington Post*, July 27, 1976.
73. Nicholas M. Horrock, "Reagan's 'Coalition' Running Mate," *New York Times*, July 27, 1976; *Time*, "The Road from Slippery Rock," August 9, 1976.
74. Cannon, *Washington Post*, July 27, 1976.
75. Sears, discussion.
76. *CBS Evening News*, 26 July 1976, CBS, White House Communications Agency Collection, Gerald Ford Presidential Library, Ann Arbor, MI.
77. James M. Naughton, "Connally Favors Ford's Candidacy As 'Better Choice,'" *New York Times*, July 28, 1976.
78. James Baker, in discussion with the author, March 25, 2004.
79. David E. Rosenbaum, "Schweiker Says He Can Help on Unity," *New York Times*, July 27, 1976.
80. Molly Ivins, "Young Conservative Convention Abuzz With Talk of Schweiker," *New York Times*, July 31, 1976.
81. James M. Naughton, "Connally Favors Ford's Candidacy As 'Better Choice,'" *New York Times*, July 28, 1976.
82. Naughton, *New York Times*, July 28, 1976.
83. Sears, discussion; Jim Lake, in discussion with the author, January 16, 2004.
84. *Washington Post*, "Gov. Reagan's Gamble," July 27, 1976.
85. Naughton, *New York Times*, July 27, 1976.
86. Jon Nordheimer, "Reagan, Says a Strategist, Had to Make Move to Left," *New York Times*, July 28, 1976.
87. *Washington Post*, "Gov. Reagan's Gamble," July 27, 1976.
88. *Washington Post*, July 27, 1976.
89. Nessen, *It Sure Looks Different From the Inside*, 224.
90. Presidential Handwriting Files, Box 39, Gerald Ford Presidential Library, Ann Arbor, MI.

91. Memorandum by Jack Marsh, 26 July 1976, Presidential Handwriting Files, Box 39, Gerald Ford Presidential Library, Ann Arbor, MI.
92. James M. Naughton, "Connally Favors Ford's Candidacy As 'Better Choice,'" *New York Times,* July 28, 1976.
93. Jon Nordheimer, "Reagan, Says a Strategist, Had to Make Move to Left," *New York Times,* July 28, 1976.
94. Jules Witcover, "Reagan Aim: Aid Drive in Northeast," *Washington Post,* July 28, 1976.
95. Charles B. Seib, "The Schweiker Choice: How the Press Reacted," *Washington Post,* August 13, 1976.
96. Jude Wanniski, "The Schweiker Gambit," *Wall Street Journal,* week of July 26, 1976.
97. *New York Times,* "On to Kansas City," August 8, 1976.
98. Greene, *The Presidency of Gerald R. Ford,* 171.
99. *Time,* "A Gamble Gone Wrong," August 9, 1976.
100. Bill McAllister, "Virginia Delegate Throws Support to Ford; Decided After Reagan's 'Blunder,'" *Washington Post,* August 5, 1976.
101. James M. Naughton, "Connally Favors Ford's Candidacy As 'Better Choice,'" *New York Times,* July 28, 1976.
102. Philip Shabecoff, "Schweiker Ready to Oppose Labor on Reagan Ticket," *New York Times,* July 31, 1976.
103. *Human Events,* "Conservatives Should Stick with Reagan," August 7, 1976.
104. Ernie Angelo, in discussion with the author, May 4, 2004.
105. *Time,* "A Gamble Gone Wrong," August 9, 1976.
106. Laxalt, discussion.
107. Kiron K. Skinner, et al, *Reagan: A Life in Letters* (New York: Free Press, 2003), 218.
108. Ivins, *New York Times,* July 31, 1976.
109. Rowland Evans and Robert Novak, "Reagan's Bitter-Enders," *Washington Post,* August 2, 1976.
110. Harry Dent, *The Prodigal South Returns to Power* (New York: John Wiley & Sons), 32.

CHAPTER THIRTEEN — Bloody Mississippi

1. David Keene, in discussion with the author, March 3, 2004.
2. Jules Witcover, *Marathon: The Pursuit of the Presidency, 1972-1976* (New York: Viking Press, 1977), 443.
3. Elizabeth Drew, *American Journal: The Events of 1976* (New York: Vintage Books, 1978), 400.
4. Keene, discussion.
5. Keene, discussion.
6. Keene, discussion.
7. Keene, discussion.
8. Witcover, *Marathon,* 488.
9. R.W. Apple Jr., "Reagan Is Assured of at Least 25 Votes Out of 30 to Be Cast by Mississippi," New York *Times,* June 30, 1976.
10. Drew, *American Journal,* 320.
11. Witcover, *Marathon,* 444.
12. Memorandum by David Keene, June 23, 1976, Mississippi and Louisiana Delegates, File 6, Box 447-446, Ronald Reagan Presidential Library, Simi Valley, CA; Memorandum by David

Keene, July 1, 1976, Telephone Calls, File 6, Box 447-446, Ronald Reagan Presidential Library, Simi Valley, CA.

13. *Human Events*, "Conservatives Angered by Ford Campaign Tactics," March 6, 1976.
14. Martin Anderson, in discussion with the author, June 23, 2004.
15. Jim Lake, in discussion with the author, January 16, 2004.
16. Billy Mounger, in discussion with the author, April 19, 2004.
17. David Keene, "Why Reagan Chose Schweiker: An Insider's Account," *The Alternative: An American Spectator*, November 1976.
18. R.W. Apple Jr., "Ford Is Found Preferred By Uncommitted Delegates," *New York Times*, May 16, 1976.
19. *Time*, "The Bruising Numbers Game," July 5, 1976, 32.
20. *Time*, "They're So Close—And Yet So Far," July 19, 1976.
21. Keene, discussion.
22. Mounger, discussion.
23. Harry S. Dent, *The Prodigal South Returns to Power* (New York: John Wiley & Sons, 1978), 31.
24. Dent, *The Prodigal South*, 21.
25. Dent, *The Prodigal South*, 42.
26. Drew, *American Journal*, 321.
27. Witcover, *Marathon*, 446.
28. Witcover, *Marathon*, 449.
29. Dent, *The Prodigal South*, 36.
30. Dent, *The Prodigal South*, 36-37.
31. Mounger, discussion.
32. James M. Naughton, "Shift of Mississippi G.O.P. To Ford Termed Imminent," *New York Times*, July 22, 1976.
33. Witcover, *Marathon*, 453.
34. Witcover, *Marathon*, 454.
35. James M. Naughton, "Mississippi Slate Delays Endorsing Until G.O.P. Meets," *New York Times*, July 26, 1976.
36. Mounger, discussion.
37. Mounger, discussion.
38. Witcover, *Marathon*, 465.
39. Witcover, *Marathon*, 465.
40. John Sears, in discussion with the author, March 18, 2004.
41. Mounger, discussion.
42. Witcover, *Marathon*, 466.
43. Keene, discussion.
44. Witcover, *Marathon*, 467; Keene, discussion.
45. Keene, discussion.
46. Witcover, *Marathon*, 467.
47. Dent, *The Prodigal South*, 43.
48. Dent, *The Prodigal South*, 43.
49. Keene, discussion.
50. Lou Cannon, "GOP Leaders In Mississippi Backs Ford," *Washington Post*, July 29, 1976.
51. *Time*, "A Gamble Gone Wrong," August 9, 1976, 14.

52. Cannon, *Washington Post*, July 29, 1976.
53. James M. Naughton, "Mississippi Slate Delays Endorsing Until G.O.P. Meets," *New York Times*, July 26, 1976.
54. Dent, *The Prodigal South*, 44.
55. *Time*, "Republicans: Down to the Wire, and Still a Horse Race," August 16, 1976, 9.
56. Drew, *American Journal*, 345.
57. R.W. Apple Jr., "Battle to Control G.O.P. Convention," *New York Times*, July 5, 1976.

CHAPTER FOURTEEN — Kansas City

1. Charles M. Roberts, "Can the GOP Unite Itself?" *Washington Post*, August 13, 1976.
2. Scott Stanley, "Mutation in Kansas City," *The Review Of The News*, September 1, 1976.
3. *Time*, "A Gracious Town in the Heartland," August 16, 1976, 11.
4. *Time*, August 16, 1976, 12.
5. Robert T. Nakamura, "Impressions of Ford and Reagan," *Political Science Quarterly*, Vol. 92, Num. 4, 652.
6. Jules Witcover, "Reagan Claims Gain of 12 Delegates," *Washington Post*, August 3, 1976.
7. Memorandum from David A. Keene to Governor Reagan, "Additional Telephone Calls," July 2, 1976, Delegate Memos, Box 447-446, Ronald Reagan Presidential Library, Simi Valley, CA.
8. Richard Cheney, in discussion with the author, June 9, 2004.
9. Lou Cannon and Edward Walsh, "Ford Unit Shakeup," *Washington Post*, August 5, 1976.
10. *Time*, "A Gamble Gone Wrong," August 9, 1976, 7.
11. Edward Walsh, "Ford, Reagan Aides Disagree On Delegate Voting Proposal," *Washington Post*, August 7, 1976.
12. *Time*, "Who Would Lose Less to Carter?" June 28, 1976, 11.
13. Margot Hornblower, "Reagan, Schweiker Pick Up 6 Delegates in Northeast," *Washington Post*, August 6, 1976.
14. Edward Walsh, "President To Delay on No. 2," *Washington Post*, August 6, 1976.
15. Hornblower, *Washington Post*, August 6, 1976.
16. Margot Hornblower, "Reagan, Schweiker Find Pa. Delegates Hard to Persuade," *Washington Post*, August 7, 1976.
17. Rowland Evans and Robert Novak, "Losing the Schweiker Gamble," *Washington Post*, August 7, 1976.
18. David Keene, in discussion with the author, March 3, 2004.
19. Cheney, discussion; John Sears, in discussion with the author, March 18, 2004.
20. Lou Cannon and Jules Witcover, "Reagan Forces Preparing Early Test of Strength," *Washington Post*, August 10, 1976.
21. Tom Ellis, in discussion with the author, May 10, 2004.
22. Sears, discussion.
23. David S. Broder, "Rules Panel Blocks Move On No. 2," *Washington Post*, August 10, 1976.
24. Cannon and Witcover, *Washington Post*, August 10, 1976.
25. Broder, *Washington Post*, August 10, 1976.
26. David S. Broder, "Ford Forces Win a Clash On Delegates," *Washington Post*, August 11, 1976.
27. Eric Sevareid, *CBS News*, August 12, 1976, White House Communications Agency Collection, Gerald Ford Presidential Library, Ann Arbor, MI.

28. Leslie Stahl, *CBS News,* August 12, 1976, White House Communications Agency Collection, Gerald Ford Presidential Library, Ann Arbor, MI.
29. Spencer Rich, "GOP Unit Backs Abortion Plank," *Washington Post,* August 11, 1976.
30. Rich, *Washington Post,* August 11, 1976.
31. Phyllis Schlafly, in discussion with the author, March 3, 2004.
32. *Time,* "A Gamble Gone Wrong," August 9, 1976, 14.
33. Edward Walsh, "President to Delay on No. 2," *Washington Post,* August 6, 1976.
34. *Time,* August 9, 1976, 15.
35. Walsh, *Washington Post,* August 6, 1976.
36. Jules Witcover, "Ford Follows Carter's Lead On No. 2 Spot," *Washington Post,* August 11, 1976.
37. *Newsweek,* "Right They Are," August 23, 1976, 21.
38. Ellis, discussion.
39. Harry Reasoner, *ABC News,* August 12, 1976, White House Communications Agency Collection, Gerald Ford Presidential Library, Ann Arbor, MI.
40. Frank Reynolds, *ABC News,* August 12, 1976, White House Communications Agency Collection, Gerald Ford Presidential Library, Ann Arbor, MI.
41. Lou Cannon, "Buckley Hints He Would Run As 'Compromise,'" *Washington Post,* August 12, 1976.
42. James A. Baker, in discussion with the author, March 25, 2004; Cannon, *Washington Post,* August 12, 1976.
43. David S. Broder and Jules Witcover, "GOP Panel Endorses ERA, Opposes Busing: Warning on Liberals," *Washington Post,* August 13, 1976.
44. Jim Lake, in discussion with the author, January 16, 2004.
45. Republican National Convention, 1976 Platform, Presidential Handwriting, Box 39, Gerald Ford Presidential Library, Ann Arbor, MI.
46. Barry Sussman and William Chapman, "Delegates Found More Conservative Than 4 Years Ago," *Washington Post,* August 15, 1976.
47. Margot Hornblower, "A Subdued Reagan Says His Destiny Rests in Hands of Uncommitteds," *Washington Post,* August 15, 1976.
48. Margot Hornblower, "The Californian: 'I'm Available for Giving That Input,'" *Washington Post,* August 16, 1976.
49. *Kansas City Times,* Chart: "Disparities in Delegate Tally," August 2, 1976.
50. Edward Walsh, "President to Begin His Most Important Political Journey," *Washington Post,* August 15, 1976.
51. Jules Witcover, "Ford Incumbency Not as Powerful as Predecessors'," *Washington Post,* August 14, 1976.
52. Hornblower, *Washington Post,* August 16, 1976.
53. John J. O'Connor, "TV: Lively Convention," *New York Times,* August 18, 1976.
54. Lou Cannon, "Running-Mate Disclosure Bid Rejected, 59-44," *Washington Post,* August 16, 1976.
55. Cannon, *Washington Post,* August 16, 1976.
56. Witcover, *Marathon,* 490-1.
57. Lou Cannon and William Claiborne, "Ford Gains Votes As Sessions Open," *Washington Post,* August 17, 1976.

58. Baker, discussion.
59. Rowland Evans and Robert Novak, "Reagan, Without Ideology," *Washington Post*, August 16, 1976.
60. Dick Wirthlin, *The Greatest Communicator: What Ronald Reagan Taught Me about Politics, Leadership, and Life* (Hoboken: John Wiley & Sons, 2004), 18.
61. Witcover, *Marathon*, 493.
62. Billy Mounger, in discussion with the author, April 19, 2004.
63. John Chancellor, *NBC News*, August 16, 1976, White House Communications Agency Collection, Gerald Ford Presidential Library, Ann Arbor, MI.
64. Don Totten, in discussion with the author, June 8, 2004.
65. Zorine Bhappu Shirley, in discussion with the author, 2004.
66. Brad Minnick, in discussion with the author, March 4, 2004.
67. Cannon and Caliborne, *Washington Post*, August 17, 1976.
68. *Washington Post*, Chart: "How Delegates View GOP Chances in November," August 18, 1976.
69. R.W. Apple Jr., "Ford Gains Edge Over Reagan; Baker or Ruckelshaus Listed As Likely Choice For No. 2 Spot," *New York Times*, August 18, 1976.
70. Cannon and Claiborne, *Washington Post*, August 17, 1976; R.W. Apple Jr., "Ford's Commitments Reach Goal On First Day of the Convention, But Reagan Presses Vote Battle," *New York Times*, August 17, 1976.
71. Witcover, *Marathon*, 494.
72. Witcover, *Marathon*, 492.
73. Witcover, *Marathon*, 495.
74. Witcover, *Marathon*, 496.
75. Witcover, *Marathon*, 496-497.
76. R.W. Apple Jr., "Ford Gains Edge Over Reagan; Baker or Ruckelshaus Listed As Likely Choice For No. 2 Spot," *New York Times*, August 18, 1976.
77. *CBS News*, August 17, 1976, CBS, White House Communications Agency Collection, Gerald Ford Presidential Library, Ann Arbor, MI.
78. Witcover, *Marathon,* 497.
79. Dan Rather, *CBS News*, August 17, 1976, CBS, White House Communications Agency Collection, Gerald Ford Presidential Library, Ann Arbor, MI.
80. Tom Pettit, *NBC News*, August 17, 1976, NBC, White House Communications Agency Collection, Gerald Ford Presidential Library, Ann Arbor, MI.
81. Apple, *New York Times*, August 18, 1976.
82. Tom Brokaw, *NBC News*, August 17, 1976, NBC, White House Communications Agency Collection, Gerald Ford Presidential Library, Ann Arbor, MI.
83. Apple, *New York Times*, August 18, 1976.
84. Carl Stern, *NBC News*, August 17, 1976.
85. Cheney, discussion.
86. David S. Broder, "Ford Passes Critical Test," *Washington Post*, August 18, 1976.
87. Cheney, discussion.
88. Cheney, discussion.
89. Witcover, *Marathon*, 500-1.
90. Frank van der Linden, *The Real Reagan: What he believes, What he has accomplished, What we can expect from him* (New York: William Morrow, 1981), 142.

91. Peter Hannaford, in discussion with the author, January 8, 2004.
92. Ellis, discussion.
93. Lyn Nofziger, in discussion with the author, 2004.
94. R.W. Apple Jr., "Ford Takes Nomination on First Ballot; Reveals Vice-Presidential Choice Today," *Washington Post*, August 19, 1976.
95. James A. Baker, in discussion with the author, March 25, 2004.
96. Hannaford, discussion; Arthur Laffer, in discussion with the author, June 8, 2004.
97. Cheney, discussion.
98. Schweiker, discussion.
99. Ernie Angelo, in discussion with the author, May 4, 2004.
100. Charles Mohr, "Ford Said to Plan Talk to Reagan," *New York Times*, August 18, 1976.
101. Chuck Tyson, in discussion with the author, May 12, 2004.
102. Apple, *New York Times*, August 19, 1976.
103. James T. Wooten, "Reagan Supporters Stage A Noisy Demonstration," *New York Times*, August 19, 1976.
104. Angelo, discussion.
105. Dale Duvall, in discussion with the author, 2004.
106. Lou Cannon, "Ford Nominated on 1st Ballot," *Washington Post*, August 19, 1976.
107. John Hart, *NBC News*, August 18, 1976, NBC, White House Communications Agency Collection, Gerald Ford Presidential Library, Ann Arbor, MI.
108. Schweiker, discussion.
109. Michael Reagan, in discussion with the author, July 2, 2004.
110. Michael Reagan, in discussion with the author.
111. Nancy Reynolds, in discussion with the author, February 25, 2004.
112. Cheney, discussion.
113. Reynolds, discussion.
114. Nofziger, discussion.
115. Jon Nordheimer, "Reagan Blames 'Machine States,'" *New York Times*, August 20, 1976.
116. Lake, discussion.
117. *New York Times*, "Tally on Vice President," August 20, 1976.
118. Tom Brokaw, *NBC News*, August 19, 1976, NBC, White House Communications Agency Collection, Gerald Ford Presidential Library, Ann Arbor, MI.
119. Kenny Klinge, in discussion with the author, May 24, 2004.

CHAPTER FIFTEEN — Reagan's Remarks

1. *New York Times*, "Transcript of Reagan's Remarks to the Convention," August 20, 1976.
2. Lou Cannon, in discussion with the author, June 28, 2004.
3. Al Cardenas, in discussion with the author, July 13, 2004.
4. Jack Germond, in discussion with the author, July 2, 2004.

CHAPTER SIXTEEN — The End of the Beginning

1. *Newsweek*, "High Noon," August 23, 1976.
2. Jerry Falwell, in discussion with the author, 2004.
3. Larry Kudlow, in discussion with the author, March 8, 2004.
4. Kiron K. Skinner, et al, *Reagan: A Life in Letters* (New York: Free Press, 2003), 218.

5. John Sears, in discussion with the author, March 18, 2004.
6. Paul Laxalt, in discussion with the author, April 21, 2004.
7. Marin Anderson, in discussion with the author, June 23, 2004.
8. Jeffrey Bell, "The Candidate and the Briefing Book," *The Weekly Standard*, February 5, 2001, 26.
9. Edwin Meese, in discussion with the author, June 23, 2004.
10. Ralph Hallow, in discussion with the author, January 9, 2004.

EPILOGUE

1. Kiron K. Skinner, et al, *Reagan: A Life in Letters* (New York: Free Press, 2003), 219.
2. Paul Weyrich, in discussion with the author, March 4, 2004.
3. Chris Matthews, e-mail message to author, September 21, 2004.
4. Rowland Evans and Robert Novak, "Reagan's Gamble," *Washington Post*, July 28, 1976.
5. *New York Times*, "After the Reagan Insurrection," August 20, 1976.
6. *Time*, Forum, August 30, 1976, 4.
7. Joseph Kraft, "'A President Who Has Not Done Badly,'" *Washington Post*, August 10, 1976.
8. Peter J. Rusthoven, "The Nation's Pulse: Remembering Reagan," *The Alternative: An American Spectator*, October 1976.
9. *New York Times*, August 20, 1976.
10. Edwin Meese, in discussion with the author, June 23, 2004.

BIBLIOGRAPHY

BOOKS

Adler, Bill and Bill Adler, Jr. *The Reagan Wit.* Aurora, IL: Caroline House, 1981.

Ambrose, Stephen E. *Nixon: The Education of a Politician 1913-1962.* New York: Simon & Schuster, 1987.

Ambrose, Stephen E. *Nixon: The Triumph of a Politician 1962-1972.* New York: Simon & Schuster, 1989.

Anderson, Martin. *Revolution.* New York: Harcourt Brace Jovanovich, 1988.

Armstrong, Richard. *The Next Hurrah: The Communications Revolution in American Politics.* New York: Beech Tree Books, 1988.

Bailey, Thomas A. *Democrats vs. Republicans: The Continuing Clash.* New York: Meredith Press, 1968.

Bakshian, Aram Jr. *The Candidates 1980.* New Rochelle, NY: Arlington House, 1980.

Barone, Michael. *Our Country: The Shaping of America from Roosevelt to Reagan.* New York: Free Press, 1990.

Bernstein, Carl and Bob Woodward. *All the President's Men.* New York: Touchstone, 1974.

Black, Earl and Merle Black. *The Rise of Southern Republicans.* Cambridge, MA: Belknap Press of Harvard University, 2002.

Boller, Paul F. Jr. *Presidential Anecdotes.* New York: Penguin Books, 1981.

Boller, Paul F. Jr. *Presidential Campaigns.* New York: Oxford University Press, 1984.

Broder, David S. *The Party's Over: The Failure of Politics in America.* New York: Harper & Row, 1972.

Buchanan, Patrick J. *Right from the Beginning.* Washington, DC: Regnery Gateway, 1990.

Buckley Jr., William F. *The Unmaking of a Mayor.* New York: Viking Press, 1966.

The Candidates 1980: Where They Stand. Washington, DC: American Enterprise Institute for Publc Policy, 1980.

Cannon, Lou. *Governor Reagan: His Rise to Power.* New York: PublicAffairs, 2003.

Cannon, Lou. *President Reagan: The Role of a Lifetime.* New York: PublicAffairs, 1991.

Cannon, Lou. *Reagan.* New York: G.P. Putnam's Sons, 1982.

Carter, Jimmy. *The Presidential Campaign 1976 (Vol. 1, Pts 1-2).* Washington, DC: United States Government Printing Office, 1978.

Carter, Jimmy. *The Presidential Campaign 1976 (Vol. 2, Pt 1).* Washington, DC: United States Government Printing Office, 1979.

Cash, Kevin. *Who the Hell Is William Loeb?* Manchester, NH: Amoskeag Press, 1975.

Casserly, John J. *The Ford White House: The Diary of a Speechwriter.* Lincoln, NE: iUniverse.com, 1977.

Chambers, Whittaker. *Witness.* Washington, DC: Regnery Gateway, 1952.

Chester, Lewis, Godfrey Hodgson, and Bruce Pag. *An American Melodrama: The Presidential Campaign of 1968.* New York: Viking Press, 1969.

Cohen, Richard M. and Jules Witcover. *A Heartbeat Away: The Investigation and Resignation of Vice President Spiro T. Agnew.* New York: Viking Press, 1974.

Collier, Peter and David Horowitz. *The Rockefellers: An American Dynasty.* New York: Summit Books, 1976.

Conason, Joe. *Big Lies: The Right-Wing Propaganda Machine and How It Distorts the Truth.* New York: Thomas Dunne Books, 2003.

Cotton, Norris. *In the Senate: Admidst the Conflict and the Turmoil.* New York: Dodd, Mead & Company, 1978.

Couch, Ernie, ed. *Presidential Trivia.* Nashville: Rutledge Hill Press, 1996.

Crane, Honorable Philip M. *Surrender in Panama: The Case against the Treaty.* Ottawa, IL: Green Hill, 1978.

Crane, Philip M. *The Sum of Good Government.* Ottawa, IL: Green Hill, 1976.

Crawford, Alan. *Thunder on the Right: The New Right and the Politics of Resentment.* New York: Pantheon Books, 1980.

Crouse, Timothy. *The Boys on the Bus.* New York: Random House, 2003.

Dallek, Robert. *An Unfinished Life: John F. Kennedy 1917-1963.* Boston: Little, Brown and Company, 2003.

Dallek, Robert. *Ronald Reagan: The Politics of Symbolism.* Cambridge, MA: Harvard University Press, 1999.

Davis, Patti. *The Way I See It.* New York: G.P. Putnam's Sons, 1992.

Deaver, Michael K. *A Different Drummer: My Thirty Years with Ronald Reagan.* New York: HarperCollins, 2001.

Dent, Harry S. *The Prodigal South Returns to Power.* New York: John Wiley and Sons, 1978.

Devine, Donald J. *Reagan Electionomics: How Reagan Ambushed the Pollsters.* Ottawa, IL: Green Hill, 1983.

Dolan, John T. *Reagan: The Revolution Continues.* Washington, DC: National Conservative Political Action Committee.

Dolan, John T. and Gregory A. Fossedal. *Reagan: A President Succeeds.* Vienna, VA: Conservative Press, 1983.

Drew, Elizabeth. *American Journal: The Events of 1976.* New York: Vintage Books, 1976.

Driscoll, James G. *Elections 1968.* Silver Springs, MD: National Observer, 1968.

Dubose, Lou, Jan Reid, and Carl M. Cannon. *Boy Genius: Karl Rove: The Brains Behind the Remarkable Political Truimph of George W. Bush.* New York: PublisAffairs, 2003.

Dugger, Ronnie. *On Reagan: The Man & His Presidency.* New York: McGraw-Hill, 1983.

Edwards, Lee. *Goldwater: The Man Who Made a Revolution.* Washington, DC: Regnery Gateway, 1995.

Edwards, Lee. *Missionary for Freedom.* New York: Paragon House, 1990.

Edwards, Lee. *Ronald Reagan: A Political Biography.* Houston, TX: Nordland Publishing International, 1981.

Edwards, Lee. *The Conservative Revolution: The Movement that Remade America.* New York: Free Press, 1999.

Ehrlichman, John. *Witness to Power: The Nixon Years.* New York: Pocket Books, 1982.

Evans, Captain G. Russell. *Death Knell of the Panama Canal?* Fairfax, VA: National Security Center, 1997.

Evans, M. Stanton. *The Future of Conservatism.* Garden City, NY: Doubleday, 1969.

Evans, M. Stanton. *The Theme Is Freedom: Religion, Politics, and the American Tradition.* Washington, DC: Regnery, 1994.

Evans, Rod L. and Irwin M. Berent. *The Quotable Conservative: The Giants of Conservatism on Liberty, Freedom, Individual Responsibility, and Traditional Virtues.* Holbrook, MA: Adams Media Corp., 1995.

Evans, Rowland and Robert Novak. *The Reagan Revolution: An Inside Look at the Transformation of the U.S. Government.* New York: E.P. Dutton, 1981.

Ford, Gerald R. *A Time To Heal: The Autobiography of Gerald R. Ford.* New York: Harper & Row, 1979.

Ford, Gerald R. *The Presidential Campaign 1976 (Vol. 2, Pt. 2).* Washington, DC: United States Government Printing Office, 1978.

Friedman, Milton and Rose Friedman. *Free To Choose.* New York: Avon Books, 1980.

Frum, David. *Dead Right.* New York: HarperCollins, 1994.

Frum, David. *How We Got Here. The 70s: The Decade that Brought You Modern Life—For Better or Worse.* New York: Basic Books, 2000.

Galston, William A. *Liberal Purposes: Goods, Virtues, and Diversity in the Liberal State.* New York: Cambridge University Press, 1991.

Gilder, George and Bruce K. Chapman. *The Party that Lost Its Head.* New York: Alfred A. Knopf, 1966.

Gold, Vic. *PR as in President.* Garden City, NY: Doubleday & Company, 1977.

Goldwater, Barry. *The Conscience of a Conservative.* New York: Hillman Books, 1960.

Gould, Lewis L. *Grand Old Party: A History of the Republicans.* New York: Random House, 2003.

Green, Mark and Gail MacColl. *There He Goes Again: Ronald Reagan's Reign of Error.* New York: Pantheon Books, 1983.

Greene, John Robert. *The Presidency of Gerald R. Ford.* Lawrence, KS: University Press of Kansas, 1995.

Haldeman, H. R. *The Haldeman Diaries: Inside the Nixon White House.* New York: G.P. Putnam's Sons, 1994.

Hallow, Ralph Z. and Bradley S. O'Leary. *Presidential Follies: Those Who Would Be President and Those Who Should Think Again.* Boerne, TX: Boru Publishing, 1995.

Hannaford, Peter. *The Reagans: A Political Portrait.* New York: Coward-McCann, 1983.

Hannaford, Peter, ed. *Recollections on Reagan: A Portrait of Ronald Reagan.* New York: William Morrow, 1997.

Hartmann, Robert T. *Palace Politics: An Inside Account of the Ford Years.* New York: McGraw-Hill, 1980.

Hayward, Stephen F. *The Age of Reagan: The Fall of the Old Liberal Order.* Roseville, CA: Forum, 2001.

Henry, John M. *Free Enterprise: An Imperative.* West Branch, IA: Herbert Hoover Presidential LibraryAssociation, 1975.

Hill, Napoleon. *Think and Grow.* Charleston, SC: Fawcett Crest, 1963.

Holmes, Joseph R., ed. *The Quotable Ronald Reagan.* San Diego: JRH & Associates, 1975.

Houston, Kerri and Patricia Fava. *Al Gore: America in the Balance.* Alexandria, VA: American Conservative Union, 2000.

Hughes, Emmet J. *The Living Presidency: The Resources and Dilemmas of the American Presidential Office.* Baltimore, MD: Penguin Books, 1973.

Jamieson, Kathleen Hall. *Everything You Think You Know about Politics—And Why You're Wrong.* New York: Basic Books, 2000.

Javits, Jacob K. *Order of Battle: A Republican's Call To Reason.* New York: Atheneum Publishers, 1964.

Josi, Christian. *Hillary Rodham Clinton: What Every American Should Know.* Alexandria, VA: American Conservative Union, 2000.

Kelley, Kitty. *Nancy Reagan: The Unauthorized Biography.* New York: Pocket Star Books, 1991.

Kennerly, David Hume. *Shooter.* New York: Newsweek Books, 1979.

Kirkpatrick, Jeane J. *The Reagan Phenomenon—And Other Speeches on Foreign Policy.* Washington, DC: American Enterprise Institute for Publc Policy, 1983.

Lasky, Victor. *It Didn't Start with Watergate.* New York: Dell Publishing, 1977.

Laxalt, Paul. *Nevada's Paul Laxalt: A Memoir.* Reno: Jack Bacon & Company, 2000.

Liddy, G. Gordon. *Will: The Autobiography of G. Gordon Liddy.* New York: Dell/St. Martin's Press, 1980.

Marlin, George J. *Fighting the Good Fight: A History of the New York Consrevative Party.* South Bend, IN: St. Augustine's Press, 2002.

Martin, Ralph G. *A Hero for Our Time.* New York: Fawcett Crest, 1983.

McGinniss, Joe. *The Selling of the President 1968.* New York: Pocket Books, 1969.

McLuhan, Marshall. *Understanding the Media: The Extensions of Man.* New York: McGraw-Hill, 1964.

Melder, Keith. *Hail to the Candidate: Presidential Campaigns from Banners to Broadcasts.* Washington, DC: Smithsonian Institution Press, 1992.

Miller, William Fishbait. *Fishbait: The Memoirs of the Congressional Doorkeeper.* New York: Warner Books, 1977.

Morris, Edmund. *Dutch: A Memoir of Ronald Reagan.* New York: Random House, 1999.

Nessen, Ron. *It Sure Looks Different from the Inside.* Chicago: Playboy Press, 1978.

Nixon, Richard. *In the Arena: A Memoir of Victory, Defeat, and Renewal.* New York: Pocket Books, 1990.

Nixon, Richard. *RN: The Memoirs of Richard Nixon: Volume I.* New York: Warner Books, 1978.

Nixon, Richard. *RN: The Memoirs of Richard Nixon: Volume II.* New York: Warner Books, 1978.

Nofziger, Lyn. *Nofziger.* Washington, DC: Regnery Gateway, 1992.

Parmet, Herbert S. *George Bush: The Life of a Lone Star Yankee.* New York: Scribner, 1997.

Perlstein, Rick. *Before the Storm: Barry Goldwater and the Unmaking of the American Consensus.* New York: Hill and Wang, 2001.

Phillips, H., ed., et al. *The New Right at Harvard.* Vienna, VA: Conservative Caucus, 1983.

Polsby, Nelson W. and Aaron Wildavsky. *Presidential Elections: Strategies of American Electoral Politics. 6th Ed.*. New York: Charles Scribner's Sons, 1984.

Pomper, Gerald, et al. *The Election of 1976: Reports and Interpretations.* New York: Longman, 1977.

Reagan, Maureen. *First Father, First Daughter: A Memoir.* Boston: Little, Brown and Company, 1989.

Reagan, Michael with Joe Hyams. *On the Outside Looking In.* New York: Kensington Publishing, 1988.

Reagan, Ronald. *Speaking My Mind.* New York: Simon & Schuster, 1989.

Reagan, Ronald. *The Politics of Symbolism.* Cambridge, MA: Harvard University Press, 1999.

The Republican Candidate's 1978 Speech Book. Washington, DC: National Republican Congressional Committee, 1978.

Reeves, Richard. *A Ford, Not a Lincoln.* New York: Harcourt Brace Jovanovich, 1975.

Roberts, James C. *The Conservative Decade.* Westport, CT: Arlington House, 1980.

Roberts, James C., ed. *A City upon a Hill: Speeches by Ronald Reagan before the Conservative Political Action Conference 1974-1988.* Washington, DC: American Studies Center, 1989.

Robinson, Michael J. and Margaret A. Sheehan. *Over the Wire and On TV: CBS and UPI in Campaign '80.* New York: Russell Sage Foundation, 1980.

Robinson, Peter. *How Ronald Reagan Changed My Life.* New York: HarperCollins, 2003.

Rusher, William A. *The Making of the New Majority Party.* Ottawa, IL: Green Hill, 1975.

Rusher, William A. *The Rise of the Right.* New York: William Morrow, 1984.

Sabato, Larry J. *The Rise of Political Consultants: New Ways of Winning Elections.* New York: Basic Books, 1981.

Schlafly, Phyllis. *A Choice Not an Echo.* Alton, IL: Pere Marquette Press, 1964.

Schlesinger, Joseph A. *Ambition and Politics: Political Careers in the United States.* Chicago: Rand McNally & Company, 1966.

Schneider, Gregory L., ed. *Conservatism in American Since 1930.* New York: New York University Press, 2003.

Schweizer, Peter. *Reagan's War.* New York: Doubleday, 2002.

Scott, Hugh. *Come to the Party.* Englewood Cliffs, NJ: Prentice-Hall, 1968.

Shadegg, Stephen C. *How To Win an Election: The Art of Political Victory. Special SUCCESS Edition.* Arlington, VA: Crestwood Books, 1964.

Shogan, Robert. *None of the Above: Why Presidents Fail—And What Can Be Done about It.* New York: New American Library, 1982.

Skinner, Kiron K., Annelise Anderson and Martin Anderson, eds. *Reagan, In His Own Hand.* New York: Free Press, 2001.

Skinner, Kiron K., Annelise Anderson and Martin Anderson, eds. *Reagan: A Life in Letters.* New York: Free Press, 2003.

Skubic, Stephen J. and Hal E. Short, eds. *Republican Humor.* Washington, DC: Acropolis, 1976.

Smith, Hedrick, et al. *Reagan the Man, the President.* New York: Macmillan Publishing, 1980.

Spada, James. *Ronald Reagan: His Life in Pictures.* New York: St. Martin's Press, 2000.

Stein, Harry. *How I Accidentally Joined the Vast Right-Wing Conspiracy.* New York: Delacorte Press, 2000.

Stockman, David A. *The Triumph of Politics: Why the Reagan Revolution Failed.* New York: Harper & Row, 1986.

Stormer, John A. *None Dare Call It Treason.* Florissant, MS: Liberty Bell Press, 1964.

Strock, James M. *Reagan on Leadership: Executive Lessons from the Great Communicator.* Rocklin, CA: Forum, 1998.

A Time for Choosing: The Speeches of Ronald Reagan 1961-1982. Chicago: Regnery Gateway, 1983.

Toobin, Jeffrey. *A Vast Conspiracy: The Real Story of the Sex Scandal that Nearly Brought Down a President.* New York: Random House, 1999.

van der Linden, Frank. *The Real Reagan: What He Believes, What He Has Accomplished, What We Can Expect from Him.* New York: William Morrow, 1981.

von Damm, Helene, ed. *Sincerely, Ronald Reagan.* New York: Berkley Books, 1983.

Wattenberg, Ben J. *The Real America.* New York: Capricorn Books and G.P. Putnam's Sons, 1976.

Whitaker, Robert W. *The New Right Papers.* New York: St. Martin's Press, 1982.

White, F. Clifton. *Politics as a Noble Calling: The Memoirs of F. Clifton White.* Ottawa, IL: Jameson Books, 1994.

White, F. Clifton and William J. Gill. *Why Reagan Won: The Conservative Movement 1964-1981.* Chicago: Regnery Gateway, 1981.

White, Theodore H. *Breach of Faith: The Fall of Richard Nixon.* New York: Atheneum Publishers, 1975.

White, Theodore H. *The Making of the President 1960.* New York: Atheneum House, 1961.

White, Theodore H. *The Making of the President 1964.* New York: Atheneum House, 1965.

White, Theodore H. *The Making of the President 1972.* New York: Atheneum House, 1973.

Wirthlin, Dick. *The Greatest Communicator: What Ronald Reagan Taught Me about Politics, Leadership, and Life.* Hoboken, NJ: John Wiley and Sons, 2004.

Witcover, Jules. *Crapshoot: Rolling the Dice on the Vice Presidency.* New York: Crown Publishers, 1992.

Witcover, Jules. *Marathon: The Pursuit of the Presidency, 1972-1976.* New York: Viking Press, 1977.

Wolfe, Tom. *Radical Chic & Mau-Mauing the Flak Catchers.* New York: Bantam Books, 1970.

Woodward, Bob and Carl Bernstein. *The Final Days.* New York: Avon Books, 1976.

Zak, Michael. *Back to Basics for the Republican Party.* Chicago: Thiessen Printing & Graphics, 2000.

PERIODICALS

Boston Globe. 1976.

Dallas Morning News. April-May 1976.

Des Moines Register. 1976.

Human Events. 1974-2004.

Kansas City Star. August 1976.

Kansas City Times. August 1976.

Manchester Union Leader. January-February 1976.

Miami Herald. March 1976.

National Journal. 1975-1976.

National Review. 1976.

New York Times. 1975-1976.

Newsweek. April-October 1976.

North Carolina Magazine. April 2004.

Political Science Quarterly. 1977-1978.

Raleigh News and Observer. March 1976.

The Alternative: An American Spectator. October 1976.

The Review of the News. September 1976.

Time. July-November 1976.

U.S. News & World Report. 1976.

Wall Street Journal. 1976.

Washington Post. 1976.

Washington Star. 1976.
Weekly Standard. February 2001.

INTERVIEWS

Ahern, Rick. Interview by Craig Shirley. 2004.
Alexander, Phil. Interview by Craig Shirley. Tape recording. June 8, 2004.
Anderson, Marty. Interview by Craig Shirley. Tape recording. June 23, 2004.
Angelo, Ernie. Interview by Craig Shirley. Tape recording. May 4, 2004.
Bailey, Doug. Interview by Craig Shirley. Tape recording. June 16, 2004.
Baker, James A. Interview by Craig Shirley. Tape recording. March 25, 2004.
Barnes, Fred. Interview by Craig Shirley. Tape recording. February 2, 2004.
Barnes, Fred. Interview by Craig Shirley. Tape recording. February 9, 2004.
Barone, Michael. Interview by Craig Shirley. January 9, 2004.
Bauer, Gary. Interview by Craig Shirley. 2004.
Bell, Jeff. Interview by Craig Shirley. Tape recording. May 5, 2004.
Black, Charles. Interview by Craig Shirley. Tape recording. 2004.
Blackwell, Morton. Interview by Craig Shirley. Tape recording. 2004.
Brock, Bill. Interview by Craig Shirley. Tape recording. 2004.
Buchanan, Bay. Interview by Craig Shirley. Tape recording. August 24, 2004.
Buchanan, Pat. Interview by Craig Shirley. 2004.
Bufkin, David. Interview by Craig Shirley. Tape recording. March 5, 2004.
Burnley, Jim. Interview by Craig Shirley. Tape recording. July 28, 2004.
Callaway, Bo. Interview by Craig Shirley. Tape recording. 2004.
Cannon, Lou. Interview by Craig Shirley. Tape recording. June 28, 2004.
Cardenas, Al. Interview by Craig Shirley. Tape recording. July 13, 2004.
Carmen, Jerry. Interview by Craig Shirley. Tape recording. February 18, 2004.
Cheney, Dick. Interview by Craig Shirley. Tape recording. June 9, 2004.
Deaver, Michael. Interview by Craig Shirley. Tape recording. December 23, 2003.
Devine, Donald J. Interview by Craig Shirley. Tape recording. 2004.
Dezenhall, Eric. Interview by Craig Shirley. 2004.
Donatelli, Becki. Interview by Craig Shirley. Tape recording. January 15, 2004.
Donatelli, Frank. Interview by Craig Shirley. Tape recording. April 2, 2004.
Dunlop, George and Becky. Interview by Craig Shirley. Tape recording. July 2004.
Duvall, C. Dale. Interview by Craig Shirley. Tape recording. June 2004.
Eberle, Bruce. Interview by Craig Shirley. Tape recording. April 28, 2004.
Eckert, Fred. Interview by Craig Shirley. August 4, 2004.
Edmonds, Tom. Interview by Craig Shirley.
Ellis, Tom. Interview by Craig Shirley. Tape recording. May 10, 2004.
Evans, M. Stanton. Interview by Craig Shirley. Tape recording. February 25, 2004.
Falwell, Jerry. Interview by Craig Shirley. 2004.
Fineman, Howard. Interview by Craig Shirley. 2004.
Finkelstein, Arthur. Interview by Craig Shirley. Tape recording. July 16, 2004.
Germond, Jack. Interview by Craig Shirley. Tape recording. July 2, 2004.
Gillespie, Ed. Interview by Craig Shirley. Tape recording. May 19, 2004.
Griffin, Bob. Interview by Craig Shirley. 2004.

Hallow, Ralph. Interview by Craig Shirley. Tape recording. January 9, 2004.
Hannaford, Peter. Interview by Craig Shirley. Tape recording. January 8, 2004.
Helms, Jesse. Interview by Craig Shirley. May 17, 2004.
Hume, Brit. Interview by Craig Shirley. March 16, 2004.
Keene, David. Interview by Craig Shirley. Tape recording. December 16, 2003.
Keene, David. Interview by Craig Shirley. Tape recording. March 3, 2004.
Kemp, Jack. Interview by Craig Shirley. Tape recording. February 6, 2004.
Klinge, Kenny. Interview by Craig Shirley. Tape recording. May 24, 2004.
Kudlow, Larry. Interview by Craig Shirley. March 8, 2004.
Kuhn, Jim. Interview by Craig Shirley. 2004.
Laffer, Art. Interview by Craig Shirley. Tape recording. June 8, 2004.
Lake, Jim. Interview by Craig Shirley. Tape recording. January 16, 2004.
Laxalt, Michele. Interview by Craig Shirley. June 8, 2004.
Laxalt, Paul. Interview by Craig Shirley. Tape recording. April 21, 2004.
Lay, Chris. Interview by Craig Shirley. Tape recording. June 25, 2004.
Leonard, Tish. Interview by Craig Shirley. 2004.
Leubsdorf, Carl. Interview by Craig Shirley. 2004.
Lewis, Drew. Interview by Craig Shirley. April 7, 2004.
Long, Mike. Interview by Craig Shirley. Tape recording. July 1, 2004.
Mahe, Eddie and Ladonna Lee. Interview by Craig Shirley. Tape recording. March 5, 2004.
Matthews, Chris. Interview by Craig Shirley. E-mail correspondence. 2004.
McPherson, Peter. Interview by Craig Shirley. Tape recording. March 7, 2004.
McShane, Michael. Interview by Craig Shirley. 2004.
Meese, Edwin. Interview by Craig Shirley. Tape recording. June 23, 2004.
Miller, Jim. Interview by Craig Shirley. February 26, 2004.
Minnick, Brad. Interview by Craig Shirley. Tape recording. March 4, 2004.
Mintz, Myron. Interview by Craig Shirley. 2004.
Monk, Peter. Interview by Craig Shirley. April 19, 2004.
Mounger, Billy. Interview by Craig Shirley. April 19, 2004.
Nofziger, Lyn. Interview by Craig Shirley. Tape recording. 2004.
Nolan, Pat. Interview by Craig Shirley. Tape recording. July 16, 2004.
Novak, Bob. Interview by Craig Shirley. Tape recording. March 10, 2004.
O'Leary, Brad. Interview by Craig Shirley. 2001.
Peden, Neal. Interview by Craig Shirley. Tape recording. 2004.
Pickering, Charles. Interview by Craig Shirley. Tape recording. April 26, 2004.
Pizzella, Pat. Interview by Craig Shirley. January 30, 2004.
Reagan, Michael. Interview by Craig Shirley. Tape recording. July 2, 2004.
Reed, Rick. Interview by Craig Shirley. March 18, 2004.
Regan, Kathie. Interview by Craig Shirley. March 21, 2004.
Reynolds, Nancy. Interview by Craig Shirley. Tape recording. February 25, 2004.
Roberts, Steve. Interview by Craig Shirley. Tape recording. 2004.
Rohrabacher, Dana. Interview by Craig Shirley. Tape recording. June 10, 2004.
Russo, Paul. Interview by Craig Shirley. 2004.
Ryskind, Allan and Tom Winter. Interview by Craig Shirley. Tape recording. March 9, 2004.
Sarasohn, Judy. Interview by Craig Shirley. July 9, 2004.

Schlafly, Phyllis. Interview by Craig Shirley. Tape recording. March 3, 2004.
Schulz, Bill. Interview by Craig Shirley. Tape recording. February 23, 2004.
Schweiker, Richard. Interview by Craig Shirley. Tape recording. April 1, 2004.
Sears, John. Interview by Craig Shirley. Tape recording. March 18, 2004.
Shirley, Zorine Bhappu. Interview by Craig Shirley. 2004.
Shuster, Bud. Interview by Craig Shirley. Tape recording. 2004.
Smith, Loren. Interview by Craig Shirley. Tape recording. July 29, 2004.
Smith, Rodney. Interview by Craig Shirley. Tape recording. February 9, 2004.
Spencer, Stuart. Interview by Craig Shirley. Tape recording. June 21, 2004.
Stone, Roger. Interview by Craig Shirley. April 5, 2004.
Totten, Don. Interview by Craig Shirley. Tape recording. June 8, 2004.
Tyson, Chuck. Interview by Craig Shirley. Tape recording. May 12, 2004.
Viguerie, Richard. Interview by Craig Shirley. Tape recording. February 2, 2004.
Wade, Terry. Interview by Craig Shirley. Tape recording. June 22, 2004.
Weyrich, Paul. Interview by Craig Shirley. March 4, 2004.
Will, George. Interview by Craig Shirley. Tape recording. February 27, 2004.
Wirthin, Dick. Interview by Craig Shirley. Tape recording. March 11, 2004.
Witcover, Jules. Interview by Craig Shirley. Tape recording. April 30, 2004.
Wrenn, Carter. Interview by Craig Shirley. Tape recording. May 12, 2004.

OTHER MATERIALS

American Conservative Union Board Meeting Minutes, June 1974-December 1976. Brigham Young University. Provo, UT.
Correspondence and notes, 1976. Duvall, C. Dale. Private Collection.
Correspondence and notes, 1976. Lacy, Jim. Private Collection.
Correspondence and notes, 1976. Lay, Chris. Private Collection.
Correspondence and notes, 1976. Minnick, Brad. Private Collection.
Correspondence, August 1975-August 1976. John M. Ashbrook Center for Public Affairs. Ashland, OH: Ashland University.
Hoyt, Austin and Adriana Bosch. *The American Experience: Reagan.* Boston: WGBH, 1998.
Newsweek Archives, 1972-1977. Center for American History. The University of Texas at Austin.
NRA Archived Information. National Rifle Association. Fairfax, VA, 2004.
Presidential records, 1974-1976. Gerald Ford Presidential Library. Ann Arbor, MI.
Presidential records, 1975-1976. Ronald Reagan Presidential Library. Simi Valley, CA.
Reagan and Ford Campaign Spots, 1976. Oklahoma University Political Communication Center. Norman, OK.
Republican Results, February 24, 1976. New Hampshire Presidential Primary. http://www.politicallibrary.org/TallState/1976rep.html.

INDEX

Y

Z

LaVergne, TN USA
20 April 2010
179887LV00001B/29/P